Jurisprudence: Tex

Jurisprudence: Texts and Commentary

Howard Davies
Lecturer in Law, University of Leeds

David Holdcroft
Professor of Philosophy, University of Leeds

Butterworths
London, Dublin, Edinburgh
1991

United Kingdom	Butterworths, a Division of Reed Elsevier (UK) Ltd, Halsbury House, 35 Chancery Lane, LONDON WC2A 1EL and 4 Hill Street, EDINBURGH EH2 3JZ
Australia	Butterworths, a Division of Reed International Books Australia Pty Ltd, CHATSWOOD, New South Wales
Canada	Butterworths Canada Ltd, MARKHAM, Ontario
Hong Kong	Butterworths Asia (Hong Kong), HONG KONG
India	Butterworths India, NEW DELHI
Ireland	Butterworth (Ireland) Ltd, DUBLIN
Malaysia	Malayan Law Journal Sdn Bhd, KUALA LUMPUR
New Zealand	Butterworths of New Zealand Ltd, WELLINGTON
Singapore	Butterworths Asia, SINGAPORE
South Africa	Butterworths Publishers (Pty) Ltd, DURBAN
USA	Lexis Law Publishing, CHARLOTTESVILLE, Virginia

© Reed Elsevier (UK) Ltd 1991
Reprinted 1993, 1994, 1995, 1996, 1999 and 2000

A CIP Catalogue record for this book is available from the British Library.

ISBN 0 406 50428 8

Typeset by Phoenix Photosetting, Chatham, Kent
Printed by Hobbs the Printers Ltd, Totton, Hampshire

Visit Butterworths LEXIS *direct* at: http://www.butterworths.com

Preface

In this book we present a series of readings which provide an introduction to some central issues in jurisprudence. We have grouped them into topics, provided a brief overview of each topic and made suggestions about further reading. We have also tried to link topics thematically to each other, and in so doing have, broadly speaking, followed a conventional view of the subject matter of jurisprudence.

Jurisprudence is the philosophy of law. Classically conceived, it has two provinces, the analytic and the normative, as John Austin the great nineteenth-century English writer on jurisprudence called them. The subject matter of the first province is, as its name suggests, the description and analysis of central legal concepts such as action, intention, responsibility, law, and a legal system. Its scope is, therefore, vast, and no book can hope to cover more than a small number of issues in this area—we shall restrict our selection of readings to ones proposing analyses of the last two concepts mentioned, those of law and of a legal system. By contrast, the second province is concerned with the discussion of normative issues, for example: should the law enforce conventional morality? What rights should a legal system recognise? Is a right action one which has better consequences than any alternative, as utilitarians maintain? And, can positive discrimination be just?

In arguing for the sharp separation of the two kinds of question Austin, following Bentham, was not simply drawing attention to what seems to be a fairly obvious distinction, but laying the groundwork for an important thesis about the nature of law itself. According to this thesis, known as legal positivism (see Chapter 1), not only should questions of analysis be sharply separated from normative ones about what ought to be, but the analysis of law itself requires no normative concepts; because this is so, the questions of what is a law and what is a legal system can be answered without any reference to what is morally desirable or right. However, acceptance of the distinction between analytic and normative questions does not itself commit one to legal positivism. One could, for instance, as does Dworkin, accept the distinction but argue that a theory of law must contain both analytic and normative elements. So we stress that our acceptance of it, and use of it as an organising principle for our selection of readings, is not intended to signal our acceptance of legal positivism—that is a thesis which must be argued for on independent grounds.

We should also make it clear that in accepting Austin's distinction between analytic and normative questions we do not want to endorse the view that these are the only kinds of question belonging to jurisprudence, so that the two provinces exhaust its domain. To accept that view would be to exclude by *fiat* those who are both critical of classical jurisprudence and its conception of its subject matter on the grounds, for instance, that in practice adjudication bears no relation to the accounts that philosophers of law have given of it, or of general scepticism about the applicability of central concepts such as those of a rule, a right, and justice. Since such grounds may be very various we have simply labelled theories which develop them 'critical' to mark their distinctiveness, and grouped selected readings from such theories together in a separate section.

So, broadly speaking, Part One is devoted to analytic theories, Part Two to normative ones, and Part Three to those that are critical. The qualification 'broadly' is, however, important; since many topics encompass both analytic and normative issues, in many cases the classification rests on a judgment about the principal source of interest in a topic. Sometimes that judgment is very finely balanced. For instance, we include a discussion of natural law in Part Two because of the distinctiveness of the normative theories that natural law theorists appeal to. But because natural law is a theory about the nature of law it is arguable that it should be included in Part One; so we have placed the readings on this topic at the beginning of Part Two so that they can be read as a transition from the predominantly analytic issues in Part One to the predominantly normative ones in Part Two.

Howard Davies
David Holdcroft

November 1990

Contents

List of extracts

Extracts from the following texts have been reproduced with the permission, where required, of the publishers concerned.

Austin	*The Lectures on Jurisprudence or the Philosophy of Positive Law* Vol I (1885) John Murray
Austin	*The Province of Jurisprudence Determined* (1954) Weidenfeld and Nicolson
Bentham	*An Introduction to the Principles of Morals and Legislation* (1823) Oxford University Press
Burrows and Veljanovski	*The Economic Approach to Law* (1981) Butterworths
Dworkin	*A Matter of Principle* (1986) Oxford University Press
Dworkin	*Law's Empire* (1986) Fontana
Dworkin	*Taking Rights Seriously* (1977) Duckworth
d'Entrèves	*Natural Law* (1970) Hutchinson & Co
Finnis	*Natural Law and Natural Rights* (1980) Oxford University Press
Finnis	*The Fundamentals of Ethics* (1983) Oxford University Press
Friedmann	*Legal Theory* (1967) Stevens and Sons
Gavison (ed)	*Issues in Contemporary Legal Philosophy* (1987) Oxford University Press
Hacker and Raz (eds)	*Law, Morality and Society, Essays in Honour of H L A Hart* (1977) Oxford University Press
Hägerström	*Inquiries into the Nature of Law and Morals* (1953) Almquist and Wiksall
Hampshire (ed)	*Public and Private Morality* (1979) Cambridge University Press
Harris	*Law and Legal Science* (1979) Oxford University Press
Hart	*Essays in Jurisprudence and Philosophy* (1983) Oxford University Press
Hart	*The Concept of Law* (1961) Oxford University Press
Hohfeld	*Fundamental Legal Conceptions as Applied in Judicial Reasoning* (1923) Yale University Press

Hume   *A Treatise of Human Nature* Book III (1874) Longmans, Green & Co

James   *Pragmatism* (1907) Longmans and Co

Kelman   *A Guide to Critical Legal Studies* (1987) Harvard University Press

Kelsen   *The Pure Theory of Law* (1967) University of California Press

Kelsen   *What is Justice?* (1957) University of California Press

Lewis (ed)   *Contemporary British Philosophy* (1976) Allen and Unwin

Llewellyn   *Jurisprudence* (1962) University of Chicago Press

Llewellyn   *My Philosophy of Law* (1941) Boston Law Co

Llewellyn   *The Common Law Tradition* (1960) Little, Brown and Company

MacCormick   *H L A Hart* (1981) Edward Arnold

MacCormick   *Legal Reasoning and Legal Theory* (1978) Oxford University Press

MacCormick   *Legal Right and Social Democracy* (1982) Oxford University Press

Martin   *The Legal Philosophy of H L A Hart: A Critical Approach* (1987) Temple University Press

Mill   *Utilitarianism, on Liberty, and Considerations on Representative Government* (1972) J M Dent & Sons

Murphy and Coleman   *The Philosophy of Law: an Introduction to Jurisprudence* (1984) Rowan & Allanheld

Nozick   *Anarchy, State and Utopia* (1974) Basil Blackwell

Olivecrona   *Law as Fact* (1971) Stevens and Sons

Paul (ed)   *Reading Nozick: Essays on Anarchy, State and Utopia* (1982) Basil Blackwell

Pettit   *Judging Justice: An Introduction to Contemporary Political Philosophy* (1980) Routledge & Kegan Paul

Polinsky   *An Introduction to Law and Economics* (1983) Little, Brown and Company

Posner   *The Economics of Justice* (1983) Harvard University Press

Rawls   *A Theory of Justice* (1972) Oxford University Press

Raz   *Practical Reason and Norms* (1975) Hutchinson & Co

Raz   *The Authority of Law* (1979) Oxford University Press

Ross   *Directives and Norms* (1968) Routledge & Kegan Paul

Ross   *On Law and Justice* (1958) Stevens and Sons

Rumble   *American Legal Realism* (1968) Cornell University Press

Further reading

Chapter 1   Legal positivism

Ago, R	'Positive Law and International Law' (1957) 51 *American Journal of International Law* 69
Detmold, M J	*The Unity of Law and Morality* (1984) Routledge & Kegan Paul
Keekok, L	*The Positivist Science of Law* (1989) Gower Publishing Group
Olivecrona, K	*Law as Fact* (2nd edn, 1971) Stevens, pp 50–62
Shuman, S I	*Legal Positivism* (1962) Wayne State University Press

Chapter 2   John Austin

Morison, W L	*John Austin* (1982) Edward Arnold
Raz, J	*Concept of a Legal System* (1970) Oxford University Press, Sections I–II
Tapper, C	'Austin on Sanctions' (1965) Cambridge University Press, p 271

Chapter 3   H L A Hart's concept of law

Hacker, P M S and Raz, J (eds)	*Law, Morality and Society, Essays in Honour of H L A Hart* (1977) Oxford University Press
Hart, H L A	*Essays in Jurisprudence and Philosophy* (1983) Oxford University Press
Leith, P and Ingram, P (eds)	*The Jurisprudence of Orthodoxy: Queen's University Essays on H L A Hart* (1988) Routledge & Kegan Paul
MacCormick, D N	*H L A Hart* (1981) Edward Arnold
Martin, M	*The Legal Philosophy of H L A Hart: A Critical Approach* (1987) Temple University Press
Moles, R N	*Definition and Rule in Legal Theory, A Reassessment of H L A Hart and the Positivist Tradition* (1987) Basil Blackwell

Chapter 7 Utilitarianism

Ayer, A J	'The Principle of Utility' in *Philosophical Essays* (1954) Macmillan
Frey, R G	*Utility and Rights* (1984) Basil Blackwell
Hare, R M	*Freedom and Reason* (1963) Oxford University Press *Moral Thinking: its Levels, Methods and Point* (1981) Oxford University Press
Harris, J W	*Legal Philosophies* (1980) Butterworths, Ch 4
Regan, D	*Utilitarianism and Cooperation* (1980) Oxford University Press
Scheffler, S	*Consequentialism and its Critics* (1988) Oxford University Press
Sen, A and Williams, B	*Utilitarianism and Beyond* (1982) Cambridge University Press
Simmonds, N E	*Central Issues in Jurisprudence* (1986) Sweet & Maxwell, Ch 1
Singer, P	*Practical Ethics* (1979) Cambridge University Press
Smart, J J C and Williams, B	*Utilitarianism: For and Against* (1973) Cambridge University Press

Chapter 8 Rights

Feinberg, J	'The Nature and Value of Rights' (1970) *Journal of Value Inquiry* 243–257
Finnis, J	*Natural Law and Natural Rights* (1980), Oxford University Press, Chs 6, 8
Frey, R G (ed)	*Utility and Rights* (1984) Basil Blackwell
Harris, J W	*Legal Philosophies* (1980) Butterworths, Ch 7
Hart, H L A	'Utilitarianism and Natural Rights' in Hart, H L A *Essays in Jurisprudence and Philosophy* (1983) Oxford University Press, pp 181–197
MacCormick, D N	'Children's Rights: A Test Case for Theories of Right' in MacCormick, D N *Legal Right and Social Democracy* (1982) Oxford University Press, pp 154–166
Martin, R and Nickel, J W	'Recent Work on the Concept of Rights' (1980) *American Philosophical Quarterly* 165–180
Murphy, J and Coleman, J	*The Philosophy of Law: An Introduction to Jurisprudence* (1984) Rowman & Allanheld, Ch 2
Simmonds, N E	*Central Issues in Jurisprudence* (1986) Sweet & Maxwell, Ch 8
Sumner, L W	*The Moral Foundation of Rights* (1987) Oxford University Press

Waldron, J   *Theories of Rights* (1984) Oxford University Press
                            The Law (1990) Routledge & Kegan Paul, Ch 5

White, A   *Rights* (1984) Oxford University Press

Chapter 9   Rawls's theory of justice

Barry, B   *The Liberal Theory of Justice* (1973) Oxford
                            University Press

Blocker, H G and   *John Rawls' Theory of Social Justice, An Introduction*
   Smith, E H   (1980) Ohio University Press

Daniels, N (ed)   *Reading Rawls* (1975) Basil Blackwell

Heath, A   *Rational Choice and Social Exchange* (1976)
                            Cambridge University Press

Kukathas, C and   *Rawls, A Theory of Justice and Its Critics* (1990)
   Pettit, P   Polity Press

Pettit, P   *Judging Justice: An Introduction to Contemporary
                            Political Philosophy* (1980) Routledge & Kegan
                            Paul, Chs 14–16

Richards, D A J   *A Theory of the Reasons for Action* (1971) Oxford
                            University Press

Sandel, M J   *Liberalism and the Limits of Justice* (1982) Cambridge
                            University Press

Wolff, R P   *Understanding Rawls: A Reconstruction and Critique of
                            a Theory of Justice* (1977) Princeton University
                            Press

Chapter 10   Dworkin's rights

Campbell, T   *Justice* (1988) Macmillan, Ch 2

Cohen, M   *Ronald Dworkin and Contemporary Jurisprudence* (1984)
                            Duckworth, Part IV

Dworkin, R   *Taking Rights Seriously* (1977) Duckworth, Chs 6–7,
                            9, 12
                            'What is Equality? Parts I & II' (1981) *Philosophy
                            and Public Affairs* 185–246, 283–345
                            A Matter of Principle (1986) Oxford University
                            Press

MacCormick, D N   'Taking the "Rights Thesis" Seriously' in
                            MacCormick, D N *Legal Right and Social Democracy*
                            (1982) Oxford University Press, pp 126–153

Mackie, J L   'Can There Be a Right-Based Moral Theory?' in
                            French, P A and Uehling Jr, T E (eds) *Studies in
                            Ethical Theory (Midwest Studies in Philosophy* Vol III)
                            (1978) University of Minnesota Press

Raz, J	'Right-Based Moralities' in Waldron, J (ed) *Theories of Rights* (1982) Oxford University Press
Sandel, M	*Liberalism and the Limits of Justice* (1982) Cambridge University Press
Simmonds, N E	*Central Issues in Jurisprudence* (1986) Sweet & Maxwell, Ch 9

Chapter 11 Nozick's theory of justice

Becker, L	*Property Rights* (1977) Routledge & Kegan Paul
von Magnus, E	'Risk, State and Nozick' in French, P et al (eds) *Midwest Studies in Philosophy* Vol VII (1982) University of Minnesota Press, pp 121–132
Paul, J (ed)	*Reading Nozick: Essays on Anarchy, State and Utopia* (1981) Rowman & Allanheld
Pettit, P	*Judging Justice: An Introduction to Contemporary Political Philosophy* (1980) Routledge & Kegan Paul, Chs 8–10
Simmonds, N E	*Central Issues in Jurisprudence* (1986) Sweet & Maxwell, Ch 3

Chapter 12 Dworkin and the interpretive theory of law

Articles on *Law's Empire* in *Law and Philosophy* Vol 6, 283–438 (1987) (by Gerald Postema, David Hoy, John Finnis, Charles Silver, Stanley Fish and Larry Alexander)

Beyleveld, D and Brownsword, R	'Practice Made Perfect' (1987) 50 Modern Law Review 662
Donato, J	'Dworkin and Subjectivity in Legal Interpretation' (1988) 40 Stanford Law Review 1517
Hutchinson, A C	'Indiana Dworkin and Law's Empire' (1987) 96 Yale Law Journal 637
Levenbrook, B B	'The Sustained Dworkin' (1986) 53 *The University of Chicago Law Review* 1108
Raz, J	'Dworkin: A New Link in the Chain' (1986) *California Law Review* 1103
Schauer, F	'Jurisprudence of Reason' (1987) 85 *Michigan Law Review* 847
Soper, P	'Dworkin's Domain' (1987) 100 *Harvard Law Review* 1166

Chapter 13 The economic theory of law

Ackerman, B	*The Economic Foundation of Property Law* (1975) Little, Brown and Company

Burrows, P and Veljanovski, C G (eds)	*The Economic Approach to Law* (1981) Butterworths
Coase, R	'The Problem of Social Cost' (1960) *Journal of Law and Economics* 1, 1–13
Dworkin, R	*A Matter of Principle* (1986) Oxford University Press, Chs 12–13 *Law's Empire* (1986) Fontana, Ch 8
Klevoric, A	'The Economics of Crime' in Pennock, J R and Chapman, J W (eds) *Nomos XXVII* (1984) New York University Press
Murphy, J and Coleman, J	*The Philosophy of Law: An Introduction to Jurisprudence* (1984) Rowan & Allanheld, Ch 5 (This is based on Coleman's paper in *Ethics*, July 1984)
Ogus, A I and Veljanovski, C G (eds)	*Readings in the Economics of Law and Regulation* (1984) Oxford University Press
Polinsky, A M	*An Introduction to Law and Economics* (1983) Little, Brown and Company
Posner, R	*The Economic Analysis of Law* (1963) Little, Brown and Company 'The Economic Approach to Law' (1975) 53 *Texas Law Review*

Chapter 14   Scandinavian legal realism

Lauridsen, P S	'On the Fundamental Problem in the Legal Theory of Prediction' (1976) 20 *Scandinavian Studies in Law* 179
MacCormack, G	'Haegerstroem's Magical Interpretation of Roman Law' (1969) 4 *Irish Jurist* 153 'Scandinavian Realism' (1970) *Judicial Review* 33
Passmore, J	'Hägerström's Philosophy of Law' (1961) 36 *Philosophy* 143
Simmonds, N E	'The Legal Philosophy of Axel Hägerström' (1976) *Juridical Review* 210

Chapter 15   American legal realism

Ackerman, B	*Reconstructing American Law* (1984) Harvard University Press
Rumble, W E	*American Legal Realism: Scepticism, Reform and the Judicial Process* (1968) Cornell University Press
Summers, R	*Instrumentalism and American Legal Theory* (1982) Cornell University Press
Twining, W	*Karl Llewellyn and the Realist Movement* (1985) Weidenfeld and Nicolson

Yntema, H E   'American Legal Realism in Retrospect' (1960–61) 14 *Vanderbilt Law Review* 317

Chapter 16   Critical legal studies

Journal of Law and Society Vols 14, 15

Kairys, D (ed)   *The Politics of Law* (1982) Pantheon

Kelman, M   *A Guide to Critical Legal Studies* (1987) Harvard University Press

Symposia   36 *Stanford Law Review* (1984)
                                   52 *George Washington Law Review* 239 (1984)
                                   34 *American University Law Review* 939 (1985)

Twining, W (ed)   *Legal Theory and Common Law* (1986) Basil Blackwell

Part One
Analytical Jurisprudence

Chapter 1

Legal positivism

THE NATURE OF LEGAL POSITIVISM

(a) Hart's five contentions

As representatives of legal positivism, we shall mainly be concerned with the ideas of John Austin, H L A Hart, Hans Kelsen, and Joseph Raz. The expression 'legal positivism' has been used in a number of ways and H L A Hart usefully differentiates several possible tenets of legal positivism.

> It may help to identify five (there may be more) meanings of 'positivism' bandied about in contemporary jurisprudence:
> (1) the contention that laws are commands of human beings;
> (2) the contention that there is no necessary connection between law and morals or law as it is and law as it ought to be;
> (3) the contention that the analysis (or study of the meaning) of legal concepts is (a) worth pursuing and (b) to be distinguished from historical inquiries into the causes or origins of laws, from sociological inquiries into the relation of law and other social phenomena, and from the criticism or appraisal of law whether in terms of morals, social aims, 'functions', or otherwise;
> (4) the contention that a legal system is a 'closed logical system' in which correct legal decisions can be deduced by logical means from predetermined rules without reference to social aims, policies, moral standards; and
> (5) the contention that moral judgments cannot be established or defended, as statements of fact can, by rational argument, evidence, or proof ('noncognitivism' in ethics).
>
> Hart *Essays in Jurisprudence and Philosophy* 57–58

Hart goes on to claim that Austin held the views expressed in (1), (2), and (3) but not those in (4) and (5); Kelsen held those in (2), (3), and (5) but not those in (1) and (4). As for Hart himself? We shall see in due course.

On the first contention, it is Austin's theory of positivism that asserts that law is a species of command and that no law can exist unless it is 'posited', that is deliberately laid down, by some human being. It will be seen that Hart does not accept the contention that all law neatly fits into this command model. His theory of legal rules as a species of social rules (infra pp 34ff) is far more sophisticated than the Austinian command theory. It is suggested that the first contention ought to be recast in the style of Raz's 'sources thesis' (infra pp 6ff).

It is the second contention that represents the quintessence of legal positivism. The separation of law and morals, the so-called 'Separation Thesis', is the defining characteristic of the positivist as is witnessed in the following extracts.

. . . general jurisprudence, or the philosophy of positive law, is concerned with law as it necessarily *is*, rather than with the law as it *ought* to be; with law as it must be, *be it good or bad*, rather than with the law as it must be, *if it be good*.

Austin *The Lectures on Jurisprudence or the Philosophy of Positive Law* Vol 1, 33

The existence of law is one thing; its merit or demerit is another.

Austin *The Province of Jurisprudence Determined* 184

[My theory is] . . . a theory of positive law . . . The theory attempts to answer the question what, and how the law *is*, and not how it ought to be. It is a science of law . . . and not legal politics.

It is called a 'pure' theory of law, because it only describes the law and attempts to eliminate from the object of this description everything that is not strictly law. Its aim is to free the science of law from alien elements.

Kelsen *Pure Theory of Law* 1

Here we shall take Legal Positivism to mean the simple contention that it is in no sense a necessary truth that laws reproduce or satisfy certain demands of morality, though in fact they have often done so.

Hart *The Concept of Law* 181–182

A jurisprudential theory is acceptable only if its tests for identifying the content of the law and determining its existence depend exclusively on the facts of human behaviour capable of being described in value-neutral terms, and applied without resort to moral argument.

Raz *The Authority of Law* 39–40

So positivism stands against blurring the distinction between law as it is and law as it ought to be: it does not follow from the mere fact that a rule violates certain standards of morality that it is not a rule of law. An iniquitous, unjust law remains a valid law. Moral evaluation is to play no role in the description of what law or a legal system is.

Note the claim is more modest than it is sometimes represented: the claim is that there is no 'necessary' connection between law and morality, thereby allowing for the conclusion that often law will, in fact, coincide with morality. However, this similarity would be through the workings of coincidence and not through the dictates of logical necessity. Again the claim is not that issues of morality and justice are comprehensively redundant and worthless. They can be described as such when the discussion centres on 'what is law?' But questions of morality and justice clearly have a role to play when discussing whether a law, correctly described as being valid, is or is not a good or just law. Consequently, positivism can be conceived of as a plea for keeping two questions separate: 'what is law?', a descriptive issue to be answered without recourse to any normative theories of justice or morality, and 'what ought the content of law to be?', a normative issue obviously raising issues of justice and morality.

It is this, Hart's second contention of positivism, that enshrines the fundamental break with the natural law tradition, the tradition that denies the 'Separation Thesis'. The natural lawyer is usually represented as posing not two questions but only one. In asking the question 'what is law?', one must look at the content of the law and any law that offends against a code of morality or a theory of justice is not a valid law but an aberration; like counterfeit currency it looks like the real thing but in reality it is not. So what is law is irretrievably involved with questions of justice and, hence, an unjust law is not a valid law. Whether this is an accurate representation of the natural law tradition will be questioned by John Finnis (infra pp 151–152, 198–200), but, in the meantime, we can treat this almost traditional representation of natural law as characteristic rather than caricature.

The third and fourth tenets of positivism identified by Hart require little dicussion. The third follows from the second, the separation of law and morals. The fourth contention, the view that a legal system is a closed logical system is often ascribed to legal positivism, but usually as a straw argument. Hart can find no good cause for this ascription.

The fifth contention represents an important qualification to the Separation Thesis of the second contention. A theory of ethics called value-noncognitivism argues for the thesis that basic ethical principles have no cognitive status. That is, moral propositions or statements about justice or injustice cannot be *known* to be either true or false; such statements are neither true nor false because they do not affirm or deny that something is the case. Hence a sentence of the type: 'doing a certain thing is morally right, good, just, etc,' makes no statement at all, because terms such as good or just designate no actual property which an activity may either have or lack. It follows that if ethical terms have no cognitive meaning no objective answer can be given to the question 'what is a just law?' The following extract from the work of Alf Ross (a Scandinavian Realist, on which see infra Chapter 14), provides a vivid illustration of value-noncognitivism.

> To invoke justice is the same thing as banging on the table: an emotional expression which turns one's demand into an absolute postulate. That is no way to mutual understanding. It is impossible to have a rational discussion with a man who mobilises 'justice', because he says nothing that can be argued for or against. His words are persuasions, not argument . . . The ideology of justice leads to implacability and conflict, since on the one hand it incites to the belief that one's demand is not merely the expression of a certain interest in conflict with opposing interests, but that it possesses a higher, absolute validity; and on the other hand it precludes all rational argument and discussion of a settlement. The ideology of justice is a militant attitude of a biological-emotional kind, to which one incites oneself for the implacable and blind defence of certain interests.

> Ross *On Law and Justice* 274–275

> Justice, therefore, cannot be a legal-political yardstick or an ultimate criterion by which a law can be judged. To assert that a law is unjust is, as we have seen, nothing but an emotional expression of an unfavourable reaction to the law. To declare a law unjust contains no real characteristic, no reference to any criterion, no argumentation. The ideology of justice has thus no place in a reasonable discussion of the value of laws.

> Ross *On Law and Justice* 280

Compare the sentiments expressed so trenchantly by Ross with Hans Kelsen's discussion of natural law (infra pp 149–151). Now to what extent must a legal positivist be committed to value-noncognitivism? Not at all. As was stressed when considering the Separation Thesis, positivism does not necessarily deny the importance of morality or justice, it merely stipulates that such matters are not relevant when considering what law is. Consequently, it is quite conceivable to be a legal positivist and yet to argue for objectively verifiable standards of morality or theories of justice when considering what law ought to be. Legal positivism does not logically entail value-noncognitivism. Therefore Austin, unquestionably a legal positivist, had a strong commitment to utilitarianism as an objective theory of ethics, when he reverted to the question of what is a just law; likewise, Hart allows a 'minimum content of natural law' when he moves from the discussion of what law is to the consideration of what law ought to be.

However, there is an extreme wing of the legal positivist approach where noncognitivism is an adjunct to positivism. Hans Kelsen fits the extremist bill.

... In its proper meaning, as distinct from that which it has in law, 'justice' connotes an absolute value. Its content cannot be ascertained by the Pure Theory of Law. Indeed it is not ascertainable by rational knowledge at all. The history of human speculation for centuries has been the history of a vain striving after a solution of the problem. That striving has hitherto led only to the emptiest of tautologies, such as the formula suum cuique or the categorical imperative. From the standpoint of rational knowledge there are only interests and conflicts of interests, the solution of which is arrived at by an arrangement which may either satisfy the one interest at the expense of the other, or institute an equivalence or compromise between them. To determine, however, whether this or that order has an absolute value, that is, is 'just', is not possible by the methods of rational knowledge. Justice is an irrational ideal. However indispensable it may be for the willing and acting of human beings it is not viable by reason. Only positive law is known, or more correctly revealed, to reason.
... The Pure Theory of Law retains its anti-ideological tendency by its attempt to isolate the positive law from every kind of natural law-justice ideology. The possibility of valid order superior to positive law it considers outside its sphere of discussion. It confines its attention to the positive law, and prevents the science of law giving itself out as a higher order or from deriving a justification from such an order; or it prevents the discrepancy between such a presupposed ideal of justice and the positive law from being misused as a juristic argument against the validity of the latter. The Pure Theory of Law is the theory of legal positivism.

Kelsen 50 LQR 482 (1934–1935)

The position, then, seems to be that although legal positivism can be conjoined with value-noncognitivism it is not a necessary conjunction.

(b) Raz and the sources thesis

In the extracts which follow Raz locates the essence of legal positivism in what he calls the 'social thesis'. He then proceeds to isolate and defend a 'strong' variant of this thesis. This is the 'sources thesis'. Essentially this thesis insists that both the existence and the content of every law is fully determined by social sources.

The perennial and inexhaustible nature of the controversy concerning the positivist analysis of the law is due in no small measure to the elusive meaning of 'positivism' in legal philosophy. True, it is well established that legal positivism is essentially independent (even though not historically unrelated) both of the positivism of nineteenth-century philosophy and of the logical positivism of the present century. But the great variation between different positivist theories of law and the large variety of philosophical motivations permeating the work of the non-positivists indicate the difficulty, perhaps the impossibility, of identifying legal positivism at its source—in a fundamental positivist philosophical outlook. The easiest approach to the continuing controversy concerning legal positivism is through the particular theses or groups of theses round which it revolves.

Three areas of dispute have been at the centre of the controversy: the identification of the law, its moral value, and the meaning of its key terms. We could identify these as the social thesis, the moral thesis, and the semantic thesis respectively. It should be understood, however, that in each area positivists (and their opponents) are identified by supporting (or rejecting) one or more of a whole group of related theses rather than any particular thesis.

In the most general terms the positivist social thesis is that what is law and what is not is a matter of social fact (that is, the variety of social theses supported by positivists are various refinements and elaborations of this crude formulation). Their moral thesis is that the moral value of law (both of a particular law and of a whole legal system) or the moral merit it has is a contingent matter dependent on the content of the law and the circumstances of the society to which it applies. The only semantic thesis which can be identified as common to most positivist theories is a negative one, namely, that terms like 'rights' and 'duties' cannot be used in the same meaning in legal and moral contexts.

Of these the social thesis is the more fundamental. It is also responsible for the name 'positivism' which indicates the view that the law is posited, is made law by the activities of human beings.

Raz The Authority of Law 37–38

So it is the social thesis and not the moral or semantic theses that constitutes the 'backbone' of the version of positivism which Raz sets out to defend. He continues with a detailed analysis of the social thesis.

The (Strong) Social Thesis. A jurisprudential theory is acceptable only if its test for identifying the content of the law and determining its existence depend exclusively on facts of human behaviour capable of being described in value-neutral terms, and applied without resort to moral argument.

Raz The Authority of Law 39–40

To clarify this he makes several points.

First, the thesis assumes that any complete theory of law includes tests for the identification of the content and determination of the existence of the law . . .

Secondly, the thesis assumes that there is a sufficiently rich vocabulary of value-neutral terms. It does not assume that there is a clear and sharp break between value-laden and value-free terms. Nor is it committed to any side in the naturalist/anti-naturalist dispute. That the test is capable of being described in value-neutral terms does not mean that no value or deontic conclusions are entailed by it. To assert that is to take an anti-naturalist position.

Thirdly, the thesis does not require disregarding the intentions, motivations, and moral views of people. Value-neutrality does not commit one to behaviourism.

Finally, it is worth noting that the social thesis can be divided into to: *A*—A social condition is necessary for identifying the existence and content of the law: A rule is a legal rule only if it meets a social condition. *B*—A social condition is sufficient for identifying the existence and content of the law: A rule is a legal rule if it meets the social condition.

Raz *The Authority of Law* 40

What argument is given for the social thesis?

. . . the main justification of the social thesis lies in the character of law as a social institution. Some social institutions may have to be understood in ways which are incompatible with an analogous social thesis applied to them. But the law, like several others, is an institution conforming to the social thesis. To see this, it is necessary to specify in a general way the main ingredients of the tests for existence and identity for a legal system and to identify those with which the social thesis is concerned. The tests for identity and existence of a legal system contain three basic elements: efficacy, institutional character, and sources.

Efficacy is the least controversial of these conditions . . . suffice it that all agree that a legal system is not the law in force in a certain community unless it is generally adhered to and is accepted or internalized by at least certain sections of the population. This condition is simply designed to assure that the law referred to is the actual law of a given society and not a defunct system or an aspiring one. It is the least important of the conditions. It is not disputed by natural lawyers . . .

More important and also more controversial is the second component of the tests for existence and identity—the institutionalized character of the law. Again, the many controversies about the precise nature of the institutional aspect of law can be side-stepped here. It is widely agreed (and by many natural lawyers as well) that a system of norms is not a legal system unless it sets up adjudicative institutions charged with regulating disputes arising out of the application of the norms of the system. It is also generally agreed that such a normative system is a legal system only if it claims to be authoritative and to occupy a position of supremacy within society, ie it claims the right to legitimize or outlaw all other social institutions.

These institutionalized aspects of law identify its character as a social type, as a kind of social institution. Put in a nutshell, it is a system of guidance and adjudication claiming supreme authority within a certain society and therefore, where efficacious, also enjoying such effective authority.

Raz *The Authority of Law* 42–44

He proceeds to discuss the social thesis in the light of natural law philosophy.

Many natural law theories are compatible with all that was said above concerning the institutional nature of law. Yet it must be pointed out that such an institutionalized conception of law is incompatible with certain natural law positions; and this for two reasons. In the first place, it is a consequence of the institutionalized character of the law that it has limits. Legal systems contain only those standards which are connected in certain ways with the operation of the relevant adjudicative institutions. This is what its institutionalized character means. Hence the law has limits: it does not contain all the justifiable standards (moral or other) nor does it necessarily comprise all social rules and conventions. It comprises only a subset of these, only those standards having the proper institutional connection. This is incompatible with the view that law does not form a separate system of standards and especially with the claim that there is no difference between law and morality or between it and social morality.

A second and perhaps more radical consequence of the conception of law as an institutional system is that one cannot impose moral qualifications as conditions for a system or a rule counting as legal which are not reflected also in its institutional features. If law is a social institution of a certain type, then all the rules which belong to the social type are legal rules, however morally objectionable they may be. Law may have necessary moral properties, but if so, then only on the ground that all or some of the rules having the required institutional connections necessarily have moral properties. To impose independent moral conditions on the identity of law will inevitably mean either that not all the rules forming a part of the social institution of the relevant type are law or that some rules which are not part of such institutions are law. Either way 'law' will no longer designate a social institution.

Raz *The Authority of Law* 44–45

At this point he introduces the distinction between a weak and a strong social thesis; it is a commitment to the latter that becomes crucial for the legal positivist.

Most positivists are ambiguous concerning one interesting point. While their general terms suggest an endorsement of the strong social thesis, their actual doctrines rest on efficacy and institutionality as the only conditions concerning the social foundation of the law. Let the combination of these two conditions be called the weak social thesis. It is easy to show that the weak and the strong theses are not equivalent. Suppose that the law requires that unregulated disputes (ie those with respect to which the law is unsettled) be determined on the basis of moral considerations (or a certain subclass of them, such as considerations of justice or moral considerations not fundamentally at odds with social morality). Suppose further that it is argued that in virtue of this law moral considerations have become part of the law of the land (and hence the law is never unsettled unless morality is). This contention runs directly counter to the strong thesis. If it is accepted, the determination of what is the law in certain cases turns on moral considerations, since one has to resort to moral arguments to identify the law. To conform to the strong thesis we will have to say that while the rule referring to morality is indeed law (it is determined by its sources) the morality to which it refers is not thereby incorporated into law. The rule is analogous to a 'conflict of law' rule imposing a duty to apply a foreign system which remains independent of and outside the municipal law.

While all this is clear enough, it is equally clear that the contrary view (according to which morality becomes part of the law as a consequence of the referring law) does not offend against the requirement of efficacy. For here too the bulk of the legal system may be conformed to. Nor is this view inconsistent with the institutional aspect of law: morality becomes law, on this view, by being tied to the relevant institutions. Finally, the allegation that morality can be thus incorporated into law is consistent with the thesis of the limits of law, for it merely asserts that source-based laws may from time to time incorporate parts of morality into law while imposing perhaps various conditions on their applicability. Having said that I should add that the result of admitting the view under consideration is that some non-source-based moral principles are part of almost every legal system, since most legal systems require judges to apply moral considerations on various occasions.

The difference between the weak and the strong social theses is that the strong one insists, whereas the weak one does not, that the existence and content of every law is fully determined by social sources. On the other hand, the weak thesis, but not the strong one, builds into the law the conditions of efficacy and institutionality. The two theses are logically independent. The weak thesis though true is insufficient to characterize legal positivism. It is compatible with—

a) sometimes the identification of some laws turns on moral arguments,

but also with—

b) in all legal systems the identification of some laws turns on moral argument.

The first view is on the borderline of positivism and may or may not be thought consistent with it. But whereas the first view depends on the contingent existence of source-based law making moral considerations into the criteria of validity in certain cases (as in the example above), the second view asserts a conceptual necessity of testing law by moral argument and is clearly on the natural law side of the historical positivist/natural law divide.

I will argue for the truth of the strong social thesis (thus excluding both (a) and (b)). I shall rename the strong social thesis 'the sources thesis'. A 'source' is here used in a somewhat technical sense (which is, however, clearly related to traditional writings on legal sources). A law has a source if its contents and existence can be determined without using moral arguments (but allowing for arguments about people's moral views and intentions, which are necessary for interpretation, for example). The sources of a law are those facts by virtue of which it is valid and which identify its content. This sense of 'source' is wider than that of 'formal sources' which are those establishing the validity of a law (one or more Acts of Parliament together with one or more precedents may be the formal source of one rule of law). 'Source' as used here includes also 'interpretative sources', namely all the relevant interpretative materials. The sources of a law thus understood are never a single Act (of legislation, etc) alone, but a whole range of facts of a variety of kinds.

Raz *The Authority of Law* 45–48

Raz offers two reasons for accepting the sources thesis. First, it reflects and explicates our conceptions of the law in that it explains and systematizes a cluster of 'distinctions' that are conventionally taken for granted. The sources thesis best fits these distinctions of ours. There are three sets of distinctions.

When discussing appointments to the Bench, we distinguish different kinds of desirable characteristics judges should possess. We value their knowledge of the law and their skills in interpreting laws and in arguing in ways showing their legal experience and expertise. We also value their wisdom and understanding of human nature, their moral sensibility, their enlightened approach, etc. There are many other characteristics which are valuable in judges. For present purposes these two kinds are the important ones. The point is that while it is generally admitted that both are very important for judges as judges, only the first group of characteristics mentioned is thought of as establishing the legal skills of the judge. The second group, though relevant to his role as a judge, is thought of as reflecting his moral character, not his legal ability. Similarly, when evaluating judgments as good or bad, lawyers and informed laymen are used to distinguishing between assessing judicial arguments as legally acceptable or unacceptable and assessing them as morally good or bad. Of many legal decisions we hear that they are legally defective, being based on a misinterpretation of a statute or a case, etc. Of others it is said that though legally the decisions are acceptable, they betray gross insensitivity to current social conditions, show how conservative judges are, that they are against trade unions, or that in their zeal to protect individuals they go too far in sacrificing administrative efficiency, etc.

These distinctions presuppose that judges are, at least on occasion, called upon to rely on arguments revealing their moral character rather than their legal ability. (It is unreasonable to suppose that the judge's moral character reveals itself only when he is wrong in law. It affects decisions too often for that to be a reasonable hypothesis.) As indicated above, the use of moral judgment is regarded not as a special case of applying law or legal arguments, but is contrasted with them. This is manifested in the way the two kinds of tests evaluating judges and judgments are related to two further distinctions. The first is that between applying the law and creating, innovating, or developing the law. It is a common view that judges both apply the law and develop it. And though their two functions are extremely hard to disentangle in many cases, yet sometimes, at least, it is clear of a case that it breaks new ground, while of many others it may be equally clear that they merely apply established law. The important point is that it is our normal view that judges use moral arguments (though perhaps not only such arguments) when developing the law and that they use legal skills when applying the law (though not only legal skills are used when they have to decide whether to apply a precedent or distinguish or overrule it . . .).

Finally, there is the distinction between settled and unsettled law. All lawyers know that on some questions the law is unsettled. Sometimes they say on such cases that no one knows what the law is—as if there is law on the question which is very difficult to discover. But most of the time they express themselves more accurately, saying that this is an open question, that the law is unsettled, etc . . . It is primarily in deciding cases regarding which the law is unsettled (as well as in distinguishing and reversing settled law) that judges are thought to develop the law using moral, social, and other non-legal arguments. It is when deciding cases where the law is settled that the judges are thought of as using their legal skills in applying the law.

Raz The Authority of Law 48–49

His conclusion to the first reason for accepting the sources thesis is the following observation.

The sources thesis explains and systemizes these distinctions. According to it, the law on a question is settled when legally binding sources provide its solution. In such cases judges are typically said to apply the law, and since it is source-based, its application involves technical, legal skills in reasoning from those sources and does not call for moral acumen. If a legal question is not answered by standards deriving from legal sources then it lacks a legal answer—the law on the question is unsettled. In deciding such cases courts inevitably break new (legal) ground and their decision develops the law (at least in precedent-based legal systems). Naturally their decisions in such cases rely at least partly on moral and other extra-legal considerations.

Raz *The Authority of Law* 49–50

Secondly, not only does the sources thesis mirror and explain these distinctions, it also captures a fundamental insight into the function of law.

If the first argument for the sources thesis was that it reflects and systemizes several interconnected distinctions embedded in our conception of the law, the second argument probes deeper and shows that the distinctions and the sources thesis which explicates them help to identify a basic underlying function of the law: to provide publicly ascertainable standards by which members of the society are held to be bound so that they cannot excuse non-conformity by challenging the justification of the standard. (Though of course, in many countries they are free to act to change it.) This is the reason for which we differentiate between the courts' applying the law, ie those standards which are publicly ascertainable and binding beyond a moral argument open to the litigants, and the activity of the courts in developing the law relying on moral and other rational considerations. In making this a test for the identification of law, the sources thesis identifies it as an example of a kind of human institution which is of decisive importance to the regulation of social life.

Raz *The Authority of Law* 52

To prevent misunderstanding let me elaborate some of the crucial steps in the argument. Many societies (large or small) have a relatively formal way of distinguishing between expressions of views, demands, etc, and authoritative rulings. Such a distinction is an essential element in our conception of government, be it in a family, in a loosely organized community, or in the state. Not all authoritative rulings are laws, not all systems of such rules are legal systems. But marking a rule as legally binding is marking it as an authoritative ruling. This marking-off of authoritative rulings indicates the existence in that society of an institution or organization claiming authority over members of the society that is holding them bound to conform to certain standards just because they were singled out by that purported authority regardless of whether or not they are justifiable standards on other grounds. Since it is of the very essence of the alleged authority that it issues rulings which are binding regardless of any other justification, it follows that it must be possible to identify those rulings without engaging in a justificatory argument, ie as issuing from certain activities and interpreted in the light of publicly ascertainable standards not involving moral argument.

Raz *The Authority of Law* 51–52

Raz insists that his version of positivism is a moderate one. To understand this it is necessary to go back to the beginning of his exposition when he discussed what he called the 'moral thesis' as a feature of positivism. Is the moral thesis, as defined by Raz, necessitated by his social thesis? If what is law is solely a matter of social fact does it not follow that conformity to moral values is not necessary and is in no way a condition for the existence of law? Therefore, it would seem, the moral thesis argues that the moral merit of the law depends on contingent factors. However, this is not his argument.

> The claim that what is law and what is not is purely a matter of social fact still leaves it an open question whether or not these social facts by which we identify the law or determine its existence do or do not endow it with moral merit. If they do, it is of necessity a moral character. But even if they do not, it is still an open question whether, given human nature and the general conditions of human existence, every legal system which is in fact the effective law of some society does of necessity conform to some moral values and ideals . . . I mention [this] only to indicate the extent to which the version of positivism that will be argued for here is a moderate one which need not conflict with the natural lawyer's view concerning . . . the relation between law and morality.
>
> Raz *The Authority of Law* 38–39

(c) A problem for legal positivism and Raz's detached legal statements

The problem: within the legal system there must be value-judgments. If a positivist theory gives only a descriptive account of what legal systems actually are, descriptions of tests for identifying the content of law which depend exclusively on facts of human behaviour described in value-neutral terms, how can this have any reference to 'justification'? How does the positivist explain statements about what ought to be done according to the law? If one says X has a legal duty to pay a debt, does not this statement collapse into the assertion that a *moral duty* to pay the debt exists?

There is no doubt that Raz (and Kelsen but not Hart) would contend that to say that a rule is valid is to say that it ought to be obeyed; to say it is valid is to say that it has the normative consequences that the rule contains (eg to pay the debt). So, it would appear that the positivist in identifying and stating what the law is on a particular matter is simultaneously endorsing its moral merit. If so, a major problem for positivism has arisen; the positivists' search for a value-neutral model of a legal system seems doomed.

The answer is found in Raz's analysis of 'statements from a point of view'—detached legal statements.

> A detached legal statement is a statement of law, of what legal rights or duties people have, not a statement about people's beliefs, attitudes, or actions, not even about their beliefs, attitudes, or actions about the law. Yet a detached normative statement does not carry the full normative force of an ordinary normative statement. Its utterance does not commit the speaker to the normative view it expresses. Lawyers' advice to their clients, law teachers' expositions in front of their students often belong to this category. I am not implying that lawyers or law teachers do not believe in the validity (ie justification) of the law with which they deal, only that often they do not commit themselves to such beliefs when acting in their professional capacity . . . [the existence of detached normative statements] shows that normative language can be used without a full normative commitment or force.
>
> Raz *The Authority of Law* 153–154

The lawyer or the teacher, or any theorist observing the legal system, is making a statement about what the law is on an issue without thereby committing himself to the values of that system. He is saying that, from the point of view of those within the system, a particular decision ought to be given, that it is justified. He is not necessarily commending or justifying the decision himself.

Two examples of statements from a point of view.

> If I go with a vegetarian friend to a dinner party I may say to him, 'You should not eat this dish. It contains meat.' Not being a vegetarian I do not believe that the fact that the dish contains meat is a reason for not eating it. I do not, therefore, believe that my friend has a reason to refrain from eating it, nor am I stating that he has. I am merely informing him what ought to be done from the point of view of a vegetarian. Of course the very same sentence can be used by a fellow vegetarian to state what ought to be done. But this is not what I am saying, as my friend who understands the situation will know.

Raz Practical Reason and Norms 175–176

> When giving legal advice a solicitor or any other person is stating what is the case from the legal point of view. He may do so because he believes that the man he is advising endorses this point of view completely or in part. But sometimes he makes no such assumption. He may know that the man he is advising is not law-abiding, that his interest is merely to find what view the police or the courts are bound to take of his behaviour. A law lecturer or a legal writer normally does the same. He states what is the case from the legal point of view without normally making any specific assumptions about the reasons which may make his audience interested in his lecture or book—they may just be interested in the information (in order to pass any examination or for any one of a variety of reasons).
>
> A barrister arguing a case before a court may do no more. He may simply state what is the case according to law in the knowledge that the judges hold themselves bound to act according to law. Naturally a barrister, a solicitor, a lecturer or any other person talking about the law may . . . state what reasons there are on account of the law. But it is important to see that they may not do this. They merely state what ought to be done according to the law.

Raz Practical Reason and Norms 176–177

The answer to the positivist's problem is evident: detached, normative statements are permissible without any commitment to normativity in a moral sense. Because a certain rule is valid (let us say, on the basis of the sources thesis) a particular decision *ought* to be given and is justified. But this conclusion does not presuppose that the law on the matter is moral. In contrast one of the key contentions of the natural law approach is that the law is essentially moral.

The importance of this detached type of statement is underlined in what follows. (Finnis's criticism of Raz's statements from a point of view and of Hart's internal point of view is considered infra pp 52ff.)

> If indeed statements from a point of view are a distinct type of statement then our view of the traditional controversy between natural lawyers and positivists is radically transformed. The main strength of the positivist's position is in its insistence that law is essentially a form of social organization. The main contention of the natural lawyer is that law is essentially moral. These

formulations suggest that the two positions are not necessarily mutually exclusive. The law may have more than one essential property. There is no denying, however, that many of the proposed natural law theories are incompatible with positivism. This impression of mutual incompatibility is enhanced by two semantic theses which are generally endorsed by natural lawyers: first, that normative terms like 'a right', 'a duty', 'ought' are used in the same sense in legal, moral, and other normative statements. For example, when one states 'It is John's legal duty to repay the debt' one is asserting that John has a (moral) duty to repay the debt arising out of the law.

Positivists reject the second semantic thesis. Even if the law is essentially moral—the cautious positivist would argue—it is clear that establishing the moral merit of a law is a different process relying on different considerations, from establishing its existence as a social fact. To the positivist the identification of the law and of the duties and rights it gives rise to is a matter of social fact. The question of its value is a further and separate question. Since one may know what the law is without knowing if it is justified, there must be a possibility of making legal statements not involving commitment to its justification. The positivist need not deny that many legal statements do carry such a commitment. First, it is admitted that whether or not the law is in fact justified, if it is in force it is held to be so by some of its subjects, and they are ready to make fully committed statements. Secondly, the law—unlike the threats of the highwayman—claims to itself legitimacy. The law presents itself as justified and demands not only the obedience but the allegiance of its subjects. The positivist need not deny that the primary kind of legal statement is the committed statement—Hart's internal statement—but he would want to allow, as we observed, for the possibility of non-committed detached statements, ie ones which though not committed are nevertheless normative. Thus the positivist is bound to reject the natural lawyer's second semantic thesis.

It may well be thought that this entails the rejection of the first thesis as well. For, if normative terms are regularly used in their ordinary sense in legal contexts, are not the statements made by their use, always committed statements? But in fact my very arguments so far show that the first semantic thesis is not essentially a natural lawyer's thesis. It is one that positivists can and should adopt, for only through it and the doctrine of statements from a point of view can we understand the possibility of detached statements which are all the same normative and not merely statements about other people's actions or beliefs, etc. Admittedly, statements from a point of view are parasitic on the full-blooded normative statements. That is, there is normally no point in making statements from a point of view unless in relation to a society in which people are often ready to make the full-blooded statements. If there is nobody whose point of view it is, why should we be interested in it? This shows how the natural lawyer's second thesis is modified rather than rejected outright. If this is another pointer that the gulf between natural lawyers and positivists need not be as unbridgeable as is sometimes imagined, then it is welcome for this reason as well.

Raz *The Authority of Law* 157–159

Chapter 2
John Austin

John Austin (1790–1859) is probably the most influential English legal positivist. In 1832 he published *The Province of Jurisprudence Determined* as an expanded version of the first part of the lectures that he had delivered at University College, London. The first complete edition of *The Lectures on Jurisprudence or the Philosophy of Positive Law*, reconstructed from his notes by his wife, was published after his death in 1863.

AUSTIN THE LEGAL POSITIVIST

Austin's credentials as a positivist have already been stressed (supra p 3). His aim is to distinguish law from other phenomena, in particular from rules of morality. For him clarity of thought about the nature of law requires a strict, watertight demarcation of the subject matter of jurisprudence. He begins his lectures thus:

> The matter of jurisprudence is positive law: law, simply and strictly so-called: or law set by political superiors to political inferiors.
>
> Austin *The Province of Jurisprudence Determined* 9

A law in its most comprehensive and literal sense is described as being a rule laid down for the guidance of an intelligent being by an intelligent being having power over him. Ignoring the fact that the word 'law' can have an extended meaning either by analogy or by metaphor, the above description of law falls into two categories: laws set by God to his human creatures and laws set by men to men. Some of the latter are established by *political* superiors.

> The aggregate of the rules thus established, or some aggregate forming a portion of that aggregate, is the appropriate matter of jurisprudence, general or particular. To the aggregate of the rules thus established, or to some aggregate forming a portion of that aggregate, the term *law*, as used simply and strictly, is exclusively applied. But, as contradistinguished to *natural* law, or to the law of *nature* (meaning, by those expressions, the law of God), the aggregate of the rules, established by the political superiors, is frequently styled *positive* law, or law existing *by position*. As contradistinguished to the rules which I style *positive morality* . . ., the aggregate of the rules, established by political superiors, may also be marked commodiously with the name of *positive law*.
>
> Austin *The Province of Jurisprudence Determined* 11

Positive law, then, is separate and distinct from the laws of God, from moral imperatives, and from any natural law philosophy. Although in the last extract he seems to characterize natural law by reference to God, clearly his aim is to distinguish positive law from morality in a wider sense. The existence of a valid, positive law is not dependent upon the goodness, the morality or the justice of its content.

AUSTIN'S SOURCES THESIS

Can it be said that Austin's tests for identifying the content of the law and determining its existence depend exclusively on facts of human behaviour capable of being described in value-neutral terms, and applied without resort to moral argument? (See Raz and the sources thesis, supra pp 6ff.)

> . . . every positive law, or every law strictly so called, is a direct or circuitous command of a monarch or sovereign number in the character of a political superior: that is to say, a direct or circuitous command of a monarch or sovereign number to a person or persons in a state of subjection to its author. And being a *command* (and therefore flowing from a *determinate* source), every positive law is a law proper, or a law properly so called.
>
> Austin *The Province of Jurisprudence Determined* 134

Therefore, the factual tests for identifying positive law are: law is a *command*; a command requires to be supported by a *sanction*; the command together with its sanction emanates from a *sovereign*.

(a) Command and sanction

> Every *law* or *rule* (taken with the largest signification which can be given to the term *properly*) is a *command*. Or, rather, laws or rules, properly so called, are a *species* of commands.
>
> Now, since the term *command* comprises the term *law*, the first is the simpler as well as the larger of the two. But, simple as it is, it admits of explanation. And, since it is the *key* to the sciences of jurisprudence and morals, its meaning should be analysed with precision.
>
> Accordingly, I shall endeavour, in the first instance, to analyse the meaning of '*command*': an analysis which, I fear, will task the patience of my hearers, but which they will bear with cheerfulness, or, at least, with resignation, if they consider the difficulty of performing it. The elements of a science are precisely the parts of it which are explained least easily. Terms that are the largest, and, therefore, the simplest of a series, are without equivalent expressions into which we can resolve them *concisely*. And when we endeavour to *define* them, or to translate them into terms which we suppose are better understood, we are forced upon awkward and tedious circumlocutions.
>
> If you express or intimate a wish that I shall do or forbear from some act, and if you will visit me with an evil in case I comply not with your wish, the *expression* or *intimation* of your wish is a *command*. A command is distinguished from other significations of desire, not by the style in which the desire is signified, but by the power and the purpose of the party commanding to inflict an evil or pain in case the desire be disregarded. If you cannot or will not harm me in case I comply not with your wish, the expression of your wish is not a command, although you utter your wish in imperative phrase. If you are able

and willing to harm me in case I comply not with your wish, the expression of
your wish amounts to a command, although you are prompted by a spirit of
courtesy to utter in the shape of a request. '*Preces* erant, sed *quibus contradici non
posset.*' Such is the language of Tacitus, when speaking of a petition by the
soldiery to a son and lieutenant of Vespasian.

A command, then, is a signification of desire. But a command is
distinguished from other significations of desire by this peculiarity: that the
party to whom it is directed is liable to evil from the other, in case he comply
not with the desire.

Being liable to evil from you if I comply not with a wish which you signify, I
am *bound* or *obliged* by your command, or I lie under a *duty* to obey it. If, in spite
of that evil in prospect, I comply not with the wish which you signify, I am said
to disobey your command, or to violate the duty which it imposes.

Command and duty are, therefore, correlative terms: the meaning denoted
by each being implied or supposed by the other. Or (changing the expression)
wherever a duty lies, a command has been signified; and whenever a
command is signified, a duty is imposed.

Concisely expressed, the meaning of the correlative expressions is this. He
who will inflict an evil in case his desire be disregarded, utters a command by
expressing or intimating his desire: He who is liable to the evil in case he
disregard the desire, is bound or obliged by the command.

The evil which will probably be incurred in case a command be disobeyed or
(to use an equivalent expression) in case a duty be broken, is frequently called
a *sanction*, or an *enforcement of obedience*. Or (varying the phrase) the command or
the duty is said to be *sanctioned* or *enforced* by the chance of incurring the evil.

Considered as thus abstracted from the command and the duty which it
enforces, the evil to be incurred by disobedience is frequently styled a
punishment. But punishments, strictly so called, are only a *class* of sanctions, the
term is too narrow to express the meaning adequately.

Austin *The Province of Jurisprudence Determined* 13–15

Some comments on the previous extract:

(a)   It is the 'evil', the power to inflict punishment (the sanction), in the case of
non-compliance which converts an expression of a wish into a command.
All law being a species of command, all law necessarily entails the presence
of punitive sanctions for non-compliance.

(b)   The commander's intention to inflict an evil or sanction is not included in
the subject matter of that which must be expressed; only the desire needs
intimation. Hence, all the commander needs to say is, 'I want you to do X';
there is no need for any imperative form of words.

(c)   The presence of the sanction leads to the conclusion that the person to
whom the command is addressed is obliged by the command or is under a
duty to obey it.

. . . it is only by the chance of incurring *evil*, that I am *bound* or *obliged* to
compliance. It is only by conditional *evil*, that duties are *sanctioned* or *enforced*. It
is the power and the purpose of inflicting eventual *evil*, and *not* the power and
the purpose of imparting eventual *good*, which gives to the expression of a wish
the name of a *command*.

Austin *The Province of Jurisprudence Determined* 17

(d)   Although a valid law must have a sanction in the case of non-compliance, the sanction itself can be feeble or insufficient.

> The truth is, that the magnitude of the eventual evil, and the magnitude of the chance of incurring it, are foreign to the matter in question. The greater the eventual evil, and the greater the chance of incurring it, the greater is the efficacy of the command, and the greater is the strength of the obligation: Or (substituting expressions exactly equivalent), the greater is the *chance* that the command will be obeyed, and that the duty will not be broken. But where there is the smallest chance of incurring the smallest evil, the expression of a wish amounts to a command, and, therefore, imposes a duty. The sanction, if you will, is feeble or insufficient; but still there is a sanction, and, therefore, a duty and a command.

Austin *The Province of Jurisprudence Determined* 16

It is because of the argument advanced in this extract that it becomes difficult to conclude that Austin is using the presence of the sanction as a reason for compliance with the content of the command. If the sanction can be feeble or insufficient, a small fine for murder, it is difficult to read the threat of such a punishment as a psychological reason for compliance with the command (for the relevance of this point see Hart, infra p 38).

(e)   A sanction in the case of non-compliance is a necessary defining characteristic of all valid law. So a prohibition on unlawful homicide is supported by the threat of a punitive punishment in the case of non-compliance. But a legal system will also include different types of valid rules: there will be laws enabling people to enter into contracts, to become married, to form companies, to make valid wills, etc. Austin must concede that these are valid laws of the system just as much as the law about unlawful homicide. If so, they must, on the Austinian definition of valid law, be supported by a sanction. What is it? What is the sanction if you fail to abide by the necessary legal conditions for making a valid will, for example? What is the punitive evil if I fail to have two witnesses for my will?

> Before I conclude I beg leave to observe, that suffering must not be confounded with physical compulsion and restraint. To suffer, is to incur an evil independently of our own consent: a pain which is inflicted upon us, independently of an act or forbearance of our own.
>
> Now, though physical compulsion or restraint, is commonly the means or instrument by which suffering is inflicted, suffering may be inflicted without it. For instance, certain obligations are sanctioned by nullities; others again are sanctioned by penalties which are purely infamising: by a declaration, pronounced by competent authority, that the party shall be held infamous or merits infamy.
>
> In these and in other cases, the sanction is applied without the consent of the party, and without physical compulsion or restraint (or, at least, without such compulsion or restraint applied to the body).
>
> In other cases, the suffering is inflicted by physical compulsion or restraint: Or at least physical compulsion or restraint may be necessary (eg Punishments which affect the body).
>
> In most of the cases, in which it may be necessary to inflict suffering by physical compulsion or restraint, the physical compulsion or restraint is, in

fact, needless: because the party, knowing it may be applied, submits voluntarily.

Austin *The Lectures on Jurisprudence or the Philosophy of Positive Law* Vol 1 471–472

Again;

Besides this principal distinction, there are other species of sanctions requiring a notice. Laws are sometimes sanctioned by nullities. The legislature annexes rights to certain transactions; for example, to contracts on condition that these transactions are accompanied by certain circumstances. If the condition be not observed, the transaction is void, that is, no right arises; or the transaction is liable to be rescinded and the right annulled. Whether the transaction is void or voidable, the sanction may be applied either directly or indirectly. The transaction may either be rescinded or an application made to the effect, or the nullity may be opposed to a demand founded on the transaction. An instance of the first kind is an application to the Court of Chancery to set aside the transaction: an instance of the second is afforded by a defendant who opposes a ground of nullity to an action at common law. The distinction in English Law between void and voidable is the same as that in the Roman Law between null ipso jure and ope exceptionis. The first conferred no right; the second conferred a right which might be rescinded or destroyed by some party interested in setting it aside. Ope exceptionis is an inadequate name, for the transaction might be rescinded, not only by exceptio, that is, a plea, but by applications analogous to an application to Chancery to set aside a voidable instrument or an instrument obtained by fraud.

Austin *The Lectures on Jurisprudence or the Philosophy of Positive Law* 505–506

(f)   In summary, valid laws are commands from superiors that, because of the threat of sanction in the case of non-compliance, and this now includes the threat of nullity, oblige or bind the inferiors. Such a model of law fits in with Raz's discussion of the essence of legal positivism (supra pp 6–13). Law is reduced to bare social fact based on power, the power wielded by the political superior.

. . . taken with the meaning wherein I here understand it, the term *superiority* signifies *might*: the power of affecting others with evil or pain, and of forcing them, through fear of that evil, to fashion their conduct to one's wishes.

Austin *The Province of Jurisprudence Determined* 24

Evidently, clubs are trumps. Furthermore, morality or theories of justice have had no role to play in this definition of law. This is Austin the positivist. The content of the command could be morally iniquitous: it is still valid law. Legal rules as such are not moral rules even if they coincide with moral rules, as they frequently do.

Now, to say that human laws which conflict with the Divine are not binding, that is to say, are not laws, is to talk stark nonsense. The most pernicious laws, and therefore those which are most opposed to the will of God, have been and are continually enforced as laws by judicial tribunals. Suppose an act innocuous, or positively beneficial, be prohibited by the sovereign under the penalty of death; if I commit this act, I shall be tried and condemned, and if I object to the sentence, that it is contrary to the law of God, who has commanded that human lawgivers shall not prohibit acts which have no evil consequences, the Court of Justice will demonstrate the inconclusiveness of my reasoning by hanging me up, in pursuance of the law of which I have impugned the validity.

Austin *The Province of Jurisprudence Determined* 185

(b) The sovereign

If law is a species of command there must be a commander. Who is this and what gives him the power to issue legal orders backed by threats of evil in the case of non-compliance? In the first extract from Austin the phrase 'political superior' was used. A political superior can only exist within an 'independent political society' and this can only exist where there is a sovereign as defined by Austin.

Sovereignty (and an independent political society) is discussed in terms of a 'habit of obedience'. In the following, notice that before an Austinian sovereign can be said to exist not only must the bulk of the society be in the habit of obeying it but also it must not be in the habit of obeying any other superior: here we have the positive and negative aspects of the sovereign.

Every positive law, or every law simply and strictly so called, is set by a sovereign person, or a sovereign body of persons, to a member or members of the independent political society wherein that person or body is sovereign or supreme. Or (changing the expression) it is set by a monarch, or sovereign member, to a person or persons in a state of subjection to its author. Even though it sprung directly from another fountain or source, it *is* a positive law, or a law strictly so called, by the institution of that present sovereign in the character of political superior. Or (borrowing the language of Hobbes) 'the legislator is he, not by whose authority the law was first made, but by whose authority it continues to be a law'.

Having stated the topic or subject appropriate to my present discourse, I proceed to distinguish sovereignty from other superiority or might, and to distinguish society political and independent from society of other descriptions.

The superiority which is styled sovereignty, and the independent political society which sovereignty implies, is distinguished from other superiority, and from other society, by the following marks or characters:—1. The *bulk* of the given society are in a *habit* of obedience or submission to a *determinate* and *common* superior: let that common superior be a certain individual person or a certain body or aggregate of individual persons. 2. That certain individual, or that certain body of individuals, is *not* in a habit of obedience to a determinate human superior. Laws (improperly so called) which opinion sets or imposes, may permanently affect the conduct of that certain individual or body. To express or tacit commands of other determinate parties, that certain individual or body may yield occasional submission. But there is no determinate person, or determinate aggregate of persons, to whose commands, express or tacit, that certain individual or body renders habitual obedience.

Or the notion of sovereignty and independent political society may be expressed concisely thus.—If a *determinate* human superior, *not* in a habit of obedience to a like superior, receive *habitual* obedience from the *bulk* of a given society, that determinate superior is sovereign in that society, and the society (including the superior) is a society political and independent.

To that determinate superior, the other members of the society are *subject*: or on that determinate superior, the other members of the society are *dependent*. The position of its other members towards that determinate superior, is *a state of subjection*, or *a state of dependence*. The mutual relation which subsists between that superior and them, may be styled *the relation of sovereign and subject*, or *the relation of sovereignty and subjection*.

Hence it follows, that it is only through an ellipsis, or an abridged form of expression, that the *society* is styled *independent*. The party truly independent (independent, that is to say, of a determinate human superior), is not the society, but the sovereign portion of the society: that certain member of the society, or that certain body of its members, to whose commands, expressed or intimated, the generality or bulk of its members render habitual obedience. Upon that certain person, or certain body of persons, the other members of the society are *dependent*: or to that certain person or certain body of persons, the other members of the society are *subject*. By 'an independent political society', or 'an independent and sovereign nation', we mean a political society consisting of a sovereign and subjects, as opposed to a political society which is merely subordinate: that is to say, which is merely a limb or member of another political society, and which therefore consists entirely of persons in a state of subjection.

In order that a given society may form a society political and independent, the two distinguishing marks which I have mentioned above must unite. The *generality* of the given society must be in the *habit* of obedience to a *determinate* and *common* superior: whilst that determinate person, or determinate body of persons must *not* be habitually obedient to a determinate person or body. It is the union of that positive, with this negative mark, which renders that certain superior sovereign or supreme, and which renders that given society (including that certain superior) a society political and independent.

Austin The Province of Jurisprudence Determined 193–195

Therefore, if it can be said that the bulk of the people are in the habit of obeying the commands set by Queen in Parliament and the latter is not itself in the habit of obeying any other superior, Queen in Parliament is an Austinian sovereign: it issues valid laws and there is an independent political society. It does not matter to Austin why the habit exists. It may be that members obey the government freely because they like it or the habit may be present through fear of death in the case of disobedience.

The concept of the sovereign and the contention that all valid law is a species of command constitute one cohesive proposition: the sovereign being the political superior whose presence is indispensable as the source of the command.

(c)   The status of custom and case law

All law takes the form of a command from a sovereign that is supported by a threat of an evil. How, then, does customary law fit into the Austinian scheme of things? Again, in what way can it be maintained that law made by a judge in his courtroom emanates from a sovereign? Austin says that 'a moment's reflection' will show that customary law is imperative and that all judge-made law is indirectly the creature of the sovereign or state.

Now when judges transmute a custom into a legal rule (or make a legal rule not suggested by a custom), the legal rule which they establish is established by the sovereign legislature. A subordinate or subject judge is merely a minister. The portion of the sovereign power which lies at his disposition is merely delegated. The rules which he makes derive their legal force from authority given by the state: an authority which the state may confer expressly, but which it commonly imparts by way of acquiescence. For, since the state may reverse the rules which he makes, and yet permits him to enforce them by the power of the political community, its sovereign will 'that his rules shall obtain as law' is clearly evinced by its conduct, though not by its express declaration.

Austin *The Province of Jurisprudence Determined* 31–32

In so far as it is not revoked, the judicial acts can be considered '*tacit* commands of the sovereign legislature'. It is to be noted that Austin has no difficulty with accepting the idea of judges actually making law.

Notwithstanding my great admiration for Mr Bentham, I cannot but think that, instead of blaming judges for having legislated, he should blame them for the timid, narrow and piecemeal manner in which they have legislated, and for legislating under cover of vague and indeterminate phrases, . . . which would be censurable in any legislator.

Austin *The Province of Jurisprudence Determined* 191

SUMMARY

Austinian positivism can be reduced to these propositions:

(1)   A superior, (S), expresses a desire that an inferior, (I), does or forbears from doing X;
(2)   S is capable of inflicting an evil if I does not do or does not forbear from doing X;
(3)   I is a member of a society, the bulk of which is in the habit of obedience to S;
(4)   S is not in the habit of obedience to any determinate, human superior.

CRITICISM

In his first lecture at University College, London, Austin said: 'Frankness is the highest compliment . . . I therefore entreat you, as the greatest favour you can do me, to demand explanation and ply me with objections—turn me inside out.' There is little doubt that he has been paid this compliment: both his method and his results have been subjected to severe and often unanswerable criticism. Indeed, it has been rather harshly said that, 'Austin's doctrine forms a very good target—we must set it up and see it clearly in order to throw bricks at it' (Jolowicz *Lectures on Jurisprudence* p 1). We need to concentrate on the criticisms levelled against Austin in Hart's *Concept of Law*. However, it is still worth referring to one of the wider range of criticisms prompted by Austinianism.

(a)   The wider criticism

There is a fundamental objection to applying the notion of a command to the concept of law. Karl Olivecrona, a Scandinavian Realist (infra Chapter 14) contends that a command is not identical with a declaration of will as Austin proposes. To argue that the law is the expression of the will of the sovereign or the command of the state manifests a basic misconception.

> From the fact that a command has been given it is possible to draw a conclusion about the will of the person who commands. But this does not imply that the command itself is a declaration of his will. If we can see a man light a match and hold it to his pipe we can conclude that he wants to smoke. But his gesture is not meant to inform us of this intention.
>
> If a command was really a declaration of will, it could be formulated as an assertion to this effect without any alteration of the meaning. But this is impossible. Compare the following two utterances to a child, 'Blow your nose!' and, 'It is a fact that I want you to blow your nose.' The *effect* of the latter may be the same as that of the former, because the child knows that the grown-up person has some means of enforcing his will. But the *meaning* of the two sentences is not identical. In the first case we have no statement of a fact at all. Instead we have an utterance that is specifically adapted to the purpose of producing an action by the person addressed and to that purpose only. It is not intended to impart knowledge but to influence the will. In the latter case, on the contrary, we have a statement about a fact, primarily intended to convey knowledge.
>
> Thus a command must be sharply distinguished from a statement or declaration of the will of the speaker. A command is an act through which one person seeks to influence the will of another.
>
> Olivecrona *Law as Fact* 1st edn, 32–33

Sovereign will as constructive metaphor

At this stage, it is worth studying J W Harris's idea that the sovereign will in Austin (and Bentham) can be conceived of as a 'constructive metaphor' (we shall also return to this idea when considering Kelsen's basic norm).

Harris starts with a familiar account of the Austinian position.

> ... Austin, like Bentham, believed that the sovereign willed all 'laws', whatever their immediate source. And his justification for the assumption of unity of will is the same, namely, unity of enforcement. He says, for example, that the state's 'sovereign will' that judge-made rules 'shall obtain as law' is evinced by the fact that it permits the judge to enforce them 'by the power of the political community'.
>
> The same is true, according to Austin and Bentham, of the laws originating from sovereigns who formerly received habitual obedience. Their wills are absorbed in the will of the sovereign person or body who now enforces what they willed.
>
> Harris *Law and Legal Science* 28–29

The idea of 'sovereign will' is itself based on acts of wishing on the part of some politically powerful individuals in the society and this conclusion carries with it a familiar objection.

> In the case, not just of some laws, but of every law that is valid at any one time in a society, the persons who are for the moment sovereign in that society have a wish directed towards its content.

A familiar objection to identifying a positive legal rule with the expression of a sovereign will is that, if 'sovereign will' is understood in a psychological sense, no such will exists so far as the bulk of legislation in a modern state is concerned. It is impossible to identify any act of wishing by which a legislative body consciously rewills the wishes of previous sovereigns, or of past judges. Nor are there any such spasms of wishing directed to the contents of laws to be issued in the future by subordinate powerholders. It is also difficult to see in what sense a legislative body, as a body, consciously addresses itself (volitionally) to the contents of a bill. Clearly the members who vote against it do not do so; and it is a contingent circumstance whether or not the majority *wish* the directive materials contained in the bill, or whether they simply *wish to vote* for some other reason. In the case of an obscure section in a taxing statute, it may be that only the bosom of the draftsman ever heaved volitionally towards what it prescribes.

Harris *Law and Legal Science* 29–30

If Austin's and Bentham's intentions were to describe laws in terms of psychological acts of wishing, why do they make no effort to reply to the above type of criticism?

Can it be then that, despite their use of pyschological-looking expressions like 'conceiving a volition' and 'conceiving a wish or desire', they intended to describe acts of wishing in some non-psychological sense?

One explanation which might be advanced is that they accepted the metaphysic of the will. To the philosophic tradition which conceives of mental processes in a trinity of thought, feeling and will, there is nothing surprising in attributing to the will the features which Bentham and Austin ascribed to the sovereign will. According to the metaphysic, the 'will' is not to be identified with any one, or any series, of psychological acts of wishing. It can operate without the consciousness of its human host. It can also splice itself with other wills into the general will of a legislative body or of any other group.

If the sovereign will is a metaphysical entity, there is nothing odd in ascribing to it the power to absorb the wills of earlier sovereigns and of subordinate powerholders. There is, indeed, nothing odd—apart from the oddness of the metaphysical conception itself—in ascribing to the sovereign will anything which the law stipulates.

Harris *Law and Legal Science* 30

But is the idea of will metaphysics an appropriate escape route? The fact is that at other parts of their work both Austin and Bentham ridicule such an idea. Therefore, as Harris points out, Austin, when discussing the difference between intentional and negligent acts, says the 'will' underlying specific volitions is 'just nothing at all'. Now comes Harris's main thesis.

... Bentham and Austin made use of this convenient and familiar metaphysical language as a constructive metaphor. Political power was organized behind the directives of the law *as if* the sovereign was willing them all. Although they were perfectly well aware that the sovereign cannot wish all the contents of all the laws in a psychological sense, and although they did not accept that there was some other (non-natural) sense in which one can conceive volitions, they none the less thought it profitable, as part of their

macroscopic analysis of political societies, to employ the conception of a
sovereign will directed towards all rules which are enforced in a state. There is
no direct authority for this suggestion in their writings. Over-all
jurisprudential aim is something about which the greatest theorists are often
unhappily silent. The ground for the suggestion is the fact that any other
interpretation attributes to these authors either fantastic empirical
assumptions, or grotesque inconsistency.

Harris *Law and Legal Science* 31–32

The conclusion is that as a conception of political theory, 'sovereign will' is of
little value; but as a conception of legal theory intended to explain the non-
contradiction of legal rules it is of value.

It can be understood as a concept, not of political, but of legal theory. As such
it would not purport to point up anything illuminating about political society
as a whole, but only about the discipline of legal science.
   Legal scientists characteristically insist on interpreting the legislative
material of a state as a non-contradictory field of meaning. In other words,
when faced with two normative stipulations which direct contradictory
behaviour, they generally insist either that there is no real contradiction, or
that the 'validity' of one entails the 'invalidity' of the other.
   Now what is the logical justification for such a practice? . . . The legal-
science principle of non-contradiction cannot be justified by reference to the
assumed non-illusoriness of nature. To discover a justification for axioms of
this sort is one of the problems faced in the recent development of 'deontic
logic'—the logic of *must, must not*, and *may* propositions. The best equivalent
truth-ground which one of its leading exponents has been able to find is the
presupposition of a rational will underlying all the norms of a consistent
system of norms. If, when we make assertions about what ought to be done, we
assume as a postulate that we are talking about the kind of instructions which
could be given by a person with a rational will, the postulate justifies us in
saying that contradictory actions cannot be directed. A rational person could
not knowingly order an individual to perform an act on a particular occasion
and at the same time excuse or prohibit him from performing it.

Harris *Law and Legal Science* 32–33

(b) Hart on Austin

(1) All law is a species of command

It is easy to see that this account of a legal system is threadbare . . . The
situation which the simple trilogy of command, sanction, and sovereign avails
to describe, if you take these notions at all precisely, is like that of a gunman
saying to his victims, 'Give your money or your life.' The only difference is that
in the case of a legal system the gunman says it to a larger number of people
who are accustomed to the racket and habitually surrender to it. Law is surely
not the gunman situation writ large, and legal order is surely not to be thus
simply identified with compulsion.

Hart *Essays in Jurisprudence and Philosophy* 59

Whereas the gunman addresses his victim face to face, a law is general in that it indicates a general type of conduct and applies to a general class of persons. Indeed it may be law before the relevant individuals know of its existence. Furthermore, whereas the gunman only has temporary superiority over his victim, laws have a 'standing' or persistent characteristic. Finally, legislatures are themselves bound by the law.

More importantly, the rules created by a legal system are of various types, some of which simply will not fit into the command model. It is true that the criminal law and the law of tort have some analogy with the theory of law as coercive orders backed by threats, however, there are other varieties of rules which do not because they perform a different social function.

> Legal rules defining the ways in which valid contracts or wills or marriages are made do not require persons to act in certain ways whether they wish to or not. Such laws do not impose duties or obligations. Instead, they provide individuals with *facilities* for realizing their wishes, by conferring legal powers upon them to create, by certain specified procedures and subject to certain conditions, structures of rights and duties within the coercive framework of the law.

> Hart *The Concept of Law* 27

These power-conferring laws are not confined to private individuals. There are rules that allow officials of government or the legal system to change laws, to create laws, and to enforce laws. All these cannot be understood as a species of command backed up by threats in the event of disobedience. They will constitute what Hart calls secondary rules.

The radical difference in function between rules that confer powers and those which impose obligations is reflected in our vocabulary. So failure to comply with the provisions of a criminal statute is described as 'breach' or 'violation' of one's duty or obligation under the statute: non-compliance is an 'offence'. On the other hand, where there is a failure, for example, to have two witnesses for a will as is required by the Wills Act, it would be quite inappropriate to use words such as 'breach', 'violation of duty', or 'offence'. The document, which we intended to be a will, through our failure to comply with the conditions will be a nullity and not an offence.

As regards public officials and bodies, there are power-conferring rules specifying the jurisdiction of judges, the manner of their appointment, the subject matter over which the legislative power may be exercised, the qualifications and the identity of the members of the legislative body, etc.

> A full detailed taxonomy of the varieties of law comprised in a modern legal system, free from the prejudice that all *must* be reducible to a single simple type, still remains to be accomplished. In distinguishing certain laws under the very rough head of laws that confer powers from those that impose duties and are analogous to orders backed by threats, we have made only a beginning. But perhaps enough has been done to show that some of the distinctive features of a legal system lie in the provision it makes, by rules of this type, for the exercise of private and public legal powers. If such rules of this distinctive kind did not exist we should lack some of the most familiar concepts of social life, since these logically presuppose the existence of such rules. Just as there could be no crimes or offences and so no murders or thefts if there were no criminal laws of the mandatory kind which do resemble orders backed by

threats, so there could be no buying, selling, gifts, wills, or marriages if there were no power-conferring rules; for these latter things, like the orders of courts and the enactments of law-making bodies, just consist in the valid exercise of legal powers.

Hart *The Concept of Law* 32

However, power-conferring rules are related to duty-imposing rules.

. . . for the powers which they confer are powers to make general rules [of the orders backed by threats] sort or to impose duties on particular persons who would otherwise not be subject to them. This is most obviously the case when the power conferred would ordinarily be termed a power to legislate. But, as we shall see, it is also true in the case of other legal powers. It might be said, at the cost of some inaccuracy, that whereas rules like those of the criminal law impose duties, power-conferring rules are recipes for creating duties.

Hart *The Concept of Law* 33

Hart's contention is that a statute that prescribes the manner in which, for example, a valid will may be made is not reducible to an analysis in terms of the simple trilogy of command, duty and sanction. He discusses one such attempted conflation of duty-imposing rules with power-conferring rules which makes use of the argument that nullity is a sanction. It will be remembered that treating nullity as a sanction was a part of the Austinian model of law (supra pp 19–20).

It is argued that nullity for failure to comply with conditions set out in a power-conferring rule is analogous to the threatened punishment attached to a criminal statute in the case of non-compliance, although it is accepted that the operation of such a sanction may amount only to slight inconvenience. After all Austin accepts that a sanction could be 'feeble or insufficient' (supra p 19). However, this extension of the notion of sanction so as to include nullity would be a confusion: nullity is a notion totally different from the punishment that follows the breach of a criminal statute.

It is possible to subtract the concept of punishment from the description of the prohibited conduct laid down, for example, in a penal statute. After such a subtraction we are still left with a comprehensible standard of behaviour. For example, subtracting the punishment from the Theft Act will still leave an understandable, intelligible standard: 'do not steal'. On the other hand, if one attempts to remove the notion of nullity from the rule that sets out the conditions for making valid wills, then nothing intelligible remains: there is no comprehensible standard remaining after the subtraction. While the sanction is only contingently related to the duty-imposing rule, that is, failure to comply may or may not be followed by a sanction, the nullity follows necessarily upon a failure to satisfy the conditions of the power-conferring rule.

In this case, if failure to comply with the essential condition did not entail nullity, the rule itself could not be intelligibly said to exist without sanctions even as a non-legal rule. The provision for nullity is *part* of this type of rule itself in a way which punishment attached to a rule imposing duties is not. If failure to get the ball between the posts did not mean the 'nullity' of not scoring, the scoring rules could not be said to exist.

Hart *The Concept of Law* 34–35

Consequently, perhaps the greater part of a legal system is comprised of rules which neither command nor forbid things to be done; instead they empower people to achieve certain ends by providing certain methods.

Two further criticisms of the command analysis of law are employed by Hart.

First, Austin's commands were wishes backed by threats that *others* do or be enjoined from doing certain things. Hart maintains that the legislation may quite properly be binding upon the legislature itself.

> It may or may not be found on interpretation to exclude those who made it, and, of course, many a law is now made which imposes legal obligations on the makers of the law. Legislation, as distinct from ordering *others* to do things under threats, may perfectly well have such a self-binding force. There is nothing *essentially* other-regarding about it. This is a legal phenomenon which is puzzling only so long as we think, under the influence of the model, of the laws as always laid down by a man or men above the law for others subjected to it.
>
> Hart *The Concept of Law* 42

This is the vertical or 'top-to-bottom' image of law making.

> For the making of a law . . . presupposes the existence of certain rules which govern the process: words said or written by the persons qualified by these rules, and following the procedures specified by them, create obligations for all within the ambit designated explicitly or implicitly by the words. These may include those who take part in the legislative process.
>
> Hart *The Concept of Law* 43

Secondly, the mode of origin of that type of law called *custom* conflicts with Austin's claim that ultimately all laws owe their status to a deliberate law-creating act (supra pp 22–23). A custom attains legal status when it is recognized as law by a particular legal system.

> . . . to attribute the legal status of a custom to the fact that a court or the legislature or the sovereign has so 'ordered' is to adopt a theory which can only be carried through if a meaning is given to 'order' so extended as to rob the theory of its point.
>
> Hart *The Concept of Law* 44

(2) *The Austinian sovereign*

In addition to the distortion produced by classifying all laws as commands backed by threats of punishment, Hart points out that the Austinian model gives an inaccurate account of a modern legal system. In particular, defining the sovereign in terms of habit of obedience, both in the positive and negative aspects, creates three major problems.

First, habit of obedience fails to account for two features of most legal systems, namely, the *continuity* of the authority to make laws by a succession of sovereigns and for the *persistence* of laws after the death of the law maker. If we interpret the Austinian model literally, on the death of the reigning sovereign, called Rex I by Hart, the bulk of the population cannot habitually have been obeying his eldest son, Rex II. Therefore, according to the Austinian model, at that moment there would be no sovereign and consequently no legal system. Such a conclusion would be absurd and one would expect a smooth transition. In reality the idea of a lawful succession involves not habit of obedience but the *acceptance of rules*. In a modern system one must attempt to explain the notion of the acceptance of certain ultimate rules, what Hart calls the ultimate rules of recognition. The character of these rules cannot be explained simply in terms of habit of obedience by the bulk of the people. These rules, like all other rules, have an *internal aspect* which is absent from the notion of mere habit. This internal aspect of acceptance of rules is going to be a pivotal concept in Hart's work (infra pp 34ff). Moreover, mere habit of obedience cannot confer any *right* on Rex II to succeed Rex I and to issue orders in his place. Why not?

> First, because habits are not 'normative'; they cannot confer rights or authority on anyone. Secondly, because habits of obedience to one individual cannot, though accepted rules can, refer to a class or line of future successive legislators as well as to the current legislator, or render obedience to them likely. So the fact that there is habitual obedience to one legislator neither affords grounds for the statement that his successor has the right to make the law, nor for the factual statement that he is likely to be obeyed.

> Hart *The Concept of Law* 58–59

If there is to be this right at the moment of succession there must have been, during the reign of Rex I, somewhere in the society a social practice more complex than a mere habit of obedience; there must have been the acceptance of the rule under which the new legislator is *entitled* to succeed. That is, there needs to be an internal attitude towards rules (infra pp 34ff).

Can anything be done to salvage the Austinian sovereign? Why not interpret Austin as saying that the habit of obedience is not owed to any particular, personal sovereign, such as Rex I, but, in complex societies, is owed to institutions such as Queen in Parliament? That is, the habit is owed to the corporation called the sovereign and, as this corporation is separate and distinct from the actual person occupying the position at any particular time, then there is perpetual succession. The corporation or institution does not die on the death of Rex I. However, Austin would have to define this institution. How? By reference to certain legal rules. But it will be remembered one of Austin's fundamental contentions is that all legal rules emanate from the sovereign. But these particular legal rules that define the institution cannot come from the sovereign; they are definitive or constitutive of the sovereign and, consequently, they cannot come from the sovereign.

Similarly with the problem of the persistence of laws. Why do laws passed by Rex II continue to be valid long after his death? Why did not the validity of his laws terminate when his subjects' habit of obedience was transferred from him to Rex III? Again the force of Hart's criticism centres on interpreting Austin as insisting on the habit of obedience being directed at a particular, personal sovereign. Surely Austin could maintain that the laws of Rex II are still valid because the habit was directed towards the institution called the sovereign which did not die on the death of Rex II. But how does Austin define this institution or corporation? We have reached the same point of the argument that we encountered above on the problem of continuity.

The conclusion for legal theory is clear. What is of the essence is an analysis of the acceptance (internal aspect) of the ultimate rules of recognition that are definitive of the sovereign. Furthermore, it is safe to conclude that these rules cannot be adequately elucidated merely by the use of the notion of habit of obedience. Of course, if Harris's discussion of the sovereign will as a 'constructive metaphor' is accepted Austin's problems on continuity and persistence would wither away (supra pp 24–26).

The second inadequacy of the Austinian sovereign relates to the negative aspect of the habit of obedience. The consequence of this feature of the sovereign is that it is legally unlimited, that it is conceived to be above the law and outside the range of application of its own laws. Hart denies that the existence of a sovereign subject to no legal limitations is a necessary condition for the existence of a legal system and, therefore, of valid law. In most modern states no one would seriously conclude that there is no legal system even though there is certainly no concept of the legal illimitability of the sovereign. A written constitution may restrict the competence of the legislature by excluding certain issues from the scope of its legislative power. Such a constitution does not impose duties on the legislature not to legislate on certain matters. It only says that such legislation is rendered void.

> It imposes not legal duties but legal disabilities. 'Limits' here implies not the presence of *duty* but the absence of legal power.
>
> Hart *The Concept of Law* 68

He proceeds to discuss the nature of such legal restrictions on sovereign power.

> Such restrictions on the legislative power of Rex may well be called constitutional: but they are not mere conventions or moral matters with which courts are unconcerned. They are parts of the rule conferring authority to legislate and they vitally concern the courts, since they use such a rule as a criterion of the validity of purported legislative enactments coming before them. Yet though such restrictions are legal and not merely moral or conventional, their presence or absence cannot be expressed in terms of the presence or absence of a habit of obedience on the part of Rex to other persons. Rex may well be subject to such restrictions and never seek to evade them; yet there may be no one whom he habitually obeys. He merely fulfils the conditions for making valid law. Or he may try to evade the restrictions by issuing orders inconsistent with them; yet if he does this he will not have disobeyed any one; he will not have broken any superior legislators' law or violated a legal duty. He will surely have failed to make (though he does not break) a valid law.
>
> Hart *The Concept of Law* 68

The third problem with the Austinian doctrine of sovereignty, according to Hart, concerns the difficulty in applying it to a modern democratic state. In Britain, where did Austin actually locate his sovereign?

> Adopting the language of most of the writers who have treated of the British Constitution, I commonly suppose that the present parliament, or the parliament for the time being, is possessed of the sovereignty: or I commonly suppose that the king and the lords, with the members of the commons' house, form a tripartite body which is sovereign or supreme. But, speaking accurately, the members of the commons' house are merely trustees for the

body by which they are elected and appointed: and, consequently, the sovereignty always resides in the king and the peers, with the electoral body of the commons.

Austin *The Province of Jurisprudence Determined* 230–231

And in the United States?

I believe that the common government, or the government consisting of the congress and the president of the united states, is merely a subject minister of the united states' governments. I believe that none of the latter is properly sovereign or supreme, even in the state or political society of which it is the immediate chief. And, lastly, I believe that the sovereignty of each of the states, and also of the larger state arising from the federal union, resides in the states' governments *as forming one aggregate body*: meaning by a state's government, not its ordinary legislature, but the body of its citizens which appoints its ordinary legislature, and which, the union apart, is properly sovereign therein.

Austin *The Province of Jurisprudence Determined* 250–251

In both cases and with an air of desperation, he attempts to identify an illimitable sovereign by using the electorate. This would lead to the uncomfortable observation that the bulk of the population is in the habit of obeying itself! As Hart says, this would mean that the original clear image of a society divided into two segments, the sovereign giving orders and the subjects who habitually obey, would blur into a society where the majority obey orders given by the majority.

To answer such criticism, Austin could draw a distinction between members of a society in their individual capacity and the same persons in their official capacity when they constitute the institution called the electorate. If so, it is perfectly reasonable to say that the bulk of the people, in their private capacity, must be in the habit of obeying themselves in their official capacity as the electorate, the point being that the individuals in their official capacity constitute a separate and distinct person who is habitually obeyed. But it is Hart's unanswerable counter-argument that, given this distinction, we need to go a step further and ask 'what counts as individuals in their official capacity?' What does it mean to say a group of individuals become a different person called the electorate? What is the electorate and when does the metamorphosis occur? To answer such questions we need to resort to certain legal rules concerning the meaning of electorate. Where did these valid rules come from? They cannot come from the sovereign because they are definitive of the sovereign and if they did not come from the sovereign, on one of the basic tenets of Austinianism, they cannot be valid laws because all law must have such an emanation. We have reached the point familiar to us after our encounter with the problems of continuity and persistence considered above.

These three inadequacies in the Austinian sovereign are fundamental: the simple idea of orders, habits, and obedience are not adequate concepts for the analysis of law. Hart will contend that what is required is the idea of a rule conferring powers, which may be limited or unlimited, on persons qualified in certain ways to legislate by following a definite procedure.

(3) A summary of Hart's criticisms

The main ways in which the theory failed are instructive enough to merit a second summary. First, it became clear that though of all the varieties of law, a criminal statute, forbidding or enjoining certain actions under penalty, most resembles orders backed by threats given by one person to others, such a statute none the less differs from such orders in the important respect that it commonly applies to those who enact it and not merely to others. Secondly, there are other varieties of law, notably those conferring legal powers to adjudicate or legislate (public powers) or to create or vary legal relations (private powers) which cannot, without absurdity, be construed as orders backed by threats. Thirdly, there are legal rules which differ from orders in their mode of origin, because they are not brought into being by anything analogous to explicit prescription. Finally, the analysis of law in terms of the sovereign, habitually obeyed and necessarily exempt from all legal limitation, failed to account for the continuity of legislative authority characteristic of a modern legal system, and the sovereign person or persons could not be identified with either the electorate or the legislature of a modern state.

Hart *The Concept of Law* 77

Chapter 3

H L A Hart's concept of law

To Hart, the basic failure of the Austinian model is its neglect of the concept of a rule. To understand the foundations of a legal system, rather than an account based on habitual obedience to the commands of an unlimited sovereign, a necessary insight will be that laws are a species of rules and ultimately the foundations of a legal system will be based on the acceptance of a fundamental rule.

> The root cause of failure [of the Austinian model] is that the elements out of which the theory was constructed, viz. the ideas of orders, obedience, habits, and threats, do not include, and cannot by their combination yield, the idea of a rule, without which we cannot hope to elucidate even the most elementary forms of law. It is true that the idea of a rule is by no means a simple one . . .
>
> Hart *The Concept of Law* 78

HART'S CONCEPT OF LAW

Hart's most systematic analysis is to be found in *The Concept of Law*, 1961, and it is upon this work that we need to concentrate. We shall approach the argument under the following headings:

(a) the nature of a rule, 'the internal aspect of rules';
(b) the idea of obligation;
(c) law as the union of primary and secondary rules;
(d) the rule of recognition;
(e) the existence of a legal system.

(a) The nature of a rule

Consider the following exhortations: 'do not commit adultery'; 'do not eat your peas with a knife'; 'you ought never to use a split infinitive'; 'when you hit the ball between the two posts you will be awarded a goal'. These are all social rules and clearly they come in many guises, including rules of morality, etiquette, grammar and sport. But the inventory of social rules is incomplete without the inclusion of legal rules, ranging from the requirement of two witnesses for a valid will to a prohibition against the intentional killing of human beings. This coalition of seemingly disparate directives is feasible because all of them can be called social rules.

For such a classification to be correct two things must be true: first, members of the relevant society must generally abide by the content of the exhortation and secondly most members of the society must exhibit an 'internal aspect' towards the relevant conduct. All social rules manifest these two dimensions. In order to understand them, consider behaviour which is not prompted by the existence of any social rule; behaviour that is merely the result of habit, what Hart calls 'convergent habitual behaviour', a feature, you will remember, that is of central significance in the Austinian analysis of a legal system. Convergent habitual behaviour only exhibits the first characteristic. The absence of the second characteristic, the internal aspect, in such behaviour as always having tea at four in the afternoon, usually going to the cinema on Fridays, sets the point of demarcation between rule-prompted and habit-based behaviour. Contrast the man who always has turkey on Christmas Day with the one who never parks on double yellow lines. The former activity is completely encapsulated in the observation that he always behaves in such a manner. Of course, this externally established feature is also present in the latter activity and it is true that both social rules and habit can be explained in terms of the fact that the standard of behaviour is generally complied with. However, in the case of the man who does not park on double yellow lines the externally observed compliance is only half the story; clearly, it would be a weak description of his case to say solely that the driver, as a matter of mere habit, never parks on the yellow lines. The recently arrived Martian would be able to come to such a conclusion after a sufficient spell of observation; but this would drastically miss the point. The point being that the car driver's conduct in connection with double yellow lines is the direct result of his attitude of mind, that is of his acceptance of traffic rules and regulations as being standards with which he ought to comply. Our friendly Martian will conclude that the yellow lines are an indication that the car driver will not park there and, indeed, if the Martian has been sufficiently assiduous in his observations, that he will be punished if he does decide to park in such a place. However, *to the driver himself*, the yellow lines are a signal not to stop. The external dimension—the Martian approach to human behaviour—is a necessary ingredient in the understanding of rule-orientated behaviour but it is not a sufficient one, as it is to the understanding of habitual behaviour. To ignore the internal attitude of the driver would be to conflate these two sentences: 'people are in the habit of taking their hats off when entering church' and 'people take their hats off when entering church because there is a social rule in existence which requires such behaviour'.

So the presence of Martian-observable, statistical regularity of behaviour entails no necessary conclusion about the existence of a social rule dictating such behavioural conformity. Here is MacCormick's pertinent illustration concerning car drivers stopping at the traffic lights when the lights turn to red: to observe or to state that the pattern 'vehicles stopping at a red light' occurs in 99% of cases is neither to see nor to say that there is a rule. The same would hold if it were observed that 99% of drivers play car radios when stopped at traffic lights (MacCormick *H L A Hart* p 30). As Hart puts it,

> By contrast [to habit] if a social rule is to exist, some at least must look upon the behaviour in question as a general standard to be followed by the group as a whole. A social rule has an 'internal' aspect, in addition to the external aspect which it shares with a social habit and which consists in the regular uniform behaviour which an observer could record.

> Hart *The Concept of Law* 55

So it is necessary to approach the standard from the vantage point of someone within the society, not a Martian but a native. The hat-wearing church-goer has a certain attitude towards hats in churches: he has a 'critical reflective attitude to the pattern of behaviour'. In other words he 'has views' about the conjunction of churches and hats in that he regards the standard as being operative for all persons within his community. He has a role-expectation of all church-goers: hats are to be removed. Contrast you and I who happen, coincidentally, to go to the same pub every Friday night: convergent habitual behaviour rather than rule-prompted.

Rules, then, have an internal aspect. This insight breeds further contrasts with mere habit-based behaviour. First, habit is established by the fact that behaviour does in fact converge and, consequentially, there need not be any criticism for a lapse of habit, for example, when you fail to turn up at the pub next Friday night. It is logically permissible to say there is a habit of doing behaviour X but no one is to be criticised for not doing X. But in the domain of social rules things are completely different: where a rule governs the behaviour, deviations are usually treated as 'lapses or faults open to criticism' and, therefore, are met with pressures of various sorts in order to instil uniformity.

Furthermore, criticism for deviation from a social rule is not only made 'but deviation from the standard is generally accepted as a *good reason* for making it'. When A criticises B for the latter's lapse from the rule-defined standard, C will not criticise A for criticising B: counter-criticism is ruled out, as it were.

A rule's rudimentary feature, then, is the internal aspect. This feature is 'implicit' in the two further characteristics noted above—criticism and justification of this criticism. In fact these latter two cannot be fully understood without the seminal concept of the internal aspect of rules.

> What is necessary is that there should be a critical reflective attitude to certain patterns of behaviour as a common standard, and that this should display itself in criticism (including self-criticism), demands for conformity, and in acknowledgements that such criticism and demands are justified, all of which find their characteristic expression in the normative terminology of 'ought', 'must', and 'should', 'right' and 'wrong'.
>
> Hart *The Concept of Law* 56

Of course, such a provocative vocabulary would be utterly inappropriate in reaction to the breaking of a habit. Finally, the internal aspect of rules is evidenced by the fact that members of the group strive to teach and intend to maintain the behaviour in question: not so in the case of mere habit.

In summary, the internal aspect of social rules is the requirement that some members of the community view the behaviour entailed in the rule as a general standard. This attitude manifests itself in certain specific ways: because of mutual demands for conformity, violations of the standard provoke criticisms, this criticism is justifiable because of the violation itself, and there is a desire to maintain and instil this standard among the members. Thus, for Hart, rules are normative, meaning they are capable of conferring rights, duties and powers; mere habits cannot.

> This internal aspect of rules may be simply illustrated from the rules of any game. Chess players do not merely have similar habits of moving the Queen in the same way which an external observer, who knew nothing about their attitude to the moves which they make, could record. In addition, they have a reflective critical attitude to this pattern of behaviour: they regard it as a

standard for all who play the game. Each not only moves the Queen in a certain way himself but 'has views' about the propriety of all moving the Queen in that way. These views are manifested in the criticism of others and the demands for conformity made upon others when deviation is actual or threatened, and in the acknowledgement of the legitimacy of such criticism and demands when received by others. For the expression of such criticisms, demands, and acknowledgements a wide range of 'normative' language is used. 'I (You) ought not to have moved the Queen like that', 'I (You) must do that', 'That is right', 'That is wrong'.

Hart *The Concept of Law* 55–56

However, there is need for clarification of this distinction between internal and external attitudes which, although touched upon by Hart, is not really confronted. Let us consider the position of an external observer, either the Martian viewing our conduct when we drive cars or the legal theorist trying to arrive at a concept of law by observing the conduct and attitudes of the members of the relevant community.

Such observers could look upon the behaviour of the group solely from the external point of view, reproducing it in terms of merely convergent habitual behaviour. So Austin falls into this category and is criticised by Hart for so doing. There is a failure to see or refusal to acknowledge the internal attitude that the members of the group have towards rule-prompted behaviour.

However, these observers could have a less extreme stance: 'the observer may, without accepting the rules himself, assert that the group accepts the rules, and thus may from the outside refer to the way in which *they* are concerned with them from the internal point of view' (p 87). This observer does explain why, for example, motorists do not park on the yellow lines in terms of their internal attitude, that is, acceptance of the traffic rules, although he does not so view the rules. Such an observer is attempting to portray the rules from the point of view of those subject to the rules. This type of observer must be treated as different from the external observer properly so called, described above. His is a type of internal attitude. These would be what Raz called 'statements from a point of view' or 'detached statements' and are discussed above (pp 13–15).

Finally there is the internal observer in the full significance of the term: the observer himself not only evaluates the members' behaviour in terms of their internal aspect towards the rules, he also accepts the rules from the internal aspect.

(b) The idea of obligation

Evidently our concern will ultimately be with one type of social rule: legal rules. The first stage of whittling down the wide catchment area of social rules, discussed under the rubric of the internal aspect, will leave us with moral and social rules, thereby discarding rules of grammar, etiquette, sport, etc. Moral and legal rules have an extra dimension that sets them apart from the others. Before looking at this extra dimension it would be wise to understand some crucial refinements.

Hart's contention is that Austin's theory fails to distinguish between the statement that one has an obligation and the statement that one is obliged to do or not do something. A person is obliged to do or refrain from doing something when the something is a necessary condition for the avoidance of some threat or punishment. A orders B to hand over the money and threatens to shoot him if he does not comply. In such a situation it would be valid to say that B, if he obeyed, was 'obliged' to disgorge the cash. In effect, the statement that one is obliged is a statement about the beliefs, motives, fears which accompany the behaviour: one believes that some unpleasant consequence would occur in the event of non-compliance and, consequently, the money is handed over to avoid this impending hostile reaction. Such statements are psychological ones referring to the beliefs and motives with which an action is done. They are really statements about the causation and motivation of acts.

But to say that one has an obligation is a statement of a very different type. To assert that someone had an obligation to tell the truth or not to park on double yellow lines is more than a statement about the person's beliefs or motives. It would remain true, even if he believed that he had nothing to fear from non-compliance. The reasonable belief that the chances of him being found out were virtually non-existent does not counter the statement that he had an obligation to tell the truth or not to park on those lines. The existence of beliefs, motives, or fears are neither necessary nor sufficient for the truth of the statement that a person had an obligation to do or refrain from doing something. According to Hart, this is the correct analysis of the concept of obligation; the conclusion that an obligation exists may be true without the subject having any particular beliefs or motives.

There is a third approach to the notion of obligation, one that seems to be favoured by Austin and some brands of Realism. Instead of defining the notion in terms of such subjective features as the actor's beliefs or motives, it can be defined in terms of the *chance* or *likelihood* of suffering some evil or punishment in the event of disobedience. This analysis of obligation concludes that a person has an obligation if, and only if, hostile reaction to deviation is predictable. The psychological underpinning of the 'being obliged' approach is irrelevant to the predictive model. It is because of the extract from Austin above (supra p 19) where he admits that the sanction can be 'feeble or insufficient', and therefore hardly a psychological inducement for compliance, that Austin best fits this third approach to obligation. Hart has two arguments against this model of the likelihood of punishment.

First, the predictive approach neglects the internal aspect of rules stressed above. It distorts the fact that where rules exist, deviations are not mere predictions that some sort of evil or punishment will ensue, but are also 'reasons and justifications' for applying that evil or punishment: it would amount to an external point of view towards rules, limited to the outward, observable regularity of social behaviour. In short, '. . . the violation of a rule is not merely a basis for the prediction that a hostile reaction will follow but a *reason* for hostility' (p 88).

Secondly, what if the person realized there was not the slightest chance of being caught or punished? According to the predictive theory, it would seem to be a contradiction to say that such a person had an obligation. In reality no such contradiction exists. It is necessary to distinguish between a general and an individual perspective. It would be acceptable to say that making statements about a person's *legal* obligations would be an exercise in futility unless *in general* sanctions or punishments were likely to be exacted from violators. Such statements presuppose belief in the continued operation of sanctions.

None the less, it is crucial for the understanding of the idea of obligation to see that in individual cases the statement that a person has an obligation under some rule and the prediction that he is likely to suffer for disobedience may diverge.

Hart *The Concept of Law* 82–83

To understand the idea of obligation we need to appreciate that it is superimposed on to a social situation that includes the existence of social rules. The existence of such rules is the normal, though unstated, background for the statement that a person has an obligation. We have seen that social rules involve not only regular conduct (the external aspect) but also a distinctive attitude towards the conduct as a standard (the internal aspect). This internal aspect together with its three manifestations (supra pp 36–37) find expression in such normative assertions as 'ought', 'must', 'should'. But within this normative vocabulary 'obligation' and 'duty' form a sub-class carrying certain manifestations over and above the internal dimension which is the hallmark of all social rules. The internal aspect is certainly a necessary condition for the conclusion that a person has an obligation; but it is not a sufficient one. 'He ought to have' is not synonymous with 'He had an obligation to'; the latter includes the former but also has three further manifestations.

> Rules are conceived and spoken of as imposing obligations when the general demand for conformity is insistent and the social pressure brought to bear upon those who deviate or threaten to deviate is great.

> Hart *The Concept of Law* 84

The *seriousness* of social pressure behind the rules is the primary characteristic of obligation prompting social rules, that is, moral and legal rules. In the case of morality, this insistent social pressure may manifest itself in feelings of shame, remorse, or guilt; when physical sanctions are evident we shall be more inclined to classify the rules as legal.

> The rules supported by this serious pressure are thought important because they are believed to be necessary to the maintenance of social life or some highly prized feature of it.

> Hart *The Concept of Law* 85

Hardly a feature of 'do not eat your peas with your knife'! In contrast, consider rules restricting the use of violence.

> . . . it is generally recognized that the conduct required by these rules may, while benefiting others, conflict with what the person who owes the duty may wish to do. Hence obligations and duties are thought of as characteristically involving sacrifice or renunciation, and the standing possibility of conflict between obligation or duty and interest is, in all societies, among the truisms of both the lawyer and the moralist.

> Hart *The Concept of Law* 85

These three manifestations—seriousness of pressure, importance, and possible conflict—must not 'trap us into a misleading conception of obligation'. If the emphasis is upon insistent, serious social pressure, is not the notion of obligation tied to feelings of pressure or compulsion or naked fear? That is, have we not succeeded in collapsing 'having an obligation' into 'being obliged' where beliefs, motives and other psychological states are of the essence?

> The fact that rules of obligation are generally supported by serious social pressure does not entail that to have an obligation under the rules is to

experience feelings of compulsion or pressure. Hence there is no contradiction in saying of some hardened swindler, and it may often be true, that he had an obligation to pay the rent but felt no pressure to pay when he made off without doing so. To *feel* obliged and to have an obligation are different though frequently concomitant things. To identify them would be one way of misrepresenting in terms of psychological feelings, the internal aspect of rules to which we drew attention . . .

Hart *The Concept of Law* 85–86

Again, what of the predictive approach which puts all the emphasis on the element of sanction, that is social pressure in all its guises? Does it not catch the essence of obligation? We already know the answer to this.

The difference may seem slight between the analysis of a statement of obligation as a prediction, or assessment of the chances, of hostile reaction to deviation, and our own contention that though this statement presupposes a background in which deviations from rules are generally met by hostile reactions, yet its characteristic use is not to predict this but to say that a person's case falls under such a rule. In fact, however, this difference is not a slight one. Indeed, until its importance is grasped, we cannot understand the whole distinctive style of human thought, speech, and action which is involved in the existence of rules and which constitutes the normative structure of society.

Hart *The Concept of Law* 86

(c)   Law as the union of primary and secondary rules

The whittling down of the vast category of social rules continues; having eliminated all social rules not involving obligation from the investigation, moral rules are now relegated so that the discussion centres upon legal rules. In the following discussion Hart distinguishes between primary and secondary legal rules and finally arrives at two conditions for the existence of a legal system. We shall consider in due course whether these features are adequate to the task of whittling down social rules so as to distinguish legal rules from moral rules (infra pp 66ff). In the meantime we shall assume this is the case.

Being a species of social rule one would have thought, on the basis of the above discussion, that all legal rules would be characterised by both internal aspect and obligation. As usual the story is not as simple as that.

Having introduced the distinction between internal and external aspects of rules, Hart puts heavy reliance on another distinction: the difference between primary legal rules and secondary legal rules. Indeed 'we shall make the general claim that in the combination of these two types of rule there lies what Austin wrongly claimed to have found in the notion of coercive orders, namely, "the key to the science of jurisprudence"' (p 79). Some rules of law do bear a strong analogy to commands backed by threats. These are primary rules which impose duties in that they require human beings to do or abstain from doing certain actions. However, a legal system will also be comprised of secondary rules which are characterised as rules which are power-conferring rules. We have already discussed the difference between these two different types of rule (supra pp 26–29).

He concedes the existence of comparisons between power-conferring rules and duty-imposing ones. Both are constitutive of standards providing a benchmark to be used in the critical appraisal of specific actions. In addition, power-conferring rules, though different from rules which impose duties, are always related to such rules (supra pp 26–29).

If the distinction between primary and secondary rules lies along the boundary of rules that impose obligations and those that confer powers, then primary rules would, for example, include criminal laws, the law of tort, and those rules of revenue law requiring the payment of income tax, whereas secondary rules would include, for example, those governing the creation of contracts, marriage laws, laws on the creation of valid wills, the formation of companies, etc.

A second account of secondary rules is offered at a later stage in the book.

> Under rules of one type, which may well be considered the basic or primary type, human beings are required to do or abstain from certain actions, whether they wish to or not. Rules of the other type are in a sense parasitic upon or secondary to the first; for they provide that human beings may by doing or saying certain things introduce new rules of the primary type, extinguish or modify old ones, or in various ways determine their incidence or control their operations. Rules of the first type impose duties; rules of the second type confer powers, public or private. Rules of the first type concern actions involving physical movement or changes; rules of the second type provide for operations which lead not merely to physical movement or change, but to the creation or variation of duties or obligations.
>
> Hart *The Concept of Law* 78–79

In this formulation of the distinction secondary rules are about primary rules. In fact, they specify the ways in which the primary rules may be ascertained, introduced, eliminated, varied, and the fact of their violation determined.

Hart accepts that it is possible to conceive of a society without legislature, courts or officials of any kind. Such a society would have only primary rules imposing obligations. Of necessity, a society exhibiting only primary rules would have to be a small, closely-knit, primitive type of community and anything more complex would need to evolve secondary rules. The community devoid of secondary rules would manifest three defects.

First, there would be no authoritative way of telling what were the primary rules of the society. The rules by which the community lives would not form a *system*, they would be a block of separate standards lacking any common identifying mark. As such they would resemble rules of etiquette. If any doubts arose as to what the rules were, there would be no authoritative procedure for settling the dispute. This is the defect of *uncertainty*.

Secondly, there would be no way of changing the primary rules. There would be no procedure for the elimination of old primary rules or for introducing new ones, other than, of course, the slow process of growth and decay. The defect is the *static nature of the rules*.

Thirdly, disputes as to whether an admitted rule had been broken would occur and there would be no agency empowered to determine the fact of violation. Similarly there would be no agency for administering punishments, other than the individuals themselves. The defect is *inefficiency*.

> The remedy for each of these three main defects in the simplest form of social structure consists in supplementing the *primary* rules of obligation with *secondary* rules which are rules of a different kind. The introduction of the

remedy for each defect might, in itself, be considered a step from the pre-legal into the legal world; since each remedy brings with it many elements that permeate law: certainly all three remedies together are enough to convert the regime of primary rules into what is indisputably a legal system.

Hart *The Concept of Law* 91

Uncertainty is remedied by the introduction of the first type of secondary rule, what Hart terms a *rule of recognition*.

This will specify some feature or features possession of which by a suggested rule is taken as a conclusive affirmative indication that it is a rule of the group to be supported by the social pressure it exerts. The existence of such a rule of recognition may take any of a huge variety of forms, simple or complex. It may, as in the early law of many societies, be no more than that an authoritative list or text of the rules is to be found in a written document or carved on some public monument. No doubt as a matter of history this step from the pre-legal to the legal may be accomplished in distinguishable stages, of which the first is the mere reduction to writing of hitherto unwritten rules. This is not itself the crucial step, though it is a very important one: what is crucial is the acknowledgement of reference to the writing or inscription as *authoritative*, ie as the *proper* way of disposing of doubts as to the existence of the rule. Where there is such an acknowledgement there is a very simple form of secondary rule: a rule for conclusive identification of the primary rules of obligation.

In a developed legal system the rules of recognition are of course more complex; instead of identifying rules exclusively by reference to a text or list they do so by reference to some general characteristic possessed by the primary rules. This may be the fact of their having been enacted by a specific body, or their long customary practice, or their relation to judicial decisions.

Hart *The Concept of Law* 92

Provision may be made for a possible conflict between these identifying criteria by arranging them in an order of superiority, such as by the subordination of custom or precedent to statute.

By providing an authoritative mark it introduces, although in embryonic form, the idea of a legal system: for the rules are now not just a discrete unconnected set but are, in a simple way, unified. Further, in the simple operation of identifying a given rule as possessing the required feature of being an item on an authoritative list of rules we have the germ of the idea of legal validity.

Hart *The Concept of Law* 93

The *static* quality of primary rules is remedied by the introduction of those secondary rules called rules of change. These empower an individual or body to introduce new and to eliminate old primary rules. It is in the light of such rules that legislation must be understood. Further, there are private power-conferring rules analogous to legislation in that they confer on individuals power to change their position under the primary rules. Rules making possible the making of wills, forming contracts, getting married, forming companies, are all illustrations.

The *inefficiency* of the primary rules is remedied by the introduction of those secondary rules empowering individuals to make authoritative determinations as to whether on a particular occasion a primary rule has been broken: *rules of adjudication*. As well as identifying the individuals who are to adjudicate, they also define the procedure to be used. These, also, provide the centralised official punishments and their administration.

(d) The rule of recognition

It is this secondary rule of recognition that provides a powerful analytic tool in that it allows us to analyse legal validity: the statement that a certain rule is valid means that it satisfies the criteria for the identification of primary rules set out in the rule of recognition.

> Wherever such a rule of recognition is accepted, both private persons and officials are provided with authoritative criteria for identifying primary rules of obligation. The criteria so provided may, as we have seen, take any one or more of a variety of forms: these include reference to an authoritative text; to legislative enactment; to customary practice; to general declarations of specified persons, or to past judicial decisions in particular cases.
>
> Hart *The Concept of Law* 97

For the most part the rule of recognition is seldom actually stated in legal argument. But its existence is *shown* by the process in which particular rules are identified by the courts, officials and private persons. Instead of being formulated on every occasion it is *used* by officials and private persons.

At this point in the discussion the *internal aspect of rules* makes a reappearance. But remember that to the internal and external statements discussed in what follows we need to add Raz's statements from a point of view (supra pp 15ff).

> The use of unstated rules of recognition, by courts, and others, in identifying particular rules of the system is characteristic of the internal point of view. Those who use them in this way thereby manifest their own acceptance of them as guiding rules and with this attitude there goes a characteristic vocabulary different from the natural expressions of the external point of view. Perhaps the simplest of these is the expression, 'It is the law that . . .', which we may find on the lips not only of judges, but of ordinary men living under a legal system, when they identify a given rule of the system. This, like the expression 'Out' or 'Goal', is the language of one assessing a situation by reference to rules which he in common with others acknowledges as appropriate for this purpose. This attitude of shared acceptance of rules is to be contrasted with that of an observer who records *ab extra* the fact that a social group accepts such rules but does not himself accept them. The natural expression of this external point of view is not 'It is the law that . . .' but 'In England they recognize as law . . . whatever the Queen in Parliament enacts . . .' The first of these forms of expression we shall call an *internal statement* because it manifests the internal point of view and is naturally used by one who, accepting the rule of recognition and without stating the fact that it is accepted, applies the rule in recognizing some particular rule of the system as valid. The second form of expression we shall call an *external statement* because it is the natural language of an external observer of the system who, without himself accepting its rule of recognition, states the fact that others accept it.
>
> Hart *The Concept of Law* 99

One can say that a rule is valid if it passes all the tests specified in the rule of recognition provided it is remembered that this is an internal statement. It follows that there is no necessary connection between the validity of a *particular* rule and *its* efficacy (unless such a provision is one of the criteria included in the rule of recognition), that is, whether the rule is generally obeyed. A rule may be valid even if it is not generally obeyed. But in a situation in which the rules of a legal system are generally disregarded it would be 'pointless' to say that certain rules were valid because of the rule of recognition. Therefore, someone who makes an internal statement concerning the validity of a particular rule of a system 'may be said to *presuppose* the truth of the external statement of fact that the system is generally efficacious' (p 101). However, in certain situations, it would not be 'pointless' to talk of the validity of a rule of a system which is inefficacious. So, Roman law may be taught by speaking *as if* the system were still efficacious. But the main point is that when a judge makes a statement to the effect that a particular rule is valid, although he is presupposing the general efficacy of the system, he does not state it to be so. The Scandinavian Realists, in contrast to Hart's argument, will argue for the identification of validity with efficacy (infra Chapter 14).

The rule of recognition is the *ultimate* rule of a system, as what follows demonstrates.

If the question is raised whether some suggested rule is legally valid, we must, in order to answer the question, use a criterion of validity provided by some other rule. Is this purported by-law of the Oxfordshire County Council valid? Yes: because it was made in exercise of the powers conferred, and in accordance with the procedure specified, by a statutory order made by the Minister of Health. At this first stage the statutory order provides the criteria in terms of which the validity of the by-law is assessed. There may be no practical need to go any farther; but there is a standing possibility of doing so. We may query the validity of the statutory order and assess its validity in terms of the statute empowering the minister to make such orders. Finally when the validity of the statute has been queried and assessed by reference to the rule that what the Queen in Parliament enacts is law, we are brought to a stop in inquiries concerning validity: for we have reached a rule which, like the intermediate statutory order and statute, provides criteria for the assessment of the validity of other rules; but it is also unlike them in that there is no rule providing criteria for the assessment of its own legal validity.

Hart *The Concept of Law* 103–104

The point is that no question as to the validity of the rule of recognition itself arises. It makes no sense to ask questions about the legal validity of the rule of recognition of a system since it is the test of legal validity in that system.

We only need the word 'validity', and commonly only use it, to answer questions which arise *within* a system of rules where the status of a rule as a member of the system depends on its satisfying certain criteria provided by the rule of recognition. No such question can arise as to the validity of the very rule of recognition which provides the criteria; it can neither be valid nor invalid but is simply accepted as appropriate for use in this way. To express this simple fact by saying darkly that its validity is 'assumed but cannot be demonstrated', is like saying that we assume, but can never demonstrate, that the standard metre bar in Paris which is the ultimate test of the correctness of all measurement in metres, is itself correct.

Hart The Concept of Law 105–106

The existence of the rule of recognition is a mere question of fact and this matter of fact is established by the practice of the courts, officials and private citizens of the system.

In a simple system of primary rules, the assertion that a given rule *exists* could only be an external question of fact that 'a given mode of behaviour was generally accepted as a standard and was accompanied by those features which, as we have seen, distinguish a social rule from mere convergent habits' (p 106). If such rules are within the actual practice of a social group, there is no separate question of their validity. We would only confuse matters by saying that we assume but cannot show their validity.

Where, on the other hand, as in a mature legal system, we have a system of rules which includes a rule of recognition so that the status of a rule as a member of the system now depends on whether it satisfies certain criteria provided by the rule of recognition, this brings with it a new application of the word 'exist'. The statement that a rule exists may now no longer be what it was in the simple case of customary rules—an external statement of the *fact* that a certain mode of behaviour was generally accepted as a standard in practice. It may now be an internal statement applying an accepted but unstated rule of recognition and meaning (roughly) no more than 'valid given the system's criteria of validity'. In this respect, however, as in others, a rule of recognition is unlike other rules of the system. The assertion that it exists can only be an external statement of fact. For whereas a subordinate rule of a system may be valid and in that sense 'exist' even if it is generally disregarded, the rule of recognition exists only as a complex, but normally concordant, practice of the courts, officials, and private persons in identifying the law by reference to certain criteria. Its existence is a matter of fact.

Hart The Concept of Law 106–107

Hart is arguing that there are two meanings of 'exist' operating. In speaking of a subordinate rule *within* the system, to say it exists within the system is simply to say that it is valid by the ultimate rule of recognition. Whether anyone accepts it is irrelevant. However to say that a rule of recognition exists in a legal system is simply to say that it is accepted by the courts and officials. Whether a rule of recognition exists and what its content is in any given legal system is a complex empirical question. Contrast Kelsen's classification of his basic norm as a presupposition (infra pp 127ff).

Therefore the existence of the rule of recognition is a matter of fact. However its existence, unlike that of a statute, must consist in the actual practice, that is the *acceptance* of it by the courts and officials. Consequently it is difficult to classify it: since it cannot be classified with other rules of law, some have concluded it is not a rule of law at all; others that it is a presupposition or meta-legal. The answer according to Hart is that the ultimate rule may be regarded from two points of view: as an external statement of fact or as an internal statement of validity. To understand the rule of recognition both points of view are necessary.

The case for calling the rule of recognition 'law' is that the rule providing criteria for the identification of other rules of the system may well be thought a defining feature of a legal system, and so itself worth calling 'law'; the case for calling it 'fact' is that to assert that such a rule exists is indeed to make an external statement of an actual fact concerning the manner in which the rules of an 'efficacious' system are identified. Both these aspects claim attention but we cannot do justice to them both by choosing one of the labels 'law' or 'fact'. Instead, we need to remember that the ultimate rule of recognition may be regarded from two points of view: one is expressed in the external statement of fact that the rule exists in the actual practice of the system; the other is expressed in the internal statements of validity made by those who use it in identifying the law.

Hart *The Concept of Law* 108

(e)   The existence of a legal system

What does it mean when it is asserted that a legal system *exists* in a given society? In the simple world of Rex I, it might well have been the case that both the officials and the bulk of the people *accepted* (meaning they had an internal aspect towards) a rule of recognition endowing Rex's word with the criterion of valid law. But this would not be the case in a complex modern state.

Here surely the reality of the situation is that a great proportion of ordinary citizens—perhaps a majority—have no general conception of the legal structure or of its criteria of validity. The law which he obeys is something which he knows of only as the 'law'. He may obey it for a variety of different reasons and among them may often, though not always, be the knowledge that it will be best for him to do so. He will be aware of the general likely consequences of disobedience: that there are officials who may arrest him and others who will try him and send him to prison for breaking the law. So long as the laws which are valid by the system's test of validity are obeyed by the bulk of the population this surely is all the evidence we need in order to establish that a given legal system exists.

Hart *The Concept of Law* 111

But such evidence, although necessary, is not sufficient for the existence of a legal system. The simple notion of general obedience was adequate to characterise the minimum in the case of ordinary citizens, but it cannot characterise the attitude of officials: in short, they need an internal attitude towards the rule of recognition.

[The evidence referred to at the end of the last extract] must be supplemented by a description of the relevant relationship of the officials of the system to the secondary rules which concern them as officials. Here what is crucial is that there should be a unified or shared official acceptance of the rule of recognition containing the system's criteria of validity.

Hart *The Concept of Law* 111

This double perspective, the ordinary citizen and the official, is critical in trying to understand what it means to say that a legal system exists.

There are therefore two minimum conditions necessary and sufficient for the existence of a legal system. On the one hand those rules of behaviour which are valid according to the system's ultimate criteria of validity must be generally obeyed, and, on the other hand, its rules of recognition specifying the criteria of legal validity and its rules of change and adjudication must be effectively accepted as common public standards of official behaviour by its officials. The first condition is the only one which private citizens *need* satisfy: they may obey each 'for his own part only' and from any motive whatever; though in a healthy society they will in fact often accept these rules as common standards of behaviour and acknowledge an obligation to obey them, or even trace this obligation to a more general obligation to respect the constitution. The second condition must also be satisfied by the officials of the system. They must regard these as common standards of official behaviour and appraise critically their own and each other's deviations as lapses. Of course it is also true that besides these there will be many primary rules which apply to officials in their merely personal capacity which they need only obey.

The assertion that a legal system exists is therefore a Janus-faced statement looking both towards obedience by ordinary citizens and to the acceptance by officials of secondary rules as critical common standards of official behaviour. We need not be surprised by this duality. It is merely the reflection of the composite character of a legal system as compared with a simpler decentralized pre-legal form of social structure which consists only of primary rules . . . In an extreme case the internal point of view with its characteristic normative language ('This is a valid law') might be confined to the official world. In this more complex system, only officials might accept and use the system's criteria of legal validity. The society in which this was so might be deplorably sheeplike; the sheep might end in the slaughter-house. But there is little reason for thinking that it could not exist or for denying it the title of a legal system.

Hart *The Concept of Law* 113–114

THE CONCEPT OF LAW: COMMENTS AND CRITICISMS

In 1961, when *The Concept of Law* was published, it was instantly received as a major contribution to the philosophy of law. Since then Hart's description of a legal system in terms of a union between two different types of rules has attained the status of a classic which no one interested in the analysis of law can afford to ignore. Such a seminal work must activate a great deal of discussion and critical comment. What follows is a sample of this discussion classified under the headings we employed earlier in this chapter but with a final, heading on the difference between legal rules and moral rules.

(a) Rules and the internal aspect

Neil MacCormick argues that there is a 'volitional element' to the internal aspect which is neglected by Hart. It is by reference to this element that we can elucidate what is denoted by Hart in such expressions as rules being generally 'accepted', 'supported' by criticism, supported by 'pressure' for conformity, etc.

In his own account of the 'internal aspect' Hart, as we saw, is anxious to reject the view that it is a matter of 'feelings' about conduct. Specifically, he argues that feelings of restriction or compulsion—'feeling bound'—are not essential to the existence of rules though some individuals may in fact experience such feelings 'where rules are generally accepted by a social group and generally supported by social criticism and pressure for conformity'. That is true, but it should not lead us, as perhaps it has led Hart, to ignore the important affective elements in the 'internal aspect' or the 'internal point of view'. There is an important, indeed essential, volitional as distinct from cognitive element in the internal aspect of rules, understanding of which is essential to an understanding of rules. When Hart himself speaks of the 'acceptance' of rules in a social group, he seems to have in view precisely such a volitional element as that which has been discussed here, though one of the weaknesses of his account taken as a whole is that he fails to give anywhere a single specific explanation of the relationship between the various intertwined conceptions which throughout the book are central to his theory—namely the 'internal aspect', the 'internal point of view', 'internal statements', and 'acceptance of rules'.

What seems beyond doubt is that the volitional element of the 'internal point of view' must be recognized as central thereto. It is the fact of people's will for conformity to a conceived pattern of action, of their preference for some rather than other possible configurations of such action in given circumstances, that is for them the primary ground of criticism and reflective appraisal of actual conduct in society. Any conceived pattern of action such as:

'People taking reasonable care to avoid harming other people'
'People marking out the perimeter of clock faces into sixty equal divisions'

could be the content of a norm; could be envisaged as a pattern for the critical appraisal of actions. But only such as are actually willed by some people as common patterns for a social group can be thought of as actual social norms.

But for the existence of a norm in a social group, not all its members need have this volitional commitment to it. Some indeed must, but others may simply 'play along' not out of conviction but from a kind of salutary hypocrisy. Different again is the 'delinquent' position, that is, the position of those who accept and prefer the common patterns, subject to exceptions for themselves, so far as they can get away with it. Thieves who are capitalists (as most are said to be) are a case in point. Again, there is the position of the 'rebels' who know and understand but actively reject the social norms willed by the more dominant groups in their society.

The 'playing along', 'delinquent', and 'rebel' positions (and any variants or intermediate types) are all comprehensible only in apposition or opposition to the volitionally committed position; it is necessarily presupposed by them while they are not presupposed by it. Of course, in the life of any complex social grouping it may be difficult or impossible to identify with confidence the members of the 'committed' group or fully to understand all the cross-currents of attitude which may be in play. But understanding the social norms and rules of a group involves an assumption of some people's will as underpinning and sustaining the patterns which thus underpinned and sustained are the norms of and for the group. Such understanding does not necessarily entail sharing in the relevant attitude.

The assumption or presupposition of that sustaining and underpinning will which is involved in understanding or *a fortiori* using and applying social rules norms and standards is of course not stated in any given judgment passed by reference to the norm; nor does the judgment *necessarily* express any such will. Understanding, using, passing judgment in terms of given social norms, are not to be thought of as acts which must themselves be accounted for in terms of an expression of the subjective will of the person who understands, passes judgment, etc. At one end of the spectrum, critical reflective attitudes are much more markedly reflective than actively critical; though at the back of them all must rest some sense of a genuinely felt preference on somebody's part against which, ultimately, the critical reflection makes sense.

There are all kinds of statements which may be made which presuppose an understanding of given norms and all that that understanding in turn presupposes. Even to say 'It is 11 o'clock', meaning it as a statement of the time, is to make a statement which presupposes an understanding of the given conventions, whose existence as a set of operative social norms in turn depends on a widely disseminated will to maintain them as such. Yet the statement itself does not express such a will. And so too for statements of, or in, the law: 'As a seller of goods by description, you must deliver goods conforming with the description', 'As occupier of these premises, you must take reasonable care for your lawful visitors', and so on. Such statements presuppose an understanding of a set of legal norms, whose existence is explicable only in terms of some volitional commitments by some members of a society, though they do not in themselves express a commitment on the speaker's part.

Such statements belong to the category of what Hart has called 'internal statements', on the ground that they can only be made 'internally' to the norm systems which they presuppose by way of truth conditions. And at least at some points in his narrative, he assumes that to make such statements is to evince the 'internal point of view'. But it will be noted that what determines the 'internality' of a statement is the *understanding*, not the *will* of the speaker. So far as that goes, indeed, an entire outsider to a given society could form an understanding of its norms, to the extent of being able to make 'internal' statements, 'internal' to the social norms of that society. I take it that that is precisely what social anthropologists try to do.

To observe that is to observe a crucial ambiguity in the internal/external distinction as drawn by Hart: is it a distinction between levels of understanding, or a distinction between degrees of volitional commitment? There are, it is submitted, two very important distinctions there; yet it seems to be the case that Hart has to some extent at least conflated them. We started this appendix by considering the 'externality' of the Lilliputian commissioner's report, which was external in the sense that it revealed a failure to understand Gulliver's conduct except in its overt behavioural manifestations. In a similar way, the study of human beings from certain scientific perspectives might involve ignoring the norms which people as agents would regard as guiding their conduct; to do so would be to study human behaviour only in its external aspect.

Whoever seeks to go beyond that level of understanding, and to appreciate conduct in terms of the categories which for the agent are crucial, is taking a radically different view of it and one which deserves to be described for some purposes at least as 'internal'. But this is 'internality' only at the level of understanding, for the observer in this case may remain entirely detached and uncommitted as regards the norms understanding of which is vital to his enterprise.

But of course that sort of detached understanding, like the not dissimilar uncommitted attitude of the person who plays along, or the delinquent, is parasitic upon and presupposes the position of volitional commitment which we have seen as essential to the existence of norms, and central to the internal point of view. For that reason it is important to draw a further line of distinction here in terms of differing dispositions of will.

To summarize the point: There is a genuine distinction as drawn by Hart between 'external' and 'internal' points of view with reference to human activity. But the 'internal' point of view as characterized by Hart contains essentially distinguishable components, which ought to be distinguished. There is the 'cognitively internal' point of view, from which conduct is appreciated and understood in terms of the standards which are being used by the agent as guiding standards: that is sufficient for an understanding of norms and the normative. But it is parasitic on—because it presupposes—the 'volitionally internal' point of view: the point of view of an agent, who in some degree and for reasons which seem good to him has a volitional commitment to observance of a given pattern of conduct as a standard for himself or for other people or for both: his attitude includes, but is not included by, 'the cognitively internal' attitude.

I do not think that in *Concept of Law* Hart has observed the need to distinguish between differences in levels of understanding and differences in degrees of commitment, and to that extent I find his account ambiguous. But if there are defects in his account, that is merely a challenge to others to improve it. That is what I have here tried to do.

MacCormick Legal Reasoning and Legal Theory 288–292

The difficulty, now, is that a volitional commitment must not be confused with a mere matter of 'feelings' because it is fundamental to Hart that it would be a misrepresentation of the internal aspect to identify it with such (supra pp 38–39). MacCormick maintains that by 'feelings' Hart means emotional elements: 'In so far as it is possible to distinguish between emotional elements and volitional elements in human attitudes, it seems correct to view the "internal aspect of" or "internal attitude to" rules as comprehending the volitional rather than the emotional' (MacCormick *H L A Hart* 34). What MacCormick is doing is distinguishing between two types of psychological states, the volitional and the emotional, and allowing the former, but not the latter, into the internal aspect. Hart did not distinguish these two and, consequently, attempted to describe the internal aspect as being free from both. It does seem a fair point to say that one can intellectually wish something without the presence of an emotional element.

Raz argues that the distinction between the internal aspect with its consequent idea of statements from a point of view and the external aspect with its consequent idea of statements from an external point of view obscure from sight the existence of a third category of statements—statements from a point of view or detached statements (supra pp 13–15). What follows is a further discussion of the relevance of this third type of statement.

If the internal statements are characteristic of the judge, and of the law-abiding citizens, this third kind of statement is characteristic of the lawyer and the law teacher (who of course often make internal and external statements as well) for they are not primarily concerned in applying the law to themselves or to others but in warning others of what they ought to do according to law. In an illuminating passage Kelsen contrasts the behaviour of the anarchist acting as a citizen making fully normative internal statements with the anarchist acting as a lawyer or scholar:

'In earlier publications I used as an example for the fact that the presupposition of the basic norm is possible but not necessary: An anarchist does not presuppose the basic norm. This example is misleading. The anarchist emotionally rejects the law as a coercive order; he objects to the law; he wants a community free of coercion, a community constituted without a coercive order. Anarchism is a political attitude, based on a certain wish. The sociological interpretation, which does not presuppose a basic norm, is a theoretical attitude. Even an anarchist, if he were a professor of law, could describe positive law as a system of valid norms, without having to approve of this law. Many textbooks in which the capitalist legal order is described as a system of norms constituting obligations, authorizations, rights, jurisdictions, are written by jurists who politically disapprove of this legal order.'

Legal scholars—and this includes ordinary practising lawyers—can use normative language when describing the law and make legal statements without thereby endorsing the law's moral authority. There is a special kind of legal statement which, though it is made by the use of ordinary normative terms, does not carry the same normative force of an ordinary legal statement. To examine its nature we should concentrate attention on the activities of lawyers. But it is a mistake to think that this kind of statement is unique to lawyers or to legal contexts. It is to be found whenever a person advises or informs another on his normative situation in contexts which make it clear that the advice or information is given from a point of view or on the basis of certain assumptions which are not necessarily shared by the speaker.

Imagine an Orthodox but relatively ill-informed Jew who asks the advice of his friend who is Catholic but an expert in Rabbinical law. 'What should I do?' he asks, clearly meaning what should I do according to *my* religion, not yours. The friend tells him that he should do so and so. The point is that both know that this is not what the friend thinks that he really ought to do. The friend is simply stating how things are from the Jewish Orthodox point of view. It is important not to confuse such statements from a point of view with statements about other people's beliefs. One reason is that there may be no one who has such a belief. The friend in our example may be expressing a very uncommon view on an obscure point of Rabbinical law. Indeed Rabbinical law may never have been endorsed or practised by anybody, not even the inquiring Jew. Nor can such statements be interpreted as conditionals: 'If you accept this point of view then you should, etc.' Rather they assert what is the case from the relevant point of view as if it is valid or on the hypothesis that it is—as Kelsen expresses the point—but without actually endorsing it.

Much of the discourse about the law falls according to Kelsen into this category which I called statement from a point of view. This is especially true of statements by legal practitioners and scholars acting in their professional capacity. The main differences between such contexts and the one of our imagined example is that the clear assumption that the Catholic does not share the point of view from which he speaks whereas the Jew does share it is missing. The lawyer—academic or practising—may or may not believe in the moral validity of the law. His reader or client may or may not share such beliefs. Such questions are irrelevant to the interpretation of such statements even though the answers to them—as in our example—may be known in some cases.

The analysis offered here of statements from a point of view is incomplete. Kelsen did not have a complete explanation of such statements. In fact what I have offered here is already an adaptation of Kelsen's position. We still await a full analysis of such statements. But Kelsen deserves the credit for drawing our attention to this most important class of statements. The discussion of the nature of normative discourse would have been saved from many confusions and mistakes had it not overlooked the prevalence of such statements.

Raz *The Authority of Law* 155–157

Hart has responded to statements from a point of view.

I drew a distinction between internal statements which manifest their authors' acceptance of a rule and external statements which simply state or predict certain regularities of behaviour whether it is rule-governed or not. But I wrongly wrote as if the normative vocabulary of 'ought', 'must', 'obligation', 'duty' were only properly used in such internal statements. This is a mistake, because, of course, such terms are quite properly used in other forms of statement, and particularly in lawyers' statements of legal obligations or duties describing the contents of a legal system (whether it be their own or an alien system) whose rules they themselves in no way endorse or accept as standards of behaviour. In so doing, lawyers report in normative form the contents of a law from the point of view of those who do accept its rules without themselves sharing that point of view. In terms of Raz's distinction, already mentioned, such statements of legal obligation or duties are 'detached', whereas the same statements made by those who accept the relevant rule are 'committed'. Of course those who make such 'detached' statements must understand the point of view of one who accepts the rule and so their point of view might well be called 'hermeneutic'. Such detached statements constitute a third kind of statement to add to the two (internal and external statements) which I distinguish. To have made all this clear I should have emphasized that as well as the distinction between mere regularities of behaviour and rule-governed behaviour we need a distinction between the acceptance of rules and the recognition of their acceptance by others.

Hart *Essays in Jurisprudence and Philosophy* 14

Finnis is critical of both Hart's internal point of view and Raz's statements from a point of view. Both ideas discuss the peripheral and fail to differentiate the central or focal description.

Rather obviously, this position of Hart and Raz is unstable and unsatisfactory. As against Austin and Kelsen they have sharply differentiated the 'internal' or 'legal' point of view from the point of view of the man who merely acquiesces in the law and who does so only because, when, and to the extent that he fears the punishment that will follow non-acquiescence. But they firmly refuse to differentiate further.

Finnis *Natural Law and Natural Rights* 3

What, then, is the central or focal case of internal point of view or statements from a legal point of view? There is only one and it is ignored by Hart and Raz.

The conclusion we should draw is clear. If there is a point of view in which legal obligation is treated as at least presumptively a moral obligation . . ., a viewpoint in which the establishment and maintenance of legal as distinct from discretionary or statically customary order is regarded as a moral ideal if

not a compelling demand of justice, then such a viewpoint will constitute the
central case of the legal viewpoint.

Finnis *Natural Law and Natural Rights* 14–15

But Finnis accepts that the term 'moral' has uncertain connotations. So it is
preferable to frame this conclusion in terms of his concept of 'practical
reasonableness' (infra p 194).

If there is a viewpoint in which the institution of the Rule of Law . . ., and
compliance with rules and principles of law according to their tenor, are
regarded as at least presumptive requirements of practical reasonableness
itself, such a viewpoint is the viewpoint which should be used as the standard
of reference by the theorist describing the features of legal order.

Finnis *Natural Law and Natural Rights* 15

But even within this viewpoint of practical reasonableness there is a central case.

Thus the central case viewpoint itself is the viewpoint of those who not only
appeal to practical reasonableness but also *are* practically reasonable, that is to
say: consistent; attentive to all aspects of human opportunity and flourishing,
and aware of their limited commensurability; concerned to remedy
deficiencies and breakdowns, and aware of their roots in the various aspects of
human personality and in the economic and other material conditions of social
interaction.

Finnis *Natural Law and Natural Rights* 15

The conclusion follows.

. . . the theorist cannot identify the central case of the practical viewpoint
which he uses to identify the central case of his subject-matter, unless he
decides what the requirements of practical reasonableness really are, in
relation to this whole aspect of human affairs and concerns. In relation to law,
the most important things which, in the judgment of the theorist, make it
important from a *practical* viewpoint to have law—the things which it is,
therefore, important in practice to 'see to' when ordering human affairs. And
when these 'important things' are (in some or even in many societies) in fact
missing, or debased, or exploited or othewise deficient, then the most
important things for the theorist to describe are those aspects of the situation
that manifest this absence; debasement, exploitation, or deficiency.

Finnis *Natural Law and Natural Rights* 16

The internal aspect of rules comes in for some general criticisms. Raz, in the
following extract, considers three fatal defects to the practice theory (or the
manifestations of the internal aspect (supra pp 34–37)).

The practice theory suffers from three fatal defects. It does not explain rules
which are not practices; it fails to distinguish between social rules and widely
accepted reasons; and it deprives rules of their normative character. Let us
consider these points one by one.
Rules need not be practised in order to be rules. It may be true that certain

types of rules must be practised. A legal rule is not a legal rule unless it is part of a legal system which is practised by a certain community. But this is necessary because it is a *legal* rule, and not because it is a rule. Likewise a rule is not a social rule unless it is practised by a certain community, but it may still be a rule. Moral rules are perhaps the clearest example of rules which are not practices. For example, many believe that it is a rule that promises ought to be kept. It may be true that this rule is practised in their communities, but what they believe when they believe that this is a rule is not that it is a practice. Nor is it a necessary condition for the correctness of their belief that the rule is practised. For one may believe that it is a rule that promises ought to be kept even if one is not, and has never been, a member of a community which practised the rule. Similarly, a person may believe in the validity of a rule that one ought to be a vegetarian even though he knows no other vegetarians.

One may be tempted to regard the cases I have referred to as cases of personal rules, but this is unlikely to solve our problem. We have not considered what the explanation of personal rules might be. It seems fairly clear, however, that to be useful at all the notion of a personal rule must mean more than simply a rule in the validity of which a person believes. If the conditions which must be satisfied before a person can be said to have a personal rule are more stringent than those on the basis of which a belief in the validity of a rule can be ascribed to him, then it is possible for a person to believe in the validity of a rule which is not his personal rule. A person may believe that a rule is valid even though he does not observe it. If so then on many occasions when a person believes in the validity of a moral rule the rule he believes in may not actually be his personal rule. Moreover, a man who follows a rule normally regards this fact as irrelevant to the correctness of his belief in the validity of the rule. We would not be surprised to hear him explain that he believes that it is a rule that such and such or that he believes that there is such a moral rule and therefore he has decided to try and follow it, or to make it his practice to follow it. Nor would we be surprised to hear him apologize and explain that despite his belief that there is such a moral rule he has never succeeded in behaving accordingly. We cannot refute him by saying that, since he is not actually following the rule, since it is not his personal rule, he must be wrong in thinking that it is a moral rule. Nor can we say that he is mistaken if it is neither his rule nor a social rule. He may admit to that and confess that neither he nor anybody he knows follows the rule, but regard this as proof of human imperfection and still believe in the validity of the moral rule. This argument does not imply that avowal of belief by a person is a sufficient condition for ascribing the belief to him. A person may sincerely declare that he believes in the validity of a rule and be mistaken. All I am arguing for is that the condition for ascribing the belief may not depend on his following the rule in practice. His belief may manifest itself, for example, in feelings of guilt and regret, and these may exist even though he invariably fails to follow the rule.

Nor can we escape from the problem by equating the holding of a personal rule with belief in the validity of the rule. If we do this it will be true, at the cost of trivializing the notion of a personal rule, that whenever a person believes in the validity of a rule it is his personal rule. Yet when he asserts that there is a rule he is not asserting that he believes in its validity. This view is no more plausible than the thesis that when a person asserts that it is raining what he is stating is that he believes it is raining.

These arguments do not, and are not designed to, prove that there are rules which are not practised. It may be that the person in my example is mistaken in believing that there are such rules, and he may be mistaken because the rules are not practised. He may be mistaken in thinking that there can be rules which are not practised. But even if he is wrong his belief is intelligible. He may be mistaken but he is not perverse or irrational or misusing language. This means that even if we believe that there can be a rule only if it is practised the word 'rule' does not mean 'a practice', and hence the explanation of what a rule is cannot be in terms of the practice theory. At best the practice theory is part of a substantive moral theory explaining when rules are valid or binding. It forms no part of the analysis of the concept of a rule.

The second major defect of the practice theory is its failure to distinguish between practised rules and accepted reasons. According to the practice theory, whenever a reason is believed in, followed and acted on by the relevant person or group, then they have a rule. If my first argument against the practice theory is sound, it follows that we can distinguish between a rule and a reason (which is not a rule) regardless of whether they are acted on and followed in practice. This suggests that there must be a distinction between the practice of acting on a general reason and that of following a rule. This distinction is in fact reflected in the way we interpret our practices. We do not regard every practice of acting on a general reason as acting on a rule. The practice theory fails to draw this distinction and it thereby fails to capture the essential feature of rules.

Consider the case of Jack. Jack believes that he ought to read all of Iris Murdoch's novels and he does usually read them not long after publication. If he fails to read one of her novels within a year of its publication he tends to reproach himself for the omission. Yet he does not think of himself as having a rule that he should read all her novels. He does have other rules. He is a vegetarian and he cleans his teeth every evening. He does this because he believes that these are good rules to have. But he does not read Murdoch because of a belief in any rule.

Consider a community in which almost everybody believes that babies should be breast-fed or that children should be encouraged to learn to read when they are three years of age. This is generally done and people tend to reproach mothers who do not breast-feed or parents who do not teach their three-year-old children to read. Yet people in the community do not regard these as rules. They merely think that they are good things to do. They do regard it as a rule, for example, that people should go to church on Sunday. Somehow they think differently of this, though the difference is not reflected in their practice (except that they would talk of a rule only in the latter case). Warnock in *The Object of Morality* makes the same point using the following example: 'Consider the situation of the spectator of a cricket match, ignorant of the game, and trying to work out what rules the players are following. He will find for instance that, when six balls have been bowled from one end, the players regularly move round and six balls are then bowled from the other end; deviations from this, he will observe, are adversely criticized. He will probably find also that, when a fast bowler is replaced by a slow one, some persons who were previously stationed quite close to the batsman are moved further away, some, probably, a lot further away; and he will find that, if this is not done, there is adverse criticism. But if he concludes that, in so acting, the players are following rules, he will of course be right in the first case, and wrong in the second. There is *no* rule that a slow bowler should not operate with exactly the same field setting as a fast one; this is indeed scarcely ever done, and it would nearly always be regarded as wrong to do it, but that is because, quite independently of any rules, it is something which there is nearly always good reason not to do.' The practice theory is at fault for failing to recognize and explain this distinction.

The third major defect of the practice theory is that it deprives rules of their normative character. We have already mentioned that a rule is a reason for action. The fact that rules are normally stated by using normative terms (and in trying to refute the practice theory I am arguing, among other things, that it can only be stated in such terms) indicates that they are operative reasons. A practice as such is not necessarily a reason for action. It may be provided that there is reason for all to behave as everyone does (to drive on the left, or follow the common rules of etiquette, etc.) or if a certain person has, generally or in particular circumstances, reason to conform to the practice (in order not to be rejected by his neighbours or not to lose his job, etc.). But the practice theory fails to account generally for the normative character of rules. At best it could claim to explain conventional rules, namely those social rules which are maintained because people believe that all have a reason to behave as everyone does. Ultimately it fails to explain even those.

To appreciate this point we should return to Hart's analysis of social rules. His fourth condition is that members of the relevant community use expressions such as 'it is a rule that one ought to . . .' to justify their own actions, and to justify demands and criticisms addressed to others. But what is it that they are actually saying when stating that one should have behaved in a certain way because it is a rule that. . .? There are three possible interpretations. According to the first they are not stating anything; they are acting. They are performing the speech act of criticizing (or demanding or justifying). The way Hart presents his analysis suggests that he does not accept this explanation, and surely he is right. For on this interpretation citing a rule does nothing to explain the demand or criticism, a view which is clearly wrong. Moreover, this interpretation does not apply at all to those cases in which one explains one's own or another person's action by saying that it was done because of a rule.

According to the second interpretation the statements under consideration invoke the practice as (an incomplete) reason for action. 'I did it because of the rule' means I did it because everybody does. 'Do it because of the rule' means do it because everybody does. There is no denying that sometimes this is what one intends to convey by making such a statement. This is the case when the rule is a conventional rule or when the speaker intends to appeal to reasons which his hearers may have for conforming to the rule, of the kind mentioned above (fear of public disapproval, etc.). But rules are invoked in other circumstances as well. When one explains a demand by reference to the rule that promises ought to be kept, one may intend to intimate that the hearer had better keep his promise or else he will have to take the consequences. But more often than not this is not the speaker's intention. And since at least sometimes this second interpretation fails, it always fails to explain what is stated, because what is stated is the same on all normal occasions on which such sentences are used. Though of course the speaker may have on occasion an additional point which he intends to convey, this cannot be part of what is stated. It is merely what is intimated or implied by the fact that he made the statement.

The third interpretation seems to be the one Hart has in mind. According to this interpretation, sentences of the form 'it is a rule that x ought to ø' and of the form 'x ought to ø' are standardly used to make the same statement. In other words, to state that it is a rule that one ought to ø is to state that one ought to ø. One can use either sentence to make this statement except that one can properly use the 'it is a rule' formulation only if the appropriate practice exists. To state that it is a rule . . ., is not to state that there is a practice. It is to assert that one ought to behave in this way, but one is entitled to use this sentence to make the assertion only if the practice exists. Both sentences are used to make the same statement with the use of the 'it is a rule' sentence presupposing that the practice exists. This seems to me to be Hart's interpretation of the use of these sentences to make statements 'from the internal point of view'. They can, according to his theory, also be used to make statements 'from the external point of view' which means statements that the practice exists.

On this interpretation rule sentences are used to make normative statements. They are not, however, statements of a reason. They are merely statements that there is a reason. But there is a more serious drawback to this view. According to it the fact that there is a rule is irrelevant to the normative import of the statement. Saying 'it is a rule that one ought, etc.' is rather like saying 'one ought, etc., and besides, though this is irrelevant from the point of view of practical reason, there is a practice of a certain kind'. To be sure, mentioning the rule is not entirely irrelevant. In so far as it implies the existence of a practice it indicates that the speaker is not alone in his view; it is, therefore, an important rhetorical device. But it is irrelevant for practical reasoning. We must, therefore, reject the practice theory and look for an alternative.

Raz Practical Reason and Norms 53–58

(b) The idea of obligation

Hoffmaster's piece is included because it presents a clear exposition of Hart's idea of obligation.

> Hart's analysis of the general notion of obligation is derived from his view of moral obligation. 'Moral rules impose obligations and withdraw certain areas of conduct from the free option of the individual to do as he likes.' This feature of requiring an individual to perform or refrain from performing some action regardless of the individual's own desires, wishes, wants, etc., is what is common to all rules of obligation. A social rule is a rule of obligation only if it has this feature. So a provisional statement of Hart's analysis of obligation can be given:
>
>> (I) *P* has an obligation to do *A* (or to refrain from doing *A*) if and only if a social rule exists in *P*'s society that dictates the performance (or non-performance) of actions of kind *A* on the part of people in situations similar to the situation *P* now is in, regardless of the wants, desires, wishes, inclinations, etc., of those people.
>
> (I) includes the notion of a social rule, but Hart already has explained what it means for a social rule to exist. This explanation can be stated:
>
>> (II) A social rule exists in a society if and only if the overt behaviour of a majority of the people in the society actually conforms to the requirements of the rule and a majority of the people in the society adopt the internal point of view to the requirements of the rule.
>
> (I) obviously will not distinguish social rules of obligation from social rules of non-obligation. One would have an obligation to speak correctly and to eat

properly according to (I). Hart therefore incorporates the three characteristics of social rules of obligation into his analysis:

(III)   *P* has an obligation to do *A* (or to refrain from doing *A*) if and only if
(1)   a social rule exists in *P*'s society that dictates the performance (or non-performance) of actions of kind *A* on the part of people in circumstances *C* regardless of wants, desires, wishes, inclinations, etc., of those people;
(2)   *P* is in circumstances *C*;
(3)   the social rule is thought to be important because it is believed to be essential to the maintenance of some valued facet of social life;
(4)   the social rule is supported by an insistent, general demand for conformity, and accompanied by the application of substantial social pressure on those who deviate or threaten to deviate; and
(5)   the social rule requires conduct that, although beneficial to some, may conflict with what the person who has the duty may want to do.

Hart wants the notion of obligation in (III) to be descriptive. He would argue that adding (3), (4), and (5) does not make the analysis evaluative because of the careful way in which these claims are qualified. The three characteristics concern people's beliefs, thoughts, demands, wishes, etc.; and whether these psychological and epistemological states exist is a factual matter.

It may seem odd to talk about a descriptive concept of obligation. The notion of obligation seems to be connected necessarily with the notion of justification. One might prefer to talk about a duty instead of obligation. A soldier, for example, may have a duty to kill, but he has no obligation to kill. The concept of duty seems closer to the concept of obligation in (III). Throughout *The Concept of Law*, however, Hart uses the terms 'duty' and 'obligation' interchangeably. Moreover, one is reluctant to substitute 'duty' for 'obligation' because one's duty often is a result of one's role, position, job, etc., and Hart's notion of obligation does not appeal to any formal or informal roles that one might play. The insight Hart wants to capture is that an action (or omission) may be obligatory not because of any intrinsic properties of the agent or the action, but rather because other people think it is obligatory or expect the agent to perform or forbear. Hart views the existence of an obligation in this sense as a factual matter.

A statement of Hart's account of legal obligation now can be attempted.

(IV)   *P* has a legal obligation to do *A* (or to refrain from doing *A*) if and only if
(1)   *P* is subject to an existing legal system *L*;
(2)   a rule that dictates the performance (or non-performance) of actions of kind *A* on the part of people in circumstances *C* regardless of the wants, desires, wishes, inclinations, etc., of those people is valid according to *L*'s rule of recognition; and
(3)   *P* is in circumstances *C*.

Whether a legal obligation exists likewise is a descriptive matter given (IV). The rule in (IV) (2) is a duty-imposing rule, so the problem of power-conferring or facilitative rules imposing obligations is avoided. But an interesting question arises about how the notion of a rule in (IV) (2) is to be understood. Must the rule be a social rule? The rule might not be a social rule, according to Hart's definition of a social rule, because people either do not conform their behaviour to the requirements of the rule or do not have the internal point of view toward the rule. This is precisely what one would say about cases in which a legislature creates an entirely new legal rule of obligation instead of merely conferring legal status on a pre-existing social rule of obligation. But if the rule is not a social rule, then Hart's account of legal obligation does not follow from his general account of obligation and (IV) collapses into Hill's claim that legal validity entails legal obligation (Hill 'Legal Validity and Legal Obligation' 80 Yale LJ 47 (1970)). In fact some of Hart's remarks support this interpretation of what legal obligation amounts to for him. In his article, *Legal and Moral Obligation*, Hart claims that the notions of duty and obligation are primarily legal notions, and he adds that 'both expressions are almost always appropriate for whatever the rules of an actually existing legal system forbid. If a statute forbids cruelty to children or animals, then we have a legal duty to forbear from such cruelty.' This suggests that for Hart legal obligation is to be understood simply in terms of a legally valid primary rule of obligation, which, as we have seen, is what Hill's interpretation comes to.

On the other hand, if the rule is a social rule, then legal obligation is understood as a special case of obligation in general. Both notions of obligation are unpacked in terms of the expectations and behaviour of others. Consequently, the term 'legal' adds nothing to our understanding of the obligation involved in legal obligation. 'Legal' merely indicates that the rule has a special formal status, namely legal validity, in addition to being a social rule of obligation.

There is an additional reason why criterion (IV) is an inadequate interpretation of Hart. According to (IV) the officials of a legal system would have no legal obligations. Hart's view is that legal obligations are imposed upon officials by social rules, which exist by virtue of the behaviour and expectations of other officials in the system, but that such social rules are not valid. So a different account is required to explain the legal obligations of officials:

(V) *P* has a legal obligation to do (or to refrain from doing) *A* if and only if
(1) *P* is an official of an existing legal system *L*;
(2) a social rule that dictates the performance (or non-performance) of actions of kind *A* on the part of officials in *L* in circumstances *C* regardless of the wants, desires, wishes, inclinations, etc., of those officials exists in *L*; and
(3) *P* is in circumstances *C*.

The upshot is that Hart has three accounts of legal obligation. Hart needs all three in order to explain (1) the legal obligation of one who is subject to a legal system as well as the legal obligation of one who is an official of a legal system, and (2) the sense in which a legal obligation is legal as well as the sense in which a legal obligation imposes an obligation. Two of the accounts pertain to the legal obligation of a subject of a legal system. Criterion (IV), when the rule in (IV) (2) is not a social rule, handles those situations in which a legislature enacts a new primary rule of obligation. This account is the same as the view that Hill wants to attribute to Hart. So Hill is correct in perceiving this account in Hart, although he does so for the wrong reasons and he goes astray in thinking it exhausts Hart's analysis of legal obligation. This account is open to the same objection that was raised in the discussion of Hill. Although it may explain the sense in which a legal obligation is legal, it does not explain the obligation involved. It amounts to the trivial claim that one has a legal obligation to do or refrain from doing an action just in case there is a legally valid rule that prescribes or proscribes the action. When the rule in (IV) (2) is a social rule, criterion (IV) handles those situations in which a legislature enacts a pre-existing primary rule of obligation. An example is a customary rule that is made legally valid. This account explains both the sense in which the obligation is legal and the nature of the obligation involved. Criterion (V) handles the legal obligation of an official. It explains the nature of the obligation involved but can explain in what sense the obligation is legal only in circular terms, namely that the social rule that imposes the *legal* obligation exists by virtue of the behaviour and expectations of other officials in the same *legal* system.

Hoffmaster *Professor Hart on Legal Obligation* 11 Georgia LR 1309–1314 (1977)

(c) Primary and secondary rules

It was noted (supra pp 40–43) that Hart seems to offer two differing descriptions of the distinction between these two types of rules. This point is taken by Martin, who goes on to question the claim that the introduction of secondary rules heralds the step from the pre-legal to a legal system.

After introducing the distinction between the internal and external aspects of rules, Hart introduces another distinction that plays a crucial role in his analysis, namely that between primary and secondary rules. Primary rules are initially described by Hart as ones that require human beings to do or abstain from certain actions. Secondary rules are characterized as rules that enable human beings to introduce new primary rules or to eliminate or modify primary rules. Primary rules impose duties; secondary rules provide power to change or modify the primary rules. Primary rules impose duties; secondary rules enable people to create duties. On this characterization primary rules would include laws, for example, prohibiting speeding and requiring the payment of income tax while secondary rules would presumably include marriage laws, laws governing the creation of wills, and laws governing the creation of contracts.

Later in his book Hart seems to conceive of the distinction between primary and secondary rules in a different way. Primary rules impose obligations, he says. But a society with only primary rules would have to be a small, closely knit primitive community. A more complex society would need and develop other types of rules. With only primary rules there would be no authoritative way of telling what was a primary rule of society; there would be no way of changing any rule and no authoritative way of telling whether any primary rule had been broken. The remedy for these defects is the introduction of secondary rules, and Hart considers the introduction of such rules as a step from the pre-legal to the legal world. Secondary rules on this view are about primary rules themselves: 'They specify the ways in which the primary rules may be conclusively ascertained, introduced, eliminated, varied, and the fact of their violation conclusively determined.'

The difference can be specified in this way:

First Account
  Primary rules: duty-imposing rules
  Secondary rules: duty-creating rules
Second Account
  Primary rules: duty-imposing rules

Secondary rules: rules that enable primary rules to be introduced, changed, identified, and so on.

The second account of secondary rules is, of course, different from the first account. Some secondary rules on Hart's second account would not be secondary rules on his first account. One important secondary rule on his second account is what Hart calls the rule of recognition, specifying how one tells which is a valid law in a legal system. Such a rule does not create duties. Indeed, the rule of recognition specifies an obligation of the officials of the legal system to judge certain rules as part of the legally valid rules of the system and certain rules as not part of the system. In fact the rule of recognition is a duty-imposing rule, not a duty-creating rule and, according to Hart's first account of the distinction between secondary and primary rules, should be classified as a primary rule.

One curious feature of Hart's second construal of the distinction between primary and secondary rules is that it seems to give no account of how rules that create obligations (what were called secondary rules in Hart's first construal) are recognized, changed, or adjudicated. Consider, for example, the following rule:

(R₁)   In order to create a contractual obligation one must do X, Y, Z.

This would be a secondary rule under Hart's first construal. Now consider a rule that specifies the way to change R₁:

(R₂)   In order to change (R₁) do A, B, C.

Clearly (R₂) is not a primary rule of obligation; nor is it a secondary rule in Hart's first construal since secondary rules are meant to enable humans to introduce new primary rules or to modify primary rules. Further, (R₂) is not a secondary rule in Hart's second construal since (R₂) does not specify the ways in which primary rules are ascertained, introduced, eliminated, or varied or in which violations are determined. In short, Hart's scheme seems to give no account of rules like (R₂).

This problem can be generalized: Given any rule (R) that is a secondary rule, Hart's theory provides no account of a rule (R') that would specify how (R) is to be changed, modified, eliminated, and so on. This may merely be an oversight on Hart's part. Nevertheless, the distinction between primary and secondary rules does not seem adequate to handle rules like (R'), let alone higher-level rules that specify how (R') itself is to be changed, modified, eliminated, and so on.

Is Hart correct in supposing that the introduction of secondary rules marks a shift from a pre-legal system to a legal system? Perhaps the idea is this: Primitive societies have a pre-legal system and civilized societies have a legal system; the essential difference between these two types of systems is that in a pre-legal system there are no secondary rules and in a legal system there are. If we interpret secondary rules that create obligation this thesis becomes:

(P₁)   No primitive societies have rules that create obligations.

However, this bit of armchair anthropology seems mistaken. For many primitive societies have marriage laws and such laws are rules creating laws. So (P₁) is false.

But Hart's position is not (P₁). He does not argue that in the introduction of secondary rules there is the step from a pre-legal society to a legal one (at least if one interprets secondary rules as rules that create obligations). What he does say at one point is that the introduction into society of rules enabling legislatures to change and add to the rules of duty and enabling judges to determine when the rules of duty have been broken is 'a step from the pre-legal into the legal world'.

This makes it sound as if what makes the crucial distinction between pre-legal and legal systems is the introduction of rules of change, rules of adjudication, and a rule of recognition. Interpreted in this way Hart is saying:

(P₂)   No primitive societies have rules of change, rules of adjudication, or rules of recognition.

However, in a footnote Hart maintains that few societies have existed in 'which legislative and adjudicative organs and centrally organized sanctions were entirely lacking'.

It is far from clear if all primitive societies are included in the few societies Hart refers to. Hart goes on in the footnote to refer the reader to works on primitive law that deal with the 'nearest approximation' to the state where there is no legislative or adjudicative organs and centrally organized sanctions. This suggests that even some primitive societies have these legal organs at least in a rudimentary form. Further, even if no primitive society had such organs, this would be compatible with the society's having rules of adjudication, change, and recognition. It is one thing for a society to have some organ that administers or enforces the laws; it is quite another thing for the society to have rules of adjudication, change, and so on that may be administered informally. An organ of adjudication presupposes a rule of adjudication; a rule of adjudication does not presume an organ of adjudication.

At other points Hart only makes the claim that one can imagine a society without a legislature, courts, or officials of any kind and that there exist many studies of primitive societies that claim that this possibility is realized. Here Hart seems only to say:

(P₃)   There are primitive societies without legislatures and courts.

As I have already argued, it is possible that there could be secondary rules of change, adjudication, and recognition without legislatures and courts. Hart admits in another footnote that in some primitive societies provisions are made for dispute settlement by rudimentary forms of adjudication although there are no centrally organized sanctions. Thus even if one admits the truth of (P₃) this is compatible with the falsehood of:

(P₄)   There are primitive societies without any rules of change, adjudication and recognition.

So (P₄) is not well supported by the evidence cited by Hart. In fact, as far as I can determine, Hart does not even cite evidence for the existence of societies that are the 'nearest approximations' to societies without rules of change, adjudication, and recognition.

We can conclude, I believe, that Hart has not shown that the step from the pre-legal to the legal system is to be understood in terms of the introduction of secondary rules in either sense of that phrase.

Martin *The Legal Philosophy of H L A Hart* 28–32

Sartorius is more blunt.

> [above] it was noted that Hart's distinction between primary and secondary rules is actually highly ambiguous, and it was further claimed that the form in which the distinction is used by Hart will depend upon the problem which Hart is discussing. If this claim is correct . . . Hart's contention that he has found in the union of primary and secondary rules 'the key to the science of jurisprudence' which eluded Austin must be rejected. The great explanatory power which this combination of elements appears to Hart to have is simply an illusion which rests upon the multiple ambiguity of the distinction between primary and secondary rules. Indeed, not only is it the case that there is no *one form* of the distinction between primary and secondary rules, and thus no such thing as *the* essence or nature of law; there are also problems in which even Hart is keenly interested in the formulation and solution of which *no form* of the distinction seems to be of the slightest relevance.

> Sartorius 'Hart's Concept of Law' *More Essays in Legal Philosophy* ed Summers 145

Whether the distinction between primary and secondary rules is the difference between duty-imposing and power-conferring rules or is the difference between rules that can exist on their own (primary rules) and rules that presuppose the existence of such rules is discussed by Raz (infra p 66).

(d) The rule of recognition

Raz, who is largely in agreement with Hart, gives a useful summary of the propositions implicit in the rule of recognition.

> In discussing Hart's doctrine I shall consider its applicability to institutionalized systems in general. Hart himself applies it only to the law and regards it as one of the distinctive features of law. But his arguments when valid apply to other institutionalized systems as well and when they fail they fail with respect to all such systems.
>
> According to Hart:
>
> (1) A rule of recognition is a rule requiring officials to apply rules identified by criteria of validity included in it.
> (2) Every legal system has at least one rule of recognition.
> (3) No legal system has more than one rule of recognition.
> (4) Every rule of recognition is accepted and practised by the officials of the system to which it belongs.
> (5) But the officials need not approve of it as a morally good or justified rule.
> (6) A legal system consists of its rule of recognition and all the rules identified by it.
>
> The considerations advanced in this section support all these theses except for (3) and (6) which have to be modified or abandoned. The first proposition is acceptable as a definition of a rule of recognition. There is just one comment which need be made: one should not confuse rules of recognition with second-order reasons to act on a reason. The rules which rules of recognition require officials to apply are not confined to rules addressed to those very same officials. They apply to such rules but also to many other rules addressed to ordinary individuals (directing them to pay their taxes, not to assault other individuals,

to keep their contracts, etc.) as well as rules granting powers and permissions to individuals. A rule of recognition is not a second-order reason requiring the officials to regard some other rules as their norm subjects should. It requires the officials to treat these rules as valid when using their powers to issue authoritative applicative determinations, for example, not to pay taxes as if the tax law applies to them but to declare that x, who is subject to the law, ought to pay the tax or that he has failed to pay the tax owed, etc.

The second proposition is clearly true. It is a direct consequence of the fact that institutionalized systems have primary organs with power to settle disputes concerning the application of their norms. This entails that such systems contain norms addressed to the primary organs requiring them to apply certain norms—and these are rules of recognition. There is no reason, on the other hand, to assume that a legal system can contain only one rule of recognition. The unity of the system does not depend on its containing only one rule of recognition. The unity of the system depends on the fact that it contains only rules which certain primary organs are bound to apply. The primary organs which are to be regarded as belonging to one system are those which mutually recognize the authoritativeness of their determinations. Some remarks in *The Concept of Law* suggest that Hart regards it as essential that the different criteria of validity will be ranked to prevent the possibility of conflicts between equally valid rules. But there is no reason to believe that valid norms belonging to one system cannot conflict . . . We should, therefore, conclude that, though every legal system must contain at least one rule of recognition, it may contain more than one.

Must rules of recognition be customary rules practised by the officials of the system? The answer is obviously yes if the system under consideration is in force, for it is part of the test for a system's being in force that primary organs apply its rules, which entails that if it is in force then its primary organs practise and follow its rules of recognition.

That the primary organs follow and apply the rules of recognition does not entail that they hold them to be morally justified. This thesis of Hart's has been so often overlooked or misinterpreted that one cannot repeat it often enough. It is normal to find that some at least of the subjects of an institutionalized system hold it be morally justified. It is even more common to find that many of its officials share this view. But it is of great importance to remember that these facts though common and widespread are not logically necessary. Moreover, it is not only logically possible but also not uncommon for an official of the system to follow its rules of recognition without regarding them as morally justified. In the first place, that a rule is followed by a person requires only that he holds it to be valid, ie, believes that the norm subjects are justified in following it—justified, perhaps, only because it already exists and is practised and despite the fact that it should not have been made and that it should even now be changed. Moreover, the official may follow the rule either without having any beliefs about why he is justified in doing so, or for prudential reasons (his best way of securing a comfortable life or of avoiding social embarrassment, etc.), or even for moral reasons which are based on his moral rejection of the system. An anarchist, for example, may become a judge on the ground that if he follows the law most of the time he will be able to disobey it on the few but important occasions when to do so will tend most to undermine it. Another may become a judge because he holds that he is justified in applying the law of which he disapproves when he is bound to do so if he makes good use of the powers judges have to make new laws and change existing laws on occasion.

Finally, though it is true that legal systems contain all the rules of recognition which apply to their primary organs and all the rules which these require the primary organs to apply, they may contain other rules as well. Basically an institutionalized system consists of the norms its primary organs are bound to apply. These include, first, all the norms addressed to them and, secondly, all the rules addressed to ordinary individuals which the primary organs are required to apply by norms addressed to them. The second class of norms consists of the norms identified by the rules of recognition of the system. The first class includes rules of recognition but may include other norms as well. There is no reason why an institutionalized system should not include rules addressed to its officials even though they are neither rules of recognition nor rules identified by the rules of recognition. The only limitation is that if the system in question is in force then those rules must not only be addressed to the primary organs, they must also be followed by them.

Raz *Practical Reason and Norms* 146–148

There is no doubt that Hart classifies the rule of recognition as a secondary rule. But there is a problem: is it a rule which confers a power, which is necessary according to one definition of secondary rules (see Martin, supra pp 60ff), or is it one which imposes an obligation?

To whom is the rule of recognition addressed? Hart speaks of private citizens using the rule of recognition to identify the law, but their use of the rule, like a spectator's use of the scoring rule of a game, does not imply that it is addressed to them. It is rather addressed to judicial officials (*CL*, p. 113), and its existence as a customary norm is to be seen in their normative behaviour. Courts have law-applying powers conferred upon them by rules of adjudication. When exercising their adjudicative powers they have a duty to apply only those laws satisfying certain criteria of validity. But the duty-imposing norm is distinct from the power-conferring norm, for the duty is not coextensive with the power (since courts may, given an appropriate rationale, refuse to adjudicate in certain kinds of cases despite being empowered to do so), and the norm imposing it is ultimate, whereas the power-conferring norm is not. Moreover, failure to comply with the rule of recognition does not nullify the adjudicative act. So a rule of recognition is a rule imposing a duty upon judicial officials to exercise their adjudicative powers by applying laws satisfying certain criteria.

Hacker 'Hart's Philosophy of Law' *Law, Morality, and Society* eds Hacker and Raz 23

A similar point is made by Raz.

[The rule of recognition] must be interpreted as duty-imposing. Besides, all the legal powers of officials are conferred upon them by the rules of change and adjudication, authorizing them to make new laws and to settle disputes. To claim that the rule of recognition is a power-conferring rule is to confuse it with either rules of change or rules of adjudication.

Raz *The Authority of Law* 93

In a footnote to the last extract, Raz returns to the distinction between primary and secondary rules.

It is commonly assumed that by secondary rules Hart means power-conferring rules. This interpretation is supported by some passages in his writings. . . . This interpretation, however, conflicts with other aspects of his theory and does not represent his present views. It is true that all the primary rules are duty-imposing, but not all the secondary rules are power-conferring. The rule of recognition is an exception. Rules of change, adjudication, and recognition are called secondary because they presuppose the existence of primary rules, whereas primary rules can exist without secondary ones, albeit not as a legal system. This is an explanation of the terminology, not a criterion for determining which rules are primary and which are secondary. This is determined by their social function—whether they are rules of change, adjudication, and recognition—not by their normative character.

Raz *The Authority of Law* 93

(e)   Legal rules and moral rules

Are the two necessary and sufficient conditions for the existence of a legal system, themselves based on the distinction between primary rules and secondary rules, adequate to the task of distinguishing legal rules from moral rules? Has Hart succeeded in what we called 'whittling down' the multiplicity of social rules so that his final discussion, the two necessary and sufficient conditions, centres exclusively upon those social rules characterized as being legal rules?

There is little doubt that moral rules can belong to a system of morality that meets the two conditions of primary moral rules that are generally obeyed and secondary moral rules that are accepted by the officials of the moral system. If this is so, Hart has failed to set any demarcation line between legal rules and moral rules. Clearly, he needs some other conditions to distinguish legal from moral rules. And, in another part of the *Concept*, he does suggest four conditions that, he claims, do just this.

We shall . . . identify under the heads of 'Importance', 'Immunity from deliberate change', 'Voluntary character of moral offences' and 'Forms of moral pressure' four cardinal features which are constantly found together in those principles, rules, and standards of conduct which are most commonly accounted 'moral'. These four features reflect different aspects of a characteristic and important function which such standards perform in social life or in the life of individuals. This alone would justify us in marking off whatever has these four features for separate consideration, and above all, for contrast and comparison with law. Moreover, the claim that morality has these four features is neutral between rival philosophical theories as to its *status* or 'fundamental' character. Certainly most, if not all, philosophers would agree that these four features were necessary in any moral rule or principle, though they would offer very different interpretations or explanations of the fact that morality possesses them. It may indeed be objected that these features though necessary are *only* necessary and not sufficient to distinguish morality from certain rules or principles of conduct which would be excluded from morality by a more stringent test. We shall refer to the facts on which such objections are based but we shall adhere to the wider sense of 'morality'. Our justification for this is both that this accords with much usage and that what the word in this wide sense designates, performs an important distinguishable function in social and individual life.

Hart *The Concept of Law* 164–165

However, it is doubtful whether these four conditions are, in themselves, capable of distinguishing legal rules from moral rules. This failure of the four conditions is demonstrated in the following extract from Michael Martin who acknowledges a Note in (1975) 84 Yale LJ 584–607.

According to Hart, legal rules can be deliberately changed, whereas moral rules cannot be; moral rules are not repealed or corrected. But one can certainly imagine a society in which the morals of some particular group are dictated by a religious leader. This moral leader can change moral rules as easily as legislatures can change legal rules. Hart is misled perhaps by thinking that all moral rules are like traditions. But they are not.

Moreover, according to Hart, legal rules unlike moral rules may be unimportant. An unimportant law remains law until it is repealed. But rules that cease to be considered important are no longer considered moral rules. However, this distinction does not always hold. One can imagine a group of people whose moral system is based on the dictates of a religious leader whose pronouncements define what is morally obligatory for the members of this group. Suppose the leader specifies at one time that going to church on Sunday is a moral obligation of the faithful. At the beginning people follow this command, and so doing is considered essential to Life Eternal. But after many years fewer and fewer people follow the command and many people in this group regard this moral command as unimportant in their total scheme of values. People high in the Church hierarchy now fail to insist that this rule be followed and the Leader is too old to know or care. This would not mean that this rule is no longer a moral rule in this system, but rather that this rule is no longer considered important.

Further, one can also imagine a legal system that contained a rule of recognition that was based in part on the criterion of importance. In terms of this rule of recognition a rule would not be considered a legal rule of the system if it was no longer considered to be important.

Moreover, according to Hart it is always an excuse for someone's breaking a moral rule that the person could not keep it. But this is not the case in the law. Some laws are based on the notion of strict liability and no excuse is possible. So in moral responsibility 'ought' always implies 'can', but in legal responsibility this implication does not always hold. However, if we understand someone's legal responsibility as including all and only those things that the law requires the person to do or refrain from doing, then 'ought' does imply 'can' even in the usual cases of strict liability. Even in strict liability the law requires that when some event E occurs, a person P_1 must do something, for example, pay damages to another person P_2, although E's occurrence was not the fault of P_1. It is a presupposition of the law that P_1 is able to pay P_2. Of course, this presupposition is not always true; P_1 may have no money and depending on the circumstances P_1 may be excused by the court. So, if interpreted in this way, even in strict liability 'ought' implies 'can'.

There is, indeed, a moral analogue to legal responsibility interpreted in this way. Sometimes people have a moral responsibility to do something about events whose occurrence was not their fault. For example, one has a moral responsibility to save a drowning child (if this can be done without danger to oneself) despite the fact that the child's desperate situation is not your fault. However, legal responsibility may be construed not in terms of what one must do, for example, pay damages, but in terms of some sanction that is imposed. On this construal someone's legal responsibility includes all and only those acts that are subject to legal sanction. Thus there may be a law making possession of a firearm punishable by a year in jail (such a law may be interpreted in terms of strict liability where no excuses are permitted). However, whether the imposition of sanctions on people without their being at fault distinguishes laws from morality remains to be seen.

This brings us to Hart's last criterion for distinguishing morals from laws. According to Hart, legal pressure is characteristically exerted by fear of punishment, while moral pressure is characteristically exerted not in this way but rather by a 'reminder of the moral character of the action and the demand of morality'. However, the distinction between law and morality in terms of sanctions cannot be drawn as sharply as Hart supposes. First, one can imagine a moral system that imposes physical sanctions for breaking moral rules. Indeed, there could be a moral system that would impose physical sanctions on people for acts or omissions that they could not help. Thus some religious sect may impose sanctions on its members who no longer believe in God although the non-believers may not be able to help their non-belief. Furthermore, although I have spoken of moral systems that impose physical sanctions in *this* world, some moral systems threaten sanctions after death, for example, in hell. Indeed, if one considers these systems, then it is plausible to suppose that the pressure many moral systems characteristically exert is the fear of punishment. In holding the opposite Hart must be talking about secular moral systems, not religious moral systems, at least not those in the Christian tradition. In addition, many people in modern society follow the law because they believe they have a moral duty to do so; the fear of punishment does not enter into their motivation.

Martin The Legal Philosophy of H L A Hart 41–43

Is there an alternative argument for Hart to use? One is suggested in the Note in the *Yale Law Journal* referred to above. Although both legal and moral systems impose sanctions there remains a distinction. A legal system has a *monopoly* over the use of physical sanctions. A moral system, it is true, may also impose physical sanctions, however, it will have no monopoly on the use of physical sanctions. Hence, if a moral system does use physical sanctions, it is because it is authorised so to do by the legal system. In other words, ultimate power resides in the legal system and not in the moral system. Perhaps it is this distinction which Hart is hinting at when he writes of 'centralized official sanctions'.

Chapter 4

Positivism and adjudication: H L A Hart v Ronald Dworkin

As we have seen, Hart maintains that a legal system is a union of primary and secondary rules where the officials of the system accept the secondary rules. But there remains the problem of legal reasoning. How does positivism fare in the arena of adjudication? After all, the officials will have to apply the primary and secondary rules. Is a particular rule to be treated as a legally valid rule of the system? How do they decide whether a rule has actually been broken? The problem is one of legal interpretation and to apply the rules to real cases will demand judicial interpretation of the wording of relevant legal materials found in cases, statutes, etc. The study of the forms of reasoning by which courts actually decide cases has been a central concern of jurists. So, for example, from the United States a number of theories concerning adjudication have emerged, most of them being sceptical about the role played by deduction from pre-existing legal material such as rules (American Realism is considered, infra Chapter 15).

So, what is involved in giving a legal interpretation and how does it fit into the Hartian model? Does his claim that law is a system of rules imply that legal adjudication is no more than the formal, automatic application of a rule to the facts of a specific case?

This chapter considers legal positivism, in particular Hart's concept of law, from the angle of the actual processes of legal adjudication and legal reasoning. It is a long and complicated chapter and it might help if the topics to be discussed are mapped out.

Hart's *The Concept of Law* and legal reasoning
Dworkin's attack on Hart
(a)   The distinction between rules and principles
(b)   The problem of judicial discretion
(c)   Principles and an apparent problem for the rule of recognition
An assessment of Dworkin's attack
(a)   The rules and principles distinction
(b)   Discretion
(c)   Legal principles and the rule of recognition
Dworkin's argument: the rights thesis
(a)   Principles v policies: rights v collective goals
(b)   The 'right answer' thesis
Comments and criticisms of Dworkin's positive contribution

HART'S *THE CONCEPT OF LAW* AND LEGAL REASONING

A theory such as Hart's, which places the emphasis on law as rules and on legal systems as the combination of primary and secondary rules, seems to flirt with formalism. Formalism or conceptualism consists in an attitude to formulated rules which seeks to minimize the element of discretion or choice in the application or interpretation of that rule.

What precisely is it for a judge to commit this error, to be a 'formalist', 'automatic', a 'slot machine'? Curiously enough the literature, which is full of the denunciation of these vices, never makes this clear in concrete terms; instead we have only descriptions which cannot mean what they appear to say; it is said that in the formalist error courts make an excessive use of logic, take a thing to 'a dryly logical extreme', or make an excessive use of analytical methods. But just how in being a formalist does a judge make an excessive use of logic? It is clear that the essence of his error is to give some general term an interpretation which is blind to social values and consequences (or which is in some other way stupid or perhaps merely disliked by critics). But logic does not prescribe interpretation of terms; it dictates neither the stupid nor intelligent interpretation of any expression. Logic only tells you hypothetically that *if* you give a certain term a certain interpretation then a certain conclusion follows. Logic is silent on how to classify particulars—and this is the heart of a judicial decision. So this reference to logic and to logical extremes is a misnomer for something else, which must be this. A judge has to apply a rule to a concrete case—perhaps the rule that one may not take a stolen 'vehicle' across State lines, and in this case an aeroplane has been taken. He either does not see or pretends not to see that the general terms of this rule are susceptible of different interpretations and that he has a choice left open uncontrolled by linguistic conventions. He ignores, or is blind to, the fact that he is in the area of the penumbra and is not dealing with a standard case. Instead of choosing in the light of social aims the judge fixes the meaning in a different way. He either takes the meaning that the word most obviously suggests in its ordinary non-legal context to ordinary men, or one which the word has been given in some other legal context, or, still worse, he thinks of a standard case and then arbitrarily identifies certain features in it—for example, in the case of a vehicle, (1) normally used on land, (2) capable of carrying a human person, (3) capable of being self-propelled—and treats these three as always necessary and always sufficient conditions for the use in all contexts of the word 'vehicle', irrespective of the social consequences of giving it this interpretation. This choice, not 'logic', would force the judge to include a toy motor car (if electrically propelled) and to exclude bicycles and the aeroplane. In all this there is possibly great stupidity, but no more 'logic', and no less, than in cases in which the interpretation given to a general term and the consequent application of some general rule to a particular case is consciously controlled by some identified social aim.

Decisions made in a fashion as blind as this would scarcely deserve the name of decisions; we might as well toss a penny in applying a rule of law.

Hart *Essays in Jurisprudence and Philosophy* 66–67

So, what is Hart's theory of legal interpretation? Clearly he is forced to walk a tightrope between American Realism and formalism; he needs to stand by his thesis that laws genuinely are rules, in contradistinction to the extreme wing of realism, and, at the same time, avoid collapsing his theory into the pitfalls of formalism.

His strategy is to maintain that, although laws are rules, it is of the essence of legal rules that they leave much scope for the discretion of judges in applying the rule to a particular case: rules are open-textured.

Whichever device, precedent or legislation, is chosen for the communication of standards of behaviour, these, however smoothly they work over the great mass of ordinary cases, will, at some point where their application is in question, prove indeterminate; they will have what has been termed an _open texture_. So far we have presented this, in the case of legislation, as a general feature of human language; uncertainty at the borderline is the price to be paid for the use of general classifying terms in any form of communication concerning matters of fact. Natural languages like English are when so used irreducibly open textured.

Hart *The Concept of Law* 124–125

127-128

He discusses three areas of indeterminacy.

In every legal system a large and important field is left open for the exercise of discretion by the courts and other officials in rendering initially vague standards determinate, in resolving the uncertainties of statutes, or in developing and qualifying rules only broadly communicated by authoritative precedents. None the less these activities, important and insufficiently studied though they are, must not disguise the fact that both the framework within which they take place and their chief end-product is one of general rules. These are rules the application of which individuals can see for themselves in case after case, without further recourse to official direction or discretion.

Hart *The Concept of Law* 132–133

First, all natural language is indeterminate, and law, being a species of natural language, manifests the same characteristic of indeterminacy. Rules are framed in ordinary language using such general words as 'vehicle', 'dwelling-house', 'intention', etc. Such words do possess a central core of certainty of meaning but also there will be a 'penumbra of doubt'. What if the issue at hand does not fall within the central core of determinate meaning: does 'vehicle' include a toy car or roller-skates?

Faced with the question whether the rule prohibiting the use of vehicles in the park is applicable to some combination of circumstances in which it appears indeterminate, all that the person called upon to answer can do is to consider (as does one who makes use of a precedent) whether the present case resembles the plain case 'sufficiently' in 'relevant' respects. The discretion thus left to him by language may be very wide; so that if he applies the rule, the conclusion, even though it may not be arbitrary or irrational, is in effect a choice. He chooses to add to a line of cases a new case because of resemblances which can reasonably be defended as both legally relevant and sufficiently close. In the case of legal rules, the criteria of relevance and closeness of resemblance depend on many complex factors running through the legal system and on the aims or purpose which may be attributed to the rule. To characterize these would be to characterize whatever is specific or peculiar in legal reasoning.

Hart *The Concept of Law* 124

Not only do rules possess an aura of uncertainty; so they should.

[One way to achieve determinacy and certainty—and incidentally to thereby stoop to formalism—] is to freeze the meaning of the rule so that its general terms must have the same meaning in every case where its application is in question. To secure this we may fasten on certain features present in the plain case and insist that these are both necessary and sufficient to bring anything which has been within the scope of the rule, whatever other features it may have or lack, and whatever may be the social consequences of applying the rule in this way. To do this is to secure a measure of certainty or predictability at the cost of blindly prejudging what is to be done in a range of future cases, about whose composition we are ignorant. We shall thus indeed succeed in settling in advance, but also in the dark, issues which can only reasonably be settled when they arise and are identified. We shall be forced by this technique to include in the scope of a rule cases which we would wish to exclude in order to give effect to reasonable social aims, and which the open textured terms of our language would have allowed us to exclude, had we left them less rigidly defined. The rigidity of our classifications will thus war with our aims in having or maintaining the rule.

Hart *The Concept of Law* 126–127

He sets out the reasons for maintaining a penumbra of uncertainty. Notice that the second handicap is contingent upon the first: the unforeseeable contingencies bring with them the relative indeterminacy of aim.

It is, however, important to appreciate why, dependence on language as it actually is, with its characteristics of open texture, we should not cherish, even as an ideal, the conception of a rule so detailed that the question whether it applied or not to a particular case was always settled in advance, and never involved, at the point of actual application, a fresh choice between open alternatives. Put shortly, the reason is that the necessity for such choice is thrust upon us because we are men, not gods. It is a feature of the human predicament (and so of the legislative one) that we labour under two connected handicaps whenever we seek to regulate, unambiguously and in advance, some sphere of conduct by means of general standards to be used without further official direction on particular occasions. The first handicap is our relative ignorance of fact: the second is our relative indeterminacy of aim. If the world in which we live were characterized only by a finite number of features, and these together with all the modes in which they could combine were known to us, then provision could be made in advance for every possibility. We could make rules, the application of which to particular cases never called for a further choice. Everything could be known, and for everything, since it could be known, something could be done and specified in advance by rule. This would be a world fit for 'mechanical' jurisprudence.

Hart *The Concept of Law* 125

Secondly, very general standards are used within the rules. So, often a rule, whether in statute or case-law, will include words such as 'reasonableness', 'fair', 'just and equitable', etc. There will be clear cases where the standard applies and clear cases where it does not. However, there will be many cases where uncertainty reigns prior to an authoritative determination by the court.
Thirdly, another area of indeterminacy is that of decisions based on precedent. There are three problem areas.

Any honest description of the use of precedent in English law must allow a place for the following pairs of contrasting facts. *First,* there is no single method of determining the rule for which a given authoritative precedent is an authority. Notwithstanding this, in the vast majority of decided cases there is very little doubt. The head-note is usually correct enough. *Secondly*, there is no authoritative or uniquely correct formulation of any rule to be extracted from cases. On the other hand, there is often very general agreement, when the bearing of a precedent on a later case is in issue, that a given formulation is adequate. *Thirdly*, whatever authoritative status a rule extracted from precedent may have, it is compatible with the exercise by courts that are bound by it of the following two types of creative or legislative activity. On the one hand courts deciding a later case may reach an opposite decision to that in a precedent by narrowing the rule extracted from the precedent, and admitting some exception to it not before considered, or, if considered, left open. This process of 'distinguishing' the earlier case involves finding some legally relevant difference between it and the present case, and the class of such differences can never be exhaustively determined. On the other hand, in following an earlier precedent the courts may discard a restriction found in the rule as formulated from the earlier case, on the ground that it is not required by any rule established by statute or earlier precedent. To do this is to widen the rule.

Hart *The Concept of Law* 131

Hart's conclusion is obvious: where there is judicial legislation in these three areas of indeterminacy, the judge uses legal reasoning to come to this conclusion—note the phrase 'legally relevant' in the last extract. Given uncertainty, his commitment to rules is witnessed in his following conclusion.

The open texture of law means that there are, indeed, areas of conduct where much must be left to be developed by courts or officials striking a balance, in the light of circumstances, between competing interests which vary in weight from case to case. None the less, the life of the law consists to a very large extent in the guidance both of officials and private individuals by determinate rules which, unlike the applications of variable standards, do *not* require from them a fresh judgment from case to case. This salient fact of social life remains true, even though uncertainties may break out as to the applicability of any rule (whether written or communicated by precedent) to a concrete case. Here at the margin of rules and in the fields left open by the theory of precedents, the courts perform a rule-producing function which administrative bodies perform centrally in the elaboration of variable standards. In a system where *stare decisis* is firmly acknowledged, this function of the courts is very like the exercise of delegated rule-making powers by an administrative body. In England this fact is often obscured by forms; for the courts often disclaim any such creative function and insist that the proper task of statutory interpretation and the use of precedent is, respectively, to search for the 'intention of the legislature' and the law that already exists.

Hart *The Concept of Law* 132

DWORKIN'S ATTACK ON HART

Ronald Dworkin succeeded Hart to the Chair of Jurisprudence at Oxford and brought with him one of the most important attacks on Hart's theory of legal reasoning. Dworkin's indictment is that legal positivism, in particular the brand espoused by Hart, is fatally flawed and induces a distortion when applied to the process of legal reasoning. Almost all rules breed unclear or problem cases for which an answer is not given merely by the logical application of the rule. It is common to say that in such 'hard' cases judges do more than find and apply law, they actually make law. So Hart would argue that although judges are bound by rules, in unclear cases they, of necessity, have a discretion. However, Dworkin argues that in any hard case where Hart supposes that judicial discretion becomes operative, in fact there exists a uniquely correct judicial decision. Although this correct answer is not furnished by the existing rules, the judge could arrive at such an answer through the use of legal principles which are implicit in the law. Hart's mistake is to assume that law is made up only of a regime of rules.

In order to understand the weight of Dworkin's attack we shall consider the following headings:

(a)　the distinction between rules and principles;
(b)　the problem of judicial discretion;
(c)　legal principles and the rule of recognition.

> My strategy will be organized around the fact that when lawyers reason or dispute about legal rights and obligations, particularly in those hard cases when our problems with these concepts seem most acute, they make use of standards that do not function as rules, but operate differently as principles, policies, and other sorts of standards. Positivism, I shall argue, is a model of and for a system of rules, and its central notion of a single fundamental test for law forces us to miss the important roles of these standards that are not rules.
>
> Dworkin *Taking Rights Seriously* 22

After considering this critical aspect of Dworkin we shall be in a position to proceed to his constructive discussion of legal reasoning in a hard case. But here is a trailer: legal principles identify *rights* of citizens as individuals; there will always be one *uniquely correct* judicial decision to a hard case provided by the legal principles, although possibly, what this is may not be known.

(a)　The distinction between rules and principles

Rules and principles are both standards. However, they differ in the character of the direction they give. Rules are applicable in an 'all-or-nothing' fashion: either an issue falls within the ambit of the rule or it does not. A rule either determines an issue or it has nothing at all to say on that issue. This is not the way principles operate. For example, the legal principle that no one may profit from his own wrong does not mean that the law never permits a person to profit from his wrong—Dworkin mentions adverse possession as such a case in point. Principles, rather than functioning in an all-or-nothing manner, merely state a reason that argues in one direction. Whereas relevant rules dictate an answer, principles merely incline towards a certain direction.

> This all-or-nothing is seen most plainly if we look at the way rules operate, not in law, but in some enterprise they dominate—a game, for example. In baseball a rule provides that if the batter has had three strikes, he is out. An official cannot consistently acknowledge that this is an accurate statement of a

baseball rule, and decide that a batter who has had three strikes is not out. course, a rule may have exceptions (the batter who has taken three strikes is not out if the catcher drops the third strike). However, an accurate statement of the rule would take this exception into account, and any that did not would be incomplete. If the list of exceptions is very large, it would be too clumsy to repeat them each time the rule is cited; there is, however, no reason in theory why they could not all be added on, and the more that are, the more accurate is the statement of the rule.

If we take baseball rules as a model, we find that rules of law, like the rule that a will is invalid unless signed by three witnesses, fit the model well. If the requirement of three witnesses is a valid legal rule, then it cannot be that a will has been signed by only two witnesses and is valid. The rule might have exceptions, but if it does then it is inaccurate and incomplete to state the rule so simply, without enumerating the exceptions. In theory, at least, the exceptions could all be listed, and the more of them that are, the more complete is the statement of the rule.

But this is not the way the sample principles in the quotations operate. Even those which look most like rules do not set out legal consequences that follow automatically when the conditions provided are met. We say that our law respects the principle that no man may profit from his own wrong, but we do not mean that the law never permits a man to profit from wrongs he commits. In fact, people often profit, perfectly legally, from their legal wrongs. The most notorious case is adverse possession—if I trespass on your land long enough, some day I will gain a right to cross your land whenever I please. There are many less dramatic examples. If a man leaves one job, breaking a contract, to take a much higher paying job, he may have to pay damages to his first employer, but he is usually entitled to keep his new salary. If a man jumps bail and crosses state lines to make a brilliant investment in another state, he may be sent back to jail, but he will keep his profits.

We do not treat these—and countless other counter-instances that can easily be imagined—as showing that the principle about profiting from one's wrongs is not a principle of our legal system, or that it is incomplete and needs qualifying exceptions. We do not treat counter-instances as exceptions (at least not exceptions in the way in which a catcher's dropping the third strike is an exception) because we could not hope to capture these counter-instances simply by a more extended statement of the principle. They are not, even in theory, subject to enumeration because we would have to include not only these cases (like adverse possession) in which some institution has already provided that profit can be gained through a wrong, but also those numberless imaginary cases in which we know in advance that the principle would not hold. Listing some of these might sharpen our sense of the principle's weight (I shall mention that dimension in a moment), but it would not make for a more accurate or complete statement of the principle.

A principle like 'No man may profit from his own wrong' does not even purport to set out conditions that make its application necessary. Rather, it states a reason that argues in one direction, but does not necessitate a particular decision. If a man has or is about to receive something, as a direct result of something illegal he did to get it, then that is a reason which the law will take into account in deciding whether he should keep it. There may be other principles or policies arguing in the other direction—a policy of securing title, for example, or a principle limiting punishment to what the legislature has stipulated. If so, our principle may not prevail, but that does not mean that it is not a principle of our legal system, because in the next case, when these contravening considerations are absent or less weighty, the principle may be decisive. All that is meant, when we say that a particular principle is a principle of our law, is that the principle is one which officials must take into account, if it is relevant, as a consideration inclining in one direction or another.

Dworkin *Taking Rights Seriously* 24–26

This distinction entails another.

> Principles have a dimension that rules do not—the dimension of weight or importance. When principles intersect (the policy of protecting automobile consumers intersecting with principles of freedom of contract, for example), one who must resolve the conflict has to take into account the relative weight of each. This cannot be, of course, an exact measurement, and the judgment that a particular principle or policy is more important than another will often be a controversial one. Nevertheless, it is an integral part of the concept of a principle that it has this dimension, that it makes sense to ask how important or how weighty it is.
>
> Rules do not have this dimension. We can speak of rules as being *functionally* important or unimportant (the baseball rule that three strikes are out is more important than the rule that runners may advance on a balk, because the game would be much more changed with the first rule altered than the second). In this sense, one legal rule may be more important than another because it has a greater or more important role in regulating behaviour. But we cannot say that one rule is more important than another within the system of rules, so that when two rules conflict one supersedes the other by virtue of its greater weight.
>
> If two rules conflict, one of them cannot be a valid rule. The decision as to which is valid, and which must be abandoned or recast, must be made by appealing to considerations beyond the rules themselves. A legal system might regulate such conflicts by other rules, which prefer the rule enacted by the higher authority, or the rule enacted later, or the more specific rule, or something of that sort. A legal system may also prefer the rule supported by the more important principles. (Our own legal system uses both of these techniques.)

Dworkin *Taking Rights Seriously* 26–27

Even in the hardest of hard cases the judge does not through the operation of his discretion determine what the law shall be; rather he is saying what the law is. For all possible cases there is a solution awaiting discovery in the form of the principles embedded in the existing law. But how are these principles disinterred? Further, when more than one principle is involved how does the judge decide which principle should be given most weight? It appears that his position as judge requires him to evolve an all-embracing philosophy of law and society. So he must extend his search in hard cases beyond the legal standards in any particular rule to those implicit in the legal system as a whole. This superhuman human enterprise requires a god-like judge; enter Mr Justice Hercules, a sort of philosopher–king in judicial garb, generously endowed with 'superhuman skill, learning, patience and acumen'.

You will now see why I call our judge Hercules. He must construct a scheme of abstract and concrete principles that provides a coherent justification for all common law precedents and, so far as these are to be justified on principle, constitutional and statutory provisions as well.

Dworkin Taking Rights Seriously 116–117

Researching precedents and statutes is just the first of Hercules' labours: he needs to construct the 'soundest theory of law' that can be provided as a justification for the explicit substantive and institutional rules of the system. A principle is only a principle of law if it figures in this soundest theory of law. To settle hard cases, then, it may be necessary for a judge to develop a comprehensive constitutional, political and legal theory consisting of a set of principles that could justify his scheme of government.

> So Hercules is driven, by the project, to a process of reasoning that is like the process of the self-conscious chess referee. He must develop a theory of the constitution, in the shape of a complex set of principles and policies that justify that scheme of government, just as the chess referee is driven to develop a theory about the character of his game. He must develop that theory by referring alternately to political philosophy and institutional detail. He must generate possible theories justifying different aspects of the scheme and test the theories against the broader institution.

Dworkin Taking Rights Seriously 107

In saying that Hercules needs to ask himself what sort of theory of law, of political theory and of justice best explains the institutions of his community, it seems an anti-positivistic argument is being presented.

Of course, in the real world, devoid of any Hercules, judges can but approximate towards what the mythological Hercules would accomplish, indeed, they may differ in their decisions. Even so, because of his commitment to the right answer thesis (infra p 99), Dworkin insists only one decision would be correct.

In seeking the soundest theory two dimensions of the task present themselves. The theory must both 'fit' and 'justify' the settled law: these are the two criteria of judgment, fit with past political decisions and justifiability or moral soundness. In *Law's Empire* Dworkin has progressed to an interpretive theory of law (infra Chapter 12) and he explains the dimensions of fit and soundness by using an analogy with the idea of a chain novel.

> In this enterprise a group of novelists writes a novel *seriatim*; each novelist in the chain interprets the chapters he has been given in order to write a new chapter, which is then added to what the next novelist receives, and so on. Each has the job of writing his chapter so as to make the novel being constructed the best it can be, and the complexity of this task models the complexity of deciding a hard case under law as integrity. The imaginary literary enterprise is fantastic but not unrecognizable. Some novels have actually been written in this way, though mainly for a debunking purpose, and certain parlor games for rainy weekends in English country houses have something of the same structure. Television soap operas span decades with the same characters and some minimal continuity of personality and plot, though they are written by different teams of authors even in different weeks. In our example, however, the novelists are expected to take their responsibilities of continuity more seriously; they aim jointly to create, so far as they can, a single unified novel that is the best it can be.

Each novelist aims to make a single novel of the material he has been given, what he adds to it, and (so far as he can control this) what his successors will want or be able to add. He must try to make this the best novel it can be construed as the work of a single author rather than, as is the fact, the product of many different hands. That calls for an overall judgment on his part, or a series of overall judgments as he writes and rewrites. He must take up some view about the novel in progress, some working theory about its characters, plot, genre, theme, and point, in order to decide what counts as continuing it and not as beginning anew. If he is a good critic, his view of these matters will be complicated and multifaceted, because the value of a decent novel cannot be captured from a single perspective. He will aim to find layers and currents of meaning rather than a single, exhaustive theme. We can, however, in our now familiar way give some structure to any interpretation he adopts, by distinguishing two dimensions on which it must be tested. The first is what we have been calling the dimension of fit. He cannot adopt any interpretation, however complex, if he believes that no single author who set out to write a novel with the various readings of character, plot, theme, and point that interpretation describes could have written substantially the text he has been given. That does not mean his interpretation must fit every bit of the text. It is not disqualified simply because he claims that some lines or tropes are accidental, or even that some events of plot are mistakes because they work against the literary ambitions the interpretation states. But the interpretation he takes up must nevertheless flow throughout the text; it must have general explanatory power, and it is flawed if it leaves unexplained some major structural aspect of the text, a subplot treated as having great dramatic importance or a dominant and repeated metaphor. If no interpretation can be found that is not flawed in that way, then the chain novelist will not be able fully to meet his assignment; he will have to settle for an interpretation that captures most of the text, conceding that it is not wholly successful. Perhaps even that partial success is unavailable; perhaps every interpretation he considers is inconsistent with the bulk of the material supplied to him. In that case he must abandon the enterprise, for the consequence of taking the interpretive attitude toward the text in question is then a piece of internal skepticism: that nothing can count as continuing the novel rather than beginning anew.

He may find, not that no single interpretation fits the bulk of the text, but that more than one does. The second dimension of interpretation then requires him to judge which of these eligible readings makes the work in progress best, all things considered. At this point his more substantive aesthetic judgments, about the importance or insight or realism or beauty of different ideas the novel might be taken to express, come into play. But the formal and structural considerations that dominate on the first dimension figure on the second as well, for even when neither of two interpretations is disqualified out of hand as explaining too little, one may show the text in a better light because it fits more of the text or provides a more interesting integration of style and content. So the distinction between the two dimensions is less crucial or profound than it might seem. It is a useful analytical device that helps us give structure to any interpreter's working theory or style. He will form a sense of when an interpretation fits so poorly that it is unnecessary to consider its substantive appeal, because he knows that this cannot outweigh its embarrassments of fit in deciding whether it makes the novel better, everything taken into account, than its rivals. This sense will define the first dimension for him. But he need not reduce his intuitive sense to any precise formula; he would rarely need to decide whether some interpretation barely survives or barely fails, because a bare survivor, no matter how ambitious or interesting it claimed the text to be, would almost certainly fail in the overall comparison with other interpretations whose fit was evident.

We can now appreciate the range of different kinds of judgments that are blended in this overall comparison. Judgments about textual coherence and integrity, reflecting different formal literary values, are interwoven with more substantive aesthetic judgments that themselves assume different literary aims. Yet these various kinds of judgments, of each general kind, remain distinct enough to check one another in an overall assessment, and it is that possibility of contest, particularly between textual and substantive judgments, that distinguishes a chain novelist's assignment from more independent creative writing. Nor can we draw any flat distinction between the stage at which a chain novelist interprets the text he has been given and the stage at which he adds his own chapter, guided by the interpretation he has settled on. When he begins to write he might discover in what he has written a different, perhaps radically different, interpretation. Or he might find it impossible to write in the tone or theme he first took up, and that will lead him to reconsider other interpretations he first rejected. In either case he returns to the text to reconsider the lines it makes eligible.

229-232

Dworkin *Law's Empire* 228–229

The following extracts rely upon and explain the interpretive method, the two dimensions and the 'in the best light thesis' (infra pp 375ff). For a much deeper consideration of these ideas and arguments, together with the idea of 'law as integrity'—referred to in the opening of the first extract, see the discussion of Dworkin's *Law's Empire* (infra Chapter 12).

Judges who accept the interpretive ideal of integrity decide hard cases by trying to find, in some coherent set of principles about people's rights and duties, the best constructive interpretation of the political structure and legal doctrine of their community. They try to make that complex structure and record the best these can be. It is analytically useful to distinguish different dimensions or aspects of any working theory. It will include convictions about both fit and justification. Convictions about fit will provide a rough threshold requirement that an interpretation of some part of the law must meet if it is to be eligible at all. Any plausible working theory would disqualify an interpretation of our own law that denied legislative competence or supremacy outright or that claimed a general principle of private law requiring the rich to share their wealth with the poor. That threshold will eliminate interpretations that some judges would otherwise prefer, so the brute facts of legal history will in this way limit the role any judge's personal convictions of justice can play in his decisions. Different judges will set this threshold differently. But anyone who accepts law as integrity must accept that the actual political history of his community will sometimes check his other political convictions in his overall interpretive judgment. If he does not—if his threshold of fit is wholly derivative from and adjustable to his convictions of justice, so that the latter automatically provide an eligible interpretation—then he cannot claim in good faith to be interpreting his legal practice at all. Like the chain novelist whose judgments of fit automatically adjusted to his substantive literary opinions, he is acting from bad faith or self-deception.

Hard cases arise for any judge, when his threshold test does not discriminate between two or more interpretations of some statute or line of cases. Then he must choose between eligible interpretations by asking which shows the community's structure of institutions and decisions—its public standards as a whole—in a better light from the standpoint of political morality. His own moral and political convictions are now directly engaged. But the political judgment he must make is itself complex and will sometimes set one department of his political morality against another: his decision will reflect not only his opinions about justice and fairness but his higher-order convictions about how these ideals should be compromised when they compete. Questions of fit arise at this stage of interpretation as well, because even when an interpretation survives the threshold requirement, any infelicities of fit will count against it, in the ways we noticed, in the general balance of political virtues. Different judges will disagree about each of these issues and will accordingly take different views of what the law of their community, properly understood, really is.

Dworkin Law's Empire 255–256

Law as integrity asks a judge deciding a common-law case to think of himself as an author in the chain of common law. He knows that other judges have decided cases that, although not exactly like his case, deal with related problems; he must think of their decisions as part of a long story he must interpret and then continue, according to his own judgment of how to make the developing story as good as it can be. (Of course the best story for him means best from the standpoint of political morality, not aesthetics.) We can make a rough distinction once again between two main dimensions of this interpretive judgment. The judge's decision—his postinterpretive conclusions—must be drawn from an interpretation that both fits and justifies what has gone before, so far as that is possible. But in law as in literature the interplay between fit and justification is complex. Just as interpretation within a chain novel is for each interpreter a delicate balance among different types of literary and artistic attitudes, so in law it is a delicate balance among political convictions of different sorts; in law as in literature these must be sufficiently related yet disjoint to allow an overall judgment that trades off an interpretation's success on one type of standard against its failure on another. I must try to exhibit that complex structure of legal interpretation, and I shall use for that purpose an imaginary judge of superhuman intellectual power and patience who accepts law as integrity.

Dworkin Law's Empire 238–239

(b)   The problem of judicial discretion

Hart argues that in a difficult case within the area of the penumbra there is no uniquely correct answer: here the operative word is 'discretion'.

In these cases it is clear that the rule-making authority must exercise a discretion, and there is no possibility of treating the question raised by the various cases as if there were one uniquely correct answer to be found, as distinct from an answer which is a reasonable compromise between many conflicting interests.

Hart *The Concept of Law* 128

Although judges are under a duty to apply the relevant rules where they are obviously applicable, of necessity they have a wider discretion where rules are not clear. In line with Austin (supra pp 22–23) but in contrast to Dworkin, Hart argues that judges do not simply find and apply the law; they make it. Hart's position is expressed clearly in the next piece.

> *Interpretation.* Laws require interpretation if they are to be applied to concrete cases, and once the myths which obscure the nature of the judicial processes are dispelled by realistic study, it is patent that the open texture of law leaves a vast field for a creative activity which some call legislative. Neither in interpreting statutes nor precedents are judges confined to the alternatives of blind, arbitrary choice, or 'mechanical' deduction from rules with predetermined meaning. Very often their choice is guided by an assumption that the purpose of the rules which they are interpreting is a reasonable one, so that the rules are not intended to work injustice or offend settled moral principles. Judicial decision, especially on matters of high constitutional import, often involves a choice between moral values, and not merely the application of some single outstanding moral principles; for it is folly to believe that where the meaning of the law is in doubt, morality always has a clear answer to offer. At this point judges may again make a choice which is neither arbitrary nor mechanical; and here often display characteristic judicial virtues, the special appropriateness of which to legal decision explains why some feel reluctant to call such judicial activity 'legislative'. These virtues are: impartiality and neutrality in surveying the alternatives; consideration for the interest of all who will be affected; and a concern to deploy some acceptable general principle as a reasoned basis for decision. No doubt because a plurality of such principles is always possible it cannot be *demonstrated* that a decision is uniquely correct: but it may be made acceptable as the reasoned product of informed impartial choice. In all this we have the 'weighing' and 'balancing' characteristic of the effort to do justice between competing interests.

Hart *The Concept of Law* 200

It will be argued below by Neil MacCormick that although Hart's views on interpretation are pointing in the right direction they do not go far enough (infra pp 87ff).

Dworkin has two arguments against discretion or 'judicial creativity'.

> The first argues that a community should be governed by men and women who are elected by and responsible to the majority. Since judges are, for the most part, not elected, and since they are not, in practice, responsible to the electorate in the way legislators are, it seems to compromise that proposition when judges make law. The second argues that if a judge makes new law and applies it retroactively in the case before him, then the losing party will be punished not because he violated some duty he had, but rather a new duty created after the event.

Dworkin *Taking Rights Seriously* 84

In *Law's Empire* the second argument has been recast in terms of law as 'integrity' (infra pp 385ff): decisions need to cohere with the most attractive principles of political theory 'and morality or justice that fit with past decisions.

However, Dworkin has a more sophisticated discussion of discretion: of the three possible varieties of discretion discussed in the next extract, it is the third that Dworkin denies a place in legal reasoning.

> We use that concept, in discussions about duty, in three different ways. First, we say that a man has discretion if his duty is defined by standards that reasonable men can interpret in different ways, as a sergeant has discretion if he is told to take the five most experienced men on patrol. Second, we say that a man has discretion if his decision is final, in the sense that no higher authority may review and set aside that decision, as when the decision whether a player is offside is left to the discretion of the linesman. Third, we say that a man has discretion when some set of standards which impose duties upon him do not in fact purport to impose any duty as to a particular decision, as when a clause in a lease gives the tenant the option in his discretion to renew.
>
> It is plain that if no social rule unambiguously requires a particular legal decision, and the profession is split on what decision is in fact required, then judges will have discretion in the first of these senses, because they will have to exercise initiative and judgment beyond the application of a settled rule. It is also plain, if these judges form the highest court of appeal, that they will have discretion in the second sense. But, unless we accept the strongest form of the social rule theory, that duties and responsibilities can be generated only by social rules, it does not follow that these judges have discretion in the third sense. A judge may have discretion in both the first and second senses, and nevertheless properly regard his decision as raising an issue of what his duty as a judge is, an issue which he must decide by reflecting on what is required of him by the varying considerations that he believes are pertinent. If so, then this judge does not have discretion in the third sense, which is the sense a positivist needs to establish if he is to show that judicial duty is defined exclusively by an ultimate social rule or set of social rules.
>
> Dworkin *Taking Rights Seriously* 69

It is discretion in this third sense, 'strong discretion', that so offends Dworkin.

> I call both of these senses weak to distinguish them from a stronger sense. We use 'discretion' sometimes not merely to say that an official must use judgment in applying the standards set him by authority, or that no one will review that exercise of judgment, but to say that on some issue he is simply not bound by standards set by the authority in question. In this sense we say that a sergeant has discretion who has been told to pick any five men for patrol he chooses or that a judge in a dog show has discretion to judge airedales before boxers if the rules do not stipulate an order of events. We use this sense not to comment on the vagueness or difficulty of the standards, or on who has the final word in applying them, but on their range and the decisions they purport to control. If the sergeant is told to take the five most experienced men, he does not have discretion in this strong sense because that order purports to govern his decision. The boxing referee who must decide which fighter has been the more aggressive does not have discretion, in the strong sense, for the same reason.
>
> Dworkin *Taking Rights Seriously* 32

To argue that the use of strong discretion is unacceptable is to say that the judge has no legislative role. It would be wrong to conclude that a judge ever legislates in the sense of making law; his function is that of finding and interpreting.

(c) Principles and an apparent problem for the rule of recognition

Principles, although genuinely legal, cannot be identified by means of a 'test of pedigree' going back to the rule of recognition. So it is Dworkin's contention that the processes of judicial decision-making are incompatible with Hart's rule of recognition and, consequently, with Hart's concept of law. What, then, according to Dworkin is the origin of legal principles?

> Most rules of law, according to Hart, are valid because some competent institution enacted them. Some were created by a legislature, in the form of statutory enactments. Others were created by judges who formulated them to decide particular cases, and thus established them as precedents for the future. But this test of pedigree will not work for principles. The origin of these as legal principles lies not in a particular decision of some legislature or court, but in a sense of appropriateness developed in the profession and the public over time. Their continued power depends upon this sense of appropriateness being sustained. If it no longer seemed unfair to allow people to profit by their wrongs, or fair to place special burdens upon oligopolies that manufacture potentially dangerous machines, these principles would no longer play much of a role in new cases, even if they had never been overruled or repealed. (Indeed, it hardly makes sense to speak of principles like these as being 'overruled' or 'repealed'. When they decline they are eroded, not torpedoed.)
>
> True, if we were challenged to back up our claim that some principle is a principle of law, we would mention any prior cases in which that principle was cited, or figured in the argument. We would also mention any statute that seemed to exemplify that principle (even better if the principle was cited in the preamble of the statute, or in the committee reports or other legislative documents that accompanied it). Unless we could find some such institutional support, we would probably fail to make out our case, and the more support we found, the more weight we could claim for the principle.
>
> Yet we could not devise any formula for testing how much and what kind of institutional support is necessary to make a principle a legal principle, still less to fix its weight at a particular order of magnitude. We argue for a particular principle by grappling with a whole set of shifting, developing and interacting standards (themselves principles rather than rules) about institutional responsibility, statutory interpretation, the persuasive force of various sorts of precedent, the relation of all these to contemporary moral practices, and hosts of other such standards. We could not bolt all of these together into a single 'rule', even a complex one, and if we could the result would bear little relation to Hart's picture of a rule of recognition, which is the picture of a fairly stable master rule specifying 'some feature or features possession of which by a suggested rule is taken as a conclusive affirmative indication that it is a rule . . .'

Dworkin Taking Rights Seriously 40–41

In the last extract, notice the discussion of 'institutional support'. According to Hart, rules are valid where there is institutional support. We also cite institutional support when arguing that a principle is a principle of law; however in this situation, for the argument advanced in the final paragraph, institutional support is inadequate. Notice also that the 'sense of appropriateness' argument would now be further elaborated in terms of law as integrity and the two dimensions (supra pp 77ff and infra Chapter 12).

Again, the rule of recognition could not simply list all the legal principles.

One more possibility must be considered, however. If no rule of recognition can provide a test for identifying principles, why not say that principles are ultimate, and *form* the rule of recognition of our law? The answer to the general question 'What is valid law in an American jurisdiction?' would then require us to state all the principles (as well as ultimate constitutional rules) in force in that jurisdiction at the time, together with appropriate assignments of weight. A positivist might then regard the complete set of these standards as the rule of recognition of the jurisdiction. This solution has the attraction of paradox, but of course it is an unconditional surrender. If we simply designate our rule of recognition by the phrase 'the complete set of principles in force', we achieve only the tautology that law is law. If, instead, we tried actually to list all the principles in force we would fail. They are controversial, their weight is all important, they are numberless, and they shift and change so fast that the start of our list would be obsolete before we reached the middle. Even if we succeeded, we would not have a key for law because there would be nothing left for our key to unlock.

I conclude that if we treat principles as law we must reject the positivists' first tenet, that the law of a community is distinguished from other social standards by some test in the form of a master rule.

Dworkin *Taking Rights Seriously* 43–44

AN ASSESSMENT OF DWORKIN'S ATTACK

(a) The rules and principles distinction

Hart in his later work continues to distinguish between cases that clearly fall under a rule and cases that cannot. However, he does seem to assume that principles are a part of the law.

It is of crucial importance that cases for decision do not arise in a vacuum but in the course of the operation of a working body of rules, an operation in which a multiplicity of diverse considerations are continuously recognized as good reasons for a decision. These include a wide variety of individual and social interests, social and political aims, and standards of morality and justice; and they may be formulated in general terms as principles, policies and standards. In some cases only one such consideration may be relevant, and it may determine decision as unambiguously as a determinate legal rule. But in many cases this is not so, and judges marshal in support of their decisions a plurality of such considerations which they regard as jointly sufficient to support their decision, although each separately would not be. Frequently these considerations conflict, and courts are forced to balance or weigh them and to determine priorities among them. The same considerations (and the same need for weighing them when they conflict) enter into the use of precedents when courts must choose between alternative rules which can be extracted from them, or when courts consider whether a present case sufficiently resembles a past case in relevant respects.

Hart *Essays in Jurisprudence and Philosophy* 107

MacCormick argues that standards other than rules can be incorporated into Hart's description of a legal system. In what follows, MacCormick explicates the difference between rules and principles in a different way from Dworkin's distinction.

> A further difficulty which was raised but not resolved earlier may be raised again in this connection. Not all of the statements (or utterances of other kinds) which people may make using normative terms do in truth presuppose the existence of a 'rule' as such. Certainly, they all presuppose *some* standard of rightness or wrongness etc. But are all such standards *rules*, let alone *social* rules? Or are rules, or social rules, merely one group among the standards of judgment of conduct that people may hold and appeal to or apply? Hart reveals himself as assuming an affirmative answer to this question, as for example, when he sets out his starting-point for clarifying the nature of morality:
>
> > 'It is . . . necessary to characterize, in general terms, those *principles, rules and standards* relating to the conduct of individuals which belong to morality and make conduct morally obligatory.' (*C.L.* p.163; italics added)
>
> Later, in the same passage, on the following page, he uses 'standards' in a way which suggests that it is in fact a general term embracing the whole group of 'rules, principles and standards'.
>
> Surely he is right in this. The vegetarian whom we thought about earlier presumably holds it as a principle that one ought not to eat the flesh of animals. But is there from his or anyone's viewpoint a rule against doing so? Being noisily drunk on a public service bus offends a widely held conception of decency or propriety or good behaviour, and this may be manifested in criticism, pressure to be quiet and behave oneself, and so on. (An incident involving noisy drunkenness occurred in the Edinburgh bus on which I travelled home on the evening I wrote this.) But this can be true without its being true that there is a social rule against being noisily drunk on buses (in Edinburgh, or anywhere else). Shared standards of propriety, decency, good behaviour are not necessarily 'rules'.
>
> The trouble is not that Hart fails to see and give some allowance for the fact that not all standards are rules, nor that principles are distinct from rules (a key point in Ronald Dworkin's criticism of Hart's theory). The trouble is that he has not himself clarified what the assumed distinction is.
>
> I shall here do no more than briefly sketch the outlines of possible Hartian clarification of that point, in the following terms. 'Principles' are, both in the legal and the moral case, according to Hart characterized as being *rational* grounds of conduct, and as being *general* in their scope. Rules, it would seem by contrast, are essentially conventional and thus may be in a sense arbitrary in the specific form they take, as with the British 'Keep Left' rule in driving—why not 'Keep Right' as elsewhere? The point or principle involved is clear, to provide safe driving conditions. That is eminently rational, but that does not make 'Keep Left' more rational than 'Keep Right', or *vice versa*. An arbitrary choice having been made or an arbitrary practice having developed, it would be irrational in anyone not to adhere to it, so long as it is indeed a *shared* standard, shared to one's best of belief and expectations by almost all or all of one's fellow drivers. So in relation to standards which are rules, it would seem important to note the point made earlier, that the element of 'preference' involved in the 'internal point of view' tends to be conditional; one's preference that a given pattern be adhered to by all may be conditional upon the pattern's

being and continuing to be supported by common or convergent preferences among all or nearly all the parties to the activity contemplated.

This may in turn remind us of another feature of rules, that we think of them as relatively 'cut and dried' often even as captured in writing. The way in which we sometimes talk of 'unwritten rules' conveys a hint that these are considered relatively unusual. An 'unwritten rule' is an instance of a conventional standard of doing which is well understood and clear cut in its provisions, as is usual with rules which are enshrined in a particular verbal formula. This expresses better the point about arbitrariness, and points to a difference between rules and broader or vaguer standards of rectitude, propriety, decency or whatever. The difference simply arises from the degree to which people do share in conceiving a reasonably cut and dried 'pattern of behaviour' as the standard, or something altogether vaguer.

These reflections are not unimportant for those whose focus of concern is law, in particular 'positive law' or 'state law'. For it is (certainly in Hart's view) a particular feature of governance under law that state legal orders are characterized by the existence of institutions and procedures for formulating in relatively clear, precise and authoritative ways those governing standards of conduct which are 'legal'. If the reflections of a moment ago were correct, then it would be a noticeable and distinctive feature of legal order that it does, through its institutions and procedures, convert vaguer standards of conduct into *rules* as such. And indeed it is significant that outwith the sphere of positive law, the other walks of life to which 'rules' as such apply tend to be those where there do exist institutions and procedures which likewise give some precision to standards and conventions, as in the case of organized games, voluntary associations, families to some degree, companies, trades unions, schools, universities and the like. In some of these cases, moreover, the rules are actually given the name of 'laws' or 'bye-laws', as in the instance of the 'Laws of Golf' or the 'Laws of Association Football' or the 'Statutes of the University' or the like.

To the extent that my sketched differentiating features of rules as against standards of conduct in general are acceptable, they do then give ground for supposing that 'rule' may be a concept particularly apposite and relevant to and in jurisprudence. What would be less convincing would be to suppose that 'rules' as such would have any great prominence in morality which (aside from some forms of religious ethics) is not in any large degree institutionalized. Indeed, according to the powerful Kantian school of ethical thought which insists on the autonomy of moral agents as such, morality cannot be authoritatively institutionalized through social agencies. The 'heteronomous' moral development of the child may be mediated through the inculcation of rules laid down by parental authority, but the adult moral agent is his or her own final authority.

Hart's own recognition of this is somewhat muted by the prominence which he gives to the concept of a rule, and by his failure to expound the distinction which he implicitly observes as holding between 'principles' and 'rules' and other 'standards'. It is however significant that it is within those chapters of the *Concept of Law* dealing with 'Justice and Morality' (Ch.8) and 'Morals and Laws' (Ch.9) that he most stresses the important part played by principles and other standards alongside of rules as such. Of the relative standing and relative importance of rules and other standards in morality there is a good deal more to be said; but it will be said in the next chapter.

MacCormick *H L A Hart* 40–43

Unless MacCormick's idea of rules being 'cut and dried' is an analogue of Dworkin's 'all-or-nothing' aspect of rules, there is little common ground between the two accounts of the difference between rules and principles: there is no necessary 'conventional' element in a Dworkinian rule; his principles need not be 'general'; MacCormick's principles, furnishing 'rational' grounds for conduct, seem to be decisive and do more than merely 'incline', as Dworkin would have it, towards one direction.

The main point, however, is that whichever distinction is accepted, Dworkin's or MacCormick's, non-rule standards can be accommodated within Hart's concept of law.

For a discussion of Dworkin's arguments as to the origin of principles (the soundest theory of law, law as integrity, the dimensions of fit and justification), refer to the analysis of *Law's Empire* (Chapter 12 and the discussion earlier in this chapter).

However, at this stage, it could be of some value to reproduce one of Hart's most recent comments on Dworkin's idea of the 'soundest theory of the law'.

. . . 'the soundest theory of the law' cannot provide an explanation of how it is that legal rules and statutes create legal rights and duties constituting prima-facie moral reasons for action, and it cannot determine the existence of such legal rights and duties where the settled law is indeterminate. The soundest theory of the law could only do these things if its principles were in themselves *sound* according to independent morality which Dworkin calls background morality, and not merely the *soundest* of those theories that could fit the settled law. But no positivist who, like myself, denies that legal rights and duties are species of moral rights and duties, would ever wish to deny that legal rights and duties arising from morally sound legal principles could provide at least prima-facie moral reasons for action and enforcement. What the positivist does claim is that there are no persuasive arguments for restricting the concepts of legal right and legal duty to such cases, and that there are persuasive arguments for employing, in a descriptive jurisprudence, concepts not so restricted.

Hart in *Issues in Contemporary Legal Philosophy* (ed Gavison) 43

(b) Discretion

Dworkin's characterisation of Hart's ideas on discretion is as follows: outside the 'core of certainty', judges use discretion in a 'strong' sense; they function in a sort of quasi-legislative capacity taking the decision which seems best to them on whatever grounds they think fit. Dworkin's contention is different: even in hard cases they must seek out legal principles and not invent them; this will require the operation of a discretion, but in a 'weak' sense, in giving weight to the various principles; in all hard cases there will be a correct decision.

In the following extract MacCormick defends and extends Hart's discussion of the role of discretion in adjudication. It is again argued that Hart's theory of rules can be extended to cover principles.

He argues that Hart's treatment of discretion points in the right direction but does not take us far enough. From what MacCormick says it would appear that Hart would accept this elaboration.

. . . there are in legal systems canons or standards of legal reasoning which establish what are satisfactory justifications of judicial decisions where justification by simple deduction from a legal rule and the established facts of the case is inapplicable for any of the reasons we have considered above. Very briefly, these can be summarized for modern legal systems as follows:

First, conformably with the principle of formal justice ('treat like cases alike') a judge ought to base the instant decision on some *ruling* which settles the *type* of case to which the instant case belongs and the proposed decision for that type of case. Secondly, he ought to *evaluate* that ruling and any possible rival rulings in the light of the *consequences* which would follow from adopting it as a ruling in general application. That evaluation should be made by reference to legally appropriate values, including justice, common sense, public policy and legal convenience, as the judge sees those. Thirdly, the ruling must be shown to be *coherent* with the rest of the legal system or the relevant branch of it. This depends upon its being either an analogical extrapolation from already settled rules of law or precedents of binding or persuasive character, or a particular application of some general principle already at least implicit in the pre-established law. Finally it must be shown to be *consistent* with the pre-established law in the sense that it does not conflict with any previously established legal rule according to some reasonable interpretation of potentially conflicting rules.

That is perhaps a ridiculously brief summary of a long and involved argument. The point of mentioning it at all in the present context is that Hart has both publicly and privately intimated that in the main he accepts the ideas put forward in *Legal Reasoning and Legal Theory* [MacCormick's 1978 book where he explores these ideas in depth] and thinks them consistent with his own views. The problem for the present work is how, if at all, such ideas do fit the Hartian theory.

On some points the 'fit' is easy. The requirement of 'consistency' simply repeats the Hartian view that judges do have to apply settled legal rules where they are applicable, adding only the corollary that it is equally obligatory for the judges to show that possibly or ostensibly conflicting rules *can* be distinguished to avoid conflict with the favoured 'ruling' in a hard case. On the other hand, one has to stress that this activity of distinguishing and reconciling ostensibly or potentially conflicting rules takes place within a wider argumentative context which is concerned *inter alia* with values and principles and other standards of conduct. That shows that the Hartian distinction between a rule's 'core of certainty' and 'penumbra of doubt' is by no means an inert and invariant 'given' arising from the purely linguistic properties of rules formulated in ordinary legal language. The possibility of ambiguity in rules is a *resource* available to the judge, who may sometimes have reason to squeeze the 'core' down to the absolute indistinguishable and unavoidable minimum, and at other times in other contexts may have reason to give a broad and liberal reading of the rule so that it captures matters within even its remotest penumbra.

That takes us . . . to considerations of the contextual variables. These bring in the very issues of valuation and of principle which figure in 'consequentialist' aspects of legal arguments from 'coherence' as sketched above. How about the matter of fit with the Hartian theory on these points?

The answer is that there is a perfectly comfortable fit with Hart's theory, provided that . . . [it is accepted] that Hart's theory of social rules admits of extension to cover principles and values as standards in themselves and various other types of social standard. Since legal rules are a species of social rules in Hart's theory, there is no reason to deny the possibility that there are legal principles, legal values-as-standards, and possibly other legal standards as well as legal rules.

That is precisely the fact of the matter. 'Law' does embrace these principles, values and other standards as well as rules of statute law and rules derived from case-law. And a study of legal reasoning reveals them in operation . . .

A particular feature of legal reasoning which points to the role and significance of general principles in law is the omnipresent resort to analogical reasoning. The instant case may not be 'covered' by a rule of statute law or by an admissible precedent. But in such cases judges and lawyers argue by analogy with settled rules, and seek to make choices between competing analogies. This exhibits a presupposition that the specific rules and rulings validated by the 'rule of recognition' are themselves instances or concretizations of more general principles, viz the principles whose observation in the law tends to promote certain valued states of affairs. These principles and values implicit in the law do then constitute legal standards to which it is considered legitimate, indeed obligatory, to have recourse where the more specific formulae of legal rules are lacking or give only weak and indeterminate guidance.

What is more, the enterprise of legal argumentation in hard cases circulates around the duty of the judge not to give any odd decision but to give a decision founded on some explicit or implicit ruling on the point(s) of law disputed by the parties. That duty depends on a legal principle of central importance, the principle of formal justice in decision-making: to decide like cases alike, and hence to make decisions on the footing that they cover any case of an envisaged generic type, not just the once-off matter in hand between the particular parties to the instant dispute.

Recognition of and adherence in some measure to the principle of formal justice is in fact a further necessary element in distinguishing the judicial role as such from that of a mere mediator or arbiter whose decision is once-off between the parties in question.

MacCormick *H L A Hart* 126–128

Standards which are not rules must be even more open-textured, with judges having a very wide discretion. And this is the point made by Hart about judicial discretion. Because of this, Dworkin's argument about judicial reasoning, based on the distinction between 'weak' and 'strong' discretion, is turned upon its head. The next extract is a convincing conclusion to the issue at hand; it also constitutes an argument against Dworkin's 'right answer' thesis yet to be considered (infra pp 99ff).

Hence there is a decided oddity in the criticism of Hart's theory of judicial discretion advanced by Ronald Dworkin. Dworkin says that *because* a legal system is always founded on principles, *therefore* judges do not really have 'strong' discretion. It is not true, he says, that when the rules fail to give a clear answer the judge has a discretion unlimited by any legal standards. That is quite correct in itself. The judge's discretion is discretion to do as seems right and proper consistently with legal principles, legal values and other relevant legal standards. But that is as strong a discretion as there can possibly be. The decision how it is right and proper to interpret and apply vague-because-general principles involves evaluating consequences of a ruling this way or that. This is a matter of *settling*, not *finding*, priorities within the legal system.

Neither is there an actual consensus within state-societies about moral and political priorities, nor is there any reason to suppose that there is some ideal judge's or observer's standpoint from which to establish the *true* moral and political priorities served by the legal system.

Even if it be the case, as Dworkin presupposes, that moral values and principles have some objective truth and universal validity, it remains also the case that people inveterately disagree about them, as he does not deny. Political principles are thus also subjects of inveterate disagreement. Legal systems result from a patchwork of historical assertions of contentious and changing political principles, political compromises and mere political muddles. That from which laws emerge is controversial, even if some or all of the controversies concern moral issues on which there may in principle be a single right answer. So the idea that judges have only a 'weak' discretion since their task is to 'find' *the* right priority ranking of legal principles and deduce from it *the* right answer is utterly unsustainable. Though the Hartian theory of judicial discretion does need amendment, and though Dworkin's criticisms do point towards the amendments needed, his own particular amendments ought not to command our assent.

In all cases, judicial discretion exists only within the framework of some predetermined standards. Where these standards are legal rules, the discretion extends only within rather a restricted field, though rarely eliminated completely. Where the rules give no guidance or give ambiguous guidance, recourse may be had to other standards of judgment. But since these standards are all less precise than rules, the discretion involved in intepreting and extrapolating from them is greater. 'Discretions' come not in differences of kind (as Dworkin supposes Hart to suppose) but in differences of degree (as Hart supposes in fact). The larger the degree of discretion the more nearly the judge approximates to a law-maker in settling his own rulings on disputed points, even though in doing so he is still interpreting and applying relatively vague legal standards. The legislature, by contrast, *can* (though it rarely does) make total innovations radically at odds with previous legal standards.

MacCormick *H L A Hart* 129–130

(c)   Legal principles and the rule of recognition

Dworkin's reason for concluding that principles are incompatible with the rule of recognition is no more than the fact that the law includes principles. As we have seen, Hart's concept of law can be generalised so as to include standards that are not rules. So, is it possible for Hart to answer Dworkin? Given the existence of principles, is it correct to say they fall outside the pale of the rule of recognition and thereby constitute a grave deficiency in Hart's scheme of things?

The answer is provided by MacCormick (supra this page, penultimate paragraph). His discussion of principles of law is based on his distinction between rules and principles (supra pp 74ff). But there is a special relationship between the two which, because of a rule's connection with the rule of recognition, brings both within the pale of the rule of recognition.

Let me restate what I believe we mean when we speak of 'principles of law' as distinct from rules of law. My opinion is that legal rules (let me for this purpose call them 'mandatory legal rules'), singly, or much more commonly, in related groups, may be conceived of as tending to secure, or being aimed at securing, some end conceived as valuable, or some general mode of conduct conceived to be desirable: to express the policy of achieving that end, or the desirability of that general mode of conduct, in a general normative statement, is, then, to state 'the principle of the law' underlying the rule or rules in question.

Thus, it is a rule of law in the U.K. that vehicles must be driven on the left-hand side of the road: there is no special reason why we should choose the left rather than the right, but there is a compelling reason, safety, why we should fix on one or the other. The principle is that safety on the roads ought to be secured by specifying codes of conduct for drivers, or that people ought to drive in a way which will minimize danger to other road users. These principles (or, that principle alternatively stated) are the underlying reason for the whole body of Road Traffic laws, not merely of the 'keep left' rule. There may of course be other principles, such as that the free and speedy movement of traffic on the roads ought to be fostered, which laws imposing parking restrictions and prohibiting obstruction are seen as embodying. So even in this simple, and almost banal case, we can identify at least two principles underlying the rules of one branch of law, which principles are obviously capable of coming into conflict with each other. The free and speedy movement of traffic is not always consonant with safety. All this is, I hope, uncontroversial.

The effect of explicating general principles in this way is to create the possibility of perceiving the Road Traffic Acts, not just as a congeries of arbitrary commands, prohibitions and permissions, but as a coherent set of rules directed at securing general ends which at least those who framed the rules conceived to be desirable. In this sense, to explicate the principles is to rationalise the rules.

MacCormick Legal Reasoning and Legal Theory 156–157

In this way principles supply a rationalisation of, and thus a justifying reason for, case-law and statute law. As such they can play a role of justification for the extension of the law in novel cases.

Conceiving of principles as relatively general norms which 'rationalise' rules or sets of rules is dependent upon one assumption: that we know what rules to rationalise. This we do because of the criteria of identification set out in the rule of recognition. The relationship between principles of law and the rule of recognition is now evident.

There is a relationship between the 'rule of recognition' and principles of law, but it is an indirect one. The rules which are rules *of law* are so in virtue of their pedigree; the principles which are principles *of law* are so because of their function in relation to those rules, that is, the function which those who use them as rationalizations of the rules thus ascribed to them.

MacCormick Legal Reasoning and Legal Theory 233

To what extent does this line of reasoning vitiate the cause of the legal positivist?

This, it may be said, suggests antipositivistically that law is not after all value free. Not so much does it suggest it, it thunderously proclaims it—but there is nothing antipositivistic about saying that law is not value free. Nobody in his right mind—and there are at least some positivists who are in their right mind—has ever suggested or would ever suggest that law itself is value free. If human beings did not value order in social life, they wouldn't have laws at all, and every legal system embodies not merely a form of social order, but that form of order which is specifically valued by those who have control of the legislative executive or adjudicative process—or at least, it is a patchwork of the rival values favoured by the various groups taking part in such processes.

The point of being a positivist is not to deny obvious truths of that sort. The point is rather in the assertion that one does not have in any sense to share in or endorse these values wholly or in part in order to know that the law exists, or what law exists. One does not have to believe that Soviet law or French law or Scots law is good law or the repository of an objectively good form of social order in order to believe that it is law, or to describe or expound or explain it for what it is.

Nor does one have to regard 'the law' as being objective or neutral or impartial as between competing interests or classes or religious groups or other groups or sexes or whatever. Historically and for all present systems that would be an absurd belief. What is more even though a good legal system (in my view) would not favour one class or race or sex or religion over others, it would be absurd to suppose that it would not favour some interests over others. The interests of those who pursue their own ends by fraud ought not be favoured against the interests of those they defraud in any circumstances. Law not merely is never, it ought never to be, neutral as between such interests.

MacCormick *Legal Reasoning and Legal Theory* 233–234

However, it would be incorrect to argue that principles are themselves determined by the rule of recognition because there may be more than one set of normative generalisations to rationalise certain rules.

What transforms a political principle held by a number of people into a legal principle?

. . . in evaluating the apprehended consequences of possible rulings on points of law the Courts take as one relevant test the bearing of 'common sense', and I have suggested that that refers in part to 'the sort of rough community consensus on social values to which judges conceive of themselves as giving effect' . . . In just that way contemporary opinion on matters of moral and political right comes to be filtered into the law, no doubt subject to the distorting lens of the judges' conceptions of 'contemporary opinion', a phrase whose nebulousness has been consciously chosen to reflect the rather nebulous quality of the reality it describes.

In this way, albeit slowly and incrementally rather than by the 'big bang' of legislation, new principles are adopted into the law through judicial decision-making.

MacCormick *Legal Reasoning and Legal Theory* 236–237

In short, when we ask what gives a principle *legal* quality we must give the answer in terms of its actual or potential explanatory and justificatory function in relation to law as already established, that is, in relation to established rules of law as identified by reference to criteria of recognition. That is thoroughly compatible with the equally true proposition that in the law-making process it is people's adherence to political and moral principles which gives them reason to enact or judicially enunciate statutes or legal rulings. In that way of course a well-framed theory of law meshes with a well-framed theory of legislation, but there is no reason to collapse the one into the other.

Does this involve drawing a sharp disjunction between principles of law and moral and political principles? Yes and no. It involves asserting that there really is a difference between principles which are and those which are not legal, subject to an intermediate *terra incognita* of principles struggling for legal recognition, like the 'neighbour principle' before 1932 and perhaps for some time after. It does not involve the assertion that a principle which is a legal principle thereby stops being a moral or political principle, on which again we are indebted to Dworkin for vigorous statement of the neglected truth.

MacCormick *Legal Reasoning and Legal Theory* 238

Sartorius uses a different argument to come to the conclusion that legal principles can be subsumed under an ultimate test along the lines of a rule of recognition. He argues that principles could be characterized as those standards that are established or implied either directly or indirectly by other standards. Therefore, he maintains that there are three stages in a rule of recognition.

Dworkin himself points out that 'not any principle will do to justify a change, or no rule would ever be safe. There must,' he thus rightly concludes, 'be some principles that count and others that do not . . .' Those that do count, I have suggested above, can be identified by something quite like Hart's ultimate rule of recognition. I see no reason, in other words, to accept Dworkin's contention that this tenet of positivism implies that standards other than rules are not binding law. Such an ultimate test, I shall argue, can provide a complex criterion by means of which it can be determined that certain principles and policies, as well as formally valid rules and judicial precedents, are binding law within a given legal system.

We may begin by loosening up a bit Hart's concept of a rule of recognition, which must include the rule of *stare decisis*, so as to take account of the fact that the doctrine of precedent gives authoritative status directly only to particular decisions, rather than to general rules. As so modified, it will identify constitutional provision, legislative enactment, and judicial decision as authoritative sources of law. Certainly Dworkin is right that there is much more here than valid legal rules; already included are broad constitutional principles, statements of policy accompanying statutory legislation, and particular judicial decisions. The additional standards which both Dworkin and I wish to identify as binding upon judges—and which I wish to identify as binding *law*—may be recursively defined as those exemplified, established, or implied by these first order standards, either directly or indirectly.

We may actually have three stages here, as can be seen if we consider that the ultimate test could identify as binding laws: (1) The statutes enacted by a particular legislative body; (2) The principles and policies embedded in (1); (3) 'Extralegal' principles and policies directly or indirectly incorporated into the law by either (1) or (2). Although the actual filling out of such an ultimate criterion would be a complex and demanding task for any mature legal system, if it is indeed a practical possibility at all, the only claim that need be made is that it is in principle possible, and that it is this possibility which in theory underlies the identification of something as an authoritative *legal* standard. Although it is perhaps a good way from Hart's version of positivism, it is in accord with the fundamental positivistic tenet as described by Dworkin: 'The law of community . . . can be identified and distinguished by specific criteria, by tests having to do not with . . . content but with . . . pedigree . . .'

Sartorius *Social Policy and Judicial Legislation* 191–192

DWORKIN'S ARGUMENT: THE RIGHTS THESIS

According to Dworkin, legal principles are a species of political principles in that they identify rights of individuals. As such they need to be distinguished from policies which identify collective goals. In a hard case there will exist a uniquely correct legal decision, a single right answer: judges have no 'strong' discretion because even in the most controversial of cases they are required to seek out and to give effect to existing legal rights. This process will require the operation of a 'weak' discretion in judging the appropriate weight to be attached to the different relevant principles. This could be controversial, resulting in genuine disagreement. But a right answer does exist—although it is possible that we will not be certain what that is.

Different judges will disagree because of the formidable complexity involved in arriving at 'the soundest theory of law, satisfying the two dimensions' (supra pp 76ff). Dworkin now characterises this as an exercise of interpretation (see the discussion of *Law's Empire* (infra Chapter 12) and we have considered his use of the chain novel as an analogy (supra pp 77ff). Here is a concise account of law as an interpretive concept.

> Propositions of law, I argued, make interpretive claims of that general character. They claim that some part of legal practice is seen in its best light if it is understood as deploying and enforcing the principle or rule the proposition reports. Judges develop, over their careers and in response to their own convictions and instincts, working theories about the best interpretation of various levels and parts of the legal practices of their jurisdiction. They expand and rely on these theories when they are confronted with new and difficult issues; they try to decide hard cases consistently, so far as they can, with what they take to be the best interpretation of the general practice of deciding hard cases. When they disagree about the law their disagreements are interpretive. If two judges disagree about how statutes should be read, or about what force should be given to precedent decisions not directly in point, this will ordinarily reflect a deeper disagreement over the best general interpretation of their community's practices of adjudication, that is, a disagreement about which account of that practice shows it in its best light from the point of view of political morality. Interpretations struggle side by side with litigants before the bar.

> Dworkin in *Issues in Contemporary Jurisprudence* (ed Gavison) 14

(a)   **Principles v policies: rights v collective goals**

In hard cases a judge's decision is and should be based on legal principles and not on the invocation of policies of social, economic or political goals. In an argument of principle, 'strong discretion' has no role to play.

> Arguments of policy justify a political decision by showing that the decision advances or protects some collective goal of the community as a whole. The argument in favour of a subsidy for aircraft manufacturers, that the subsidy will protect national defence, is an argument of policy. Arguments of principle justify a political decision by showing that the decision respects or secures some individual or group right. The argument in favour of anti-discrimination statutes, that a minority has a right to equal respect and concern, is an argument of principle.

> Dworkin *Taking Rights Seriously* 82

Arguments of policy, specifying what is in the public interest and general welfare, are not normally the concern of judges; they are for legislatures.

> In fact . . . judges neither should be nor are deputy legislators, and the familiar assumption, that when they go beyond political decisions made by someone else they are legislating, is misleading. It misses the importance of a fundamental distinction within political theory . . . This is the distinction between arguments of principle on the one hand and arguments of policy on the other.
>
> <div align="right">Dworkin <i>Taking Rights Seriously</i> 82</div>

He does not dispute that people believe that certain principles are enshrined in their legal system because they promote the collective welfare. However this does not mean that judges do or ought to make their decisions in terms of collective welfare.

In what follows, note: rights are individuated; rights have a threshold weight to be trumped only by a goal of special urgency.

> Arguments of principle are arguments intended to establish an individual right; arguments of policy are arguments intended to establish a collective goal. Principles are propositions that describe rights; policies are propositions that describe goals. But what are rights and goals and what is the difference? It is hard to supply any definition that does not beg the question. It seems natural to say, for example, that freedom of speech is a right, not a goal, because citizens are entitled to that freedom as a matter of political morality, and that increased munitions manufacture is a goal, not a right, because it contributes to collective welfare, but no particular manufacturer is entitled to a government contract. This does not improve our understanding, however, because the concept of entitlement uses rather than explains the concept of a right.
>
> I shall distinguish rights from goals by fixing on the distributional character of claims about rights, and on the force of these claims, in political argument, against competing claims of a different distributional character. I shall make, that is, a formal distinction that does not attempt to show which rights men and women actually have, or indeed that they have any at all. It rather provides a guide for discovering which rights a particular political theory supposes men and women to have. The formal distinction does suggest, of course, an approach to the more fundamental question: it suggests that we discover what rights people actually have by looking for arguments that would justify claims having the appropriate distributional character. But the distinction does not itself supply any such arguments.
>
> I begin with the idea of a political aim as a generic political justification. A political theory takes a certain state of affairs as a political aim if, for that theory, it counts in favor of any political decision that the decision is likely to advance, or to protect, that state of affairs, and counts against the decision that it will retard or endanger it. A political right is an individuated political aim. An individual has a right to some opportunity or resource or liberty if it counts in favor of a political decision that the decision is likely to advance or protect the state of affairs in which he enjoys the right, even when no other political aim is served and some political aim is disserved thereby, and counts against that decision that it will retard or endanger that state of affairs, even when

some other political aim is thereby served. A goal is a nonindividuated political aim, that is, a state of affairs whose specification does not in this way call for any particular opportunity or resource or liberty for particular individuals.

Collective goals encourage trade-offs of benefits and burdens within a community in order to produce some overall benefit for the community as a whole. Economic efficiency is a collective goal: it calls for such distribution of opportunities and liabilities as will produce the greatest aggregate economic benefit defined in some way. Some conception of equality may also be taken as a collective goal; a community may aim at a distribution such that maximum wealth is no more than double minimum wealth, or, under a different conception, so that no racial or ethnic group is much worse off than other groups. Of course, any collective goal will suggest a particular distribution, given particular facts. Economic efficiency as a goal will suggest that a particular industry be subsidized in some circumstances, but taxed punitively in others. Equality as a goal will suggest immediate and complete redistribution in some circumstances, but partial and discriminatory redistribution in others. In each case distributional principles are subordinate to some conception of aggregate collective good, so that offering less of some benefit to one man can be justified simply by showing that this will lead to a greater benefit overall.

Collective goals may, but need not, be absolute. The community may pursue different goals at the same time, and it may compromise one goal for the sake of another. It may, for example, pursue economic efficiency, but also military strength. The suggested distribution will then be determined by the sum of the two policies, and this will increase the permutations and combinations of possible trade-offs. In any case, these permutations and combinations will offer a number of competing strategies for serving each goal and both goals in combination. Economic efficiency may be well served by offering subsidies to all farmers, and to no manufacturers, and better served by offering double the subsidy to some farmers and none to others. There will be alternate strategies of pursuing any set of collective goals, and, particularly as the number of goals increases, it will be impossible to determine in a piecemeal or case-by-case way the distribution that best serves any set of goals. Whether it is good policy to give double subsidies to some farmers and none to others will depend upon a great number of other political decisions that have been or will be made in pursuit of very general strategies into which this particular decision must fit.

Rights also may be absolute: a political theory which holds a right to freedom of speech as absolute will recognize no reason for not securing the liberty it requires for every individual; no reason, that is, short of impossibility. Rights may also be less than absolute; one principle might have to yield to another, or even to an urgent policy with which it competes on particular facts. We may define the weight of a right, assuming it is not absolute, as its power to withstand such competition. It follows from the definition of a right that it cannot be outweighed by all social goals. We might, for simplicity, stipulate not to call any political aim a right unless it has a certain threshold weight against collective goals in general; unless, for example, it cannot be defeated by appeal to any of the ordinary routine goals of political administration, but only by a goal of special urgency. Suppose, for example, some man says he recognizes the right of free speech, but adds that free speech must yield whenever its exercise would inconvenience the public. He means, I take it, that he recognizes the pervasive goal of collective welfare, and only such distribution of liberty of speech as that collective goal recommends in particular circumstances. His political position is exhausted by the collective goal; the putative right adds nothing and there is no point to recognizing it as a right at all.

Dworkin *Taking Rights Seriously* 90–92

In *Law's Empire*, this distinction becomes pivotal in Dworkin's interpretive thesis of law as integrity (infra Chapter 12).

Integrity is about principle and does not require any simple form of consistency in policy. The legislative principle of integrity demands that the legislature strive to protect for everyone what it takes to be their moral and political rights, so that public standards express a coherent scheme of justice and fairness. But the legislature makes many decisions that favor a particular group, not on the ground that the best conception of justice declares that that group has a right to that benefit, but only because benefiting that group happens to work for the general interest. If the legislature provides subsidies for farmers who grow wheat, for example, in order to ensure an adequate crop, or pays corn farmers not to plant because there is too much corn, it does not recognize any right of the farmers to these payments. A blind form of consistency would require the legislature to offer subsidies or payments for not planting to all farmers, or at least to all farmers whose crops were essential or who produced crops now in oversupply. But there might be sound reasons of policy—perhaps of a very different sort—why the legislature should not generalize these policies in that way. Integrity is not violated just by accepting these reasons and refusing to make the policy of subsidy more general.

We shall notice an argument that might seem to threaten this distinction because it shows that integrity has force even in these decisions of policy. A government that accepts what I shall there call the abstract egalitarian principle that it must treat its citizens as equals, needs a conception of equal concern, and integrity demands that the government settle on a single conception that it will not disavow in any decision, including those of policy. Many politicians, for example, think that treating people as equals means counting the welfare of each in some overall utilitarian calculation; an institution that used that conception of equal concern to justify some laws could not use a contradictory conception—that equal concern requires material equality among citizens, for instance—to justify other laws. But in ordinary politics legislators must take a long view of these requirements. They would be paralyzed if they undertook to ensure that each decision, one by one, left each citizen with exactly what the most sensitive utilitarian calculation, for example, would assign him. A working political theory must be more relaxed: it requires only that government pursue general strategies that promote the overall good as defined roughly and statistically to match what equal concern requires according to the conception in play. So a government committed to the utilitarian conception aims at legislative strategies that, as a whole and in the long run, improve average welfare better than alternate strategies would; a government committed to material equality adopts programs that make sections and classes more equal in material wealth as groups, and so forth. Decisions in pursuit of these strategies, judged one by one, are matters of policy, not principle; they must be tested by asking whether they advance the overall goal, not whether they give each citizen what he is entitled to have as an individual. Subsidies to one set of farmers may be justified on that test, even though subsidies to a different set, as part of a different overall strategy, would also have improved the general welfare, perhaps just as much.

Most working political theories also recognize, however, distinct individual rights as trumps over these decisions of policy, rights that government *is* required to respect case by case, decision by decision. These may be grand political rights, like the right of each citizen to have his vote counted as equal to any other citizen's, or not to be denied freedom of speech or conscience, even when violating these rights would contribute to the general welfare. Or rights drawn more directly from personal morality, like the right to be compensated for injuries caused by another's carelessness. Integrity fixes its gaze on these matters of principle: government must speak with one voice about what these rights are and so not deny them to anyone at any time. Integrity's effect on decisions of policy is more diffuse. It requires, as I said, that government pursue some coherent conception of what treating people as equals means, but this is mainly a question of general strategies and rough statistical tests. It does not otherwise require narrow consistency within policies: it does not require that particular programs treat everyone the same way. Integrity's concern with rights and principle does, however, sometimes disqualify inconsistency of a certain special kind. An American legislature could not decide that no Catholic farmer should receive subsidies even if, incredibly, there were sound reasons of policy for this discrimination.

The distinction between policy and principle and the direct connection between integrity and principle are important outside legislation as well. Consider prosecutor's discretion and other policy decisions in the criminal process. Consistency might be thought to argue that if some people who commit a particular crime have been and will be punished, all such people should be, and that punishments should be uniform, given an equal level of culpability. Integrity is more discriminating. If a prosecutor's reason for not prosecuting one person lies in policy—if the prosecution would be too expensive, for example, or would for some reason not contribute effectively to deterrence—integrity offers no reason why someone else should not be prosecuted when these reasons of policy are absent or reversed. But if the reasons that argue against prosecution in one case are reasons of principle— that the criminal statute did not give adequate notice, for example—then integrity demands that these reasons be respected for everyone else. Obviously integrity would also condemn prosecutors' decisions that discriminate, even for reasons of ostensible policy, on grounds that violate rights otherwise recognized, as if our prosecutors saved expense by prosecuting only blacks for a kind of crime that was particularly prevalent in mainly black communities.

Dworkin Law's Empire 221–224

Although what the judge is required to interpret may have been influenced by policy arguments, policy does not figure in his judgment.

A legislature may justify its decision to create new rights for the future by showing how these will contribute, as a matter of sound policy, to the overall good of the community as a whole . . . the legislature need not show that citizens already have a moral right to compensation for injury under particular circumstances in order to justify a statute awarding damages in those circumstances.

Law as integrity assumes, however, that judges are in a very different position from legislators. It does not fit the character of a community of principle that a judge should have authority to hold people liable in damages for acting in a way he concedes they had no legal duty not to act. So when judges construct rules of liability not recognized before, they are not free in the way I just said legislators are. Judges must make their common-law decisions on grounds of principle, not policy: they must deploy arguments why the parties actually had the 'novel' legal rights and duties they enforce at the time the parties acted or at some other pertinent time in the past . . . [Hercules] follows law as integrity and therefore wants an interpretation of what judges did in the earlier . . . cases that shows them acting in the way he approves, not in the way he thinks judges must decline to act. It does not mean he must dismiss [an interpretation of the cases that supposes] that past judges acted to protect a general legal right to compensation when this would make the community richer. For if people actually have such a right, others have a corresponding duty, and judges do not act unjustly in ordering the police to enforce it. The argument disqualifies [such an interpretation] only when this is read to deny any such general duty and to rest on grounds of policy alone.

Dworkin *Law's Empire* 244

(b) A uniquely correct decision

Legal positivism argues that a court could be confronted with a case to which there is no answer which can be described as being the one and only answer open to the court. Judges must use their discretion. There is no right answer so they have to do the best they can. Dworkin dissents.

Is there always a right answer to a question of law? Suppose the legislature has passed a statute stipulating that 'sacrilegious contracts shall henceforth be invalid'. The community is divided as to whether a contract signed on Sunday is, for that reason alone, sacrilegious. It is known that very few of the legislators had that question in mind when they voted, and that they are now equally divided on the question of whether it should be so interpreted. Tom and Tim have signed a contract on Sunday, and Tom now sues Tim to enforce the terms of the contract, whose validity Tim contests. Shall we say that there is a right answer to the question of whether Tom's contract is valid, even though the community is deeply divided about what the right answer is? Or is it more realistic to say that there simply is no right answer to that question?

That issue is central to a large number of controversies about what law is. It has been debated under many titles, including the question of whether judges always have discretion in hard cases, and whether there are what some legal philosophers call 'gaps' in the law. For some time the weight of opinion has been on one side of the issue. I myself am often accused of thinking that there is almost always a right answer to a legal question; the accusation suggests that if I were to confess to that opinion anything else I said about legal reasoning could safely be ignored. In fact the issue is much more complex than is often supposed. I now wish to defend the unpopular view, that in the circumstances just described the question of Tom's contract has a right answer, against certain arguments on which its opponents knowingly or unknowingly rely. I shall also try to show what sense there is in the no-right-answer thesis, and why the occasions in which a legal question has no right answer in our own legal system must be much rarer than is generally supposed. I shall begin, however, by insisting upon a clarification of the issue that removes a troublesome ambiguity.

Dworkin in *Law, Morality and Society* (ed Hacker and Raz) 58–59

So 'the seamless web' of the law will yield a right answer. His strategy is to consider two arguments, which, if valid, would militate *against* Dworkin's position.

(i)   The first version of the 'no right answer' thesis

This rests on the assumption that two concepts which appear to be contradictories are not so. A pair of propositions is not exhaustive because of the possibility of a logical gap existing between them.

> The first version argues that the surface linguistic behaviour of lawyers just described is misleading because it suggests that there is no logical space between the proposition that a contract is valid and the proposition that it is not valid; that is, because it does not contemplate that both propositions may be false. In fact, however, if we look deeper into the matter, we find that it might be false both that a contract is valid and that it is not valid, false both that a person is liable and that he is not liable for some act, and false both that a particular act constitutes a crime and that it does not. In each case both propositions may be false because in each case they do not exhaust the logical space they occupy; in each case there is a third independent possibility that occupies the space between the other two. On this first version of the thesis the question 'Is Tom's contract valid or invalid?' makes a mistake like the question 'Is Tom a young man or an old man?' The latter question may have no right answer because it ignores a third possibility, which is that Tom is a middle-aged man. According to the first version, the legal question also ignores a third possibility, which is that an exchange of promises may constitute neither a valid contract, such that judges have a duty to enforce the exchange, nor a contract that is not valid, with the consequence that judges have a duty not to enforce it, but something else that might be called, for example, an 'inchoate' contract.

Dworkin in *Law, Morality and Society* (ed Hacker and Raz) 59–60

If this thesis is correct, cases will occur in which neither party is entitled to a decision and the judge has a discretion to decide the case either way: there would be no right answer. Dworkin concedes that many decisions do exist where it would be a mistake to say the judge has a duty to make a decision either way.

> . . . when the defendant has been convicted of a crime for which the statute provides a sentence of from three to five years, and the prosecution asks for the maximum, while the defence asks for the minimum, sentence. The concept of duty provides a space between the proposition that the judge has a duty to decide one way and the proposition that he has to decide in another; this space is occupied by the proposition that he has no duty to decide either way, but rather a permission, or as lawyers say a 'discretion', to decide either way.

Dworkin in *Law, Morality and Society* (ed Hacker and Raz) 62

But the first version of the no-right-answer thesis argues that this is the case in a legal system generally: there is a gap between a concept and its apparent negation that is filled by a distinct concept, like an inchoate contract, although 'we do not have a separate name for that distinct concept'.

To maintain that there is no right answer on the issue of the validity of a contract or the existence of liability in tort is to maintain that there is a discretion within the concept. It would be maintaining that the law says there is a valid contract or tortious liability if the judge so finds. This must be wrong: validity or liability is given as a reason why the judge ought to make his decision.

> It would plainly be fallacious, for example, to argue for the first version in the following way. There is logical space between the proposition that a judge has a duty to enforce the contract and the proposition that he has a duty not to. That space is occupied by the proposition that he has discretion to enforce it or not. Since it is a consequence of the proposition that the contract is valid that a judge has a duty to enforce it, and a consequence of the proposition that the contract is not valid that he has a duty not to enforce it, there must therefore be a parallel space between these two propositions about the contract, which is left available for the proposition that the contract is inchoate.
>
> That would be a fallacious argument because it does not follow from the fact that the concept of duty has, in this sense, three values, that the concepts used to define occasions of duty must also have three values. In tennis, for example, judges have a duty to call a fault if a serve falls wholly outside the service court, and a duty not to call a fault if it does not. There is space between the propositions that a judge has a duty to call a fault and that he has a duty not to, but it does not follow that there is space between the propositions that the serve fell wholly without the service court and that it did not. Dispositive concepts are used to describe the occasions of official duty, but it does not follow that these concepts must themselves have the same structure as the concept of duty.
>
> Dworkin in *Law, Morality and Society* (ed Hacker and Raz) 63

His concluding remarks on the first version refer to a 'dispositive' concept, viz, if the concept holds in a particular situation, then judges have a duty, at least prima facie, to decide some legal claim one way; but if the concept does not hold then judges have a duty, at least prima facie, to decide the same claim in the opposite way.

> The semantic theory which simply translates statements about contracts into statements about official duties therefore obscures the interesting and distinctive role of dispositive concepts in legal argument. These concepts provide a special kind of bridge between certain sorts of events and the conclusory claims about rights and duties that hold if these events can be demonstrated to have occurred. They both designate tests for conclusory claims and insist that if the tests they designate are not met, then the opposite conclusory claim, not simply the denial of the first, holds instead. The need for concepts having that function in legal argument arises because the concepts of right and duty in which conclusory claims are framed are structured, that is because there is space between the opposite conclusory claims. The function is the function of denying that the space thus provided may be exploited by rejecting both the opposing claims. Dispositive concepts are able to fill this function just because the first version of the no-right-answer thesis is false; if there were space between the propositions that a

contract is and is not valid, that concept could not close the space the concepts of right and duty provide.

Dworkin in *Law, Morality and Society* (ed Hacker and Raz) 65

(ii)   The second version of the 'no right answer' thesis

The second version of the no-right-answer thesis, on the other hand, does not suppose that there is any logical space, in that sense, between the propositions that a contract is valid and that it is not valid, or that a person is liable or that he is not, or that an act is a crime or that it is not. It does not suppose that there is any third possibility, and yet it denies that there is always a right answer to the question of which of the two possibilities it does recognise holds, because it may not be true that either does. On this second version of the thesis, the question 'Is Tom's contract valid or not valid?' is like the question 'Is Tom middle-aged or not?' There may be no right answer to the latter question if Tom is of an age that lies on the border between youth and middle age, not because we recognise categories of age distinct from both middle age and non-middle age, but because, at the border, it is a mistake to say of someone either that he is or that he is not middle-aged.

Dworkin in *Law, Morality and Society* (ed Hacker and Raz) 60

Under this version two propositions are not mutually exclusive so that there is an overlap between them into which a case may fall. Again, if this is correct, we would not be able to say that either party is entitled to a decision and we would be made to concede that the judge had a discretion to go either way.

Dworkin considers that the most influential argument in support of this version is 'the argument from controversy' and this itself rests on what he calls the 'demonstrability thesis'. If the demonstrability thesis holds, then there is no right answer.

The argument may be put in the form of a doctrine which I shall call the demonstrability thesis. This thesis states that if a proposition cannot be demonstrated to be true, after all the hard facts that might be relevant to its truth are either known or stipulated, then it cannot be true. By 'hard facts' I mean physical facts and facts about behaviour (including the thoughts and attitudes) of people. By 'demonstrated' I mean backed by arguments such that anyone who understood the language in which the proposition is formed must assent to its truth or stand convicted of irrationality.

If the demonstrability thesis holds, then there must be legal questions to which no right answer can be given because neither the proposition that some dispositive concept holds nor the proposition that it does not hold can be true. If reasonable lawyers can disagree whether Sunday contracts are sacrilegious within the meaning of the statute, because they hold different views about how statutes containing vague terms should be interpreted or construed, then the proposition that Tom's contract is valid cannot be demonstrated to be true, even when all facts about what the legislators had in mind are known or stipulated. Therefore, on the determinacy thesis, it cannot be true. But the same holds for the proposition that Tom's contract is not valid. Since neither of these propositions can be true, and since they are assumed to exhaust the range of possible answers, then there is no right answer to the question.

Dworkin in *Law, Morality and Society* (ed Hacker and Raz) 76–77

If hard facts are all the facts there are, the demonstrability thesis succeeds and he would be forced to concede that, at least in some cases, no right answer can be given. Needless to say he proceeds to argue for the existence of facts other than the hard variety: the most important being facts that are revealed by analogy with a literary exercise. Imagine we are debating an issue about the details of the life of David Copperfield, details which are not directly revealed by Dickens: for example, did David have an homosexual affair with Steerforth? An answer is the right answer if it gives better consistency than the other.

> [Debaters in this literary exercise] assert a proposition about David as true (or deny it as false) if that proposition provides a better (or worse) fit than its negation with propositions already established, because it explains in a more satisfactory way why David did what he did, or said what he said, or thought what he thought, according to the established propositions.
>
> . . . it does require the assumption, I think, that there are facts of narrative consistency, like the fact that the hypothesis that David had a sexual relationship with Steerforth provides a more satisfactory explanation of what he subsequently did and thought than the hypothesis that he did not.
>
> Dworkin in *Law, Morality and Society* (ed Hacker and Raz) 77–78

The assumption is that there is a right answer. The debaters would advance reasons for their views in terms of a better fit with what Dickens actually did reveal about the life of David. A proposition is true if it is in accord with the hard facts and it satisfies narrative consistency with the hard facts. This exercise in literary interpretation may be helpful as furnishing a comparison with the exercise of legal reasoning. Although there are differences between consistency in legal reasoning and narrative consistency in the literary exercise, the comparison may help to explain why it is sensible to suppose that there is a right answer to many legal problems even when the right answer cannot be demonstrated. For similar arguments, see the 'chain novel' (supra pp 77ff) and the general discussion of interpretation in *Law's Empire* (infra Chapter 12).

However, as a qualification, we can imagine questions that would have no right answer.

> We can imagine questions that might be raised within a legal system that would have no right answer for the same sort of reason. We must concede the theoretical possibility that the political theory that provides the best justification for the settled law is for some reason entirely neutral on the question whether, in some particular case, an exchange of promises must be taken to constitute a contract or not. We must also concede the theoretical possibility that two different political theories, which suggest different answers to that question, for some reason each provide exactly as good a justification of the settled law as the other. We can also imagine a case in which the issue of whether one or another of these grounds of neutrality holds is itself in dispute, with one party contending for one answer, another for the other, and a third for no answer at all.
>
> Dworkin in *Law, Morality and Society* (ed Hacker and Raz) 83

But, for all practical purposes, the 'seamless web' of the law will provide a right answer.

COMMENTS AND CRITICISMS OF DWORKIN'S POSITIVE CONTRIBUTION

(a) The rights thesis

Critics of Dworkin dispute the distinction that is pivotal to his thesis: the distinction between principles and policies. They contend that in hard cases the decision is often dictated by policy considerations; so, for example, in the law of nuisance courts take into account the benefit to the community of certain kinds of activities before deciding whether or not they are to be prohibited.

> But for Professor Dworkin, a judge who thus steps into the area of what he calls policy, as distinct from principles determining individual rights, is treading forbidden ground reserved for the elected legislature. This is so because for him not only is the law a gapless system, but it is a gapless system of rights or entitlements, determining what people are entitled to have as a matter of distributive justice, not what they should have because it is to the public advantage that they should have it. This exclusion of 'policy considerations' will, I think, again run counter to the convictions of many lawyers that it is perfectly proper and indeed at times necessary for judges to take account of the impact of their decisions on the general community welfare.
>
> Hart *Essays in Jurisprudence and Philosophy* 141

Hart continues with the observation that this exclusion of policy from judicial decisions is symptomatic of Dworkin's general hostility to utilitarianism.

Dworkin, in championing this distinction, is not only claiming that judicial reasoning ought to proceed on the basis of this distinction; his claim is that this is the case. Hence, all the examples advanced by his critics as instances of policy encroachment into judges' reasoning are said not to be true counter-examples to the rights thesis. What the courts are actually doing is weighing the rights of some claimants against the rights of others. The following extract from John Umana shows Dworkin wrestling with the problems resulting from his insistence upon this distinction. References to Greenawalt are to his 'Discretion and Judicial Decision' (75 Columbia Law Review 359 (1975)); references to Dworkin are to *Taking Rights Seriously* pp 98–100 and 108–111.

> A further difficulty with the rights thesis, aside from its inability to resolve jurisprudential dilemmas that Dworkin himself considers crucial, is that it conflicts with the common-sense intuition that it is sometimes appropriate for judges to consider social policies in adjudicating. It seems reasonable to suppose that most people would be surprised by the suggestion that judges characteristically are and ought to be oblivious to social policies. For indeed, there are a variety of circumstances in which judges typically are thought to include policy considerations in their adjudications. Consider, for example, the following kinds of cases suggested by Kent Greenawalt: (1) '[S]ome legal standards such as "unreasonable search" and "nuisance" appear to build in notions of competing costs and benefits. . . . [I]n these instances [a judge] is properly weighing competing social interests in deciding cases.' (2) Judges should also take account of social consequences 'in the sense of administrability and likely effectiveness of proposed rules'; and (3) '[W]hen the court knows that the legislature will not soon address a small problem within a large area covered by legislation, again it is harder to argue that it

should refuse to take into account considerations that would be important for a legislative body.' The remainder of this section explores these three kinds of cases in which judicial consideration of policy seems particularly appropriate. The conclusion reached is that Dworkin is able to accommodate these apparent counterexamples to his rights thesis only by engaging in a conceptual 'gerrymandering' that abandons his original formulations of the principle-policy distinction.

Dworkin explicitly considers the first of these possible counterexamples in discussing the implications of Learned Hand's formula for negligence:

'[Hand] said, roughly, that the test of whether the defendant's act was unreasonable, and therefore actionable, is the economic test which asks whether the defendant could have avoided the accident at less cost to himself than the plaintiff was likely to suffer if the accident occurred, discounted by the improbability of the accident. It may be said that this economic test provides an argument of policy rather than principle, because it makes the decision turn on whether the collective welfare would have been advanced more by allowing the accident to take place or by spending what was necessary to avoid it. If so, then cases in which some test like Hand's is explicitly used, however few they might be, would stand as counterexamples to the rights thesis.'

Dworkin's rejoinder is that Hand's test is really not an argument of policy at all, but rather a method of 'compromising competing rights.' This can be understood, he says, once the distinction between 'abstract' and 'concrete rights' is drawn. 'Abstract rights . . . take no account of competing rights; concrete rights, on the other hand, reflect the impact of such competition.' Hand's test, he urges, is not a simple cost-benefit formula but rather 'a mechanism for compromising competing claims of abstract right.'

Dworkin applies his distinction between abstract and concrete rights to a broad range of cases:

'Negligence cases are not the only cases in which judges compromise abstract rights in defining concrete ones. If a judge appeals to public safety or the scarcity of some vital resource, for example, as a ground for limiting some abstract right, then *his appeal might be understood as an appeal to the competing rights* of those whose security will be sacrificed, or whose just share of that resource will be threatened if the abstract right is made concrete. His argument is an argument of principle if it respects the distributional requirements of such arguments, and if it observes the restriction . . . that the weight of a competing principle may be less than the weight of the appropriate parallel policy.'

Thus, Dworkin's view is much more sophisticated than it first appears to be. On one hand, he wishes to maintain the position that judges should not adjudicate on the basis of policy arguments. Yet on the other hand, he is forced to concede that much of what *looks* like adjudication by policy arguments is quite appropriate after all. Dworkin seeks to reconcile these two views by suggesting that ostensible policy considerations are actually appeals to competing abstract rights. In the quoted passage, for example, appeals to public safety—what most people would consider a paradigm instance of a collective goal—are viewed by Dworkin as appeals to a right. Unfortunately, Dworkin can only manipulate his original definitions of rights and goals in this manner by conceding much ground to his opponents. If policy considerations can be 'understood as an appeal to competing rights,' what force remains behind his original distinction between principles and policies? When is an ostensible policy consideration to count as a 'hard core' policy consideration and when not? Dworkin's response, apparently, is that an argument is one of principle if it respects the distributional requirement of principles—that rights be consistently enforced—and if it has greater weight than the parallel or cognate argument of policy. This response is unconvincing, however, when something like public safety, which seems so plainly a goal, can be so readily understood as a right. Indeed, Dworkin seems to have committed himself in his examples to the somewhat elusive position that a judge can be attentive to what is commonly called a 'policy' just in case the 'policy' has sufficient importance in his political theory—in which case it is really a principle rather than a policy.

To be sure, Dworkin attempts to bolster his principle–policy distinction by providing an example of what he considers a true argument of policy. He suggests the situation in which one man is drowning, and another man, with little personal risk, can save him:

> 'Suppose someone argued that the principle requiring rescue at minimal risk should be amended so as to make the decision turn, not on some function of the collective utilities of the victim and rescuer, but on marginal utility to the community as a whole so that the rescuer must take into account not only the relative risks to himself and the victim, but the relative social importance of the two. It might follow that an insignificant man must risk his life to save a bank president but that a bank president need not even tire himself to save a nobody. The argument is no longer an argument of principle, because it supposes the victim to have a right to nothing but his expectations under general utility.'

But is it so clear that this must count as a true argument of policy under Dworkin's model? Cannot this example too be accommodated as an appeal to competing abstract rights? Arguably, the bank's employees as well as members of the community at large have an abstract right to economic security. These rights might be jeopardized should the bank president drown in an attempted rescue. They would be jeopardized much less if the 'insignificant man' happened to drown. The decision to risk only the life of the 'insignificant man' can thus be reached by appealing to competing abstract rights. Indeed, as this example and Dworkin's treatment of Hand's formula demonstrate, it should ordinarily be a simple matter to transform what appears to be an argument of policy into an argument of principle. If the transformation can always be so easily accomplished, as seems to be the case, then nothing counts conceptually as an argument of policy, and the concept is, hence, *logically vacuous*.

Greenawalt's second situation in which a judge is deemed justified in considering social consequences occurs when a judge considers the administrability or workability of a proposed rule. Dworkin has not discussed this possibility, but as Greenawalt projects, Dworkin probably would not deny that judges properly take such considerations into account. Perhaps Dworkin would feel that judicial consideration of administrability is permissible in light of the fairness requirement that rights be consistently enforced. Under this view, a judge could properly estimate whether or not a rule could be enforced in a consistent manner. Dworkin might well insist, however, that a judge consider the enforceability of a rule from the viewpoint of fairness, and not from that of utility.

According to Greenawalt, the third situation in which judges should properly weigh social policies occurs when a legislature leaves some areas in a piece of legislation largely open for subsequent development by the courts. Under such circumstances, he suggests, judges must calculate social consequences in much the same way as do legislators. Dworkin explicitly contradicts such a view: 'It would be inaccurate . . . to say that [a judge] supplemented what the legislature did in enacting the statute, or that he tried to determine what it would have done if it had been aware of the problem presented by the case . . . [Rather, a judge] constructs his political theory as an argument about what the legislature has, on this occasion, done.' Though the foregoing statement is not free of ambiguity, it does at least make clear Dworkin's rejection of the notion that a judge should put himself in the place of the legislature and should try to determine how that body would have responded to the facts of the case before the court; statutory construction, Dworkin states, does not call for 'hypotheses about the mental state of particular legislators. . . .' But then, is a judge to weigh social policies or not?

In a note appended to his article, Dworkin explains that a judge must consider collective goals in such cases, yet not in the same capacity as would a legislator: 'When [a judge] interprets statutes he fixes to some statutory language . . . arguments of principle or policy that provide the best justification of that language in the light of the legislature's responsibilities. His argument remains an argument of principle; he uses policy to determine what rights the legislature has already created.' So a judge must turn to his political theory to determine which principles and which policies best justify, or best rationalize, the particular language of the act. But a judge performing this task, Dworkin would mean to say, is not simply weighing policies *ab initio*. Instead, he must determine '[w]hich arguments of principle and policy might properly have persuaded the legislature to enact just that statute' in light of the legislature's 'general duty to pursue collective goals defining the public welfare.' In making arguments of policy to construe a statute, a judge is further limited by the 'canonical terms' of the statute; he cannot extend an argument of policy beyond the limits of the actual language of the statute.

Yet these weak restrictions obviously afford judges considerable leeway in choosing which policies to include in their calculations and in determining how they should be balanced. It would thus seem that the calculation of social policies is more than a peripheral task of a judge engaged in statutory interpretation, particularly where the language is of a very general nature. This observation reaffirms the preliminary judgment reached above that the balancing of social policies, Dworkin's theory notwithstanding, is at times an important and proper aspect of adjudication.

Umana 74 Michigan Law Review 1167, 1179–83 (1976)

(b) The 'right answer' thesis

Two extracts from Hart that question the idea of a uniquely correct answer will conclude this chapter.

It is right and illuminating to speak of the existing law as exerting a gravitational pull over the judge, but that there will not quite often be equal gravitational pulls in different directions seems to me something still to be shown. It is plain from Professor Dworkin's exposition that the underlying justificatory theory of the existing law from which the judges are to extract rules of decision includes principles that are hugely general and abstract and I find it difficult to believe that among these just one principle or set of principles can be shown to fit the existing settled law better than any other.

Hart *Essays in Jurisprudence and Philosophy* 157

Professor Dworkin's theory will, I am sure, much excite and stimulate both jurists and philosophers for a long time on both sides of the Atlantic. It has indeed already added much to the stock of valuable jurisprudential ideas. But if I may venture a prophecy, I think the chief criticism that it will attract will be of his insistence that, even if there is no way of demonstrating which of two conflicting solutions, both equally well warranted by the existing law, is correct, still there must always be a single correct answer awaiting discovery. Lawyers might think that if a judge has conformed before he decides to all those constraints which distinguish judicial law-making from law-making by a legislator, above all if he has considered conscientiously and impartially what Professor Dworkin well calls the 'gravitational force' of the clearly established law and has arrived at a conclusion as to which of the alternatives open to him is most fair or just, no purpose is served by insisting that if a brother judge arrives after the same conscientious process at a different conclusion there is a unique right answer which would show which of the two judges, if either, is right, though this answer is laid up in a jurist's heaven and no one can demonstrate what it is.

Similarly, philosophers may dispute the claim that as a matter of logical coherence anyone who attempts to answer a question of value, whether it be the question which of two legal answers to a litigant's claims is more just or fair, or which of two competitors in a beauty competition is more beautiful, or which of Shakespeare's comedies is the funniest, must, in order to give sense to such questions, assume that there is a single objective right answer in all such cases. The corollary in the case of law is that what litigants are always entitled to have from the judge is the right answer (though there is no means of demonstrating what it is), just as they would be entitled to have a right answer to the question which of two buildings is the taller, where of course the correctness of the answer can be demonstrated by a public objective test. Perhaps both philosophers and lawyers might agree with Professor Kent Greenawalt of Columbia Law School who, after a patient examination of Professor Dworkin's attack on the idea that judges have a discretion in hard cases, concludes that '[d]iscretion exists so long as no practical procedure exists for determining if a result is correct, informed lawyers disagree about the proper result, and a judge's decision either way will not widely be considered a failure to perform his judicial responsibilities'.

Hart *Essays in Jurisprudence and Philosophy* 139–140

(Note: this passage ends with a reference to Greenawalt's article, 'Discretion and the Judicial Decision: The Elusive Quest for the Fetters that Bind Judges', in (1975) 75 Columbia Law Review 359, 386.)

Chapter 5

Hans Kelsen and the pure theory of law

Kelsen (1881–1973), in what he calls the pure theory of law, argues that every legal activity can be traced back to an authoritative standard, which he calls a *norm*. As we shall see, it is the norm which gives validity to the behaviour contained in that activity. Since it is a theory of positive law he is concerned with what is the law and not with what ought the law to be. His programme is the description and analysis of the subject matter of law; any ethical or moral judgments are to be sublimated from this analysis.

We have reached the high water mark of legal positivism. Kelsen asks us to consider law as it is, without reference to ideology or ethics; the adjective 'pure' requires the relegation of ethics, politics, ideology, sociology, religion, history etc, to the status of mere adulterants that obscure and thwart the structural analysis of the positive law. Needless to say, all varieties of natural law are characterised as anathemas, as the results of 'metajuristic' speculation, all contaminating the pure science of law.

THE PURE THEORY AS A THEORY OF POSITIVE LAW

One of the reasons for the postulate of 'purity' appears in the opening piece.

> The Pure Theory of Law is a theory of positive law. It is a theory of positive law in general, not of a specific legal order. It is a general theory of law, not an interpretation of specific national or international legal norms; but it offers a theory of interpretation.
>
> As a theory, its exclusive purpose is to know and to describe its object. The theory attempts to answer the question what and how the law *is*, not how it ought to be. It is a science of law (jurisprudence), not legal politics.
>
> It is called a 'pure' theory of law, because it only describes the law and attempts to eliminate from the object of this description everything that is not strictly law: Its aim is to free the science of law from alien elements. This is the methodological basis of the theory.
>
> Such an approach seems a matter of course. Yet, a glance upon the traditional science of law as it developed during the nineteenth and twentieth centuries clearly shows how far removed it is from the postulate of purity; uncritically the science of law has been mixed with elements of psychology, sociology, ethics, and political theory. This adulteration is understandable, because the latter disciplines deal with subject matters that are closely connected with law. The Pure Theory of Law undertakes to delimit the cognition of law against these disciplines, not because it ignores or denies the connection, but because it wishes to avoid the uncritical mixture of methodologically different disciplines (methodological syncretism) which

obscures the essence of the science of law and obliterates the limits imposed upon it by the nature of its subject matter.

Kelsen *The Pure Theory of Law* 1

LAW AS NORMS AND NORMS ACTING AS A SCHEME OF INTERPRETATION

Take any act. It can be seen as a natural event. However, any body of fact that can also be interpreted as *legal* can be viewed in a different manner; it can be viewed in terms of its legal meaning, the meaning that law has imputed to it.

> For if you analyze any body of facts interpreted as 'legal' or somehow tied up with law, such as a parliamentary decision, an administrative act, a judgment, a contract, or a crime, two elements are distinguishable: one, an act or series of acts—a happening occurring at a certain time and in a certain place, perceived by our senses: an external manifestation of human conduct; two, the legal meaning of this act, that is, the meaning conferred upon the act by the law. For example: People assemble in a large room, make speeches, some raise their hands, others do not—this is the external happening. Its meaning is that a statute is being passed, that law is created. We are faced here with the distinction (familiar to jurists) between the process of legislation and its product, the statute. To give other illustrations: A man in a robe and speaking from a dais says some words to a man standing before him; legally this external happening means: a judicial decision was passed. A merchant writes a letter of a certain content to another merchant, who, in turn, answers with a letter; this means they have concluded a legally binding contract. Somebody causes the death of somebody else; legally, this means murder.

Kelsen *The Pure Theory of Law* 2

In order to understand something in terms of its legal meaning it is necessary to understand it as being a legally valid *norm*. And to interpret an act in such a normative manner is to view the act in relation to a norm which prescribes something, the norm being understood as a legally valid norm. So, viewing an act from the perspective of a natural phenomenon is to conclude that it can be perceived by the senses—it can be determined by causality. What brings about the metamorphosis of this act into a legal or illegal act is its *objective meaning* which is the consequence of its interpretation; and it is the fact that a legally valid norm exists that functions as this *scheme of interpretation*. In other words, the specific, *legal* meaning of an act, such as those listed in the last extract, lies in the fact that the conduct the act specifies corresponds to the content of a norm—a norm understood as being legally valid (when will this be so? Keep reading!).

The meaning of 'norm'

> Those norms then, which have the character of legal norms and which make certain acts legal or illegal, are the objects of the science of law. The legal order which is the object of this cognition is a normative order of human behavior—a system of norms regulating human behavior. By 'norm' we mean that something *ought* to be or *ought* to happen, especially that a human being ought to behave in a specific way. This is the meaning of certain human acts directed

toward the behavior of others. They are so directed, if they, according to their content, command such behavior, but also if they permit it, and—particularly—if they authorize it. 'Authorize' means to confer upon someone else a certain power, specifically the power to enact norms himself. In this sense the acts whose meaning is a norm are acts of will. If an individual by his acts expresses a will directed at a certain behavior of another, that is to say, if he commands, permits, or authorizes such behavior—then the meaning of his acts cannot be described by the statement that the other individual *will* (future tense) behave in that way, but only that he *ought* to behave in that way. The individual who commands, permits, or authorizes *wills*; the man to whom the command, permission, or authorization is directed *ought to*. The word 'ought' is used here in a broader than the usual sense. According to customary usage, 'ought' corresponds only to a command, while 'may' corresponds to a permission, and 'can' to an authorization. But in the present work the word 'ought' is used to express the normative meaning of an act directed toward the behavior of others; this 'ought' includes 'may' and 'can'. If a man who is commanded, permitted, or authorized to behave in a certain way asks for the reason of such command, permission, or authorization, he can only do so by saying: Why 'ought' I behave in this way? Or, in customary usage: Why may I or why can I behave in this way?

Kelsen *The Pure Theory of Law* 4–5

Accordingly, a norm is a rule whose meaning is that something ought to be or to be done and it can have the character of a command or prescription when it will usually be expressed linguistically in the imperative mood. But the 'ought' has an extended meaning: it may have not only the character of a command but the character of an authorisation or the character of a permission. More on these later.

But norms are 'oughts' interpreted *objectively* and this will not be the case when the 'ought' is merely treated as the wish of someone.

'Norm' is the meaning of an act by which a certain behavior is commanded, permitted, or authorized. The norm, as the specific meaning of an act directed toward the behavior of someone else, is to be carefully differentiated from the act of will whose meaning the norm is: the norm is an *ought*, but the act of will is an *is*. Hence the situation constituted by such an act must be described by the statement: The one individual wills that the other individual ought to behave in a certain way. The first part of this sentence refers to an *is*, the existing fact of the first individual's act of volition; the second part to an *ought*, to a norm as the meaning of that act. Therefore it is incorrect to assert—as is often done—that the statement: 'an individual ought' merely means that another individual wills something; that the *ought* can be reduced to an *is*.

Kelsen *The Pure Theory of Law* 5

He offers an illustration of the distinction between subjective and objective meaning.

A criminal code might contain the sentence: Theft is punished by imprisonment. The meaning of this sentence is not, as the wording seems to indicate, a statement about an actual event; instead, the meaning is a norm: it is a command or an authorization, to punish theft *by* imprisonment. The legislative process consists of a series of acts which, in their totality, have the meaning of a norm. To say that acts, especially legislative acts, 'create' or 'posit' a norm, is merely a figure of speech for saying that the meaning or the significance of the act or acts that constitute the legislative process, is a norm. It is, however, necessary to distinguish the subjective and the objective meaning of the act. 'Ought' is the subjective meaning of every act of will directed at the behavior of another. But not every such act has also objectively this meaning; and only if the act of will has also the objective meaning of an 'ought,' is this 'ought' called a 'norm.'

Kelsen *The Pure Theory of Law* 7

But what is involved in interpreting an 'ought' as having an objective meaning? What is it that makes a norm valid?

If the 'ought' is also the objective meaning of the act, the behavior at which the act is directed is regarded as something that *ought* to be not only from the point of view of the individual who has performed the act, but also from the point of view of the individual at whose behavior the act is directed, and of a third individual not involved in the relation between the two. That the 'ought' is the objective meaning of the act manifests itself in the fact that it is supposed to exist (that the 'ought' is valid) even if the will ceases to exist whose subjective meaning it is—if we assume that an individual ought to behave in a certain way even if he does not know of the act whose meaning is that he ought to behave in this way. Then the 'ought,' as the objective meaning of an act, is a valid *norm* binding upon the addressee, that is, the individual at whom it is directed. The ought which is the subjective meaning of an act of will is also the objective meaning of this act, if this act has been invested with this meaning, if it has been authorized by a norm, which therefore has the character of a 'higher' norm.

Kelsen *The Pure Theory of Law* 7–8

The idea seems to be that a norm is objectively valid when it is authorized by a higher norm, and the latter will be objectively valid only if it is itself similarly authorized by an even higher norm.
We need another illustration.

The command of a gangster to turn over to him a certain amount of money has the same subjective meaning as the command of an income-tax official, namely that the individual at whom the command is directed ought to pay something. But only the command of the official, not that of the gangster, has the meaning of a valid norm, binding upon the addressed individual. Only the one order, not the other, is a norm-positing act, because the official's act is authorized by a tax law, whereas the gangster's act is not based on such an authorizing norm. The legislative act, which subjectively has the meaning of *ought*, also has the objective meaning—that is, the meaning of a valid norm—because the constitution has conferred this objective meaning upon the legislative act. The act whose meaning is the constitution has not only the subjective but also the objective meaning of 'ought,' that is to say, the character of a binding norm, if—in case it is the historically first constitution—we presuppose in our juristic thinking that we ought to behave as the constitution prescribes.

Kelsen *The Pure Theory of Law* 8

In the last extract it can be seen that the validity of a norm depends on its authorization by a higher norm and exactly the same reason provides for the validity of the higher norm. This is a process of concatenation and we can go on and on up the ladder of validity. What could be called Kelsen's definitional stop to this infinite regress is the 'historically first constitution' which is described as a *presupposition*. It is this basic norm that brings an abrupt end to the process of finding a yet higher validating norm. Again, there will be much more on this basic norm later on. But the next extract serves as another introduction to the idea of a basic norm or *Grundnorm*, the point where the validity buck stops.

> If a man in need asks another man for help, the *subjective* meaning of this request is that the other ought to help him. But in an objective sense he ought to help (that is to say, he is morally obliged to help) only if a general norm—established, for instance, by the founder of a religion—is valid that commands, 'Love your neighbor.' And this latter norm is objectively valid only if it is presupposed that one ought to behave as the religious founder has commanded. Such a presupposition, establishing the objective validity of the norms of a moral or legal order, will here be called a *basic norm* (*Grundnorm*). Therefore, the objective validity of a norm which is the subjective meaning of an act of will that men ought to behave in a certain way, does not follow from the factual act, that is to say, from an *is*, but again from a norm authorizing this act, that is to say, from an *ought*.
>
> Kelsen *The Pure Theory of Law* 8–9

Norms command, authorise or permit

This was introduced in the previous extracts. What follows is a more detailed account.

> The behavior regulated by a normative order is either a definite action or the omission (nonperformance) of such an action. Human behavior, then, is either positively or negatively regulated by a normative order. Positively, when a definite action of a definite individual or when the omission of such an action is commanded. (When the omission of an action is commanded, the action is forbidden.) To say that the behavior of an individual is commanded by an objectively valid norm amounts to the same as saying the individual is obliged to behave in this way. If the individual behaves as the norm commands he fulfills his obligation—he obeys the norm; if he behaves in the opposite way, he 'violates' the norm—he violates his obligation. Human behavior is positively regulated also, when an individual is authorized by the normative order to bring about, by a certain act, certain consequences determined by the order. Particularly an individual can be authorized (if the order regulates its own creation) to create norms or to participate in that creation; or when, in case of a legal order providing for coercive acts as sanctions, an individual is authorized to perform these acts under the conditions stipulated by the legal order; or when a norm permits an individual to perform an act, otherwise forbidden—a norm which limits the sphere of validity of a general norm that forbids the act. An example for the last-mentioned alternative is self-defense: although a general norm forbids the use of force of one individual against another, a special norm permits such use of force in self-defense. When an individual acts as he is authorized by the norm or behaves as he is permitted by a norm, he 'applies' the norm. The judge, authorized by a statute (that is, a general norm)

to decide concrete cases, applies the statute to a concrete case by a decision which constitutes an *individual* norm. Again, authorized by a judicial decision to execute a certain punishment, the enforcement officer 'applies' the individual norm of the judicial decision. In exercising self-defense, one applies the norm that permits the use of force. Further, a norm is also 'applied' in rendering a judgment that an individual does, or does not, behave as he is commanded, authorized, or permitted by a norm.

In the broadest sense, any human behavior determined by a normative order as condition or consequence, can be considered as being authorized by this order and in this sense as being positively regulated. Human behavior is regulated negatively by a normative order if this behavior is not forbidden by the order without being positively permitted by a norm that limits the sphere of validity of a forbidding norm, and therefore is permitted only in a negative sense. This merely negative function of permitting has to be distinguished from the positive function of permitting—'positive,' because it is the function of a positive norm, the meaning of an act of will. The positive character of a permission becomes particularly apparent when the limitation of the sphere of validity of a norm that forbids certain conduct is brought about by a norm that permits the otherwise forbidden conduct under the condition that the permission has to be given by an organ of the community authorized thereto. The negative as well as positive function of permitting is therefore fundamentally connected with the function of commanding. A definite human behavior can be *permitted* only within a normative order that *commands* different kinds of behavior.

'To permit' is also used in the sense of 'to entitle (*berechtigen*).' If A is commanded to endure that B behaves in a certain way, it is said that B is permitted (that is, entitled) to behave in this way. And if A is commanded to render a certain service to B, it is said that B is permitted (that is, entitled) to receive the service of A. In the first example, then, the sentence: 'B is permitted to behave in a certain way' says the same as the sentence: 'A is commanded to endure that B behaves in a certain way.' And in the second example, the sentence: 'B is permitted to receive a certain service from A' says the same as the sentence: 'A is commanded to render a service to B.' The quality of B's behavior 'to be permitted' is merely the reflex of the quality of A's behavior 'to be commanded.' This kind of 'permitting' is not a function of the normative order different from its function of 'commanding.'

Kelsen The Pure Theory of Law 15–17

In contrast to his earlier efforts, these extracts show that a norm is far wider than a command; the 'ought' not only includes commands but also embraces 'may' and 'can'. It is also clear, in contrast to earlier efforts, that the command is directed towards citizens and not to officials only. We are well away from his original notion that law is a command to officials and this is no more apparent than in his above discussion of authorising and permitting. The inclusion of these two types of norm allows him to describe a complex legal system in more satisfactory terms than reducing it to a criminal law model with everything discussed in terms of commands.

Legal positivism and the emphasis on 'ought'

The 'ought' in the norm is a 'descriptive' ought. There is no question of 'ought' being used in an evaluative sense which would, in Kelsen's view, pollute the purity of the method. The theorist is saying something like this: 'from the point of view of those within the system, that decision ought to be made or is justified'. No ethics is involved: the 'ought' is merely 'a functional connection', the normative form used to express legal propositions. Compare Raz and statements from a point of view (supra pp 13ff). Notice in what follows that whereas legal science *describes*, it is only the legal authority that *prescribes*.

The science of law, by comprehending human behavior only to the extent that it is the content of—which means, determined by—legal norms, represents a normative interpretation of its object. The science of law describes the legal norms created by acts of human behavior and to be applied and obeyed by such acts; and thereby describes the norm-constituted relations between the facts determined by the norms. The sentences by which the science of law describes these norms and relationships must be distinguished as 'rules of law' from the legal *norms* that are created by the legal authorities, applied by them, and obeyed by the legal subjects. Rules of law (in a descriptive sense), on the other hand, are hypothetical judgments stating that according to a national or international legal order, under the conditions determined by this order, certain consequences determined by the order ought to take place. Legal *norms* are not judgments, that is, they are not statements about an object of cognition. According to their meaning they are commands; they may be also permissions and authorizations; but they are not instructions as is often maintained when law and jurisprudence are erroneously equated. The law commands, permits, or authorizes, but it does not 'teach.' However, when legal norms are linguistically expressed in words and sentences, they may appear in the form of assertions stating facts. For example, the norm that theft ought to be punished is frequently formulated by the legislator in the sentence: 'Theft is punished by imprisonment'; the norm that the head of state is authorized to conclude treaties is expressed by saying: 'The head of state concludes treaties.' Important, however, is not the linguistic form, but the meaning of the law-creating, norm-positing act. The meaning of the act is different from the meaning of the law-describing rule of law. The differentiation between 'rule of law' (in German: Rechts-*Satz*) and 'legal norm' (in German Rechts-*Norm*) expresses the difference between the function of legal cognition and the entirely different function of legal authority represented by the organs of the legal community. The science of law has to know the law—as it were from the outside—and to describe it. The legal organs, as legal authorities, have to create the law so that afterward it may be known and described by the science of law. It is true that the law-applying organs also have to know—as it were from the inside—the law they are applying. The legislator who applies the constitution ought to know the constitution, and the judge who applies the law ought to know the law. But this knowledge is not the essential element of their functions; it is only the preparation for their functions.

It is further true that, according to Kant's epistemology, the science of law as cognition of the law, like any cognition, has constitutive character—it 'creates' its object insofar as it comprehends the object as a meaningful whole. Just as the chaos of sensual perceptions becomes a cosmos, that is, 'nature' as a unified system, through the cognition of natural science, so the multitude of general and individual legal norms, created by the legal organs, becomes a unitary system, a legal 'order', through the science of law. But this 'creation' has a purely epistemological character. It is fundamentally different from the creation of objects by human labor or the creation of law by the legal authority.

The difference between the function of the science of law and the function of the legal authority, and thereby the difference between the product of the one and that of the other, is frequently ignored. Linguistically law and science of law are often used synonymously. For example by speaking of 'classical international law' one actually means a certain theory of international law; or by speaking of science of law as source of law, one means that the science of law can make a binding decision of a law case. But the science of law can only *describe* the law, it cannot *prescribe* a certain behavior like the law created by the legal authority (in the form of general or individual norms). No jurist can deny the essential difference between a law published in the official legal gazette and a scientific commentary to this law—between the penal code and a textbook on criminal law. The statements formulated by the science of law that, according to a legal order, something ought to be done or not to be done, do not impose obligations nor confer rights upon anybody; they may be true or false. But the norms enacted by the legal authority, imposing obligations and conferring rights upon the legal subjects, are neither true nor false, but only valid or invalid; just as facts are neither true nor false, but only existent or nonexistent, and only *statements about* facts can be true or false. For example, the statement contained in a text on civil law that a person who does not fulfil a promise of marriage has to compensate for the damage caused or else a civil execution ought to be directed into his property, is false if the law of the state, which is described in this legal text, does not establish such an obligation because it does not prescribe such a civil execution. The answer to the question of whether such a legal norm is valid within a legal order can be—indirectly— verified, because the norm, to be valid, must have been created by an empirically identifiable act. But the norm enacted by the legal authority (prescribing compensation for the damage and civil execution in case of nonfulfilment) cannot be true or false, because it is not an assertion about a fact—not a *de*scription of an object but a *pre*scription—and is as such the object to be described by the science of law. The norm constituted by the legislator (prescribing execution against a person who does not fulfil a marriage promise and does not compensate for the damage) and the statement formulated by the science of law and describing this norm (that execution ought to be carried out against a person who does not fulfil his marriage promise and does not compensate for the damage caused)—these expressions are logically different. It is therefore convenient to differentiate them terminologically as 'legal norm' and 'rule of law.' It follows from what has been said that the rules of law formulated by the science of law are not simply repetitions of the legal norms created by the legal authority. The objection that rules of law are superfluous is not so obviously unfounded, however, as the view that a natural science is superfluous beside nature, for nature does not manifest itself in spoken and written words, as the law does. The view that a rule of law formulated by the science of law is superfluous beside the legal norm created by the legislator can be met only by pointing out that such a view would amount to the opinion that a scientific presentation of a criminal law is superfluous beside this criminal law, that the science of law is superfluous beside the law.

Since legal norms, being prescriptions (that is, commands, permissions, authorizations), can neither be true nor false, the question arises: How can logical principles, especially the Principle of the Exclusion of Contradiction and the Rules of Inference, be applied to the relation between legal norms, if, according to traditional views these principles are applicable only to assertions that can be true or false. The answer is: Logical principles are applicable, indirectly, to legal norms to the extent that they are applicable to the rules of law which describe the legal norms and which can be true or false. Two legal norms are contradictory and can therefore not both be valid at the same time, if the two rules of law that describe them are contradictory; and one legal norm may be deduced from another if the rules of law that describe them can form a logical syllogism.

This is not incompatible with the fact that these rules of law are ought-statements and must be ought-statements, because they describe norms prescribing that something ought to be. The statement describing the validity of a norm of criminal law that prescribes imprisonment for theft would be false if it were to say that according to that norm theft is punished by imprisonment—it would be false, because there are circumstances in which despite the validity of that norm theft is, in fact, not punished; for example, when the thief is not caught. The rule of law describing this norm can be formulated only in this way: If somebody steals, he ought to be punished. But the 'ought' of the legal rule does not have a prescriptive character, like the 'ought' of the legal norm—its meaning is descriptive. This ambiguity of the word 'ought' is overlooked when ought-statements are identified with imperative statements.

Kelsen *The Pure Theory of Law* 71–75

LAW AS A COERCIVE ORDER

The law as coercive order and the role of the basic norm is emphasised in the next passage.

Because, when we compare the objects that have been designated by the word 'law' by different peoples at different times, we see that all these objects turn out to be *orders of human behavior*. An 'order' is a system of norms whose unity is constituted by the fact that they all have the same reason for their validity; and the reason for the validity of a normative order is a basic norm—as we shall see—from which the validity of all norms of the order are derived. A single norm is a valid legal norm, if it corresponds to the concept of 'law' and is part of a legal order; and it *is* part of a legal order, if its validity is based on the basic norm of that order.

Kelsen *The Pure Theory of Law* 31

What distinguishes a legal order of norms from a moral order, which also uses norms as the mode of expression, is that a legal order is a positive, by and large effective, coercive order. He emphasises the difference between coercive sanction and mere disapproval in the next extract.

The first characteristic, then, common to all social orders designated by the word 'law' is that they are orders of human behavior. A second characteristic is that they are *coercive orders*. This means that they react against certain events, regarded as undesirable because detrimental to society, especially against human behavior of this kind, with a coercive act; that is to say, by inflicting on the responsible individual an evil—such as deprivation of life, health, liberty, or economic values—which, if necessary, is imposed upon the affected individual even against his will by the employment of physical force. By the coercive act an evil is inflicted in the sense that the affected individual ordinarily regards it as such, although it may occasionally happen that this is not so. For example, somebody who has committed a crime may regret his action so much that he actually wishes to suffer the punishment of the law and therefore does not regard it as an evil; or somebody commits a crime in order to go to jail where he can be sure of food and shelter. But these are, of course, exceptions. Since, ordinarily, the affected individual regards the coercive act as an evil, the social orders, designated as 'law' are coercive orders of human behavior. They command a certain human behavior by attaching a coercive act to the opposite behavior. This coercive act is directed against the individual who behaves in this way (or against individuals who are in some social relation to him). That means: the coercive order authorizes a certain individual to direct a coercive act as a sanction against another individual. The sanctions prescribed by the legal order are socially immanent (as distinguished from transcendental) sanctions; besides, they are socially organized (as distinguished from mere approval or disapproval).

By prescribing coercive acts, a legal order may not only react against a certain human behavior, but also against other socially detrimental facts, as will be described later. In other words: Whereas the coercive act prescribed by the legal order is always the behavior of a certain individual, the condition to which the coercive act is attached need not necessarily be the behavior of an individual but may be another fact, regarded as socially detrimental. As we shall see, the coercive act prescribed by the legal order may be interpreted as an action of the community constituted by the legal order and especially as a reaction of the legal community against a socially detrimental fact. That means that the coercive act may be *attributed* to this community; which is a figurative expression of the mental operation by which we refer the coercive act prescribed by the legal order to this legal order, the unity of which we personify as an acting entity. If the socially detrimental fact against which the community reacts with a coercive act is a definite human behavior, the reaction is interpreted as a sanction. That the law is a coercive order means that the legal norms prescribe coercive acts which may be attributed to the legal community. This does not mean that the execution of the sanctions each time requires the application of physical force; this is necessary only if execution meets resistance, which ordinarily does not happen.

Modern legal orders sometimes contain norms that provide for rewards, such as titles or decorations, for certain meritorious acts. But rewards are not an element common to all social orders designated as law; they are not an essential function of these orders. Within these coercive orders they play a subordinate role. Besides, these norms authorizing certain organs to confer titles or decorations on individuals who have distinguished themselves in some way or another have a fundamental connection with the sanction-prescribing norms: For the use of a title or the display of a decoration is either legally not prohibited, that is, negatively permitted; or—and this is the usual situation—it is positively permitted, which means it is forbidden, unless expressly permitted. The legal situation, then, can only be described as a norm-stipulated restriction of the validity of a prohibitive norm; in other words, by referring to a coercive norm.

As a coercive order, the law is distinguished from other social orders. The decisive criterion is the element of force—that means that the act prescribed by the order as a consequence of socially detrimental facts ought to be executed even against the will of the individual and, if he resists, by physical force.

Kelsen *The Pure Theory of Law* 33–34

The sanction

The coercive act has the character of a sanction.

Insofar as the coercive act prescribed by the legal order has the function of a reaction against a human behavior determined by the legal order, then this coercive act has the character of a sanction. The human behavior against which the coercive act is directed is to be considered as prohibited, illegal—as a delict. It is the opposite of *that* behavior that is regarded as commanded or legal, namely the behavior that avoids the application of the sanction. That the law is characterized as a 'coercive order' does not mean—as is sometimes asserted—that it 'enforces' the legal, that is, the commanded, behavior. This behavior is not enforced by the coercive act, because the coercive act is to be executed precisely when an individual behaves in the prohibited, not the commanded, manner. It is exactly for this case that the coercive act as a sanction is prescribed. Perhaps, however, the mentioned assertion should be taken to mean that the law, by prescribing sanctions, tries to induce men to behave in conformity with its command, in that the wish to avoid the sanctions becomes the motive that brings about this behavior. However, the motivation in question is only a possible, not a necessary, function of the law; the legal— that is, the commanded—behavior may be brought about by other motives also, especially by religious and moral ones. And this happens frequently enough. The coercion that is implied in the motivation is a psychic coercion, which is a possible effect of the idea an individual has of the law, and which takes place within this individual. And this psychic coercion must not be confused with the prescription of the coercive act, which takes place within the legal order. Every effective social order exerts some kind of psychic coercion, and some orders—such as the religious order—in much higher degree than the legal order. This psychic coercion, then, is not a characteristic that distinguishes the law from other social orders. The law is not a coercive order in the sense that it exerts a psychic coercion; but in the sense that it prescribes coercive acts, namely the forcible deprivation of life, freedom, economic and other values as a consequence of certain conditions. These conditions are in the first place—but not exclusively—a definite human behavior, which precisely by being a condition of a sanction assumes the character of legally prohibited (illegal) behavior—a delict.

Kelsen *The Pure Theory of Law* 34–35

Coercive acts other than sanctions

The more sophisticated analysis in the later work in terms of commanding, authorising and permitting is used to note that some 'coercive orders' do not fit the earlier sanction/delict correlative.

As the state develops from a judicial to an administrative community, the sphere of facts that are made conditions for coercive acts grows. Now not only socially undesirable actions and omissions but also other facts, not having the character of delicts, are included. Among those facts is the suspicion that a definite individual has committed a delict. Special organs, having the character of police agents, may be legally authorized to deprive the suspected individual of his liberty in order to safeguard legal proceedings against him, in which it will be decided whether he has, in fact, committed the delict of which he is suspected. The condition for the deprivation of liberty is not a definite behavior of the individual, but the suspicion of such a behavior. Similarly, the police may be authorized by the legal order to take persons in so-called protective custody, that is, to deprive them of their liberty, in order to protect them against illegal aggression that threatens them. Further, modern legal orders prescribe the forced internment in institutions of insane individuals constituting a public danger, and in hospitals of persons with contagious diseases. Further, property may be expropriated if necessary in the public interest, domestic animals may be destroyed if infected with an epidemic illness, buildings may be torn down by force to prevent their collapsing or the spread of a conflagration. The legal order of totalitarian states authorizes their governments to confine in concentration camps persons whose opinions, religion, or race they do not like; to force them to perform any kind of labor; even to kill them. Such measures may morally be violently condemned; but they cannot be considered as taking place outside the legal order of these states. All these acts constitute the same forced deprivation of life, liberty, and property as the sanctions of the death penalty, imprisonment, and civil execution. But, as we have said, they differ from sanctions insofar as they are not the consequence of a legally ascertained, socially undesirable action or omission of an individual; the condition is not a legally ascertained delict committed by an individual. Delict is a definite human behavior (an action or omission) which, because socially undesirable, is prohibited by the legal order; and it is prohibited insofar as the legal order attaches to it (or, more correctly formulated: to the fact that it is ascertained in a legal procedure) a coercive act, as this fact is made by the legal order the condition of a coercive act. And this coercive act is a sanction (in the sense of a reaction against a delict) and as such distinguishable from other legally established coercive acts only in that the conditioning fact of the former is a legally ascertained human behavior, whereas the coercive acts which have not the character of sanctions are conditioned by other facts. Some of the coercive acts belonging to the second category may be interpreted as sanctions, if the concept of 'sanction' is not limited to reactions against a definite human behavior whose actual existence is legally ascertained, but is extended to situations in which the coercive act is provided for as reaction against a delict—but against a delict whose commission by a definite individual has not yet been legally ascertained, though the individual may be suspected of having committed it and may therefore be arrested by the police; and to situations in which the coercive act is a reaction against a delict that has not even been committed yet, but is expected in the future as a possibility—as in the cases of internment of dangerous psychopaths or persons of undesired opinions, religions, and races, insofar as they are interned in concentration camps to prevent them from a socially undesired behavior of which, rightly or wrongly, in the opinion of the legal authority, they are considered capable. Apparently, this motive is the basis for the limitations of liberty to which, in a war, the citizens of the one belligerent party living on the territory of the other are subjected by the latter. If we extend the concept of 'sanction' in this sense, it is no longer congruent with 'consequence of a delict.' Sanction in this wider sense of the word does not necessarily *follow* the delict.

Finally, the concept of sanction may be extended to include all coercive acts established by the legal order, if the word is to express merely that the legal order reacts with this action against socially undesirable circumstances and qualifies in this way the circumstances as undesirable. This, indeed, is the common characteristic of all coercive actions commanded or authorized by legal orders. The concept of 'sanction,' understood in this broadest sense, then, the force monopoly of the legal community, may be formulated by the alternative: 'The use of force of man against man is either a delict or a sanction.'

Kelsen The Pure Theory of Law 40–42

With coercion included in the definition of law, it may be asked, where is the coercion in constitutional law? In the next extract, in the last three sentences, he uses two separate arguments to establish the link with coercion—the dependent norm argument and an explanation based on 'authorization'.

Against the definition of law as a coercive order, that is, against the inclusion of the element of coercion into the concept of law, the objections have been raised (1) that legal orders actually contain norms that do not stipulate coercive acts: norms that permit or authorize a behavior, and also norms that command a behavior without attaching to the opposite behavior a coercive act; and (2) that the nonapplication of the norms that stipulate coercive acts are frequently not made the condition for coercive acts functioning as sanctions.

The second objection is not valid, because the definition of law as a coercive order can be maintained even if the norm that stipulates a coercive act is not itself essentially connected with a norm that attaches, in a concrete case, a sanction to the nonordering or nonexecuting of the coercive act—if, therefore, the coercive act stipulated in the general norm is to be interpreted objectively not as commanded but only as authorized or positively permitted (although the subjective meaning of the act by which the general norm stipulates the coercive act is a commanding). As for the first objection, the definition of law as a coercive order can be maintained even with respect to norms that authorize a behavior not having the character of a coercive act; or norms that positively permit such a behavior insofar as they are *dependent* norms, because they are essentially connected with norms that stipulate the coercive acts. A typical example for norms cited as arguments against the inclusion of coercion into the definition of law are the norms of constitutional law. It is argued that the norms of the constitution that regulate the procedure of legislation do not stipulate sanctions as a reaction against nonobservance. Closer analysis shows, however, that these are dependent norms establishing only one of the conditions under which coercive acts stipulated by other norms are to be ordered and executed. Constitutional norms authorize the legislator to create norms—they do not command the creation of norms; and therefore the stipulation of sanctions does not come into question at all. If the provisions of the constitution are not observed, valid legal norms do not come into existence, the norms created in this way are void or voidable. This means: the subjective meaning of the acts established unconstitutionally and therefore not according to the basic norm, is not interpreted as their objective meaning or such a temporary interpretation is annulled.

Kelsen The Pure Theory of Law 50–51

The nature of dependent norms deserves a more extensive analysis, and this is just what it gets.

It was pointed out earlier that: if one norm commands a certain behavior and a second norm stipulates a sanction as reaction against nonobservance, the two norms are tied to each other. This is particularly true if a social order—as the legal order—commands a certain behavior specifically by attaching a coercive act as sanction to the opposite behavior. Therefore a behavior according to such an order may be regarded as commanded—and in case of a legal order as legally commanded—only so far as the opposite behavior is the condition of a sanction. If a legal order, such as a statute passed by parliament, contains one norm that prescribes a certain behavior and a second norm that attaches a sanction to the nonobservance of the first, then the first norm is not an independent norm, but fundamentally tied to the second; the first norm merely designates—negatively—the condition under which the second stipulates the sanction; and if the second one positively designates the condition under which it stipulates the sanction, then the first one is superfluous from the point of view of legislative technique. For example: If a civil code contains the norm that a debtor ought to pay back the received loan to the creditor; and the second norm that a civil execution ought to be directed into the property of the debtor if the debtor does not repay the loan; then everything prescribed by the first norm is contained conditionally in the second. Modern criminal codes usually do not contain norms that prohibit, like the Ten Commandments, murder, adultery, and other crimes; they limit themselves to attach penal sanctions to certain behavior. This shows clearly that a norm: 'You shall not murder' is superfluous, if a norm is valid: 'He who murders ought to be punished'; it shows, further, that the legal order indeed prohibits a certain behavior by attaching to it a sanction or that it commands a behavior by attaching a sanction to the opposite behavior.

Dependent are also those legal norms that positively permit a certain behavior. For—as shown before—they merely limit the sphere of validity of a legal norm that prohibits this behavior by attaching a sanction to the opposite. The example of self-defense has been cited earlier. Another example is found in the United Nations Charter. Article 2, paragraph 4, forbids all members to use force: the Charter attaches to the use of force the sanctions stipulated in Article 39. But the Charter permits in Article 51 the use of force as individual or collective self-defense by limiting the general prohibition of Article 2, paragraph 4. The named articles form a unit. The Charter could have combined them all in a single article forbidding all members to use force which does not have the character of individual or collective self-defense by making the thus restricted use of force the condition of a sanction. Yet another example: A norm prohibits the sale of alcoholic beverages; that is, makes it punishable; but this prohibition is restricted by another norm according to which the sale of these beverages, if a licence is obtained, is not forbidden; that means that the sale is not punishable.

The second norm, restricting the sphere of validity of the first, is a dependent norm; it is meaningful only in connection with the first; both form a unit. Their contents may be expressed in the single norm: 'If somebody sells alcoholic beverages without a state license, he ought to be punished.' The function of the merely negative permission, consisting in the nonprohibition by the legal order of a certain behavior, need not be considered here because negative permission is not granted by a positive norm.

A legal norm may not only restrict the sphere of validity of another norm, but may entirely annul the validity. These derogating norms too are dependent norms, meaningful only in connection with other, sanction-stipulating norms. Further, legal norms authorizing a certain behavior are dependent norms likewise, if 'authorizing' is understood to mean: confer upon an individual a legal power, that is, the power to create legal norms. These authorizing norms designate only one of the conditions under which—in an independent norm—the coercive act is prescribed. These are the norms that authorize the creation of general norms: (1) the norms of the constitution which regulate legislation or institute custom as a law-creating fact; and (2) the norms that regulate judicial and administrative procedures in which the general norms created by statute or custom are applied by authorized courts and administrative officials through individual norms created by these organs.

To give an example: Suppose the legal order of a state prohibits theft by attaching to it in a statute the penalty of imprisonment. The condition of the punishment is not merely the fact that a man has stolen. The theft has to be ascertained by a court authorized by the legal order in a procedure determined by the norms of the legal order; the court has to pronounce a punishment, determined by statute or custom; and this punishment has to be executed by a different organ. The court is authorized to impose, in a certain procedure, a punishment upon the thief, only if in a constitutional procedure a general norm is created that attaches to theft a certain punishment. The norm of the constitution, which authorizes the creation of this general norm, determines a condition to which the sanction is attached. The rule of law that describes this situation says: 'If the individuals authorized to legislate have issued a general norm according to which a thief is to be punished in a certain way; and if the court authorized by the Code of Criminal Proceedings in a procedure prescribed by this code has ascertained that an individual has committed theft; and if that court has ordered the legally determined punishment; then a certain organ ought to execute the punishment.' By thus phrasing the rule of law that describes the law, it is revealed that the norms of the constitution which authorize the creation of general norms by regulating the organization and procedure of legislation; and the norms of a Code of Criminal Procedure which authorize the creation of the individual norms of the judicial court decisions by regulating the organization and procedure of the criminal courts, are dependent norms; for they determine only conditions under which the punitive sanctions are to be executed. The execution of all coercive acts stipulated by a legal order—including those that are ordered by an administrative procedure and those that do not have the character of sanctions—is conditioned in that manner. The constitutional creation of the general norms to be applied by courts and administrative agencies, and the creation of the individual norms by which these organs have to apply the general norms, are as much conditions of the execution of the coercive act as the ascertainment of the fact of the delict or as other circumstances which the legal norms have made the condition of coercive acts that are not sanctions. But the general norm that stipulates the coercive act under all these conditions is an independent legal norm—even if the coercive act is not commanded because its nonexecution is not made the condition of a further coercive act. If we say that in this case the coercive act is authorized, then the word 'authorized' is used in a wider sense. It then does not merely mean conferring a legal power in the sense of a power to create legal norms, but also conferring the power to perform the coercive acts stipulated by the legal norms. In a wider sense, then, this power may also be designated as a legal power.

Dependent norms are, finally, also those that further determine the meaning of other norms, by defining a concept used in a second norm or by authentically interpreting a second norm otherwise. For example, a Criminal Code might contain an article saying: 'By murder is to be understood the behavior of an individual which intentionally causes the death of another individual.' This article defines murder; however, the article has normative character only in connection with another article that says: 'If a man commits murder, the authorized court ought to impose the death penalty.' And this article, again, is inseparably connected with a third article that says: 'The death penalty is to be carried out by hanging.'

It follows, that a legal order may be characterized as a coercive order, even though not all its norms stipulate coercive acts; because norms that do not themselves stipulate coercive acts (and hence do not command, but authorize the creation of norms or positively permit a definite behavior) are dependent norms, valid only in connection with norms, that *do* stipulate coercive acts. Again, not all norms that stipulate a coercive act but only those that stipulate the coercive act as a reaction against a certain behavior (that is, as a sanction), command a specific, namely the opposite, behavior. This, therefore, is another reason why the law does not have exclusively a commanding or imperative character. Since a legal order, in the sense just described, is a coercive order, it may be described in sentences pronouncing that under specific conditions (that is, under conditions determined by the legal order) specific coercive acts ought to be performed. All legally relevant material contained in a legal order fits in this scheme of the rule of law formulated by legal science—the *rule of law* which is to be distinguished from the *legal norm* established by the legal authority.

Kelsen The Pure Theory of Law 54–57

THE VALIDITY AND THE EFFECTIVENESS OF NORMS

Legal validity is not the same thing as effectiveness, but neither is it wholly independent of effectiveness: effectiveness acts as a condition of legal validity.

By the word 'validity' we designate the specific existence of a norm. When we describe the meaning or significance of a norm-creating act, we say: By this act some human behavior is ordered, commanded, prescribed, forbidden, or permitted, allowed, authorized. If we use the word *ought* to comprise all these meanings, as has been suggested, we can describe the validity of a norm by saying: Something ought to, or ought not to, be done. If we describe the specific existence of a norm as 'validity,' we express by this the special manner in which the norm—in contradistinction to a natural fact—is existent. The 'existence' of a positive norm—that is to say, its 'validity'—is not the same as the existence of the act of will, whose objective meaning the norm is. A norm can be valid, even if the act of will whose meaning the norm is, no longer exists. Indeed, the norm does not become valid until the act of will whose meaning the norm is has been accomplished and hence has ceased to exist. The individual who has created a legal norm by an act directed at the behavior of others, need not continue to will this conduct in order that the norm be valid. When the men who act as legislators have passed a statute regulating certain affairs and have put this statute into 'force' (i.e., into validity), they turn in their decisions to the regulation of other affairs; and the statutes put into validity may be valid long after these men have died and therefore are unable to will anything. It is incorrect, therefore, to characterize norms in general, and legal norms in particular, as the 'will' or the 'command' of the legislator or state, if by 'will' or 'command' a psychological act of will is meant. The norm is the *meaning* of an act of will, not the act of will.

Since the validity of a norm is an *ought* and not an *is*, it is necessary to distinguish the validity of a norm from its effectiveness. Effectiveness is an 'is-fact'—the fact that the norm is actually applied and obeyed, the fact that people actually behave according to the norm. To say that a norm is 'valid,' however, means something else than that it is actually applied and obeyed; it means that it *ought* to be obeyed and applied, although it is true that there may be some connection between validity and effectiveness. A general legal norm is regarded as valid only if the human behavior that is regulated by it actually conforms with it, at least to some degree. A norm that is not obeyed by anybody anywhere, in other words a *norm* that is not effective at least to some degree, is not regarded as a valid legal norm. A minimum of effectiveness is a condition of validity. 'Validity' of a legal norm presupposes, however, that it is possible to behave in a way contrary to it: a norm that were to prescribe that something ought to be done of which everyone knows beforehand that it must happen necessarily according to the laws of nature always and everywhere would be as senseless as a norm which were to prescribe that something ought to be done of which one knows beforehand that it is impossible according to the laws of nature.

Nor do validity and effectiveness coincide in time. A legal norm becomes valid before it becomes effective, that is, before it is applied and obeyed; a law court that applies a statute immediately after promulgation—therefore before the statute had a chance to become 'effective'—applies a valid legal norm. But a legal norm is no longer considered to be valid, if it remains permanently ineffective. Effectiveness is a condition of validity in the sense that effectiveness has to join the positing of a legal norm if the norm is not to lose its validity.

By effectiveness of a legal norm, which attaches a sanction to a certain behavior and thus qualifies the behavior conditioning the sanction as illegal, that is, as 'delict,' two facts may be understood: (1) that this norm is *applied* by the legal organs (particularly the law courts), which means, that the sanction in a concrete case is ordered and executed; and (2) that this norm is *obeyed* by the individuals subjected to the legal order, which means, that they behave in a way which avoids the sanction. If the stipulation of sanctions intends to prevent the commission of delicts, we are faced with the ideal case of the validity of a legal norm if this norm is never applied, because the awareness among those subjected to the legal order of the sanction to be executed in case of the commission of a delict has become the motive to refrain from committing the delict. In this situation, the effectiveness of the legal norm is confined to obedience to it. But obedience to the legal norm can be induced by other motives. If, for instance, the legal delict is at the same time a religious delict, obedience to the law may be caused not by the wish to avoid the legal sanction, but to avoid the religious sanction. In this case the law is effective, that is, actually obeyed, because religion is effective. The relation between validity and effectiveness will be discussed later.

Let us take the statement: 'The norm refers to a certain human behavior.' If by this behavior we mean the behavior that constitutes the content of the norm, then the norm can also refer to other facts than human behavior—however, only to the extent that these are *conditions* or (if existent in reality) *effects* of human behavior. For example: A legal norm can prescribe that in the event of a natural catastrophe those not immediately affected are obliged to render aid to the victims as much as possible. If a legal norm establishes the death penalty for murder, then the delict as well as the sanction do not only consist in a certain human behavior—directed toward the death of another human being—but also in a specific effect of such behavior, namely the death of a human being, which is a physiological event, not a human behavior. Since human behavior, as well as its conditions and effects, occur in space and time, the legal norm must refer to space and time. The validity of norms regulating human behavior in general, and the validity of legal norms in particular, therefore, must be defined in terms of space and time, since these norms refer to spatial and temporal events in their content. That a norm is 'valid' means always that it is valid for some specified space and time; it means that it relates to a behavior that can take place only somewhere and sometime (although it may perhaps not actually take place).

Kelsen *The Pure Theory of Law* 10–12

The reason for the validity of norms

If the law is a normative system, this question suggests itself: 'What constitutes the unity of a multitude of norms—why does a certain norm belong to a certain order? And this question is closely tied to the question: Why is a norm valid, what is the reason for its validity? Such questions cannot be answered by any statement to the effect that something *is*. The reason for the validity of a norm can only be the validity of a higher norm. Only a competent authority can create valid norms, and such competence can only be based on a norm that authorises the issuing of norms.

But a hierarchical system of norms ultimately leads to the *presupposed* starting point. Why?

The norm which represents the reason for the validity of another norm is called, as we have said, the 'higher' norm. But the search for the reason of a norm's validity cannot go on indefinitely like the search for the cause of an effect. It must end with a norm which, as the last and highest, is presupposed. It must be *presupposed*, because it cannot be 'posited,' that is to say: created, by an authority whose competence would have to rest on a still higher norm. This final norm's validity cannot be derived from a higher norm, the reason for its validity cannot be questioned. Such a presupposed highest norm is referred to in this book as basic norm. All norms whose validity can be traced back to one and the same basic norm constitute a system of norms, a normative order. The basic norm is the common source for the validity of all norms that belong to the same order—it is their common reason of validity. The fact that a certain norm belongs to a certain order is based on the circumstance that its last reason of validity is the basic norm of this order. It is the basic norm that constitutes the unity in the multitude of norms by representing the reason for the validity of all norms that belong to this order.

Kelsen *The Pure Theory of Law* 194–195

A legal norm is not valid because it has a certain content, in fact, any kind of content might be law.

> The norm system that presents itself as a legal order has essentially a dynamic character. A legal norm is not valid because it has a certain content, that is, because its content is logically deducible from a presupposed basic norm, but because it is created in a certain way—ultimately in a way determined by a presupposed basic norm. For this reason alone does the legal norm belong to the legal order whose norms are created according to this basic norm. Therefore any kind of content might be law. There is no human behavior which, as such, is excluded from being the content of a legal norm. The validity of a legal norm may not be denied for being (in its content) in conflict with that of another norm which does not belong to the legal order whose basic norm is the reason for the validity of the norm in question. The basic norm of a legal order is not a material norm which, because its content is regarded as immediately self-evident, is presupposed as the highest norm and from which norms for human behavior are logically deduced. The norms of a legal order must be created by a specific process. They are posited, that is, positive, norms, elements of a positive order. If by the constitution of a legal community is understood the norm or norms that determine how (that is, by what organs and by what procedure—through legislation or custom) the general norms of the legal order that constitute the community are to be created, then the basic norm is that norm which is presupposed when the custom through which the constitution has come into existence, or the constitution-creating act consciously performed by certain human beings, is objectively interpreted as a norm-creating fact; if, in the latter case, the individual or the assembly of individuals who created the constitution on which the legal order rests, are looked upon as norm-creating authorities. In this sense, the basic norm determines the basic fact of law creation and may in this respect be described as the constitution in a logical sense of the word (which will be explained later) in contradistinction to the constitution in the meaning of positive law.
>
> Kelsen *The Pure Theory of Law* 198–199

The basic norm

In the next, critical passage, the illustration concerning the coercive act of hanging leads him to the 'historically first constitution' the validity of which must be presupposed.

> The basic norm is the presupposed starting point of a procedure: the procedure of positive law creation. It is itself not a norm created by custom or by the act of a legal organ; it is not a positive but a presupposed norm so far as the constitution-establishing authority is looked upon as the highest authority and can therefore not be regarded as authorized by the norm of a higher authority.
>
> If the question as to the reason for the validity of a certain legal norm is raised, then the answer can only consist in the reduction to the basic norm of this legal order, that is, in the assertion that the norm was created—in the last instance—according to the basic norm. In the following pages we would like to consider only a national legal order, that is, a legal order limited in its validity to a specific space, the so-called territory of the state, and which is regarded as 'sovereign,' that is, as not subordinated to any higher legal order. We shall

discuss the problem of the validity of the norms of a national legal order, at first without considering an international legal order superordinated to or included in it.

The question of the reason for the validity of a legal norm belonging to a specific national legal order may arise on the occasion of a coercive act; for example, when one individual deprives another of his life by hanging, and now the question is asked why this act is legal, namely the execution of a punishment, and not murder. This act can be interpreted as being legal only if it was prescribed by an individual legal norm, namely as an act that 'ought' to be performed, by a norm that presents itself as a judicial decision. This raises the questions: Under what conditions is such an interpretation possible, why is a judicial decision present in this case, why is the individual norm created thereby a legal norm belonging to a valid legal order and therefore ought to be applied? The answer is: Because this individual norm was created in applying a criminal law that contains a general norm according to which (under conditions present in the case concerned) the death penalty ought to be inflicted. If we ask for the reason for the validity of this criminal law, then the answer is: the criminal law is valid because it was created by the legislature, and the legislature, in turn, is authorized by the constitution to create general norms. If we ask for the reason of the validity of the constitution, that is, for the reason of the validity of the norms regulating the creation of the general norms, we may, perhaps, discover an older constitution; that means the validity of the existing constitution is justified by the fact that it was created according to the rules of an earlier constitution by way of a constitutional amendment. In this way we eventually arrive at a historically first constitution that cannot have been created in this way and whose validity, therefore, cannot be traced back to a positive norm created by a legal authority; we arrive, instead, at a constitution that became valid in a revolutionary way, that is, either by breach of a former constitution or for a territory that formerly was not the sphere of validity of a constitution and of a national legal order based on it. If we consider merely the national legal order, not international law, and if we ask for the reason of the validity of the historically first constitution, then the answer can only be (if we leave aside God or 'nature') that the validity of this constitution—the assumption that it is a binding norm—must be *presupposed* if we want to interpret (1) the acts performed according to it as the creation or application of valid general legal norms; and (2) the acts performed in application of these general norms as the creation or application of valid individual legal norms. Since the reason for the validity of a norm can only be another norm, the presupposition must be a norm: not one posited (i.e., created) by a legal authority, but a presupposed norm, that is, a norm presupposed if the subjective meaning of the constitution-creating facts and the subjective meaning of the norm-creating facts established according to the constitution are interpreted as their objective meaning. Since it is the basic norm of a legal order (that is, an order prescribing coercive acts), therefore this norm, namely the basic norm of the legal order concerned, must be formulated as follows: Coercive acts ought to be performed under the conditions and in the manner which the historically first constitution, and the norms created according to it, prescribe. (In short: One ought to behave as the constitution prescribes.) The norms of a legal order, whose common reason for their validity is this basic norm, are not a complex of valid norms standing coordinatedly side by side, but form a hierarchical structure of super- and subordinate norms.

Clearly, his basic norm is something different from 'the constitution' as we customarily use the phrase. He distinguishes between 'the constitution in a transcendental-logical sense' (or what he sometimes calls 'constitution in a legal-logical sense'—as in the next extract), that is the basic norm, from 'constitution in a positive-legal sense', that is the actual rules of the constitution. To clear up some of the many potential confusions it is worth quoting a small excerpt from Kelsen's reply to Julius Stone (Kelsen's article is in response to Stone's attack in [1963] 26 MLR 34).

One of the main objects of Professor Stone's criticism is my theory of the *basic norm*. Professor Stone says with respect to this concept that it conceals

an ambiguity, swinging between, on the one hand, a norm that is at the top of the pyramid of norms of each legal order, and on the other, some other norm which remains outside this pyramid, and is thus wholly meta-legal, and amounts to a general presupposition requiring that in each and every legal order 'the constitution' shall be obeyed.

In the following sentence Professor Stone maintains that I 'now,' that is, not earlier than in the second edition of my *Reine Rechtslehre*, insist 'that the basic norm is outside the legal system,' but nevertheless 'has legally relevant functions.' That means that—according to Professor Stone—I understand by the 'basic norm' a norm which is not a norm of positive law, and at the same time a norm which is a norm of positive law. This interpretation is without any foundation in my writings. I have always and not only in the second edition of my *Reine Rechtslehre* clearly distinguished between the basic norm presupposed in juristic thinking as the constitution in a legal-logical sense and the constitution in a positive legal sense, and I have always insisted that the basic norm as the constitution in a legal-logical sense—not the constitution in a positive legal sense—is *not* a norm of positive law, that it is not a norm 'posited,' i.e., created by a real act of will of a legal organ, but a norm *presupposed in juristic thinking*. It is, unfortunately, not possible to translate adequately into English the German terms by which the difference between the basic norm and a norm of positive law is characterized, namely, that the basic norm is not *gesetzt* by a real act of will, but *vorausgesetzt* in juristic thinking. I refer in this respect to my *Reine Rechtslehre* and my *General Theory of Law and State* which was published in 1945, fifteen years before the second edition of the *Reine Rechtslehre*. It is as a norm presupposed in juristic thinking that the basic norm (*if* it is presupposed) is 'at the top of the pyramid of norms of each legal order.' It is 'meta-legal' if by this term is understood that the basic norm is not a norm of positive law, that is, not a norm created by a real act of will of a legal organ. It is 'legal' if by this term we understand everything which has legally relevant functions, and the basic norm presupposed in juristic thinking has the function to found the *objective* validity of the subjective meaning of the acts by which the constitution of a community is created.

Kelsen (1965) 17 Stan LR 1130, 1141

The basic norm as transcendental-logical presupposition

To understand the nature of the basic norm it must be kept in mind that it refers directly to a specific constitution, actually established by custom or statutory creation, by and large effective, and indirectly to the coercive order created according to this constitution and by and large effective; the basic norm thereby furnishes the reason for the validity of this constitution and of the coercive order created in accordance with it. The basic norm, therefore, is not the product of free invention. It is not presupposed arbitrarily in the sense that there is a choice between different basic norms when the subjective meaning of a constitution-creating act and the acts created according to this constitution are interpreted as their objective meaning. Only if this basic norm, referring to a specific constitution, is presupposed, that is, only if it is presupposed that one ought to behave according to this specific constitution—only then can the subjective meaning of a constitution-creating act and of the acts created according to this constitution be interpreted as their objective meaning, that is, as objectively valid legal norms, and the relationships established by these norms as legal relations.

In presupposing the basic norm referring to a specific constitution, the contents of this constitution and of the national legal order created according to it is irrelevant—it may be a just or unjust order; it may or may not guarantee a relative condition of peace within the community established by it. The presupposition of the basic norm does not approve any value transcending positive law.

Insofar as only the presupposition of the basic norm makes it possible to interpret the subjective meaning of the constitution-creating act (and of the acts established according to the constitution) as their objective meaning, that is, as objectively valid legal norms, the basic norm as represented by the science of law may be characterized as the transcendental-logical condition of this interpretation, if it is permissible to use by analogy a concept of Kant's epistemology. Kant asks: 'How is it possible to interpret without a metaphysical hypothesis, the facts perceived by our senses, in the laws of nature formulated by natural science?' In the same way, the Pure Theory of Law asks: 'How is it possible to interpret without recourse to meta-legal authorities, like God or nature, the subjective meaning of certain facts as a system of objectively valid legal norms describable in rules of law?' The epistemological answer of the Pure Theory of Law is: 'By presupposing the basic norm that one ought to behave as the constitution prescribes, that is, one ought to behave in accordance with the subjective meaning of the constitution-creating act of will—according to the prescriptions of the authority creating the constitution.' The function of this basic norm is to found the objective validity of a positive legal order, that is, to interpret the *subjective* meaning of the acts of human beings by which the norms of an effective coercive order are created, as their *objective* meaning. The foundation of the validity of a positive norm, that is, one established by an act of will and prescribing a certain behavior, is the result of a syllogistic procedure. In this syllogism, the major premise is the assertion about a norm regarded as objectively valid, according to which one ought to obey the commands of a certain person, that is, one ought to behave according to the subjective meaning of these commands; the minor premise is the assertion of the fact that this person has commanded to behave in a certain way; and the conclusion is the assertion of the validity of the norm: that one ought to behave in this particular way. Thus the norm whose validity is stated in the major premise legitimizes the subjective meaning of the command, whose existence is asserted in the minor premise, as the command's objective meaning. For example: One ought to obey God's commands. God has commanded to obey the commands of the parents. Hence, one ought to obey the commands of the parents. Thus the subjective meaning of the act by which a father commands a certain behaviour of his son is legitimized as its objective meaning, that is, as a binding norm.

The norm whose validity is asserted in the major premise is a basic norm if its objective validity is not questioned. It is not questioned if its validity cannot be based on a syllogistic procedure. And it cannot be so based, if the statement of the fact that this norm was established by an individual's act of will is not possible as the minor premise of a syllogism. This is the case when the person whose commands one ought to obey according to the norm now in question, is regarded as a highest authority, for example, God. Then the norm prescribing to obey the commands of this person has to be placed at the top of the syllogism as its major premise without it being possible that the norm itself is stated in the form of a conclusion of a further syllogism. This means: the norm is *presupposed* as a basic norm.

For this reason, the norm: 'One ought to obey the commands of God' is a basic norm on which the validity of the norm: 'One ought to obey the commands of one's parents,' is based. A theological ethics that regards God as the highest norm-creating authority cannot state that somebody else has ordered to obey the commands of God—because this would have to be an authority higher than God. And if the norm: 'One ought to obey the commands of God' were presumed to be posited by God, it could not be the reason for the validity of God-created norms, because it would itself be a God-created norm. Nor can theological ethics in itself create such a norm (that is, command to obey the commands of God) because as cognition it cannot be a norm-creating authority. Therefore, the norm: 'One ought to obey the commands of God,' as the basic norm, cannot be the subjective meaning of an act of will; it can only be the meaning of an act of thinking. That means: Theological ethics can only state: 'The command of the parents has the character of an objectively binding norm if we presuppose in our thinking the norm: "One ought to obey the commands of God" (who has commanded to obey the commands of the parents).'

Since a positivistic science of law regards the creator of the historically first constitution as the highest legal authority and therefore cannot maintain that the norm to obey the commands of the creator of the constitution is the subjective meaning of the act of will of an authority higher than the creator of the constitution—such as God's or nature's—so therefore, the science of law cannot base the validity of this norm on a syllogistic procedure. A positivistic science of law can only state that this norm is presupposed as a basic norm in the foundation of the objective validity of the legal norms, and therefore presupposed in the interpretation of an effective coercive order as a system of objectively valid legal norms. Since this basic norm cannot be the meaning of an act of will; and since this norm (rather: the statement about it) is logically indispensable for the foundation of the objective validity of positive legal norms, it can only be the meaning of an act of thinking; the science of law can state no more than: the subjective meaning of the acts by which legal norms are created can be interpreted as their objective meaning only if we presuppose in our juristic thinking the norm: 'One ought to obey the prescriptions of the historically first constitution.'

The science of law does not prescribe that one ought to obey the commands of the creator of the constitution. The science of law remains a merely cognitive discipline even in its epistemological statement that the basic norm is the condition under which the subjective meaning of the constitution-creating act, and the subjective meaning of the acts performed in accordance with the constitution, are interpreted as their objective meaning, as valid norms, even if the meaning of these acts is so interpreted by the legal science itself.

By offering this theory of the basic norm, the Pure Theory of Law does not inaugurate a new method of legal cognition. It merely makes conscious what most legal scientists do, at least unconsciously, when they understand the mentioned facts not as causally determined, but instead interpret their subjective meaning as objectively valid norms, that is, as a normative legal order, without basing the validity of this order upon a higher, meta-legal norm, that is, upon a norm enacted by an authority superior to the legal authority; in other words, when they consider as law exclusively positive law. The theory of the basic norm is merely the result of an analysis of the procedure which a positivistic science of law has always applied.

Kelsen The Pure Theory of Law 201–205

What follows is a translation of an essay published by Kelsen in German in 1964. In it the basic norm is described as a 'fiction', thereby appearing to accept that the basic norm does not correspond to reality. Thus the basic norm is to be seen as fiction in the sense of the doctrine of 'as if'. This modification rests on his new idea that there is 'a very important correlation between ought and willing (between Sollen and Wollen)'.

The basic norm may be termed the constitution in a transcendental-logical sense, as distinct from the constitution in a positive-legal sense. The latter is the constitution posited by·human acts of will, whose validity is grounded through the presupposed basic norm.

The basic norm may, but need not, be presupposed. What ethics and legal science have to say about the basic norm is: only once it is presupposed can the subjective meaning of acts of will directed toward the conduct of others come to be interpreted also as their objective meaning, these meaning-contents [Sinngehalte] come to be interpreted as moral or legal norms. Since this interpretation is conditioned by the presupposing of the basic norm, it must be admitted that ought-propositions [Soll-Sätze] can be interpreted as objectively valid moral or legal norms only in this conditioned sense.

To the acceptance of a norm merely presupposed [vorausgesetzt] in juristic thinking, and not posited [gesetzt] through a real act of will, one can validly object that a norm can be the meaning only of an act of will [Willensakt] and not of an act of thinking [Denkakt], that there is a very important correlation between 'ought' and 'willing' [Sollen und Wollen]. One can meet this objection only by conceding that along with the supposed [gedacht] basic norm one must also come to suppose an imaginary authority whose (fancied [fingiert]) act of will has the basic norm as its meaning.

With this fiction, the acceptance of the basic norm becomes contradictory to accepting that the constitution whose validity is grounded by the basic norm is the meaning of the act of will of a supreme authority over which no higher authority can be admitted. Thus the basic norm comes to be seen as a genuine [echt] fiction in the sense of the Vaihingerian philosophy of As-If. A fiction in this sense is characterized by its not only contradicting reality but also containing contradiction within itself. And the acceptance of a basic norm— such as, for instance, the basic norm of a religious moral order, 'One ought to pay heed to the ordinances of God,' or the basic norm of a legal order, 'One ought to conduct oneself as the historically first constitution determines'—not only contradicts reality, in which no such norm exists as the meaning of an actual act of will, but also contains contradiction within itself, for it presents [darstellt] the authorization of a supreme moral or legal authority, and hence authority issues from an authority lying beyond that authority, even though the further authority is merely fancied.

For Vaihinger a fiction is an aid to thought, of which one avails oneself when one cannot reach the aim of one's thoughts with the materials available. The thought-aim of the basic norm is the grounding of the validity of norms composing a positive moral or legal order; that is, the interpreting of the subjective meaning of the acts positing these norms as their objective meaning, *i.e.* as valid norms, and the corresponding acts as acts positing norms. This object is to be reached only by means of a fiction. Therefore one has to keep in mind that the basic norm in the sense of the Vaihingerian As-If philosophy is not a hypothesis—as I myself have sometimes characterized it—but a fiction, which distinguishes itself from a hypothesis in that it comes, or should come, to be accompanied by an awareness that reality does not correspond to it.

Kelsen (1980) Juridical Review 199, 121–122, translated by I Stewart

Therefore, he seems to accept that the basic norm as fiction contradicts reality; but more than that, it also contains a contradiction within itself because it is now defined as the meaning of an act of will that cannot exist, that 'is merely fancied'.

Harris is worth quoting on the so-called transition from basic norm as presupposition to basic norm as fiction. Does it really represent a major change in Kelsen's pure theory?

Kelsen at times expressed misgivings about the adequacy of his characterizations of the basic norm as a 'presupposition' or 'hypothesis'. [In later articles] he stated that 'the presupposition of the basic norm is a typical case of a fiction in the sense of Vaihinger's *Philosophie des Als-Ob*'. [See 'as if' in the last extract.] Vaihinger sought to distinguish between two senses in which the term 'hypothesis' is used. In one sense, he said, it refers to a presupposition about reality which is in principle verifiable; in the other sense (which he preferred to designate 'fiction'), it refers to a construct which is 'of service to discursive thought'. Hence, by terming the basic norm a 'fiction' in Vaihinger's sense, Kelsen merely reiterated the view which had always permeated his writings, namely, that this mental construct ('presupposition', 'hypothesis') is needed to explain the logic of legal science.

Harris *Law and Legal Science* 78–79

Have we returned to the idea of a fictive act of will being nothing more or less than Harris's 'constructive metaphor' which, although largely valueless in political theory, becomes useful in the realm of legal theory by explaining the logical basis of descriptive legal science? Harris came to the same conclusion in connection with Austin's reliance upon 'sovereign will' (supra pp 24ff).

THE NATURE OF THE BASIC NORM

Legitimacy and effectiveness: the basic norm and the problem of revolution

The function of the basic norm becomes particularly apparent if the constitution is not changed by constitutional means but by revolution; when the existence—that is, the validity—of the entire legal order directly based on the constitution, is in question.

It was said earlier that a norm's sphere of validity, particularly its temporal sphere of validity, may be limited; the beginning and end of its validity may be determined by the norm itself or by a higher norm regulating the creation of the lower one. The norms of a legal order are valid until their validity is terminated according to the rules of this legal order. By regulating its own creation and application, the legal order determines the beginning and end of the validity of the legal norms. Written constitutions usually contain special rules concerning the method by which they can be changed. The principle that a norm of a legal order is valid until its validity is terminated in a way determined by this legal order or replaced by the validity of another norm of this order, is called the principle of legitimacy.

This principle is applicable to a national legal order with one important limitation only: It does not apply in case of a revolution. A revolution in the broader sense of the word (that includes a coup d'état) is every not legitimate change of this constitution or its replacement by another constitution. From the point of view of legal science it is irrelevant whether this change of the legal situation has been brought about by the application of force against the legitimate government or by the members of that government themselves, whether by a mass movement of the population or by a small group of individuals. Decisive is only that the valid constitution has been changed or replaced in a manner not prescribed by the constitution valid until then. Usually a revolution abolishes only the old constitution and certain politically important statutes. A large part of the statutes created under the old constitution remains valid, as the saying goes; but this expression does not fit. If these statutes are to be regarded as being valid under the new constitution, then this is possible only because they have been validated expressly or tacitly by the new constitution. We are confronted here not with a creation of new law but with the reception of norms of one legal order by another; such as the reception of the Roman Law by the German Law. But such reception too is law creation, because the direct reason for the validity of the legal norms taken over by the new revolutionary established constitution can only be the new constitution. The content of these norms remains unchanged, but the reason for their validity, in fact the reason for the validity of the entire legal order, has been changed. As the new constitution becomes valid, so simultaneously changes the basic norm, that is, the presupposition according to which are interpreted as norm-creating and norm-applying facts the constitution-creating fact and the facts established according to the constitution. Suppose the old constitution had the character of an absolute monarchy and the new one of a parliamentary democracy. Then the basic norm no longer reads: 'Coercive acts ought to be carried out under the conditions and in the manner as determined by the old, no longer valid, constitution,' and hence by the general and individual norms created and applied by the constitutionally functioning monarch and the organs delegated by him; instead, the basic norm reads: 'Coercive acts ought to be carried out under the conditions and in the manner determined by the new constitution,' and hence by the general and individual norms created and applied by the parliament elected according to that constitution and by the organs delegated in these norms. The new basic norm does not make it possible—like the old one—to regard a certain individual as the absolute monarch, but makes it possible to regard a popularly elected parliament as a legal authority. According to the basic norm of a national legal order, the government, which creates effective general and individual norms based on an effective constitution, is the legitimate government of the state.

The change of the basic norm follows the change of the facts that are interpreted as creating and applying valid legal norms. The basic norm refers only to a constitution which is actually established by legislative act or custom, and is effective. A constitution is 'effective' if the norms created in conformity with it are by and large applied and obeyed. As soon as the old constitution loses its effectiveness and the new one has become effective, the acts that appear with the subjective meaning of creating or applying legal norms are no longer interpreted by presupposing the old basic norm, but by presupposing the new one. The statutes issued under the old constitution and not taken over are no longer regarded as valid, and the organs authorized by the old constitution no longer as competent. If the revolution is not successful there would be no reason to replace the old basic norm by a new one. Then, the revolution would not be regarded as procedure creating new law, but— according to the old constitution and the criminal law based on it and regarded as valid—would be interpreted as high treason. The principle applied here is the principle of effectiveness. The principle of legitimacy is limited by the principle of effectiveness.

Kelsen The Pure Theory of Law 208–211

Validity and effectiveness of the basic norm

Two points about the next piece: first, in the very last sentence of the extract, he comes to the conclusion that effectiveness is only one 'condition' of validity; secondly, although he does address the problem of the effectiveness of the whole legal system as a condition for the validity of each individual norm, he also, in the third paragraph from the end, considers the status of an individual norm that is not obeyed and not followed.

It should also be pointed out that this extract needs to be read in conjunction with his initial discussion of validity and effectiveness (supra pp 24ff).

This limitation reveals the repeatedly emphasized connection (so important for a theory of positive law) between the validity and the effectiveness of law. The correct determination of this relationship is one of the most important and at the same time most difficult problems of a positivistic legal theory. It is only a special case of the relationship between the 'ought' of the legal norm and the 'is' of natural reality. Because the act by which a positive legal norm is created, too, is an 'is-fact' (German: *Seinstatsache*) just as the effectiveness of the legal norm. A positivistic legal theory is faced by the task to find the correct middle road between two extremes which both are untenable. The one extreme is the thesis that there is no connection between validity as something that ought to be and effectiveness as something that is; that the validity of the law is entirely independent of its effectiveness. The other extreme is the thesis that validity and effectiveness are identical. An idealistic theory of law tends to the first solution of this problem, a realistic theory to the second. The first is wrong for it is undeniable that a legal order in its entirety, and an individual legal norm as well, lose their validity when they cease to be effective; and that a relation exists between the *ought* of the legal norm and the *is* of physical reality also insofar as the positive legal norm, to be valid, must be created by an act which exists in the reality of being. The second solution is wrong because it is equally undeniable that there are many cases—as has been shown before—in which legal norms are regarded as valid although they are not, or not yet, effective. The solution proposed by the Pure Theory of Law is this: Just as the norm (according to which something *ought* to be) as the meaning of an act is not identical with the act (which actually *is*), in the same way is the validity of a legal norm not identical with its effectiveness; the effectiveness of a legal order as a whole and the effectiveness of a single legal norm are—just as the norm-creating act—the condition for the validity; effectiveness is the condition in the sense that a legal order as a whole, and a single legal norm, can no longer be regarded as valid when they cease to be effective. Nor is the effectiveness of a legal order, any more than the fact of its creation, the reason for its validity. The reason for the validity—that is, the answer to the question why the norms of this legal order ought to be obeyed and applied— is the presupposed basic norm, according to which one ought to comply with an actually established, by and large effective, constitution, and therefore with the by and large effective norms, actually created in conformity with that constitution. In the basic norm the fact of creation and the effectiveness are made the condition of the validity—'effectiveness' in the sense that it has to be added to the fact of creation, so that neither the legal order as a whole nor the individual legal norm shall lose their validity. A condition cannot be identical with that which it conditions. Thus, a man, in order to live, must have been born; but in order that he remain alive other conditions must also be fulfilled, for example, he must receive nutrition. If this condition is not fulfilled, he will lose his life. But life is neither identical with birth nor with being nourished.

In the normative syllogism leading to the foundation of the validity of a legal order, the major premise is the ought-sentence which states the basic norm: 'One ought to behave according to the actually established and effective constitution'; the minor premise is the is-sentence which states the facts: 'The constitution is actually established and effective'; and the conclusion is the ought-sentence: 'One ought to behave according to the legal order, that is, the legal order is valid.' The norms of a positive legal order are valid *because* the fundamental rule regulating their creation, that is, the basic norm, is presupposed to be valid, not because they are effective; but they are valid only *as long as* this legal order is effective. As soon as the constitution loses its effectiveness, that is, as soon as the legal order as a whole based on the constitution loses its effectiveness, the legal order and every single norm lose their validity.

However, a legal order does not lose its validity when a single legal norm loses its effectiveness. A legal order is regarded as valid, if its norms are *by and large* effective (that is, actually applied and obeyed). Nor does a single legal norm lose its validity if it is only exceptionally not effective in single cases. As mentioned in another connection, the possibility of an antagonism between that which is prescribed by a norm as something that ought to be and that which actually happens must exist; a norm, prescribing that something *ought* to be, which, as one knows beforehand *must* happen anyway according to a law of nature, is meaningless—such a norm would not be regarded as valid. On the other hand, a norm is not regarded as valid which is never obeyed or applied. In fact, a legal norm may lose its validity by never being applied or obeyed— by so-called *desuetudo*. *Desuetudo* may be described as negative custom, and its essential function is to abolish the validity of an existing norm. If custom is a law-creating fact at all, then even the validity of statutory law can be abolished by customary law. If effectiveness in the developed sense is the condition for the validity not only of the legal order as a whole but also of a single legal norm, then the law-creating function of custom cannot be excluded by statutory law, at least not as far as the negative function of *desuetudo* is concerned.

The described relation between validity and effectiveness refers to general legal norms. But also individual legal norms (judicial decisions, administrative decrees) that prescribe an individual coercive act lose their validity if they are permanently unexecuted and therefore ineffective, as has been shown in the discussion of a conflict between two legal decisions.

Effectiveness is a condition for the validity—but it is not validity. This must be stressed because time and again the effort has been made to identify validity with effectiveness; and such identification is tempting because it seems to simplify the theoretical situation. Still, the effort is doomed to failure, not only because even a partly ineffective legal order or legal norm may be regarded as valid, and an absolutely effective norm which cannot be violated as invalid because not being regarded as a norm at all; but particularly for this reason: if the validity, that is, the specific existence of the law, is considered to be part of natural reality, one is unable to grasp the specific meaning in which the law addresses itself to reality and thereby juxtaposes itself to reality, which can be in conformity or in conflict with the law only if reality is not identical with the validity of the law. Just as it is impossible in determining validity to ignore its relation to reality, so it is likewise impossible to identify validity and reality. If we replace the concept of reality (as effectiveness of the legal order) by the concept of power, then the problem of the relation between validity and effectiveness of the legal order coincides with the more familiar problem of the relationship between law and power or right and might. And then, the solution attempted here is merely the scientifically exact formulation of the old truism that right cannot exist without might and yet is not identical with might. Right (the law), according to the theory here developed, is a certain order (or organization) of might.

Kelsen *The Pure Theory of Law* 211–214

Kelsen here recognises that a norm is valid from the moment of its enactment, before it can attain effectiveness. But he also maintains that it must cease to be valid if it remains permanently inefficacious. It should be noted that this would be the case only in jurisdictions where *desuetudo* is an accepted constitutional doctrine; this is not so in common law jurisdictions. Hart's view is that although efficacy and validity are closely related they are not identical. However, it would be 'generally *pointless*' to ascribe validity to rules where the legal system to which they belong was inefficacious. He suggests two exceptions: where the object was to describe a set of laws valid in the past ('One vivid way of teaching Roman Law is to speak *as if* the system were efficacious still and to discuss the validity of particular rules and solve problems in their terms') and where the object of ascribing validity to what was an ineffective system was to encourage political opposition to the regime.

The basic norm and the rule of recognition

According to Hart, the judgment that a rule is valid is different from the Kelsenite response that validity is to be equated with the judgment that it ought to be obeyed. To Hart a rule is valid if it passes all the tests provided by the rule of recognition. Kelsen is prepared to ask the ultimate question: 'When you concatenate back to the ultimate constitution or, in Hartian terminology, to the rule of recognition, what is it that makes this top rule valid?' To Hart such a question would be meaningless; it would make no more sense than asking whether the metre-bar in Paris is really a metre in length (refer to Hart's discussion of the rule of recognition, supra pp 43ff). The only appropriate question, having scaled the pyramid, is whether the rule of recognition is accepted (internal aspect) by the officials. Acceptance seems to be a question of fact. As usual, it is more complicated; the fact of official acceptance can be viewed from two angles—external or internal statements (supra pp 45–46). Therefore, in a sense, the rule of recognition is both law and fact: externally it is a social fact that officials are acting according to the requirements of the rule of recognition; internally, it is the attitude of mind of the officials towards the rule.

In contrast, Kelsen's commitment to a presupposition requires no such quest for an ultimate legal rule, in actually existing legal systems, that injects validity into all the other rules of the system. The *Grundnorm*, in order to abide by the requirements of purity, is a theoretical construct, indeed a fiction, acting out a theoretical function; it is the norm that stands behind the actual rule of recognition or the historically first constitution. MacCormick has commented on the difference between two committed legal positivists.

> Kelsen's pure theory of law aims to establish what makes possible knowledge of the law as an objective normative order. His answer is that in juristic thinking there is a presupposition of a non-positive 'basic norm', according to which the human act of creating the historically first constitution of a given legal order is valid—crudely, according to which that constitution ought to be obeyed. Such a presupposition has a rational foundation if the legal norms which the constitution itself validates are effectively in force in a given territory. Within this scheme, the task of the jurist is concerned with 'pure' legal cognition, having no concern with descriptive sociology, psychology, politics, economics or ethics. The juristic task is to produce a rationally structured representation of all the norms of law which are valid norms given the presupposed basic norm. Kelsen's theory in effect sets out the framework for such a rationally structured representation of a legal order, given his further assumption that an identifying characteristic of law is the way in which it authorizes particular legal 'organs' to apply coercive sanctions to persons in the event of their acting in certain ways. Hart has several times acknowledged his debt to the analysis of legal order which Kelsen establishes on the above premises. His own hermeneutic concerns however lead him to give an account of rules, duties, authority etc. which relates these concepts both to particular social contexts and to individual or group attitudes. In doing so, he rejects Kelsen's programme for a 'pure' theory of law; his own debt here is, ultimately, to Hume.

> MacCormick *H L A Hart* 165

Raz has attempted a conciliation between Hart's and Kelsen's views on the nature of ultimate rules.

> The claim that legal sources are reasons for action raises as many questions as it solves. Are legal sources moral reasons or prudential reasons, or is there a

special and distinct kind of reasons which legal reasons exemplify? Do ordinary legal statements import moral approval of the law? These questions cannot be explored here. . . . But suppose one asks why is a certain legislative act a reason for action? Is it not because of moral grounds that a policeman's order, for example, is a reason for action? Be that as it may, some of these grounds are legal while others may not be. The policeman's order is a valid reason because, generally, policemen act to preserve the peace and are reliable. This is not a legal ground. Another ground for accepting that the policeman's order is a reason for action is that Parliament conferred on him power to give such orders. There may or may not be non-legal grounds for accepting legal sources as reasons, but there are always such legal grounds. Or almost always, for in the end one gets to ultimate legal rules.

Suppose it is asked of English law why is it true that parliamentary legislation is binding on the courts. The answer is that this is so because of the practice of the courts which follows a rule to that effect and because the rules practised by the courts of a legal system are rules of that system according to the doctrine of identity. Here (as in the case of all ultimate rules) the courts' practice is what makes the rule a legal rule and is thus its source. But the relation of source to rule and to the action the rule requires is different in the case of ultimate rules from that relation in the rest of the law.

With the rest of the law both the rule and its source could with equal justice be regarded as the reason for doing as the rule prescribes. Ultimate rules are likewise reasons for the action they require, but not so their source. That the English courts hold themselves bound to apply statutes is not the reason why they ought to do so. The rule that they should apply statutes is such a reason. The practice is no more than proof (constitutive proof) that the rule is a legal rule. It is neither a ground for the validity of the rule nor for the action it prescribes. It is this fact which establishes the character of the rule as an ultimate *legal* rule. The fact that a rule is an ultimate legal rule means no more than that there is no legal ground, no legal justification for its validity. It does not imply that there is no ground or justification for the rule, only that if such ground exists it is not a legal one. With ordinary legal rules their source is the legal ground of their validity and a reason for behaving as they prescribe. That Parliament so enacted is a ground for the validity of the law and a reason for the required behaviour. These are legal reasons for their character as grounds of validity is itself determined by another law. By definition ultimate legal rules are not similarly grounded on legal reasons. The absence of a further law determining the grounds of validity of the ultimate rules is precisely what makes them *ultimate* legal rules.

Because further legal rules (themselves grounded in social facts) determine which facts create rules and are thus, with those facts, the grounds of validity of the rules, they can be used to identify the rules for the validity of which they are a ground. Since all the grounds are social facts or legal rules grounded in social facts, this identification is in accord with the sources thesis. There are no legal grounds for the validity of ultimate rules; no justification of them is provided by law. If they are identifiable by social facts, i.e. if they have sources, these facts cannot be the legal grounds for their validity. Therefore they cannot be legal reasons for doing as they require. They are identifying criteria only. The courts themselves use them as such. English courts look for their own practices when asking whether they are bound by a fraudulently obtained Private Act or by an Act of Parliament binding future Parliaments. But they refer to the source of the law in the practice of the courts in order to identify the precise content of the ultimate legal rule which binds them, not in order to justify it.

Therefore, though the ultimate rule itself is the reason for the action it requires, its sources are not.

Raz *The Authority of Law* 68–69

In a footnote to the last sentence of this extract, Raz writes: 'Hart was right in asserting that the rule of recognition, like all other rules, rests on social sources. Kelsen, however, was right in insisting that the relation between ultimate rules and their sources is different from that between ordinary rules and their sources. Positivists often claim that controversy is proof that the law is unsettled. By the analysis presented here, this is true of ultimate rules but not of others.'

The form of the grundnorm: Kelsen's thesis applied to a country without a written constitution

This problem does not receive any detailed consideration in Kelsen's work. He tells us only that where there is no written constitution, as in the United Kingdom, the grundnorm authorises the norm-creating effect of custom. It is Harris who has tried to apply Kelsen's schema to such a system.

> But what is the form of the grundnorm which is presupposed in the case of a national legal order whose constitutional norms have been established by custom? Kelsen himself does not answer this question.
>
> Where the constitution is contained in a written document promulgated at some date in the past, Kelsen tells us, in *General Theory of Law and State*, that the schematic form of the grundnorm of a national legal order is as follows: 'Coercive acts ought to be carried out only under the conditions and in the way determined by the 'fathers' of the constitution or the organs delegated by them.' In the case of any particular such national system, words referring to the actual individuals responsible for promulgating the constitution—either their names or a generic description of them—are apparently to be substituted in this formulation for the word 'fathers.' Hence, in contemporary France, the 'fathers' are General de Gaulle and those who assisted him in the preparation and promulgation of the Constitution of the Fifth Republic.
>
> In *The Pure Theory of Law*, the formula expressing the grundnorm is stated thus: 'Coercion of man against man ought to be exercised in the manner and under the conditions determined by the historically first constitution.' The grundnorm of any given national order must apparently be found, in terms of this formulation, by substituting for the words 'the historically first constitution' some words by which the written constitution now in force can be identified, such as 'the constitution of the Fifth Republic' in the case of contemporary France. But that there is no shift in theory on this point between the two works is made clear when, later in *The Pure Theory of Law*, we read that, where a basic norm is presupposed in the case of a consciously created constitution, the individuals who created it 'are looked upon as norm-creating authorities.'
>
> Where there is no written constitution, as in the United Kingdom, Kelsen tells us only that the grundnorm authorises the norm-creating effect of custom. (It may do this even where there is a written constitution which does not stipulate custom as a source of law; in which case, the 'constitution in a material sense'—which includes all ultimate sources authorised by the grundnorm—will not be confined to the written constitution.)

In the latest version of his theory, Kelsen tells us that custom is created by an act of will 'individual or collective.' What he means by this is not clear, but the following interpretation is suggested: the norms of an entirely or partially customary constitution could not have attained their constitutional normative status if, at various times in the past, influential individuals had not specifically wanted such norms to operate on the constitutional level and if their wishes had not received general acquiescence. Accordingly, the grundnorm of the United Kingdom legal system authorises the population at large from time to time to fashion the ultimate norms of the constitution in any way which meets with general approval.

The following example is suggested to illustrate Kelsen's schema for the cognition of law, as applied to the national legal system of the United Kingdom.

(A) Grundnorm of United Kingdom legal order:	Coercive acts ought to be applied only under the conditions and in the ways customarily recognised as constitutional from time to time by the population at large.
(B) One of the ultimate constitutional norms:	Coercive acts ought to be applied in accordance with statutes enacted by the Queen in Parliament.
(C) General norm:	Where, pursuant to a contract of sale of goods, the seller neglects or refuses to deliver the goods to the buyer, and the buyer elects to sue, the seller ought to be condemned to pay damages.
(D) Particular norm created by contract between Smith and Brown:	If Smith neglects or refuses to deliver his horse (Dobbin) to Brown, and Brown elects to sue, Smith ought to be condemned to pay damages.
(E) Particular concretised norm created by a county court Judge on Brown's suing Smith for breach of contract:	If Smith fails to pay damages of £100 within 28 days of this order, and Brown issues a warrant of execution, the bailiff ought to levy execution upon the goods of Smith.
(F) Particular fully concretised norm created by Brown's issuing a warrant of execution:	'Bailiff, levy execution upon the goods of Smith.'

Harris [1971] Cambridge Law Journal 109–110

In this extract Harris refers to only one of the ultimate constitutional norms. Elsewhere in his article he gives a more complete description of these ultimate norms.

In the United Kingdom there are at least two norms which authorise the creation of general norms. These are, giving them the form stipulated by Kelsen: (i) coercive acts ought to be applied in accordance with statutes enacted by the Queen in Parliament; (ii) coercive acts ought to be applied in accordance with judge-made rules established in conformity to the doctrine of binding precedents. A third such authorising constitutional norm would have to be postulated if custom is still regarded as an independent source of law.

Harris [1971] Cambridge Law Journal 109

Harris's analysis of the basic norm and the problem of revolutions

Austin's analysis of positive law is ultimately dependent upon the existence of a sovereign which exhibits both the positive and negative aspects (supra pp 21–22). It is a socio-political phenomeon described in terms of 'habit of obedience'. Hart's analysis of the concept of law is dependent upon the idea of an ultimate rule, the rule of recognition, which is accepted by, and motivates the action of, officials within the system. Again this is a social phenomenon. The vital point when we turn to the grundnorm is that it is not a socio-political phenomenon. It is hypothesis, presupposition or fiction. We need to consider the nature, identity, and status of the grundnorm in the aftermath of revolution.

Being merely a hypothesis of juristic thinking, the grundnorm does not change the moment the revolutionaries shoot the King. It cannot change until jurists change their thinking, that is, until lawyers begin to make post-revolutionary assertions to the effect: 'The law in the country *now* is . . .,' where 'now' refers to some revolutionary, established source of law.

While attitudes of commitment and even rule-ideas may gradually develop, the grundnorm will not change at all so long as legal scientists give primacy to the same ultimate sources in their logical arrangement of legal material.

Kelsen generally distinguishes ultimate sources into two kinds only: written constitutions and customary constitutions. This entails that there can be only two kinds of grundnorm: one authorising the 'fathers' to promulgate the written constitution at some past date, and one which authorises the population at large from time to time to create a material constitution by custom.

Hence, where the constitution is written, there will be a change in the grundnorm (a revolution) if jurists begin to deduce laws from some newly promulgated constitution. The new basic norm will differ formally from the old only in that the personnel constituting the 'fathers' will be different, for they will be the promulgators of the new written constitution. There will also be a change in the grundnorm if the written constitution is abandoned and jurists begin to refer to as 'laws' acts of legislation made in some new way sanctioned by custom.

If the constitution is customary to begin with, a change in the grundnorm will only occur if a written constitution is substituted. Thus, in Kelsen's terms, the decision of the House of Lords in 1966 not to be bound by its own decisions did not constitute a change in the grundnorm (revolution), and neither did the 'revolution' of 1688. In the terminology suggested above, however, the 1966 decision did represent a change in an important 'rule-idea,' and the 1688 revolution did represent a change in a basic 'attitude of commitment.'

To achieve a more discriminating logic for revolutions, it would be necessary to make a more detailed taxonomy of ultimate sources and grundnorms than Kelsen's formal distinction between written and customary constitutions. For instance, customary constitutions could be subdivided according to the kind of social group which the grundnorm effectively authorised to dictate constitutional developments; and written constitutions, by reference to the kind of group which promulgated them—were they, for instance, socialist or non-socialist 'fathers'?

Harris [1971] Cambridge Law Journal 117–118

So there will be no change in the grundnorm until the legal scientist makes a new presupposition and, as we have seen, this they cannot do without the precondition of efficacy. But what is efficacy or effectiveness in this context? In the following piece Harris outlines Kelsen's answer to this and then attempts a reformulation of this answer.

The effectiveness of each individual norm is to be measured, according to Kelsen, by two criteria: first, by whether the norm is 'obeyed,' that is, by whether the conduct (the opposite of which is made the condition of the sanction stipulated by the norm) is performed; secondly, by whether, if the norm is not obeyed, the sanction is applied by the official whom the norm directs to apply it. These are questions of fact. It is true that soon after the occurrence of a revolution they may be future questions of fact, but that does not make apolitical judgments about them impossible or impracticable, only more subject to error.

What is meant by saying that norms, to be effective, must be obeyed or applied 'by and large?' It would be impracticable to say, in the case of many norms, whether the sanction was applied *more often than not* when disobedience to the norm occurred, because statistical evidence of the number of cases of disobedience could not be obtained. It would be impossible to say whether the norm was obeyed more often than not, without first postulating what was to count as obedience. Kelsen says: 'Law is observed by that behaviour to whose opposite is attached the coercive act of the sanction' and that motive is irrelevant. Then laws which prohibit the performing of acts which most people do not in any case perform (such as laws against witchcraft) must always be generally 'obeyed'; in other words, one of Kelsen's criteria of obsolescence can never apply to them.

It is submitted that the 'by and large' test should be reformulated in the following way. The first criterion (obedience) should be eliminated, and the test should run: 'a norm is to be judged effective if the official acts of application of sanctions bear a socially significant ratio to the recorded acts of disobedience.'

The test need be no more precise in order to choose between the effectiveness of competing norms issued by rival legislative authorities.

Harris [1971] Cambridge Law Journal 120–121

Whether or not this reformulation is an acceptable description of efficacy, there is a further problem: what implications, if any, does Kelsen's theory have for the judge? Harris points out that the pure theory assumes that legal science is a socially useful activity and being such it must purport to describe law which is not only positive, in the sense of being laid down by human beings, but also by and large effective. Hence the legal scientist will presuppose the grundnorm only if there exists a coercive order by and large effective. However, given that the legal scientist, if he is to act in a socially useful way, needs must presuppose the effective grundnorm, what warrant does his theory give the *judge* to presuppose it? Answer: none. But Harris argues that the role of the judge can be equated with that of the legal scientist. If this is so, and it must be regarded as an extension to what Kelsen did write, it would be acceptable for judges deciding post-revolution issues in the courtroom to rely on the pure theory of law.

The pure theory of law is intended to describe the science of law—its aims, its *a priori* formal assumptions, and the logical status of the judgments contained in it. Kelsen says that every act of law-application is an act of law-creation, in the process of concretisation and individualisation of norms. The judgment of a court is therefore simultaneously an act applying the law and an act creating law and, to the extent that it creates law, it is an act of the will. The act of presupposing the grundnorm, on the other hand, he describes as an act of cognition. 'The science of law has to know the law—as it were from the outside—and to describe it. The legal organs, as legal authorities, have to create the law so that afterwards it may be known and described by the science of law.'

Thus the theory does not directly warrant the judge in presupposing any grundnorm; for jurisprudence, says Kelsen, is not a source of law.

Nevertheless, it is submitted, the pure theory does have indirect social suggestive force for judges. The theory assumes that legal science is socially useful, which is precisely the reason for insisting that legal science should follow efficacy. Clearly legal science of the sort described by the pure theory can only continue to be socially useful so long as judges also indulge in it. If judges ceased altogether to think of their decisions as subsumptions under general rules, if they persistently ignored the hierarchy of constitution, statute, contract, etc., this sort of legal science would become pointless.

To assert that at the present time judges in developed legal systems do act as legal scientists is a correct description of their verbal behaviour, although to what extent their actual decisions are determined by factors other than what they say about 'the law' is uncertain and controversial. The pure theory assumes that this legal-science verbal behaviour is not only what judges do indulge in, but also what they ought to indulge in. Kelsen's assertion that: 'What sociological jurisprudence predicts that the courts will decide, normative jurisprudence maintains that they ought to decide,' is true if we understand 'say' for 'decide.'

Thus, in so far as judgments are acts of law-application, the judges are assumed to act as legal scientists, and in that capacity they do and ought to presuppose the grundnorm.

A further implication of the theory, as of all positivist theories of law, is that, to the extent that the solution of a particular case given by the science of law is clear (that is, to the extent that the judge has no discretion within the meaning of the relevant higher norms), the judge ought to apply that solution. If judges acted as legal scientists up to the point at which they found that solution X was given, and then regularly opted for solution Y, again legal science would become pointless. Hence, that it would be inconsistent with the role of a judge to do this, is implied by a theory which assumes that legal science is useful.

The pure theory of law therefore has three relevant implications for the role of a judge: (a) judges do act as legal scientists; (b) they ought so to act; (c) to the extent that legal science gives a clear solution to a particular case, the judge ought to accept that solution as the basis for his decision.

Thus, where a revolution is, or is predicted to be going to be, successful, Kelsen's theory (directly) requires the legal scientist, acting in his role as legal scientist, to presuppose a new grundnorm, and (indirectly) suggests that a judge, acting in his role as judge, ought to do the same. It does therefore seem that the theory warrants a judge, who wishes to avoid express political commitment ('joining the revolution'), in accepting the laws of a successful revolutionary régime.

Harris [1971] Cambridge Law Journal 125–127

Harris's conclusion is, therefore, quite predictable.

It is true that Kelsen's theory does not directly authorise a judge to make any particular decision. But indirectly it suggests that, when legal science gives a clear solution to a case, the judge ought to adopt that solution, and this is true when, soon after the occurrence of a revolution, the question arises: has the grundnorm changed? The reason why it has this suggestive force for a judge is that the theory assumes that legal science is a socially useful activity, which it could not be if it were not an essential part of the role of a judge to act as a legal scientist and to apply the conclusions of legal science.

Harris [1971] Cambridge Law Journal 132

Part Two
Normative Jurisprudence

Chapter 6

Natural law

Natural law is an unwieldly subject and it might help if, at the outset, we itemize the various headings under which the subject will be explained and discussed.

The meaning of natural law
The history of natural law doctrine
Classical natural law: Thomas Aquinas (1225–1274)
(a) The four species of law and the problem of derivation
(b) The self-evidential nature of the precepts of natural law, the doctrine of natural inclinations and the teleological framework to the argument
(c) The distinction between primary precepts and secondary precepts of natural law
(d) The problem of immutability
Criticism of traditional natural law doctrine
(a) The illogical inference from fact to value
Modern theories of natural law
(a) H L A Hart and the 'minimum content of natural law'
(b) John Finnis and a restatement of natural law

THE MEANING OF NATURAL LAW

Natural law has a long and illustrious history. In all its epochs it has been subjected to the most virulent attacks and, in the aftermath, it has been common practice to describe its condition as terminal. Nevertheless, it has the habit of bouncing back, leading one to conclude that it represents one of the most durable motifs in the development of moral and political theory.

Although in the last 2,500 or so years it has manifested itself in various guises, it is possible to detect a common theme at the centre of most theories of natural law. It is the assertion that there exists in nature, in particular human nature, a rational order. This order furnishes value-statements independently of human will which are usually said to be universal and eternal. The value-statements are expressed in the form of moral imperatives providing an objective stance from which the legal and political structures can be critically evaluated. So the prescriptions of natural law are closely associated with reality in that the starting point of the process of reasoning is to be found in nature or human nature.

In all its diverse forms, natural law philosophy stands for the possibility of having objective standards and these are to be found by looking for the rational order in nature and in man. The presuppositions behind the implications of this process are considered by Hans Kelsen, a legal positivist with little time for the natural law approach.

> The natural-law doctrine undertakes to supply a definitive solution to the eternal problem of justice, to answer the question as to what is right and wrong

in the mutual relations of men. The answer is based on the assumption that it is possible to distinguish between human behavior which is natural, that is to say which corresponds to nature because it is required by nature, and human behavior which is unnatural hence contrary to nature and forbidden by nature. This assumption implies that it is possible to deduce from nature, that is to say from the nature of man, from the nature of society, and even from the nature of things, certain rules which provide an altogether adequate prescription for human behavior, that by a careful examination of the facts of nature we can find the just solution of our social problems. Nature is conceived of as a legislator, the supreme legislator.

This view presupposes that natural phenomena are directed toward an end or shaped by a purpose, that natural processes or nature conceived of as a whole are determined by final causes. It is a thoroughly teleological view, and as such does not differ from the idea that nature is endowed with will and intelligence. This implies that nature is a kind of superhuman personal being, an authority to which man owes obedience. At the lower stage of human civilization this interpretation of nature manifests itself in so-called animism. Primitive man believes that natural things—animals, plants, rivers, the stars in the sky—are animated, that spirits or souls dwell within or behind these phenomena, and that consequently these things react toward man like personal beings according to the same principles that determine the relations of man to his fellow men. It is a social interpretation of nature, for primitive man considers nature to be a part of his society. Since the spirits or souls animating the natural phenomena are believed to be very powerful and able to harm as well as to protect man, they must be worshipped. Animism is consequently a religious interpretation of nature. At a higher stage of religious evolution, when animism is replaced by monotheism, nature is conceived of as having been created by God and is therefore regarded as a manifestation of his all powerful and just will. If the natural-law doctrine is consistent, it must assume a religious character. It can deduce from nature just rules of human behavior only because and so far as nature is conceived of as a revelation of God's will, so that examining nature amounts to exploring God's will. As a matter of fact, there is no natural-law doctrine of any importance which has not a more or less religious character. Grotius, for example, defines the law of nature as a dictate of rational nature by which certain acts are forbidden or enjoined 'by the author of nature, God.' He states that the law of nature proceeding from the 'essential traits implanted in man can rightly be attributed to God, because of His having willed that such traits exist in us.' Hobbes declares that the law of nature is a dictate of reason, but the dictates of reason are 'conclusions, or theorems concerning what conduces to the conservation and defense of themselves; whereas law properly is the word of him that by right has command over others. But yet if we consider the same theorems, as delivered in the word of God, that by right commands all things, then are they properly called laws.' Following Hobbes, Pufendorf states that if the dictates of reason—that is, the principles of natural law—are to have the force of law it must 'under all circumstances be maintained that the obligation of natural law is of God.' Only thus can it be assumed that the law deduced from nature is an eternal and immutable law, in contradistinction to positive law which, created by man, is only a temporary and changeable order; that the rights established by natural law are sacred rights inborn in man because implanted in man by a divine nature; and that positive law can neither establish nor abolish these rights, but only protect them. This is the essence of the natural-law doctrine.

Kelsen *What is Justice?* 137–138

Again:

> The so-called doctrine of natural law is a variety of certain theories of law, which may be designated *idealistic*, and which, in contrast to a *realistic* theory of law, assume that there is, beside and above the real or *positive* law established by human acts—custom or legislation—an *ideal* law, just or correct. The validity of positive law is therefore traced back to ideal law, ie, according to these theories, positive law may be regarded as valid in so far as it corresponds to ideal law. And thus these theories seek to justify positive law. The idealistic theories of law, of which the doctrine of natural law is only a particular case, are characterized by a *dualism* of two legal orders, one ideal and one real, whereas the realistic theory of law recognizes only one form of law, *positive* law, and by not seeking the reason for its validity in a superior normative order thus dispenses with a justification for positive law. Its proponents confine themselves to description and structural analysis.
>
> The so-called doctrine of natural law is characterized by its assertion that it is able to find ideal law, ie, the rules for the correct and just conduct not only of men but also of things; hence norms commanding the good and prohibiting the evil, in nature in general and in human nature in particular. By 'nature' is meant *empirical reality*, and by 'human nature', the actual human condition. The main thesis of all doctrines of natural law is based on this foundation: all good is in accordance with nature, all evil is contrary to nature. Since man is looked on as an essentially reasonable being, and since it is assumed that the natural law controlling his conduct is to be found in his reason, the norms of the correct, just human conduct are also represented as a law of reason.
>
> Kelsen 'Plato and Natural Law' 1960 Vanderbilt Law Review 24

In the preceding extracts one can detect a certain characterisation of natural law philosophy that has been common currency: any law that offends the prescriptions of natural law is unjust and, as such, is not law—*lex injusta non est lex*. As a corrective to this characterisation Finnis's discussion of the issue needs to be considered. (The quotations from Raz are from 'Kelsen's Theory of the Basic Norm' [1972] 19 American Journal of Jurisprudence 94 at 100 and from *Practical Reason* 162.)

> Here we have to deal with the image of natural law entertained by jurists such as Kelsen, Hart, and Raz. This image should be reproduced in their own words, since they themselves scarcely identify, let alone quote from, any particular theorist as defending the view that they describe as the view of natural law doctrine. Joseph Raz usefully summarizes and adopts Kelsen's version of this image:
>
> > Kelsen correctly points out that according to natural law theories there is no specific notion of legal validity. The only concept of validity is validity according to natural law, i.e., moral validity. Natural lawyers can only judge a law as morally valid, that is, just or morally invalid, i.e., wrong. They cannot say of a law that it is legally valid but morally wrong. If it is wrong and unjust, it is also invalid in the only sense of validity they recognise.
>
> In his own terms, Raz later defines 'Natural Law theorists' as 'those philosophers who think it a criterion of adequacy for theories of law that they show . . . that it is a necessary truth that every law has moral worth'.
>
> For my part, I know of no philosopher who fits, or fitted, such a description,

or who would be committed to trying to defend that sort of theoretical or meta-theoretical proposal . . . Suffice it here to say that the root of the misunderstanding seems to be the failure of the modern critics to interpret the texts of natural law theorists in accordance with the principles of definition which those theorists have, for the most part, consistently and self-consciously used. I have already given a sketch of these principles . . . under the rubric 'central cases and focal meaning'.

Finnis *Natural Law and Natural Rights* 26–27

The distinction between 'central case and focal meaning' on the one hand and peripheral meaning on the other hand is an important device introduced and regularly employed by Aristotle. The focal conception of law is an ideal or pure form to which existing forms are but inadequate approximations. As will be seen when we discuss his theory in depth, the focal meaning is something in the nature of an ordering of a community aimed at the realisation of the common good (infra pp 186ff). In this context, from the focal meaning of law, it would be valid to conclude that unjust law is not law. But from the point of view of law actually existing within legal systems the equating of unjust with invalid is not appropriate. Therefore, the definitions of law by natural lawyers which equate invalidity with the unjust content of the law are to be construed as statements about the focal meaning of the concept of law. But there are other meanings of law, secondary meanings, where there is no point in denying the status of law to an unjust law.

By exploiting the systematic multi-significance of one's theoretical terms [the difference between the focal and the penumbral meanings] . . . one can differentiate the mature from the undeveloped in human affairs, the sophisticated from the primitive, the flourishing from the corrupt, the fine specimen from the deviant case, the 'straightforwardly', 'simply speaking' (*simpliciter*), and 'without qualification' from the 'in a sense', 'in a manner of speaking', and 'in a way' (*secundum quid*)—but all without ignoring or banishing to another discipline the undeveloped, primitive, corrupt, deviant or other 'qualified sense' or 'extended sense' instances of the subject-matter.

Finnis *Natural Law and Natural Rights* 10–11

Consequently, when he provides his own focal meaning of law (infra pp 198–200), he can say the following of it.

I have by now sufficiently stressed that one would be simply misunderstanding my conception of the nature and purpose of explanatory definitions of theoretical concepts if one supposed that my definition 'rules out as non-laws' laws which failed to meet, or meet fully, one or other of the elements of the definition.

Finnis *Natural Law and Natural Rights* 278

In addition, he asserts that this is how natural lawyers have usually understood their conclusions. It follows that the shibboleth '*lex injusta non est lex*' has been misrepresented by its detractors, such as Kelsen. There is no doubt that natural law is conceived of as a higher law. But this claim is open to two interpretations. First, it can mean that natural law, as a higher law, is definitive of what is a valid human law so that any law that offends the higher law is unjust and consequently is invalid. Finnis argues that this is not the main claim of natural lawyers. The second meaning of higher law treats it as providing a role other than a definitional one. It provides an evaluative function; it acts as a sort of moral barometer of human laws: given that a decree is a valid law, natural law informs whether that is a just law, whether it is a good law that is morally binding in conscience. So an unjust law is not a nullity, a non-law; it is a valid law which fails to come up to the demands revealed by the natural law.

It follows that many of the claims of the legal positivist to the effect that they are setting out a definition of law without recourse to any theories of ethics or natural law are misguided in their understanding of the true role of natural law which is, and has been, evaluative of rather than definitive of the law (for statements to this effect by Austin, Kelsen, Hart, and Raz see supra).

THE HISTORY OF NATURAL LAW DOCTRINE

It would be far beyond the scope of this book to go into the history of natural law in great detail. Instead we shall focus on the work of a representative natural lawyer—Aquinas. But as a necessary preliminary here is a brief excursus into the embarrassment of riches to be found in the history of the doctrine.

Anyone interested in moral philosophy or the development of political theory must examine this theory which has been a major theme in political thought from the fifth century BC to the present day.

> A great jurist of the last century who devoted his life to the historical study of law, once wrote that the undying spirit of natural law can never be extinguished. 'If it is denied entry into the body of positive law, it flutters around the room like a ghost and threatens to turn into a vampire which sucks the blood from the body of the law' (von Gierke *Natural Law and the Theory of Society* vol 1, 226).
>
> d'Entrèves *Natural Law* 108

In fact from the earliest days there has been philosophical speculation concerning the existence of a set of immutable and eternal axioms governing the affairs of nature and of man. As a philosophy it played a central role in three momentous historical episodes: the conquest of Western Europe by Roman civilisation, the infilteration of Greek thought into Christianity, and the flourishing of individualism in the seventeenth and eighteenth centuries. The claim is monumental: in these different epochs natural law furnished an ubiquitous, immutable, rational ordering which defined the parameters of the concept of political obligation, constituted a critical morality as a benchmark for the evaluation of the system and methods of government, and determined the relationship between law and morality. To demonstrate the wealth and complexity of the natural law tradition here is a summary of contents of a book that specialises in the historical aspects of the subject: natural law in Greek thought, including the sophists; Aristotle and the stoics; natural law in Roman thought, including Cicero and the *ius gentium*; medieval theories of natural law, with the emphasis on St Thomas Aquinas; natural law in the sixteenth to eighteenth centuries, including Bodin, Hooker, Suarez, Grotius, Hobbes, Pufendorf, Spinoza, Locke, Montesquieu, and Rousseau; the revival of natural law, including Köhler, Stammler, Duguit, Gény, Dabin, Le Fur, Rommen, Maritain, Renard, Radbruch, and Del Vecchio; modern accounts, including Fuller, Finnis, and Hart. The inventory is unending; the amount of scholarship, breathtaking. It would be inconceivable and an inevitable distortion of the scholarship involved to attempt slick summaries of this welter of thought. As a second best, we shall concentrate on the work of a few jurists appearing in this galaxy. However, before doing so it is worth reading the account by Friedmann of the divergent if not antinomous uses to which the doctrine has been put.

The history of natural law is a tale of the search of mankind for absolute justice and of its failure. Again and again, in the course of the last 2,500 years, the idea of natural law has appeared, in some form or other, as an expression of the search for an ideal higher than positive law after having been rejected and derided in the interval. With changing social and political conditions the notions about natural law have changed. The only thing that has remained constant is the appeal to something higher than positive law. The object of that appeal has been as often the justification of existing authority as a revolt against it.

Natural law has fulfilled many functions. It has been the principal instrument in the transformation of the old civil law of the Romans into a broad and cosmopolitan system; it has been a weapon used by both sides in the fight between the medieval Church and the German emperors; in its name the validity of international law has been asserted, and the appeal for freedom of the individual against absolutism launched. Again it was by appeal to principles of natural law that American judges, professing to interpret the Constitution, resisted the attempt of state legislation to modify and restrict the unfettered economic freedom of the individual.

It would be simple to dismiss the whole idea of natural law as a hypocritical disguise for concrete political aspirations and no doubt it has sometimes exercised little more than this function. But there is infinitely more in it. Natural law has been the chief though not the only way to formulate ideals and aspirations of various peoples and generations with reference to the principal moving forces of the time. When the social structure itself becomes rigid and absolute, as at the time of the Schoolmen, the ideal too will take a static and absolute content. At other times, as with most modern natural law theories, natural law ideals become relative or merely formal, expressing little more than the yearning of a generation which is dissatisfied with itself and the world, which seeks something higher, but is conscious of the relativity of values. It is as easy to deride natural law as it is to deride the futility of mankind's social and political life in general, in its unceasing but hitherto vain search for a way out of the injustice and imperfection for which Western civilisation has found no other solution but to move from one extreme to another.

The appeal to some absolute ideal finds a response in men, particularly at a time of disillusionment and doubt, and in times of simmering revolt. Therefore natural law theories, far from being theoretical speculations, have often heralded powerful political and legal developments.

Many distinctions of natural law theories are possible, depending on the criterion adopted. They may be divided into authoritarian and individualistic, into progressive and conservative, into religious and rationalistic, into absolute and relativist theories. For a juristic consideration the most important distinction would appear to be that between natural law as a higher law, which invalidates any inconsistent positive law, and natural law as an ideal to which positive law ought to conform without its legal validity being affected. Broadly speaking, ancient and medieval law theories are of the first type, modern law theories of the second. This change coincides on the whole with the rise of the modern state and its claim to absolute sovereignty.

Natural law has, at different times, been used to support almost any ideology; but the most important and lasting theories of natural law have undoubtedly been inspired by the two ideas, of a universal order governing all men, and of the inalienable rights of the individual. When used in the service of either of these ideas, natural law has formed an organic and essential part in a hierarchy of legal values. As the basis of an international order, it has, in a continuous line of development, inspired the Stoics, Roman jurisprudence and philosophy, the Fathers of the Church, the legal order of medieval Western society and Grotius' system of International Law. Through the theories of Locke and Paine, it has provided the foundation for the individualist philosophy of the American and other modern constitutions. The growing supremacy of the national state, on the one hand, and the growth of collective discipline on the other, have not favoured natural law ideology, nor has an effective combination of these two main trends of natural law thinking been as yet achieved. This remains a challenge to be taken up by a society which would combine an effective international legal order with the protection of individual rights.

At the same time, closer social and legal organisation means an increasing measure of incorporation of natural law principles into positive law. The natural law principle of scholastic philosophy became the highest positive law within the Church; the natural law ideas of Locke and Paine became the highest positive law of the United States through their incorporation in the Bill of Rights of the Constitution. Moreover, the general clauses of the Constitution came to be interpreted in the light of natural law principles which thus became part of positive law.

The interlocking of an unwritten higher law and 'posited' fundamental principles becomes particularly complex when certain principles of a written constitution are held to be higher in rank than other parts of the same constitution. In a basic decision of 1953, the West German Constitutional Court held that the principle of separation of powers and the principles governing the relations between husband and wife on the basis of general equality were 'supra-positive' ('uebergesetzliche') principles governing the Constitution, and could be declared by the Constitutional Court to invalidate a 'simple' constitutional norm. Again, the modern controversy between theories of national and international sovereignty reduces itself juridically to an endeavour to transform certain natural law principles binding all nations into positive law. If and when the whole of mankind becomes legally organised, certain principles described by Grotius and others as natural law, and today described by more modest names such as 'general principles of law,' will become the foundation of the highest positive law emanating from the international sovereign.

Friedmann *Legal Theory* 95–97

CLASSICAL NATURAL LAW:THOMAS AQUINAS (1225–1274)

(a) The four species of law and the problem of derivation

Natural law, being the part of the eternal law which man is capable of apprehending and appreciating by means of his unaided reason, produces in man conformity to the eternal law which is an act of will. Furthermore, Aquinas clearly distinguishes natural law from divine law, which is God's direct revelation to man through Christ and the scriptures, functioning not only as confirmation of, but also as supplementation to the natural law, with precepts that are not susceptible to discovery by man's reason.

> A law is nothing else but a dictate of practical reason emanating from the ruler who governs a perfect community. Now it is evident, granted that the world is ruled by divine providence, that the whole community of the universe is governed by divine reason. Wherefore the very idea of the government of things in God the Ruler of the universe has the nature of a law. And since the divine reason's conception of things is not subject to time but is eternal, according to Proverbs viii 23, therefore it is that this kind of law must be called eternal.
>
> Aquinas *Summa Theologica* Q91 A1

> Law, being a rule and measure, can be in a person in two ways: in one way, as in him that rules and measures; in another way, as in that which is ruled and measured, since a thing is ruled and measured in so far as it partakes of the rule or measure. Wherefore, since all things subjected to divine providence are ruled and measured by the eternal law, it is evident that all things partake somewhat of the eternal law, in so far as, namely, from its being imprinted on them, they derive their respective inclinations to their proper acts and ends. Now among all others the rational creature is subject to divine providence in the most excellent way, in so far as it partakes of a share of providence, by being provident both for itself and for others. Wherefore it has a share of the eternal reason, whereby it has a natural inclination to its proper act and end: and this participation of the eternal law in the rational creature is called the natural law. Hence the Psalmist after saying: 'Offer up the sacrifice of justice,' as though someone asked what the works of justice are, adds: 'Many say, Who showeth us good things?' in answer to which question he says: 'The light of Thy countenance, O Lord, is signed upon us'; thus implying that the light of natural reason, whereby we discern what is good and what is evil, which is the function of the natural law, is nothing else than an imprint on us of the divine light. It is therefore evident that the natural law is nothing else than the rational creature's participation of the eternal law.
>
> Aquinas *Summa Theologica* Q91 A2

Human law is the final species of law discussed by Aquinas.

> A law is a dictate of the practical reason. Now it is to be observed that the same procedure takes place in the practical and in the speculative reason, for each proceeds from principles to conclusions. Accordingly we conclude that just as, in the speculative reason, from naturally known indemonstrable principles we draw the conclusions of the various sciences, the knowledge of which is not imparted to us by nature, but acquired by the efforts of reason; so, too, it is from the precepts of the natural law, as from general and indemonstrable principles, that the human reason needs to proceed to the more particular determination of certain matters. These particular determinations, devised by human reason, are called human laws, provided the other essential conditions of law be observed. Wherefore Cicero says in his *Rhetoric* that 'justice has its source in nature; there certain things came into custom by reason of their

utility; afterwards these things which emanated from nature and were approved by custom were sanctioned by fear and reverence for the law.'

Aquinas *Summa Theologica* Q92 A3

In maintaining that human law is the application of the maxims of natural law to particular cases, he seems to be arguing that human law is made up of determinations derived from the natural law. However, in the next extract he considers the relationship between the two in more depth and sophistication.

But it must be noted that something may be derived from natural law in two ways: first, as a conclusion from premises; secondly, by way of determination of certain generalities. The first way is like to that by which, in the sciences, demonstrated conclusions are drawn from the principles, while the second mode is likened to that whereby, in the arts, general forms are particularized as to details: thus the craftsman needs to determine the general form of a house to some particular shape. Some things are therefore derived from the general principles of the natural law by way of conclusions, e.g., that 'one must not kill' may be derived as a conclusion from the principle that 'one should do harm to no man'; while some are derived therefrom by way of determination, e.g., the law of nature has it that the evildoer should be punished; but that he be punished in this or that way is not directed by natural law but is a derived determination of it.

Accordingly, both modes of derivation are found in the human law. But those things which are derived in the first way are contained in human law, not as emanating therefrom exclusively, but having some force from the natural law also. But those things which are derived in the second way have no other force than that of human law.

Aquinas *Summa Theologica* Q95 A2

Derivation in the first sense produces a conclusion which, strictly speaking, would not be a species of human law unless some legal consequences, such as the imposition of a sanction, were added; it would remain in the category of natural law, although admittedly more concrete than the broader natural law premise from which it is deduced. Such a conclusion is a division of natural law precept (a secondary precept of natural law) rather than a complete axiom of the human law. When considering the relationship between natural and human law, it is the second process of derivation, the 'determination of particulars', which is of importance. In the illustration used it would be impossible to derive the most satisfactory type of punishment from the premise given. Certainly, in the sense that the punishment decided upon ought to be reasonable, it could be said to be derived from natural law. But it is derivation by determination of particulars, not of conclusions from premises. Rules of human law so derived 'have no other force than that of human law', whereas conclusions derived from premises, although present in human law, obtain their force from being a secondary division of natural law precepts. In another passage he employs the familiar division of laws into the *ius gentium* and the *ius civile* to distinguish the two processes of derivation.

A thing can of itself be divided in respect of something contained in the notion of that thing. Thus a soul either rational or irrational is contained in the notion of animal; and therefore animal is divided properly and of itself in respect of its being rational or irrational, but not in the point of its being white or black, which are entirely beside the notion of animal. Now, in the notion of human law, many things are contained in respect of any of which human law can be divided properly and of itself. For in the first place it belongs to the nature of human law to be derived from the law of nature. In this respect positive law is divided into the 'law of nations' and 'civil law', according to the two ways in which something may be derived from the law of nature. Because to the law of nations belong those things which are derived from the law of nature as conclusions from premises, e.g., just buyings and sellings, and the like, without which men cannot live together, which is a point of the law of nature, since man is by nature a social animal, as is proved in *Politics* i.2. But those things which are derived from the law of nature by way of particular determination belong to the civil law, according as each state decides on what is best for itself.

Aquinas Summa Theologica Q95 A4

Therefore, conclusions derived from premises make up the *ius gentium* which, although a part of human law, is intimately connected with the natural law. These secondary precepts of natural law will need some sanction or legal consequence to be added in order for them to become effective rules of human law, and this is achieved by derivation from the natural law by way of particular determination.

From this discussion it follows that human law must be compatible with the natural law although not deduced from it in the sense of conclusions from premises. It is not given to us, as is natural law, but is the expression and result of a creative use of human reason. It is for this reason that a human law which fails this compatibility test is to be catalogued as an act of violence rather than as a human law.

There is a further discussion of the status of a human law that offends the precepts of natural law. This needs to be read in the light of the argument advanced by Finnis (supra pp 151–153).

As Augustine says, 'that which is not just seems to be no law at all', wherefore the force of a law depends on the extent of its justice. Now in human affairs a thing is said to be just from being right according to the rule of reason. But the first rule of reason is the law of nature. Consequently, every human law has just so much of the nature of law as it is derived from the law of nature. But if in any point it deflects from the law of nature, it is no longer a law but a perversion of law.

Aquinas Summa Theologica Q95 A2

Laws framed by man are either just or unjust. If they be just, they have the power of binding in conscience, from the eternal law whence they are derived, according to Proverbs viii 15: 'By Me kings reign, and lawgivers decree just things.' Now laws are said to be just—from the end, when, to wit, they are ordained to the common good—and from their author, that is to say, when the law that is made does not exceed the power of the lawgiver—and from their form, when, to wit, burdens are laid on the subjects, according to an equality of proportion and with a view to the common good. For, since one man is a part of the community, each man, in all that he is and has, belongs to the community, just as a part, in all that it is, belongs to the whole; wherefore nature inflicts a loss on the part in order to save the whole, so that on this account such laws as these which impose proportionate burdens are just and binding in conscience and are legal laws.

On the other hand, laws may be unjust in two ways: first, by being contrary to human good, through being opposed to the things mentioned above—either in respect of the end, as when an authority imposes on his subjects burdensome laws, conducive, not to the common good, but rather to his own cupidity or vainglory; or in respect of the author, as when a man makes a law that goes beyond the power committed to him; or in respect of the form, as when burdens are imposed unequally on the community, although with a view to the common good. The like are acts of violence rather than laws, because, as Augustine says, 'A law that is not just, seems to be no law at all.' Wherefore such laws do not bind in conscience, except perhaps in order to avoid scandal or disturbance, for which cause a man should even yield his right, according to Matthew v. 40, 41: 'If a man . . . take away thy coat, let go thy cloak also unto him; and whosoever will force thee one mile, go with him another two.'

Secondly, laws may be unjust through being opposed to the divine good: such are the laws of tyrants inducing to idolatry or to anything else contrary to the divine law; and laws of this kind must nowise be observed because, as stated in Acts v. 29, 'we ought to obey God rather than men.'

Aquinas *Summa Theologica* Q96 A4

First, it is worth referring to Finnis's contention concerning the treatment of the unjust law in natural law doctrine. More specifically, in connection with Aquinas's treatment, Finnis supports his main contention.

We may refer again to Thomas Aquinas—as always, not because there is any presumption that whatever he asserts is true, but simply because he is unquestionably a paradigm 'natural law theorist' and dominates the period 'from the church fathers down to Kant', by synthesizing his patristic and early medieval predecessors and by fixing the vocabulary and to some extent the doctrine of later scholastic and, therefore, early modern thought. Now Aquinas indeed asserts that positive law derives its validity from natural law; but in the very same breath he shows how it is *not* a mere emanation from or copy of natural law, and how the legislator enjoys all the creative freedom of an architect: the analogy is Aquinas's. Aquinas thinks that positive law is needed for two reasons, of which one is that the natural law 'already somehow in existence' does *not* itself provide all or even most of the solutions to the co-ordination problems of communal life. On any reasonable view, Aquinas's clear elaborations of these points (based on a hint from Aristotle) must be considered one of the more successful parts of his not always successful work on natural law.

Finnis *Natural Law and Natural Rights* 28

The reference to the architect takes us back to the discussion of derivation in Q95 A2 (supra p 15).

Secondly, disobedience is urged only in the case of the second type of unjust law—where there is an offence against the divine good such as idolatry. In other situations primacy is given to the avoidance of social disruption over the injustice of any particular law. Consequently the position appears to be this: human law acquires its validity from its conformity with natural law, so if it conflicts with natural law it has no validity. But this does not mean that one has a right to refuse to obey every unjust law: the right to rebel is trumped by the continuation of order and allegiance to the State. In this way, religious support is given to the State and the status quo, although the Church, as the interpreter of the maxims of natural law, retains the right of censure and denunciation.

However, a different interpretation could be argued. Laws against the divine good, which 'must nowise be observed' could be given a broad interpretation so as to include not only idolatry but also all laws that conflict with the dictates of natural law (or at least, against the primary, self-evidential dictates—infra p 161). If so, the right, or indeed duty, of everyone to offer resistance to the unjust law is wider than first appears.

A final point on Aquinas's classification of the different types of laws can be made. On various occasions he speaks of positive law, meaning laws enacted and promulgated. An enacted law which offends against the natural law is unjust, although in assessing one's right to rebel it is necessary to weigh up the social disturbance that will be caused by the exercise of that right. However, he does not say that such a rule is not to be treated as a part of the positive law. The point is that positive law may be enacted with or without regard for the natural law. But when there is lack of conformity with natural law, the law cannot be regarded as a part of the *human* law. It is the validity of *human* law that depends on the conformity to natural law: positive law is valid although unjust.

(b)   The self-evidential nature of the precepts of natural law, the doctrine of natural inclinations and the teleological framework to the argument

At last we turn to the precepts of natural law themselves. The next important passage will be followed by some observations but first it is necessary to wrestle with the meaning of what follows.

The precepts of natural law are to the practical reason what the first principles of demonstrations are to the speculative reason, because both are self-evident principles. Now a thing is said to be self-evident in two ways: first, in itself; secondly, in relation to us. Any proposition is said to be self-evident in itself if its predicate is contained in the notion of the subject, although to one who knows not the definition of the subject it happens that such a proposition is not self-evident. For instance, this proposition, 'Man is a rational being,' is, in its very nature, self-evident, since who says 'man' says 'a rational being'; and yet to one who knows not what a man is, this proposition is not self-evident. Hence it is that, as Boethius says, certain axioms or propositions are universally self-evident to all; and such are those propositions whose terms are known to all, as, 'Every whole is greater than its part,' and, 'Things equal to one and the same are equal to one another.' But some propositions are self-evident only to the wise who understand the meaning of the terms of such propositions; thus to one who understands that an angel is not a body, it is self-evident that an angel is not circumspectively in a place; but this is not evident to the unlearned, for they cannot grasp it.

Now a certain order is to be found in those things that are apprehended universally. For that which, before aught else, falls under apprehension, is *being*, the notion of which is included in all things whatsoever a man apprehends. Wherefore the first indemonstrable principle is that *the same thing cannot be affirmed and denied at the same time*, which is based on the notion of *being* and *not-being*: and on this principle all others are based, as is stated in *Metaph.* iv., text 9. Now as *being* is the first thing that falls under the apprehension simply, so *good* is the first thing that falls under the apprehension of the practical reason, which is directed to action: since every agent acts for an end under the aspect of good. Consequently the first principle in the practical reason is one founded on the notion of good, *viz*., that *good is that which all things seek after*. Hence this is the first precept of law, that *good is to be done and ensued, and evil is to be avoided*. All other precepts of the natural law are based upon this: so that whatever the practical reason naturally apprehends as man's good (or evil) belongs to the precepts of the natural law as something to be done or avoided.

Since, however, good has the nature of an end, and evil, the nature of a contrary, hence it is that all those things to which man has a natural inclination, are naturally apprehended by reason as being good, and consequently as objects of pursuit, and their contraries as evil, and objects of avoidance. Wherefore according to the order of natural inclinations, is the order of the precepts of the natural law. Because in man there is first of all an inclination to good in accordance with the nature which he has in common with all substances; inasmuch as every substance seeks the preservation of its own being, according to its nature: and by reason of this inclination, whatever is a means of preserving human life, and of warding off its obstacles, belongs to the natural law. Secondly, there is in man an inclination to things that pertain to him more specially, according to that nature which he has in common with other animals: and in virtue of this inclination, those things are said to belong to the natural law, *which nature has taught to all animals*, such as sexual intercourse, education of offspring and so forth. Thirdly, there is in man an inclination to good, according to the nature of his reason, which nature is proper to him: thus man has a natural inclination to know the truth about God, and to live in society: and in this respect, whatever pertains to this inclination belongs to the natural law; for instance, to shun ignorance, to avoid offending those among whom one has to live, and other such things regarding the above inclination.

Aquinas *Summa Theologica* Q94 A2

(i)   A proposition can be claimed to be self-evident in two ways: propositions can be objectively self-evident in themselves even though the proposition in question is not immediately known to everyone; alternatively a proposition which is self-evident in relation to us is subjectively self-evident, in the sense that its truth is grasped without reflection as soon as the terms employed are understood. Aquinas's point is that natural law precepts also fall into these two categories of self-evidence.

(ii)   An analogy is drawn between the precepts of natural law and the first principles of demonstration. Just as, in the province of speculative reason, 'being' is apprehended before anything else, 'good' is the basic notion that falls under the apprehension of practical reason, the latter meaning the type of reasoning when the mind is working out what ought to be done. So nothing can be understood by practical reason without the notion of 'good' being included in it and the reason for the fundamental importance of good is that all things attempt to attain it.

(iii) The first principle of natural law is introduced in the last extract. It is self-evident to all people because it is a part of the very nature of man and so, because of his 'natural inclinations', man immediately apprehends 'good' as something to be pursued. So the principle that good is to be done and evil to be avoided is similar to the proposition that the whole is greater than any of its parts, because both are known to us immediately.

(iv)   The other principles of natural law are based on this first principle. But be careful; it does not 'spin the whole of natural law out of itself' in the way of conclusions deduced from the first principle. 'As regards deduction, Aquinas did not think we can deduce the proposition that to have sexual intercourse with someone else's wife is wrong from the precept that good is to be pursued and evil avoided simply by contemplating, as it were, this latter precept' (Copleston *Aquinas* 231). It would be better to consider this first principle as a 'directive', with which the precepts of natural law must be in accord.

(v)   As the precepts of natural law are not deduced from the first principle, how, then, do we acquire knowledge of them? The answer is to be found in the doctrine of 'natural inclinations'. To attain a knowledge and understanding of the principles of natural law that man ought to follow, first, it is necessary to attain an understanding. What corresponds to the basic drives of human nature is understood as being good, and in this sense, a natural law based on natural inclinations, although not deduced from the first principle, is in accord with it. The first principle, being a 'directive principle' can only signpost towards objects which are commensurate with man's basic inclination, towards the end for which humans were made. In this way the doctrine of natural inclinations provides a basis for our knowledge of the self-evident principles of natural law. It should be noted that it is human reason which discovers and proclaims the capabilities of human nature. This does not mean that man has the power to alter the natural law, but it does mean that man has the capacity to discern the content of the natural law: 'he promulgates it to himself'.

(vi)   The content of the natural inclinations are set out towards the end of the extract. Each inclination has a principle embedded within itself. So, the inclination of self-preservation enshrines the principle of respect for human life. Having stated that the natural inclination suggests the principle of natural law, the connection is often not an obvious one. What, for example, is the principle conjured up by the inclination to have sexual intercourse and the care of offspring? Perhaps, the relevant principles that correspond to the natural inclinations can be summarised as follows: one ought to respect all life; sexual intercourse has a dignity and a significance and therefore ought to be subject to some form of regulation; in order for children to be nursed, cared for and educated the family group ought to comply with some fixed pattern, eg polygamous, polyandrous or monogamous. Notice the final inclination: to live in society. The corresponding principle, presumably, would be that we ought to live together in obedience to certain rules.

(vii)   A significant point is that the inclinations and the corresponding principles, while not self-evident to all, are self-evident in themselves. Therefore, while everybody would be able to see immediately what is 'good' and hence 'what ought to be done', everyone might not immediately grasp that, for example, we ought to live together under regulations. This failure would be because of a lack of understanding of terms such as 'family'. Nevertheless, these principles are a species of self-evident propositions, objectively self-evident in that this characterisation does not depend upon the universal understanding of the terms used.

(viii) There is yet another important feature in this extract: teleology. What is good for man is the activation of his true self. This good is the fulfilment of his nature, and it is towards this end that he naturally tends. To realise man's essential nature is to do good; and it is the doctrine of natural inclinations which provides man's reason with the way to actualise this essential nature. Furthermore an act is either morally good or morally bad according to whether it is compatible with the realisation of man's final end or supreme good. Ultimately this argument must lead to the belief in a purposive divine being who invests man with certain natural inclinations which function as guides to fulfilment. Returning to the meaning of eternal law, it can now be described as the plan of divine wisdom directing all things to the attainment of their ends. All human beings act for an end, and to the extent that acting for an end is acting for a good, all human beings act for a good. But, of course, what a particular person chooses for his end may not correspond with the objective good for mankind. It follows that a concept of 'right reason' or objective good needs to be introduced to evaluate the various ends actually pursued.

(c) The distinction between primary precepts and secondary precepts of natural law

Whereas the last extract was concerned with the primary precepts of natural law corresponding to the natural inclinations, the next passage reveals the existence of secondary precepts, covering 'matters of detail'. Again the extract will be followed by some notes.

To the natural law belong those things to which a man is inclined naturally; and among these it is a special property of man to be inclined to act according to reason. Now reason proceeds from what is common, or general, to what is proper, or special. But there is a difference in this regard between the speculative reason and the practical reason. The speculative reason is concerned primarily with what is necessary, that is, with those things which cannot be other than they are; and therefore, in the case of speculative reason, both the common principles and the special conclusions are necessarily true. In the case of the practical reason, on the other hand, which is concerned with contingent matters, such as human actions, even though there be some necessary truth in the common principles, yet the more we descend to what is proper and peculiar, the more deviations we find. Therefore in speculative matters the same truth holds among all men both as to principles and as to conclusions, even though all men do not discern this truth in the conclusions but only in those principles which are called axiomatic notions. In active matters, on the other hand, all men do not hold to the same truth or practical rectitude in what is peculiar and proper, but only in what is common. And even among those who hold to the same line of rectitude in proper and peculiar matters, such rectitude is not equally known to all. It is clear, therefore, that as far as common principles are concerned in the case of speculative as well as of practical reason the same truth and the same rectitude exists among all and is equally known to all. In the case, however, of the proper or peculiar conclusions of speculative reason, the same truth obtains among all, even though it is not known equally to all. For it is true among all men that the three angles of a triangle are equal to two right angles, even though not all men know this. But in the case of the proper or peculiar conclusions of the practical reason there is neither the same truth and rectitude among all men, nor, where it does exist, is it equally known to all. Thus it is true and right among all men that action proceed in accordance with reason. From this principle there follows as a proper conclusion that deposits should be restored to the owner. This conclusion is indeed true in the majority of cases. But a case may possibly arise in which such restitution is harmful and consequently contrary to reason; so, for example, if things deposited were claimed so that they might be used against the fatherland. This uncertainty increases the more particular the cases become: as, for example, if it were laid down that the restitution should take place in a certain way, with certain *definite* precautions; for as the limiting particular conditions become more numerous, so do the possibilities decrease that render the principle normally applicable, with the result that neither the restitution nor the failure to do so can be rigorously presented as right.

It follows therefore that natural law in its first common principle is the same among all men, both as to validity and recognition (something is right for all and is so by all recognised). But as to certain proper or derived norms, which are, as it were, conclusions of these common principles, they are valid and are so recognised by all men only in the majority of cases. For in special cases they may prove defective both as to validity because of certain particular impediments (just as things of nature in the sphere of generation and corruption prove to be defective because of impediments) and also as to recognition. And this because some men have a reason that has been distorted by passion, or by evil habits, or by bad natural relations. Such was the case among the ancient Germans, who failed to recognise theft as contrary to justice, as Julius Caesar relates, even though it is an explicit violation of natural law.

Aquinas Summa Theologica Q94 A4

(i)   These secondary precepts are more detailed moral principles derived from the primary precepts. Their existence makes the claim that natural law acts as a guide to human action more feasible.

(ii) The mode of derivation from the primary precepts is the first type of derivation considered above in Q95 A2 (supra p 157).

(iii) Some secondary precepts are an obvious step from the primary precepts. So, for example, the Ten Commandments would be secondary precepts with a close affinity to the primary precepts. However, other secondary precepts would not be so proximate and would require a more arduous process of reasoning. The category of secondaries, therefore, will include all principles which can be seen by reason to be in step with human nature. The following has been offered as an illustration (see Armstrong *Primary and Secondary Precepts in Thomist Natural Law Teaching*). That 'one ought not to bomb the innocent in time of war' is a precept requiring a more prolonged process of reasoning for its truth to be grasped. Nevertheless it would be a secondary precept arrived at by logical deduction from the primary precept that one should do harm to no man (the first primary precept considered above). It would not simply be a human law arrived at by a 'determination of particulars'.

(iv) Neither the obvious nor the more remote secondary precepts are self-evident in either of the meanings considered in Q94 A2. So, it follows that all secondary precepts, even the more obvious, require some reasoning over and above the knowledge of self-evident primary precepts. Therefore, whereas primary precepts are immediately known and appreciated as soon as the terms are understood, the category of secondary precepts includes principles of which some people are unaware.

(d) The problem of immutability

It is a standard claim of natural lawyers that the principles of natural law are unchangeable. In the light of what Aquinas says, this needs qualification. In fact the last extract appears to support the possibility of a secondary precept being modified for two reasons. First, there is the admission that the application of natural law can vary from situation to situation because of the variation in the relevant circumstances. So, while it is a general rule that one ought to return borrowed articles, there are certain circumstances where this ought not to be the case; therefore, the moral rule is not necessarily correct for every conceivable situation. Furthermore, the more remote the secondary precept the more frequent will be the modification of the moral standard in the precept. Hence, in certain cases, the circumstances of an act may be such that it no longer falls under the class of actions prohibited by the precept. This characteristic of the secondaries is clearly articulated by Rommen: 'Correct deductive reasoning thereupon yields additional norms; such, for instance, is the rule that what is borrowed must be returned. However, this principle does not apply with the same universality as, for instance, the prohibition against a direct killing of an innocent person. For should a weapon be demanded back by the lender because in a fit of rage he is preparing to slay his adversary . . . with it, the borrower's refusal to give it back then and there is justified. That private property must be respected follows from its validity in natural law, which is presupposed in the norm, "Thou shalt not steal". Yet a person who find himself in dire need may make use of another's relatively surplus property to meet the emergency; by the same token the owner is obliged to suffer this action and may not appeal to the principle of self-defence, since it is not a question of an unjust, unwarranted invasion of property' (*Natural Law* 224–225).

However, Armstrong has something interesting to say on this point. He argues that this recognition of the modification of secondary precepts does not amount to saying that natural law can vary or is relative. The situations where one is not under a moral duty to return borrowed goods to the owner are not exceptions to the general precept: merely, the general precept failed to state all the conditions. There is now a reformulation so as to include the relevant condition. It is not the enunciation of a new precept which contrasts with the old, but rather the filling out of the old precept so as to include the relevant condition. Therefore the issue is not one of variability, but rather one of reformulation, particularly in the case of the remote conclusions.

The second ground for a possible modification or reformulation of secondary precepts discussed in this extract is the fact that there can be disagreement about the content of secondary precepts when 'the reason is perverted by passion'; for example, the ancient German attitude to theft. But, of course, this would not lead to the conclusion that natural law is mutable and varies with the progress of time. Natural law remains the same, despite the fact that there are differing manifestations of it. This position is reiterated in the following extract.

> There belong to the natural law, first, certain most general precepts, that are known to all; and secondly, certain secondary and more detailed precepts, which are, as it were, conclusions following closely from first principles. As to those general principles, the natural law, in the abstract, can nowise be blotted out from men's hearts. But it is blotted out in the case of a particular action, in so far as reason is hindered from applying the general principle to a particular point of practice, on account of concupiscence or some other passion. But as to

the other, ie, the secondary precepts, the natural law can be blotted out from the human heart either by evil persuasions, just as in speculative matters errors occur in respect of necessary conclusions, or by vicious customs and corrupt habits, as among some men theft and even unnatural vices, as the Apostle states, were not esteemed sinful.

. Aquinas *Summa Theologica* Q94 A6

This passage, which speaks for itself, makes clear the position on the changeability of primary and secondary precepts. However, Aquinas further discusses the possibility of variation or modification based on an ever-improving understanding of human nature.

A change in the natural law may be understood in two ways. First, by way of addition. In this sense nothing hinders the natural law from being changed, since many things, for the benefit of human life, have been added over and above the natural law, both by the divine law and by human laws.

Secondly, a change in the natural law may be understood by way of subtraction, so that what previously was according to the natural law ceases to be so. In this sense the natural law is altogether unchangeable in its first principles, but in its secondary principles, which are certain special conclusions drawn from the first principles, the natural law is not changed so that what it prescribes be not right in most cases. But it may be changed in some particular cases of rare occurrence, through some special causes hindering the observance of such precepts.

Aquinas *Summa Theologica* Q94 A5

Therefore because an understanding of the nature of man has developed, our understanding of natural law apparently changes. This certainly admits the existence of constant progress in the content of natural law: but again, it does not argue for the variability of natural law. The change is only in the various manifestations of natural law, brought about by an improved understanding of human nature.

Although the claim that natural law is universal and immutable must be read in the light of the above extracts and discussion, one can safely conclude that Aquinas did not consider that natural law can vary. There can be variation in the existing codes of morality, but not in natural law itself; there are different manifestations of natural law without there being any variation of natural law; natural law precepts can be reformulated without the introduction of exceptions to the general precepts.

CRITICISM OF TRADITIONAL NATURAL LAW DOCTRINE

In a combative piece of writing Alf Ross attacks natural law philosophy.

A searching criticism of the philosophy of natural law would lead into depths far beyond the limits of a general theory of law. But perhaps a glance at the history of natural law will be more helpful than epistemological argumentation to see the arbitrariness and emptiness of metaphysical speculation. Strictly speaking, metaphysical assertions do not admit of being disproved, precisely because they disport themselves in a sphere beyond the reach of verification. One learns simply to by-pass them as something that has no rightful place or function in scientific thought. Has anyone ever proved that it is not Zeus or the fate goddesses who ordain the path of the sun? All that we can say is that modern astronomy manages without this assumption. Similarly the most effective way to vanquish metaphysics in law is simply to create a scientific theory of law whose self-sufficiency will push metaphysical speculations into oblivion along with other myths and legends of the childhood of civilisation.

The history of natural law reveals two striking points: the arbitrariness of the fundamental postulates concerning the nature of existence and of man; and the arbitrariness of the moral-legal ideas that are evolved on this basis. Natural law seeks the absolute, the eternal, that shall make of law something more than the handiwork of human beings and exempt the legislator from the pains and responsibility of decision. The source of the transcendent validity of law has been sought in a magical law of fate, in the will of God, or in the insight of absolute reason. But experience shows that the doctrines men have built on these sources, far from being eternal and immutable, have changed according to time, place and person. The noble guise of natural law has been used in the course of time to defend or fight for every conceivable kind of demand, obviously arising from a specific situation in life or determined by economic and political class interests, the cultural traditions of the era, its prejudices and aspirations—in short, all that goes to make what is generally called an ideology.

Is it nature's bidding that men shall be as brothers, or is it nature's law that the strong shall rule over the weak, and that therefore slavery and class distinctions are part of God's meaning for the world? Both propositions have been asserted with the same support and the same 'right'; for how should anyone be able to make a choice between these absolutes except by an absolute assertion elevated above all rational argumentation: It is so, because I know that it is so! The ideology of equality was preached by the Sophists in the fifth century BC and by Rousseau in the eighteenth century, by both as the expression of the political aspirations of a class; likewise by the Stoics and Christians, but there against a background of religion without political intent. Plato, on the other hand, postulated the innate inequality of men, and advocated slavery and a community strictly divided into classes. Aristotle followed him with regard to the natural justification of slavery, and since then the postulate concerning the natural inequality of men has been the point of departure for many conservative doctrines of natural law and organic or totalitarian theories of government.

Carl Ludwig von Haller, a Swiss teacher of constitutional law at the beginning of the nineteenth century, maintains it is the law of nature that the strong shall rule over the weak, the husband over the wife, the father over the child, the leader over his men and the teacher over his pupils. In the same way Thomas Dew, the American political theorist, declared that 'it is ordained by nature and by God that the being who has the greatest abilities and learning and therefore the greater power shall rule and dispose over him who is inferior.' On this basis he upheld the institution of slavery in the Southern States, and others went so far as to maintain that slavery assures the natural rights of the slaves. Liberty in its true sense is not licence. 'For this reason slavery secures them in their natural rights and endows them with real liberty to the extent to which they are capable of receiving it. Were the institution of slavery to be abolished they would no longer enjoy their natural rights.'

In the political field it is well known how natural law combined with the doctrine of the contract of government has been used happily to justify every kind of government from absolute power (Hobbes) to absolute democracy (Rousseau). Natural law has also similarly lent itself equally to those who wished to consolidate the existing order (Heraclitus, Aristotle, Thomas Aquinas and others) and to those who wished to advocate revolution (Rousseau).

In the social and economic fields the natural law of the eighteenth century advocated an extreme individualism and liberalism. The inviolability of private ownership and the unfettered freedom of contract were the two dogmas which the nineteenth century inherited from natural law, and which were asserted in the practice of the American courts to obtain the reversal of a number of laws in the sphere of social welfare. As recently as 1922 the United States Supreme Court (in the *Adkin's* case) reversed the validity of a law concerning minimum wages for women in the District of Columbia on the grounds that this law—which had been enacted in order to assure the worst-paid women a degree of acceptable minimum subsistence and free them from the necessity of semi-prostitution—was an infringement of the natural right of these women to make contracts freely. On the other hand, natural law has also been used to provide a basis for a morality of solidarity (Grotius, Comte and other 'sociologists') and, even, in Duguit's interpretation, in support of the denial of all individual rights to make way for a system of social services.

The chapter on family law always makes amusing reading in the systems of natural law, because it so clearly reflects the moral prejudices of the age. For Thomas Aquinas the indissolubility of marriage ('thou shalt not commit adultery') was of course an evident truth of reason. The ludicrous dryness of rationalism is reflected in Kant's definition of marriage as a contract between two persons of different sexes for the lifelong mutual possession of their sexual capacities; sexual intercourse is only permitted in wedlock; if one of the marriage partners gives himself or herself into another's possession, the other marriage partner is invariably entitled to 'recover' the runaway, like a material object, into his possession.

It would be easy to go on, but let me close by recalling St. Paul's Epistle to the Corinthians: 'Judge it yourselves: is it comely that a woman pray unto God uncovered? Does not even nature itself teach you, that, if a man have long hair, it is a shame unto him? But if a woman have long hair it is a glory to her: for her hair is given to her for a covering.'

Like a harlot, natural law is at the disposal of everyone. The ideology does not exist that cannot be defended by an appeal to the law of nature. And, indeed, how can it be otherwise, since the ultimate basis for every natural right lies in a private direct insight, as evident contemplation, an intuition. Cannot my intuition be just as good as yours? Evidence as a criterion of truth explains the utterly arbitrary character of the metaphysical assertions. It raises them up above any force of inter-subjective control and opens the door wide to unrestricted invention and dogmatics.

The historical variability of natural law supports the interpretation that metaphysical postulates are merely constructions to buttress emotional attitudes and the fulfilment of certain needs. It must, however, be admitted that the variability is not a decisive proof for this interpretation. It can be argued that scientific theories also change, and (with Thomas Aquinas) that reason can be led astray by passions, and that not all that appears as evident is necessarily true evidence. This, however, raises the difficult problem of what is the criterion of true evidence, a problem that can only be solved by recourse to evidence in the power, and so on continuing *ad infinitum*.

A strong argument supporting the view that natural-law doctrines are arbitrary and subjective constructions is that evidence cannot be a criterion of truth. What we mean by calling a proposition true is obviously different from the psychological fact that the assertion of the proposition is accompanied by a feeling of certainty. The assumption that evidence guarantees the truth of a proposition cannot therefore be true analytically, that is, as a definition of what truth means. The assumption must be taken synthetically, that is, as asserting that the feeling of evidence always occurs together with such a state of affairs which makes the proposition true. But what is the proof that these two phenomena always should go together? There is none. A feeling of evidence, to be sure, accompanies many true assertions, but there is no reason why the same feeling could not attach also to errors and fallacies. The firm belief in the truth of a proposition always needs justification and can never be its own justification.

The historic variability is not in itself decisive. The argument adduced applies independently of it. Even if we all admitted the same interpretation of the law of nature, indeed even if these ideas should obtrude themselves upon us with the automatism of a law of nature, the criticism would still remain unmoved. If under the influence of poison all mankind should see visions, these fantasies would still not be true, as long as by truth we mean something other than psychological coercion.

Ross *On Law and Justice* 258–262

Psychological considerations supplement the epistemological criticism. The picture becomes clearer if we understand not only that moral-metaphysical speculations are empty and meaningless, but also the reasons why men persist in them.

The driving force of metaphysics in the field of morals and religion is the fear of the vicissitudes of life, the transitoriness of all things; the inexorability of death; or, conversely, the desire for the absolute, the eternally immutable which defies the law of corruption. This fear, in moral matters, is associated with the fear of having to make choices and decisions under changing circumstances and on one's own responsibility. Therefore, by seeking justification for our actions in immutable principles outside ourselves, we try to relieve ourselves of the burden of responsibility. If there is a law, independent of our own choices and pleasure, given to us as an eternal truth based in the will of God or an *a priori* insight of reason, and dictating to us the 'right' course of action, then we ourselves, obeying this universal law, are but obedient parts of a cosmic order and relieved from all responsibility.

The desire for the absolute that bestows freedom from responsibility and brings peace that passeth all understanding has in the moral life of man the best conditions for developing into metaphysical beliefs, hardly to be broken down by critical thinking. The reason for this is the peculiar psychological mechanism from which the moral consciousness (the conscience) emanates, presenting itself in a set of apparently blindly imperative impulses. Since these impulses make themselves felt independently of our conscious needs and desires, they are well suited to force upon us the illusionary view that in our conscience speaks a voice of a law telling us about 'validity' or 'rightness' radically different from, and independent of, our physical nature, its instincts, and desires. From there the way lies open to all sorts of metaphysical constructions of the nature of moral validity and the content of the moral law.

But just as an illusion of the senses is dispelled when I observe the object of it more clearly, so the *fata morgana* of the moral consciousness vanishes before a more intense psychological observation. A fuller account of the psychological mechanism which gives rise to the moral consciousness is outside the scope of this book. Here it can merely be said that the moral consciousness with its mystical pathos is like manna from Heaven to the metaphysically hungry; and that it is not after all so mystical that it is not amenable to scientific explanation on a psychological basis.

What has been said here about morality and the moral consciousness similarly applies to law and legal consciousness. The law, too, is experienced as validly 'binding,' that is, something which I obey, not merely because of fear of the external compulsion (the sanction), but also because of respect for the inner authority (validity) of the law. The legal consciousness, therefore, just like the moral consciousness, gives rise to superempirical interpretations. Natural law and moral philosophy are closely connected, whether natural law is thought of as a part of morality, or as an independent province, co-ordinate with morality, of ethics.

Ross *On Law and Justice* 262–263

Politically, natural law can be conservative, evolutionary or revolutionary. Of course, its political orientation cannot be adduced as an argument for or against the theoretical tenability of the doctrine of natural law, but a person's political views will determine his sympathy for, or opposition to, the doctrine.

Although all three types occur, natural law in history has primarily fulfilled the conservative function of endowing the existing power relations with the halo of validity. Natural law is first and foremost an ideology created by those in power—statesmen, jurists, the clergy—to legitimise and reinforce their position of authority.

A natural law that was originally revolutionary will ordinarily become conservative once the social classes whose interests it asserted have prevailed. An example of this is the individualist and liberalist natural law which led to the American Revolution. The principles concerning ownership, economic freedom and freedom of contract which made possible the tremendous expansion of the American community in the early part of the nineteenth century, became in the latter half of the century a reactionary power which, to preserve the advantages of the propertied classes, hindered the evolution toward social levelling and welfare. The United States Supreme Court used its constitutional power—often by straining its interpretation of the Constitution—in order to overrule the validity of a series of laws resulting from the needs of this evolution but in conflict with the natural-law principles of liberty. This occurred, for example, in the laws for the regulation of work hours or the establishment of minimum wages; laws concerning child labour in mines and factories; laws forbidding employers to interfere in their employees' membership in trade unions; laws for the restriction of the owner's unlimited right over his property. Even a law proposing a modest income tax was overruled by the Supreme Court (1895) with the result that no income tax could be introduced until after an amendment to the Constitution had been adopted as late as 1913. This battle against advancing social principles in legislation reached a dramatic climax when after the great depression of 1929

President Roosevelt began his New Deal in the thirties. The Supreme Court overruled the validity of several laws aiming at a constructive restoration of the economic life of the country, and the president found he had no choice but to break the resistance in the Supreme Court by the appointment of a sufficient number of new judges who were in favour of progress. In 1937 the president put before Congress a plan for a general reform of the organisation of the courts, the real, although veiled, purpose of which was to make possible the appointment of six new Supreme Court judges. The plan aroused violent opposition and was never carried out. There had for some time been a growing minority within the Supreme Court who were willing to follow the Government in its economic policy. This group now won ascendancy, possibly as a result of the president's threat to increase the number of judges, but no drastic measures were taken. Since about 1937 the American Supreme Court has accepted the new economic ideology and restrained the exercise of its power of judicial review in dealing with Acts of Congress. Since that time, in only one case has an Act of Congress been declared unconstitutional.

Ross *On Law and Justice* 263–265

There must be some sort of response to one of the arguments in the preceding extract: that there has, and never will be, any commonly agreed content to the moral-legal ideas that emanate from natural law philosophy: Finnis to the rescue.

H. L. A. Hart has said that 'natural law theory in all its protean guises attempts to assert that human beings are equally devoted to and united in their conception of aims (the pursuit of knowledge, justice to their fellow men) other than that of survival.' For my part, I know of no one who has ever asserted this. Certainly the classical theorists of natural law all took for granted, and often enough bluntly asserted, that human beings are not all equally devoted to the pursuit of knowledge or justice, and are far from united in their conception of what constitutes worthwhile knowledge or a demand of justice. There is much to be said for Leo Strauss's judgment that 'knowledge of the indefinitely large variety of notions of right and wrong is so far from being incompatible with the idea of natural right that it is the essential condition for the emergence of the idea: realization of the variety of notions of right is *the* incentive for the quest for natural right.'

Thomas Aquinas frequently tackled the question of the extent of human recognition of the natural law. When his remarks are taken together, it can be seen that he is working with a threefold categorization of the principles or precepts of natural law. *First* there are the most general (*communissima*) principles, which are 'not so much precepts as, so to speak, the ends or point of the precepts'; they state the basic forms of human good; at least to the extent that they concern his own good, they are recognized by anyone who reaches the age of reason and who has enough experience to know what they refer to, and in this sense they 'cannot, as general principles [*in universali*], be eliminated from the human heart'. This is the nearest Aquinas gets to making the assertion which Hart suggests is the core of natural law theorizing. It amounts to no more than saying that any sane person is capable of seeing that life, knowledge, fellowship, offspring, and a few other such basic aspects of human existence are, as such, good, ie worth having, leaving to one side all particular predicaments and implications, all assessments of relative importance, all moral demands, and in short, all questions of whether and how one is to devote oneself to these goods.

For, *secondly*, even the most elementary and easily recognizable moral implications of those first principles are capable of being obscured or distorted for particular people and, indeed, for whole cultures, by prejudice, oversight, convention, the sway of desire for particular gratifications, etc.; for example, many people (in Aquinas's day, as now) think that morality touches only interpersonal relations and that 'everyone is free to do what he will in those matters that concern only himself', while others cannot see that they have any obligations to other people. And *thirdly*, there are many moral questions which can only be rightly answered by someone who is wise, and who considers them searchingly.

So when Hart objects that the conception of 'the human end or good for man' which was entertained by 'the classical exponents' of natural law was 'complex', 'debatable', and 'disputable', the classical exponents would have replied that indeed it was complex, debated, and disputed, and that they had made rather extensive contributions to the debate. For the real problem of morality, and of the point or meaning of human existence, is not in discerning the basic aspects of human well-being, but in integrating those various aspects into the intelligent and reasonable commitments, projects, and actions that go to make up one or other of the many admirable forms of human life. And by no means everybody can see these things steadily and whole, let alone put them into practice. The fact that there is controversy is not an argument against one side in that controversy. A genuine requirement of practical reasonableness is not the less a part of natural law (to use the classical phrase) just because it is not universally recognized or is actively disputed.

Finnis *Natural Law and Natural Rights* 29–31

The illogical inference from fact to value

One of the most frequently encountered attacks on natural law philosophy is what can be called the deductive fallacy. In accepting that the starting point of natural law theories is natural reality, in particular human nature, they proceed to arrive at value judgments. If this is the case it would be an example of the illegitimate reasoning by which an 'ought' statement is derived from an 'is' statement. In a celebrated passage David Hume argues that any deductive argument is invalid if its conclusion is a value judgment and all its premises are facts.

> I cannot forbear adding to these reasonings an observation, which may, perhaps, be found of some importance. In every system of morality, which I have hitherto met with, I have always remark'd, that the author proceeds for some time in the ordinary way of reasoning, and establishes the being of a God, or makes observations concerning human affairs: when of a sudden I am surpriz'd to find, that instead of the usual copulations of propositions, *is* and *is not*, I meet with no proposition that is not connected with an *ought*, or an *ought not*. This change is imperceptible: but is, however, of the last consequence. For as this *ought*, or *ought not*, expresses some new relation or affirmation, 'tis necessary that it shou'd be observ'd and explain'd; and at the same time that a reason should be given, for what seems altogether inconceivable, how this new relation can be a deduction from others, which are entirely different from it. But as authors do not commonly use this precaution, I shall presume to

recommend it to the readers; and am persuaded, that this small attention wou'd subvert all the vulgar systems of morality, and let us see, that the distinction of vice and virtue is not founded merely on the relations of objects, nor is perceiv'd by reason.

Hume *A Treatise of Human Nature* Book III. Part 1, section i

In more modern terminology: in all systems of morality we start with certain statements of fact which contain no trace of judgments of value and no moral words. From the point of view of natural law these would involve statements about human nature describing what men *are* or *do*. Think of Aquinas's use of natural inclinations. We are then told that because these things are so we ought to act in a certain manner; in this way normative, evaluative or prescriptive statements are deduced from empirical statements alone. This must be illegitimate reasoning, since the conclusion of an argument can contain nothing which is not in the premises, and there are no 'oughts' in the premises.

Does natural law fall foul of Hume's guillotine? Clearly there are many critics who think just so. Here is a representative sample.

The first objection which must be made from the point of view of science is that this doctrine obliterates the essential difference which exists between scientific laws of nature, the rules by which the science of nature describes its object, and the rules by which ethics and jurisprudence describe their objects, which are morality and law. A scientific law of nature is the rule by which two phenomena are connected with each other according to the principle of causality, that is to say, as cause and effect. Such a rule is, for example, the statement that if a metallic body is heated it expands. The relation between cause and effect, whether it is considered as a relation of necessity or of mere probability, is not attributed to any act of human or superhuman will. If we speak of morality or law, on the other hand, we refer to norms prescribing human behavior, norms which are the specific meaning of acts of human or superhuman beings. Such a norm is, for instance, the moral norm issued by Christ enjoining that one help a fellow man in need, or a legal norm issued by a legislator prescribing punishment for a murderer. Ethics describes the situation which exists under moral norms by the statement: If a man is in need, his fellow men ought to help him; jurisprudence describes the situation under the legal norm: If a man commits murder, he ought to be punished. It is evident that a rule of morality or a rule of law connects the condition with its consequence not according to the principle of causality, but according to a totally different principle. A law of nature is a statement to the effect that if there is A, there *is* B, whereas a rule of morality or a rule of law is a statement to the effect that if there is A, there *ought* to be B. It is the difference between the 'is' and the 'ought,' the difference between causality and normativity (or imputation).

If we presuppose a general norm prescribing a certain type of human behavior, we may characterize concrete behavior which is in conformity with the presupposed norm as good, right, correct, and behavior which is not in conformity with the presupposed norm, as wrong, bad, incorrect. These statements are called value judgments, the term being used in an objective sense. Value, in this sense of the term, is conformity with a presupposed norm. It is a positive value, in contradistinction to a negative value, which is nonconformity with a presupposed norm. Since the statement that the concrete behavior of a definite individual is good or bad (or, what amounts to the same, has a positive or negative value) means that his behaviour is in conformity or not in conformity with a presupposed general norm, we may express this value judgment by the statement that the individual ought or ought not to behave as he actually does. Without presupposing a general norm prescribing (or forbidding) something, we cannot make a value judgment in the objective sense of this term. The value attributed to an object is not given with the properties of this object without reference to a presupposed norm. The value is not inherent in the object judged as valuable, it is the relation of this object to a presupposed norm. We cannot find the value of a real thing or of actual behavior by analyzing these objects. Value is not immanent in natural reality. Hence value cannot be deduced from reality. It does not follow from the fact that something is, that it ought to be or to be done, or that it ought not to be or not to be done. The fact that in reality big fish swallow small fish does not imply that the behavior of the fish is good, nor yet that it is bad. There is no logical inference from the 'is' to the 'ought,' from natural reality to moral or legal value.

If we compare the rules by which ethics or jurisprudence describe their objects (rules referring to moral or legal norms) with the rules by which natural science describes its object, that is, causal rules, we must take into consideration the fact that the norms to which the rules of morality and the rules of law refer are, as previously stated, the meaning of acts of a moral or legal authority. So far as this authority is a human being, these norms are subjective in character, that is, they express the intention of their author. That which such a human authority prescribes or forbids depends on the end at which he aims. That at which somebody aims as an end is also called a value, but in a subjective sense of this term; and if it is an ultimate end, not a means to an end, it is called a highest value. There are great variances of opinion about ultimate ends or highest values in this subjective sense of the term, and frequently one highest value is in conflict with another, as, for instance, personal freedom with social security, the welfare of the single individual with the welfare of the whole nation, in situations where the one can be reached only at the expense of the other. Then arises the question which end is preferable, or which value is superior and which is inferior—which is in truth the highest value? This question cannot be answered in the same way as the question whether iron is heavier than water or water heavier than wood. This latter question can be resolved by experience in a rational scientific way, but the question as to the highest value in the subjective sense of the term can be decided only emotionally, by the feelings or the wishes of the deciding subject. One subject may be led by his emotions to prefer personal freedom; another, social security; one, the welfare of the single individual; the other, the welfare of the whole nation. By no rational consideration can it be proved that the one is right or the other wrong. Consequently there are, as a matter of fact, very different systems of morality and very different systems of law, whereas there is only one system of nature. What according to one system of morality is good may, under another system of morality, be bad; and what under one legal order is a crime may be under another legal order perfectly right. This means that the values which consist in conformity or nonconformity with an existing moral or legal order are relative values. Only if the authority issuing the norms is supposed to be God, an absolute and transcendental being, is there an exclusive moral and legal system, and then the values which consist in compliance with these norms are supposed to be absolute values.

The natural-law doctrine presupposes that value is immanent in reality and that this value is absolute, or, what amounts to the same thing, that a divine will is inherent in nature. Only under this presupposition is it possible to maintain the doctrine that the law can be deduced from nature and that this law is absolute justice. Since the metaphysical assumption of the immanence of value in natural reality is not acceptable from the point of view of science, the natural-law doctrine is based on the logical fallacy of an inference from the 'is' to the 'ought.' The norms allegedly deduced from nature are—in truth—tacitly presupposed, and are based on subjective values, which are presented as the intentions of nature as a legislator. By identifying the laws of nature with rules of law, pretending that the order of nature is or contains a just social order, the natural-law doctrine, like primitive animism, conceives of nature as a part of society. But it can be easily proved that modern science is the result of a process characterized by the tendency of emancipating the interpretation of nature from social categories. Before the tribunal of science, the natural-law doctrine has no chance. But it may deny the jurisdiction of this tribunal by referring to its religious character.

Kelsen *What is Justice?* 139–142

For an answer to this indictment, again, we turn to Finnis.

Another of the three 'decisive issues' formulated by Stone was this: 'Have the natural lawyers shown that they can derive ethical norms from facts?' And the answer can be brisk: They have not, nor do they need to, nor did the classical exponents of the theory dream of attempting any such derivation.

This answer will doubtless give widespread dissatisfaction. For if it is correct, the most popular image of natural law has to be abandoned. The corresponding and most popular objection to all theories of natural law has to be abandoned, too, and the whole question of natural law thought through afresh by many.

Thus it is simply not true that 'any form of a natural-law theory of morals entails the belief that propositions about man's duties and obligations can be inferred from propositions about his nature'. Nor is it true that for Aquinas 'good and evil are concepts analysed and fixed in metaphysics before they are applied in morals'. On the contrary, Aquinas asserts as plainly as possible that the first principles of natural law, which specify the basic forms of good and evil and which can be adequately grasped by anyone of the age of reason (and not just by metaphysicians), are *per se nota* (self-evident) and indemonstrable. They are not inferred from speculative principles. They are not inferred from facts. They are not inferred from metaphysical propositions about human nature, or about the nature of good and evil, or about 'the function of a human being', nor are they inferred from a teleological conception of nature or any other conception of nature. They are not inferred or derived from anything. They are underived (though not innate). Principles of right and wrong, too, are derived from these first, pre-moral principles of practical reasonableness, and not from any facts, whether metaphysical or otherwise. When discerning what is good, to be pursued (*prosequendum*), intelligence is operating in a different way, yielding a different logic, from when it is discerning what is the case (historically, scientifically, or metaphysically); but there is no good reason for asserting that the latter operations of intelligence are more rational than the former.

Of course, Aquinas would agree that 'were man's nature different, so would be his duties'. The basic forms of good grasped by practical understanding are what is good for human beings with the nature they have. Aquinas considers that practical reasoning begins not by understanding this nature from the outside, as it were, by way of psychological, anthropological, or metaphysical observations and judgments defining human nature, but by experiencing one's nature, so to speak, from the inside, in the form of one's inclinations. But again, there is no process of inference. One does not judge that 'I have [or everybody has] an inclination to find out about things' and then infer that therefore 'knowledge is a good to be pursued'. Rather, by a simple act of non-inferential understanding one grasps that the object of the inclination which one experiences is an instance of a general form of good, for oneself (and others like one).

There are important objections to be made to Aquinas's theory of natural law. O'Connor rightly identifies the main one: Aquinas fails to explain 'just how the specific moral rules which we need to guide our conduct can be shown to be connected with allegedly self-evident principles'. But the objection that Aquinas's account of natural law proposes an illicit inference from 'is' to 'ought' is quite unjustified.

How can this objection have become so popular? There are a number of probable reasons, of which I may mention three. The first is that the very phrase 'natural law' can lead one to suppose that the norms referred to, in any theory of natural law, are based upon judgments about nature (human and/or otherwise). And the second reason is that this supposition is in fact substantially correct in relation to the Stoic theory of natural law and, as we shall shortly see, in relation to some Renaissance theories, including some that claimed the patronage of Thomas Aquinas and have been influential almost to the present day.

And thirdly, Aquinas himself was a writer not on ethics alone but on the whole of theology. He was keen to show the relationship between his ethics of natural law and his general theory of metaphysics and the world-order. He wished to point out the analogies running through the whole order of being. Thus human virtue is analogous to the 'virtue' that can be predicated of anything which is a fine specimen of things of its nature, in good shape, *bene disposita secundum convenientiam suae naturae*. So he is happy to say that human virtue, too, is in accordance with the nature of human beings, and human vice is *contra naturam*. If we stopped here, the charge against him would seem to be proved, or at least plausible (and certain later philosophical theologians would seem to have been justified in claiming his patronage). But in fact Aquinas takes good care to make his meaning, his order of explanatory priorities, quite clear. The criterion of conformity with or contrariety to human nature is reasonableness.

> 'And so whatever is contrary to the order of reason is contrary to the nature of human beings as such; and what is reasonable is in accordance with human nature as such. *The good of the human being is being in accord with reason, and human evil is being outside the order of reasonableness.* . . . So human virtue, which makes good both the human person and his works, is in accordance with human nature *just* in *so* far as [*tantum . . . inquantum*] it is in accordance with reason; and vice is contrary to human nature just in so far as it is contrary to the order of reasonableness.'

In other words, for Aquinas, the way to discover what is morally right (virtue) and wrong (vice) is to ask, not what is in accordance with human nature, but what is reasonable. And this quest will eventually bring one back to the *underived* first principles of practical reasonableness, principles which make no reference at all to human nature, but only to human good. From end to end of his ethical discourses, the primary categories for Aquinas are the 'good' and the 'reasonable'; the 'natural' is, from the point of view of his ethics, a speculative appendage added by way of metaphysical reflection, *not* a counter with which to advance either to or from the practical *prima principia per se nota.*

Since Aquinas's Aristotelian distinction between 'speculative' and practical reason corresponds so neatly with the modern (but not only modern!) distinction which we (roughly!) indicate by contrasting 'fact' and 'norm' or 'is' and 'ought', it will be helpful to examine in greater depth the historical process by which the theory of natural law has come to be associated with a fundamental disregard of this distinction. To this examination the next two sections are devoted; they are, however, no more than an introduction to a much-needed investigation, still to be made.

Finnis *Natural Law and Natural Rights* 33–36

In his *Fundamentals of Ethics* he elaborates on his thesis and the following passages are to be read in relation to his own version of natural law (infra pp 186ff) which he claims is free from any fallacious reasoning.

I shall say that one is thinking practically, or exercising practical understanding, when one is considering what to be, to get, to have or to do. And that can also be expressed as follows, using the term 'good' in that informal, idiomatic sense which is not tied to 'morality': one is thinking practically, or exercising practical understanding, when one is considering what it is (or would be, under relevantly possible conditions) good to be, to get, to have or to do. Such thinking or understanding is practical *simpliciter* [without qualification] when my consideration is of my own predicament with a view to undertaking my own commitments and/or actions here and now. It is practical *secundum quid* [in a qualified sense] (but still primarily practical rather than theoretical) when my consideration is more reflective, reviewing my present commitments and past actions, contemplating future commitments and actions, or assessing the commitments, actions and characters of other persons . . .

My thesis, then, is this: one's primary understanding of human good, and of what it is worthwhile for human beings to seek to do, to get, to have and to be, is attained when one is considering what it would be good, worthwhile to do, to get, to have and to be—ie, by definition, when one is thinking practically. My thesis does not for a moment deny that the understanding thus attained can be integrated into a general account of human nature, ie of human potentialities and their various forms of fulfilment. What I do assert is that our primary grasp of what is good for us (or: really a fulfilment of our potentialities) is a practical grasp.

Finnis *The Fundamentals of Ethics* 11–12

Now any thesis about what is in this sense supremely good for you or me, or any other human being, can helpfully be expressed in various sorts of ways. It can be expressed as a thesis about what a human being should do or be; or what it is the business (not necessarily the *peculiar* function) of a human being to do or be; or what fulfils a human being; or what fully actualizes the

potentialities of human nature; or what is in keeping with human nature . . .
These last formulae, referring explicitly to human nature, can thus be a way of
expressing the conclusions of an openly evaluative, practical, ethical
investigation. Such references to what is (humanly) natural *need* not be
regarded as an appeal to, or expression of, some independent, 'value-free'
investigation of the sort that Veatch would call (Aristotelian) physics, and that
we might call general anthropology.

Finnis *The Fundamentals of Ethics* 20

There is a legitimate, theoretical (non-practical) investigation and description
of human nature, and it cannot be a satisfactory description unless it
incorporates results *which cannot be obtained except by that practical pursuit that
Aristotle called ethics*. In our theoretical descriptions of the nature of other types
of beings, we have to be content with what we can discover by the use of rather
'external' techniques; and those techniques will doubtless tell us much about
human beings, too. But why suppose that our techniques for developing a
description of *human* nature are limited to those available for describing beings
whose nature we do not share?

Finnis *The Fundamentals of Ethics* 20

Epistemologically, (knowledge of) human nature is not 'the basis of ethics';
rather, ethics is an indispensable preliminary to a full and soundly based
knowledge of human nature. What one can and should say about human
nature, as the result of one's ethical inquiries, is not mere rhetorical addition; it
finds a place in the sober and factual account of what it is to be a human being.

Finnis *The Fundamentals of Ethics* 21–22

I am not for a moment saying that everything that we know about human
nature comes from our ethical understanding. Nor am I saying that our ethical
understanding can be acquired independently of all 'factual', descriptive,
'theoretical' knowledge; I am not proposing a kind of ethical 'intuitionism' . . .
As I have said elsewhere:

> There is thus a mutual though not quite symmetrical *interdependence*
> between the project of describing human affairs by way of theory and the
> project of evaluating human options with a view, at least remotely, to
> acting reasonably and well. The evaluations are in no way deduced from
> the descriptions . . .; but one whose knowledge of the facts of the human
> situation is very limited is unlikely to judge well in discerning the
> practical implications of the basic values [which indeed cannot be
> grasped at all without a knowledge of possibilities]. Equally, the
> descriptions are not deduced from the evaluations; but without the
> evaluations one cannot determine what descriptions are really
> illuminating and significant.

Ethics is not deduced or inferred from metaphysics or anthropology. But a
mistaken metaphysics or anthropology will block one's reflective
understanding of the way in which one participates in the human goods
(particularly the good of practical reasonableness itself). If, for example, one
supposes that reason is the slave of the passions, a mere instrument for
efficiently sorting out and attaining wants that are simply given prior to all

understanding one will find no reason to give the requirements of practical reasonableness their architectonic and conclusive force.

Finnis The Fundamentals of Ethics 22

MODERN THEORIES OF NATURAL LAW

(a) H L A Hart and the 'minimum content theory of natural law'

Hart, a legal positivist, accepts that there is a 'core of good sense' within natural law doctrines.

> For it is a truth of some importance that for the adequate description not only of the law but of many other social institutions, a place must be reserved, besides definitions and ordinary statements of fact, for a third category of statements: those the truth of which is contingent on human beings and the world they live in retaining the salient characteristics which they have.

Hart The Concept of Law 195

There are certain rules which are essential if individuals are to live together. He places emphasis on an assumption of survival as a principal human goal; we are not members of a suicide club. This assumption constitutes the premise of his argument. The minor premise is supplied by certain indisputable facts, he calls them truisms, about man and the world. First, men are mutually vulnerable. Secondly, they are approximately equal in their abilities either to harm or help each other. Thirdly, being neither devils nor angels, it is a fact that they have limited altruism. Fourthly, the world has but limited resources. Last, they have limited intelligence and weakness of will.

Because of these factual, universal truisms, all societies must, of necessity, have certain rules that restrict violence, rules that protect property, and some rules which provide a system of promising. Notice he does not proceed to state the actual minimum universal rules.

Martin has subjected this version of natural law to close scrutiny.

HART'S ARGUMENT EXPOUNDED

Hart's argument for a natural law with minimum content is based on what he calls 'simple truisms.' These are:

- (T_1) Human beings are vulnerable to physical attack.
- (T_2) Human beings are approximately equal in mental and physical abilities.
- (T_3) Human beings have limited altruism.
- (T_4) Human beings have limited resources.
- (T_5) Human beings have limited understanding and strength of will.

Hart argues that things could have been different, that (T_1)–(T_5) are not logically necessary truths. For example, humans could have been built so as not to be vulnerable to attack from members of their own species and people might have been more like angels than they are. But although these things are logically possible, in our world human beings are vulnerable and are not angels.

Further Hart assumes that

(W)   Humans want to survive.

This is a contingent fact about human nature. This too could have been different, but in our world survival is a basic human desire. Survival, then, is a minimum goal for human law. As Hart puts it, 'Our concern is with social arrangements for continued existence, not with those of a suicide club.'

Given truisms (T_1)–(T_5) and the goal of survival, Hart argues that a certain minimum content of law is a 'natural necessity.' This minimum content is specified by Hart as follows:

(V)   Laws must have restrictions on the free exercise of violence.
(M)   Laws must be based on mutual forbearance.
(P)   Laws must regulate the use of property.
(D)   Laws must provide for the creation of obligations.
(S)   Laws must provide for sanctions if they are not obeyed.

What precisely is the connection between (T_1)–(T_5) and (W) on the one hand, and (V), (M), (P), (D), and (S) on the other? Hart does not claim that the facts specified by (T_1)–(T_5) and (W) cause the rules of law to have the content specified by (V), (M), (P), (D), and (S). The connection is rational, not causal. The facts specified by (T_1)–(T_5) 'afford a *reason* why, given survival as an aim, laws and morals should include a specific content. The general form of the argument is simply that without such a content laws and morals could not forward the minimum purpose of survival which men have in associating with each other.'

Hart stresses that the causal connections between certain child-rearing practices and the successful function of the law are not what he is concerned with. 'Connexions of this sort . . . are not mediated by *reasons*; for they do not relate the existence of certain rules to the conscious aims or purpose of those whose rules they are. Being fed in infancy in a certain way may well be shown to be a necessary condition or even a *cause* of a population developing or maintaining a moral or legal code, but it is not a *reason* for their doing so.' According to Hart, causal connections do not rest on truisms but are established by the sciences through observation and where possible experimentation.

Given this rational connection between the goal of survival, the truisms, and the minimum content of law, one can speak of the minimum content of law as a 'natural necessity.' By this term Hart wants to contrast his position with two others. Hart is not saying that it is logically necessary for law to have this minimum content. This would make the connection too strong, for given a different world in which the truisms (T_1)–(T_5) did not hold and given the aim of survival, laws without minimum content might be rational. Or given a different world in which people did not want to survive and the truisms (T_1)–(T_5) still held, it would not be rational to have laws with the minimum content required by Hart's theory. Nor is Hart just saying that as a matter of fact most legal systems have rules with minimum content. This makes the connection too weak, for, given the truisms and the goal of survival, it is rational for the legal system to have rules with minimum content.

However, Hart is not claiming that it is a natural necessity that the laws governing every group in society must have this minimum content. He argues that this minimum content may be extended to 'different ranges of persons' in different societies. In a slave society, for example, laws governing slaves would not have this minimum content. Hart's position seems to be that given

(1) $(T_1)-(T_5)$ and (W)

it is a natural necessity that

(2)   For every society there is at least one group in the society whose laws have minimum content (specified by (V), (M), (P), (D), and (S) above)

and that there is a rational connection between (1) and (2).

Hart's Argument Explicated

Hart is surely correct that $(T_1)-(T_5)$ and (W) provide a reason why (2) should be true. If this were all Hart is saying when he speaks of a rational connection between (1) and (2), there would be no disagreement. Hart's thesis would be uncontroversial and rather uninteresting. After all, $(T_1)-(T_5)$ and (W) might be one among many reasons for (2), and not a very important reason at that. So in taking this as well as other reasons into account it might not be rational (all things considered) to suppose that (2) should be true.

However, Hart seems to be saying more than this. He says that the 'general form of the argument is simply that without such a content law and morals could not forward the minimum purpose of survival.' He also says that given $(T_1)-(T_5)$ and (W) laws with minimum content are a 'natural necessity.' How can this stronger interpretation of Hart be understood?

One suggestion is that Hart is saying that (1) is a conclusive reason why (2) should be true. By 'conclusive reason,' I mean this. Assume:

(R)   People are rational.
(K_1) People know that (1).
(N)   People are not prevented from carrying out their plans.

Then to say that (1) is a conclusive reason why (2) should be the case is to say that (R) and (K_1) and (N) entail (2) and that (1) is true.

We may assume that (1) is true since (1) consists of the truisms $(T_1)-(T_5)$ and the uncontroversial (W). To say that the conjunction of (R) and (K_1) and (N) entails (2) is to say that the statement

(3)   If (R) and (K_1) and (N), then (2)

is a necessary truth.

It is important that what I am saying not be confused with the claim that

(3')   If (1), then (2)

is a necessary truth. It is clearly not. Furthermore, it is important to see that my explication does not conflict with Hart's insistence that (2) is a natural necessity given (1) and not a logical necessity. Statement (3), not (2), is logically necessary on the present interpretation and the claim that (3) is logically necessary is compatible with the claim that (2) is not.

This explication of Hart makes good sense of two rather obscure statements of his mentioned above: (a) Given (1), (2) is a natural necessity but not a logical necessity. (b) There is a rational (but not a causal) connection between (1) and (2). Statement (a) is simply an elliptical way of calling attention to the idea that (2) is neither logically necessary nor accidentally true. Statement (2) is a nomological statement that allegedly follows from (R) and (K) and (N). Statement (b) is an elliptical way of calling our attention to the idea that rational people with knowledge of (1) will construct societies with certain kinds of laws if they are not prevented. It does not mean that the facts described by (1) cause societies with laws of a certain kind to be constructed.

HART'S THEORY EVALUATED

Given this interpretation. Hart's argument is wrong, for (2) is not a logical consequence of (R) and (K$_1$) and N. One can imagine a case in which the conjunction of (R) and (K$_1$) and N is true but (2) is false. Put less formally, Hart is mistaken to suppose that rational people who knew that (1) would construct societies with laws with a natural law minimum content unless they were prevented from doing so. It is important to see that I am not attacking Hart's truisms. I will question the truth of (3), not (1).

Consider a world in which people have a desire to survive, where (T$_1$)–(T$_5$) hold true, where people are rational and know that they want to survive and know that (T$_1$)–(T$_5$), but where human nature is such that laws with the minimum content specified above are not the best way to further survival. Suppose, for example, that in this world positive reinforcement is a much more effective way of getting people not to break the law than the use of sanctions and that people know this. Indeed, suppose that in this world it is well known that the use of sanctions would so outrage the population that it would indirectly cause civil strife. So far from sanctions' inducing obedience to law, they would cause disobedience. Thus (R) and (K$_1$) and (N) do not entail (2) and consequently (1) cannot provide a conclusive reason why (2) should be true.

This suggests another interpretation of the relationship of (1) to (2). Since (R) and (K$_1$) and (N) combined do not entail (2) straightaway, perhaps R and (K$_1$) and (N) in combination with other premises entail (2). What would these other premises be? Consider:

(4)   In all societies sanctions are the most effective ways to prevent people from breaking the law

and

(K$_2$)   People know that (4).

Then we can say that (1) and (4) together provide a conclusive reason for

(2′)   Every society has at least one group of people in the society governed by laws with sanctions for breaking the law.

This means only that the conjunction (R) and (K$_1$) and (K$_2$) and (N) entails (2′) and that (1) and (4) are true.

The trouble with this suggestion is that it is by no means clear that (4) is true. In fact, some psychologists such as B. F. Skinner have maintained that positive reinforcement is more effective than sanctions.

When Hart contrasts causal and rational connections he seems to be suggesting that rational connections, unlike causal connections, rest upon truisms and that evidence from the social sciences is not needed to establish them. But on the present interpretation evidence that presumably is not available is needed to establish (4). Thus, (1) and (4) combined cannot provide a conclusive reason why (2) should be true, since (4) is dubious.

Could a similar argument be used against other aspects of the minimum content of natural law? I believe so. Consider rules governing property. (R) and (K$_1$) and (N) in conjunction do not entail

(2″)   For every society there is at least one group of people in the society that has rules governing its use of property.

Consequently, (1) cannot provide a conclusive reason why (2) should be true.

To see this, imagine a world in which people have the desire to survive and in which (T_1)–(T_5) hold, but in which psychological, sociological, and economic factors different from ours are present. Consider a world of pacifist communists. They believe that the land and material goods belong to no one or perhaps to everyone. Anyone can help themselves to anything, including what anyone produces. Everyone is expected to do their share, but if some people do not, that is something the others believe one must live with. These people believe that it is far better that people should help themselves without doing their share than that there should be rules forbidding their behavior. In such a society there would be no institution of property, at least as Hart seems to understand it. There would be, to use Hart's example, no rules 'excluding persons generally other than the "owner" from entry on, or the use of the land, or from taking or using material things.'

Could people survive in this society? It may be suggested that they could not; that without rules to stop them, people would want more and more, would acquire more land and more material goods in their insatiable greed; that their uncontrolled greed, given limited resources, would make survival in this world impossible. But in the world I am imagining people are not greedy. This seems to be quite compatible with Hart's truisms. Thus, the truism that human beings have limited altruism refers to people's desire to inflict violence on one another, not to their greed. In fact, one can imagine that, given people's psychological make-up, in this world rules regulating property might cause such greed that no sanctions could stop it. So, rather than furthering survival, rules of property might hinder it.

Consider, however, the following:

(5) People are greedy in all social and economic systems.
(6) Because of limited resources, uncontrolled greed makes survival impossible.

Let us suppose:

(K_3) = People know that (5) and (6).

Then it might be argued that (R) and (K_1) and (N) entail $(2'')$ and, consequently that (1), (5), and (6) combined provide a conclusive reason why $(2'')$ should be true.

But even if one accepts (6), the truth of (5) is by no means obvious. Some theorists have suggested that greed is a function of the social and economic system people live in and that those who lived in a non-capitalistic system would not be greedy. Whether this is true or not remains to be shown, of course, but the important point for our discussion is that the truth of (5) is not known. Consequently, the fact that (1) and (5) and (6) combined provide a conclusive reason for (2) and (5) is dubious.

Consider now the laws restricting the free exercise of violence. Again we may question if (1) is a conclusive reason why it should be the case that

$(2''')$ Every society has at least one group of people in the society governed by laws restricting the free exercise of violence.

Do (R) and (K_1) and (N) entail $(2''')$? I think not. One can imagine a society in which there are no laws forbidding the free exercise of violence (just as in our society there are no laws forbidding people from hurting other people's feelings or being impolite) and yet the chance of survival is close to ours. In this imaginary society, of course, people are in general opposed to violence and take steps to protect themselves from it. Someone who desires to hurt or kill someone else might be deterred from doing so by private self-defense measures. But there would be no laws against violence and people in this society might well be appalled at the very idea of such laws. (Compare people's reaction in our society to the very idea of laws forbidding hurting other people's feelings or being rude.)

What would be the individual survival rate in such a society? I imagine a society in which the survival rate is close to ours. I construct this imaginary society in such a way that makes this possible. First, in such a society everyone is trained in self-defense from childhood; people are always armed. Housing and clothing are designed with self-defense in mind. People who attack others can be fairly well assured that they will meet stiff and sophisticated resistance. Second, people in such a society are psychologically prepared for violent attack and are determined to defend themselves. Third, people in this society have a sophisticated defense technology. For example, they might have metal detectors built into their clothing to warn them that someone with a gun is nearby.

It might be argued that the above considerations neglect the possibility of many people banding together in order to hurt or kill some individual person, that self-defense training and weapons would be powerless against large numbers of violent people working in unison. However, there is nothing in this imaginary society, as I have conceived it, that necessitates people's protecting themselves individually.

A defender of Hart may argue that, once this last step is taken, Hart's point must be granted. For if groups band together for mutual protection there must be rules restricting the free exercise of violence among members of this group. This is tantamount to granting (2'''). Consequently (1) *is* a conclusive reason for (2''') once the need for mutual protection societies is granted. However, there is nothing inevitable about large groups of people banding together to hurt individuals. Whether violent people work individually or in groups is a function of certain psychological and sociological factors operating in a particular society. In the society I imagine violent people are always loners. This is compatible with Hart's truisms.

Moreover, even if large numbers of people are needed to protect someone from group violence it does not follow that a mutual protection society is essential. If I have ten people to protect me and my house from my enemies, who have banded together to kill me, it is not necessary that my ten guards and I form a mutual protection society. My guards may protect me just because they are getting good pay and not because I will protect them in turn. There need be no rules restricting the free exercise of violence in order to hire bodyguards. The bodyguards know, of course, that if they attack me or one another they will not get paid, and that if I attack them they will no longer want to protect me. Such restraint is not based on rules, but on economic advantages. Whatever may be the case in ours, I assume that in this society considerations of economic advantages are paramount.

The above considerations suggest other premises that need to be added to (1) to provide a conclusive reason. Consider:

(7)   In every society, there is no adequate individual self-protection against group violence.

(8)   In every society there will be group violence.

(9)   In every society without a public police force the only adequate protection against group violence is mutual protection sub-societies.

If

(K_4)   People know that (7), (8), and (9)

then we could say that (1), (7), (8) and (9) provide a conclusive reason for (2'''). But, for the reasons given above, even if one accepts (7), (8) and (9) are not obviously true. Consequently, it is not clear that (1), (7), (8) and (9) do provide a conclusive reason for (2''').

COULD HART MEET THE CRITICISM?

Can Hart's theory be reformulated to meet my objections? The various reformulations that suggest themselves either trivialize his theory or else are implausible.

One proposal has in a way already been considered. Hart might say that (1) provides *a* reason why (2) should be the case but not a conclusive reason. Given this formulation of his position, my criticism that rational people who believe (1) would not necessarily bring about (2) if they were not prevented would be irrelevant. Since rational people would simply take (1) into account in constructing their laws, their laws would not necessarily have the minimum content specified by Hart.

The problem with this suggestion is that it trivializes Hart's thesis. Who would want to deny that (1) is something rational people would take into account in constructing their laws? But, of course, rational people take all sorts of things into account in constructing their laws. Statement (1) may have no particular significance and may have little importance.

Another proposal would be to say that only under *some* conditions would rational people who know (1) construct societies with laws with minimum content unless they were prevented. In our terms the claim would be that

(3'') There is some condition C such that if (R) and (K_1) and (N) and C, then (2).

Such a claim would be trivial since C could be (2) itself, consequently (3'') would be the barest tautology.

Yet another suggestion would be to specify condition C in some particular way. But how could it be so specified without granting the very point raised above, namely that (R) and (K_1) and (N) entail (2) *only* given certain particular assumptions about the society in which people live and the psychological motivation of the people and so on? More importantly, this would be to give up Hart's major idea that the minimum content of natural law is based on truisms and the desire to survive; it would undercut completely the generality of his theory and his own perception of it. As I have stressed, Hart intends his theory to apply to all societies—not just societies of a certain kind—and to all people—not just people motivated in certain ways—for which (1) holds true. He envisions his theory as being in the tradition of natural law theory, which certainly had these broad and general aims.

Finally, it might be proposed that (1) would provide rational people with a *prima facie* conclusive reason for (2). Rational people who knew (1) would have conclusive reasons to construct laws with minimum content unless there were special and abnormal circumstances that prevailed in their society. Thus on the assumption

(A) There are no known abnormal or special circumstances prevailing in any society

the following would be entailed:

(3''') If (R) and (K_1) and (N) and (A), then (2).

The trouble with this suggestion is that it is unclear why it is supposed that the circumstances that might induce rational people not to construct laws with minimum content are special or abnormal. The hypothesis that reinforcement and not sanctions is the most effective way to prevent people from breaking the law is not dependent on any special or abnormal circumstances. Furthermore, what one takes to be special or abnormal may vary from one perspective to another. A society of pacifist communists may appear abnormal to us. To them our society of aggression and capitalism would appear abnormal.

I conclude that the suggestion that Hart could easily meet the above criticism is implausible.

Martin *The Legal Philosophy of H L A Hart* 181–190

(b)　John Finnis and a restatement of natural law

John Finnis's book, *Natural Law and Natural Rights* (1980), in attempting a restatement of natural law philosophy, is probably the most important, as well as the most erudite, work to appear on this subject for some time. Consequently, we intend a relatively detailed coverage, particularly of the early sections of the book. We shall also have occasion to refer to his later book, *The Fundamentals of Ethics* (1983).

Ethics is practical

The sophistication of Finnis's natural law philosophy will not be fully appreciated unless a wider question is confronted: what does reflection about ethics or questions concerning correct human conduct entail? Clearly such reflection has common ground with other investigations, for example, in mathematics, history or science. They are all theoretical pursuits in that they are prompted by a concern with truth, or an approximation thereto, with the 'right' answers, with knowledge for its own sake. Ethics, however, is unique in that it encompasses an additional dimension: it is also practical. What does this mean?

> . . . one chooses to seek that truth not only 'for its own sake', nor simply for the sake of becoming a person who knows the truth about that subject-matter, but rather (and equally primarily) in order that one's choices, actions and whole way of life will be (and known by oneself to be) good, worthwhile.

Finnis *The Fundamentals of Ethics* 4

Academic investigation into this subject matter, therefore, has two objectives in view:

> It is indeed hard to focus steadily on the fact that this academic pursuit, alone amongst all academic pursuits, has two formal, primary objects (objectives, goods in view); (i) truth about a certain subject-matter, and (ii) the instantiation of that truth in choices and actions—choices and actions of which the first, but only the first, is the investigation and affirmation of that truth (and acceptance of it as the good which discloses all the other real goods to be attained and participated in by my action).

Finnis *The Fundamentals of Ethics* 4

The singular quality of practicality is the formative use to which my theoretical search for the 'right' answer is put. It becomes participating in *my* life decisions: I will practise its precepts, whereas after a successful theoretical investigation into science etc, the 'I', the theorist, 'disappears from view'.

It follows that the slogan 'ethics is practical' has far deeper meaning than the assertion that it is practical because its subject involves human conduct, an assertion that would be a truism in a whole range of other disciplines.

> Notice: ethics is not practical merely by having as its subject-matter human action (*praxis*). Large parts of history and of psychology and of anthropology have human *praxis* as their subject-matter; but these pursuits are not practical. No: ethics is practical because my choosing and acting and living in a certain sort of way (and thus my becoming a certain sort of person . . .) is not a secondary (albeit inseparable and welcome) objective and side-effect of success in the intellectual enterprise; rather it is *the very objective primarily envisaged* as well as the subject-matter about which I hope to be able to affirm true propositions.
>
> Finnis *The Fundamentals of Ethics* 3

The relevance of this claim will emerge while unravelling the steps in this theory of natural law, a theory which furnishes 'the rational foundations for moral judgment'.

The basic goods for human beings

There are certain objective goods or values which we need to promote and realise in our lives if our lives are to be worthwhile. As with all natural law philosophy, the claim is that an understanding of law, morality, justice, authority, etc rests ultimately on a real comprehension of human good or well-being. All these storm-centres of legal philosophy emanate from a theory of basic human goods. The inventory of basic goods is: life, knowledge, play, aesthetic experience, sociability (friendship), practical reasonableness, religion.

The value of *life* is the first basic value manifesting itself in the drive for self-preservation. As well as including anything done by man to further this preservation (eg medicine, agriculture) it also encompasses the continuation of life by procreation. *Knowledge* corresponds to the drive of curiosity and this takes in an impressive terrain from the 'intellectual cathedrals' of science and philosophy to the more mundane satisfaction derived in 'detective stories, daily newspapers, and gossip'. Knowledge, or truth, as this good could be renamed, is considered desirable for its own sake and not merely instrumentally to some other end, for example, as being useful in pursuit of survival, power, popularity or passing examinations: it is 'speculative' rather than 'instrumental'.

Play, for its own sake, is an undeniable feature in human existence. *Beauty*, unlike play, need not involve any action of one's own. *Sociability* ranges from a mere minimum of peace and harmony to its 'strongest form in the flowering of full friendship', which involves an active concern with the well-being of the friend.

Practical reasonableness becomes a seminal concept. How are we to make practical decisions in the pursuit of these basic human goods?

> . . . the basic good of being able to bring one's own intelligence to bear effectively in practical reasoning that issues in action on the problems of choosing one's actions and life-style and shaping one's own character. Negatively, this involves that one has a measure of effective freedom:

positively, it involves that one seeks to bring an intelligent and reasonable order into one's own actions and habits and practical attitudes. . . . This value is thus complex, involving freedom and reason, integrity and authenticity. But it has a sufficient unity to be treated as one; and for a label I choose 'practical reasonableness' . . .

Finnis *Natural Law and Natural Rights* 88–89

Although its area of operation is mapped out by the other basic goods, it is itself one of the seven.

Practical reasonableness is an opportunity. Being reasonable in one's choices, commitments, actions and habits is a form of life in which one can participate to a greater or lesser degree. In short, it is a good, indeed a basic good, neither reducible to nor superior or alternative to any of the other basic goods: life, knowledge, play, creativity, friendship . . .

Practical reasonableness makes its claims upon us because it is a basic aspect of human flourishing. Its claim is: to direct the way in which we seek to participate in each and all of the basic human goods. It is architectonic: directive, in charge . . .

Finnis *The Fundamentals of Ethics* 70

Religion has a wider meaning than usual. It corresponds to any concern for the relationship between basic goods and the cosmos, including the origins, if any, of the cosmos. An atheist, who after all has views about such matters, does value this good.

The basic goods are objective, basic, fundamental, pre-moral and self-evident

The objectivity of the basic goods evidences itself from a survey of anthropological research, which leads to 'some rather confident assertions':

All human societies show a concern for the value of human life; in all, self-preservation is generally accepted as a proper motive for action, and in none is the killing of other human beings permitted without some fairly definite justification. All human societies regard the procreation of a new human life as in itself a good thing unless there are special circumstances. No human society fails to restrict sexual activity; in all societies there is some prohibition of incest, some opposition to boundless promiscuity and to rape, some favour for stability and permanence in sexual relations. All human societies display a concern for truth, through education of the young in matters not only practical (eg avoidance of dangers) but also speculative or theoretical (eg religion). Human beings, who can survive infancy only by nurture, live in or on the margins of some society which invariably extends beyond the nuclear family, and all societies display a favour for the values of co-operation, of common over individual good, of obligation between individuals, and of justice within groups. All know friendship. All have some conception of *meum* and *tuum*, title or property, and of reciprocity. All value play, serious and formalized, or relaxed and recreational. All treat the bodies of dead members of the group in some traditional and ritual fashion different from their procedures for rubbish disposal. All display a concern for powers or principles which are to be respected as suprahuman; in one form or another, religion is universal.

Finnis *Natural Law and Natural Rights* 83–84

They are basic because all other values that exist are subordinate to these.

> ... there are countless aspects of human self-determination and self-realization besides the seven basic aspects which I have listed. But these other aspects, such as courage, generosity, moderation, gentleness, and so on, are not themselves basic values; rather, they are ways, not means, but modes: of pursuing the basic values, and fit (or are deemed by some individual, or group, or culture, to fit) a man for their pursuit.
>
> Finnis *Natural Law and Natural Rights* 90–91

What is the difference between a 'means' and a 'mode'?

> ... it seems to me that those seven purposes are all of the basic purposes of human action, and that any other purpose which you or I might recognize and pursue will turn out to represent, or be constituted of, some aspect(s) of some or all of them.
>
> Finnis *Natural Law and Natural Rights* 92

All seven are equally fundamental. Consequently, there is no hierarchy within the structure of basic values.

> If one focuses on the value of speculative truth, it can reasonably be regarded as more important than anything; knowledge can be regarded as the most important thing to acquire; life can be regarded as merely a pre-condition, of lesser or no intrinsic value; play can be regarded as frivolous; one's concern about 'religious' questions can seem just an aspect of the struggle against error, superstition, and ignorance; friendship can seem worth forgoing, or be found exclusively in sharing and enhancing knowledge; and so on. But one can shift one's focus. If one is drowning, or, again, if one is thinking about one's child who died soon after birth, one is inclined to shift one's focus to the value of life simply as such. The life will not be regarded as a mere pre-condition of anything else; rather, play and knowledge and religion will seem secondary, even rather optional extras. But one can shift one's focus, in this way, one-by-one right round the circle of basic values that constitute the horizon of our opportunities. We can focus on play, and reflect that we spend most of our time working simply in order to afford leisure: play is performances enjoyed for their own sake as performances and thus can seem to be the point of everything; knowledge and religion and friendship can seem pointless unless they issue in the playful mastery of wisdom, or participation in the play of the divine puppetmaster (as Plato said), or in the playful intercourse of mind or body that friends can most enjoy.
>
> Thus I have illustrated this point in relation to life, truth, and play; the reader can easily test and confirm it in relation to each of the other basic values. Each is fundamental. None is more fundamental than any of the others, for each can reasonably be focused upon, and each, when focused upon, claims a priority of value. Hence there is no objective priority of value amongst them.
>
> Finnis *Natural Law and Natural Rights* 92–93

Although fundamental, there is freedom of choice.

Of course, each one of us can reasonably *choose* to treat one or some of the values as of more importance in *his* life. A scholar chooses to dedicate himself to the pursuit of knowledge, and thus gives its demands priority, to a greater or lesser degree (and perhaps for a whole lifetime), over the friendships, the worship, the games, the art and beauty that he might otherwise enjoy. He might have been out saving lives through medicine or famine relief, but he chooses not to. But he may change his priorities: he may risk his life to save a drowning man, or give up his career to nurse a sick wife or to fight for his community. The change is not in the relation between the basic values as that relation might reasonably have seemed to him before he chose his life-plan (and as it should always seem to him when he is considering human opportunity and flourishing in general); rather, the change is in his chosen life-plan. That chosen plan *made* truth more important and fundamental for him. His new choice changes the status of that value *for him*; the change is in him. Each of us has a subjective order of priority amongst the basic values; this ranking is no doubt partly shifting and partly stable, but is in any case essential if we are to act at all to some purpose. But one's reasons for choosing the particular ranking that one does choose are reasons that properly relate to one's temperament, upbringing, capacities and opportunities, not to differences of rank of intrinsic value between the basic values.

Finnis *Natural Law and Natural Rights* 93–94

By 'good' or 'basic value' he does not yet mean 'moral good'.

Certainly, there seems to be no practical principle which has the specificity we expect of a 'moral rule' and which is accepted, even 'in principle' or 'in theory', amongst all human beings. But my present concern is not at all with 'morals' or 'ethics'.

Finnis *Natural Law and Natural Rights* 84

Therefore, taking for example knowledge as a basic value:

To think of knowledge as a value is not, as such, to think of it as a 'moral' value; 'truth is a good' is not, here, to be understood as a moral proposition, and 'knowledge is to be pursued' is not to be understood, here, as stating a moral obligation, requirement, prescription, or recommendation. In our reflective analysis of practical reasonableness, morality comes later.

Finnis *Natural Law and Natural Rights* 62

Although, in themselves, pre-moral, they furnish 'the evaluative substratum of all moral judgments'.

How are we to identify these seven as being 'good' in a pre-moral sense? Is he saying that because of their universality they must be 'good'? Is he arguing that because they constitute an irrefutable component of human existence, they are good? Again, taking knowledge as our example:

Is it not the case that knowledge is really a good, an aspect of authentic human flourishing, and that the principle which expresses its value formulates a real (intelligent) reason for action? It seems clear that such indeed is the case, and that there are no sufficient reasons for doubting it to be so. The good of knowledge is self-evident, obvious. It cannot be demonstrated, but equally it needs no demonstration.

Finnis Natural Law and Natural Rights 64–65

Does self-evidence mean they are obvious to everyone? Is it synonymous with innateness?

> This is not to say that everyone actually does recognize the value of knowledge, or that there are no pre-conditions for recognizing that value. The principle that truth (and knowledge) is worth pursuing is not somehow innate, inscribed on the mind at birth. On the contrary, the value of truth becomes obvious only to one who has experienced the urge to question, who has grasped the connection between question and answer, who understands that knowledge is constituted by correct answers to particular questions, and who is aware of the possibility of further questions and of other questioners who like himself could enjoy the advantage of attaining correct answers. A new-born child, for example, has presumably not had any such set of felt inclinations, memories, understandings, and (in short) experiences.

Finnis Natural Law and Natural Rights 65

We must distinguish the concept of self-evidence from depth of feelings.

> Nowadays, any claim that something is self-evident is commonly misunderstood by philosophers. They think that any such claim either asserts or presupposes that the criterion of the truth of the allegedly self-evident principle, proposition, in fact is one's *feeling of certitude* about it. This is indeed a misunderstanding. Self-evident principles such as those I have been discussing are not validated by feelings. On the contrary, they are themselves the criteria whereby we discriminate between feelings, and discount some of our feelings (including feelings of certitude), however intense, as irrational or unwarranted, misleading or delusive.

Finnis Natural Law and Natural Rights 69

Then comes his most revealing description of self-evidence: the buck stops here.

> Non-derivability in some cases amounts to lack of justification and of objectivity. But in other cases it betokens self-evidence; and these cases are to be found in every field of inquiry. For in every field there is and must be, at some point or points, an end to derivation and inference. At that point or points we find ourselves in face of the self-evident, which makes possible all subsequent inferences in that field.

Finnis Natural Law and Natural Rights 70

Consequently, he claims that he is not commencing with a factual observation or assertion from which he deduces a normative conclusion.

> In asking oneself whether knowledge is indeed a value for its own sake: thus, a basic value, one should not be deflected by the fact that one's inclination to seek truth has psychological roots. It may well be that at an early stage in the life of the mind the urge to know is scarcely differentiated from other urges, such as

the sexual drive. This early lack of differentiation may be never wholly surmounted, so that the one urge remains capable not only of deflecting but also of reinforcing the other. Such facts, interesting and important as they may be in some contexts, are not relevant to the question 'Is knowledge indeed a good, objectively worth pursuing'. In considering the question: 'Is the psychologist's opinion that curiosity is a form of sexuality a true or at least a warranted opinion?', it is relevant to attend to the coherence of the psychologist's hypothesis, to the pertinence of his evidence, to the soundness of his inferences. But it is *not* relevant to ask whether the psychologist's opinion emerged in his psyche at the call of his sexuality or as a reflection of his organic constitution or under the influence of any other such sub-rational cause. The soundness of an answer to a particular question is never established or disconfirmed by the answer to the *entirely different* question of what are the physical, biological, and psychological pre-conditions and concomitants of the raising of that question (or any question) and of the proposing of that answer (or any answer). And all this holds true of the answer 'Yes, obviously' to the question 'Is knowledge worth having?'.

Just as we should not appeal to causes, pre-conditions, and concomitants in order to raise an illegitimate doubt about the self-evidence of the value of knowledge, so we should not seek a deduction or inference of that value from facts. If one is to go beyond the felt urge of curiosity to an understanding grasp of the value of knowledge, one certainly must know at least the fact that some questions can be answered. Moreover, one certainly will be assisted if one also knows such facts as that answers tend to hang together in systems that tend to be illuminating over as wide a range as the data which stimulate one's questions. But, one who, thus knowing the possibility of attaining truth, is enabled thereby to grasp the value of that possible object and attainment is not inferring the value from the possibility. No such inference is possible. No value can be deduced or otherwise inferred from a fact or set of facts.

Nor can one validly infer the value of knowledge from the fact (if fact it be) that 'all men desire to know'. The *universality* of a desire is not a sufficient basis for inferring that the object of that desire is really desirable, objectively good. Nor is such a basis afforded by the fact that the desire or inclination manifests, or is part of, a *deep* structure shaping the human mind, or by the fact that the desire, or the structure, is *ineradicable*, or by the fact that in whole or part the desire is (or is not) *common* to all animals, or by the fact that it is (or is not) *peculiar* to human beings.

Finnis Natural Law and Natural Rights 65–66

The claim is: no 'ought' from 'is' deduction is deployed in his theory of natural law. Indeed:

For the moment let us reflect on the fact that, for one who considers something like knowledge to be a good, the true expression of his opinion and attitude is *not* 'it is good because or in so far as I desire it', *but* 'I desire it because and in so far as it is good'.

Finnis Natural Law and Natural Rights 70

This is his conclusion:

> What *are* the basic aspects of my well-being? Here each one of us, however extensive his knowledge of the interests of other people and other cultures, is alone with his own intelligent grasp of the indemonstrable, because self-evident, first principles of his own practical reasoning. From one's capacity to grasp intelligently the basic forms of good as 'to-be-pursued' one gets one's ability, in the descriptive disciplines of history and anthropology, to sympathetically (though not uncritically) see the point of actions, life-styles, characters, and cultures that one would not choose for oneself. And one's speculative knowledge of other people's interests and achievements does not leave unaffected one's practical understanding of the forms of good that lie open to one's choice. But there is no inference from fact to value. At this point in our discourse (or private meditation), inference and proof are left behind (or left until later), and the proper form of discourse is: '. . . is a good, in itself, don't you think?'

> Finnis *Natural Law and Natural Rights* 85–86

This characterisation of human goods is a direct result of his contention that ethics is practical. The importance of natural inclination and desires is stressed, but it is by an 'insight' that one understands some inclinations as being 'towards desirable objects'. This is the process of practical reasoning that avoids any 'ought' from 'is' deduction.

> . . . one proceeds by reflecting on one's own wanting, deciding and acting; and this reflection must not be an attempt to peer inside oneself, or to catch oneself as it were in a mirror out of the corner of one's eye: those empiricist methods, based on the uncritical fancy that understanding is just a matter of opening one's eyes (or other senses) and looking, yield nothing but illusions. Reflection on practical reasoning and human action is truly empirical when it seeks to understand human capacities by understanding human acts and to understand those acts by understanding their object(ive)s. Thus the revealing question is the question 'Why?', not interpreted blankly as if one were investigating iron filings jumping to a magnet or the ricochet of billiard balls, but humanly and intelligently as 'What for?' Only thus will one be able to describe one's actions as they really are, and oneself as the agent one really is. And only thus will the relations between desire and understanding in the identification and pursuit of human goods be accurately known.

> Finnis *The Fundamentals of Ethics* 51–52

He continues:

> . . . when one pursues the question 'What for?' to the point where no further such question is intelligent, one arrives, not at a 'contingent desire' or state of feeling . . . to be explained in turn by the mechanics, biology and/or psychology of 'human nature'. Rather, one arrives at the perception (ie the understanding or intelligent discernment) of a basic form of human flourishing in which, not one human being on one occasion, but somehow all human beings in appropriate circumstances can participate.

> Finnis *The Fundamentals of Ethics* 52

There can be a legitimate theoretical (non-practical) analysis of human nature, eg anthropology, but the connection between practical reasoning and a true undertaking of human good lies at the heart of Finnis.

Knowledge as a basic good attracts an argument separate from self-evidence, although this argument 'may help to undermine sceptical doubts about all and any of the basic goods'.

> In the case of the basic values and practical principles to be identified in the next chapter, the discussion of their self-evidence and objectivity would have to rest at this point. But in the case of the basic value of knowledge we can go one step further. We can show that *any* argument raised by the sceptic is going to be self-defeating. To show this is not to show that the basic value of knowledge is self-evident or objective; it is only to show that counter-arguments are invalid.
>
> Finnis *Natural Law and Natural Rights* 73

This is the concept of retorsiveness.

> The sceptical assertion that knowledge is not a good is operationally self-refuting. For one who makes such an assertion, intending it as a serious contribution to rational discussion, is implicitly committed to the proposition that he believes his assertion is worth making, and worth making *qua* true; he thus is committed to the proposition that he believes that truth is a good worth pursuing or knowing. But the sense of his original assertion was precisely that truth is not a good worth pursuing or knowing. Thus he is implicitly committed to formally contradictory beliefs.
>
> One can certainly toy with the notion that knowledge is not a good worth pursuing. But the fact that to *assert* this whether to an audience, or as the judgment concluding one's own inner cogitations, would be operationally self-refuting should persuade the sceptic to cut short idle doubting. Self-defeating positions should be abandoned. The sceptic, on this as on other matters, can maintain coherence by *asserting* nothing; but coherence is not the only requirement of rationality.
>
> Finnis *Natural Law and Natural Rights* 74–75

Practical reasonableness

The ten principles that comprise the basic requirement of practical reasonableness, although they are themselves prior to morality, transform the seven pre-moral goods into a theory of morality; they lead to moral requirements. The ten principles distinguish between social and unsocial practical thinking. Sound practical thinking then distinguishes between morally right and wrong action.

> Thus, speaking very summarily, we could say that the requirements to which we now turn express the 'natural law method' of working out the (moral) 'natural law' from the first (pre-moral) 'principles of natural law'. Using only the modern terminology (itself of uncertain import) of 'morality', we can say that the following . . . concern the sorts of reasons why (and thus the ways in which) there are things that morally ought (not) to be done.
>
> Finnis *Natural Law and Natural Rights* 103

He places great importance on these ten 'intermediate principles'.

> The history of moral philosophy, especially in the centuries during which it
> has sought to distinguish its method from the method proper to theology, is the
> history of a search for the missing *intermediate principles*. This search for
> principles, to guide the transition from judgments about human goods to
> judgments about the right thing to do here and now, has been waylaid by all
> sorts of intellectual, spiritual and cultural confusions.

Finnis The Fundamentals of Ethics 70

A theory of morality emerges:

> Ordinary 'moral principles', about murder, stealing, promise-keeping,
> calumny, and so on, can be reached by arguments which start from one or
> more of the intermediate principles and have as their middle term one or other
> of the basic human goods. That is why I have called these intermediate
> principles the *basic* requirements of practical reasonableness.

Finnis The Fundamentals of Ethics 74

The 'intermediate principles' of practical reasonableness are: to form a rational
plan of life; to have no arbitrary preferences among the values, recognising the
importance of all seven; to have no arbitrary preferences among persons;
recognising impartiality among persons; to maintain some degree of detachment
from one's projects; not to abandon projects too lightly; to pursue the goods
efficiently; to respect every basic value recognising that one should not choose to
do any act which *of itself does nothing but* damage a realisation of or participation in
any one of the basic forms of human good; to seek the good of the community; to
follow one's conscience; not to pick mere simulations of real goods.

> The first three respond to the multiplicity of basic goods, of opportunities of
> participating in them, of persons who can participate in them . . .: (1) have a
> harmonious set of orientations, purposes and commitments; (2) do not leave
> out of account, or arbitrarily discount or exaggerate, any of the basic human
> goods; (3) do not leave out of account, or arbitrarily discount or exaggerate,
> the goodness of other people's participation in human goods. The next two
> respond to the emotional pull of immoderate and one-eyed enthusiasm and of
> apathy, inertia, laziness . . .: (4) do not attribute to any particular project the
> overriding and unconditional significance which only a basic human good and
> a general commitment can claim; (5) pursue one's general commitments with
> creativity and do not abandon them lightly. The next calls for more than mere
> well-meaning and good intentions: (6) do not waste your opportunities by
> using needlessly inefficient methods, and do not overlook the foreseeable bad
> consequences of your choices . . . The next is the requirement insisted upon by
> St Paul and, as the second formulation of this categorical imperative, by Kant;
> I formulate it thus: (7) do not choose directly against any basic human
> good . . . The next acknowledges that the human goods are realized and
> protected by, *inter alia*, the actions of groups and of group members acting as
> such: (8) foster the common good of your communities. The last of the
> requirements . . . responds to the problem of extending reasonable judgment
> into reasonable choice, in the face of conformism and other temptations: (9) do
> not act contrary to your conscience, ie against your best judgment about the

implications for your own action of these requirements of practical reasonableness and the moral principles they generate or justify.

To those I would now add another . . . do not choose apparent goods, knowing them to be only the simulations of real goods, even when the simulation brings real emotions or experiences, real satisfactions.

Finnis *The Fundamentals of Ethics* 75

The fact that there are seven equally fundamental values and not just one is the reason for these abstract requirements of method. Therefore taking the first requirement, because there is an infinite number of ways in which we are capable of participation in each one of the seven, we are forced to unite decisions about projects through which we pursue the goods: a rational plan becomes a necessity.

It will be apparent that these requirements are expressions of the most general moral principle—that one remain open to integral human fulfilment—in the various normative and existential contexts in which choice must respond to that most general principle. Hence the evident overlap between many of the requirements. Hence, too, the possibility of other formulations or other intermediate principles . . .

Finnis *The Fundamentals of Ethics* 76

The idea of community and the common good

Why not pursue the basic goods solely for ourselves? How do the objective goods provide a basis for a theory of morality? The human goods and the manner in which they are to be sought need to be considered in the context of a community of human beings. Only in such a context of communal life are there the necessary conditions for the pursuit of the goods.

For there is a 'common good' for human beings, inasmuch as life, knowledge, play, aesthetic experience, friendship, religion, and freedom in practical reasonableness are good for any and every person. And each of these human values is itself a 'common good' inasmuch as it can be participated in by an inexhaustible number of persons in an inexhaustible variety of ways or on an inexhaustible variety of occasions. These two senses of 'common good' are to be distinguished from a third, from which, however, they are not radically separate. This third sense of 'common good' is the one commonly intended throughout this book, and it is: a set of conditions which enables the members of a community to attain for themselves reasonable objectives, or to realize reasonably for themselves the value(s), for the sake of which they have reason to collaborate with each other (positively and/or negatively) in a community.

Finnis *Natural Law and Natural Rights* 155

There is a warning.

Notice that this definition neither asserts nor entails that the members of a community must all have the same values or objectives (or set of values or objectives); it implies only that there be some set (or set of sets) of conditions which needs to obtain if each of the members is to attain his own objectives. And that there is, in human communities, some such set (or set of sets) of conditions is no doubt made possible by the fact that human beings have a 'common good' in the first sense mentioned in the last paragraph. The common good in the first sense thus explains the availability and relevance of a common good in the third sense. In this respect we can speak of the common good on different explanatory levels.

Finnis Natural Law and Natural Rights 156

This concept of community begins at its lowest in the simply physical need for others but, at its highest, it develops into a sense of community, which evolves through the various stages of diminishing self-interest until it peaks, as it were, in the idea of friendship. It will be remembered that friendship is itself an objective good, a form of the objective good or sociability.

> In the fullest sense of 'friendship', A is the friend of B when (i) A acts (or is willing to act) for B's well-being, for the sake of B, while (ii) B acts (or is willing to act) for A's well-being, for the sake of A, (iii) each of them knows of the other's activity and willingness and of the other's knowledge, and (iv) each of them co-ordinates (at least some of) his activity with the activity (including acts of friendship) of the other so that there is a sharing, community, mutuality, and reciprocity not only of knowledge but also of activity (and thus, normally, of enjoyment and satisfaction). And when we say that A and B act 'for the sake of each other', we mean that the concern of each for the other is founded, not in devotion to some principle according to which the other (as a member of a class picked out by that principle) is entitled to concern, but in regard or affection for that individual person as such.

Finnis Natural Law and Natural Rights 142

Furthermore, there is the third requirement of practical reasonableness—no arbitrary preferences among persons.

> My own well-being (. . . includes a concern for the well-being of others, my friends: . . . but ignore this for the moment) is reasonably the first claim on my interest, concern, and effort. Why can I so regard it? Not because it is of more value than the well-being of others, simply because it is mine: intelligence and reasonableness can find no basis in the mere fact that A is A and is not B (that I am I and am not you) for evaluating his (our) well-being differentially. No: the only *reason* for me to prefer my well-being is that it is through *my* self-determined and self-realizing participation in the basic goods that I can do what reasonableness suggests and requires, viz. favour and realize the forms of human good indicated in the first principles of practical reason.
>
> There is, therefore, reasonable scope for self-preference. But when all allowance is made for that, this third requirement remains, a pungent critique of selfishness, special pleading, double standards, hypocrisy, indifference to the good of others whom one could easily help ('passing by on the other side'), and all the other manifold forms of egoistic and group bias. So much so that many have sought to found ethics virtually entirely on this principle of impartiality between persons. In the modern philosophical discussion, the principle regularly is expressed as a requirement that one's moral judgments and preferences be *universalizable*.

Finnis Natural Law and Natural Rights 107

Law

The common good requires a legal system.

> . . . the term 'law' has been used with a focal meaning so as to refer primarily to rules made, in accordance with regulative legal rules, by a determinate and effective authority (itself identified and, standardly, constituted as an institution by legal rules) for a 'complete' community, and buttressed by sanctions in accordance with the rule-guided stipulations of adjudicative institutions, this ensemble of rules and institutions being directed to reasonably resolving any of the community's co-ordination problems (and to ratifying, tolerating, regulating, or overriding co-ordination solutions from any other institutions or sources of norms) for the common good of that community, according to a manner and form itself adapted to that common good by features of specificity, minimization of arbitrariness, and maintenance of a quality of reciprocity between the subjects of the law both amongst themselves and in their relations with the lawful authorities.

> Finnis *Natural Law and Natural Rights* 276–277

But he acknowledges that law can work against the common good. So what is the status of an unjust law? Finnis's views on this have already been canvassed (supra pp 151–153). He reiterates and extends his argument in the following extracts.

> All my analyses of authority and obligation can be summed up in the following theorem: the ruler has, very strictly speaking, no right to be obeyed . . . but he has the authority to give directions and make laws that are morally obligatory and that he has the responsibility of enforcing. He has this authority for the sake of the common good (the needs of which can also, however, make authoritative the opinions—as in custom—or stipulations of men who have no authority). Therefore, if he uses his authority to make stipulations against the common good, or against any of the basic principles of practical reasonableness, those stipulations altogether lack the authority they would otherwise have *by virtue of being his.* More precisely, stipulations made for partisan advantage, or (without emergency justification) in excess of legally defined authority, or imposing inequitable burdens on their subjects, or directing the doing of things that should never be done, simply fail, of themselves, to create any moral obligation whatever.

> Finnis *Natural Law and Natural Rights* 359–360

> . . . for the purpose of assessing one's legal obligations in the moral sense, one is entitled to discount laws that are 'unjust' in any of the ways mentioned. Such laws lack the moral authority that in other cases comes simply from their origin, 'pedigree', or formal source. In this way, then, *lex injusta non est lex* and *virtutem obligandi non habet* . . .

> Finnis *Natural Law and Natural Rights* 360

It may be the case, for example, that if I am *seen* by fellow citizens to be disobeying or disregarding this 'law', the effectiveness of other laws, and/or the general respect of citizens for the authority of a generally desirable ruler or constitution, will probably be weakened, with probable bad consequences for the common good. Does not this collateral fact create a moral obligation? The obligation is to comply with the law, but it should not be treated as an instance for what I have called 'legal obligation in the moral sense'. For it is not based on the good of *being* law-abiding, but only on the desirability of not rendering ineffective the just parts of the legal system. Hence it will not require compliance with unjust laws according to their tenor or 'legislative intent', but only such degree of compliance as is necessary to avoid bringing 'the law' (as a whole) 'into contempt'. This degree of compliance will vary according to time, place, and circumstance; in some limiting cases (eg of judges, or other officials administering the law) the morally required degree of compliance may amount to full or virtually full compliance, just *as if* the law in question had been a just enactment.

So, if an unjust stipulation is, in fact, homogeneous with other laws in its formal source, in its reception by courts and officials, and in its common acceptance, the good citizen may (not always) be morally required to conform to that stipulation to the extent necessary to avoid weakening 'the law', the legal system (of rules, institutions, and dispositions) as a whole. The ruler still has the responsibility of repealing rather than enforcing his unjust law, and in this sense has no right that it should be conformed to. But the citizen, or official, may meanwhile have the diminished, collateral, and in an important sense extra-legal, obligation to obey it.

Finnis *Natural Law and Natural Rights* 361–362

So, sometimes, there may be a moral obligation to comply with unjust laws and the reason for this will be the ideal of a legal order. Notice how this obligation is variable. What of the maxim *lex injusta non est lex*?

Thus Aquinas carefully avoids saying flatly that 'an unjust law is not a law: *lex injusta non est lex*'. But in the end it would have mattered little had he said just that. For the statement either is pure nonsense, flatly self-contradictory, or else is a dramatization of the point more literally made by Aquinas when he says that an unjust law is not law in the focal sense of the term 'law' [ie *simpliciter*] notwithstanding that it is law in a secondary sense of that term [ie *secundum quid*].

Perhaps we can dwell on this a little. The central tradition of natural law theorizing in which the 'lex injusta . . .' doctrine is embedded has not chosen to use the slogans attributed to it by modern critics, for example that '*what is utterly immoral* cannot be law', or that '*certain rules* cannot be law because of their moral iniquity', or that '*these evil things* are not law', or that '*nothing iniquitous* can *anywhere* have the status of law', or that '*morally iniquitous demands* . . . [are] *in no sense* law', or that '*there cannot be* an unjust law'. On the contrary, the tradition, even in its most blunt formulations, has affirmed that unjust LAWS are not law. Does not this formula itself make clear, beyond reasonable question, that the tradition is not indulging in 'a refusal, made *once and for all*, to recognize evil laws as valid *for any purpose*'? Far from 'denying legal validity to iniquitous rules', the tradition explicitly (by speaking of 'unjust *laws*') accords to iniquitous rules legal validity, whether on the ground and in the sense that these rules are accepted in the courts as guides to judicial decision, or on the ground and in the sense that, in the judgment of the speaker, they satisfy the criteria of validity laid down by constitutional or other legal rules, or on both these grounds and in both these senses. The tradition goes so far as to say that there may be an obligation to conform to some such unjust laws in order to uphold respect for the legal system as a whole (what I called a 'collateral obligation' . . .)

Finnis *Natural Law and Natural Rights* 364–365

In this repudiation of a view that is frequently equated with mainstream natural law theory, Finnis has a further complication. On his own reasoning he is forced to maintain that in the focal or central sense (supra p 152) unjust 'laws' are really not laws. But the basis of the above extract is to insist on the relevance of characterising unjust laws as being valid, albeit in a peripheral sense.

The book is rich with discussions of issues that are perhaps outside the reach of a book such as this. The connection between law and practical reasonableness manifests itself in his discussion of justice and rights. Again, the ideas of obligation and of authority receive detailed analysis.

In the final section of the book, 'Nature, Reason, God', he claims that the theory of natural law is viable on its own without recourse to the existence of God. However, he maintains that if the arguments he has offered in the book are accepted, then this will furnish a strong reason for establishing the existence of a God—the uncaused Cause of the universe.

A comment on Finnis's restatement

In what follows Weinreb raises some fundamental questions about Finnis's version of natural law with its reliance on the notion of self-evidence.

The scale of the argument and the confidence with which Finnis states his conclusions divert attention from detail. Even as a straightforward moral theory, however, without regard to its credentials as a theory of natural law, everything depends on the capacity of the lists of basic goods and methodological requirements together to yield usably specific, self-evidently true moral principles. Although the lists articulate our unformed judgments with subtlety and insight, they do nothing to resolve the genuine ambiguities and uncertainties that may attend moral choice. The basic goods are not more than clusters of related human experiences usually thought to be valuable, stated with sufficient generality to include anything one may want to include. Finnis observes that they 'lay down for us the outlines of everything one could reasonably want to do, to have, and to be' and concedes that neither his terminology nor his precise categories are essential to the argument. But if that is so, especially because the methodological requirements prescribe respect for all the basic goods and allow no 'arbitrary' preferences among them, the catalogue of basic goods is scarcely more informative or helpful for the solution of moral issues than Aquinas' injunction, 'Do good and avoid evil.' Finnis gives us a powerful analysis of the ways in which human experience acquires value: as life (or life-sustaining), as knowledge, as play, and so forth. He helps us to understand the variousness of human good, without limiting the manner in which we may seek it.

The same is true about the methodological requirements of practical reasonableness. They are thoughtful, convincing prescriptions for the good life. Most of us would probably subscribe to them generally and instruct our children, less articulately, along the same lines. But it is whistling in the dark to suppose that they allow only one moral solution to a problem. For the most part, Finnis' elaborations of them are no more definite than the general moral precepts on which we usually rely. (The 'classical non-philosophical expression' of the third requirement is, 'of course, the so-called Golden Rule.') When he indicates concretely how they are to be applied, the result does not inspire confidence in his method as a path to certain truth. If we look far enough beyond our own society, even the cases that do not trouble us begin to look uncertain at the edges.

The sixth and seventh methodological requirements, as Finnis elaborates them, reject consistent consequentialism or utilitarianism as a ground of moral decision and prescribe that one not commit any act that itself damages a basic good without promoting a basic good, however beneficial the act's consequences. Conceding that everything depends on how we distinguish the act itself from its consequences, Finnis is nevertheless clear about some implications of these requirements. (Finnis makes the distinction along lines indicated by the concept of intention. His analysis closely resembles the doctrine of 'double effect' of the Roman Catholic Church.) One is that it is never morally correct to sacrifice the life of a person (which is the act) in order to save the life of however many other persons or to accomplish whatever other goal (the consequences). Finnis does not say so, but he would presumably conclude that suicide is never justified. Another implication is that abortion and, evidently, artificial contraception are never morally correct except to save the life of the mother. Lying is apparently another act that is never morally correct, whatever the consequences of telling the truth. Finnis recognizes that his conclusions will often be hard and unwelcome. The course he rejects, he says, 'will often accord with our feelings, our generosity, our sympathy, and with our commitments and projects in the forms in which we undertook them. But it can never be justified in reason.'

The conclusions that Finnis reaches may be correct. But, contrary to what he repeatedly suggests, arguments opposed to his own are not accepted only by persons who have not thought carefully or are blinded by bias or self-interest or convention. It is certain, at least, that each of his conclusions is contested by many thoughtful, morally committed persons, in principle and in practice, and that contrary conclusions have been endorsed in the law after prolonged, serious debate. If Finnis believes that his conclusions are self-evident, he is using the term in a special sense of his own. Even those who agree with him on the merits may suppose that he has confused self-evidence with personal conviction.

Finnis identifies his theory with natural law on the ground that it provides the basic principles of any legal system that is conformable to reason. He does not suggest that such principles are found unchanged in the law; rather they are embodied in an elaborate and complex body of rules invoking and involving remote aspects of the legal order. So the taking of human life 'may be a crime (and one of several procedurally significant classes of offence), and/or a tort, and/or an act which effects automatic vacation or suspension of office or forfeiture of property and/or an act which insurers and/or public officials may properly take into account in avoiding a contract or suspending a license . . . etc. . . . . Thus, in a well-developed legal system, the integration of even an uncontroversial requirement of practical reasonableness into the law will not be a simple matter.' As Finnis also points out, the process of formulating rules of conduct that have bounds and consequences raises additional considerations of stability, predictability, and so forth. Taking all this into account, we cannot expect that practical reasonableness will yield the detail of a statutory code.

On the other hand, if Finnis' claim is to be supported at all, his principles of practical reasonableness must indicate in a not inconsiderable number of cases what the law ought to be, with certainty. Finnis believes they do. He says: 'The central principle of the law of murder, of theft, of marriage, of contract . . . may be a straightforward application of universally valid requirements of reasonableness,' although their full integration into a legal system requires 'countless elaborations' that are not all obvious or determinate. He writes as if there were 'central' principles of law, ascertainable with certainty by his method, that determine a core of basic legal obligations, while other, less basic obligations are indeterminate matters of detail. The discussion resembles Aquinas' treatment of human law, which Finnis explicitly invokes. The law, however, does not contain central principles of that kind. The only principles that might plausibly be said to arise from reason (let alone reason unaided by evidence or inference) are so general and abstract that they leave even the most basic legal obligations for further determination.

The law of murder, Finnis says, 'from the layman's point of view . . . can be regarded as a directive not to intentionally kill (or attempt to kill) any human being, unless in self-defense . . .'; this, he says, corresponds 'rather closely to the requirement of practical reason . . . that one is not to deliberately kill the innocent (in the relevant sense of "innocent").' Is it then a requirement of practical reason that one ought not kill a person if it is necessary to prevent him from inflicting a serious but not mortal injury on oneself; to prevent him from inflicting a mortal (or serious but not mortal) injury on a near relation, or a friend, or a stranger; to repel an unjustified, or felonious, entry into one's house or theft of one's property? Does practical reason allow one to kill another person who innocently threatens one's life or is in possession of the one means to save one's life? Does it allow one to kill (or to let die) one or several persons in order to save many lives? Does practical reason prohibit abortion to save the life or health of the mother or simply to avoid having an unwanted child? Does it prohibit killing in defense of one's country, or capital punishment? One might suppose that laws protective of human life are as likely as any to satisfy Finnis' requirements of objectivity and certainty. Yet none of the preceding questions, which Finnis' principle by itself either leaves unanswered or in some cases appears to answer contrary to the prevailing law in the United States, is remote from or peripheral to 'the central principle of the law of murder.' Separate from answers to such questions, the principle he provides is radically incomplete. The answers do not depend only on a complex interweaving with other (known) principles and procedures of the legal order. They depend on a resolution of uncertainties about the meaning and application of underlying moral values that do not all point in the same direction.

Similar puzzles attend Finnis' references to the central principles of the law of theft, marriage, and contract. One may be able to imagine what such principles would be: of theft, 'do not take the property of another against his will'; of contract, 'perform the obligations that one has freely undertaken' (but—only if there was consideration, or not?), of marriage, 'cleave to one's spouse' (but—for how long, and how many spouses, wife or husband, at the same time?). Finnis might state the central principles differently. The point is now how he or I or someone else would state them. It is whether they can be stated beyond reasonable disagreement in such a way that they fix actual obligations. The central principle of the law of theft depends, at any rate, on the bases of private ownership, at least if it is not to be a vacuous abstraction; more particularly, it depends on complex judgments about what methods of acquiring property should be allowed or encouraged and what methods should be prohibited. No one familiar with the history of Anglo-American criminal law could suppose that such judgments are provided definitively by reason alone. The law of contract requires us to decide whether and, if so, what consideration for a promise is necessary to create an obligation to perform, what formalities and what degree of equality of bargaining power are necessary, and what deception or nondisclosure is permissible. The law of marriage depends on a host of questions about relations between men and women (and why not also relations between persons of the same sex?), and relation between parents and children, and the familial relation generally. Finnis does not begin to show that the principles of practical reason dispose of such questions so that conscientious disagreement is eliminated. If he thinks otherwise, he must believe that most of the most difficult, troubling, and controversial legal issues would vanish if we only thought carefully and seriously about them.

Finnis' book contains much compelling argument. He suggests ways of thinking about purposive human activity that help us to recognize how much agreement there is about human ends and how properly to achieve them. That is a shelter from the wind of moral relativism and an antidote to excessive skepticism. Hard cases of moral uncertainty and conflict understandably attract our attention; but they are so troubling partly because more often the moral course is unproblematic. Finnis rightly insists that reflection about the nature of law should begin with the central core of standard cases, in which the obligations of law and morality reinforce one another. Nevertheless, he does not provide a convincing natural law theory even as he himself would define it. The weakness of his argument is not simply that one can find complex counterexamples. The belief that, if one reflects carefully about the human condition, the principles of moral action are a self-evident basis for the determination of concrete obligations, is itself mistaken. One is led to suspect that Finnis believes that there are ascertainable principles determinative of moral obligations because he believes that, at a deep level, unless there are such principles, none of our moral judgments makes any sense—and of course, they do make sense. If he does in fact hold this belief, in that as in much else he and I agree. But the puzzle cannot be solved as he proposes.

Weinreb *Natural Law and Justice* 111–115

Weinreb makes the following comment on Finnis's characterisation of the natural law tradition in general and Thomas Aquinas in particular.

Finnis believes that the description of natural law as an ontological theory is historically inaccurate. It is evident from what I have said . . . that he and I disagree about that. Stating, as all would agree, that Thomas Aquinas is 'unquestionably a paradigm "natural law theorist"' (*Natural Law and Natural Rights*, p 28), Finnis observes that Aquinas, like Finnis himself, regarded the first principles of natural law as self-evident and indemonstrable. That is true enough as far as it goes. But to extract Aquinas' doctrine of natural law from its context and treat it as separable from the idea of a universal order according to the Eternal Law of God not only radically distorts Aquinas' philosophy as a whole but misconceives the doctrine of natural law itself. It is because the universe is ordered by divine Providence that there is a natural law, and because we know that it is so ordered that we know that there is natural law. These propositions much more than the specific content of any principles of conduct are the heart of Aquinas' philosophy, as his wholly abstract first principle, 'Do good and avoid evil,' sufficiently indicates. Natural law was not so much a body of moral principles as part of an ontological explanation of the possibility of human freedom in a universe wholly subject to the will of God. Finnis evidently believes that 'the existence and nature of God' explain how there happen to be objective principles of morality, but regards the content of the principles, for Aquinas as for himself, as separable and a sufficient subject for study. . . . As I indicate below, I agree with Finnis that his theory is properly classified as natural law, but for entirely different reasons, which do not require one to make the remarkable claim that Aquinas' doctrine of natural law was not ontological.

Weinreb *Natural Law and Justice* 109

foundation of that system, the object of which is to rear the fabric of felicity by the hands of reason and of law. Systems which attempt to question it, deal in sounds instead of sense, in caprice instead of reason, in darkness instead of light.

But enough of metaphor and declamation: it is not by such means that moral science is to be improved.

2. The principle of utility is the foundation of the present work: it will be proper therefore at the outset to give an explicit and determinate account of what is meant by it. By the principle[b] of utility is meant that principle which approves or disapproves of every action whatsoever, according to the tendency which it appears to have to augment or diminish the happiness of the party whose interest is in question: or, what is the same thing in other words, to promote or to oppose that happiness. I say of every action whatsoever; and therefore not only of every action of a private individual, but of every measure of government.

Principle of utility, what

3. By utility is meant that property in any object, whereby it tends to produce benefit, advantage, pleasure, good, or happiness (all this in the present case comes to the same thing), or (what comes again to the same thing) to prevent the happening of mischief, pain, evil, or unhappiness to the party whose interest is considered: if that party be the community in general, then the happiness of the community: if a particular individual, then the happiness of that individual.

Utility, what

4. The interest of the community is one of the most general expressions that can occur in the phraseology of morals: no wonder that the meaning of it is often lost. When it has a meaning, it is this. The community is a fictitious *body*, composed of the individual persons who are considered as constituting as it were its *members*. The interest of the community then is, what?—the sum of the interests of the several members who compose it.

Interest of the community, what

sufficiently manifest connexion between the ideas of *happiness* and *pleasure* on the one hand, and the idea of *utility* on the other, I have every now and then found operating, and with but too much efficiency, as a bar to the acceptance, that might otherwise have been given, to this principle.

  [b] (Principle) The word principle is derived from the Latin *principium*: which seems to be compounded of the two words *primus*, first, or chief, and *cipium*, a termination which seems to be derived from *capio*, to take, as in *mancipium*, *municipium*; to which are analogous *auceps*, *forceps*, and others. It is a term of very vague and very extensive signification: it is applied to any thing which is conceived to serve as a foundation or beginning to any series of operations: in some cases, of physical operations; but of mental operations in the present case.

The principle here in question may be taken for an act of the mind; a sentiment; a sentiment of approbation; a sentiment which, when applied to an action, approves of its utility, as that quality of it by which the measure of approbation or disapprobation bestowed upon it ought to be governed.

*An action
conformable
to the prin-
ciple of
utility, what*

*A measure of
government
conformable
to the prin-
ciple of
utility, what*

*Laws or
dictates of
utility, what*

*A partisan of
the principle
of utility,
who*

*Ought,
ought not,
right and
wrong, &c.
how to be
understood*

*To prove
the rectitude
of this prin-
ciple is at
once unneces-
ary and
impossible*

5.   It is in vain to talk of the interest of the community, without understanding what is the interest of the individual.[c] A thing is said to promote the interest, or to be *for* the interest, of an individual, when it tends to add to the sum total of his pleasures: or, what comes to the same thing, to diminish the sum total of his pains.

6.   An action then may be said to be conformable to the principle of utility, or, for shortness sake, to utility (meaning with respect to the community at large), when the tendency it has to augment the happiness of the community is greater than any it has to diminish it.

7.   A measure of government (which is but a particular kind of action, performed by a particular person or persons) may be said to be conformable to or dictated by the principle of utility, when in like manner the tendency which it has to augment the happiness of the community is greater than any which it has to diminish it.

8.   When an action, or in particular a measure of government, is supposed by a man to be conformable to the principle of utility, it may be convenient, for the purposes of discourse, to imagine a kind of law or dictate, called a law or dictate of utility: and to speak of the action in question, as being conformable to such law or dictate.

9.   A man may be said to be a partisan of the principle of utility, when the approbation or disapprobation he annexes to any action, or to any measure, is determined by, and proportioned to the tendency which he conceives it to have to augment or to diminish the happiness of the community: or in other words, to its conformity or unconformity to the laws or dictates of utility.

10.   Of an action that is conformable to the principle of utility, one may always say either that it is one that ought to be done, or at least that it is not one that ought not to be done. One may say also, that it is right it should be done; at least that it is not wrong it should be done: that it is a right action; at least that it is not a wrong action. When thus interpreted, the words *ought*, and *right* and *wrong*, and others of that stamp, have a meaning: when otherwise, they have none.

11.   Has the rectitude of this principle been ever formally contested? It should seem that it had, by those who have not known what they have been meaning. Is it susceptible of any direct proof? It should seem not: for that which is used to prove every thing else, cannot itself be proved: a chain of proofs must have their commencement somewhere. To give such proof is as impossible as it is needless.

Bentham *An Introduction to the Principles of Morals and Legislation* Ch 1

---

[c] (Interest, &c.) Interest is one of those words, which not having any superior *genus*, cannot in the ordinary way be defined.

Bentham's theory is a classical statement of act-utilitarianism. The three components of a utilitarian theory distinguished above can be readily identified. His claim about what makes a good state of affairs good and a bad one bad—see claim (a) above—is that it depends directly on the amount of happiness it contains. In turn, happiness is explained in terms of pleasure and pain, so that to increase a person's happiness is to increase the 'sum total of his pleasures: or what comes to the same thing, to diminish the sum total of his pains'.

Assuming that the quantities of pleasure and pain in different states of affairs can be measured and compared, then Bentham's theory also provides a principle for ranking states of affairs. There are, he thought, a number of different dimensions in which the quantity of pleasure in a given state of affairs can be measured. One of these was duration; for other things being equal, if one pleasure lasts longer than another it is preferable. Another factor Bentham considered was purity; some pleasures are less pure than others because they have unpleasant side effects, so that other things being equal a pleasure which does not have such effects is preferable to one that does. In all there were seven such factors distinguished by Bentham which are summarised below:

VALUE OF A LOT OF PLEASURE OR PAIN, HOW TO BE MEASURED

1. Pleasures then, and the avoidance of pains, are the *ends* which the legislator has in view: it behoves him therefore to understand their *value*. Pleasures and pains are the *instruments* he has to work with: it behoves him therefore to understand their force, which is again, in another point of view, their value. — *Use of this chapter*

2. To a person considered *by himself*, the value of a pleasure or pain considered *by itself*, will be greater or less, according to the four following circumstances:[a]
  1. Its *intensity*.
  2. Its *duration*.
  3. Its *certainty* or *uncertainty*.
  4. Its *propinquity* or *remoteness*.

3. These are the circumstances which are to be considered in estimating a pleasure or a pain considered each of them by itself. But when the value of any pleasure or pain is considered for the purpose of estimating the tendency of any *act* by which it is produced, there are two other circumstances to be taken into the account; these are,

Circumstances to be taken into the account in estimating the value of a pleasure or pain considered with reference to a single person, and by itself—considered as connected with other pleasures or pains

---

[a] These circumstances have since been denominated *elements* or *dimensions* of *value* in a pleasure or a pain.

Not long after the publication of the first edition, the following memoriter verses were framed, in the view of lodging more effectually, in the memory, these points, on which the whole fabric of morals and legislation may be seen to rest.

Intense, long, certain, speedy, fruitful, pure—
Such marks in *pleasures* and in *pains* endure.
Such pleasures seek, if *private* be thy end:
If it be *public*, wide let them *extend*.
Such *pains* avoid, whichever be thy view:
If pains *must* come, let them *extend* to few.

5. Its *fecundity*, or the chance it has of being followed by sensations of the *same* kind: that is, pleasures, if it be a pleasure: pains, if it be a pain.

6. Its *purity*, or the chance it has of *not* being followed by sensations of the *opposite* kind: that is, pains, if it be a pleasure: pleasures, if it be a pain.

These two last, however, are in strictness scarcely to be deemed properties of the pleasure or the pain itself; they are not, therefore, in strictness to be taken into the account of the value of that pleasure or that pain. They are in strictness to be deemed properties only of the act, or other event, by which such pleasure or pain has been produced; and accordingly are only to be taken into the account of the tendency of such act or such event.

–considered with reference to a number of persons

4. To a *number* of persons, with reference to each of whom the value of a pleasure or a pain is considered, it will be greater or less, according to seven circumstances: to wit, the six preceding ones; viz.

1. Its *intensity*.
2. Its *duration*.
3. Its *certainty* or *uncertainty*.
4. Its *propinquity* or *remoteness*.
5. Its *fecundity*.
6. Its *purity*.

And one other; to wit:

7. Its *extent*; that is, the number of persons to whom it *extends*; or (in other words) who are affected by it.

Bentham *An Introduction to the Principles of Morals and Legislation* ch 4

Bentham's answer to the question, what makes a right action right, is also clear (cf claim (b) above): right actions are those whose tendency is to promote the happiness of those whose interests are affected by that action. So if one has to choose between two actions, then the action one should perform is the one which produces the most happiness; ie, assuming that we can rank states of affairs in the way sketched above, then the action that should be performed is the one which has the highest ranked outcome.

Note also that the relation between a right action and its outcome envisaged by Bentham is a direct one. That is, it is the specific consequences of the action and those alone which determine whether it is right. Suppose, for instance, that the consequences of telling the truth on a particular occasion would be less good than those of telling a lie; then, according to Bentham one should tell a lie, even though in general truth-telling is to be preferred and indeed encouraged. The following passage contains Bentham's description of the calculations involved in estimating the tendency of an action to produce pleasure and pain:

Process for estimating the tendency of any act or event

5. To take an exact account then of the general tendency of any act, by which the interests of a community are affected, proceed as follows. Begin with any one person of those whose interests seem most immediately to be affected by it: and take an account,

1. Of the value of each distinguishable *pleasure* which appears to be produced by it in the *first* instance.

2. Of the value of each *pain* which appears to be produced by it in the *first* instance.

3. Of the value of each pleasure which appears to be produced by it *after* the first. This constitutes the *fecundity* of the first *pleasure* and the *impurity* of the first *pain*.

4. Of the value of each *pain* which appears to be produced by it after the first. This constitutes the *fecundity* of the first *pain*, and the *impurity* of the first pleasure.

5. Sum up all the values of all the *pleasures* on the one side, and those of all the *pains* on the other. The balance, if it be on the side of pleasure, will give the *good* tendency of the act upon the whole, with respect to the interests of that *individual* person; if on the side of pain, the *bad* tendency of it upon the whole.

6. Take an account of the *number* of persons whose interests appear to be concerned; and repeat the above process with respect to each. *Sum up* the numbers expressive of the degrees of *good* tendency, which the act has, with respect to each individual, in regard to whom the tendency of it is *good* upon the whole: do this again with respect to each individual, in regard to whom the tendency of it is *good* upon the whole: do this again with respect to each individual, in regard to whom the tendency of it is *bad* upon the whole. Take the *balance*; which, if on the side of *pleasure*, will give the general *good tendency* of the act, with respect to the total number or community of individuals concerned; if on the side of pain, the general *evil tendency*, with respect to the same community.

6. It is not to be expected that this process should be strictly pursued previously to every moral judgment, or to every legislative or judicial operation. It may, however, be always kept in view: and as near as the process actually pursued on these occasions approaches to it, so near will such process approach to the character of an exact one. *Use of the foregoing process*

7. The same process is alike applicable to pleasure and pain, in whatever shape they appear: and by whatever denomination they are distinguished: to pleasure, whether it be called *good* (which is properly the cause or instrument of pleasure) or *profit* (which is distant pleasure, or the cause or instrument of distant pleasure), or *convenience*, or *advantage, benefit, emolument, happiness*, and so forth: to pain, whether it be called *evil* (which corresponds to *good*), or *mischief*, or *inconvenience*, or *disadvantage*, or *loss*, or *unhappiness*, and so forth. *The same process applicable to good and evil, profit and mischief, and all other modifications of pleasure and pain*

8. Nor is this a novel and unwarranted, any more than it is a useless theory. In all this there is nothing but what the practice of mankind, wheresoever they have a clear view of their own interest, is perfectly conformable to. An article of property, an estate in land, for instance, is valuable, on what account? On account of the pleasures of all kinds which it enables a man to produce, and what comes to the same thing the pains of all kinds which it *Conformity of men's practice to this theory* enables him to avert. But the value of such an article of property is universally understood to rise or fall according to the length or shortness of the time which a man has in it: the certainty or uncertainty of its coming into possession: and the nearness or remoteness of the time at which, if at all, it is to come into possession. As to the *intensity* of the pleasures which a man may derive from it, this is never thought of, because it depends upon the use which each particular person may come to make of it; which cannot be estimated till the particular pleasures he may come to derive from it, or the particular pains he may come to exclude by means of it, are brought to view. For the same reason, neither does he think of the *fecundity* or *purity* of those pleasures.

Thus much for pleasure and pain, happiness and unhappiness, in *general*. We come now to consider the several particular kinds of pain and pleasure.

Bentham *An Introduction to the Principles of Morals and Legislation* ch 4

Finally, Bentham's answer to the question of who should be taken into consideration when evaluating and comparing states of affairs should be clear from his answer to the question what makes a right act right. We are to take into consideration everyone whose interests are affected. No one is to be ignored, and if they have been then they should not have been. This principle has, on the face of it, a strong anti-discriminatory tendency, for much discrimination has consisted of excluding the interests of others from consideration.

ATTRACTIONS OF UTILITARIANISM

There are a number of things that make utilitarianism an attractive theory. As a committed critic of utilitarianism, Bernard Williams points out that, since it has no transcendental elements of the kind that, rightly or wrongly, many people associate with natural law (Chapter 6) it has an obvious appeal in a predominantly secular society to those who are looking for a moral theory which is rooted in human nature, and which makes no religious presuppositions (B Williams, *Morality: An Introduction to Ethics*, 97). Moreover, it is hard to dispute that its overall value, happiness, is something that people do value.

To this one might add that a related attraction is that utilitarianism seems to be an individualistic theory, which tries to take the well-being of each person into account. In other words, it offers the possibility of combining a respect for individual development with a concern for the public welfare, which is very attractive to liberals. Indeed, it might seem that it is no more than the generalisation of a commonsense conception of individual rationality. For, as Rawls points out, we certainly regard it as rational for a man to maximise his interests setting his losses off against his gains. For instance, it may be necessary for him to incur a short-term loss, in order to achieve the largest possible long-term gains:

Now why should not a society act on precisely the same principle applied to the group and therefore regard that which is rational for one man as right for an association of men? . . . Since the principle for an individual is to advance as far as possible his own welfare, the principle for society is to advance as far as possible the welfare of the group, to realize to the greatest possible extent the most comprehensive system of desire arrived at from the desires of its members. Just as an individual balances present and future gains against present and future losses, so a society may balance satisfactions and dissatisfactions between different individuals. And so by these reflections one reaches the principle of utility in a natural way . . .

Rawls *A Theory of Justice* 22

Nevertheless, many, including Rawls himself (cf Chapter 9), have thought that there are overwhelming objections in principle to utilitarianism, and it is to some of these that we now turn.

SOME OBJECTIONS TO ACT-UTILITARIANISM

It is natural to separate these into three groups: those to the standard of evaluation; those to the consequentialist component; and those to the utilitarian theory of the weight to be given to each individual's interests when deciding what to do.

(a)   The standard of evaluation

Because of its emphasis on pleasure and pain, Bentham's theory is called 'hedonistic', and that has been the source of perhaps the most easily met objections to it. These objections centre round the question of whether pleasure is inherently good. Are not some pleasures, on the contrary, thoroughly bad, eg, those of the voyeur, the sadist, the torturer? And are not some pleasures simply better than others; are not the intellectual pleasures of reading poetry and listening to music, for instance, better than those of eating a Big Mac or drinking a Coke? Bentham's response to these points was admirably consistent in that he did not try to exclude sadistic pleasures from the scope of his theory, and maintained, in response to the second point, that quantities of pleasure being equal, pushpin, a popular game of his day, is as good as poetry.

However, apart from noting that Bentham clearly has something to say in his own defence, we shall not try to defend him here. For if this is the only criticism someone has of Bentham's version of act-utilitarianism, then there is a simple response to it, namely, replace his evaluative criterion by your own. The resulting theory is still an act-utilitarian theory, but one which answers the question what makes a good state of affairs good differently from Bentham (cf claim (a) above).

Many reasons for proposing a different standard of evaluation might be given, but one mentioned by Simmonds is of particular interest. Discussing a standard of evaluation which involves considering the degree to which individuals get their preferences satisfied in a state of affairs, so that a state of affairs in which more individual preferences are satisfied is better than one in which fewer are, Simmonds argues that the adoption of this standard of evaluation ought to be appealing to those who favour liberalism. This is so because those who, like Bentham, take as the basis of their theory a certain conception of the good, are at odds with liberal political theories which reject this approach on the grounds that it does precisely what liberals are opposed to, namely imposes a set of values on others. On the contrary, liberals argue that:

. . . our account of the principles of justice and moral right (and our choice of laws and institutions) should not presuppose any particular conception of what is a good and worthwhile life. The mere fact that we believe that one way of life is valuable and ought to be aspired to, while another way of life is not, does not justify us in imposing that view on others by making it the presupposed basic value of our legal and political system. Rather than seeking to inculcate and encourage one conception of the good life, the law should, so far as possible, provide a framework within which everyone has the opportunity to pursue his own life . . . the legal order of a liberal society should be neutral between different conceptions of the good.

Simmonds *Central Issues in Jurisprudence* 27

This is not the only reason why people have opted for a version of preference utilitarianism—that is, a consequentialist theory which takes the maximisation of individual preferences as its standard of evaluation, but it is certainly an important one. The attraction of this view is that utilitarianism is compatible with wide variations in the values of individuals, and many modern versions of utilitarianism in fact advocate some form of preference utilitarianism.

(b) Calculating consequences

A different set of objections to Bentham's theory cluster round his version of the consequence condition (cf claim (b) above), which assumes that states of affairs can be evaluated and compared, and that there is a calculus which enables us to sum the quantities of pleasure and pain in states of affairs and then rank them. But is this really possible? Can one in fact compare the pleasure one person gets from drinking a fine wine with that another gets from drinking a Coke and calculate which is the greater?

Another objection is that the consequences of an action might conceivably go on to infinity, as it were, so that we are never in a position to do the calculations, even if the calculus is available. A third objection would be that the principle that we are to take into consideration everyone whose interests are affected does not guarantee that the preferred outcome according to a utilitarian is a fair one. In our next extract an advocate of act-utilitarianism, J J C Smart, discusses these objections and tries to defend utilitarianism against them:[1]

I shall now state the act-utilitarian doctrine. Purely for simplicity of exposition I shall put it forward in a broadly hedonistic form. If anyone values states of mind such as knowledge independently of their pleasurableness he can make appropriate verbal alterations to convert it from hedonistic to ideal utilitarianism. And I shall not here take sides on the issue between hedonistic and quasi-ideal utilitarianism. I shall concern myself with the evaluation signified by 'ought' in 'one ought to do that which will produce the best consequences', and leave to one side the evaluation signified by the word 'best'.

Let us say, then, that the only reason for performing an action *A* rather than an alternative action *B* is that doing *A* will make mankind (or, perhaps, all sentient beings) happier than will doing *B*. (Here I put aside the consideration that in fact we can have only probable belief about the effects of our actions,

---

[1] Originally published in 1961, our extract from Smart's essay is from the revised version which appeared in J J C Smart and Bernard Williams *Utilitarianism For and Against*, 30–37 (1972) Cambridge University Press. In the other essay in that volume, 'A Critique of Utilitarianism', Bernard Williams develops a number of important criticisms of utilitarianism.

and so our reason should be more precisely stated as that doing *A* will produce more probable benefit than will doing *B*. For convenience of exposition I shelve this question of probability for a page or two.) This is so simple and natural a doctrine that we can surely expect that many of my readers will have at least some propensity to agree. For I am talking, as I said earlier, to sympathetic and benevolent men, that is, to men who desire the happiness of mankind. Since they have a favourable attitude to the general happiness, surely they will have a tendency to submit to an ultimate moral principle which does no more than express this attitude. It is true that these men, being human, will also have purely selfish attitudes. Either these attitudes will be in harmony with the general happiness (in cases where everyone's looking after his own interests promotes the maximum general happiness) or they will not be in harmony with the general happiness, in which case they will largely cancel one another out, and so could not be made the basis of an interpersonal discussion anyway. It is possible, then, that many sympathetic and benevolent people depart from or fail to attain a utilitarian ethical principle only under the stress of tradition, of superstition, or of unsound philosophical reasoning. If this hypothesis should turn out to be correct, at least as far as these readers are concerned, then the utilitarian may contend that there is no need for him to defend his position directly, save by stating it in a consistent manner, and by showing that common objections to it are unsound. After all, it expresses an ultimate attitude, not a liking for something merely as a means to something else. Save for attempting to remove confusions and discredit superstitions which may get in the way of clear moral thinking, he cannot, of course, appeal to argument and must rest his hopes on the good feeling of his readers. If any reader is not a sympathetic and benevolent man, then of course it cannot be expected that he will have an ultimate pro-attitude to human happiness in general. Also some good-hearted readers may reject the utilitarian position because of certain considerations relating to justice. I postpone discussion of these until [later].[a]

The utilitarian's ultimate moral principle, let it be remembered, expresses the sentiment not of altruism but of benevolence, the agent counting himself neither more nor less than any other person. Pure altruism cannot be made the basis of a universal moral discussion because it might lead different people to different and perhaps incompatible courses of action, even though the circumstances were identical. When two men each try to let the other through a door first a deadlock results. Altruism could hardly commend itself to those of a scientific, and hence universalistic, frame of mind. If you count in my calculations why should I not count in your calculations? And why should I pay more attention to my calculations than to yours? Of course we often tend to praise and honour altruism even more than generalized benevolence. This is because people too often err on the side of selfishness, and so altruism is a fault on the right side. If we can make a man try to be an altruist he may succeed as far as acquiring a generalized benevolence.

Suppose we could predict the future consequences of actions with certainty. Then it would be possible to say that the total future consequences of action *A* are such-and-such and that the total future consequences of action *B* are so-and-so. In order to help someone to decide whether to do *A* or to do *B* we could say to him: 'Envisage the total consequences of *A*, and think them over carefully and imaginatively. Now envisage the total consequences of *B*, and

[a] Ed. See next extract, p 219 of this vol.

think them over carefully. As a benevolent and humane man, and thinking of yourself just as one man among others, would you prefer the consequences of *A* or those of *B*?' That is, we are asking for a comparison of one (present and future) *total* situation with another (present and future) *total* situation. So far we are not asking for a *summation* or *calculation* of pleasures or happiness. We are asking only for a comparison of total situations. And it seems clear that we can frequently make such a comparison and say that one total situation is better than another. For example few people would not prefer a total situation in which a million people are well-fed, well-clothed, free of pain, doing interesting and enjoyable work, and enjoying the pleasures of conversation, study, business, art, humour, and so on, to a total situation where there are ten thousand such people only, or perhaps 999,999 such people plus one man with toothache, or neurotic, or shivering with cold. In general, we can sum things up by saying that if we are humane, kindly, benevolent people, we want as many people as possible now and in the future to be as happy as possible. Someone might object that we cannot envisage the total future situation, because this stretches into infinity. In reply to this we may say that it does not stretch into infinity, as all sentient life on earth will ultimately be extinguished, and furthermore we do not normally in practice need to consider very remote consequences, as these in the end approximate rapidly to zero like the furthermost ripples on a pond after a stone has been dropped into it.

But do the remote consequences of an action diminish to zero? Suppose that two people decide whether to have a child or remain childless. Let us suppose that they decide to have the child, and that they have a limitless succession of happy descendants. The remote consequences do not seem to get less. Not at any rate if these people are Adam and Eve. The difference would be between the end of the human race and a limitless accretion of human happiness, generation by generation. The Adam and Eve example shows that the 'ripples on the pond' postulate is not needed in every case for a rational utilitarian decision. If we had some reason for thinking that every generation would be more happy than not we would not (in the Adam and Eve sort of case) need to be worried that the remote consequences of our action would be in detail unknown. The necessity for the 'ripples in the pond' postulate comes from the fact that usually we do not know whether remote consequences will be good or bad. Therefore we cannot know what to do unless we can assume that remote consequences can be left out of account. This can often be done. Thus if we consider two actual parents, instead of Adam and Eve, then they need not worry about thousands of years hence. Not, at least, if we assume that there will be ecological forces determining the future population of the world. If these parents do not have remote descendants, then other people will presumably have more than they would otherwise. And there is no reason to suppose that my descendants would be more or less happy than yours. We must note, then, that unless we are dealing with 'all or nothing' situations (such as the Adam and Eve one, or that of someone in a position to end human life altogether) we need some sort of 'ripples in the pond' postulate to make utilitarianism workable in practice. I do not know how to prove such a postulate, though it seems plausible enough. If it is not accepted, not only utilitarianism, but also deontological systems like that of Sir David Ross, who at least admits beneficence as one *prima facie* duty among the others, will be fatally affected.

Sometimes, of course, more needs to be said. For example one course of action may make some people very happy and leave the rest as they are or perhaps slightly less happy. Another course of action may make all men rather more happy than before but no one very happy. Which course of action makes mankind happier on the whole? Again, one course of action may make it highly probable that everyone will be made a little happier whereas another course of action may give us a much smaller probability that everyone will be made very much happier. In the third place, one course of action may make everyone happy in a pig-like way, whereas another course of action may make a few people happy in a highly complex and intellectual way.

It seems therefore that we have to weigh the maximizing of happiness against equitable distribution, to weigh probabilities with happiness, and to weigh the intellectual and other qualities of states of mind with their pleasurableness. Are we not therefore driven back to the necessity of some calculus of happiness? Can we just say: 'envisage two total situations and tell me which you prefer'? If this were possible, of course there would be no need to talk of summing happiness or of a calculus. All we should have to do would be to put total situations in an order of preference. Since this is not always possible there is a difficulty, to which I shall return shortly.

We have already considered the question of intellectual versus non-intellectual pleasures and activities. This is irrelevant to the present issue because there seems to be no reason why the ideal or quasi-ideal utilitarian cannot use the method of envisaging total situations just as much as the hedonistic utilitarian. It is just a matter of envisaging various alternative total situations, stretching out into the future, and saying which situation one prefers. The non-hedonistic utilitarian may evaluate the total situations differently from the hedonistic utilitarian, in which case there will be an ultimate ethical disagreement. This possibility of ultimate disagreement is always there, though we have given reasons for suspecting that it will not frequently lead to important disagreement in practice.

Let us now consider the question of equity. Suppose that we have the choice of sending four equally worthy and intelligent boys to a medium-grade public school or of leaving three in an adequate but uninspiring grammar school and sending one to Eton. (For sake of the example I am making the almost certainly incorrect assumption that Etonians are happier than other public-school boys and that these other public-school boys are happier than grammar-school boys.) Which course of action makes the most for the happiness of the four boys? Let us suppose that we can neglect complicating factors, such as that the superior Etonian education might lead one boy to develop his talents so much that he will have an extraordinary influence on the well-being of mankind, or that the unequal treatment of the boys might cause jealousy and rift in the family. Let us suppose that the Etonian will be as happy as (we may hope) Etonians usually are, and similarly for the other boys, and let us suppose that remote effects can be neglected. Should we prefer the greater happiness of one boy to the moderate happiness of all four? Clearly one parent may prefer one total situation (one boy at Eton and three at the grammar school) while another may prefer the other total situation (all four at the medium-grade public school). Surely both parents have an equal claim to being sympathetic and benevolent, and yet their difference of opinion here is not founded on an empirical disagreement about facts. I suggest, however, that there are not in fact many cases in which such a disagreement could arise. Probably the parent who wished to send one son to Eton would draw the line at sending one son to Eton plus giving him expensive private tuition during the holidays plus giving his other sons no secondary education at all. It is only within rather small limits that this sort of disagreement about equity can arise. Furthermore the cases in which we can make one person *very* much happier without increasing *general* happiness are rare ones. The law of diminishing returns comes in here. So, in most practical cases, a disagreement about what should be done will be an empirical disagreement about what total situation is likely to be brought about by an action, and will not be a disagreement about which total situation is preferable. For example the inequalitarian parent might get the other to agree with him if he could convince him that there was a much higher probability of an Etonian benefiting the human race, such as by inventing a valuable drug or opening up the mineral riches of Antarctica, than there is of a non-Etonian doing so. (Once more I should like to say that I do not myself take such a possibility very seriously!) I must again stress that since disagreement about what causes produce what effects is in practice so much the most important sort of disagreement, to have intelligent moral discussion with a person we do not in fact need complete agreement with him about ultimate ends: an approximate agreement is sufficient.

> Smart 'An Outline of a Utilitarian System of Ethics' in Smart and Williams
> *Utilitarianism For and Against* 30–37

Smart's answers to some of the difficulties mentioned above are clear. Perhaps the least convincing is his reply to the objection that a utilitarian distribution may well be very unfair; but since this raises important issues to be discussed later, we will postpone discussion of it until then.

More interesting are his replies to the alleged difficulties about calculating consequences. His reply to the objection that we cannot calculate them because they go on to infinity is that, on the contrary, they often seem to diminish rapidly in significance, like the ripples on a pond. For instance, the consequences for the lives of a couple who want children but cannot have them are obviously serious, but it is difficult to see how they could be serious from the point of view of future generations. Smart does not claim to be able to prove that there is a ripple effect, but argues that it is plausible, and that any system, not just utilitarianism, that takes the welfare of others into account needs a similar assumption. It is, of course, true that in the kind of situation studied by the epidemiologist the very reverse of a ripple effect would seem to occur. But Smart's point would presumably be that once an epidemic has reached its equilibrium point, its consequences become of decreasing significance.

As for the argument that the kind of calculus assumed by Bentham is impossible, he by-passes this issue in the extract by arguing that assuming that we can predict the consequences of alternative actions with certainty, then all we need to do is to compare one total situation with another, and decide which we prefer. As he says, we in fact often seem to do this. For instance, on the day after the monetary union of the two Germanies the West German Finance Minister said it would be a great success since no one would be worse off, and most people would be better. Supposing that he was right, then clearly the state of affairs resulting from monetary union is preferable to that existing previously.[2]

---

[2] If the Finance Minister is correct, then the post-monetary union state of affairs is what is called *Pareto Superior* to the previous situation. Pareto superiority is defined as follows:
  'A state of affairs S' is Pareto Superior to another S, if and only if, no one is worse off in S' than in S, and at least one person is better off in S' than in S.'
For an interesting discussion see J Murphy and J Coleman *The Philosophy of Law* p 212.

However, as Smart goes on to admit, there is a serious problem arising from the facts that often we cannot either specify what the total situation aising from any given action will be, or assign rough probabilities to the likelihood of its occurrence. He sketches a method, which assumes that we can assign numerical probabilities to the effects of our actions. But though we can sometimes do this,

> . . . can we give a numerical value to the probability that a new war will break out, that a proof of Fermat's last theorem will be found, or that our knowledge of genetical linkage in human chromosomes will be much improved in the next five years? Surely it is meaningless to talk of a numerical value for these probabilities, and it is probabilities of this sort with which we have to deal in our moral life.
>
> Smart 'An Outline of a Utilitarian System of Ethics' in Smart and Williams
> *Utilitarianism For and Against* 39

So Smart concludes that what utilitarianism badly needs is a method for assigning a probability in principle to any future event.

(c) Does everyone count equally?

The contention that we are to consider the happiness of everyone whose interests are affected by an action when calculating consequences might seem to guarantee that the result of such a calculation is just. But this first impression is perhaps deceptive. For utilitarianism also requires us to maximise happiness (or preference satisfaction, etc). And it might seem that sometimes the most effective way of doing this will involve sacrificing the interests of someone, or some group. For it seems that sometimes the alternative in which those interests are sacrificed will be the one which maximises happiness, because it is better than any of the alternatives in which those interests are not sacrificed. So those whose interests are sacrificed cannot claim that they have not had their interests taken into account. They have been; it is just unfortunate that when the calculations have been made it turns out that the best outcome is one in which those interests have been set aside for the greater good. The next passage illustrates this difficulty vividly:

> It is not difficult to show that utilitarianism could, in certain exceptional circumstances, have some very horrible consequences. In a very lucid and concise discussion note,[a] H J McCloskey has considered such a case. Suppose that the sheriff of a small town can prevent serious riots (in which hundreds of people will be killed) only by 'framing' and executing (as a scapegoat) an innocent man. In actual cases of this sort the utilitarian will usually be able to agree with our normal moral feelings about such matters. He will be able to point out that there would be some possibility of the sheriff's dishonesty being found out, with consequent weakening of confidence and respect for law and order in the community, the consequences of which would be far worse even than the painful deaths of hundreds of citizens. But as McCloskey is ready to point out, the case can be presented in such a way that these objections do not apply. For example, it can be imagined that the sheriff could have first-rate empirical evidence that he will not be found out. So the objection that the sheriff *knows* that the man he 'frames' will be killed, whereas he has only probable belief that the riot will occur unless he frames the man, is not a sound

[a] H J McCloskey, 'A note on utilitarian punishment', *Mind* 72 (1963) 599.

one. Someone like McCloskey can always strengthen his story to the point that we would just have to admit that if utilitarianism is correct, then the sheriff must frame the innocent man. (McCloskey also has cogently argued that similar objectionable consequences are also implied by rule-utilitarianism. That is, an unjust *system* of punishment might be more *useful* than a just one. Hence even if rule-utilitarianism can clearly be distinguished from act-utilitarianism, a utilitarian will not be able to avoid offensive consequences of his theory by retreating from the 'act' form to the 'rule' form.) Now though a utilitarian might argue that it is empirically unlikely that some such situation as McCloskey envisages would ever occur, McCloskey will point out that it is *logically* possible that such a situation will arise. If the utilitarian rejects the unjust act (or system) he is clearly giving up his utilitarianism. McCloskey then remarks: 'But as far as I know, only J J C Smart among the contemporary utilitarians, is happy to adopt this "solution".' Here I must lodge a mild protest. McCloskey's use of the word 'happy' surely makes me look a most reprehensible person. Even in my most utilitarian moods I am not *happy* about this consequence of utilitarianism. Nevertheless, however unhappy about it he may be, the utilitarian must admit that he draws the consequence that he might find himself in circumstances where he ought to be unjust. Let us hope that this is a logical possibility and not a factual one. In hoping thus I am not being inconsistent with utilitarianism, since any injustice causes misery and so can be justified only as the lesser of two evils. The fewer the situations in which the utilitarian is forced to choose the lesser of two evils, the better he will be pleased. One must not think of the utilitarian as the sort of person who you would not trust further than you could kick him. As a matter of untutored sociological observation, I should say that in general utilitarians are more than usually trustworthy people, and that the sort of people who might do you down are rarely utilitarians.

It is also true that we should probably dislike and fear a man who could bring himself to do the right utilitarian act in a case of the sort envisaged by McCloskey. Though the man in this case might have done the right utilitarian act, his act would betoken a toughness and lack of squeamishness which would make him a dangerous person. We must remember that people have egoistic tendencies as well as beneficent ones, and should such a person be tempted to act wrongly he could act very wrongly indeed. A utilitarian who remembers the possible moral weakness of men might quite consistently prefer to be the sort of person who would not always be able to bring himself to do the right utilitarian act and to surround himself by people who would be too squeamish to act in a utilitarian manner in such extreme cases.

No, I am not happy to draw the conclusion that McCloskey quite rightly says that the utilitarian must draw. But neither am I happy with the anti-utilitarian conclusion. For if a case really *did* arise in which injustice was the lesser of two evils (in terms of human happiness and misery), then the anti-utilitarian conclusion is a very unpalatable one too, namely that in some circumstances one must choose the greater misery, perhaps the *very much* greater misery, such as that of hundreds of people suffering painful deaths.

Still, to be consistent, the utilitarian must accept McCloskey's challenge. Let us hope that the sort of possibility which he envisages will always be no more than a logical possibility and will never become an actuality. At any rate, even though I have suggested that in ethics we should test particular feelings by general attitudes, McCloskey's example makes me somewhat sympathetic to the opposite point of view. Perhaps indeed it is too much to hope that there is *any* possible ethical system which will appeal to all sides of our nature and to all our moods.[b] It is perfectly possible to have conflicting attitudes within oneself. It is quite conceivable that there is *no* possible ethical theory which will be conformable with all our attitudes. If the theory is utilitarian, then the possibility that sometimes it would be right to commit injustice will be felt to be acutely unsatisfactory by someone with a normal civilized upbringing. If on the other hand it is not utilitarian but has deontological elements, then it will have the unsatisfactory implication that sometimes avoidable misery (perhaps very great avoidable misery) ought not to be avoided. It might be thought that some compromise theory, on the lines of Sir David Ross's, in which there is some 'balancing up' between considerations of utility and those of deontology, might provide an acceptable compromise. The trouble with this, however, is that such a 'balancing' may not be possible: one can easily feel pulled sometimes one way and sometimes the other. How can one 'balance' a serious injustice, on the one hand, and hundreds of painful deaths, on the other hand? Even if we disregard our purely self-interested attitudes, for the sake of interpersonal discussions, so as to treat ourselves neither more nor less favourably than other people, it is still possible that there is no ethical system which would be satisfactory to all men, or even to one man at different times. It is possible that something similar is the case with science, that no scientific theory (known or unknown) is correct. If so, the world is more chaotic than we believe and hope that it is. But even though the world is not chaotic, men's moral feelings may be. On anthropological grounds it is only too likely that these feelings are to some exent chaotic. Both as children and as adults, we have probably had many different moral conditionings, which can easily be incompatible with one another.

Meanwhile, among possible options, utilitarianism does have its appeal. With its empirical attitude to questions of means and ends it is congenial to the scientific temper and it has flexibility to deal with a changing world. This last consideration is, however, more self-recommendation than justification. For if flexibility is a recommendation, this is because of the utility of flexibility.

Smart 'A Utilitarian System of Ethics' in Smart and Williams
Utilitarianism For and Against 69–73

[b] J W N Watkins considers this matter in his 'Negative utilitarianism', Aristotelian Society Supp. Vol. 67 (1963) 95–114. It is now apparent to me that my paper 'The methods of ethics and the methods of science', Journal of Philosophy, 62 (1965) 344–9, on which the present section of this monograph is based, gives a misleading impression of Watkins's position in this respect.

Smart's acceptance of the conclusion that it could be right to sacrifice an innocent man is disconcerting. For it has seemed to many both that utilitarianism is committed to such a conclusion, and that the fact that it is so committed reveals a fatal flaw in it, namely, that in setting as its overall goal the maximisation of the general happiness, it is committed to treating individuals or groups unjustly, if so doing does indeed produce the best overall result. In other words, it has seemed to many that utilitarianism is completely at odds with our intuitions about justice; that is why Smart's continued adherence to utilitarianism in spite of his acceptance of this point is disconcerting. Consider again Rawls's argument for utilitarianism. It is all right for me to trade off some of my losses against my gains, because I am not doing this at anyone else's expense. But a quite different situation arises, when group A's losses are traded off against group B's gains; group B gains its advantage only at the expense of group A. How could that be fair?

Certainly, an act-utilitarian need not be indifferent to issues of fairness. In Smart's example about education, for instance, he could argue that it would be right to send the one boy to Eton, with whatever advantages that entails, only if the general happiness was improved. If by that he means that often a utilitarian could not approve of a grossly unequal distribution of happiness, because the gains to the minority could not offset the losses to the majority, that is quite plausible. For not only do we have to consider the unhappiness of the disadvantaged, but we also have to consider the costs to social harmony arising from perceived inequalities. But the case of the sacrifice of the innocent man is not like that; the unjust course of action is to the advantage of the majority, or so it seems.

Now since Smart's conclusion about the innocent man seems to be unavoidable from the point of view of act-utilitarianism, then unless there is a different version of utilitarianism which yields a different verdict about the case in question, we shall have to conclude that utilitarianism is indeed fatally flawed.

We now turn to consider a version of utilitarianism which claims to respond differently than does act-utilitarianism at this point.

INDIRECT UTILITARIANISM

Consider to begin with the following extract:[3]

> The creed which accepts as the foundation of morals, Utility, or the Greatest Happiness Principle, holds that actions are right in proportion as they tend to promote happiness, wrong as they tend to produce the reverse of happiness. By happiness is intended pleasure, and the absence of pain; by unhappiness, pain, and the privation of pleasure. To give a clear view of the moral standard set up by the theory, much more requires to be said; in particular, what things it includes in the idea of pain and pleasure; and to what extent this is left an open question. But these supplementary explanations do not affect the theory of life on which this theory of morality is grounded—namely, that pleasure, and freedom from pain, are the only things desirable as ends; and that all desirable things (which are as numerous in the utilitarian as in any other scheme) are desirable either for the pleasure inherent in themselves, or as means to the promotion of pleasure and the prevention of pain.

Mill *Utilitarianism* ch 2

At first sight this is an orthodox exposition of Bentham's theory. Mill's version of the consequence condition (cf claim (b)) is that actions are right to the degree that they promote happiness; while his standard of evaluation (cf claim (a)) is the amount of happiness and unhappiness involved in a state of affairs; and his answer to the question (claim (c)) who is to be taken into consideration for the purposes of a utilitarian calculation is clear from what he says elsewhere, namely, that '. . . everyone is to count as one and no more than one'. So it is important to stress that despite the apparent similarities, Mill's theory differs from Bentham's

[3] Originally appearing in 1861 as three articles in Fraser Magazine, *Utilitarianism* is a relatively late work of Mill's (1806–1873). Educated by his father, a disciple and friend of Bentham's, Mill knew Bentham intimately. He suffered a severe nervous breakdown in 1826, perhaps in part because of a reaction against the teachings of his father and of Bentham. So though Mill continued to describe himself as a utilitarian, he had a number of major reservations about Bentham's formulation of the doctrine.

in a number of respects. In particular, he thought that the evaluation of the consequences of an action should apply indirectly, that is, that the question whether a particular action is right should be settled not by considering its consequences alone, but by drawing on past experience of the tendency of actions of that kind. In the following passage, Mill replies to the objection that utilitarianism is incapable of providing guidance in particular cases, because we cannot make the necessary calculations there and then:

Again, defenders of utility often find themselves called upon to reply to such objections as this—that there is not time, previous to action, for calculating and weighing the effects of any line of conduct on the general happiness. This is exactly as if any one were to say that it is impossible to guide our conduct by Christianity, because there is not time, on every occasion on which anything has to be done, to read through the Old and New Testaments. The answer to the objection is, that there has been ample time, namely, the whole past duration of the human species. During all that time, mankind have been learning by experience the tendencies of actions; on which experience all the prudence, as well as all the morality of life, are dependent. People talk as if the commencement of this course of experience had hitherto been put off, and as if, at the moment when some man feels tempted to meddle with the property or life of another, he had to begin considering for the first time whether murder and theft are injurious to human happiness. Even then I do not think that he would find the question very puzzling; but, at all events, the matter is now done to his hand. It is truly a whimsical supposition that, if mankind were agreed in considering utility to be the test of morality, they would remain without any agreement as to what *is* useful, and would take no measures for having their notions on the subject taught to the young, and enforced by law and opinion. There is no difficulty in proving any ethical standard whatever to work ill, if we suppose universal idiocy to be conjoined with it; but on any hypothesis short of that, mankind must by this time have acquired positive beliefs as to the effects of some actions on their happiness; and the beliefs which have thus come down are the rules of morality for the multitude, and for the philosopher until he has succeeded in finding better. That philosophers might easily do this, even now, on many subjects; that the received code of ethics is by no means of divine right; and that mankind have still much to learn as to the effects of actions on the general happiness, I admit, or rather, earnestly maintain. The corollaries from the principle of utility, like the precepts of every practical art, admit of indefinite improvement, and, in a progressive state of the human mind, their improvement is perpetually going on. But to consider the rules of morality as improvable, is one thing; to pass over the intermediate generalisations entirely, and endeavour to test each individual action directly by the first principle, is another. It is a strange notion that the acknowledgment of a first principle is inconsistent with the admission of secondary ones. To inform a traveller respecting the place of his ultimate destination, is not to forbid the use of landmarks and direction-posts on the way. The proposition that happiness is the end and aim of morality, does not mean that no road ought to be laid down to that goal, or that persons going thither should not be advised to take one direction rather than another. Men really ought to leave off talking a kind of nonsense on this subject, which they would neither talk nor listen to on other matters of practical concernment. Nobody argues that the art of navigation is not founded on astronomy, because sailors cannot wait to calculate the Nautical Almanack. Being rational creatures, they go to sea with it ready calculated; and all rational creatures go out upon the sea of life with their minds made up on the common questions of right and wrong, as well as on many of the far more difficult questions of wise and foolish. And this, as long as foresight is a human quality, it is to be presumed they will continue to do. Whatever we adopt as the fundamental principle of morality, we require subordinate principles to apply it by; the impossibility of doing without them, being common to all systems, can afford no argument against any one in particular; but gravely to argue as if no such secondary principles could be had, and as if mankind had remained till now, and always must remain, without drawing any general conclusions from the experience of human life, is as high a pitch, I think, as absurdity has ever reached in philosophical controversy.

Mill *Utilitarianism* ch 2

One advantage of having 'intermediate generalisations', ie, rules, is as Mill says that often we do not have time to calculate, and so we must have something else to fall back on. What Mill proposes we should fall back on is a rule that has stood the test of time, in the sense that the consequences of following the rule have been better than those of not following it.

The importance of this distinction has been stressed in a sophisticated modern version of the distinction between act and indirect utilitarianism, to which distinction it is argued correspond different levels of thinking about moral issues:

We have now, therefore, to make an important distinction between two kinds or 'levels' of moral thinking. It has some affinities with a distinction made by Rawls in his article 'Two Concepts of Rules'[a] (in which he was by way of defending utilitarianism), though it is not the same; it also owes something to Sir David Ross, and indeed to others. I call it the difference between level-1 and level-2 thinking, or between the principles employed at these two levels.[b] Level-1 principles are for use in practical moral thinking, especially under conditions of stress. They have to be general enough to be impartable by education (including self-education), and to be 'of ready application in the emergency', but are not to be confused with rules of thumb (whose breach excites no compunction). Level-2 principles are what would be arrived at by leisured moral thought in completely adequate knowledge of the facts, as the right answer in a specific case. They are universal but can be as specific (the opposite of 'general', not of 'universal') as needs be. Level-1 principles are inculcated in moral education; but the selection of the level-1 principles for this purpose should be guided by leisured thought, resulting in level-2 principles for specific considered situations, the object being to have those level-1 principles whose general acceptance will lead to actions in accord with the best level-2 principles in most situations that are actually encountered. Fantastic and highly unusual situations, therefore, need not be considered for this purpose.

I have set out this distinction in detail elsewhere;[c] here we only need to go into some particular points which are relevant. The thinking that I have been

---

[a] Philosophical Review, 64, 3–32.

[b] See Hare 'Critical Study–Rawls' Theory of Justice', Philosophical Quarterly, 1973, 153; 'Principles', *Proceedings of the Aristotelian Society*, 1972–1973, 1–18; and *Freedom and Reason*, Oxford University Press, 1963, 43–5.

[c] See note b.

talking about so far in this paper, until the preceding paragraph, and indeed in most of my philosophical writings until recently, is level-2. It results in a kind of act-utilitarianism which, because of the universalisability of moral judgments, is practically equivalent to a rule-utilitarianism whose rules are allowed to be of any required degree of specificity. Such thinking is appropriate only to 'a cool hour', in which there is time for unlimited investigation of the facts, and there is no temptation to special pleading. It can use hypothetical cases, even fantastic ones. In principle it can, given superhuman knowledge of the facts, yield answers as to what should be done in any cases one cares to describe.

The commonest trick of the opponents of utilitarianism is to take examples of such thinking, usually addressed to fantastic cases, and confront them with what the ordinary man would think. It makes the utilitarian look like a moral monster. The anti-utilitarians have usually confined their own thought about moral reasoning (with fairly infrequent lapses which often go unnoticed) to what I am calling level 1, the level of everyday moral thinking on ordinary, often stressful, occasions in which information is sparse. So they find it natural to take the side of the ordinary man in a supposed fight with the utilitarian whose views lead him to say, if put at the disconcertingly unfamiliar standpoint of the archangel Gabriel, such extraordinary things about these carefully contrived examples.

To argue in this way is entirely to neglect the importance for moral philosophy of a study of moral education. Let us suppose that a fully-informed archangelic act-utilitarian is thinking about how to bring up his children. He will obviously not bring them up to practise on every occasion on which they are confronted with a moral question the kind of archangelic thinking that he himself is capable of; if they are ordinary children, he knows that they will get it wrong. They will not have the time, or the information, or the self-mastery to avoid self-deception prompted by self-interest; this is the real, as opposed to the imagined, veil of ignorance which determines our moral principles.

So he will do two things. First, he will try to implant in them a set of good general principles. I advisedly use the word 'implant'; these are not rules of thumb, but principles which they will not be able to break without the greatest repugnance, and whose breach by others will arouse in them the highest indignation. These will be the principles they will use in their ordinary level-1 moral thinking, especially in situations of stress. Secondly, since he is not always going to be with them, and since they will have to educate *their* children, and indeed continue to educate themselves, he will teach them, as far as they are able, to do the kind of thinking that he has been doing himself. This thinking will have three functions. First of all, it will be used when the good general principles conflict in particular cases. If the principles have been well chosen, this will happen rarely; but it will happen. Secondly, there will be cases (even rarer) in which, though there is no conflict between general principles, there is something highly unusual about the case which prompts the question whether the general principles are really fitted to deal with it. But thirdly, and much the most important, this level-2 thinking will be used to *select* the general principles to be taught both to this and to succeeding generations. The general principles may change, and should change (because the environment changes). And note that, if the educator were not (as we have supposed him to be) archangelic, we could not even assume that the best level-1 principles were imparted in the first place; perhaps they might be improved.

How will the selection be done? By using level-2 thinking to consider cases, both actual and hypothetical, which crucially illustrate, and help to adjudicate, disputes between rival general principles. But, because the general principles are being selected for use in actual situations, there will have to be a careful proportioning of the weight to be put upon a particular case to the probability of its actually occurring in the lives of the people who are to use the principles. So the fantastic cases that are so beloved of anti-utilitarians will have very little employment in this kind of thinking (except as a diversion for philosophers or to illustrate purely logical points, which is sometimes necessary). Fantastic unlikely cases will never be used to turn the scales as between rival general principles for practical use. The result will be a set of general principles, constantly evolving, but on the whole stable, such that their use in moral education, including self-education, and their consequent acceptance by the society at large, will lead to the nearest possible approximation to the prescriptions of archangelic thinking. They will be the set of principles with the highest acceptance-utility. They are likely to include principles of justice.

It is now necessary to introduce some further distinctions, all of which, fortunately, have already been made elsewhere, and can therefore be merely summarised. The first, alluded to already, is that between specific rule-utilitarianism (which is practically equivalent to universalistic act-utilitarianism) and general rule-utilitarianism.[d] Both are compatible with act-utilitarianism if their rules are carefully distinguished. Specific rule-utilitarianism is appropriate to level-2 thinking, general rule-utilitarianism to level-1 thinking; and therefore the rules of specific rule-utilitarianism can be of unlimited specificity, but those of general rule-utilitarianism have to be general enough for their role. The thinking of our archangel will thus be of a specific rule-utilitarian sort; and the thinking of the ordinary people whom he has educated will be for the most part of a general rule-utilitarian sort, though they will supplement this, when they have to and when they dare, with such archangelic thinking as they are capable of.

The second distinction is that between what Professor Smart[e] calls (morally) 'right' actions and (morally) 'rational' actions. Although Smart's way of putting the distinction is not quite adequate, as he himself recognises, I shall, as he does, adopt it for the sake of brevity. Both here, and in connexion with the 'acceptance-utility' mentioned above, somewhat more sophisticated calculations of probability are required than might at first be thought. But for simplicity let us say that an action is rational if it is the action most likely to be right, even if, when all the facts are known, as they were not when it was done, it turns out not to have been right. In such a society as we have described, the (morally) rational action will nearly always be that in accordance with the good general principles of level 1, because they have been selected precisely in order to make this the case. Such actions may not always turn out to have been (morally) right in Smart's sense when the cards are turned face upwards; but the agent is not to be blamed for this.

Hare 'Ethical Theory and Utilitarianism' in Lewis (ed) *Contemporary British Philosophy*

---

[d] See Hare, 'Principles', *Proceedings of the Aristotelian Society* 1972–1973, 1–18.
[e] See J J C Smart & Bernard Williams, *Utilitarianism For and Against* (1972) Cambridge University Press.

Other reasons why rules are needed could be mentioned; for in.
from the difficulty of making calculations on each occasion, there
involved in making them which it is desirable to avoid, if we are not to spe.
our time on reflection, leaving none for action. Further, if everyone calculated ι
himself on every occasion, it would be very hard to know what to expect others to
do, and so difficult, if not impossible, to decide what to do oneself, since to decide
this one has to know what others are likely to do. So the inculcation of rules that
have been critically accepted, ie have stood the test of time, makes utilitarianism
possible. But another powerful argument for indirect utilitarianism remains: it is
that it is the only version of utilitarianism that provides an account of why a
particular action which is to the advantage of the majority of those whose
interests are directly affected by that action may, nevertheless, not be what Hare
calls the (morally) rational action to perform. To set his case up Smart has to
suppose that the sheriff has good empirical evidence that he will not be found out,
since Smart acknowledges that if he was found out, the cost of weakening respect
for law and order would outweigh the benefit of the lives saved by framing the
innocent man. But one wonders what evidence the sheriff could have that would
make him certain that he would not be found out; how, for instance, could he be
sure that the guilty man would not confess later? So it looks as though the
supposition that the sheriff will not be found out is just the sort of supposition that
makes the case one which Hare calls 'fantastic'; that is the sort of case in which
the level-1 rule that the innocent should not be punished should not be set aside.

UTILITARIANISM TODAY

We must stress again that there are as many versions of utilitarianism as there are
standards of evaluation; that it is important to distinguish act-utilitarianism from
indirect utilitarianism; that the respects in which utilitarianism has seemed to be
most objectionable to many of its critics have involved its treatment of rights and
justice; and that it would seem that only indirect utilitarianism has any chance of
meeting those objections. We shall not discuss any more criticisms of
utilitarianism here, because many of the further extracts on normative
jurisprudence that follow will involve discussions critical of it, so that we can
evaluate them *in situ*. However, to provide a reference point we would like to end
with an extract from an influential paper by Hart in which he summarises the
main contemporary objections to utilitarianism. The theory referred to in the first
sentence is Nozick's, and it is discussed in Chapter 11:

> For a just appraisal of the first of these two theories it is necessary to gain a
> clear conception of what precisely is meant by the criticism, found in different
> forms in very many different modern writers, that unqualified utilitarianism
> fails to recognize or abstracts from the separateness of persons when, as a
> political philosophy, it calls on governments to maximize the total or the
> average net happiness or welfare of their subjects. Though this accusation of
> ignoring the separateness of persons can be seen as a version of the Kantian
> principle that human beings are ends in themselves, it is none the less the
> distinctively modern criticism of utilitarianism. In England Bernard Williams[a]
> and in America John Rawls[b] have been the most eloquent expositors of this

[a] 'A Critique of Utilitarianism', in J Smart and B Williams, *Utilitarianism For and Against* 108–118 (1973); and 'Persons, Character and Morality' in *The Identity of Persons* (Rorty edn., 1977).
[b] See J Rawls, *A Theory of Justice* 22–4, 27, 181, 183, 187 (1971).

form of criticism; and John Rawls's claim that 'Utilitarianism does not take seriously the distinction between persons'[c] plays a very important role in his *A Theory of Justice*. Only faint hints of this particular criticism flickered through the many different attacks made in the past on utilitarian doctrine, ever since Jeremy Bentham in 1776 announced to the world that both government and the limits of government were to be justified by reference to the greatest happiness of the greatest number, and not by reference to any doctrine of natural rights: such doctrines he thought so much 'bawling upon paper',[d] and he first announced them in 1776 in a brief rude reply[e] to the American Declaration of Independence.

What then does this distinctively modern criticism of utilitarianism, that it ignores the moral importance of the separateness of individuals, mean? I think its meaning is to be summed up in four main points, though not all the writers who make this criticism would endorse all of them.

The first point is this: In the perspective of classical maximizing utilitarianism separate individuals are of no intrinsic importance but only important as the points at which fragments of what *is* important, i.e. the total aggregate of pleasure or happiness, are located. Individual persons for it are therefore merely the channels or locations where what is of value is to be found. It is for this reason that as long as the totals are thereby increased there is nothing, if no independent principles of distribution are introduced, to limit permissible trade-offs between the satisfactions of different persons. Hence one individual's happiness or pleasure, however innocent he may be, may be sacrificed to procure a greater happiness or pleasure located in other persons, and such replacements of one person by another are not only allowed but required by unqualified utilitarianism when unrestrained by distinct distributive principles.

Secondly, utilitarianism is not, as sometimes it is said to be, an individualistic and egalitarian doctrine, although in a sense it treats persons as equals, or of equal worth. For it does this only by in effect treating individual persons as of *no* worth; since not persons for the utilitarian but the experiences of pleasure or satisfaction or happiness which persons have are the sole items of worth or elements of value. It is of course true and very important that, according to the utilitarian maxim, 'everybody [is] to count for one, nobody for more than one',[f] in the sense that in any application of the greatest happiness calculus the equal pains or pleasures, satisfactions or dissatisfactions or preferences of different persons are given the same weight whether they be Brahmins or Untouchables, Jews or Christians, black or white. But since utilitarianism has no direct or intrinsic concern but only an instrumental concern with the relative *levels* of total well-being enjoyed by different persons, its form of equal concern and respect for persons embodied in the maxim 'everybody to count for one, nobody for more than one' may license the grossest form of inequality in the actual treatment of individuals, if that is required in order to maximize aggregate or average welfare. So long as that condition is satisfied, the situation in which a few enjoy great happiness

[c] Ibid., at 187.

[d] Bentham, *Anarchical Fallacies*, in 2 *Works* 494 (Bowring edn., 1838–43).

[e] For an account of this reply included in *An Answer to the Declaration of the American Congress* (1776) by Bentham's friend John Lind, see my 'Bentham and the United States of America', 19 *J.L. & Econ.* 547, 555–6 (1976), reprinted in my *Essays on Bentham* (Oxford, 1982), ch. III.

[f] See J S Mill, *Utilitarianism* (ch 5), in 10 *Collected Works of John Stuart Mill* 157 (1969); Bentham, *Plan of Parliamentary Reform*, in 3 *Works* 459 (Bowring edn. 1838–43).

while many suffer is as good as one in which happiness is more equally distributed.

Of course in comparing the aggregate economic welfare produced by equal and unequal distribution of resources account must be taken of factors such as diminishing marginal utility and also envy. These factors favour an equal distribution of resources, but by no means always favour it conclusively. For there are also factors pointing the other way, such as administrative and transaction costs, loss of incentives and failure of the standard assumption that all individuals are equally good pleasure or satisfaction machines, and derive the same utility from the same amount of wealth.

Thirdly, the modern critique of utilitarianism asserts that there is nothing self-evidently valuable or authoritative as a moral goal in the mere increase in totals of pleasure or happiness abstracted from all questions of distribution. The collective sum of different persons' pleasures, or the net balance of total happiness of different persons (supposing it makes sense to talk of adding them), is not in itself a pleasure or happiness which anybody experiences. Society is not an individual experiencing the aggregate collected pleasures or pains of its members; no person experiences such an aggregate.

Fourthly, according to this critique, maximizing utilitarianism, if it is not restrained by distinct distributive principles, proceeds on a false analogy between the way in which it is rational for a single prudent individual to order his life and the way in which it is rational for a whole community to order its life through government. The analogy is this: it is rational for one man as a single individual to sacrifice a present satisfaction or pleasure for a greater satisfaction later, even if we discount somewhat the value of the later satisfaction because of its uncertainty. Such sacrifices are amongst the most elementary requirements of prudence and are commonly accepted as a virtue, and indeed a paradigm of practical rationality, and, of course, any form of saving is an example of this form of rationality. In its misleading analogy with an individual's prudence, maximizing utilitarianism not merely treats one person's pleasure as replaceable by some greater pleasure of that same person, as prudence requires, but it also treats the pleasure or happiness of one individual as similarly replaceable without limit by the greater pleasure of other individuals. So in these ways it treats the division between persons as of no more moral significance than the division between times which separates one individual's earlier pleasure from his later pleasure, as if individuals were mere parts of a single persisting entity.

Hart 'Between Utility and Rights' 78 Columbia Law Review (1979), 828–846

Chapter 8
Rights

To have the right to do X is to be in a strong position when someone questions whether one should be allowed to do X.[1] For the fact that one has the right normally defeats the challenge. Thus, if a student has the right to resit an examination which he has failed, then arguments that he should not resit because he has been lazy and did not make a serious effort at the first attempt are normally defeated by the existence of his right. The right in question may not seem a very important one; but it is a good example of an institutional right which is unquestionably of importance to the members of that institution. We have many institutional rights, among the most important of which are of course the legal rights conferred by statutes and the decisions of courts, such as the right to make a will, to dispose of property that is lawfully owned, and to stand on a picket line when on strike, etc.

But as well as institutional rights many claim that there are moral rights, such as the right to freedom of speech or worship, which though they may be recognised by a constitution or legal system under which we live do not owe their existence or authority to the constitution or legal system in question. These rights, it is argued, are ones that people have whether or not they are recognised by a given constitution or legal system; so that if they are not recognised, they ought to be. Further, it is claimed that such rights have the special value that they do, because they rest on a moral conception of persons as separate individuals of equal worth, who should, in Kant's phrase, be treated as ends and not as means.[2] To signify the special importance of these rights they have been called variously 'natural', 'fundamental', 'background', etc, and it is rights of this kind that the American Declaration of Independence of 1776 invokes when it asserts that all men are created equal and have the inalienable natural rights of man to life, liberty, and the pursuit of happiness.

The existence of institutional rights, in many cases anyway, would seem to admit of a utilitarian explanation; for instance, the right of a police officer to break the speed limit when pursuing a suspect is one which could be plausibly justified on consequentialist grounds. But the existence of fundamental rights would seem to be another matter; for the importance of these resides precisely in the fact that they act as constraints on collective goals, so that if to maximise welfare one would have to violate a fundamental right, one should not try to maximise welfare. It is not surprising, therefore, that those who believe that there are fundamental rights believe that utilitarianism is fatally flawed because it does not and cannot recognise their importance as constraints on collective goals.

[1] For an excellent discussion of the issues raised in this chapter see the introduction to J Waldron (ed) *Theories of Rights* Oxford University Press, 1984; and R Martin and J W Nickel, 'Recent Work on the Concept of Rights', American Philosophical Quarterly, 17, 1980, 165–180.
[2] For an interesting discussion see J Murphy and J Coleman *The Philosophy of Law* 74–86.

Theorists who believe that there are fundamental rights which both constrain collective goals and cannot be justified on utilitarian grounds are sometimes described as 'right-based'. In an important discussion Dworkin has argued that political theories differ not only in the kinds of goals, duties, and rights that they recognise, but in the interconnections they claim exist between them (*Taking Rights Seriously* 171). Normally, a theory will take one of these categories as fundamental, and the others as derivative. For instance, utilitarianism is a goal-based theory which takes the maximisation of individual preference satisfaction as its goal, and acknowledges those rights and duties whose existence furthers that goal. By contrast, a right-based theory will treat certain rights as fundamental, and acknowledge those duties and goals which are necessary to secure the rights in question for individuals; and the theorists discussed in the following chapters, Rawls, Dworkin, and Nozick, are sometimes all classified as right-based theorists. But, apart from the fact that it is at least arguable whether this classification is defensible,[3] it is sufficient for our purposes to note one crucial respect in which all of these theorists differ from utilitarians. For while the latter believe that rights can be justified only instrumentally, on the grounds that their existence maximises welfare, they believe that fundamental rights cannot be justified in this way at all, and so treat them as things of value in their own right (J Murphy and J Coleman *The Philosophy of Law* 77). Thus, as MacCormick has argued, '. . . a theory which asserts the primacy of rights must necessarily postulate that there are goods or values which in their character as goods-which-ought-to-be-secured-to-individuals therefore count as rights' (N MacCormick *Legal Right and Social Democracy* 144).

However, while those who believe that there are fundamental rights are united in their rejection of utilitarianism, there is considerable disagreement as to which rights are fundamental. Some rights-theorists such as Dworkin believe that the defence of individual rights sometimes requires vigorous intervention by the State and other bodies, and the adoption of programmes such as positive discrimination, while others, such as Nozick, believe that a proper appreciation of what rights we have and the weight that should be given to them leads to the conclusion that such policies would be wrong. This is so because any State with powers greater than those of the so-called 'Night Watchman' State, which is 'limited to the functions of protecting all its citizens against violence, theft, and fraud, and to the enforcement of contracts, and so on' (R Nozick *Anarchy, State and Utopia* 26), has powers which will inevitably lead to the violation of rights. Clearly, these very different conclusions rest on different views of the nature and kinds of fundamental rights we have, which raises the question of how precisely claims about the existence of fundamental rights should be settled in the absence of agreement about what fundamental rights we have.

So the topic of rights raises a number of very important issues: are there any fundamental rights, and if there are, is it really true that their existence cannot be accounted for by utilitarianism? Further, if there are fundamental rights, what precisely are the rights we have? And given the lack of agreement among rights-theorists themselves in the answers they give to this last question, how are claims about the existence of fundamental rights to be justified?

Many of these issues will be touched on only lightly in this chapter; detailed

---

[3] For instance, Waldron argues convincingly that Nozick's theory of justice, which is based on a conception of rights as side-constraints, in fact has many agent-relative concerns indicating the dominance of a duty-based approach (J Waldron ed *Theories of Rights* 16).

discussion of them will, for reasons that will become clear later, be reserved for the chapters which follow devoted to the work of Rawls, Dworkin, and Nozick. But before turning to them there are a number of important questions to be considered about the analysis of the concept of a right, and the relation between rights and duties.

HOHFELD'S ANALYSIS[4]

Although concerned only with legal rights Hohfeld's analysis is a justly famous one, which continues to influence and shape contemporary discussions, not only because of the intrinsic interest of the distinctions he makes about legal rights, but also because it would seem that his distinctions, if sound, apply to other kinds of rights, including fundamental rights.

Two points about Hohfeld's analysis are of special interest: first, he raises the question whether the claim made by 'X has a right to A' is unequivocal, as he argues many had believed, or ambiguous, as he himself believed. In fact, he maintains that the term right is multiply ambiguous, and that the result of the failure to detect these ambiguities is frequent equivocation in legal arguments due to the confusion of one sense of the term with another. Analysis reveals, he claims, that there are four basic distinctions which traditional discussions of rights obscured and to which all other relevant distinctions are reducible:

(i)   privileges (which are now usually called 'liberties');
(ii)   claim-rights, which, as we shall see, are for him the only rights there are in a strict sense;
(iii) powers; and
(iv)   immunities.

We shall question later whether Hohfeld was correct to treat the distinctions he made as evidence that the term right is ambiguous; but whether or not he was correct the distinctions themselves are of great interest, and it is them rather than the 'ambiguity thesis' that we are primarily interested in.

Second, Hohfeld's account is important because of his insight that a proper analysis is a relational one which describes the relation in which a right-holder stands to another person or persons, and hence in what correlative relation they stand to him. Thus privileges, claim-rights, etc are to be distinguished by the differences that obtain in the relations between the person who has them and the other party.

(a)   Claim-rights and privileges

For ease of exposition we shall consider the distinction between claim-rights and privileges first; in the following extract Hohfeld explains how they are to be distinguished from each other by describing the differences between the correlative relations involved:[5]

[4] For discussions of Hohfeld's views see L W Sumner *The Moral Foundation of Rights* Oxford University Press, 1987, 18–31; N E Simmonds *Central Issues in Jurisprudence* 129–135; and J W Harris *Legal Philosophies* Butterworths, 1980, 76–86.
[5] Publishing details: New Haven, Yale University Press. The extensive footnotes have been omitted.

FUNDAMENTAL JURAL RELATIONS CONTRASTED WITH ONE ANOTHER

One of the greatest hindrances to the clear understanding, the incisive statement, and the true solution of legal problems frequently arises from the express or tacit assumption that all legal relations may be reduced to 'rights' and 'duties,' and that these latter categories are therefore adequate for the purpose of analyzing even the most complex legal interests, such as trusts, options, escrows, 'future' interests, corporate interests, etc. Even if the difficulty related merely to inadequacy and ambiguity of terminology, its seriousness would nevertheless be worthy of definite recognition and persistent effort toward improvement; for in any closely reasoned problem, whether legal or non-legal, chameleon-hued words are a peril both to clear thought and to lucid expression. As a matter of fact, however, the above mentioned inadequacy and ambiguity of terms unfortunately reflect, all too often, corresponding paucity and confusion as regards actual legal conceptions. That this is so may appear in some measure from the discussion to follow.

The strictly fundamental legal relations are, after all, *sui generis*; and thus it is that attempts at formal definition are always unsatisfactory, if not altogether useless. Accordingly, the most promising line of procedure seems to consist in exhibiting all of the various relations in a scheme of 'opposites' and 'correlatives,' and then proceeding to exemplify their individual scope and application in concrete cases. An effort will be made to pursue this method:

Jural Opposites	right	privilege	power	immunity
	no-right	duty	disability	liability
Jural Correlatives	right	privilege	power	immunity
	duty	no-right	liability	disability

Rights and Duties. As already intimated, the term 'rights' tends to be used indiscriminately to cover what in a given case may be a privilege, a power, or an immunity, rather than a right in the strictest sense; and this looseness of usage is occasionally recognized by the authorities. As said by Mr Justice Strong in *People v Dikeman*:

'The word "right" is defined by lexicographers to denote, among other things, *property, interest, power, prerogative, immunity, privilege* (Walker's Dict. word "Right"). In law it is most frequently applied to property in its restricted sense, but it is often used to designate *power, prerogative,* and *privilege* . . .'

Recognition of this ambiguity is also found in the language of Mr Justice Jackson, in *United States v Patrick*:

'The words "right" or "privilege" have, of course, a variety of meanings, according to the connection or context in which they are used. Their definitions, as given by standard lexicographers, include "that which one has a *legal claim to do*," "*legal power*," "*authority*," "*immunity* granted by authority," "the investiture with special or peculiar rights."'

And, similarly, in the language of Mr Justice Sneed, in *Lonas v State*:

'The state, then, is forbidden from making and enforcing any law which shall abridge the *privileges* and *immunities* of citizens of the United States. It is said that the words *rights, privileges* and *immunities*, are abusively used, as if they were synonymous. The word *rights* is generic, common, embracing whatever may be lawfully claimed.'

It is interesting to observe, also, that a tendency toward discrimination may be found in a number of important constitutional and statutory provisions. Just how accurate the distinctions in the mind of the draftsman may have been it is, of course, impossible to say.

Recognizing, as we must, the very broad and indiscriminate use of the term 'right,' what clue do we find, in ordinary legal discourse, toward limiting the word in question to a definite and appropriate meaning? That clue lies in the correlative 'duty,' for it is certain that even those who use the word and the conception 'right' in the broadest possible way are accustomed to thinking of 'duty' as the invariable correlative. As said in *Lake Shore & M. S. R. Co. v Kurtz*:

'A duty or a legal obligation is that which one ought or ought not to do. "Duty" and "right" are correlative terms. When a right is invaded, a duty is violated.'

In other words, if X has a right against Y that he shall stay off the former's land, the correlative (and equivalent) is that Y is under a duty toward X to stay off the place. If, as seems desirable, we should seek a synonym for the term 'right' in this limited and proper meaning, perhaps the word 'claim' would prove the best. The latter has the advantage of being a monosyllable. In this connection, the language of Lord Watson in *Studd v Cook* is instructive:

'Any words which in a settlement of moveables would be recognized by the law of Scotland as sufficient to create a right *or claim* in favor of an executor . . . must receive effect if used with reference to lands in Scotland.'

Privileges and 'No-Rights.' As indicated in the above scheme of jural relations, a privilege is the opposite of a duty, and the correlative of a 'no-right.' In the example last put, whereas X has a *right* or *claim* that Y, the other man, should stay off the land, he himself has the *privilege* of entering on the land; or, in equivalent words, X does not have a duty to stay off. The privilege of entering is the negation of a duty to stay off. As indicated by this case, some caution is necessary at this point; for, always, when it is said that a given privilege is the mere negation of a *duty*, what is meant, of course, is a duty having a content or tenor precisely *opposite* to that of the privilege in question. Thus, if, for some special reason, X has contracted with Y to go on the former's own land, it is obvious that X has, as regards Y, both the privilege of entering and the *duty of entering*. The privilege is perfectly consistent with this sort of duty,—for the latter is of the *same* content or tenor as the privilege;—but it still holds good that, as regards Y, X's privilege of entering is the precise negation of a duty *to stay off*. Similarly, if A has not contracted with B to perform certain work for the latter, A's privilege of *not* doing so is the very negation of a duty of *doing* so. Here again the duty contrasted is of a content or tenor exactly opposite to that of the privilege.

Passing now to the question of 'correlatives,' it will be remembered, of course, that a duty is the invariable correlative of that legal relation which is most properly called a right or claim. That being so, if further evidence be needed as to the fundamental and important difference between a right (or claim) and a privilege, surely it is found in the fact that the correlative of the latter relation is a 'no-right,' there being no single term available to express the latter conception. Thus, the correlative of X's right that Y shall not enter on the land is Y's duty not to enter; but the correlative of X's privilege of entering himself is manifestly Y's 'no-right' that X shall not enter.

In view of the considerations thus far emphasized, the importance of keeping the conception of a right (or claim) and the conception of a privilege quite distinct from each other seems evident; and, more than that, it is equally clear that there should be a separate term to represent the latter relation. No doubt, as already indicated, it is very common to use the term 'right' indiscriminately, even when the relation designated is really that of privilege; and only too often this identity of terms has involved for the particular speaker or writer a confusion or blurring of ideas. Good instances of this may be found even in unexpected places. Thus Professor Holland, in his work on *Jurisprudence*, referring to a different and well-known sort of ambiguity inherent in the Latin '*Ius*,' the German '*Recht*,' the Italian '*Diritto*,' and the French '*Droit*,'—terms used to express 'not only a "right," but also "Law" in the abstract,'—very aptly observes:

'If the expression of widely different ideas by one and the same term resulted only in the necessity for . . . clumsy periphrases, or obviously inaccurate paraphrases, no great harm would be done; but unfortunately the identity of terms seems irresistibly to suggest an identity between the ideas expressed by them.'

Curiously enough, however, in the very chapter where this appears,—the chapter on 'Rights,'—the notions of right, privilege and power seem to be blended, and that, too, although the learned author states that 'the correlative of . . . legal right is legal duty,' and that 'these pairs of terms express . . . in each case the same state of facts viewed from opposite sides.' While the whole chapter must be read in order to appreciate the seriousness of this lack of discrimination, a single passage must suffice by way of example:

'If . . . the power of the State will protect him in so carrying out his wishes, and will compel such acts or forbearances on the part of other people as may be necessary in order that his wishes may be so carried out, then he has a "legal right" so to carry out his wishes.'

The first part of this passage suggests privileges, the middle part rights (or claims), and the last part privileges.

Similar difficulties seem to exist in Professor Gray's able and entertaining work on *The Nature and Sources of Law*. In his chapter on 'Legal Rights and Duties' the distinguished author takes the position that a right always has a duty as its correlative; and he seems to define the former relation substantially according to the more limited meaning of 'claim.' Legal privileges, powers, and immunities are *prima facie* ignored, and the impression conveyed that all legal relations can be comprehended under the conceptions 'right' and 'duty.' But, with the greatest hesitation and deference, the suggestion may be ventured that a number of his examples seem to show the inadequacy of such mode of treatment. Thus eg, he says:

'The eating of shrimp salad is an interest of mine, and, if I can pay for it, the law will protect that interest, and it is therefore a right of mine to eat shrimp salad which I have paid for, although I know that shrimp salad always gives me the colic.'

This passage seems to suggest primarily two classes of relations: *first*, the party's respective privileges, as against A, B, C, D and others in relation to eating the salad, or, correlatively, the respective 'no-rights' of A, B, C, D and others that the party should not eat the salad; *second*, the party's respective rights (or claims) as against A, B, C, D and others that they should not interfere with the physical act of eating the salad, or, correlatively, the respective duties of A, B, C, D and others that they should not interfere.

These two groups of relations seem perfectly distinct; and the privileges could, in a given case, exist even though the rights mentioned did not. A, B, C and D, being the owners of the salad, might say to X: 'Eat the salad, if you can; you have our license to do so, but we don't agree not to interfere with you.' In such a case the privileges exist, so that if X succeeds in eating the salad, he has violated no rights of any of the parties. But it is equally clear that if A had succeeded in holding so fast to the dish that X couldn't eat the contents, no right of X would have been violated.

Hohfeld *Fundamental Legal Conceptions as Applied in Judicial Reasoning* 35–41

As Hohfeld makes clear, an important difference between a claim-right and a privilege is that while in the first case there is a correlative duty, there is none in the second. For instance, if Y has promised to pay X £10, then X can claim £10 from Y as a matter of right, and the correlative duty is, of course, Y's duty to pay X £10. But if X has a liberty against Y to smoke in his presence, because doing this is not forbidden—so that in Hohfeld's terminology he has a privilege—Y does not have a corresponding duty to facilitate X's smoking. Indeed, since X's liberty consists only in the absence of a duty to refrain from smoking in Y's presence, Y would not be at fault if he tried to dissuade X from smoking. Of course, there are ways in which it would be wrong for Y to try to stop X smoking in his presence, for instance, by taking the cigarette from his mouth. However, these are ruled out not by X's liberty to smoke in Y's presence, but by X's right not to be physically assaulted.

Of course, X may be at liberty to smoke in Y's presence but not in Z's, because there is a prohibition in the latter case but not the former. Similarly, X's claim-right to £10 discussed above is a right against Y which clearly does not give him a similar right against anyone else, since it originated in a specific transaction between X and Y. Such rights have been called by Hart *special rights*, on the grounds that they arise out of special transactions between specific individuals, or from some special relationship between them, such as the recognition by X of Y's authority as a result of which Y acquires the right to direct certain aspects of X's behaviour.[6] But as well as rights which are in this sense special, Hart distinguishes ones which are *general* in the sense that they are possessed equally by all members of a society; for instance, the right to vote in elections, or the right to park by the roadside in an unrestricted area. The existence of general as well as special rights raises some difficult issues for Hohfeld's correlativity thesis. For there seem to be duties, including those which Bentham called 'public', such as the duty not to counterfeit money, to pay one's taxes, or to do military service, which are not owed to anyone in particular.[7] But whether or not the existence of general rights means that Hohfeld's theory has to be modified in some respects, his main distinctions would seem to apply to general rights as well as to special

[6] See H L Hart, 'Are There Any Natural Rights?', Philosophical Review, LXIV (1955) 175–191.
[7] For discussion of these see L W Sumner, *The Moral Foundation of Rights* 39–42.

ones. For while the right to vote is a claim-right imposing on others the correlative duty of not using coercive means to stop those with the right exercising it, the right to park by the roadside if there are no restrictions is simply a liberty. If you park in a place I had hoped to use, you have not violated my right, since its correlative is in Hohfeldian terms only a 'no-right' on your part that I should not park there, ie you are in no position to demand that I should not park there, but at the same time you are at liberty to do so yourself.

Many important 'rights' involve liberties, but not claim-rights. For instance, the existence of X's right to manufacture and sell a certain product does not mean that others violate that right if they go into competition with him and try to put him out of business, provided, of course, that they do not use means which violate his other rights. As Simmonds says, 'It is therefore a fallacy to argue that if X has a right to run a business, Y has a duty not to interfere with him. The argument would be valid only if by "a right" we meant a claim-right; but X enjoys only a *liberty* to run a business, and such a liberty does not entail any duty on Y's part' (N E Simmonds *Central Issues in Jurisprudence* 131). Another example of a 'right' which is not a claim-right under English law is the right to picket, which does not impose a duty on others to stop and listen (J W Harris *Legal Philosophies* 78). It does not follow, of course, that therefore it is merely a liberty, since there are other possible ways of classifying it in the Hofeldian scheme which we have yet to consider; but the fact that it is not a claim-right is important, because many people think that rights such as this are more substantial than they are, which supports Hohfeld's claim that this is an area in which important distinctions are easily confused.

In this connection a distinction within the category of claim-rights itself is important. For some impose only a duty of non-interference, while others impose a requirement of assistance, eg welfare rights. Thus 'I have a right to work' can be interpreted either as a claim that others have a duty not to prevent me forcibly from so doing, or as a claim that others ought to provide the means to make it possible for me to work. But many who argue that claim-rights of the first kind are important, have severe reservations about those of the second kind; Nozick, for instance, argues that the nature of the claim made on others in such cases violates their rights by redistributing goods to which they are entitled.

(b) Powers and immunities

We saw earlier that as well as claim-rights and liberties Hohfeld distinguished two further categories, powers and immunities, and our next extract considers these.

> *Powers and Liabilities.* As indicated in the preliminary scheme of jural relations, a legal power (as distinguished, of course, from a mental or physical power) is the opposite of legal disability, and the correlative of legal liability. But what is the intrinsic nature of a legal power as such? Is it possible to analyze the conception represented by this constantly employed and very important term of legal discourse? Too close an analysis might seem metaphysical rather than useful; so that what is here presented is intended only as an approximate explanation, sufficient for all practical purposes.
>
> A change in a given legal relation may result (1) from some superadded fact or group of facts not under the volitional control of a human being (or human beings); or (2) from some superadded fact or group of facts which are under the volitional control of one or more human beings. As regards the

second class of cases, the person (or persons) whose volitional control is paramount may be said to have the (legal) power to effect the particular change of legal relations that is involved in the problem.

This second class of cases—powers in the technical sense—must now be further considered. The nearest synonym for any ordinary case seems to be (legal) 'ability,'—the latter being obviously the opposite of 'inability,' or 'disability.' The term 'right,' so frequently and loosely used in the present connection, is an unfortunate term for the purpose,—a not unusual result being confusion of thought as well as ambiguity of expression. The term 'capacity' is equally unfortunate; for, as we have already seen, when used with discrimination, this word denotes a particular group of operative facts, and not a legal relation of any kind.

Many examples of legal powers may readily be given. Thus, X, the owner of ordinary personal property 'in a tangible object' has the power to extinguish his own legal interests (rights, powers, immunities, etc.) through that totality of operative facts known as abandonment; and—simultaneously and correlatively—to create in other persons privileges and powers relating to the abandoned object,—eg, the power to acquire title to the latter by appropriating it. *Similarly*, X has the power to transfer his interest to Y,—that is, to extinguish his own interest and concomitantly create in Y a new and corresponding interest. So also X has the power to create contractual obligations of various kinds. Agency cases are likewise instructive. By the use of some *metaphorical* expression such as the Latin, *qui facit per alium, facit per se*, the true nature of agency relations is only too frequently obscured. The creation of an agency relation involves, *inter alia*, the grant of legal powers to the so-called agent, and the creation of correlative liabilities in the principal. That is to say, one party, P, has the power to create agency powers in another party, A,—for example, the power to convey P's property, the power to impose (so-called) contractual obligations on P, the power to discharge a debt owing to P, the power to 'receive' title to property so that it shall vest in P, and so forth. In passing, it may be well to observe that the term 'authority,' so frequently used in agency cases, is very ambiguous and slippery in its connotation. Properly employed in the present connection, the word seems to be an abstract or qualitative term corresponding to the concrete 'authorization,'—the latter consisting of a particular group of operative facts taking place between the principal and the agent. All too often, however, the term in question is so used as to blend and confuse these operative facts with the powers and privileges thereby created in the agent. A careful discrimination in these particulars would, it is submitted, go far toward clearing up certain problems in the law of agency.

Essentially similar to the powers of agents are powers of appointment in relation to property interests. So, too, the powers of public officers are, intrinsically considered, comparable to those of agents,—for example, the power of a sheriff to sell property under a writ of execution. The power of a donor, in a gift *causa mortis*, to revoke the gift and divest the title of the donee is another clear example of the legal quantities now being considered, also a pledgee's statutory power of sale. . . .

In view of what has already been said, very little may suffice concerning a *liability* as such. The latter, as we have seen, is the correlative of power, and the opposite of immunity (or exemption). While no doubt the term 'liability' is often loosely used as a synonym for 'duty,' or 'obligation,' it is believed, from an extensive survey of judicial precedents, that the connotation already adopted as most appropriate to the word in question is fully justified. A few cases tending to indicate this will now be noticed. In *McNeer v McNeer*, Mr Justice Magruder balanced the conceptions of power and liability as follows:

'So long as she lived, however, his interest in her land lacked those *elements of property*, such as *power of disposition* and *liability to sale on* execution which had formerly given it the character of a vested estate.'

In *Booth v Commonwealth*, the court had to construe a Virginia statute providing 'that all free white male persons who are twenty-one years of age and not over sixty, shall be *liable* to serve as jurors, except as hereinafter provided.' It is plain that this enactment imposed only a *liability* and not a *duty*. It is a liability to have a duty created. The latter would arise only when, in exercise of their powers, the parties litigant and the court officers had done what was necessary to impose a specific duty to perform the functions of a juror. The language of the court, by Moncure, J., is particularly apposite as indicating that liability is the opposite, or negative, of immunity (or exemption):

'The word both expressed and implied is "liable," which has a very different meaning from "qualified" . . . Its meaning is "bound" or "obliged." . . . A person exempt from serving on juries is not liable to serve, and a person not liable to serve is exempt from serving. The terms seem to be convertible.'

A further good example of judicial usage is to be found in *Emery v Clough*. Referring to a gift *causa mortis* and the donee's liability to have his already vested interest divested by the donor's exercise of his power of revocation, Mr Justice Smith said:

'The title to the gift *causa mortis* passed by the delivery, defeasible only in the lifetime of the donor, and his death perfects the title in the donee by terminating the donor's right or *power of defeasance*. The property passes from the donor to the donee directly . . . and after his death it is *liable* to be *divested* only in favor of the donor's creditors. . . . His right and power ceased with his death.'

Perhaps the nearest synonym of 'liability' is 'subjection' or 'responsibility.' As regards the latter word, a passage from Mr Justice Day's opinion *McElfresh v Kirkendall* is interesting:

'The words "debt" and "liability" are not synonymous, and they are not commonly so understood. As applied to the pecuniary relations of the parties, liability is a term of broader significance than debt. . . . Liability is responsibility.'

While the term in question has the broad generic connotation already indicated, no doubt it very frequently indicates that specific form of liability (or complex of liabilities) that is correlative to a power (or complex of powers) vested in a party litigant and the various court officers. Such was held to be the meaning of a certain California statute involved in the case of *Lattin v Gillette*. Said Mr Justice Harrison:

'The word "liability" is the condition in which an individual is placed after a breach of his contract, or a violation of any obligation resting upon him. It is defined by Bouvier to be responsibility.'

Immunities and Disabilities. As already brought out, immunity is the correlative of disability ('no-power'), and the opposite, or negation, of liability. Perhaps it will also be plain, from the preliminary outline and from the discussion down to this point, that a power bears the same general contrast to an immunity that a right does to a privilege. A right is one's affirmative claim against another, and a privilege is one's freedom from the right or claim of another. Similarly, a power is one's affirmative 'control' over a given legal relation as against another; whereas an immunity is one's freedom from the legal power or 'control' of another as regards some legal relation.

A few examples may serve to make this clear. X, a landowner, has, as we have seen, power to alienate to Y or to any other ordinary party. On the other hand, X has also various immunities as against Y, and all other ordinary parties. For Y is under a disability (ie, has no power) so far as shifting the legal interest either to himself or to a third party is concerned; and what is true of Y applies similarly to everyone else who has not by virtue of special operative facts acquired a power to alienate X's property. If, indeed, a sheriff has been duly empowered by a writ of execution to sell X's interest, that is a very different matter: correlative to such sheriff's power would be the *liability* of X,—the very opposite of immunity (or exemption). It is elementary, too, that as against the sheriff, X might be immune or exempt in relation to certain parcels of property, and be liable as to others. Similarly, if an agent has been duly appointed by X to sell a given piece of property, then, as to the latter, X has, in relation to such agent, a liability rather than an immunity.

For over a century there has been, in this country, a great deal of important litigation involving immunities from powers of taxation. If there be any lingering misgivings as to the 'practical' importance of accuracy and discrimination in legal conceptions and legal terms, perhaps some of such doubts would be dispelled by considering the numerous cases on valuable taxation exemptions coming before the United States Supreme Court. Thus, in *Phoenix Ins. Co. v Tennessee*, Mr Justice Peckham expressed the views of the court as follows:

'In granting to the De Soto Company "all the rights, privileges, and immunities" of the Bluff City Company, all words are used which could be regarded as necessary to carry the exemption from taxation possessed by the Bluff City Company; while in the next following grant, that of the charter of the plaintiff in error, the word "immunity" is omitted. Is there any meaning to be attached to that omission, and if so, what? We think some meaning is to be attached to it. The word "immunity" expresses more clearly and definitely an intention to include therein an exemption from taxation than does either of the other words. Exemption from taxation is more accurately described as an "immunity" than as a privilege, although it is not to be denied that the latter word may sometimes and under some circumstances include such exemptions.'

In *Morgan v Louisiana* there is an instructive discussion from the pen of Mr Justice Field. In holding that on a foreclosure sale of the franchise and property of a railroad corporation an immunity from taxation did not pass to the purchaser, the learned judge said:

'As has been often said by this court, the whole community is interested in retaining the power of taxation undiminished. . . . The exemption of the property of the company from taxation, and the exemption of its officers and servants from jury and military duty, were both intended for the benefit of the company, and its benefit alone. In their personal character they are analogous to exemptions from execution of certain property of debtors, made by laws of several of the states.'

So far as immunities are concerned, the two judicial discussions last quoted concern respectively problems of interpretation and problems of alienability. In many other cases difficult constitutional questions have arisen as the result of statutes impairing or extending various kinds of immunities. Litigants have, from time to time, had occasion to appeal both to the clause against impairment of the obligation of contracts and to the provision against depriving a person of property without due process of law. This has been especially true as regards exemptions from taxation and exemptions from execution.

If a word may now be permitted with respect to mere terms as such, the first thing to note is that the word 'right' is overworked in the field of immunities as elsewhere. As indicated, however, by the judicial expressions already quoted, the best synonym is, of course, the term 'exemption.' It is instructive to note, also, that the word 'impunity' has a very similar connotation. This is made evident by the interesting discriminations of Lord Chancellor Finch in *Skelton v Skelton*, a case decided in 1677:

'But this I would by no means allow, that equity should enlarge the restraints of the disabilities introduced by act of parliament; and as to the granting of injunctions to stay waste, I took a distinction where tenant hath only *impunitatem*, and where he hath *jus in arboribus*. If the tenant have only a bare indemnity or *exemption* from an action (at law), if he committed waste, there it is fit he should be restrained by injunction from committing it.'

Hohfeld *Fundamental Legal Conceptions as Applied in Judicial Reasoning* 50–63

To have a legal power is to be in a position to change certain of the legal rights, duties, and obligations of others. Legal powers are important precisely because they make such changes possible, for if there were no such changes a legal system would rapidly ossify. As the owner of my car I have a variety of legal powers, for instance, the power to leave it in my will to another, or to give it to him, or to sell it, etc. And if I exercise these powers, the rights I have at present in the car pass to someone else, so that I not only cease to be in a position to make certain claims, but also acquire new duties. The correlative to a power is, according to Hohfeld, a liability on the part of others to be affected by its exercise. For example, a board of examiners has the power to pass or fail the students who present themselves to it, and they are thus liable to be judged accordingly. But that liability does not extend to those over whom the board has no jurisdiction. At first sight Hohfeld's point might seem to be no more than a truism; but its importance will become clearer when we have considered what he has to say about his remaining category, that of immunities.

If X has an immunity with respect to a matter A against Y, then Y not only lacks the power to change X's interest in A, but cannot legitimately acquire such a power while the immunity is in force. So, for instance, if I have obtained an exemption from a local bye-law, then I at the same time obtain an immunity against prosecution for violating it. Constitutional rights such as freedom of speech involve important immunities; for the existence of such a right is a barrier not only to a government trying to stop me speaking my mind now, but also to its taking powers that would entitle it to do so in the future. The correlative of an immunity is a disability; for if X has an immunity with respect to A against Y, then Y lacks the ability in X's case to affect A. So in countries in which there is a constitutional right to free speech, the legislature does not have the ability to pass legislation which infringes the right. Finally, we can now see more clearly why Hohfeld said that the correlative of a power is a liability; for if X lacks an immunity with respect to A against Y, then he is clearly liable to have his interest in A affected by Y.

(c)   Problems with Hohfeld's analysis

In this section we want briefly to discuss two sets of issues. The first set involves the correlativity thesis,[8] while the second set concerns the broader applicability of Hohfeld's distinctions and of his claim that in a strict sense of 'right' only claim-rights are rights.

(i)   Correlativity

If there are duties which do not have correlative rights, then the claim made by Hohfeld's correlativity thesis that claim-rights and duties are correlative would seem to be open to a knock-down objection. But if it is, then so is the thesis, which various philosophers have argued for, that rights and duties are correlative, even though their grounds for maintaining this may have differed from Hohfeld's which were, of course, that strictly speaking only claim-rights are rights, and claim-rights have correlative duties.

We have already mentioned Bentham's public duties of not counterfeiting money, paying taxes, and performing military service as examples of duties which do not have correlative individual rights, and it has been argued that there are many other examples. White, for instance, maintains that moral and religious codes such as the Decalogue impose duties without conferring rights:

> Such duties to do something, which are nevertheless not duties to anyone, may even include duties to do something to someone, as when it is my duty to punish an offender, to stop the opposing centre forward, to expose someone's felony or, in a totalitarian country, to inform on my parents. It would be queer to suggest that, because of my duty, the offender has a right to be punished, the centre forward a right to be stopped, or the felon or my parents a right to be informed on.
>
> White *Rights* 60

White goes on to argue that there are also many examples of legal duties which do not have correlative rights: for instance, the duty not to carry offensive weapons in a public place, to insure a car, and to observe road signs are all duties '. . . which contain no reference to duties to other people and, therefore, in no way imply corresponding rights in others' (A R White *Rights* 63).

Though one might quarrel with some of these examples, they are so numerous that it is clear that the correlativity thesis is false if it claims that to every duty there corresponds a claim-right. However, this still leaves a way of defending a

---

[8] For a critical discussion of the correlativity thesis see A R White *Rights* Clarendon Press, 55–73. For an interesting discussion of the issues see J W Harris *Legal Philosophies* 81–84.

version of the correlativity thesis. Note, to begin with, that even supposing that apparent counter-examples to the thesis can be accounted for, a puzzling question arises about right-based theories, particularly if they claim, as Hohfeld did, that the only genuine rights are claim-rights. For if claim-rights and duties are strictly correlative, and the only rights there are are claim-rights, then it is difficult to see how we can make a meaningful distinction between right-based and duty-based theories. Surely, on Hohfeld's account to take rights seriously is to take duties seriously, and vice-versa, and to give pride of place to one of these categories is simply a mistake?

Part of the answer to this argument is that the difference between the theories resides in the grounds for positing the correlation; the two types of theory appeal to different grounds, and, as a result the correlativity thesis has to be understood differently in the two cases. In a helpful discussion Waldron has described the different grounds which a right-based and a duty-based theorist might cite for prohibiting the use of torture by the police and others:

> Most of us think that the reason for this requirement has to do with the profound and traumatic suffering that torture necessarily involves. If so, that is if our recognition of this requirement is generated by a concern for the interests of those who might be tortured, we may say that the requirement is *right*-based. But some people think there are other grounds for concern in this case: it may be thought that the deliberate infliction of suffering debases and degrades the torturer, derogating from his humanity and undermining his rational integrity. If this is what we think, then to that extent our concern about torture is *duty*-based. Now, of course, most people feel both sorts of concern. But if it is possible to identify one sort of concern as more basic than another in a theory, to that extent the *theory* may be called right-based or duty-based.
>
> Waldron *Theories of Rights* 13

So, in so far as a theory is right-based, it will argue that correlative duties are required to protect the rights of individuals, which are things of value in their own right; whereas the rationale of the correlative duties is such that they are of value not in their own right but simply because of their function of protecting things of value, viz individual rights. But though the theory is thus committed to maintaining that the rationale of many duties is the fact that they protect rights, it could perfectly well admit that there are other duties which have an independent rationale, so that there is no reason to suppose that these duties have correlative rights. Hence, though the theory would be committed to the claim that every right, or at least every one of a certain kind, has a correlative duty, it need not be committed to the claim that every duty has a corresponding right; so that it is now much less clear that White's examples constitute a counter-example to the version of the correlativity thesis to which the theory is committed.

Of course, if there are reasons for thinking, contrary to what Hohfeld argues, that claim-rights are not the only sort of rights there are, then the thesis that to every right there corresponds a duty may still be false. For instance, if immunities can constitute the core of certain important rights, then there will be rights which do not have correlative duties; for the correlative of an immunity is not a duty but a disability. Hence, the importance of the question to be discussed in the next section of whether all rights are claim-rights.

(ii)   Rights and claim-rights

We said earlier that if Hohfeld's distinctions apply in the legal domain, then it is plausible to suppose that they apply more widely both to discussions of institutional rights in general and to ones of fundamental rights. Since the claim is plausible, though difficult to substantiate, we shall not argue it here. But if it is conceded, it becomes important to ask whether Hohfeld was right to claim that in a strict sense all genuine legal-rights are claim-rights. For if this is so, then it would seem reasonable to claim that all genuine rights, whether institutional or fundamental, are claim-rights also.

Before we turn to a discussion of this claim it is important to underline the fact that its rejection, which we think is correct, does not entail the rejection of Hohfeld's distinctions themselves. For it is possible to combine a rejection of Hohfeld's thesis that strictly speaking the only legal rights there are are claim-rights, with the thesis that rights are what Sumner has called bundles of Hohfeldian positions which confer normative advantages on those who occupy them. Moreover, in the light of the discussion at the end of the previous section it is interesting to note that Sumner's argument supports the conclusion that '. . . at least some rights are just immunities'.

Whatever rights may be, everyone agrees that they too are normatively advantageous. Thus we may limit the materials out of which they are to be constructed to those Hohfeldian positions which are advantages. But which of them? Here we can broadly distinguish two hypotheses. One is that rights are simple, thus that every right consists of just one position. The other is that rights are complex, thus that every right consists of some bundle of different positions. These two hypotheses do not, of course, exhaust the possibilities; some rights might be simple while others are complex. Further, we can easily distinguish between monistic and pluralistic versions of each hypothesis. A monistic version of the first hypothesis would hold that every right consists of the same normative position, while a pluralistic version would allow different rights to consist of different positions (though only one in each case). Likewise, a monistic version of the second hypothesis would hold that every right consists of the same bundle of positions, while a pluralistic version would allow different rights to consist of different bundles. Given the variety of possible analyses, it will be out of the question to give a full hearing to each. Thus I will confine myself to offering some considerations in favour of a view which is both complex and pluralistic.

Let us begin, however, with the idea that rights are simple, thus that every right is identical to some single Hohfeldian advantage. Which one (or ones)? As we have seen, Hohfeld himself identified rights 'in the strictest sense' with claims, thus holding a monistic version of the simple view. Certainly it seems likely that if all rights are to be identified with the same simple position then claims will have, as it were, the strongest claim. But it will be instructive to postpone consideration of Hohfeld's proposals a little, until we have had an opportunity to examine the credentials of the other contenders. Could rights, then, be just liberties? Hobbes thought so:

'For though they that speak of this subject, use to confound *Jus*, and *Lex*, *Right* and *Law*; yet they ought to be distinguished; because RIGHT, consisteth in liberty to do, or to forbeare; whereas LAW, determineth, and bindeth to one of them: so that Law, and Right, differ as much, as

Obligation, and Liberty; which in one and the same matter are inconsistent.'[a]

It is immediately noticeable, however, that Hobbes identified the right to do something not with the mere (half) liberty to do it but with the (full) liberty 'to do, or to forbear'. Technically, therefore, he held that every right is a bundle of two related Hohfeldian positions, thus defending a (monistic) version of the complex view. Still, since both of the positions in question are liberties, it is probably more illuminating to treat Hobbes's analysis of rights as a (slightly deviant) simple one.

Certainly if rights are just liberties then there is little plausibility in the idea that they are mere half liberties. One element present in at least many rights is the agent's opportunity to choose, free of deontic constraints, among alternative courses of action. Since a half liberty to do something is compatible with, because entailed by, a duty to do it, it cannot by itself capture this feature of deontically unhindered choice. Thus at least some rights either are, or at least contain, full liberties. Indeed it is questionable whether any right can consist of only one liberty without its complementary half. Imagine that some rule system imposes on you the duty to bleep. Knowing this, would I then want to say that you have a right to bleep? Ordinarily, conventions of conversational implicature would dictate otherwise. In saying that you have a right to bleep I conversationally imply that I have given a full account of your normative position with respect to bleeping, thus that you do not also have a duty to bleep. Saying that you have a right when I know that you have a duty would then be akin to saying that you have two children when I know that you have three. However, if it would be conversationally deviant in this latter case for me to say that you have two children this fact does nothing to show that what I say is false; after all, if you have three children then you do also have two. Likewise, even if it would be conversationally deviant for me to say that you have the right to bleep, you may have the right for all that. And in some cases it is not even conversationally deviant. Thus, for example, I might quite intelligibly say that you have the right to chair the meeting when I know that you have the duty to do so. In such instances of what Feinberg has called 'mandatory rights' the background presupposition is generally either that the duty in question is a mark of some desirable rank or privilege (as in the case of the right and duty to vote or to serve as a juror, both of which can be regarded as privileges of citizenship) or that it can otherwise be seen as a benefit as well as a burden (as in the case of a child's right and duty to attend school). For all we have said thus far, there might be good reasons for thinking that the notion of a mandatory right is deviant or oxymoronic. But at this stage of our inquiry it would be arbitrary to insist that rights must contain full liberties.

The special case of mandatory rights is, however, instructive in one respect. Where we are tempted to ascribe such rights there are normative elements in the picture besides the right-holder's duty and consequent half liberty. If you have a genuine right to chair the meeting then the other members are obliged not to interfere with your doing so. Likewise, if I have a legal right to vote then private individuals are required not to prevent me from doing so (eg, by impeding my access to the polling station) and electoral officials are required to assist me in doing so (eg, by offering me a ballot). A similar framework of duties imposed on others is visible in each of the other cases of mandatory

---

[a] Hobbes *Leviathan* 189.

rights. This fact suggests something important, namely that a mere half liberty by itself, without any supporting duties of assistance or non-interference imposed on others, does not constitute a right. And if this is so, then the same seems to hold of full liberties. Hobbes's natural rights, which are fully enjoyed by everyone in the state of nature, are notoriously lacking in such supporting duties. My possession of them therefore imposes no normative constraint on others. But if the choice which is provided by a full liberty seems to be one ingredient in our ordinary concept of a right, another such ingredient seems to be the imposition of some constraints on others. As we have seen, this ingredient, however vague it might be, is especially prominent in the case of those rights which play a role in moral/political argument. If rights are to constrain others, however, they must contain something more than mere liberties (whether half or full). The view that rights are full liberties nicely captures the idea of deontically unencumbered choice which is central to at least some rights. But it omits the idea of insulation against the liberties of others which is just as central. In order to capture this latter idea liberties must be surrounded by what H L A Hart has usefully called a 'protective perimeter' of duties imposed on others.[b] But the structure of a right which we assemble in this manner will be necessarily complex.

Since powers are the higher-order counterparts of liberties the proposal that (at least some) rights are just powers requires little independent assessment. As in the case of liberties, we can distinguish half powers and full powers. The counterpart of a mandatory right will therefore be something like a 'necessary power'—ie, the power to affect some normative relation in some particular way without the power not to do so, or vice versa.[c] Just as we can question whether mandatory rights are genuine rights, we could also question whether necessary powers are genuine rights. But anyone who chose to identify rights with powers in the first place would be thinking of those cases in which someone has both the power to affect some relation and the power not to do so. The holder of such a (full) power has the alethic analogue of deontic freedom of choice. If I have a full liberty then there are different options among which I may choose (which are permissible for me). If I have a full power then there are different options among which I can choose (which are possible for me). Thus both full liberties and full powers are capable of being *exercised*, since in each case exercising them means selecting one of the available (permissible/possible) options.

To the extent that (deontically or alethically) unencumbered choice is one important ingredient in our common conception of a right, then the idea that at least some rights are simply full powers will hold some attraction. Thus we might think that my right to make a will consists solely of my power (or capacity) to do so or not as I choose, or that a police officer's right to make an arrest consists solely of her power (or authority) to do so or not as she chooses. But a little further reflection reveals that in such cases, just as in the parallel cases of full liberties, we invariably attribute to the right-holder some additional normative advantages. The most obvious of these is the one which we added to liberty, namely a protective perimeter of duties borne by others. Thus we would not think much of my 'right' to make a will if, while I have the power to do so or not as I choose, others are permitted to prevent me from

---

[b] See p 249 of this vol.
[c] I have a necessary power whenever some particular alteration of a relation is impossible for me. I then lack the power to alter it, but (trivially) have the power not to alter it.

exercising this power. A mere power, which by itself can impose no constraints on others, seems too defenceless to count as a genuine right.

In the case of powers, however, there are two further ingredients whose addition to the package is necessitated by the fact that powers are second-order normative positions. The first is an immunity against the like powers of others. We would also not think much of my 'right' to make a will if, while I have the power to do so or not as I choose, others have the same power (to make a will for me or not as they choose). We ordinarily assume that my right to make a will confers on me exclusive control over whether anything will come to count as *my* will. But my (full) power to make a will does not by itself assure me of this control. To do so it must be accompanied by a guarantee that no one else has a power with the same content. Thus the protective perimeter of powers consists not just of claims (ie, duties borne by others) but also of immunities (ie, disabilities borne by others). Since immunities are the higher-order counterparts of claims, this is exactly what we should expect. Meanwhile, the second additional ingredient is one which we need not add to a liberty because it is itself a liberty. We would also not think much of my 'right' to make a will if, while I have the power to do so or not as I choose, I also have the duty not to do so. Thus we must add to a power at least the higher-order liberty to exercise it. Must we also add the liberty not to exercise it? If I am to have full control over whether anything will come to count as my will, then my full power must be accompanied by a full liberty to exercise it or not as I choose. But just as we can make some sense of first-order mandatory rights (ie, mandatory or directed liberties), so we can also make some sense of second-order mandatory rights (ie, mandatory or directed powers). Thus, for instance, a university registrar may be empowered to issue academic transcripts but also required to do so in the case of any applicant who satisfies some specified conditions. It would not be a gross abuse of language to say that the registrar has the right to issue transcripts, despite the fact that (when these conditions are satisfied) he lacks the liberty not to.

Whatever we may think of second-order mandatory rights, it is clear that when we think of powers as rights we are normally thinking of them as ingredients in some complex package. Interestingly, the same need not hold for immunities. We are less tempted to identify rights with immunities if only because immunities tend to be both less common and less visible than other normative positions. But some high-profile rights are arguably just immunities. Consider, for example, a constitutionally guaranteed right of free speech. The normative effect of entrenching such a right in the constitution of a municipal legal system might be to disable the legislature from regulating speech in certain ways (eg, on grounds of content rather than occasion). If so, then the right confers an immunity against legislative restriction of a first-order liberty (or bundle of liberties). The right therefore entails the liberty, which might seem to show that once again it is a package consisting at least of an immunity plus a liberty. But closer inspection reveals that this is not (necessarily) the case. The liberty which is entailed by the right is also entailed by the immunity, since it is an immunity against legislative restriction of *that* liberty. The relationship between the liberty and the immunity is thus logical rather than normative: the liberty is part of the content of the immunity. Since every second-order normative position must take some first-order position as part of its content, there is a sense in which no second-order position is simple. But the logical complexity of second-order positions is irrelevant to the issue of whether at least some rights consist solely of such positions. Since the first-order liberty which is insulated from abridgement by a second-order immunity is already included in that immunity, we need not add it as part of a more complex package. Furthermore, since we can easily imagine the immunity also insulating the protective perimeter of the liberty against legislative interference, we need not add that either. Indeed, it may be that once we have fully spelled out the content of the immunity (ie, the full set of first-order deontic positions which it insulates against change), nothing more will be needed in order for it to qualify as a genuine right. Certainly since the immunity is not a power it cannot require further protection by an immunity; nor, for the same reason, does it require a higher-order liberty to exercise it. An immunity thus appears not to need supplementation by any of the ingredients which we have found reason to add to bare liberties and powers. It seems reasonable to think that at least some immunities, all by themselves, are rights, and thus that at least some rights are just immunities.

Let us take stock of results so far. There seems little merit in the idea that a bare liberty (even a full liberty) can constitute a right since it can impose no normative constraints on others. There is even less merit in the idea that a bare power can constitute a right since it requires supplementation by a number of further ingredients. On the other hand, it seems reasonable to think that a bare immunity can constitute a right since it does impose a normative constraint (a disability) on others. However, we have no reason to suppose that all rights are just immunities, or even that all rights include immunities. We have thus not got far with defending the simple view that every right is identical with precisely one normative advantage. This is not surprising, however, for we have not yet considered the strongest version of this view. There still remains the possibility that (some or all) rights are just claims.

As we have seen, Hohfeld defended the view that rights 'in the strictest sense' are just claims. A similar view has been defended by Feinberg. Since claims impose deontic constraints on others it is easy to see why they have been singled out as capturing the insistent or peremptory quality of rights. Indeed, the plausibility in the idea that some rights are just immunities seems to derive from the fact that immunities, being the second-order analogues of claims, impose alethic constraints which are the analogues of deontic constraints. None the less, we already have decisive evidence against the (monistic) hypothesis that all rights are nothing but claims. If some rights are full liberties with a protective perimeter of duties, while others are full powers with a similar protective perimeter (plus additional ingredients), and still others are bare immunities, then some rights are not just claims. Indeed, surprisingly few rights consist of nothing but claims. The standard model for illustrating the claim-duty normative relation is that of two-party agreements in which the first party's claim against the second hooks up directly with the second party's duty to the first. But the making of agreements involves the power to impose duties on oneself (thereby conferring claims on the other party), while the terms of most agreements also involve the power to waive one's claims (thereby extinguishing the duties of the other party). Contractual rights are thus unintelligible without the notion of a power (and doubtless that of an immunity as well).

Sumner *The Moral Foundation of Rights* 32–39

Sumner goes on to raise the question whether some rights are bare claims, but argues that the answer to this question depends on the answer to the issue to be discussed in the following section of whether there is some common feature possessed by the different bundles in virtue of which they are all rights.

PROTECTED CHOICES v PROTECTED INTERESTS

Sumner's argument that rights are bundles of Hohfeldian positions which confer a normative advantage on those who occupy them is persuasive. But if different bundles can constitute rights as he claims, the question arises of what it is about the different bundles which leads us to classify them all as rights. If some rights are full liberties with a protective perimeter, others are powers also with a protective perimeter, and yet others are immunities, what is the source of our perception that there is a unity underlying this diversity? Without an answer to this question we may have an account of rights which is descriptively adequate, but we certainly have not got one which is intellectually satisfying.

In the rest of this section we shall consider two conflicting answers to this question. According to the first, the choice-theory (sometimes called the 'will theory')—if X has a right against Y to do A, then X's decision as to whether A shall be done or not is decisive. So the existence of the right recognises the autonomy of his choice to do A or not as the case may be. According to the second, the interest-theory (sometimes called the 'benefit theory')—if X has a right against Y to do A, then X has an interest which is, or ought to be, protected by the imposition on Y of a duty, a disability, or a liability.

Hart's development of the choice-theory in the next extract is of great interest because he develops his own theory in conscious opposition to a version of the interest-theory defended by Bentham. Much of the detailed exposition of Bentham's theory has been omitted, but some preliminary comments are called for. Bentham distinguishes between two sorts of rights, liberty-rights, and rights correlative to an obligation. The former are rights either to do or abstain from some action, and arise from the absence of an obligation. Hence, if I have a liberty-right to do A I am neither obliged to do A nor obliged not to do it. By contrast, as their name suggests, rights of the second kind arise from obligations imposed by law whose non-performance by others violates that right.

But while Hart agrees with Bentham that liberty-rights are important, he argues that '. . . the notion of a liberty right needs some further characterisation beyond that given to it by Bentham's phrase, "right resulting from the absence of obligation"'.[9] This is so because he thinks that a bare liberty which is not protected in some way by the imposition of general obligations on others does not deserve the title of a right, and that it only does so when it is protected by a perimeter of protective obligations or duties.[10] In some cases the law may regard a liberty as so important that it imposes a strictly correlative obligation. Normally, however, liberties are not protected in this way, but by the imposition of general obligations not to restrict the exercise of a liberty in certain ways:

> Two people walking in an empty street see a purse lying on the pavement: each has a liberty so far as the law is concerned to pick it up and each may prevent the other doing so if he can race him to the spot. But though each has this liberty there are also several specific things which each has a right that the other should not do; these are rights with correlative obligations and these correlative obligations together with the duties of the criminal law protect (and also restrict) each party's liberty. Thus neither of the competitors may hit or trip up the other, or threaten him with violence in order to get the prize. The

[9] H L Hart, 'Bentham on Legal Rights', in A W B Simpson (ed) *Oxford Essays in Jurisprudence*, Second Series, 175.
[10] Ibid 182.

perimeter of obligations to abstain from such actions constitutes the ring within which the competitors compete in the exercise of their liberties.

Hart 'Bentham on Legal Rights' in Simpson (ed) *Oxford Essays in Jurisprudence* 175

How severe a criticism this is of Bentham depends, of course, on how specific the obligations in the perimeter are in particular cases, for the obligations of the criminal law are always operative, so that even on Bentham's account a liberty always has a perimeter of general obligations.

But Hart's main stalking horse is Bentham's account of rights correlative to obligations. According to Bentham, every legal obligation has a correlative right, with the exception of two classes of obligation: self-regarding ones, such as the now-repealed obligation not to commit suicide, and those which are imposed by a legislator in disregard of the dictates of utility and so benefit no one. So with these exceptions every offence is the violation of a right which denies the right-holder an intended benefit; and Hart characterises the benefit theory of rights as that theory which identifies a right-holder 'by reference to the person intended to benefit by the performance of an obligation'.[11] This of course leaves the very difficult question of what we mean when we say that a law is intended to benefit an individual, but Hart argues that we may interpret this to mean 'no more than that to establish its breach an assignable individual must be shown to have suffered an individual detriment'.[12] But, so understood, the benefit theory is, Hart argues, seriously deficient:

Absolute and relative duties

The principal advocates of benefit or 'interest' theories of rights correlative to obligations have shown themselves sensitive to the criticism that, if to say that an individual has such a right means no more than that he is the intended beneficiary of a duty, then 'a right' in this sense may be an unnecessary, and perhaps confusing, term in the description of the law; since all that can be said in a terminology of such rights can be and indeed is best said in the indispensable terminology of duty. So the benefit theory appears to make nothing more of rights than an alternative formulation of duties: yet nothing seems to be gained in significance or clarity by translating, eg the statement that men are under a legal duty not to murder, assault, or steal from others into the statement that individuals have a right not to be murdered, assaulted, or stolen from, or by saying, when a man been murdered, that his right not to be killed has been violated.[a]

Ihering as I have said was visited by just such doubts. Bentham confronted them in his codification proposals in the form of an inquiry whether the law should be expounded at length in a list of rights or a list of obligations. The test which he proposed was 'Present the entire law to that one of the parties that has most need to be instructed'[b] and he thought that the law should generally be expounded at length in terms of obligations but need 'only to be mentioned' in a list of rights; his principal reason for this was that because of the penalties

[a] Under the American Civil Rights Act 1964 suits were brought against white men who had murdered negroes alleging 'that they had deprived their victims of their civil rights'. This desperate expedient was necessary because murder is a state crime and prosecutions in such cases were not likely to succeed in Southern state courts. I owe this point to Mrs Carolyn Irish.
[b] Bowring III, 195.

[11] Ibid 178.
[12] Ibid 187.

imposed the party on whom the law imposed the obligation had most need for instruction.[c]

(a) *Criminal* versus *civil law*. The most cogent criticisms of the benefit theory are those that on the one hand press home the charge of redundancy or uselessness to a lawyer of the concept of right correlative to obligation defined simply in terms of the intended beneficiary of the obligation, and on the other hand constructively present an alternative selective account of those obligations which are for legal purposes illuminatingly regarded as having correlative rights. This latter task amounts to a redrawing of the lines between 'absolute' and relative duties which for Bentham merely separated 'barren' and self-regarding duties from duties 'useful to others'. This has been done sometimes in too sweeping a fashion as a distinction precisely coinciding with that between the criminal and civil law, and on the assumption, which seems dogmatic, if not plainly mistaken, that the purpose of the criminal law is not to secure the separate interests of individuals but 'security and order', and that all its duties are really duties not to behave in certain ways which are prejudicial to the 'general interests of society'.[d]

None the less a line may be drawn between most duties of the criminal law and those of the civil law which does not depend on this assumption, but would, on principles quite distinct from those of the benefit theory, reserve the notion of relative duties and correlative rights mainly for the obligations of the civil law, such as those which arise under contracts or under the law of tort, and other civil wrongs. For what is distinctive about these obligations is not their content which sometimes overlaps with the criminal law, since there are some actions, eg assault, which are both a crime and a civil wrong; nor is the only distinction of importance the familiar one that crime has as its characteristic consequence liability to punishment, and civil wrong liability to pay compensation for harm done. The crucial distinction, according to this view of relative duties, is the special manner in which the civil law as distinct from the criminal law provides for individuals: it recognizes or gives them a place or *locus standi* in relation to the law quite different from that given by the criminal law. Instead of utilitarian notions of benefit or intended benefit we need, if we are to reproduce this distinctive concern for the individual, a different idea. The idea is that of one individual being given by the law exclusive control, more or less extensive, over another person's duty so that in the area of conduct covered by that duty the individual who has the right is a small-scale sovereign to whom the duty is owed. The fullest measure[e] of control comprises three distinguishable elements: (i) the right holder may waive or extinguish the duty or leave it in existence; (ii) after breach or threatened breach of a duty he may leave it 'unenforced' or may 'enforce' it by suing for compensation or, in certain cases, for an injunction or mandatory order to restrain the continued or further breach of duty; and (iii) he may

[c] Ibid.

[d] Allen, *Legal Duties*, pp 184–6.

[e] The right holder will have less than the full measure of control if, as in the case of statutory duties, he is unable to release or extinguish the duty or if principles of public policy prevent him, even after breach of the duty, making a binding agreement not to sue for injury caused by its breach (see eg *Bowmaker Ltd v Tabor* (1942) 2 KB 1). In such cases the choice left to him is only to sue or not to sue. There are suggestions, never fully developed, that such a choice is a necessary element in a legal system in Bentham's *A Fragment on Government* Ch. V para 6 n 1 s 2.

waive or extinguish the obligation to pay compensation to which the breach gives rise. It is obvious that not all who benefit or are intended to benefit by another's legal obligation are in this unique sovereign position in relation to the duty. A person protected only by the criminal law has no power to release anyone from its duties, and though, as in England, he may in theory be entitled to prosecute along with any other member of the public he has no unique power to determine whether the duties of the criminal law should be enforced or not.

These legal powers (for such they are) over a correlative obligation are of great importance to lawyers: both laymen and lawyers will need, in Bentham's phrase, 'to be instructed' about them; and their exercise calls for the specific skills of the lawyer. They are therefore a natural focus of legal attention, and there are I think many signs of the centrality of those powers to the conception of a legal right. Thus it is hard to think of rights except as capable of *exercise* and this conception of rights correlative to obligations as containing legal powers accommodates this feature.[f] Moreover, we speak of a breach of duty in the civil law, whether arising in contract or in tort, not only as wrong, or detrimental to the person who has the correlative right, but as *a wrong to* him and a breach of an obligation *owed to* him; we also speak of the person who has the correlative right as *possessing* it or even *owning* it. The conception suggested by these phrases is that duties with correlative rights are a species of normative property belonging to the right-holder, and this figure becomes intelligible by reference to the special form of control over a correlative duty which a person with such a right is given by the law. Whenever an individual has this special control, as he has in most cases in the civil law but not over the duties of the criminal law, there is a contrast of importance to be marked and many jurists have done so by distinguishing the duties of the criminal law as 'absolute duties' from the 'relative' duties of the civil law.[g]

It is an incidental, though substantial merit of this approach that it provides an intelligible explanation of the fact that animals, even though directly protected by the duties of the criminal law prohibiting cruelty to them, are not spoken or thought of as having rights. However it is to be observed that if the distinction between absolute and relative duties is drawn as above suggested, this does not entail that only duties of the civil law have correlative rights. For there are cases made prominent by the extension of the welfare functions of the state where officials of public bodies are under a legal duty to provide individuals, if they satisfy certain conditions, with benefits which may take the

---

[f] Where infants or other persons not *sui juris* have rights, such powers and the correlative obligations are exercised on their behalf by appointed representatives and their exercise may be subject to approval by a court. But since (a) what such representatives can and cannot do by way of exercise of such power is determined by what those whom they represent could have done if *sui juris* and (b) when the latter become *sui juris* they can exercise these powers without any transfer or fresh assignment; the powers are regarded as belonging throughout to them and not to their representatives, though they are only exercisable by the latter during the period of disability.

[g] It is sometimes argued that in the case of persons not *sui juris* eg infants, it is only the fact that they are direct beneficiaries of the correlative duties which explains the ascription of rights to them, rather than to their representatives who alone can exercise the powers over the correlative duties. But the explanation offered above in the previous note seems adequate; even if it is not, this would only show that being the direct beneficiary of a duty was a *necessary* condition of a person not *sui juris* having a right. Hence it would still be possible, so far as this argument goes, to distinguish the duties of the criminal law (over which there are no such powers of control exercisable by the beneficiaries' representatives) as not having correlative rights.

form of money payments (eg public assistance, unemployment relief, farming subsidies) or supply of goods or services, eg medical care. In such cases it is perfectly common and natural to speak of individuals who have satisfied the prescribed conditions as being legally entitled to and having a right to such benefits. Yet it is commonly not the case that they have the kind of control over the official's duties which, according to the view suggested above, is a defining feature of legal rights correlative to obligations. For though such obligations are not always supported by criminal sanctions they cannot be extinguished or waived by beneficiaries, nor does their breach necessarily give rise to any secondary obligation to make compensation which the beneficiaries can enforce, leave unenforced or extinguish. None the less there are in most of such cases two features which link them to the paradigm cases of rights correlative to obligations as these appear in the civil law. In most cases here such public duties are thought of as having correlative rights, the duty to supply the benefits are conditional upon their being demanded and the beneficiary of the duty is free to demand it or not. Hence, though he has no power to waive or extinguish the duty he has a power by presenting a demand to substitute for a conditional duty not requiring present performance an unconditional duty which does, and so has a choice. Secondly, though breach of such duties may not give rise to any secondary duties of compensation, there are in many such cases steps which the beneficiary if he has suffered some peculiar damage may take to secure its performance, and in regard to which he has a special *locus standi* so that on his application a court may make a peremptory or mandatory order or injunction directing the official body to carry out the duty or restraining its breach.[h] These two features of the case differentiate the beneficiary of such public duties from that of the ordinary duties of the criminal law. This explains why, though it is generally enough to describe the criminal law only in terms of duties, so to describe the law creating these public welfare duties would obscure important features. For the necessity that such beneficiaries if they wish the duty to be performed must present demands, and the availability to them of means of enforcement, make their position under the law a focus for legal attention needing separate description from that of the duties beneficial to them.[i]

(b) *Contracts and third parties.* The identification of a right-holder with the person who is merely benefited by the performance of a duty not only obscures a very important general dividing line between criminal and civil law, but is ill adapted to the law relating to contract. Whereas in the last paragraph it was urged that to be an intended beneficiary of an obligation is not a satisfactory *sufficient* condition of having a right, the present criticism is that it is not satisfactory as a *necessary* condition. For where there is a contract between two people, not all those who benefit and are intended to benefit by the performance of its obligations have a legal right correlative to them. In many jurisdictions contracts expressly made for the benefit of third parties, eg a contract between two people to pay a third party a sum of money, is not enforceable by the third party and he cannot waive or release the obligation. In such a case although the third party is a direct beneficiary since breach of the contracts constitutes a direct detriment to him, he has no legal control over the

[h] Difficult questions may arise concerning the nature of the interest which a successful applicant for such relief must possess. See *R v Manchester Corp* [1911] 1 KB 560.
[i] But so far as such public welfare duties are thought of as providing for essential human needs they may on that ground alone be regarded as constituting legal rights. See below.

duty and so no legal right. On the other hand the contracting party having the appropriate control has the legal right, though he is not the person intended to benefit by the performance of the contract.[j] Where, however, the law is modified as it is in some jurisdictions so as to give the third party power to enforce the contract then he is consistently with the view presented here spoken of as having legal right.

The analysis of a right correlative to obligation which is suggested by the foregoing criticisms of the benefit theory is that for such a right to exist it is neither sufficient nor necessary for the person who had the right to be the beneficiary of the obligation; what is sufficient and necessary is that he should have at least some measure of the control, described above, over the correlative obligation.

IV. THE LIMIT OF A GENERAL THEORY

If the arguments of the last section are accepted and if we substitute for the utilitarian idea of benefit, as a defining feature of a right correlative to obligation, the individual's legal powers of control, full or partial, over that obligation, a generalization may be made concerning all three kinds of right distinguished by Bentham. This is attractive because it imposes a pattern of order on a wide range of apparently disparate legal phenomena. Thus in all three kinds of right the idea of a bilateral liberty is present and the difference between the kinds of right lies only in the kind of act which there is liberty to do. In the case of liberty-rights such as a man's right to look at his neighbour, his act may be called a natural act in the sense that it is not endowed by the law with a special legal significance or legal effect. On the other hand in the case of rights which are powers, such as the right to alienate property, the act which there is a bilateral liberty[k] to do is an act-in-the-law, just in the sense that it is specifically recognized by the law as having legal effects in varying the legal position of various parties. The case of a relative correlative to obligation then emerges as only a special case of legal power in which the right-holder is at liberty to waive or extinguish or to enforce or leave unenforced another's obligation. It would follow from these considerations that in each of these three types of case one who has a right has a choice respected by the law. On this view there would be only one sense of legal right—a legally respected choice— though it would be one with different exemplifications, depending on the kind of act or act-in-the-law which there is liberty to do.

The merits of this analysis are therefore threefold. First, it coincides with a very wide area of common and legal usage. Secondly it explains why liberty-rights, powers, and rights correlative to obligations are all described as rights and does so by identifying as common to three superficially diverse types of

---

[j] It is sometimes argued that the fact that in some jurisdictions a third-party beneficiary may sue shows this point against the beneficiary theory of rights to be mistaken. But of course a third party entitled to sue or not to sue would on *that* account be recognized as having a legal right and this does nothing to confirm the beneficiary theory.

[k] As in the case of liberty-rights, duties may be superimposed on rights which are powers and such duties will render the liberty to exercise the power unilateral (a simple example from property law is where an owner of property binds himself by contract either to sell it or not to sell it). In general where there is a duty to exercise a power the resultant unilateral liberty is not described as a right nor is there usually any point in so describing it. Exceptions to this are again cases such as that of a trustee whose legal rights are theoretically distinguishable from his equitable duties (see above, p 183, n 56) and are thought of as coexisting even where they in fact conflict.

case, an element which, on any theory of law or morals, is of great importance; namely an individual choice respected by the law. Thirdly, the concept which it defines is well adapted to a lawyer's purpose; for it will lead him to talk in terms of rights only where there is something of importance to the lawyer to talk about which cannot be equally well said in terms of obligation or duty, and this is pre-eminently so in the case of the civil law.

However, in spite of its attractions, this theory, centred on the notion of a legally respected individual choice, cannot be taken as exhausting the notion of a legal right: the notion of individual benefit must be brought in, though *not* as the benefit theory brings it in, to supplement the notion of individual choice. Unless this is done no adequate account can be given of the deployment of the language of rights, in two main contexts, when certain freedoms and benefits are regarded as essential for the maintenance of the life, the security, the development, and the dignity of the individual. Such freedoms and benefits are recognized as rights in the constitutional law of many countries by Bills of Rights, which afford to the individual protection even against the processes of legislation. In countries such as our own, where the doctrine of legislative sovereignty is held to preclude limiting the powers of the legislature by Bills of Rights, they are, though given only the lesser measure of legal protection in the form of duties of the criminal law, thought and spoken of as legal rights by social theorists or critics of the law who are accustomed to view the law in a wider perspective than the lawyer concerned only with its day-to-day working.

IMMUNITY RIGHTS

Both the benefit theory of rights and the alternative theory of a right as a legally respected choice are designed primarily as accounts of the rights of citizen against citizen; that is of rights under the 'ordinary' law. From that point of view the benefit theory was criticized above (*inter alia*) for offering no more than a redundant translation of duties of the criminal law into a terminology of rights, eg not to be murdered or assaulted. But this accusation of redundancy is no longer pertinent when what is to be considered are not rights under the ordinary law, but fundamental rights which may be said to be against the legislature, limiting its powers to make (or unmake) the ordinary law, where so to do would deny to individuals certain freedoms and benefits now regarded as essentials of human well-being, such as freedom of speech and of association, freedom from arbitrary arrest, security of life and person, education, and equality of treatment in certain respects.

The various elements which the benefit theory uses to analyse rights correlative to obligations and those which the rival 'choice' theory uses to analyse these and other kinds of right (that is: duty, absence of duty, benefit, act, and act-in-the-law) are not sufficient to provide an analysis of such constitutionally guaranteed individual rights. These require for their analysis the notion of an immunity. Bentham, unlike Hohfeld, did not isolate this notion in distinguishing different kinds or meanings of legal right, and indeed his attention was never seriously given to the analysis of fundamental legal rights. This was, no doubt, because, although, unlike Austin, he did not think that there were logical or conceptual objections to the notion of legal limitations of a sovereign legislature[1] he viewed with extreme suspicion any legal arrangements which would prevent the legislature enacting whatever

[1] See for his discussion of such limitations, *OLG*, pp 18, 64–71, 306, and *A Fragment of Government*, ch IV, paras 23–36, and my 'Bentham on Sovereignty' (1967) Irish Jurist 327.

measures appeared from time to time to be required by the dictates of general utility; and suspicion became contempt at the suggestion that such arrangements should be used to give legal form to doctrines of natural or fundamental individual rights. Hohfeld, who identified among the various 'loose' uses of the expression 'a right' its use to refer to an immunity, defined an immunity as the correlative of 'disability' or 'no power'; so that to say that a man, X, had a certain immunity meant that someone else lacked legal power to alter X's legal position in some respect. But, plainly, even in the loosest usage, the expression 'a right' is not used to refer to the fact that a man is thus immune from an *advantageous* change; the facts that the City Council cannot legally, ie has 'no power', to award me a pension, and my neighbour has no power to exempt me from my duty to pay my income-tax, do not constitute any legal rights for me. An individual's immunity from legal change at the hands of others is spoken and thought of as a right only when the change in question is *adverse*, that is, would deprive him of legal rights of other kinds (liberty-rights, powers, rights correlative to obligations) or benefits secured to him by law.

The chief, though not the only employment[m] of this notion of an immunity from adverse legal change which we may call an 'immunity right' is to characterize distinctively the position of individuals protected from such adverse change by constitutional limitations or, as Hohfeld would say, by disabilities of the legislature. Such immunity rights are obviously of extreme importance to individuals and may usually be asserted in the form of justiciable claims that some purported enactment is invalid because it infringes them. There is here an illuminating contrast with the redundancy of rights as defined by the beneficiary theory; for whereas, as I have urged above, nothing is to be gained for the lawyer, either in clarity or the focusing of legal attention, by expounding, say, the law of murder or assault in terms of rights, the case is altered if a constitutional Bill of Rights precludes the legislature from depriving individuals of the protections of the criminal law. For then there is every reason why lawyers and others should have picked out for them, as rights to life or security of the person, legal immunities the assertion of which on behalf of the individual calls for their advice and skill. That is why I said above that though certain legally secured individual benefits would have to be brought in to any adequate account of legal rights, they would not be brought in as the benefit theory brings them in.

WIDER PERSPECTIVES

Law is however too important a thing to leave to lawyers—even to constitutional lawyers; and the ways of thinking about rights common among serious critics of the law and social theorists must be accommodated even though they are different from and may not serve any of the specific purposes of the lawyer. Here also a concept of legal rights limited to those cases where the law, in the ways described above, respects the choice of individuals, would be too narrow. For there is a distinct form of the moral criticism of law which, like the constitutional immunity rights already described, is inspired by regard for the needs of the individual for certain fundamental freedoms and protections or benefits. Criticism of the law for its failure to provide for such individual needs is distinct from, and sometimes at war with, the criticism with which

---

[m] Immunities against divestment of various kinds of rights are involved in the notion of ownership. See A M Honoré, 'Ownership' in *Oxford Essays in Jurisprudence*, First Series (1961), p 119.

Bentham was perhaps too exclusively concerned, that the law often fails to maximize aggregate utility. A critic of the former, individualistic, kind will of course not address himself only to those legal systems in which there are immunity rights guaranteed by Bills of Rights; but in scrutinizing systems like our own, where the maximum form of provision for such individual needs must fall short of constitutional immunity rights, he will count the measure of protection afforded by the ordinary criminal law as a provision for those needs, together with the duties to provide for them which fall on public bodies or officials. Viewed in this light the law against murder and assault will be considered and described quite properly as securing rights to life and security of the person; though if it were a question simply of expounding the criminal law this would be redundant and even confusing.

Hence in cases where the criminal law provides for such essential human needs the individualistic critic of the law would agree with the benefit-theorist in speaking of rights corresponding to certain duties of the criminal law. They would however differ in two ways: first the critic need entertain no *general* theory that every direct beneficiary of a legal obligation had a corresponding legal right and he could therefore consistently subscribe to all the criticisms of the beneficiary theory made above; secondly the individualistic critic implicitly draws a distinction quite foreign to the letter and the spirit of the beneficiary theory between the legal provision of benefits simply as a contribution to general utility and as a contribution to the satisfaction of individual needs. It is the latter which leads him to talk of rights secured by the duties of the criminal law.

The upshot of these considerations is that instead of a general analytical and explanatory theory covering the whole field of legal rights I have provided a general theory in terms of the notion of a legally respected individual choice which is satisfactory only at one level—the level of the lawyer concerned with the working of the 'ordinary' law. This requires supplementation in order to accommodate the important deployment of the language of rights by the constitutional lawyer and the individualistic critic of the law, for whom the core of the notion of rights is neither individual choice nor individual benefit but basic or fundamental individual needs. This result may be felt as distressingly untidy by some, and they may be tempted to combine the perspectives which I have distinguished of the ordinary lawyer, the constitutional lawyer, and the individualistic critic of the law in some general formula embracing all three. Such a general formula is suggested by Hohfeld's statement that the generic sense of a right means 'any legal advantage'.[n] But I fear that, behind the comfortable appearance of generality, we would have only an unilluminating combination or mere juxtaposition of the choice theory together with the benefit theory; and this would fail to be sensitive to the important reasons for describing only some legally secured benefits, only in some contexts, as legal rights.

Hart 'Bentham on Legal Rights' in Simpson (ed) *Oxford Essays in Jurisprudence* 190–201

[n] Cf also Bentham's discussion in *OLG*, pp 55–9 of the inclusion in the idea of a 'party favoured by the law' of two kinds of favour: favour in 'point of interest' and 'in point of agency'. A party is 'favoured in point of agency' when he has an *exceptional* liberty, ie a liberty to do some act generally prohibited.

Though Hart is careful to point out that his theory is only a theory of legal rights, and even so, not an exhaustive one, it would be odd if it was not generalisable, so that we had to give a completely different account of moral rights. The account of legal rights given by Hart argues for an internal connection between rights and choice, and hence individual liberty. Since a right is a protected choice it follows that if in exercising it one limits the freedom of another, one has not done any wrong from a legal point of view. It is interesting therefore that in an earlier paper in which he argues that if there are any moral rights at all there is at least one natural right, namely the equal right of all men to be free, Hart describes a moral right in terms similar to those in which he characterised legal rights. He argues that there is an essential connection between the notion of a right and the justified limitation of another's freedom (H L Hart, 'Are There Any Natural Rights', Philosophical Review, LSIV, 1955) and that to have a right involves having a moral justification of a certain sort for limiting the freedom of another and determining how he should act. Exactly how close the two accounts are is not easy to determine, but clearly there are substantial similarities, which is what one would expect, since it would be very odd if the account of legal rights was not generalisable at all.

But whether or not his theory is generalisable to cover moral rights, Hart concedes that it is not an exhaustive one even of legal rights, since it requires supplementation to deal with constitutional rights for whose analysis Hohfeld's notion of an immunity is required. It is on this concession that MacCormick seizes in his critique of Hart's theory, in the course of which he develops his own version of the interest theory.

> There is something, on the face of it, odd about Hart's concession that immunities cannot be properly taken into account within the four corners of the 'will theory' as propounded by himself. For it is often the case that A's immunity is waivable by A's choice. If A owns a car, B cannot divest him of ownership by any unilateral act (if B is another private citizen); in other words, A's rights over the car are in this respect protected by (or do they simply include?) an immunity against B. But, of course, A's immunity from being divested of ownership in favour of B is not absolute, but conditional on his own choice to transfer or not transfer the property—otherwise sale, exchange, and gift would be impossible.
>
> That being so, it follows that there is a class of immunities which could comfortably be brought within the Hartian version of the will theory, namely, the whole class of those immunities in relation to which the immunity-holder has a power of waiver. Looked at from the other party's point of view, from the point of view of the party B who is under a disability to alter A's legal position in some respect, such a disability may be absolute (B cannot enslave A, even if A should consent to be enslaved); or it may be conditional upon A's will; A has a right not to be assaulted by B, and B can't take that away from A, unless A agrees—for example, in a boxing match.
>
> In the light of those facts, the reasonable extrapolation to make from Hart's thesis in relation to claims, liberties, and powers would be along the lines of including within the genus 'rights' only those immunities which lie within the immunity-holder's own power, those which he can waive or assert at will. Such would be 'immunity rights' (a species of the genus 'rights'); unwaivable immunities would belong outside of the genus 'rights'.
>
> But surely the moment we make that extrapolation we hit upon the fundamental implausibility of the 'will theory'. It seems to me unproblematic

to say that I have (legally and morally) a right not to be deprived of my personal freedom and a right not to be deprived of my property. The two rights seem to me to be on all fours with each other, at any rate when we are concerned with the propriety of using the noun 'right' in the statement of such propositions of law (or of morals); in my view, which I believe to be widely held, the former right is of greater importance than the latter—I would rather, if it came to the bit, be propertyless than be a slave. The laws of the UK certainly place a higher value on the right of freedom than on the right of property in a certain highly important respect: the former is regarded as absolute in the sense that no person can enslave any other, not even a person willing to be enslaved; whereas the latter is conditional upon the property-holder's will—no person can deprive another of his property *without his consent*.

Let us take note of the point. *A*'s right to personal freedom involves *B* in having (a) a duty not to reduce *A* to a servile condition, eg by clapping him in irons; and (b) a disability to impose upon *A* the status of a slave; and (c) a disability to change the relation (a) and (b) *even with A's consent*. *A* does not himself have power to waive his immunities in these respects—he too is under a disability here, though it may well be said that the disability is to his own advantage in preventing him ever from bartering away his freedom, whatever the temptation. That, indeed, is one of the grounds upon which untutored common sense would found the assertion that the right to personal freedom is yet more securely protected in our law than any right of property.

But there's the rub, there, for the 'will theory', the paradox. For it appears that this legal dispensation, be it ever so advantageous from the point of view of securing liberty, is so forceful as to thrust liberty beyond the realm of 'right' altogether. If there be no power to waive or assert the immunity, the claim, or whatever, upon some matter, upon that matter there is, *by definition*, no right either. In the matter of non-enslavement no person in any contemporary western legal system can *de jure* waive his immunity; the same is true of other interests characteristically protected by Bills of Rights (whence, perhaps, Hart's embarrassment over these in connection with the notion of 'immunity'). Are we really to conclude that here the terminology of 'rights' is inapposite? Really to conclude that the language of the practical lawyer does such violence to common understanding as to exclude such protections of human interests, when arguably at their most efficacious, from the category which it is interesting or useful to describe as 'rights'? The paradox would seem to me altogether too violent; the ascription of concerns to the practical lawyer, unconvincingly ethnocentric.

Admittedly, we are to some extent in the realms of stipulative definition when we enter into contention over the essential characteristics of the concept 'right'. Yet we are entitled to ask somebody who stipulates that there shall be held to be 'rights' only where there are choices, whether that stipulation does not go wholly against common understanding, and whether there is any profit derived from it.

What seems to me strangest is the way in which the will theory seems to cut off the use of 'rights'-language at a predetermined point on the scale of protection which the law may confer upon people's interests. To take a somewhat trivial case: the law relating to assault prohibits any person from offering or inflicting physical interference or harm on another. *A* has a duty not to interfere with *B*. So far as concerns the 'will theory', *B* has a 'right not to be harmed' *only* if and in so far as he, *B*, can in some way regulate *A*'s duty not to interfere with him. That seems all very well: in relation to minor interference, or manly sports, or bona-fide surgical operations, *B* can waive *A*'s duty. So, for the 'will theory', *B* has a right not to be trivially assaulted, or assaulted in the course of manly sports, or assaulted by a surgeon conducting an operation. Yet in relation to serious assaults, or 'unmanly' pastimes (eg flagellation by or of a prostitute),[a] or operations by unqualified persons, no valid consent can be given which releases the assaulting party from the duty of non-interference.[b] It is rather bewildering to suppose that none of us has a right not to be thus grievously assaulted, simply because for various reasons of policy the law denies us the power to consent to these graver interferences with our physical security.

Students of Dicey's *Law and Opinion* will recall his ill-disguised disapproval of those collectivist measures which were introduced in the later nineteenth century in order to protect various elements in the poorer sections of the population.[c] The technique which he deplored was as follows: first, the legislature conferred protection on people which they could have conferred on themselves by contract, eg in matters of safety at work; secondly, the legislators, discovering that too many of the protected class exercised the power 'voluntarily' to contract out of the protection, removed the matter from the option of the protected party altogether by depriving of legal effect such waivers of the statutory protection. Perhaps such legislation was as disgracefully paternalistic as Dicey so evidently thought it (though it cannot be said that this century has seen any reversal of its increase, far from it) but can it really be said that the second stage of protection is a stage at which a 'right' disappears? At stage one, the employer is obliged to take steps to protect his employee's safety, unless his employee 'contracts out'—here, for the 'will theory', is a classic case of 'right'. At stage two, the employer's duty is made unconditional upon the employee's will, and that with a view to protecting better the interests of employees individually and as a class—and now, for the will theory, the 'right' has gone. How odd that, as the protection is strengthened, the right disappears![d]

There is no point in multiplying such examples, of which there is certainly an abundance; the ones here given reinforce the particular case of the legal and moral protections of children which I have discussed in my recent paper on 'Children's Rights'.[e] If I may immodestly quote, and adopt from, that argument, I should like to repeat what I said in relation to what I conceive to be a child's (legal and moral) right to care and nurture:

> 'We are put . . . to our election. Either we abstain from ascribing to children a right to care and nurture [on the ground that no one has discretion to waive the responsible adult's duty of care and nurture] or we abandon the will theory. For my part I have no inhibitions about abandoning the latter. It causes me no conceptual shock or mental cramp

---

[a] See *R v Donovan* [1934] 2 KB 498 for discussion of this instance, and of consent generally.

[b] G H Gordon, *Criminal Law* (Edinburgh, 1967), pp 773–6; J C Smith and B Hogan, *Criminal Law*, 3rd edn (London, 1973), pp 287–90.

[c] A V Dicey, *Law and Opinion in England during the Nineteenth Century*, 2nd edn (London, 1924), pp 260–9.

[d] But note that in 'BLR' at p 192 Hart shows that the 'fullest measure of control' by one person over another's duty need not be present in every case of a right; there are several distinguishable elements in that 'fullest measure' of which powers of waiver or enforcement are only one (remedial powers and powers of waiver of remedial rights being others). But it must be at least embarrassing to him if measures conceived of as strengthening rights standardly involve derogation from the fullest forms of control.

[e] A paper read to the conference of the Association of Legal and Social Philosophy in Cambridge, April 1975, and published in 1976 *Archiv für Rechts und sozial Philosophie.*

to say that children have that right. What is more, I will aver that it is *because* children have that right that it is good that legal provision should be made in the first instance to encourage and assist parents to fulfil their duty of care and nurture, and secondarily to provide for its performance by alternative foster parents when natural parents are disqualified by death, incapacity, or wilful and persistent neglect. *Ubi ius, ibi remedium.* So far from its being the case that the remedial provision is constitutive of the right, the fact is rather that recognition of the right justifies the imposition of the remedial provision.'

We are all accustomed to talking and thinking about some rights as 'inalienable'. But if the will theory is correct, the more they are inalienable, the less they are rights. So far at least as concerns claim rights and immunities, I find the paradoxes with which the will theory is faced so great that, rather than swallow them, I am driven to seek an alternative. As a first step towards doing so, I should like to probe some of the grounds which have been suggested as foundations for the will theory with a view to showing that they are not as sound as they sound. In doing so I shall resume consideration of the statutory provisions referred to in my opening section.

IV

'The principal advocates of benefit or "interest" theories of rights correlative to obligations have shown themselves sensitive to the criticism that, if to say that an individual has such a right means no more than that he is the intended beneficiary of a duty, then "a right" in this sense may be an unnecessary, and perhaps confusing, term in the description of the law; since all that can be said in a terminology of such rights can be and indeed is, best said in the indispensable terminology of duty.'[f]

In that statement we find one of the principal grounds of Hart's case in favour of this theory, and against any version of interest theory. By introducing 'the idea . . . of one individual being given by the law exclusive control, more or less extensive, over another person's duty so that in the area of conduct covered by that duty the individual who has the right is a small-scale sovereign to whom the duty is owed', Hart claims to have shown us an idea by reference to which the 'terminology of . . . rights' can be used without redundancy to say things which cannot be said in the 'indispensable terminology of duty' by itself.[g]

This argument of Hart's perhaps has a certain force as against Bentham's account of rights—even in the brilliant polished version of it expounded by Hart in his essay thereon. To rest an account of claim rights *solely* on the notion that they exist whenever a legal duty is imposed by a law intended to benefit assignable individuals (in which case all the beneficiaries of the law have rights as against all the duty bearers) is to treat rights as being simply the 'reflex' of logically prior duties. Accordingly, for any statement about rights there could always be substituted a statement about duties which would be at a more fundamental level analytically and which yet would say just the same as the 'rights statement'.

It is however no part of my intention here to advance a theory according to

---

[f] 'BLR', p 190.
[g] Ibid.

which even 'claim rights' are conceived as being merely the reflex of duties,[h] as though the latter must always be understood as being in every way prior to rights. Here I return to the importance of my introductory point, that legal rights are conferred by laws, and that scrutiny of those laws which confer rights must therefore be profitable, not to say essential, for understanding rights. In relation to the point in hand, let me refer again to section 2(1) of the Succession (Scotland) Act 1964: '(a) Where an intestate is survived by children, they shall have right to the whole of the intestate estate.'

It is worth taking a few moments (and repeating a point which I have made elsewhere)[i] in explaining the context and effects of that provision. Under it, whenever a person domiciled in Scotland dies intestate leaving children, there automatically vests in those children a right to the whole of that part of his estate statutorily entitled 'the intestate estate' (ie the residue after certain statutorily established prior claims have been satisfied). At the moment at which the right vests, it is not a 'real right' involving ownership of the estate or any particular assets included in it. Rather, each child's right is a right to receive in due course an equal share in the assets remaining in the executor's hands after satisfaction of prior claims. So it seems that we have a normal right–duty relationship, which could as well have been stated in the 'indispensable terminology of duty' as in the terminology which commended itself to the draftsman.

The problem, however, is that whereas the right vests at the moment of the intestate's death, there is not at that moment an executor to bear a correlative duty. Vesting of the right is temporally prior to the vesting in any other individual of the correlative duty, which can occur only when an executor has in due course been judicially confirmed or appointed. The executor dative has then the duty to wind up the estate and to transfer appropriate shares in the intestate estate to those having right thereto. What is more, when the question of confirmation of an executor dative is raised before the relevant court, a person who has beneficial rights in the estate is normally *on that ground* to be preferred to other parties, at least if the estate appears to be solvent. So one of the intestate's children may, *because of this right conferred on him by the Act*, have a resultant preferential right to be confirmed as executor. His confirmation as such will in turn result in his incurring the duties of executor, including the duty of distributing the intestate estate to those (including himself) who have right thereto under section 2(1)(a) of the 1964 Act.

In this case, therefore, it is not only the case that the vesting of a given right is temporally prior to the vesting of the correlative duty, but it is also the case that the vesting of the right in a given individual is a ground for confirming him in that office to which is attached the duty correlative to the like rights of his brothers and sisters; so that in this context right is logically prior to duty as well. Here then we have a concrete instance of a 'right of recipience' which correlates with 'duty' indeed, but in a much more interesting way than as being a mere 'reflex' of a duty which the legislator might have as readily imposed in simpler and more straightforward terms. An 'interest theory' of rights which can take account of such subtleties as this may well avoid the reproach of redundancy, as well as escaping the paradoxes in which (as the last section showed) the will theory is inevitably drawn.

[h] To this exent disagreeing with Geoffrey Marshall 'Rights, Options, and Entitlements' (in Simpson, ed, op cit, pp 228–41) with which otherwise I substantially agree. Cf A M Honoré, 'Rights of Exclusion and Immunities against Divesting', 34, Tulane Law Review 453 (1959–60).
[i] Op cit. For a general account of the matters sketched here, see M C Meston, *The Succession (Scotland) Act 1964*, 2nd edn (Edinburgh, 1970).

In drafting a law to deal with intestate succession, a legislator might indeed be very likely to regard the crucial and primary question, as being who is to take the benefit of the estate left by the intestate, and to treat as secondary the means (appointment of executors or administrators, and imposition of appropriate duties upon them) of securing that the benefit in view should actually reach the hands of the intended beneficiary. It is the end which makes sense of the means, not vice versa. This is as obvious in relation to section 46 of the (English) Administration of Estates Act 1925, which likewise confers rights of succession on intestacy though without saying so expressly, as in relation to Section 2 of the Succession (Scotland) Act 1964.

In such a case, given that the legal system recognizes and establishes a system of private property, there is necessarily a vacant 'estate' whenever somebody dies possessed of property. The system must make *some* provision as to the destination of that estate. Whoever gets it, to him will be owed all the duties which are owed to property owners, and to him will ensue also the various liberties, powers, and immunities which accrue to property owners, but *that* person gets all that only because—only if—the law has already vested in him the right of ownership of the property in question. And the step before that is the conferment on some generically identified type of person(s) of the right to have ownership of some part of or share of the property comprising the estate invested in him. What is essentially at stake is, who is to get the more or less substantial advantage of inheriting what share of what part of the estate. It is a quite secondary question to settle by what precise means (imposition of duties and disabilities on *whom?*) that advantage shall be secured to him.

It seems obviously—even trivially—true that at least one function, and that a prominent one, of such laws as those concerning succession, is that they are concerned with the conferment and securing of advantages to individuals; or, rather, to members of given classes severally.[j] To explain the idea of 'members of given classes severally': section $2(1)(a)$ of the Succession (Scotland) Act protects and promotes the interests of a certain class, the class of children of a parent who has died intestate but possessed of some property. But the protection is not of the interests of the class indiscriminately, taking them all together as a group—as, perhaps, aircraft-noise-control legislation indiscriminately protects everybody living or working or doing anything else in the near vicinity of airports. The protection, in the succession case, is rather of each and every individual who is within that class each in respect of some separate share of an identified estate.

It is not necessarily the case that each individual acquiring a right under the law should experience it as a benefit, an advantage, an advancement or protection of his interests. Perhaps there are some people who have been more harmed than benefited by an inheritance. Perhaps in some cases property inherited—eg slum properties subject to statutory tenancies at controlled rents—are literally more trouble than they are worth, and, besides, something of an embarrassment to their proprietor. None of that is in any way inconsistent with the proposition that the function of the law is to confer what is considered to be normally an advantage on a certain class by granting to each of its members a certain legal right.

---

[j] For Hart's account of an essentially similar view of Bentham's see 'BLR', pp 186–8. For another similar account, see John Austin on 'absolute' and 'relative' duties in the seventeenth chapter of *Lectures in Jurisprudence* (London, 1862).

The case of the mortgagor's entitlement (under s 96(1) of the Law of Property Act 1925) to inspect and make copies of title-deeds, also quoted as an example in the introductory section of the present paper, further indicates the way in which a legislator's concern with protecting what are conceived to be legitimate interests of the members of a given class of individuals leads naturally to the framing of legislation in terms of the rights or entitlements of the given class rather than in terms of the correlative obligations of the mortgagee. In just this sense, what is essential to a clear and comprehensible law relating to mortgages is that the relevant legislation should make clear the respective advantages, protections, and powers accruing to each of the parties to any mortgage. Judicial enforcement of the legislation may then proceed by elucidation and enforcement of duties etc. as necessarily consequential upon conferment of the relevant rights.

By contrast with this branch of the law, the criminal law is no doubt primarily concerned with duties,[k] with laying down in clear and precise terms the prohibitions infraction of which may expose the citizen to prosecution and punishment. This of course follows from a respect for the right of individuals to freedom from interference by the state save for breach of clear rules of the criminal law. Thus, in so far as it is an important function of the criminal law to protect important individual rights—to freedom, to physical and mental security, and so on—it is nevertheless not surprising that the law is not expressly framed in terms of rights, but rather in terms of duties, or through the imposition of duties by the denomination of offences. Even at that, however, there is a large part of the criminal law which deals with crimes against property, and which therefore necessarily presupposes the existence of that elaborate and interlocking set of laws which define and regulate the institution of property and the many and various rights in relation thereto which the law confers. Rights of, and rights in relation to, property—eg a mortgagor's right to redeem, a child's right of intestate succession—are on the face of it much too complex to be dissoluble into a set of bare reflexes of correlative duties. But that is not an objection to the thesis that right-conferring laws are best understood in terms of a standard intention to confer some form of benefit or advantage or protection of interests upon the members of a class severally rather than collectively. There may indeed be simple cases in which some general duty—eg a duty not to assault—is imposed upon everyone at large with a view to protecting the physical security of each and every person in society, and where the 'right not to be assaulted' is simply the correlative of the duty not to assault; no doubt in such simple cases the 'terminology of rights' does not enable us to say very much more than can be said in the terminology of duty. But it may be well adapted even in this simple case to expressing a reason why people aggrieved by breaches of certain duties *should* be empowered to take various measures and actions at law to secure remedies therefor, and why they *should* be permitted, at least when there are no strong countervailing reasons of policy, to waive other people's duties in this respect. If I'm allowed to be the best judge of my own good, and if such laws (being right-conferring) are aimed at securing what's good for me, why should I not be allowed to have a say over their operation when only my own protection is at stake?

What is more, there are other, more complex, cases in which the legislative decision to confer certain benefits on individuals who satisfy certain generic

[k] Cf 'BLR', pp 191–5.

qualifications ('institutive' or 'investitive' facts) is logically prior to the vesting or the enforcement of a correlative duty. Taken as a whole, there is no reason to suppose that an 'interest theory' so defines 'rights' as to make the term redundant.

In another context, I have expressed as follows the conclusion which follows from arguments such as the foregoing:[1]

'to ascribe to all members of a class C a right to treatment T is to presuppose that T is, in all normal circumstances, a good for every member of C, and that T is a good of such importance that it would be wrong to deny it to or withhold it from any member of C. That deals with moral rights; as for legal rights, I should say this: when a right to T is conferred by law on all members of C, the law is envisaged as advancing the interests of each and every member of C, and the law has the effect of making it legally wrongful to withhold T from any member of C.'

That is certainly not a perfect or watertight formulation, nor am I sure that I can at present make it so. But it does bring out the three features which must be included in any characterization of rules which confer rights.

First, they concern 'goods' (or 'advantages', or 'benefit', or 'interests', or however we may express the point). Whatever *x* may be, the idea of anyone's having a right to *x* would be absurd unless it were presupposed that *x* is normally a good for human beings, at any rate for those people who qualify as having the 'right' in question. That does not mean that in every case the *x* which is subject matter of a right need be beneficial to a particular potential right-holder, or be thought so by him. Some *hereditates* may be *damnosae*, but our general view of the law of succession as conceding '*rights*' of succession is founded on the firm supposition that most are not.

Secondly, they concern the enjoyment of goods by individuals separately, not simply as members of a collectivity enjoying a diffuse common benefit in which all participate in indistinguishable and unassignable shares. But since necessarily the qualifications and conditions which must be satisfied for the application of such a rule of law in favour of any given individual have to be expressible and expressed in generic terms, it is therefore correct to say that such rules of law must be concerned with classes of individuals, but the benefit secured is secured to each and every individual severally upon satisfaction of the 'institutive' or 'investitive' conditions.

Thirdly, benefits are secured to individuals in that the law provides normative protection for individuals in their enjoyment of them. No doubt it is too narrow to envisage such protection purely in terms of its being 'legally wrongful to withhold T from any member of C'. 'Normative protection' may be understood as involving any or all of the various modes identified by Hohfeld and others. Thus an individual *A* may in the relevant sense be 'protected' in his enjoyment of *x* if

    (a) some or all other people are under a duty not to interfere with him in relation to *x* or his enjoyment of *x*,

or (b) he is himself not under any duty to abstain from enjoyment of, or avoid or desist from *x* (being therefore protected from any complaint as to alleged wrongful use, enjoyment, etc. of *x*),

or (c) some or all other individuals lack legal power to change the legal situation to the prejudice of *A*'s advantage in respect of *x* (the case of disability/immunity),

[1] Op cit.

or (d) *A* himself is in some respect enabled by law to bring about changes in legal relations concerning *x* in pursuit of whatever he conceives to be his advantage.

Not every right entails protection at all these levels or in all these modes simultaneously, though more than one may be and all sometimes are (this being contrary to the Hohfeldian picture of rights as atomic relations between paired individuals). Consider section 5(1) of the Trade Union and Labour Relations Act 1974: '. . . [E]very worker shall have the right not to be—(a) excluded from membership (b) expelled from membership, of a trade union . . . by way of arbitrary or unreasonable discrimination.' That confers protection of at least the first three kinds; it being presumed that membership of a union is beneficial to any worker in normal circumstances (a) people at large are put under a duty not to injure any worker by getting him excluded or expelled from a trade union, (b) every worker is in law free to apply for membership of a union of his choice, and (c) any act of purported expulsion of a worker from his union lacks legal effect if it is judged to be 'by way of arbitrary or unreasonable discrimination'. Consequentially, of course, *A* has various legal remedies which he may pursue for alleged infractions of the primary right conferred by the Act.

Thus using the terminology (in my view indispensable) of 'rights' the legislature can in short and simple words achieve complex legal protections for the several members of a given class. What is more, it can do so in a way which draws attention to the end in view, the protection of those people in relation to a supposedly advantageous condition of things. This serves better than would any alternative formulation the function of conveying to the population in general and to the judiciary in particular the intended aim and object of the measure.

> MacCormick 'Rights in Legislation' in Hacker and Raz (eds)
> *Law, Morality and Society* 195–207

It is clear that MacCormick sees no difficulty in generalising his account to cover moral rights also, for according to him

> To ascribe to all members of a class C a right to treatment T is to presuppose that T is, in all normal circumstances, a good for every member of C, and that T is a good of such importance that it would be wrong to deny it or withhold it from any member of C.

> MacCormick 'Rights in Legislation' in Hacker and Raz (eds)
> *Law, Morality and Society* 204

Of course, this account is a formal one which does not itself determine what rights we have; that can be determined only on the basis of substantial moral and political arguments, as MacCormick is, of course, aware. But he has elsewhere argued, for instance, that in the sense of right in question children do indeed have rights—a claim, incidentally, which brings him into sharp disagreement with the choice-theorist who is committed to rejecting it on the grounds that children do not have the requisite kind of control over the correlative obligation.

Both the choice-theory and the interest-theory agree that to possess a right is to possess a normative advantage which is, or ought to be, normatively protected. So each of them is able to explain why someone who has a right to do X is in a strong position when someone questions whether he should do X. Moreover, each of them is in a position to explain why different bundles of Hohfeldian positions should constitute rights, though the explanations given differ of course. For the choice-theory the leading idea is that the function of rights is to protect individual freedom and autonomy, whereas for the interest-theory it is that their function is to protect individual welfare. It is not surprising therefore that the two theories differ in a number of important respects. For instance, the choice-theorist insists that rights are capable of being exercised, and so doubts the intelligibility of claims that children, let alone animals, have rights, whereas, as we have seen, the interest-theorist may have no such doubts about children's rights, and can at least concede that talk of animal rights is intelligible.[13]

Clearly the question of which theory is correct is an important one. However, it would not be appropriate to try to answer it here for two reasons. First, because it is clear that they are not the only possible theories which could explain why certain bundles of Hohfeldian positions are rights. Dworkin, for instance, has argued that 'the rights which have traditionally been described as consequences of a general right to liberty are in fact the consequences of equality instead'. (R Dworkin *A Matter of Principle* 372), so for him the function of rights is to protect an individual's claim to equal concern and respect. On the other hand, one would expect a natural-rights theorist such as Finnis (see Chapter 6) to argue that the primary function is to make human flourishing possible. So the number of possible views about the functions of rights means that a debate about which one is the correct one would have to be a very wide one indeed. Second, it is clear that which view is accepted is not going to depend simply on analysis of cases since, as we have seen, there are disputed cases, such as those involving children and animals, in which there is not even a consensus that talk about rights is intelligible. In such cases different intuitions can only be defended by substantive moral and political arguments which raise issues of quite different kinds from the analytical ones we have been considering in this chapter, and it is to the consideration of the theories of Rawls, Dworkin, and Nozick which have developed such arguments that we turn in the following three chapters.

These theories differ in important respects, but whatever the differences between them, they all share a conception of individual rights as normatively protected values which confer normative advantages on their possessors, and are, as a result, united in their condemnation of utilitarianism on the grounds that fundamental rights are constraints on collective goals. Where the theories differ is in the accounts they offer of why the values in question are important and should be protected, and over the weight to be attached to the normative advantage that is conferred and, correlatively, the degree of protection of it that is warranted.

---

[13] For a valuable discussion of this and other differences between the two theories see L W Sumner *The Moral Foundation of Rights* 45–53.

Chapter 9
Rawls's theory of justice

The critical acclaim accorded John Rawls's *A Theory of Justice* (1971) is attested to by the avalanche of books and articles that it has spawned since publication. It has initiated a renascence in social philosophy unparalleled in this century, stretching across academic subjects that have traditionally been isolated and kept distinct from one another: philosophy, jurisprudence, economics, and social history. The work of this American will have a major impact on social theory and public policy issues for generations to come. To give a flavour of what is involved, here is a description of the book from another American professor of philosophy.

> The book contains three elements. One is a vision of men and society as they should be. Another is a conception of moral theory. The third is a construction that attempts to derive principles expressive of the vision, in accordance with methods that reflect the conception of moral theory. In that construction, Rawls has pursued the contractarian tradition in moral and political philosophy. His version of the social contract, a hypothetical choice situation called the original position, was first presented in 1958 and is here developed in great and explicit detail. The aim is to provide a way of treating the basic problems of social choice, for which no generally recognized methods of precise solution exist, through the proxy of a specially constructed parallel problem of individual choice, which can be solved by the more reliable intuitions and decision procedures of rational choice.
>
> Thomas Nagel (1973) Vol LXXXII Philosophical Review 220

INTRODUCTION

Rawls has two interrelated reasons for producing a theory of justice. His overriding motivation is to provide a theory which acts as a radical alternative to arguments structured on utilitarianism, which, at least in its classical manifestation, depicts a society as being rightly ordered, and therefore just, when its social institutions, such as law, serve, and only serve, to maximise aggregate utility. Justice is satisfied when a society's institutions are arranged so as to achieve the greatest net balance of satisfaction (or happiness or preferences as revealed through choices) summed over all the individuals belonging to that society: justice becomes 'the principle of rational prudence applied to an aggregate conception of the welfare of the group' *(A Theory of Justice* p 24). He strenuously argues that his theory is far more successful than utilitarianism in explaining our 'considered judgments' about what constitutes justice. And this is his second aim: to articulate a concept of justice that accounts for moral judgments that we make about the justice or injustice of laws, policies, or actions. Not the instantaneous, reflex judgment but the considered, reflective judgment arrived at after a process of deliberation. For example, 'we are confident that religious intolerance and racial discrimination are unjust' (p 19). Such judgments are provisional 'fixed points' which he presumes any theory of justice must fit. If he succeeds in demonstrating that it is his theory of justice, in stark contrast to utilitarianism, which underpins our reflective moral judgments about the content of justice, he also provides a superior theory of justice as a radical alternative to utilitarianism.

JUSTICE'S DOMAIN

his concern is social justice

What things can appropriately be characterised as being just or unjust? There is a considerable catchment area that includes specific decisions, judgments or attitudes. But his theory is targeted at something even more fundamental. His concern is social justice: laws, institutions and social systems rather than particular decisions, judgments or attitudes. His domain will be nothing less than the basic structure of society, meaning the political constitution together with its partner, the legal system.

This is the agenda: to agree on a set of principles which a basic structure of any society, if it is to be just, must satisfy. It is the search for principles that will determine how the basic structure is to distribute fundamental rights and duties in a manner that can be described as just.

THE MAIN IDEA OF THE THEORY OF JUSTICE

embarkation

social contract

At the outset Rawls gives a useful compendium of the convolutions to come. His point of embarkation is the theory of the social contract: the familiar doctrine that social cooperation rests on a contract or compact which people have made among themselves. The principles of justice are to be viewed as the result of a binding contract among the members of a society. But this helpful and traditional idea is generalised and taken to a 'higher level of abstraction' (p 11). We are not to think of the original position as an agreement entered into to gain admission to any particular society. Instead the guiding idea is that the principles of justice are themselves the actual object and reason for the contract. Consider a hypothetical situation in which a group of rational persons need to agree on a set of principles to govern the 'basic structure' of their society. Imagine this hypothetical position in which we the contractors decide in advance a 'fundamental charter' (p 11) that will dictate the basic structure of our society. In one joint act we are to decide in advance the principles upon which the assignment of the basic rights and duties are to be determined. It is claimed that the social contract concept has the advantage of conveying the idea that the principles of justice are those that would be chosen by rational persons; that the theory of justice is a part of the theory of rational choice.

The following introductory extract serves two purposes. First, it makes clear that any such heavy reliance on a hypothetical, contractual starting-point necessitates a careful description of the conditions which Rawls is going to impose upon the contractors.

Secondly, there is an initial, although incomplete, statement of the two principles of justice which rational persons under these conditions would agree upon: the principles of justice that would govern the basic structure of the contractors' society. In this extract look for these points:

(a)   the contractual starting-point is called the original position;
(b)   the original position is hypothesis not history;
(c)   the relevance of the veil of ignorance;
(d)   justice as fairness being the consequence of the veil of ignorance;
(e)   a society based upon a concept of justice arrived at by this argument comes as close as a society can to being a voluntary scheme;
(f)   people in the original position have the characteristics of rationality and mutual disinterestedness;
(g)   the reason why utilitarianism would be a non-starter for parties in the original position;
(h)   the two principles of justice chosen by the parties in the original position.

In justice as fairness the original position of equality corresponds to the state of nature in the traditional theory of the social contract. This original position is not, of course, thought of as an actual historical state of affairs, much less a primitive condition of culture. It is understood as a purely hypothetical situation characterized so as to lead to a certain conception of justice. Among the essential features of this situation is that no one knows his place in society, his class position or social status, nor does any one know his fortune in the distribution of natural assets and abilities, his intelligence, strength, and the like. I shall even assume that the parties do not know their conception of the good or their special psychological propensities. The principles of justice are chosen behind a veil of ignorance. This ensures that no one is advantaged or disadvantaged in the choice of principles by the outcome of natural choice or the contingency of special circumstances. Since all are similarly situated and no one is able to design principles to favour his particular condition, the principles of justice are the result of fair agreement or bargain. For given the circumstances of the original position, the symmetry of everyone's relations to each other, this initial situation is fair between individuals as moral persons, that is, as rational beings with their own ends and capable, I shall assume, of a sense of justice. The original position is, one might say, the appropriate initial status quo, and thus the fundamental agreements reached in it are fair. This explains the propriety of the name 'justice as fairness': it conveys the idea that the principles of justice are agreed to in an initial situation that is fair, the name does not mean that the concepts of justice and fairness are the same, any more than the phrase 'poetry as metaphor' means that the concepts of poetry and metaphor are the same.

Justice as fairness begins, as I have said, with one of the most general of all choices which persons might make together, namely, with the choice of the first principles of a conception of justice which is to regulate all subsequent criticism and reform of the institutions. Then, having chosen a conception of justice, we can suppose that they are to choose a constitution and a legislature to enact laws, and so on, all in accordance with the principles of justice initially agreed upon. Our social situation is just if it is such that by this sequence of hypothetical agreements we would have contracted into the general system of rules which define it. Moreover, assuming that the original position does determine a set of principles (that is, that a particular conception of justice would be chosen), it will then be true that whenever social institutions satisfy these principles those engaged in them can say to one another that they are cooperating on terms to which they would agree if they were free and equal persons whose relations with respect to one another were fair. They could all view their arrangements as meeting the stipulations which they would acknowledge in an initial situation that embodies widely accepted and reasonable constraints on the choice of principles. The general recognition of this fact would provide the basis for a public acceptance of the corresponding principles of justice. No society can, of course, be a scheme of cooperation which men enter voluntarily in a literal sense; each person finds himself placed at birth in some particular position in some particular society, and the nature of this position materially affects his life prospects. Yet a society satisfying the principles of justice as fairness comes as close as a society can to being a voluntary scheme, for it meets the principles which free and equal persons would assent to under circumstances that are fair. In this sense its members are autonomous and the obligations they recognize self-imposed.

One feature of justice as fairness is to think of the parties in the initial situation as rational and mutually disinterested. This does not mean that the parties are egoists, that is, individuals with only certain kinds of interests, say in wealth, prestige, and domination. But they are conceived as not taking an interest in another's interests. They are to presume that even their spiritual aims may be opposed, in the way that the aims of those of different religions may be opposed. Moreover, the concept of rationality must be interpreted as far as possible in the narrow sense, standard in economic theory, of taking the most effective means to given ends. I shall modify this concept to some extent . . . but one must try to avoid introducing any controversial ethical elements. The initial situation must be characterized by stipulations that are widely accepted.

In working out the conception of justice as fairness one main task clearly is to determine which principles of justice would be chosen in the original position . . . It may be observed, however, that once the principles of justice are thought of as arriving from an original agreement in a situation of equality, it is an open question whether the principle of utility would be acknowledged. Offhand it hardly seems likely that persons who view themselves as equals, entitled to press their claims upon one another, would agree to a principle which may require lesser life prospects for some simply for the sake of a greater sum of advantages enjoyed by others. Since each desires to protect his interests, his capacity to advance his conception of the good, no one has a reason to acquiesce in an enduring loss for himself in order to bring about a greater net balance of satisfaction. In the absence of strong and lasting benevolent impulses, a rational man would not accept a basic structure merely because it maximized the algebraic sum of advantages irrespective of its permanent effects on his own basic rights and interests. Thus it seems that the principle of utility is incompatible with the conception of social cooperation among equals for mutual advantage. It appears to be inconsistent with the idea of reciprocity implicit in the notion of a well-ordered society. Or, at any rate, so I shall argue.

I shall maintain instead that the persons in the initial position would choose two rather different principles: the first requires equality in the assignment of basic rights and duties, while the second holds that social and economic inequalities, for example inequalities of wealth and authority, are just only if they result in compensating benefits for everyone, and in particular for the least advantaged members of society. These principles rule out justifying institutions on the grounds that the hardships of some are offset by a greater good in the aggregate. It may be expedient but it is not just that some should have less in order that others may prosper. But there is no injustice in the greater benefits earned by a few provided that the situation of persons not so fortunate is thereby improved. The intuitive idea is that since everyone's well-being depends upon a scheme of cooperation without which no one could have a satisfactory life, the division of advantages should be such as to draw forth the willing cooperation of everyone taking part in it, including those less well situated. Yet this can be expected only if reasonable terms are proposed. The two principles mentioned seem to be a fair agreement on the basis of which those better endowed, or more fortunate in their social position, neither of which we can be said to deserve, could expect the willing cooperation of others when some workable scheme is a necessary condition of the welfare of all. Once we decide to look for a conception of justice that nullifies the accidents of natural endowment and the contingencies of social circumstance as counters in quest for political and economic advantage, we are led to these principles. They express the result of leaving aside those aspects of the social world that seem arbitrary from a moral point of view.

Rawls *A Theory of Justice* 12–15

The two principles of justice which receive their first expression in this introductory extract need to be highlighted. First principle: each person is to have an equal right to the most extensive total system of equal basic liberties compatible with a similar system of liberty for all. This is called the principle of greatest equal liberty. Basic liberties include various freedoms such as freedom of speech, freedom of conscience, and freedom from arbitrary arrest. A fuller account will be given later. Second principle: social and economic inequalities are fair and just but only if they work for the benefit of the least advantaged in society. This is the so-called difference principle. Rather than being concerned with the distribution of liberties, its subject matter is the distribution of wealth and social position within a society and in marked contrast to the first principle inequalities are permissible provided they improve the lot of the worst off.

Rawls claims to have ascertained those principles of justice which it would be rational for persons in the original position to choose. The essential point is that it is through the device of the notional social contract, the original position, that a connection between the theory of justice and a theory of rational choice is achieved. This pivotal device must be examined in depth. It contains several related elements: the veil of ignorance, the circumstances of justice, the rationality of the parties and the formal constraints.

THE ORIGINAL POSITION

(a) The veil of ignorance

Precisely what species of information is denied the parties in the original position? Is there any information which pierces the veil of ignorance and which consequently the parties in the original position are deemed to know?

The idea of the original position is to set up a fair procedure so that any principles agreed to will be just. The aim is to use the notion of pure procedural justice as a basis of theory. Somehow we must nullify the effects of specific contingencies which put men at odds and tempt them to exploit social and natural circumstances to their own advantage. Now in order to do this I assume that the parties are situated behind a veil of ignorance. They do not know how the various alternatives will affect their own particular case and they are obliged to evaluate principles solely on the basis of general considerations.

It is assumed, then, that the parties do not know certain kinds of particular facts. First of all, no one knows his place in society, his class position or social status; nor does he know his fortune in the distribution of natural assets and abilities, his intelligence and strength, and the like. Nor, again, does anyone know his conception of the good, the particulars of his rational plan of life, or even the special features of his psychology such as his aversion to risk or liability to optimism or pessimism. More than this, I assume that the parties do not know the particular circumstances of their own society. That is, they do not know its economic or political situation, or the level of civilization and culture it has been able to achieve. The persons in the original position have no information as to which generation they belong. These broader restrictions on knowledge are appropriate in part because questions of social justice arise between generations as well as within them, for example, the question of the appropriate rate of capital saving and the conservation of natural resources and the environment of nature. There is also, theoretically anyway, the question of a reasonable genetic policy. In these cases too, in order to carry through the idea of the original position, the parties must not know the contingencies that set them in opposition. They must choose principles the consequences of which they are prepared to live with whatever generation they turn out to belong to.

As far as possible, then, the only particular facts which the parties know is that their society is subject to the circumstances of justice and whatever this implies [the circumstances of justice are considered below]. It is taken for granted, however, that they know the general facts about human society. They understand political affairs and the principles of economic theory; they know the basis of social organization and the laws of human psychology. Indeed, the parties are presumed to know whatever general facts affect the choice of the principles of justice. There are no limitations on general information, that is, on general laws and theories, since conceptions of justice must be adjusted to the characteristics of the system of social cooperation which they are to regulate, and there is no reason to rule out these facts. It is, for example, a consideration against a conception of justice that in view of the laws of moral psychology, men would not acquire a desire to act upon it even when the institutions of their society satisfied it. For in this case there would be difficulty in securing the stability of social cooperation. It is an important feature of a conception of justice that it would generate its own support. That is, its principles should be such that when they are embodied in the basic structure of society men tend to acquire the corresponding sense of justice [discussed below under the characteristic of rationality]. Given the principles of moral learning, men develop a desire to act in accordance with its principles. In this case a conception of justice is stable. This kind of general information is admissible in the original position.— *virtual reality* →

Rawls *A Theory of Justice* 136–138

It has already been argued by Rawls that this type of constraint on certain information ensures a conception of justice as fairness. Unanimity is another consequence. However, can it be rational to determine principles of justice from behind such a constraint upon information?

These remarks show that the original position is not to be thought of as a general assembly which includes at one moment everyone who will live at

why do people leave wills & testament.

some time; or, much less, as an assembly of everyone who could live at some time. It is not a gathering of all actual or possible persons. To conceive of the original position in either of these ways is to stretch fantasy too far; the conception would cease to be a natural guide to intuition. In any case, it is important that the original position be interpreted so that one can at any time adopt its perspective. It must make no difference when one takes up this viewpoint, or who does so: the restrictions must be such that the same principles are always chosen. The veil of ignorance is a key condition in meeting this requirement. It ensures not only that the information available is relevant, but that it is at all times the same.

It may be protested that the condition of the veil of ignorance is irrational. Surely, some may object, principles should be chosen in the light of all the information available. There are various replies to this contention. Here I shall sketch those which emphasize the simplifications that need to be made if one is to have any theory at all . . . To begin with, it is clear that since the differences among the parties are unknown to them, and everyone is equally rational and similarly situated, each is convinced by the same arguments. Therefore, we can view the choice in the original position from the standpoint of one person selected at random. If anyone after due reflection prefers a conception of justice to another, then they all do, and a unanimous agreement can be reached. We can, to make the circumstances more vivid, imagine that the parties are required to communicate with each other through a referee as intermediary, and that he is to announce which alternatives have been suggested and the reasons offered in their support. He forbids the attempt to form coalitions, and he informs the parties when they have come to an understanding. But such a referee is actually superfluous, assuming that the deliberations of the parties must be similar.

Rawls A Theory of Justice 139

The radical significance of the veil of ignorance manifests itself in the following excerpts.

Thus there follows the very important consequence that the parties have no basis for bargaining in the usual sense. No one knows his situation in society nor his natural assets, and therefore no one is in a position to tailor principles to his advantage. We might imagine that one of the contractees threatens to hold out unless the others agree to principles favourable to him. But how does he know which principles are especially in his interest? The same holds for the formation of coalitions: if a group were to decide to band together to the disadvantage of others, they would not know how to favour themselves in the choice of the principles. Even if they could get everyone to agree to their proposal, they would have no assurance that it was to their advantage, since they cannot identify themselves either by name or description.

Rawls A Theory of Justice 139–140

The restrictions on particular information in the original position are, then, of fundamental importance. Without them we would not be able to work out any definite theory of justice at all. We would have to be content with a vague formula stating that justice is what would be agreed to without being able to say much, if anything, about the substance of the agreement itself. . . . The veil of ignorance makes possible a unanimous choice of a particular conception of

Rawls theory can be viewed as a personal attack on the achievement of the real world conception of justice. Which is the achievement...

justice. Without these limitations on knowledge the bargaining problem of the original position would be hopelessly complicated. Even if theoretically a solution were to exist, we would not, at present anyway, be able to determine it.

that should be celebrated a pride some sense of pride despite the current situation of knowledge lacking here... on the other hand it shows how much societies have managed justice close to...

veil of ignorance

Rawls *A Theory of Justice* 140

Now the reasons for the veil of ignorance go beyond mere simplicity. We want to define the original position so that we get the desired solution. If a knowledge of particulars is allowed, then the outcome is biased by arbitrary contingencies. As already observed, to each according to his threat [*sic*—own?] advantage is not a principle of justice. If the original position is to yield agreements that are just, the parties must be fairly situated and treated equally as moral persons. The arbitrariness of the world must be corrected for by adjusting the circumstances of the initial contractual situation. Moreover, if in choosing principles we require unanimity even when there is full information, only a few rather obvious cases could be decided. A conception of justice based on unanimity in these circumstances would indeed be weak and trivial. But once knowledge is excluded, the requirement of unanimity is not out of place and the fact that it can be satisfied is of great importance. It enables us to say of the preferred conception of justice that it represents a genuine reconciliation of interests.

unfair and blow to the current conception of justice

Rawls *A Theory of Justice* 140–141

playing God? Who??

(b) The circumstances of justice

Questions concerning justice do not arise in all circumstances. It follows that if Rawls is to derive principles of justice from the original position, the latter needs to be defined in such a way as to guarantee that questions of justice do in fact arise. Consequently, there are both objective and subjective 'background conditions' in the original position without which a theory of justice would be both redundant and unattainable; they are 'the normal conditions under which human cooperation is both possible and necessary' (p 126). The objective conditions are encapsulated in the concept of 'moderate scarcity'. If a society is endowed with a superabundance of readily available resources all questions about how they are to be distributed become superfluous. Equally, if scarcity is extreme it would be unreasonable to expect it to be dealt with by voluntary social cooperation. Therefore, parties in the original position need to be aware of the existence of a moderate scarcity otherwise there would be no stimulus to engage in any search for principles of justice. There are also subjective conditions in the sense that there are certain attitudes which the parties in the original position have towards the objective conditions. Most relevant is the fact that parties have different interests and ends. They each have different life plans and consequently make different demands on the available resources. Notice each person in the original position will have some conception of the good, some life plan, but, of course, because of the veil of ignorance, knowledge of the specific content of the conception of the good will be blotted out. In addition to the diversity of life plans, the parties in the original position are mutually disinterested; they are concerned to advance their own conception of the good and no one else's. In fact mutual disinterest is the paramount subjective condition.

to apply to world of conflict wealthy poor society

brain washing gimmick that the OP puts people in a position whereby they have to conform to these views that are not their own

Thus, one can say, in brief, that the circumstances of justice obtain whenever mutually disinterested persons put forward conflicting claims to the diversion

Principle of liberty defies itself since everyone is imprisoned in this sack of named equality

of social advantages under conditions of moderate scarcity. Unless these circumstances existed there would be no occasion for the virtue of justice, just as in the absence of threats of injury to life and limb there would be no occasion for physical courage.

Rawls *A Theory of Justice* 128

(c)   The rationality of the parties

The parties in the original position are motivated to pursue their life plans in a rational manner. In the excerpt that follows the concept of 'primary social goods' is introduced. These are the goods to which the two principles of justice address themselves. In other words they include basic liberties such as freedom of speech (the first principle) and wealth (the second principle). A fuller examination of primary social goods comes later. In the meantime what is the meaning and significance of the rationality of the parties?

I have assumed throughout that the persons in the original position are rational. In choosing between principles each tries as best he can to advance his interests. But I have also assumed that the parties do not know their conception of the good. This means that while they know they have some rational plan of life, they do not know the details of this plan, the particular ends and interests which it is calculated to promote. How, then, can they decide which conceptions of justice are most to their advantage? Or must we suppose that they are reduced to mere guessing? To meet this difficulty, I postulate that they accept [this] account of the good . . . they assume that they would prefer more primary social goods rather than less. Of course, it may turn out, once the veil of ignorance is removed, that some of them for religious or other reasons may not, in fact, want more of these goods. But from the standpoint of the original position, it is rational for the parties to suppose that they want a larger share, since in any case they are not compelled to accept more if they do not wish to, nor does a person suffer from a greater liberty. Thus even though the parties are deprived of information about their particular ends, they have enough knowledge to rank the alternatives. They know that in general they must try to protect their liberties, widen their opportunities, and enlarge their means for promoting their aims whatever these are. Guided by the theory of the good and the general facts of moral psychology, their deliberations are no longer guesswork. They can make a rational decision in the ordinary sense.

The concept of rationality invoked here . . . is the standard one familiar in social theory. Thus in the usual way, a rational person is thought to have a coherent set of preferences between the options open to him. He ranks these options according to how well they further his purposes; he follows the plan that will satisfy more of his desires than less, and which has the greater chance of being executed. The special assumption I make is that a rational individual does not suffer from envy. He is not ready to accept a loss for himself if only others have less as well. He is not downcast by the knowledge or perception that others have a larger index of primary social goods. Or at least this is true as long as the differences between himself and others do not exceed certain limits, and he does not believe that the existing inequalities are founded on injustice or are the result of letting chance work itself out for no compensating social purpose . . .

Rawls *A Theory of Justice* 142–143

Therefore the concept of mutual disinterest includes the assumption of a lack of envy. This assumption is important in connection with the second principle of justice. If envy were a characteristic of parties in the original position, presumably, equality in the distribution of wealth would be preferred to Rawls's second principle of justice.

The following extract examines rationality in conjunction with the primary subjective circumstance of justice.

> The assumption of mutually disinterested rationality, then, comes to this: the persons in the original position try to acknowledge principles which advance their scheme of ends as far as possible. They do this by attempting to win for themselves the highest index of primary social goods, since this enables them to promote their conception of the good most effectively whatever it turns out to be. The parties do not seek to confer benefits or to impose injuries on one another; they are not moved by affection or rancour. Nor do they try to gain relative to each other; they are not envious or vain. Put in terms of a game, we might say: they strive for as high an absolute score as possible. They do not wish a high or low score for their opponents, nor do they seek to maximize or minimize the differences between their successes and those of others. The idea of a game does not really apply, since the parties are not concerned to win but to get as many points as possible judged by their own system of ends.
>
> Rawls *A Theory of Justice* 144–145

The condition of rationality subsumes a further assumption: 'a sense of justice'. It needs to be noted that this assumption is itself conditional upon the principles not being chosen in disregard of general facts of human psychology, information which pierces the veil of ignorance and which, consequently, the parties in the original position are deemed to know (supra p 273).

> There is one further assumption to guarantee strict compliance. The parties are presumed to be capable of a sense of justice and this fact is public knowledge to them. This condition is to insure the integrity of the agreement made in the original position. It does not mean that in their deliberations the parties apply some particular conception of justice, for this would defeat the motivation assumption. Rather, it means that the parties can rely on each other to understand and to act in accordance with whatever principles are finally agreed to. Once principles are acknowledged the parties can depend on one another to conform to them. In reaching an agreement, then, they know that their undertaking is not in vain: their capacity for a sense of justice insures that the principles chosen will be respected. It is essential to observe, however, that this assumption still permits the consideration of men's capacity to act on the various conceptions of justice. The general facts of human psychology and the principles of moral learning are relevant matters for the parties to examine. If a conception of justice is unlikely to generate its own support, or lacks stability, this fact must not be overlooked. For then a different conception of justice might be preferred. The assumption only says that the parties have a capacity for justice in a purely formal sense: taking everything into account, including the general facts of moral psychology, the parties will adhere to the principles eventually chosen [the other matters to be taken into account are the formal constraints, infra pp 278ff]. They are rational in that they will not enter into agreements they know they cannot keep, or can do so

only with great difficulty. Along with other considerations they count the strains of commitment . . . Thus in assessing conceptions of justice the persons in the original position are to assume that the one they adopt will be strictly complied with. The consequences of their agreement are to be worked out on this basis.

Rawls *A Theory of Justice* 145

This is the important constraint of commitment. Just as the conditions of the veil of ignorance ensures justice will be fair, equal, and unanimous, the sense of justice ensures commitment to the principles of justice decided upon. The assumption is that the parties in the original position are capable of adhering to principles which in fact constrain the pursuit of self-interest. The principles are moral in the sense that, having determined on the principles of justice, the parties in the original position must abide by them, and, furthermore they can expect others to abide by them, even when it is not in the best interests of such persons so to do. This needs to be read in conjunction with the formal constraints considered below.

The final extract in this section vividly demonstrates the combined consequences of two essential conditions of the original position: the veil of ignorance and the rationality of the parties.

Finally, if the parties are conceived as themselves making proposals, they have no incentive to suggest pointless or arbitrary principles. For example, none would urge that special privileges be given to those exactly six feet tall or born on a sunny day. Nor would anyone put forward the principle that basic rights should depend on the color of one's skin or the texture of one's hair. No one can tell whether such principles would be to his advantage. Furthermore, each such principle is a limitation of one's liberty of action, and such restrictions are not to be accepted without a reason. Certainly we might imagine peculiar circumstances in which these characteristics are relevant. Those born on a sunny day might be blessed with a happy temperament, and for some positions of authority this might be a qualifying attribute. But such distinctions would never be proposed in first principles, for they must have some rational connection with the advancement of human interests broadly defined. The rationality of the parties and their situation in the original position guarantees that ethical principles and conceptions of justice have this general content. Inevitably, then, racial and sexual discrimination presupposes that some hold a favoured place in the social system which they are willing to exploit to their advantage. From the standpoint of persons similarly situated in an initial situation which is fair, the principles of explicit racist doctrines are not only unjust. They are irrational. For this reason we could say that they are not moral conceptions at all, but simply means of suppression. They have no place on a reasonable list of traditional conceptions of justice. Of course, this contention is not at all a matter of definition. It is rather a consequence of the conditions characterizing the original position, especially the conditions of the rationality of the parties and the veil of ignorance. That conceptions of right have a certain content and exclude arbitrary and pointless principles is, therefore, an inference from the theory.

Rawls *A Theory of Justice* 149–150

(d) The formal constraints of justice

These five constraints seriously limit the choice of principles of justice that are available to the parties in the original position: the principles of justice must be general in the sense that they must be capable of serving as a 'public charter of a well-ordered society in perpetuity' (p 131); they must be universal in application, applying to everyone in virtue of their being moral persons; they need to be publicisable, this arising naturally from a contractarian standpoint; they must be adjudicative, given that the role of the principles of justice must be efficiently adjusting competing demands; and they must be final, in the sense that the buck stops with the principles because they are the final court of appeal.

These five formal constraints need to be satisfied if the principles of justice are to provide a 'public charter' which is conducive to social cooperation in that we have a set of principles, general in form and universal in application, that is to be publicly recognized as a final court of appeal for ordering the conflicting claims of moral persons.

THE PRIMARY SOCIAL GOODS *being) - unforeseeable*

Rawls is formulating and justifying two principles of justice which a basic structure, if it is to be just, must satisfy. The principles specify how the basic structure is to distribute what he calls primary social goods. These are 'things which every rational man is presumed to want. These goods normally have a use whatever a person's rational life plan' (p 62). This being so, the panoramic view of Rawls's theory is something like this: the veil of ignorance ensures equality and unanimity; the rationality of the parties and the formal constraints ensure a commitment to the principles, and the idea of primary social goods desired by all rational men whatever else they may want, together with the circumstances of justice, provide the motivation necessary to get the problem of rational choice going in the first place.

The first principle of justice, the principle of greatest equal liberty, is targeted at those primary social goods which can be described as basic rights, liberties or powers. They encompass the freedom to participate in the political process (the right to vote and to be eligible for public office), freedom of speech and assembly (including freedom of the press), liberty of conscience and freedom of thought (including religious freedom), freedom of the person (as defined by the rule of law) and the right to hold personal property, and freedom from arbitrary arrest and seizure (as defined by the rule of law). The second principle of justice, the difference principle, distributes a different species of primary social goods. It is targeted at 'the distribution of income and wealth and . . . the design of organizations that make use of differences in authority and responsibility . . .' (p 61): the primary goods of wealth, income, power and responsibility.

In what follows notice the means-to-ends role of the primary goods and the 'more rather than less' assumption. Needless to say this must be read in conjunction with the condition of the veil of ignorance as the penultimate sentence of the extract makes clear.

> Now primary goods . . . are things which it is supposed a rational man wants whatever else he wants. Regardless of what an individual's rational plans are in detail, it is assumed that there are various things which he would prefer more of rather than less. With more of these goods men can generally be assured of greater success in carrying out their intentions and advancing their ends, whatever these ends may be. The primary social goods, to give them in broad categories, are rights and liberties, opportunities and powers, income and wealth . . . It seems evident that in general these things fit the description of

primary goods. They are social goods in view of their connection with the basic structure; liberties and powers are defined by the rules of the major institutions and the distribution of income and wealth is regulated by them.

. . . The main idea is that a person's good is determined by what is for him the most rational long-term plan of life given reasonably favorable circumstances. A man is happy when he is more or less successfully in the way of carrying out this plan. To put it briefly, the good is the satisfaction of rational desire. We are to suppose, then, that each individual has a rational plan of life drawn up subject to the conditions that confront him. This plan is designed to permit the harmonious satisfaction of his interests. It schedules activities so that various desires can be fulfilled without interference. It is arrived at by rejecting other plans that are either less likely to succeed or do not provide for such an inclusive attainment of aims. Given the alternatives available, a rational plan is one which cannot be improved upon; there is no other plan which, taking everything into account, would be preferable.

Now the assumption is that though men's rational plans do have different final ends, they nevertheless all require for their execution certain primary goods, natural and social. Plans differ since individual abilities, circumstances, and wants differ; rational plans are adjusted to these contingencies. But whatever one's system of ends, primary goods are necessary means. Greater intelligence, wealth and opportunity, for example, allow a person to achieve ends he could not rationally contemplate otherwise. The expectations of representative men are, then, to be defined by the index of primary social goods available to them. While the persons in the original position do not know their conception of the good, they do know, I assume, that they prefer more rather than less primary goods. And this information is sufficient for them to know how to advance their interests in the initial position.

Rawls A Theory of Justice 92–93

Later in his book Rawls adds to the inventory of primary goods within the domain of the first principle; indeed, this addition could be the most important of the primary goods.

On several occasions I have mentioned that perhaps the most important primary good is that of self-respect. We must make sure that the conception of goodness as rationality explains why this should be so. We may define self-respect (or self-esteem) as having two aspects. First of all . . . it includes a person's sense of his own value, his secure conviction that his conception of his good, his plan of life, is worth carrying out. And second, self-respect implies a confidence in one's ability, so far as it is within one's power, to fulfil one's intentions. When we feel that our plans are of little value, we cannot pursue them with pleasure or take delight in their execution. Nor plagued by failure and self-doubt can we continue in our endeavors. It is clear then why self-respect is a primary good. Without it nothing may seem worth doing, or if some things have value for us, we lack the will to strive for them. All desire and activity becomes empty and vain, and we sink into apathy and cynicism. Therefore the parties in the original position would wish to avoid at almost any cost the social conditions that undermine self-respect. The fact that justice as fairness gives more support to self-esteem than other principles is a strong reason for them to adopt it.

Rawls A Theory of Justice 440

The idea of primary social goods is significant in that it represents Rawls's answer to a self-inflicted dilemma. Primary goods are conceived of as those things which any rational people would desire for themselves. However, the veil of ignorance precludes the parties in the original position from knowing what it is in particular they desire, what their specific conception of the good is. Consequently, how is it that they have the potential to know that they will want the primary goods? How do they know what things are a means to fulfilling other desires? The theory of primary social goods is dependent upon what he calls 'the thin theory of the good'. The purpose of the thin theory of the good is to allow him to argue that even though people outside the veil of ignorance will have a diversity of desires and conceptions of the good, there are certain common, standard features of all desires and conceptions and these are known by the parties in the original position. So the thin theory of the good comprises certain minimal assumptions about those things likely to be useful, if not essential, to all full theories of the good outside the original position, whatever their specific design. In short, parties behind the veil are deemed to know that they will want the primary social goods, now including self-respect, and more rather than less, whatever their individual desires and ends will be in the real, unveiled world. It is in this way that the thin theory of the good formulates the minimal motivation necessary to the problem of rational choice.

But why should this be so? So far the only argument for the thin theory of the good and, consequently, the primary social goods themselves which are dependent upon it, has been argument by assertion only. What is the basis of the thin theory of the good? How do the parties in the original position work out what the primary goods are? What argument, other than assertion, is used to establish that these things are indeed primary goods and as such the minimal requirements for all conceptions of the good? In the following extract, leaving aside the Aristotelian Principle, there are three different types of general facts about human nature that answer these questions. But again, is this really anything more than mere assertion? Notice the last sentence.

> First of all, there are the broad features of human desires and needs, their relative urgency and cycles of recurrence, and their phases of development as affected by physiological and other circumstances. Second, plans must fit the requirements of human capacities and abilities, their trends of maturation and growth, and how they are best trained and educated for this or that purpose. Thirdly, I shall postulate a basic principle of motivation which I shall refer to as the Aristotelian Principle. Finally, the general facts of social interdependency must be reckoned with. The basic structure of society is bound to encourage and support certain kinds of plans more than others by rewarding its members for contributing to the common good in ways consistent with justice. Taking account of these contingencies narrows down the alternative plans so that the problem of decision becomes, in some cases anyway, reasonably definite . . .
>
> The general facts about human needs and abilities are perhaps clear enough and I shall assume that common sense knowledge suffices for our purposes here.
>
> Rawls *A Theory of Justice* 425–426

It seems, therefore, that a lot depends on the Aristotelian Principle; this 'deep psychological fact' (p 432).

[The Aristotelian Principle] says only that we prefer, other things being equal, activities that depend upon a larger repertoire of realized capacities and that they are more complex . . . What the Aristotelian Principle says is that whenever a person engages in an activity belonging to some chain (and perhaps to several chains) he tends to move up the chain. In general, he will prefer doing the nth to doing the n–1th activity; and this tendency will be stronger the more his capacity is yet to be realized and the less onerous he finds the strains of learning and training. Presumably there is a preference for ascending the chain or chains which offer the better prospects of exercising the higher abilities with the least strain . . . By itself the principle simply asserts a propensity to ascend whatever chains are chosen. It does not entail that a rational plan includes any particular aims, nor does it imply any special form of society.

Rawls A Theory of Justice 429–430

What arguments are advanced to support the Aristotelian Principle?

We must assume, then, that the list of primary goods can be accounted for by the conception of goodness as rationality in connection with the general facts about human wants and abilities, their characteristic phases and requirements of nurture, the Aristotelian Principle, and the necessities of social interdependence . . . I shall not argue the case for the list of primary goods here, since their claims seem evident enough.

Rawls A Theory of Justice 434

Such heavy reliance on self-evidence will not convince everyone. But he does have another argument: perhaps, at the basis of the thin theory of the good, the primary social goods and the Aristotelian Principle is the good of self-respect.

The conception of goodness as rationality allows us to characterize more fully the circumstances that support the first aspect of self-esteem, the sense of our own worth. These are essentially two: (1) having a rational plan of life, and one in particular that satisfies the Aristotelian Principle; and, (2) finding our person and deeds appreciated and confirmed by others who are likewise esteemed and their association enjoyed. I assume then that someone's plan of life will lack a certain attraction for him if it fails to call upon his natural capacities in an interesting fashion. When activities fail to satisfy the Aristotelian Principle, they are likely to seem dull and flat, and to give us no feeling of competence or a sense that they are worth doing. A person tends to be more confident of his value when his abilities are both fully realized and organized in ways of suitable complexity and refinement.

But the companion effect of the Aristotelian Principle also enters into the fact that others confirm and take pleasure in what we do. For while it is true that unless our endeavors are appreciated by our associates it is impossible for us to maintain the conviction that they are worthwhile, it is also true that others tend to value them only if what we do elicits their admiration or gives them pleasure. Thus activities that display intricate and subtle talents, and manifest discrimination and refinement, are valued by both the person himself and those around him. Moreover the more someone experiences his own way of life as worth fulfilling, the more likely he is to welcome our attainments . . . The application of the Aristotelian Principle is always relative to the individual and therefore to his natural assets and particular situation. It normally suffices that for each person there is some association (one or more) to which he belongs and within which the activities that are rational for him are publicly affirmed by others. In this sense we acquire a sense that what we do in everyday life is worthwhile.

Rawls *A Theory of Justice* 440–441

THE THREE STAGES

The structure of Rawls's theory of justice that emerges from the original position can be viewed as a three-stage development. From the thin theory of the good the two principles of justice evolve and they, in their turn, evaluate as just or unjust the particular ends and values, that is the conception of the good, that people in the real, unveiled world actually have. The sequence is: the thin theory of the good in the original position leading to the two principles of justice leading to a just full theory of the good.

... to establish these principles it is necessary to rely on some notion of goodness, for we need assumptions about the parties' motives in the original position. Since these assumptions must not jeopardize the prior place of the concept of right, the theory of the good used in arguing for the principles of justice is restricted to the bare essentials. This account of the good I call the thin theory: its purpose is to secure the premises about primary goods required to arrive at the principles of justice. Once this theory is worked out and the primary goods accounted for, we are free to use the principles of justice in the further development of what I shall call the full theory of the good.

Rawls *A Theory of Justice* 396

THE TWO PRINCIPLES

We now need to consider in some detail the two principles of justice decided upon by the parties in the original position. Rawls's introductory account of them is set out above (p 271); here is his final statement of the principles.

First Principle   Each person is to have an equal right to the most extensive total system of equal basic liberties compatible with a similar system of liberty for all.

Second Principle   Social and economic inequalities are to be arranged so that they are both:
(a)   to the greatest benefit of the least advantaged, consistent with the just savings principle, and
(b)   attached to offices and positions open to all under conditions of fair equality of opportunity.

(a) The first principle

The equal liberties under this principle are described above (p 279); they are the familiar rights and liberties of liberal democratic regimes and they are to be protected from encroachments. Liberty ought to be maximized by a system of liberties calculated to create the greatest possible freedom of speech, freedom of conscience, etc for all. There are two ways of contravening this principle: liberty is unequal when one class of persons has a greater liberty than another, or liberty is less extensive than it should be. In fact 'liberty can be restricted only for the sake of liberty' and two situations are envisaged. First, where a less extensive liberty strengthens the overall liberty shared by all. The point is that no individual liberty can be completely untrammelled and remain equally held by all: for example, if freedom of speech is to be equally available, there must be rules governing debate and inquiry (p 203). Clearly, 'when the liberties are left unrestricted they collide with one another'; liberty of conscience, for example, is limited by the common interest in public order and security. Now it is important for Rawls to justify such restrictions without employing a utilitarian calculation in the sense of arguing that such restrictions on individual liberty enhance the aggregate, public good. Rather his justification for these restrictions is that they would be accepted from the premise of the original position.

> . . . it now seems evident that, in limiting liberty (of conscience) by reference to the common interest in public order and security, the government act on a principle that would be chosen in the original position. For in this position each recognizes that the disruption of these conditions is a danger for the liberty of all. This follows once the maintenance of public order is understood as a necessary condition for everyone's achieving his ends whatever they are . . .

Rawls A Theory of Justice 212–213

Secondly, a less than equal liberty can be justified if it is acceptable to those with the lesser liberty. But he insists that 'acceptable to those with the lesser liberty' means not acceptable for any reason, but only acceptable because the less than equal liberty produces a greater protection of their other liberties (p 233). It must be shown that the inequalities would be accepted by the less favoured in return for the greater protection of their other liberties that results from the restriction.

> The problem of paternalism deserves some discussion here, since it . . . concerns a lesser freedom. In the original position the parties assume that in society they are rational and able to manage their own affairs. Therefore they do not acknowledge any duties to self, since this is unnecessary to further their good. But once the ideal conception is chosen, they will want to insure themselves against the possibility that their powers are undeveloped and they cannot rationally advance their interests, as in the case of children; or that through some misfortune or accident they are unable to make decisions for their good, as in the case of those seriously injured or mentally disturbed. It is also rational for them to protect themselves against their own irrational inclinations by consenting to a scheme of penalties that may give them a sufficient motive to avoid foolish actions and by accepting certain impositions designed to undo the unfortunate consequences of their imprudent behavior. For these cases the parties adopt principles stipulating when others are authorized to act in their behalf and to override their present wishes if necessary; and this they do recognizing that sometimes their capacity to act rationally for their good may fail, or be lacking altogether . . . Thus the principles of paternalism are those that the parties would acknowledge in the original position to protect themselves against the weakness and infirmities of their reason and will in society.

Rawls A Theory of Justice 248–249

This is the greatest equal liberty principle. But what is meant by liberty or freedom?

> The general description of liberty, then, has the following form: this or that person (or persons) is free (or not free) from this or that constraint (or set of constraints) to do (or not to do) so and so.
>
> Rawls *A Theory of Justice* 202

Constraints upon liberty take one of two forms: either they are duties or prohibitions present within the rules and principles of the law or they result from the coercive influences arising from public opinion and social pressure. Our liberty is restricted by the presence of either of these constraints. But what of poverty, which can exist even after the operation of the difference principle (the second principle of justice)? If, like legal restrictions and public opinion, lack of wealth was a constraint on liberty, then it would not be rational for parties in the original position to accept Rawls's second principle of justice.

Rawls does accept that economic disadvantage can have an effect upon liberty. For example, freedom of speech under the first principle is guaranteed to both the wealthy and the poor. However, the wealthy are in a position to voice their opinions more effectively through their access to, if not control of, the media. Again freedom under the rule of law is equal to all; but those with the necessary money can afford the top legal representation. In short the wealthy can do more with their liberties; their freedom is greater. But Rawls wishes to draw a distinction between liberty and the worth of liberty. Whereas constraints which manifest themselves in the form of legal restrictions and public opinion do embarrass liberty itself, economic disadvantages affect the worth of liberty leaving liberty itself intact. In this way it is quite rational for a person in the original position to choose a principle which allows for inequality in wealth distribution together with a principle that enshrines equality of certain basic liberties.

> Thus liberty and the worth of liberty are distinguishable as follows: liberty is represented by the complete system of the liberties of equal citizenship, while the worth of liberty to persons and groups is proportional to their capacity to advance their ends within the framework the system defines. Freedom as equal liberty is the same for all; the question of compensating for a lesser than equal liberty does not arise. But the worth of liberty is not the same for everyone. Some have greater authority and wealth, and therefore greater means to achieve their aims. The lesser worth of liberty is, however, compensated for, since the capacity for the less fortunate members of society to achieve their aims would be even less were they not to accept the existing inequalities whenever the difference principle is satisfied.
>
> Rawls *A Theory of Justice* 204

(b) The second principle

The second principle has acquired two accretions since its first, introductory statement. The first part of this principle, the so-called difference principle (2a), is now conditioned by the just savings rule, and there is an entirely new second section (2b): the principle of fair equality of opportunity. Both these additions will be examined in due course, but we shall first consider the familiar difference principle itself.

(i)   The difference principle

Economic and social inequalities are to be arranged in such a manner that they result in the greatest advantage for the worst off as far as the primary social goods of wealth, income, power and authority are concerned.

What is the meaning of 'worst off'? It seems there are two possibilities and either will do.

> Here it seems possible to avoid a certain arbitrariness. One possibility is to choose a particular social position, say that of the unskilled worker, and then to count as the least advantaged all those with the average income and wealth of this group, or less. The expectation of the lowest representative man is defined as the average taken over this whole class. Another alternative is a definition solely in terms of relative income and wealth with no reference to social position. Thus all persons with less than half of the median income and wealth may be taken as the least advantaged segment. This definition depends only upon the lower half of the distribution and has the merit of focusing attention on the social distance between those who have least and the average citizen. Surely this gap is an essential feature of the situation of the less favored members of society. I suppose that either of these definitions, or some combination of them, will serve well enough.
>
> Rawls *A Theory of Justice* 98

The stringent conditions of the original position provide the reason for the choice of the difference principle. The choice of principles of justice is conceived of as an issue of rational choice. But it is a rational choice which is denied certain types of information: like going blind in poker, there is a self-inflicted uncertainty. Furthermore, the parties know they will be bound by whatever principles they agree to in perpetuity (the sense of justice and the formal constraints). An issue of such paramountcy determined upon in a state of such amnesia gives the parties but one choice: they will employ the 'maximin' rule. They will opt for the insurance and security of the best worst off position.

> There is an analogy between the two principles and the maximin rule for choice under uncertainty. This is evident from the fact that the two principles are those a person would choose for the design of a society in which his enemy is to assign him his place. The maximin rule tells us to rank alternatives by their worst possible outcomes; we are to adopt the alternative the worst outcome of which is superior to the worst outcomes of the others. The persons in the original position do not, of course, assume that their initial place in society is decided by a malevolent opponent . . . But that the two principles of justice would be chosen if the parties were forced to protect themselves against such a contingency explains the sense in which this conception is the maximin solution. And this analogy suggests that if the original position has been described so that it is rational for the parties to adopt the conservative attitude expressed by this rule, a conclusive argument can indeed be constructed for these principles.
>
> Rawls *A Theory of Justice* 152–153

The maximin strategy not only accounts for the choice of the difference principle, it also rationalises the first principle, together with the two situations when liberty can be restricted, and the two additions to the second principle yet to be considered.

Rawls's contention is that there are three features implicit in the original position which give plausibility to the maximin rule. First, because of the informational constraint of the veil, the situation is one in which knowledge of the likelihoods of the possible circumstances is impossible, meaning that the probabilities of outcomes cannot be estimated. Secondly, the parties in the original position care little for what they might gain above the 'minimum stipend' which is guaranteed them under the difference principle. In such a gamble, the party can conceivably lose much that is important to him. Thirdly, any alternative choices, in particular one based on some form of utilitarianism, can have 'outcomes that we can hardly accept' (p 154).

... let us review briefly the nature of this situation with these three special features in mind. To begin with, the veil of ignorance excludes all but the vaguest knowledge of likelihoods. The parties have no basis for determining the probable nature of their society, or their place in it. Thus they have strong reasons for being wary of probability calculations if any other course is open to them. They must also take into account the fact that their choice of principles should seem reasonable to others, in particular their descendants, whose rights will be deeply affected by it. There are further grounds for discounting that I shall mention as we go along. For the present it suffices to note that these considerations are strengthened by the fact that the parties know very little about the gain-and-loss table. Not only are they unable to conjecture the likelihoods of the various possible circumstances, they cannot say much about what the possible circumstances are, much less enumerate them and foresee the outcome of each alternative available. Those deciding are much more in the dark than the illustration by a numerical table suggests. It is for this reason that I have spoken of an analogy with the maximin rule.

Several kinds of arguments for the two principles of justice illustrate the second feature. Thus if we can maintain that these principles provide a workable theory of social justice, and that they are compatible with reasonable demands of efficiency, then this conception guarantees a satisfactory minimum. There may be, on reflection, little reason for trying to do better. Thus much of the argument . . . is to show, by their application to the main questions of social justice, that the two principles are a satisfactory conception. These details have a philosophical purpose . . .

Finally, the third feature holds if we can assume that other conceptions of justice may lead to institutions that the parties would find intolerable. For example, it has sometimes been held that under some conditions the utility principle (in either form) justifies, if not slavery or serfdom, at any rate serious infractions of liberty for the sake of greater social benefits. We need not consider here the truth of this claim, or the likelihood that the requisite conditions obtain. For the moment, this contention is only to illustrate the way in which conceptions of justice may allow for outcomes which the parties may not be able to accept. And having the ready alternative of the two principles of justice which secure a satisfactory minimum, it seems unwise, if not irrational, for them to take a chance that these outcomes are not realized.

Rawls *A Theory of Justice* 155–156

It follows that the most prodigious disparities in wealth and income are possible and are just, provided the expectations of the worst off are improved by the tiniest amount. Likewise any substantial increase favouring the more advantaged is precluded if the position of the worst off deteriorates by the tiniest amount. But these comments must be read in conjunction with the principle of fair equal opportunity, below.

(ii)   *The just savings principle*

The concern for justice between generations is introduced as conditioning the operation of the difference principle. The parties in the original position are deemed to know that they have a degree of paternalistic concern for, at least, the members of the next generation. This assumption is the result of one of those general laws of human psychology that pierce the veil of ignorance (supra p 273). The principle which encompasses both savings and conservation is formulated as follows: in applying the difference principle, consideration will be shown for the long-term prospects of the least advantaged extending over future generations, or, at the least, over the next generation. Therefore each generation will not only preserve the gains of culture and civilisation but also save a suitable amount of capital. The level of savings needs to be sufficient to improve the lot of the worst off of future generations, to the highest possible level that is acceptable to the worst off of the present generation. As we have seen, this principle is based on an assumption resulting from a general law piercing the veil; parties do care about the welfare of their descendants. Such an assumption would not offend against the subjective circumstance of justice, mutual disinterestedness among the parties in the original position, because offspring are not parties to the contract. But, surely Rawls does not need such a cumbersome, motivational assumption to justify the just savings principle; the principle fits the condition of the veil of ignorance. Because of the black-out of information behind the veil no one knows what generation he will end up in, therefore there is motivation for something along the lines of the just savings principle to condition the operation of the difference principle.

(iii)   *The principle of fair equality of opportunity*

This comprises the second subsection to the second principle, which now reads:

2(a)—the difference principle;
2(b)—the principle of fair equality of opportunity.

Economic and social inequalities acceptable under the operation of the difference principle will only be just if they are attached to offices and positions that are open to all. A formal equality of opportunity requires that all have the same legal rights of access to all advantaged social positions. Rawls's principle goes considerably further than this; there must be 'fair' equality of opportunity. Not only are jobs to be open to all with the necessary qualifications, but also, to achieve fairness, the best possible education needs to be open to all, including remedial education to counteract disadvantages due to family or social background. All are to be given the chance to develop their potential.

Obviously, this is an important separate and distinct principle within the second principle, acting as a vital restriction on the operation of the difference principle.

For it may be possible to improve everyone's situation by assigning certain powers and benefits to positions despite the fact that certain groups are excluded from them. Although access is restricted, perhaps these offices can still attract superior talent and encourage better performance. But the principle of open positions forbids this. It expresses the conviction that if some places were not open on a basis fair to all, those kept out would be right in feeling unjustly treated even though they benefited from the greater efforts of those who were allowed to hold them. They would be justified in their complaint not only because they were excluded from certain external rewards of office such as wealth and privilege, but because they would be debarred from experiencing the realization of self which comes from a skillful and devoted exercise of social duties. They would be deprived of one of the main forms of human good.

Rawls *A Theory of Justice* 84

Notice in the above extract that the primary social good of self-respect, which Rawls discusses as one of the most important of the primary goods that are within the province of the first principle, is here extended to underpin this part of the second.

It has already been observed that the unimpeded operation of the difference principle could result in gross disparities between the wealthy and the poor. This principle is invoked to qualify the problem.

While nothing guarantees that inequalities will not be significant, there is a persistent tendency for them to be leveled down by the increasing availability of educated talent and ever widening opportunities. The conditions established by the other principles insure that the disparities likely to result will be much less than the differences that men have often tolerated in the past.

Rawls *A Theory of Justice* 158

JUSTIFICATIONS FOR THE TWO PRINCIPLES OF JUSTICE

There are three different justifications for his principles of justice.

First, if a principle would be chosen under conditions which, according to our considered moral judgments, are appropriate conditions for choosing principles of justice, then this is an acceptable reason for accepting the principle. The conditions are those contained in the concept of the original position: 'We shall say that certain principles of justice are justified because they would be agreed to in the [original position]' (p 21).

Secondly, there is the notion of 'reflective equilibrium'. From what has just been said it would be thought that the two principles of justice are to be deduced from the original position. But at times he seems to be arguing in the opposite direction. Instead of arguing from the original position to the two principles he seems to argue from the two principles back to the original position. Therefore, he defines the original position in terms of the desired outcome rather than deducing principles from the original position: 'We want to define the original position so that we get the desired solution' (p 141). To understand this methodology we need to grasp the significance of the notion of 'reflective equilibrium'.

The intuitive idea of justice as fairness is to think of the first principles of justice as themselves the object of an original agreement in a suitably defined initial situation. These principles are those which rational persons concerned to advance their interests would accept in this position of equality to settle the basic terms of their association. It must be shown, then, that the two principles of justice are the solution for the problem of choice presented by the original position. In order to do this, one must establish that, given the circumstances of the parties, and their knowledge, beliefs, and interests, an agreement on these principles is the best way for each person to secure his ends in view of the alternatives available.

Now obviously no one can obtain everything he wants; the mere existence of other persons prevents this. The absolutely best for any man is that everyone else should join with him in furthering his conception of the good whatever it turns out to be. Or failing this, that all others are required to act justly but that he is authorized to exempt himself as he pleases. Since other persons will never agree to such terms of association these forms of egoism would be rejected. The two principles of justice, however, seem to be a reasonable proposal. In fact, I should like to show that these principles are everyone's best reply, so to speak, to the corresponding demands of the others. In this sense, the choice of this conception of justice is the unique solution to the problem set by the original position.

By arguing in this way one follows a procedure familiar in social theory. That is, a simplified situation is described in which rational individuals with certain ends and related to each other in certain ways are to choose among various courses of action in view of their knowledge of the circumstances. What these individuals will do is then derived by strictly deductive reasoning from these assumptions about their beliefs and interests, their situation and the options open to them. Their conduct is, in the phrase of Pareto, the resultant of tastes and obstacles. In the theory of price, for example, the equilibrium of competitive markets is thought of as arising when many individuals each advancing their own interests give way to each other what they can best part with in return for what they most desire. Equilibrium is the result of agreements freely struck between willing traders. For each person it is the best situation that he can reach by free exchange consistent with the right and freedom of others to further their interests in the same way. It is for this reason that this state of affairs is an equilibrium, one that will persist in the absence of further changes in the circumstances. No one has any incentive to alter it. If a departure from this situation sets in motion tendencies which restore it, the equilibrium is stable.

Of course, the fact that a situation is one of equilibrium, even a stable one, does not entail that it is right or just. It only means that given men's estimate of their position, they act effectively to preserve it. Clearly a balance of hatred and hostility may be a stable equilibrium; each may think that any feasible change will be worse. The best that each can do for himself may be a condition of lesser injustice rather than of greater good. The moral assessment of equilibrium situations depends upon the background circumstances which determine them. It is at this point that the conception of the original position embodies features peculiar to moral theory. For while the theory of price, say, tries to account for the movements of the market by assumptions about the actual tendencies at work, the philosophically favored interpretation of the initial situation incorporates conditions which it is thought reasonable to impose on the choice of principles. By contrast with social theory, the aim is to characterize this situation so that the principles that would be chosen, whatever they turn out to be, are acceptable from a moral point of view. The original position is defined in such a way that it is a status quo in which any agreements reached are fair. It is a state of affairs in which the parties are equally represented as moral persons and the outcome is not conditioned by arbitrary contingencies or the relative balance of social forces. Thus justice as fairness is able to use the idea of pure procedural justice from the beginning.

It is clear, then, that the original position is a purely hypothetical situation. Nothing resembling it need ever take place, although we can by deliberately following the constraints it expresses simulate the reflections of the parties. The conception of the original position is not intended to explain human conduct except insofar as it tries to account for our moral judgments and helps to explain our having a sense of justice. Justice as fairness is a theory of our moral sentiments as manifested by our considered judgments in reflective equilibrium. These sentiments presumably affect our thought and action to some degree. So while the conception of the original position is part of the theory of conduct, it does not follow at all that there are actual situations that resemble it. What is necessary is that the principles that would be accepted play the requisite part in our moral thought and action.

One should note also that the acceptance of these principles is not conjectured as a psychological law or probability. Ideally anyway, I should like to show that their acknowledgment is the only choice consistent with the full description of the original position. The argument aims eventually to be strictly deductive. To be sure, the persons in the original position have a certain psychology, since various assumptions are made about their beliefs and interests. These assumptions appear along with other premises in the description of this initial situation. But clearly arguments from such premises can be fully deductive, as theories in politics and economics attest. We should strive for a kind of moral geometry with all the rigor which this name connotes. Unhappily the reasoning I shall give will fall far short of this, since it is highly intuitive throughout. Yet it is essential to have in mind the ideal one would like to achieve.

Rawls *A Theory of Justice* 118–121

Therefore the key to the idea of reflective equilibrium is that moral justification is a process of reasoning that has two starting points, both of which are open to modification in the process of reasoning. The two starting points are, first, the conditions of the original position, which accord with our considered moral judgments, and secondly, our intuitions about justice. The process of reasoning begins at both these end points and works towards each other. Which principles of justice would be chosen when we think of both the acceptable conditions of choice in the original position and given certain strongly held intuitive notions about the content of justice? The process will involve modification of the idea of the conditions of choice in the light of our intuitions about justice and the modification of our intuitions about the content of justice in the light of the conditions of choice. Reflective equilibrium is achieved when there is a fit between the two ends. His claim is that if we go through this process in relation to our intuitive judgments about social justice, for example, liberty, distribution of wealth etc, we shall find that his two principles of justice are the closest approximation to our intuitively held moral judgments considered in reflective equilibrium.

What Rawls has done is to show that the conditions of the original position will lead to two principles of justice that we already intuitively accept. The original position provides an explanation of why these two principles are held intuitively: the rational person, stripped of all knowledge of the features that distinguish one person from another, would pick these two principles. So the veil of ignorance is vital to this process; it is this which allows a person unhampered by 'specific contingencies', not knowing his colour, sex, relative wealth, religion etc, to pick principles of justice. This is why the choice made by such a relatively flawless persona corresponds to intuitively felt versions of justice by those who are not in the original position.

Thirdly, there is a justification based upon 'philosophical reflection'. This section of the book is called the 'Kantian Interpretation' and it provides a justification for the conditions of the original position. It is based on Kant's concept of the autonomous agent, or 'noumenal self'. Such an agent sets about the process of choice unhampered by particular desires and it is accepted that the ensuing rational principles will serve as principles for everyone, not merely for the agent.

> My suggestion is that we think of the original position as the point of view from which noumenal selves see the world. The parties qua noumenal selves have complete freedom to choose whatever principles they wish; but they also have a desire to express their nature as rational and equal members of the intelligible realm with precisely this liberty to choose, that is, as beings who can look at the world in this way and express this perspective in their life as members of society. They must decide, then, which principles when consciously followed and acted upon in everyday life will best manifest this freedom in their community, most fully reveal their independence from natural contingencies and social accident. Now if the argument of the contract doctrine is correct, these principles are indeed those defining the moral law, or more exactly, the principles of justice for institutions and individuals. The description of the original position interprets the point of view of noumenal selves, of what it means to be a free and equal rational being. Our nature as such beings is displayed when we act from the principles we would choose when this nature is reflected in the conditions determining the choice. Thus men exhibit their freedom, their independence from the contingencies of nature and society, by acting in ways they would acknowledge in the original position.
>
> Properly understood, then, the desire to act justly derives in part from the desire to express most fully what we are or can be, namely free and equal rational beings with a liberty to choose.
>
> Rawls *A Theory of Justice* 255–256

It is when people accept the two principles that were chosen by people in the original position that they are acting autonomously and expressing themselves as noumenal selves. Of course, it is the formal constraint (supra pp 278ff) on the choice of the two principles that renders them universalisable.

CRITICISM

Since its publication *A Theory of Justice* has been subjected to numerous assessments and evaluations, including three full-length books. The next extract from Philip Pettit gives an indication of the range of criticisms that have been levelled against Rawls. By 'POP' he means the people in the original position.

> Should we find unsurprising the idea that the charter chosen by the parties in the original position is the just arrangement of social affairs? Many commentators have thought so and in pressing the point they have variously

emphasized the narrow sense in which the POP's are rational, their exclusive concern with their own interests, and the stultifying ignorance under which they labour. This is scarcely fair criticism, however, for there surely is something plausible in the general idea that a charter chosen by people in a situation that eliminates the effects of bias and self-interest is a just charter. Rawls insists on this aspect of his enterprise.

> The aim is to characterize this situation so that the principles that would be chosen, whatever they turn out to be, are acceptable from a moral point of view. The original position is defined in such a way that it is a status quo in which any agreements reached are fair. It is a state of affairs in which the parties are equally represented as moral persons and the outcome is not conditioned by arbitrary contingencies or the relative balance of social forces. (TJ, p 120)

At the source of Rawls's contractarian approach is a powerful egalitarian intuition, as Ronald Dworkin has stressed. The original position is an appealing device for filtering out the requirements of justice because it is a decision procedure in which the equality of people is given institutional expression. What it lifts out is the charter which we, were we forced to respect one another's equality, would choose. Against this it has recently been suggested that the device deals only in ciphers: decision-makers whose essence is wholly contained in Rawls's specification of them as rational, mutually disinterested POP's. The idea is that it does not tell us what we, were we in the original position, would choose, on the grounds that if that were what it was telling us then questions such as the following would at least be sensible: 'Might we not get frustrated with the decision problem and end up sulking at one another?', 'Might we not refuse to go through the required deliberations?', 'Might we not just fall asleep?'. This objection is ill-conceived, for it may well be argued on behalf of Rawls that to go through with a piece of speculation which entertained questions like these would be practically impossible, and that the only way of getting at what we would choose in the original position is to find out what certain cipher surrogates would select in that situation.

But if we agree that there is something satisfyingly intuitive in the idea of the original position, we must still ask whether Rawls's specification of it is justified. This is the second question that I want to raise in regard to the organization of the contractarian criterion. There are many aspects of Rawls's account of the original position to which it might be addressed but I will consider it only in relation to his specification of the primary goods. The point at issue is whether or not Rawls succeeds in giving a convincing picture of the original position, and the parties who exercise choice there; the background suspicion is that the picture is merely a projection of culture-bound prejudice.

It will be recalled that for Rawls the primary goods are things that the POP's desire as conditions the fulfilment of which is necessary if they are going to be able to satisfy whatever individually variable goals they turn out to have. The conditions are certain rights and liberties, opportunities and powers, income and wealth, and self-respect (TJ, p 92). Does Rawls do anything to establish that these things are indeed primary goods? Well, he certainly sets out a strategy for arguing that they are. The items on his list are meant to be the goods to which the POP's are directed by certain general facts about human beings (TJ, p 424). These include facts about human desires and wants, capacities and abilities, and social interdependence, but such matters are not discussed, on the ground that they are items of common sense knowledge (TJ, p 425). The only relevant matter that is examined is something described as a deep psychological fact (TJ, p 432). 'It says only that we prefer, other things equal, activities that depend upon a larger repertoire of realized capacities and that are more complex' (TJ, pp 429–30). Rawls calls it the Aristotelian principle.

Rawls suggests that from the general facts at which he gestures the parties in the original position should be able to work out the primary goods and thus should be able to get their calculations going. Unfortunately, however, he does very little to give the suggestion argumentative weight. At the point where we might have expected the required deduction we are treated to a rather disappointing invocation of self-evidence.

> 'We must assume, then, that the list of primary goods can be accounted for by the conception of goodness as rationality in connection with the general facts about human wants and abilities, their characteristic phases and requirements of nurture, the Aristotelian principle, and the necessities of social interdependence. I shall not argue the case for the list of primary goods here, since their claims seem evident enough.' (TJ, p 434)

The absence of a deduction of the primary goods raises a natural doubt in the mind of a reader. Perhaps the conditions that appear on Rawls's list are regarded as natural goals, both by him and by us, only because of our habituation in a certain contemporary style of life. Rawls appeals rather blandly to facts that are meant to hold of people in all cultures and he assumes as a matter of course that there are general psychological principles (TJ, pp 24, 456), which include unspecified laws of motivation (TJ, p 26). We may reasonably complain about his suppositions in this respect. There is serious question about the existence of universal facts and principles such as he invokes and we may well suspect that the mention of them merely conceals his parochialism. Nothing has been said to still the feeling that the POP's have been ascribed a locally specific mentality.

But it is unfair to say that Rawls offers no argument for his list of primary goods. He does make a case out for the necessity of one item on his list, self-respect. This he defines as (a) having a sense of the value of one's plan in life and (b) having confidence in one's ability to carry it out. He appeals to intuition in defence of the idea that it ranks as a primary good. 'Without it nothing may seem worth doing, or if some things have value for us, we lack the will to strive for them' (TJ, p 440). But here, as much as in the cases where no argument is provided, the thought is irresistible that Rawls is allowing himself to be carried away uncritically by his own historically local experience, and that he is not isolating something that inevitably matters to human beings. He writes: 'what is necessary is that there should be for each person at least one community of shared interests to which he belongs and where he finds his endeavors confirmed by his associates' (TJ, p 442, see also pp 178–9). Is this something that necessarily holds for people of all cultures, even for those who are raised to put more importance than contemporary western society does on the tradition or nation or church to which the individual belongs? Perhaps it is; but perhaps again, it is not.

How are we to judge the question that is raised against Rawls? Well we can reasonably complain that little is done to assure us that the primary goods really are what they claim to be, and not just the projections of an anthropologically narrow imagination. But should the complaint be pressed further? Can one argue that the whole idea of the original position is undermined by the alleged relativity to culture of the things that people desire? I think not. If desires really are culture-bound in the suggested sense then all that the people of any culture can be interested in is the decision that their kind would make in the original position, and in this case there can be no objection to the postulation of primary goods that are locally distinctive. It is only because of the possibility that there are persuasive candidates for the role of universal primary goods that we can really complain at Rawls's easy appeals to common sense and psychology and at his lack of argument for the list of primary goods that he puts forward.

It appears then that while the original position device does have an undoubted intuitive appeal, we may at least complain against Rawls that he is less than his usual conscientious self in justifying his account of it, in particular his version of the primary goods which persons in the original position are said to pursue. So much by way of comment on the organization of the contractrarian criterion. We now have to submit the criterion to some questioning in regard to its mode of operation. Here again there are two queries that I wish to raise. First, is Rawls's argument for the maximin strategy convincing? And second, does he establish that maximinning would lead the POP's to choose the two principles?

It will be recalled that Rawls's first two arguments for the rationality of maximinning in the original position bore on the relation between the options presented. They were: that the best promised by alternatives to the two principles charter is not of significantly greater value than the worst guaranteed by that arrangement, and that the worst that such alternatives allow is downright intolerable. If such conditions are fulfilled then certainly we must say that the choice of the two principles, a maximin strategy, is the uniquely rational one. As we saw, Rawls believes that at least so far as the utilitarian alternative goes the conditions are indeed satisfied. However, he does not set out to prove this explicitly, the reasons which he develops for the choice of the two principles having to do only with the maximin nature of that choice.

But in any case Rawls's specification of alternatives to the two principles is scarcely rich enough for us to be impressed by the claim that his preferred charter meets such powerful constraints. The list is restricted to some variations on the two principles, and some traditional conceptions of the just society. And it is further marred by the fact that in considering a traditional conception such as the utilitarian charter Rawls takes this to mean: not that charter, whatever it is, which promises to secure maximum happiness; but rather the charter which is fully characterized in the injunction to maximize happiness. This representation of the utilitarian's ideal society seems scarcely charitable, especially when one considers that the charter is expected to meet the constraints of right, and in particular that it is to be the publicly recognized means of resolving any issues that come up. The utilitarian system envisaged by Rawls is a brave new world in which the solutions to political issues are constantly adjusted and amended as new information comes in on the state of want-satisfaction in the community. This is not necessarily the charter which a utilitarian would prefer; it is the charter that would obtain were the legal authorities practising utilitarians, something that the utilitarian philosopher might wish they were not.

Rawls offers only one argument for maximinning that is independent of the alternatives presented in the original position, and that is unaffected therefore by the inadequacy of his list of alternatives. This is the argument from the unavailability of the probability figures required if the POP's are to consider maximizing expected utility rather than maximinning. Unfortunately, however, this piece of reasoning is not very persuasive in view of the fact that such figures would be available under a thin veil of ignorance, and a thin veil would serve the contractarian purpose of eliminating the effects of self-interest and bias. As we saw, Rawls opts for a thick veil, but he does nothing to justify this option; indeed he scarcely shows any awareness of the possibility of construing the veil of ignorance otherwise than he does. Under the thin veil the POP's suppose that they will be accorded their respective social positions in the system chosen, by a process of random distribution; under the thick they take it that they will accede to such positions in accordance with their talent, effort and fortune. The thin veil would allow the POP's to reason that they each have the same chance of being in any given social station, the thick would force them to recognize that their chances vary, although in an unknown pattern. Rawls does nothing to establish that the original position makes probability calculations impossible because he gives no reason for thinking that a thick rather than a thin veil ought to be dropped over that situation of choice.

It seems then that Rawls fails to make his case for the maximinning strategy. His argument from the unavailability of probabilities looks to be a dead-end, and his arguments from the nature of the alternatives need to be backed by a more careful account of the options between which the POP's have to choose. Our second question in regard to the operation of the contractarian criterion has to do with whether maximinning would in any case lead to the choice of the two principles but before we take that up we may just mention the likely reason why Rawls is anxious to make a case for the maximin strategy. It is that if the POP's maximize expected utility in their choice of system then there is every reason to believe that what they choose will coincide with the preference of the unreformed utilitarian. In particular they will not necessarily shrink from a charter that does badly by a minority, since the gambling value of that system may yet be very high. But in that case the contractarian criterion will fall foul of reflective equilibrium in just the way that utilitarianism does: it will fail to guard against inequalities that we intuitively find intolerable. If contractarianism is to sail by those rocks on which the welfare criterion flounders it is vital that the parties in the original position be taken to behave like pessimists rather than gamblers.

It may be that maximinning can be justified in a fuller consideration of the options put before the POP's, or on some grounds not mentioned by Rawls. Where then would maximinning lead the parties? Would it necessarily support the choice of the two principles, as Rawls maintains? This question, like the preceding one, is impossible to judge with any confidence in the absence of a thoroughly worked out list of the alternative charters with which the POP's are presented. My own feeling is that something like the two principles would indeed be selected but I do not intend to try to justify this other than by reminding the reader of the sorts of grounds that Rawls quotes in his case against utilitarianism, and in his intuitive account of the reasoning that the POP's might go through.

However, there is one unexamined assumption in Rawls's work which threatens his argument that the two principles are the maximin solution and we may usefully draw attention to this. Rawls supposes that each party in the original position compares the worst off positions within the different systems presented to him, and ranks them ordinarily for the extent to which they satisfy primary goods (TJ, pp 91–2). The crucial element in this supposition is the idea that each person will want more rather than less of the goods in question.

> Regardless of what an individual's rational plans are in detail, it is assumed that there are various things which he would prefer more of rather than less. With more of these goods men can generally be assured of greater success in carrying out their intentions and in advancing their ends, whatever these ends may be. (TJ, p 92, see also pp 396–7)

But as Brian Barry has pointed out, an individual may not want the greatest liberty or wealth available to him if the circumstances under which he gets this are ones where everyone else has a similar abundance: when the abundance is collective, the situation may radically change, as will be clear from a moment's reflection on the characteristics of the extremely libertarian or affluent society. It would seem then that in maximinning the POP will not necessarily go for the system whose worst off position gives maximal satisfaction of the primary goods on Rawls's list. These goods may be wanted in maximum supply, only under the condition that certain social patterns are realized. The appropriate sort of constraint needs to be written into the list of primary goods before we can be sure where maximinning would lead the parties in the original position. Thus we return to the point of criticism made in relation to the organization of the contractarian criterion, that Rawls does not pay sufficient attention to the justification of his list of primary goods.

So far our criticisms of the contractarian approach can be read, not as deeply subversive comments, but only as complaints that Rawls, however heroic his efforts, has not done important parts of his job well enough: in particular that he has not devoted enough care either to the construction of the list of primary goods or to the devising of the list of alternatives with which the parties in the original position are presented. We come finally to the crucial count on which a criterion of justice has to be assessed: that of whether its normative output is satisfactory, the recommendations that it supports being in reflective equilibrium with our intuitive judgments of justice. Assuming that the contractarian criterion does support the two principles as the just charter for the organization of society, does this mean that the criterion passes the test of reflective equilibrium? . . .

The most direct challenge that has been made to Rawls's charter, and it applies to any regime that imposes a structural ideal of distribution, is that which comes from Nozick, to the effect that such an arrangement is indistinguishable from slavery. It will be recalled that Nozick tells the tale of a slave whose lot is gradually improved, until the slave finds himself in much the position of a citizen in a redistributive state, and that he then challenges the reader to give a reason for drawing the line between slavery and non-slavery somewhere along the continuum of improvements. Against Nozick's challenge, however, we made the point that whether or not one finds reason for drawing such a line depends precisely on one's background philosophy and that someone of a redistributivist outlook will have no difficulty in justifying the appropriate demarcation to himself.

Does any equally central challenge to the two principles have some plausibility? Well, Rawls might be accused of endorsing a curiously rigid dispensation in arguing that no amount of socio-economic advantage would compensate for a diminution in the most extensive system of equal liberties, especially since these liberties are not particularly restricted: they include political freedom, freedom of thought, speech and assembly, freedom of person and (personal) property, and freedom from arbitrary arrest (TJ, p 61), but apparently they also extend to such privileges as 'the important liberty of free choice of occupation' (TJ, p 274). Any assault on this count, however, is likely to be parried by the open-ended qualification which Rawls puts on the priority of liberty, that if a society is not sufficiently well-off to ensure the effective realization of equal liberties, then liberty may be traded for socio-economic advantage (TJ, p 152). No society that I know of has been able effectively to realize the equal liberty of people to choose their occupations and at least in respect of that freedom then the priority rule would not seem to apply. It is not clear how widely Rawls means to use the qualification: as we have seen, he stipulates rather strictly that the circumstances for which the POP's are choosing a social charter do admit of the effective realization of equal liberties. However, one suspects that if pressure is put on the two principles arrangement for its consecration and indeed idolization of liberty, the qualification can always be invoked to stave off criticism.

There is a second point at which the two principles may also seem to be open to fairly basic challenge but here again Rawls proves to be something of a moving target. It may be said that the principles pay absurd attention to the position of the worst off person, and that they have the following intolerable results: that so long as the worst off are at the same level the principles would be indifferent between two systems in one of which people other than the worst off are much better treated than they are in the other, and that so long as it improved by a tittle the position of the worst off person, the principles would prefer a system that greatly impaired the lot of those other than the worst off. Rawls's general response to these difficulties is to say that they are empirically unlikely, in view of the connections between the welfare levels of different positions in a society (TJ, pp 80–3). This rebuttal makes for an effective stalemate, since the empirical question is not one that allows of easy resolution. It may be mentioned that the second is the more pressing problem since, as Rawls notices, he is free to respond to the first with an amendment to the second principle, suggested by Amartya Sen (TJ, p 83). This amendment would replace the simple difference principle with an ordered one: a principle that would rank systems initially by the welfare of the worst off positions, as in the simple case, but which would break the tie between two equally ranked systems by the welfare of the second worst off positions, and so on up the hierarchy until all ties are settled.

The lesson to be learned from these tentative assaults on Rawls's two principles is surely that, unlike the charters recommended by the rival criteria of justice, the charter which these comprise is not in flagrant conflict with our native intuitions as to how political issues ought to be resolved. If the dispensation fails the test of reflective equilibrium then it does not do so in any obvious way. At this point the task which lies before the political philosopher is to follow Rawls in explicating the exact content of the two principles and in expanding on their implementation. What he has to judge is whether the consequences of the contractarian criterion, as they are brought to light in this process, achieve the desired degree of equilibrium with his considered judgments on the demands of justice . . .

In this chapter we set out to examine the contractarian criterion on the usual scores of organization, operation and output. We found under the heading of organization that the criterion is an intuitively compelling one but that the specification of the original position, particularly in the identification of primary goods, requires more careful handling than that which Rawls gives it. Under the title of operation we urged that both the argument for maximinning and the argument for the two principles suffer from the inadequate account provided of the alternatives with which the POP's are presented. We also saw that, as Brian Barry has emphasized, Rawls is rash to assume that the parties will always be concerned to maximize the payoff accruing to them in primary goods; this gave us another reason for thinking that greater care is needed in the specification of those goods. Finally, we argued that the two principles, if indeed they are the output most naturally forthcoming from the contractarian criterion, have the conspicuous merit of not offending against our intuitions on justice in a flagrant manner. The brunt of these criticisms then is that while contractarianism may not be up and kicking, it cannot be laid to rest in the fashion in which we despatched its proprietarian and (unmodified) utilitarian competitors. There is life in the young dog yet.

Pettit *An Introduction to Contemporary Political Philosophy* 169–178

THE IDEA OF AN OVERLAPPING CONSENSUS

In 1987 Rawls wrote an article which explains, justifies and develops the main thesis of his book and also answers some of the critical comments that were provoked by it. He maintains that the aim of political philosophy is not only to present a political conception of justice that provides a shared public basis for the justification of the political and social institutions, but also to contribute to the maintenance of stability from one generation to the next.

> Now a basis of justification that rests on self- or group-interests alone cannot be stable; such a basis must be, I think, even when moderated by skillful constitutional design, a mere *modus vivendi*, dependent on a fortuitous conjunction of contingencies. What is needed is a regulative political conception of justice that can articulate and order in a principled way the political ideals and values of a democratic regime, thereby specifying the aims the constitution is to achieve and the limits it must respect. In addition, this political conception needs to be such that there is some hope of its gaining the support of an overlapping consensus, that is, a consensus in which it is affirmed by the opposing religious, philosophical and moral doctrines likely to thrive over generations in a more or less just constitutional democracy, where the criterion of justice is that political conception itself.

Rawls *The Idea of an Overlapping Consensus* (1987) 7 Oxford Journal of Legal Studies 1

What is being offered is a political conception of justice and such a conception has three features.

> The first feature of a political conception of justice is that, while such a conception is, of course, a moral conception, it is a moral conception worked out for a specific kind of subject, namely, for political, social and economic institutions. In particular, it is worked out to apply to what we may call the 'basic structure' of a modern constitutional democracy. (I shall use 'constitutional democracy', and 'democratic regime', and similar phrases interchangeably.) By this structure I mean a society's main political, social

and economic institutions, and how they fit together into one unified scheme of social cooperation. The focus of a political conception of justice is the framework of basic institutions and the principles, standards and precepts that apply to them, as well as how those norms are expressed in the character and attitudes of the members of society who realize its ideals. One might suppose that this first feature is already implied by the meaning of a political conception of justice: for if a conception does not apply to the basic structure of society, it would not be a political conception at all. But I mean more than this, for I think of a political conception of justice as a conception framed in the first instance solely for the special case of the basic structure.

The second feature complements the first: a political conception is not to be understood as a general and comprehensive moral conception that applies to the political order, as if this order was only another subject, another kind of case, falling under that conception. Thus, a political conception of justice is different from many familiar moral doctrines, for these are widely understood as general and comprehensive views. Perfectionism and utilitarianism are clear examples, since the principles of perfection and utility are thought to apply to all kinds of subjects ranging from the conduct of individuals and personal relations to the organization of society as a whole, and even to the law of nations. Their content as political doctrines is specified by their application to political institutions and questions of social policy. Idealism and Marxism in their various forms are also general and comprehensive. By contrast, a political conception of justice involves, so far as possible, no prior commitment to any wider doctrine. It looks initially to the basic structure and tries to elaborate a reasonable conception for that structure alone.

Rawls *The Idea of an Overlapping Consensus* (1987) 7 Oxford Journal of Legal Studies 3–4

He proceeds to the third feature of a political conception of justice and it is here that he refers to the political conception he developed in his book. He stresses that the fundamental intuitive ideas in his theory must not be read as religious, philosophical or metaphysical ideas.

. . . we come to a third feature of a political conception of justice, namely, it is not formulated in terms of a general and comprehensive religious, philosophical or moral doctrine but rather in terms of certain fundamental intuitive ideas viewed as latent in the public political culture of a democratic society. These ideas are used to articulate and order in a principled way its basic political values. We assume that in any such society there exists a tradition of democratic thought, the content of which is at least intuitively familiar to citizens generally. Society's main institutions, together with the accepted forms of their interpretation, are seen as a fund of implicitly shared fundamental ideas and principles. We suppose that these ideas and principles can be elaborated into a political conception of justice, which we hope can gain the support of an overlapping consensus. Of course, that this can be done can be verified only by actually elaborating a political conception of justice and exhibiting the way in which it could be thus supported. It's also likely that more than one political conception may be worked up from the fund of shared political ideas; indeed, this is desirable, as these rival conceptions will then compete for citizens' allegiance and be gradually modified and deepened by the contest between them.

Here I cannot, of course, even sketch the development of a political conception. But in order to convey what is meant, I might say that the conception I have elsewhere called 'justice as fairness' is a political conception of this kind. It can be seen as starting with the fundamental intuitive idea of political society as a fair system of social cooperation between citizens regarded as free and equal persons, and as born into the society in which they are assumed to lead a complete life. Citizens are further described as having certain moral powers that would enable them to take part in social cooperation. The problem of justice is then understood as that of specifying the fair terms of social cooperation between citizens so conceived. The conjecture is that by working out such ideas, which I view as implicit in the public political culture, we can in due course arrive at widely acceptable principles of political justice.

The details are not important here. What is important is that, so far as possible, these fundamental intuitive ideas are not taken for religious, philosophical or metaphysical ideas. For example, when it is said that citizens are regarded as free and equal persons, their freedom and equality are to be understood in ways congenial to the public political culture and explicable in terms of the design and requirements of its basic institutions. The conception of citizens as free and equal is, therefore, a political conception, the content of which is specified in connection with such things as the basic rights and liberties of democratic citizens. The hope is that the conception of justice to which this conception of citizens belongs will be acceptable to a wide range of comprehensive doctrines and hence supported by an overlapping consensus.

But, as I have indicated and should emphasize, success in achieving consensus requires that political philosophy try to be, so far as possible, independent and autonomous from other parts of philosophy, especially from philosophy's long-standing problems and controversies. For given the aim of consensus, to proceed otherwise would be self-defeating. But as we shall see . . . we may not be able to do this entirely when we attempt to answer the objection that claims that aiming for consensus implies scepticism or indifference to religious, philosphical or moral truth. Nevertheless, the reason for avoiding deeper questions remains. For as I have said above, we can present a political view either by starting explicitly from within a general and comprehensive doctrine, or we can start from fundamental intuitive ideas regarded as latent in the public political culture. These two ways of proceeding are very different, and this difference is significant even though we may sometimes be forced to assert certain aspects of our own comprehensive doctrine. So while we may not be able to avoid comprehensive doctrines entirely, we do what we can to reduce relying on their more specific details, or their more disputed features. The question is: what is the least that must be asserted; and if it must be asserted, what is its least controversial form?

Rawls *The Idea of an Overlapping Consensus* (1987) 7 Oxford Journal of Legal Studies 6–8

Rawls continues with a consideration of four possible objections to the idea of social unity based on an overlapping consensus of a political conception of justice.

The first objection argues that an overlapping consensus is a mere modus vivendi.

To begin with the objection: some will think that even if an overlapping consensus should be sufficiently stable, the idea of political unity founded on an overlapping consensus must still be rejected, since it abandons the hope of political community and settles instead for a public understanding that is at bottom a mere *modus vivendi*. To this objection, we say that the hope of political community must indeed be abandoned, if by such a community we mean a political society united in affirming a general and comprehensive doctrine. This possibility is excluded by the fact of pluralism together with the rejection of the oppressive use of state power to overcome it. I believe there is no practicable alternative superior to the stable political unity secured by an overlapping consensus on a reasonable political conception of justice. Hence the substantive question concerns the significant features of such a consensus and how these features affect social concord and the moral quality of public life. I turn to why an overlapping consensus is not a mere *modus vivendi*.

Rawls *The Idea of an Overlapping Consensus* (1987) 7 Oxford Journal of Legal Studies 10

Now, that an overlapping consensus is quite different from a *modus vivendi* is clear . . . Note two aspects: first, the object of consensus, the political conception of justice, is itself a moral conception. And second, it is affirmed on moral grounds, that is, it includes conceptions of society and of citizens as persons, as well as principles of justice, and an account of the cooperative virtues through which those principles are embodied in human character and expressed in public life. An overlapping consensus, therefore, is not merely a consensus on accepting certain authorities, or on complying with certain institutional arrangements, founded on a convergence of self- or group-interests. . . .

The preceding two aspects (moral object and moral grounds) of an overlapping consensus connect with a third aspect, that of stability: that is, those who affirm the various views supporting the political conception will not withdraw their support of it should the relative strength of their view in society increase and eventually become dominant. So long as the three views are affirmed and not revised, the political conception will still be supported regardless of shifts in the distribution of political power. We might say: each view supports the political conception for its own sake, or on its own merits, and the test for this is whether the consensus is stable with respect to changes in the distribution of power among views. This feature of stability highlights a basic contrast between an overlapping consensus and a *modus vivendi*, the stability of which does depend on happenstance and a balance of relative forces.

Rawls *The Idea of an Overlapping Consensus* (1987) 7 Oxford Journal of Legal Studies 11

The second objection he discusses and then rejects is that the overlapping consensus, in so far as it involves the avoidance of general and comprehensive doctrines, implies indifference or scepticism as to whether a political conception of justice is true.

This avoidance may appear to suggest that such a conception might be the most reasonable one of us even when it is known not to be true, as if truth were simply beside the point. In reply, it would be fatal to the point of a political conception to see it as sceptical about, or indifferent to, truth, much less as in conflict with it. Such scepticism or indifference would put political philosophy in conflict with numerous comprehensive doctrines, and thus defeat from the outset its aim of achieving an overlapping consensus. In following the method of avoidance, as we may call it, we try, so far as we can, neither to assert nor to deny any religious, philosophical or moral views, or their associated philosophical accounts of truth and the status of values. Since we assume each citizen to affirm some such view or other, we hope to make it possible for all to accept the political conception as true, or as reasonable, from the standpoint of their own comprehensive view, whatever it may be.

Properly understood, then, a political conception of justice need be no more indifferent, say, to truth in morals than the principle of toleration, suitably understood, need be indifferent to truth in religion. We simply apply the principle of toleration to philosophy itself. In this way we hope to avoid philosophy's long-standing controversies, among them controversies about the nature of truth and the status of values as expressed by realism and subjectivism. Since we seek an agreed basis of public justification in matters of justice, and since no political agreement on those disputed questions can reasonably be expected, we turn instead to the fundamental intuitive ideas we seem to share through the public political culture. We try to develop from these ideas a political conception of justice congruent with our considered convictions on due reflection. Just as with religion, citizens situated in thought and belief within their comprehensive doctrines, regard the political conception of justice as true, or as reasonable, whatever the case may be.

Rawls *The Idea of an Overlapping Consensus* (1987) 7 Oxford Journal of Legal Studies 12–13

He addresses the third objection.

A third objection is the following: even if we grant that an overlapping consensus is not a *modus vivendi*, it may be said that a workable political conception must be general and comprehensive. Without such a doctrine on hand, there is no way to order the many conflicts of justice that arise in public life. The idea is that the deeper the conceptual and philsophical bases of those conflicts, the more general and comprehensive the level of philosophical reflection must be if their roots are to be laid bare and an appropriate ordering found. It is useless, the objection concludes, to try to work out a political conception of justice expressly for the basic structure apart from any comprehensive doctrine. And as we have just seen, we may be forced to refer, at least in some way, to such a view.

This objection is perfectly natural: we are indeed tempted to ask how else could these conflicting claims be adjudicated. Yet part of the answer is found . . . Namely, a political conception of justice regarded not as a consequence of a comprehensive doctrine but as in itself sufficient to express values that normally outweigh whatever other values oppose them, at least under the reasonably favourable conditions that make a constitutional democracy possible. Here the criterion of a just regime is specified by that political conception; and the values in question are seen from its principles and standards, and from its account of the cooperative virtues of political justice, and the like. Those who hold this conception have, of course, other views as well, views that specify values and virtues belonging to other parts of life; they differ from citizens holding the two other views in our example of an overlapping consensus in having no fully (as opposed to partially) comprehensive doctrine within which they see all values and virtues as being ordered. They don't say such a doctrine is impossible, but rather practically speaking unnecessary. Their conviction is that, within the scope allowed by the basic liberties and the other provisions of a just constitution, all citizens can pursue their way of life on fair terms and properly respect its (non-public) values. So long as those constitutional guarantees are secure, they think no conflict of values is likely to arise that would justify their opposing the political conception as a whole, or on such fundamental matters as liberty of conscience, or equal political liberties, or basic civil rights, and the like.

Those holding this partially comprehensive view might explain it as follows. We should not assume that there exist reasonable and generally acceptable answers for all or even for many questions of political justice that might be asked. Rather, we must be prepared to accept the fact that only a few such questions can be satisfactorily resolved. Political wisdom consists in identifying those few, and among them the most urgent. That done, we must frame the institutions of the basic structure so that intractable conflicts are unlikely to arise; we must also accept the need for clear and simple principles, the general form and content of which we hope can be publicly understood. A political conception is at best but a guiding framework of deliberation and reflection which helps us reach political agreement on at least the constitutional essentials. If it seems to have cleared our view and made our considered convictions more coherent; if it has narrowed the gap between the conscientious convictions of those who accept the basic ideas of a constitutional regime, then it has served its practical political purpose. And this remains true even though we can't fully explain our agreement: we know only that citizens who affirm the political conception, and who have been raised in and are familiar with the fundamental ideas of the public political culture, find that, when they adopt its framework of deliberation, their judgments converge sufficiently so that political cooperation on the basis of mutual respect can be maintained. They view the political conception as itself normally sufficient and may not expect, or think they need, greater political understanding than that.

But here we are bound to ask: how can a political conception of justice express values that, under the reasonably favourable conditions that make democracy possible, normally outweigh whatever other values conflict with them? One way is this. As I have said, the most reasonable political conception of justice for a democratic regime will be, broadly speaking, liberal. But this means, as I will explain in the next section, that it protects the familiar basic rights and assigns them a special priority; it also includes measures to ensure that all persons in society have sufficient material means to make effective use of those basic rights. Faced with the fact of pluralism, a liberal view removes from the political agenda the most divisive issues, pervasive uncertainty and serious contention about which must undermine the bases of social cooperation.

The virtue of political cooperation that makes a constitutional regime possible are, then, *very great* virtues. I mean, for example, the virtues of tolerance and being ready to meet others halfway, and the virtue of reasonableness and the sense of fairness. When these virtues (together with the modes of thought and sentiments they involve) are widespread in society and sustain its political conception of justice, they constitute a very great public good, part of society's political capital. Thus, the values that conflict with the political conception of justice and its sustaining virtues may be normally outweighed because they come into conflict with the very conditions that make fair social cooperation possible on a footing of mutual respect.

Moreover, conflicts with political values are much reduced when the political conception is supported by an overlapping consensus, the more so the more inclusive the consensus. For in this case the political conception is not viewed as incompatible with basic religious, philosophical and moral values.

We avoid having to consider the claims of the political conception of justice against those of this or that comprehensive view; nor need we say that political values are intrinsically more important than other values and that's why the latter are overridden. Indeed, saying that is the kind of thing we hope to avoid, and achieving an overlapping consensus enables us to avoid it.

To conclude: given the fact of pluralism, what does the work of reconciliation by free public reason, and thus enables us to avoid reliance on general and comprehensive doctrines, is two things: first, identifying the fundamental role of political values in expressing the terms of fair social cooperation consistent with mutual respect between citizens regarded as free and equal; and second, uncovering a sufficiently inclusive concordant fit among political and other values as displayed in an overlapping consensus.

Rawls *The Idea of an Overlapping Consensus* (1987) 7 Oxford Journal of Legal Studies 15–17

The last difficulty I shall consider is that the idea of an overlapping consensus is utopian; that is, there are not sufficient political, social, or psychological forces either to bring about an overlapping consensus (when one does not exist), or to render one stable (should one exist). Here I can only touch on this intricate question and I merely outline one way in which such a consensus might come about and its stability be made secure. For this purpose I use the idea of a liberal conception of political justice, the content of which I stipulate to have three main elements (noted previously): first, a specification of certain basic rights, liberties and opportunities (of the kind familiar from constitutional democratic regimes); second, an assignment of a special priority to those rights, liberties and opportunities, especially with respect to the claims of the general good and of perfectionist values; and third, measures assuring to all citizens adequate all-purpose means to make effective use of their basic liberties and opportunities.

Now let's suppose that at a certain time, as a result of various historical events and contingencies, the principles of a liberal conception have come to be accepted as a mere *modus vivendi*, and that existing political institutions meet their requirements. This acceptance has come about, we may assume, in much the same way as the acceptance of the principle of toleration as a *modus vivendi* came about following the Reformation: at first reluctantly, but nevertheless as providing the only alternative to endless and destructive civil strife. Our question, then, is this: how might it happen that over generations the initial acquiescence in a liberal conception of justice as a *modus vivendi* develops into a stable and enduring overlapping consensus? In this connection I think a certain looseness in our comprehensive views, as well as their not being fully comprehensive, may be particularly significant. To see this, let's return to our model case.

One way in which that example is atypical is that two of the three doctrines were described as fully general and comprehensive, a religious doctrine of free faith and the comprehensive liberalism of Kant or Mill. In these cases the acceptance of the political conception was said to be derived from and to depend solely on the comprehensive doctrine. But how far in practice does the allegiance to a political conception actually depend on its derivation from a comprehensive view? There are several possibilities. For simplicity distinguish three cases: the political conception is derived from the comprehensive doctrine; it is not derived from but is compatible with that doctrine; and last, the political conception is incompatible with it. In everyday life we have not usually decided, or even thought much about, which of these cases hold. To decide among them would raise highly complicated issues; and it is not clear that we need to decide among them. Most people's religious, philosophical and moral doctrines are not seen by them as fully general and comprehensive, and these aspects admit of variations of degree. There is lots of slippage, so to speak, many ways for the political conception to cohere loosely with those (partially) comprehensive views, and many ways within the limits of a political conception of justice to allow for the pursuit of different (partially) comprehensive doctrines. This suggests that many if not most citizens come to affirm their common political conception without seeing any particular connection, one way or the other, between it and their other views. Hence it is possible for them first to affirm the political conception and to appreciate the public good it accomplishes in a democratic society. Should an incompatibility later be recognized between the political conceptions and their wider doctrines, then they might very well adjust or revise these doctrines rather than reject the political conception.

At this point we ask: in virtue of what political values might a liberal conception of justice gain an allegiance to itself? An allegiance to institutions and to the conception that regulates them may, of course, be based in part on long-term self- and group-interests, custom and traditional attitudes, or simply on the desire to conform to what is expected and normally done. Widespread allegiance may also be encouraged by institutions securing for all citizens the political values included under what Hart calls the minimum content of natural law. But here we are concerned with the further bases of allegiance generated by a liberal conception of justice.

Now when a liberal conception effectively regulates basic political institutions, it meets three essential requirements of a stable constitutional regime. First, given the fact of pluralism—the fact that necessitates a liberal regime as a *modus vivendi* in the first place—a liberal conception meets the urgent political requirement to fix, once and for all, the content of basic rights and liberties, and to assign them special priority. Doing this takes those guarantees off the political agenda and puts them beyond the calculus of social interests, thereby establishing clearly and firmly the terms of social cooperation on a footing of mutual respect. To regard that calculus as relevant in these matters leaves the status and content of those rights and liberties still unsettled; it subjects them to the shifting circumstances of time and place, and by greatly raising the stakes of political controversy, dangerously increases the insecurity and hostility of public life. Thus, the unwillingness to take these matters off the agenda perpetuates the deep divisions latent in society; it betrays a readiness to revive those antagonisms in the hope of gaining a more favourable position should later circumstances prove propitious. So, by contrast, securing the basic liberties and recognizing their priority achieves the work of reconciliation and seals mutual acceptance on a footing of equality.

The second requirement is connected with a liberal conception's idea of free public reason. It is highly desirable that the form of reasoning a conception specifies should be, and can publicly be seen to be, correct and reasonably reliable in its own terms. A liberal conception tries to meet these desiderata in several ways. As we have seen, in working out a political conception of justice it starts from fundamental intuitive ideas latent in the shared public culture; it detaches political values from any particular comprehensive and sectarian (non-public) doctrine; and it tries to limit that conception's scope to matters of political justice (the basic structure and its social policies). Further, . . . it recognizes that an agreement on a political conception of justice is to no effect without a companion agreement on guidelines of public enquiry and rules for assessing evidence. Given the fact of pluralism, these guidelines and rules must be specified by reference to the forms of reasoning available to common sense, and by the procedures and conclusions of science when not controversial. The role of these shared methods and this common knowledge in applying the political conception makes reason *public*; the protection given to freedom of speech and thought makes it *free*. The claims of religion and philosophy (as previously emphasized) are not excluded out of scepticism or indifference, but as a condition of establishing a shared basis for free public reason.

A liberal conception's idea of public reason also has a certain simplicity. To illustrate: even if general and comprehensive teleological conceptions were acceptable as political conceptions of justice, the form of public reasoning they specify would be politically unworkable. For if the elaborate theoretical calculations involved in applying their principles are publicly admitted in questions of political justice (consider, for example, what is involved in applying the principle of utility to the basic structure), the highly speculative nature and enormous complexity of these calculations are bound to make citizens with conflicting interests highly suspicious of one another's arguments. The information they presuppose is very hard if not impossible to obtain, and often there are insuperable problems in reaching an objective and agreed assessment. Moreover, even though we think our arguments sincere and not self-serving when we present them, we must consider what it is reasonable to expect others to think who stand to lose when our reasoning prevails. Arguments supporting political judgments should, if possible, not only be sound but such that they can be publicly seen to be sound. The maxim that justice must not only be done, but be seen to be done, holds good not only in law but in free public reason.

The third requirement met by a liberal conception is related to the preceding ones. The basic institutions enjoined by such a conception, and its conception of free public reason—when effectively working over time—encourage the cooperative virtues of political life: the virtue of reasonableness and a sense of fairness, a spirit of compromise and a readiness to meet others halfway, all of which are connected with the willingness if not the desire to cooperate with others on political terms that everyone can publicly accept consistent with mutual respect. Political liberalism tests principles and orders institutions with an eye to their influence on the moral quality of public life, on the civic virtues and habits of mind their public recognition tends to foster, and which are needed to sustain a stable constitutional regime. This requirement is related to the preceding two in this way. When the terms of social cooperation are settled on a footing of mutual respect by fixing once and for all the basic liberties and opportunities with their priority, and when this fact itself is publicly recognized, there is a tendency for the essential cooperative virtues to develop. And this tendency is further strengthened by successful conduct of free public reason in arriving at what are regarded as just policies and fair understandings.

The three requirements met by a liberal conception are evident in the fundamental structural features of the public world it realizes, and in its effects on citizens' political character, a character that takes the basic rights and liberties for granted and disciplines its deliberations in accordance with the guidelines of free public reason. A political conception of justice (liberal or otherwise) specifies the form of a social world—a background framework within which the life of associations, groups and individual citizens proceeds. Inside that framework a working consensus may often be secured by a convergence of self- or group-interests; but to secure stability that framework must be honoured and seen as fixed by the political conception, itself affirmed on moral grounds.

The conjecture, then, is that as citizens come to appreciate what a liberal conception does, they acquire an allegiance to it, an allegiance that becomes stronger over time. They come to think it both reasonable and wise for them to confirm their allegiance to its principles of justice as expressing values that under the reasonably favourable conditions that make democracy possible normally counterbalance whatever values may oppose them. With this an overlapping consensus is achieved.

Rawls *The Idea of an Overlapping Consensus* (1987) 7 Oxford Journal of Legal Studies 18–22

Chapter 10

Dworkin's rights

One powerful intuition about justice is that it essentially involves the adjudication of an individual's rights, so that, for instance, what a judge has to determine is what the rights of the parties to a dispute are and whose were violated. This intuition is forcefully and subtly developed in the writings of Ronald Dworkin, who argues that individual rights have priority over policies designed to promote the general welfare. For instance, if all we had to consider was the general welfare, then it would be right to prohibit a march by Nazi sympathisers. But if the sympathisers have as individuals the right to march, then it would be wrong to ban them on the grounds that the general welfare would suffer. In this respect rights are like trumps; a trump, however small, is a more powerful card than one of any other suit.

Clearly, Dworkin's theory has a strong anti-utilitarian thrust, and it is primarily as a powerful critic of utilitarianism that we shall consider him in this chapter. However, his theory of rights provides the underpinning not only for his critique of utilitarianism and other goal-directed theories, but also for his attack on Hart's *Concept of Law* which we discuss in Chapter 4. Our separation of the normative and critical aspects of Dworkin's theory is at times rather arbitrary; but the important thing to note here is that the two chapters are closely connected.

Since the notion of an individual right is central to Dworkin's argument, we shall begin our discussion of his views by considering his *formal* definition of rights, and some of the distinctions he makes between *kinds* of rights which are important for his overall argument.

RIGHTS AS TRUMPS

In his introduction to *Taking Rights Seriously* Dworkin introduces the metaphor of individual rights as trumps:[1]

> Individual rights are political trumps held by individuals. Individuals have rights when, for some reason, a collective goal is not a sufficient justification for denying them what they wish, as individuals, to have or to do, or not a sufficient justification for imposing some loss or injury upon them. That characterization of a right is, of course, formal in the sense that it does not indicate what rights people have or guarantee, indeed, that they have any. But it does not suppose that rights have some special metaphysical character, and the theory defended in these essays therefore departs from older theories of rights that do rely on that supposition.
>
> Dworkin *Taking Rights Seriously* xi

[1] The extracts from *Taking Rights Seriously* are from the fourth impression which includes Dworkin's replies to a number of criticisms.

As Dworkin rightly stresses this is not a proof of the existence of rights, but a definition of the concept. It is clear that rights as defined have a strong anti-utilitarian thrust, since the fact that the maximisation of welfare would be impeded by someone's exercising his right does not entail that he should not exercise it. On this account, if I have the right to publish pornography, then the fact that the general welfare will suffer if I do publish it is not a reason for stopping me. However, it is important to note that on Dworkin's account there would be exactly the same objection to any collective goal which violated an individual's rights. Hence, there is, in his view, an important distinction to be made between the promotion of individual rights as one of our aims, and the pursuit of a collective goal; and, of course, genuine rights must have priority over at least some collective goals.

Dworkin goes on to define the weight of a right in terms of the sort of goals over which it has priority, so that different rights have different weights. For instance, the right to freedom of speech may well be so important that it is arguable that it should be restricted only in very exceptional circumstances, such as those arising in time of war when the collective goal of survival is judged to be of overriding importance; whereas many property rights may well be justifiably restricted for weaker reasons, eg, because of the need to reduce pollution. A further theoretical complication arises because not only do rights have different weights, but they are also of very differing kinds, and in that respect of differing degrees of importance. Differences between rights and goals, between kinds of rights and between the weights of rights have been discussed earlier. The passage cited goes on to make an important distinction between background and institutional rights.[2]

> These definitions and distinctions make plain that the character of a political aim – its standing as a right or goal – depends upon its place and function within a single political theory. The same phrase might describe a right within one theory and a goal within another, or a right that is absolute or powerful within one theory but relatively weak within another. If a public official has anything like a coherent political theory that he uses, even intuitively, to justify the particular decisions he reaches, then this theory will recognize a wide variety of different types of rights, arranged in some way that assigns rough relative weight to each.
>
> Any adequate theory will distinguish, for example, between background rights, which are rights that provide a justification for political decisions by society in the abstract, and institutional rights, that provide a justification for a decision by some particular and specified political institution. Suppose that my political theory provides that every man has a right to the property of another if he needs it more. I might yet concede that he does not have a legislative right to the same effect; I might concede, that is, that he has no institutional right that the present legislature enact legislation that would violate the Constitution, as such a statute presumably would. I might also concede that he has no institutional right to a judicial decision condoning theft. Even if I did make these concessions, I could preserve my initial background claim by arguing that the people as a whole would be justified in amending the Constitution to abolish property, or perhaps in rebelling and overthrowing the present form of government entirely. I would claim that each man has a residual background right that would justify or require these acts,

[2] See Ch 4, p 95.

even though I concede that he does not have the right to specific institutional decisions as these institutions are now constituted.

Any adequate theory will also make use of a distinction between abstract and concrete rights, and therefore between abstract and concrete principles. This is a distinction of degree, but I shall discuss relatively clear examples at two poles of the scale it contemplates, and therefore treat it as a distinction in kind. An abstract right is a general political aim the statement of which does not indicate how that general aim is to be weighed or compromised in particular circumstances against other political aims. The ground rights of political rhetoric are in this way abstract. Politicians speak of a right to free speech or dignity or equality, with no suggestion that these rights are absolute, but with no attempt to suggest their impact on particular complex social situations.

Concrete rights, on the other hand, are political aims that are more precisely defined so as to express more definitely the weight they have against other political aims on particular occasions. Suppose I say, not simply that citizens have a right to free speech, but that a newspaper has a right to publish defense plans classified as secret provided this publication will not create an immediate physical danger to troops. My principle declares for a particular resolution of the conflict it acknowledges between the abstract right of free speech, on the one hand, and competing rights of soldiers to security or the urgent needs of defense on the other. Abstract rights in this way provide arguments for concrete rights, but the claim of a concrete right is more definitive than any claim of abstract right that supports it.[a]

Dworkin *Taking Rights Seriously* 92–94

[a] A complete political theory must also recognize two other distinctions that I use implicitly in this chapter. The first is the distinction between rights against the state and rights against fellow citizens. The former justify a political decision that requires some agency of the government to act; the latter justify a decision to coerce particular individuals. The right to minimum housing, if accepted at all, is accepted as a right against the state. The right to recover damages for a breach of contract, or to be saved from great danger at minimum risk of a rescuer, is a right against fellow citizens. The right to free speech is, ordinarily, both. It seems strange to define the rights that citizens have against one another as political rights at all; but we are now concerned with such rights only insofar as they justify political decisions of different sorts. The present distinction cuts across the distinction between background and institutional rights; the latter distinguishes among persons or institutions that must make a political decision, the former between persons or institutions whom that decision directs to act or forbear. Ordinary civil cases at law, which are the principal subject of this essay, involve rights against fellow citizens; but I also discuss certain issues of constitutional and criminal law and so touch on rights against the state as well.

The second distinction is between universal and special rights; that is, between rights that a political theory provides for all individuals in the community, with exceptions only for phenomena like incapacity or punishment, and rights it provides for only one section of the community, or possibly only one member. I shall assume, in this essay, that all political rights are universal.

The distinction which Dworkin makes between background rights and institutional rights, which are different kinds of rights, is an important one for the development of his thought. However, it should be noted that though it is tempting to think of background rights as moral rights, and institutional rights as non-moral ones, this is not Dworkin's position. For, as we shall see, he wants to argue that legal rights, which are a species of institutional rights, sometimes have a moral dimension. For instance, the constitutional right to free speech guaranteed by the First Amendment is, he argues, representative of the moral right to free speech that citizens have (*Taking Rights Seriously* 191). And whether this is correct or not, simply to assume that no legal rights have a moral dimension is clearly to beg some crucial questions in jurisprudence.

Finally, it is important to note that though, of course, every right must, on Dworkin's theory, have priority over *some* collective goal, since they have differing degrees of priority, and hence weights, many rights, including fundamental ones, must be less than absolute. The question therefore arises of the circumstances in which it would be legitimate to extend or restrict a right:

> I can think of only three sorts of grounds that can consistently be used to delimit the definition of a particular right. First, the Government must show that the values protected by the original right are not really at stake in the marginal case, or at stake only in some attenuated form. Second, it might show that if the right is defined to include the marginal case, then some competing right, in the strong sense I defined earlier, would be abridged. Third, it might show that if they were so defined, then the cost to society would not be simply incremental, but would be of a degree far beyond the cost paid to grant the original right, a degree great enough to justify whatever assault on dignity or equality might be involved.
>
> Dworkin *Taking Rights Seriously* 200

Thus, one might argue that the right to free speech should not be extended to cover defamation for the first reason; that the freedom of the press should not be defined to include intrusions into privacy on the second; and that the right to health care cannot be defined in a way that is totally unrestricted for the third reason. This is not implausible; but the fact that for Dworkin most rights are not absolute not only introduces considerable complexity into his discussions about the concrete rights we in fact have, but sharply distinguishes his theory of rights from that both of traditional natural rights theorists, such as John Locke, and those who, like Nozick, take as their starting point the existence of the kind of natural rights described by Locke. For though Dworkin speaks of natural rights, the basis of his argument for their existence is quite different from that of traditional theorists.

WHY WE SHOULD TAKE RIGHTS SERIOUSLY

One of the clearest statements of Dworkin's argument for taking rights seriously is to be found in a thoughtful account he gives of the meaning of liberalism. Written in 1978, at a time when the cause of liberalism was in some disarray, the paper acknowledges that a number of developments of the 1970s and 1980s raised the question whether liberalism is a distinct policy after all:[3]

> One of these was the war. John F Kennedy and his men called themselves liberals; so did Johnson, who retained the Kennedy men and added liberals of his own. But the war was inhumane and discredited the idea that liberalism was the party of humanity.
>
> Dworkin 'Liberalism' in Hampshire (ed) *Public and Private Morality* 113

Another was that many contemporary political issues, such as pollution and consumer protection, were not clearly identifiable with familiar liberal or conservative positions. Moreover, some politicians became difficult to classify in

---

[3] R Dworkin's 'Liberalism' has been reprinted as Chapter 8 of *A Matter of Principle* Cambridge University Press.

terms of the traditional categories – Carter, for instance, seemed to combine liberal positions on human rights with conservative positions about the importance of balancing the budget. It might, therefore, be suggested that there is no common core to the causes traditionally classed as liberal, and that there is only an historical explanation why particular clusters of these causes were important at particular times, eg, during the period of the New Deal. But Dworkin rejects this suggestion:

> In any coherent political program there are two elements: constitutive political positions that are valued for their own sake, and derivative positions that are valued as strategies, as means of achieving the constitutive positions. The sceptic believes that the liberal package of ideas had no constitutive political morality at all; it was a package formed by accident and held together by self interest. The alternative account argues that the package had a constitutive morality and has come apart, to the extent it has, because it has become less clear which derivative positions best serve that constitutive morality.
>
> Dworkin 'Liberalism' in Hampshire (ed) *Public and Private Morality* 116

In other words, Dworkin argues that there is a constitutive core to liberalism, and that apparent deep policy differences between liberals at different times are not evidence of differences about the core, but of different beliefs about the strategies to be adopted to implement them. In the following extract, he argues that the constitutive core consists of treating a certain ideal of equal concern and respect as central, and that the importance of individual rights becomes clear when we reflect on the question of what economic and political strategies will best implement that ideal. For when we do reflect, we see that unless individual rights are recognised, the idea of equal concern and respect is unrealisable:

> What does it mean for the government to treat its citizens as equals? That is, I think, the same question as the question of what it means for the government to treat all its citizens as free, or as independent, or with equal dignity. In any case, it is a question that has been central to political theory at least since Kant.
>
> It may be answered in two fundamentally different ways. The first supposes that government must be neutral on what might be called the question of the good life. The second supposes that government cannot be neutral on that question, because it cannot treat its citizens as equal human beings without a theory of what human beings ought to be. I must explain that distinction further. Each person follows a more-or-less articulate conception of what gives value to life. The scholar who values a life of contemplation has such a conception; so does the television-watching, beer-drinking citizen who is fond of saying 'This is the life', though of course he has thought less about the issue and is less able to describe or defend his conception.
>
> The first theory of equality supposes that political decisions must be, so far as is possible, independent of any particular conception of the good life, or of what gives value to life. Since the citizens of a society differ in their conceptions, the government does not treat them as equals if it prefers one conception to another, either because the officials believe that one is intrinsically superior, or because one is held by the more numerous or more powerful group. The second theory argues, on the contrary, that the content of equal treatment cannot be independent of some theory about the good for man

or the good of life, because treating a person as an equal means treating him the way the good or truly wise person would wish to be treated. Good government consists in fostering or at least recognizing good lives; treatment as an equal consists in treating each person as if he were desirous of leading the life that is in fact good, at least so far as this is possible.

This distinction is very abstract, but it is also very important. I shall now argue that liberalism takes, as its constitutive political morality, the first conception of equality. I shall try to support that claim in this way. In the next section of this essay I shall show how it is plausible, and even likely, that a thoughtful person who accepted the first conception of equality would, given the economic and political circumstances of America in the last several decades, reach the positions I identified as the familiar core of liberal positions. If so, then the hypothesis satisfies the second of the conditions I described for a successful theory. In the following section I shall try to satisfy the third condition by showing how it is plausible and even likely that someone who held a particular version of the second theory of equality would reach what are normally regarded as the core of American conservative positions. I say 'a particular version of' because American conservatism does not follow automatically from rejecting the liberal theory of equality. The second (or non-liberal) theory of equality holds merely that the treatment government owes citizens is at least partly determined by some conception of the good life. Many political theories share that thesis, including theories as far apart as, for example, American conservatism and various forms of socialism or Marxism, though these will of course differ in the conception of the good life they adopt, and hence in the political institutions and decisions they endorse. In this respect, liberalism is decidedly not some compromise or half-way house between more forceful positions, but stands on one side of an important line that distinguishes it from all competitors taken as a group.

I shall not provide arguments in this essay that my theory of liberalism meets the first condition I described—that the theory must provide a political morality that it makes sense to suppose people in our culture hold—though I think it plain that the theory does meet this condition. The fourth condition requires that a theory be as abstract and general as the first three conditions allow. I doubt there will be objections to my theory on that account.

I now define a liberal as someone who holds the first, or liberal, theory of what equality requires. Suppose that a liberal is asked to found a new state. He is required to dictate its constitution and fundamental institutions. He must propose a general theory of political distribution, that is, a theory of how whatever the community has to assign, by way of goods or resources or opportunities, should be assigned. He will arrive initially at something like this principle of rough equality: resources and opportunities should be distributed, so far as possible, equally, so that roughly the same share of whatever is available is devoted to satisfying the ambitions of each. Any other general aim of distribution will assume either that the fate of some people should be of greater concern than that of others, or that the ambitions or talents of some are more worthy, and should be supported more generously on that account.

Someone may object that this principle of rough equality is unfair because it ignores the fact that people have different tastes, and that some of these are more expensive to satisfy than others, so that, for example, the man who prefers champagne will need more funds if he is not to be frustrated than the man satisfied with beer. But the liberal may reply that tastes as to which people differ are, by and large, not afflictions, like diseases, but are rather cultivated, in accordance with each person's theory of what his life should be like.[a] The most effective neutrality, therefore, requires that the same share be devoted to each, so that the choice between expensive and less expensive tastes can be made by each person for himself, with no sense that his overall share will be enlarged by choosing a more expensive life, or that, whatever he chooses, his choice will subsidize those who have chosen more expensively.[b]

But what does the principle of rough equality of distribution require in practice? If all resources were distributed directly by the government through grants of food, housing, and so forth; if every opportunity citizens have were provided directly by the government through the provisions of civil and criminal law; if every citizen had exactly the same talents; if every citizen started his life with no more than what any other citizen had at the start; and if every citizen had exactly the same theory of the good life and hence exactly the same scheme of preferences as every other citizen, including preferences between productive activity of different forms and leisure, then the principle of rough equality of treatment could be satisfied simply by equal distributions of everything to be distributed and by civil and criminal laws of universal application. Government would arrange for production that maximized the mix of goods, including jobs and leisure, that everyone favored, distributing the product equally.

Of course, none of these conditions of similarity holds. But the moral relevance of different sorts of diversity are very different, as may be shown by the following exercise. Suppose all the conditions of similarity I mentioned did hold except the last: citizens have different theories of the good and hence different preferences. They therefore disagree about what product the raw materials and labor and savings of the community should be used to produce, and about which activities should be prohibited or regulated so as to make others possible or easier. The liberal, as lawgiver, now needs mechanisms to satisfy the principles of equal treatment in spite of these disagreements. He will decide that there are no better mechanisms available, as general political institutions, than the two main institutions of our own political economy: the economic market, for decisions about what goods shall be produced and how they shall be distributed, and representative democracy, for collective decisions about what conduct shall be prohibited or regulated so that other conduct might be made possible or convenient. Each of these familiar institutions may be expected to provide a more egalitarian division than any other general arrangement. The market, if it can be made to function efficiently, will determine for each product a price that reflects the cost in resources of material, labor and capital that might have been applied to produce something different that someone else wants. That cost determines, for anyone who consumes that product, how much his account should be charged in computing the egalitarian division of social resources. It provides a measure of how much more his account should be charged for a house than a

[a] See Scanlon, 'Preference and Urgency', J. Phil., LXXII, 655.

[b] A very different objection calls attention to the fact that some people are afflicted with incapacities like blindness or mental disease, so that they require more resources to satisfy the *same* scheme of preferences. That is a more appealing objection to my principle of rough equality of treatment, but it calls, not for choosing a different basic principle of distribution, but for corrections in the application of the principle like those I consider later.

book, and for one book rather than another. The market will also provide, for the laborer, a measure of how much should be credited to his account for his choice of productive activity over leisure, and for one activity rather than another. It will tell us, through the price it puts on his labor, how much he should gain or lose by his decision to pursue one career rather than another. These measurements make a citizen's own distribution a function of the personal preferences of others as well as of his own, and it is the sum of these personal preferences that fixes the true cost to the community of meeting his own preferences for goods and activities. The egalitarian distribution, which requires that the cost of satisfying one person's preferences should as far as is possible be equal to the cost of satisfying another's, cannot be enforced unless those measurements are made.

We are familiar with the anti-egalitarian consequences of free enterprise in practice; it may therefore seem paradoxical that the liberal as lawgiver should choose a market economy for reasons of equality rather than efficiency. But, under the special condition that people differ only in preferences for goods and activities, the market is more egalitarian than any alternative of comparable generality. The most plausible alternative would be to allow decisions of production, investment, price and wage to be made by elected officials in a socialist economy. But what principles should officials use in making those decisions? The liberal might tell them to mimic the decisions that a market would make if it was working efficiently under proper competition and full knowledge. This mimicry would be, in practice, much less efficient than an actual market would be. In any case, unless the liberal had reason to think it would be much more efficient, he would have good reason to reject it. Any minimally efficient mimicking of a hypothetical market would require invasions of privacy to determine what decisions individuals would make if forced actually to pay for their investment, consumption and employment decisions at market rates, and this information gathering would be, in many other ways, much more expensive than an actual market. Inevitably, moreover, the assumptions officials make about how people would behave in a hypothetical market reflect the officials' own beliefs about how people should behave. So there would be, for the liberal, little to gain and much to lose in a socialist economy in which officials were asked to mimic a hypothetical market.

But any other instructions would be a direct violation of the liberal theory of what equality requires, because if a decision is made to produce and sell goods at a price below the price a market would fix, then those who prefer those goods are, *pro tanto*, receiving more than an equal share of the resources of the community at the expense of those who would prefer some other use of the resources. Suppose the limited demand for books, matched against the demand for competing uses for wood-pulp, would fix the price of books at a point higher than the socialist managers of the economy will charge; those who want books are having less charged to their account than the egalitarian principle would require. It might be said that in a socialist economy books are simply valued more, because they are inherently more worthy uses of social resources, quite apart from the popular demand for books. But the liberal theory of equality rules out that appeal to the inherent value of one theory of what is good in life.

In a society in which people differed only in preferences, then, a market would be favored for its egalitarian consequences. Inequality of monetary wealth would be the consequence only of the fact that some preferences are more expensive than others, including the preference for leisure time rather than the most lucrative productive activity. But we must now return to the real world. In the actual society for which the liberal must construct political institutions, there are all the other differences. Talents are not distributed equally, so the decision of one person to work in a factory rather than a law firm, or not to work at all, will be governed in large part by his abilities rather than his preferences for work or between work and leisure. The institutions of wealth, which allow people to dispose of what they receive by gift, means that children of the successful will start with more wealth than the children of the unsuccessful. Some people have special needs, because they are handicapped; their handicap will not only disable them from the most productive and lucrative employment, but will incapacitate them from using the proceeds of whatever employment they find as efficiently, so that they will need more than those who are not handicapped to satisfy identical ambitions.

These inequalities will have great, often catastrophic, effects on the distribution that a market economy will provide. But, unlike differences in preferences, the differences these inequalities make are indefensible according to the liberal conception of equality. It is obviously obnoxious to the liberal conception, for example, that someone should have more of what the community as a whole has to distribute because he or his father had superior skill or luck. The liberal lawgiver therefore faces a difficult task. His conception of equality requires an economic system that produces certain inequalities (those that reflect the true differential costs of goods and opportunities) but not others (those that follow from differences in ability, inheritance, etc.). The market produces both the required and the forbidden inequalities, and there is no alternative system that can be relied upon to produce the former without the latter.

The liberal must be tempted, therefore, to a reform of the market through a scheme of redistribution that leaves its pricing system relatively intact but sharply limits, at least, the inequalities in welfare that his initial principle prohibits. No solution will seem perfect. The liberal may find the best answer in a scheme of welfare rights financed through redistributive income and inheritance taxes of the conventional sort, which redistributes just to the Rawlsian point, that is, to the point at which the worst-off group would be harmed rather than benefited by further transfers. In that case, he will remain a reluctant capitalist, believing that a market economy so reformed is superior, from the standpoint of his conception of equality, to any practical socialist alternative. Or he may believe that the redistribution that is possible in a capitalist economy will be so inadequate, or will be purchased at the cost of such inefficiency, that it is better to proceed in a more radical way, by substituting socialist for market decisions over a large part of the economy, and then relying on the political process to insure that prices are set in a manner at least roughly consistent with his conception of equality. In that case he will be a reluctant socialist, who acknowledges the egalitarian defects of socialism but counts them as less severe than the practical alternatives. In either case, he chooses a mixed economic system—either redistributive capitalism or limited socialism—not in order to compromise antagonistic ideals of efficiency and equality, but to achieve the best practical realization of the demands of equality itself.

Let us assume that in this manner the liberal either refines or partially retracts his original selection of a market economy. He must now consider the second of the two familiar institutions he first selected, which is representative democracy. Democracy is justified because it enforces the right of each person to respect and concern as an individual; but in practice the decisions of a democratic majority may often violate that right, according to the liberal theory of what the right requires. Suppose a legislature elected by a majority decides to make criminal some act (like speaking in favor of an unpopular political position, or participating in eccentric sexual practices) not because the act deprives others of opportunities they want, but because the majority disapproves of those views or that sexual morality. The political decision, in other words, reflects not simply some accommodation of the *personal* preferences of everyone, in such a way as to make the opportunities of all as nearly equal as may be, but the domination of one set of *external* preferences, that is, preferences people have about what others shall do or have.[c] The decision invades rather than enforces the right of citizens to be treated as equals.

How can the liberal protect citizens against that sort of violation of their fundamental right? It will not do for the liberal simply to instruct legislators, in some constitutional exhortation, to disregard the external preferences of their constituents. Citizens will vote for these preferences in electing their representatives, and a legislator who chooses to ignore them will not survive. In any case, it is sometimes impossible to distinguish, even by introspection, the external and personal components of a political position: this is the case, for example, with associated preferences, which are the preferences some people have for opportunities, like the opportunity to attend public schools, but only with others of the same 'background'.

The liberal, therefore, needs a scheme of civil rights, whose effect will be to determine those political decisions that are antecedently likely to reflect strong external preferences, and to remove those decisions from majoritarian political institutions altogether. Of course, the scheme of rights necessary to do this will depend on general facts about the prejudices and other external preferences of the majority at any given time, and different liberals will disagree about what is needed at any particular time.[d] But the rights encoded in the Bill of Rights of the United States Constitution, as interpreted (on the whole) by the Supreme Court, are those that a substantial number of liberals would think reasonably well suited to what the United States now requires (though most would think that the protection of the individual in certain important areas, including sexual publication and practice, are much too weak).

The main parts of the criminal law, however, present a special problem not easily met by a scheme of civil rights that disable the legislature from taking certain political decisions. The liberal knows that many of the most important decisions required by an effective criminal law are not made by legislators at all, but by prosecutors deciding whom to prosecute for what crime, and by juries and judges deciding whom to convict and what sentences to impose. He also knows that these decisions are antecedently very likely to be corrupted by the external preferences of those who make these decisions because those they judge, typically, have attitudes and ways of life very different from their own. The liberal does not have available, as protection against these decisions, any strategy comparable to the strategy of civil rights that simply remove a decision from an institution. Decisions to prosecute, convict and sentence

---

[c] *Taking Rights Seriously*, pp 234ff, 275.
[d] See Dworkin, 'Social Sciences and Constitutional Rights', The Educational Forum, XLI (March 1977), 271.

must be made by someone. But he has available, in the notion of procedural rights, a different device to protect equality in a different way. He will insist that criminal procedure be structured to achieve a margin of safety in decisions, so that the process is biased strongly against the conviction of the innocent. It would be a mistake to suppose that the liberal thinks that these procedural rights will improve the *accuracy* of the criminal process, that is, the probability that any particular decision about guilt or innocence will be the right one. Procedural rights intervene in the process, even at the cost of inaccuracy, to compensate in a rough way for the antecedent risk that a criminal process, especially if it is largely administered by one class against another, will be corrupted by the impact of external preferences that cannot be eliminated directly. This is, of course, only the briefest sketch of how various substantive and procedural civil rights follow from the liberal's initial conception of equality; it is meant to suggest, rather than demonstrate, the more precise argument that would be available for more particular rights.

So the liberal, drawn to the economic market and to political democracy for distinctly egalitarian reasons, finds that these institutions will produce inegalitarian results unless he adds to his scheme different sorts of individual rights. These rights will function as trump cards held by individuals; they will enable individuals to resist particular decisions in spite of the fact that these decisions are or would be reached through the normal workings of general institutions that are not themselves challenged. The ultimate justification for these rights is that they are necessary to protect equal concern and respect; but they are not to be understood as representing equality in contrast to some other goal or principle served by democracy or the economic market. The familiar idea, for example, that rights of redistribution are justified by an ideal of equality that overrides the efficiency ideals of the market in certain cases, has no place in liberal theory. For the liberal, rights are justified, not by some principle in competition with an independent justification of the political and economic institutions they qualify, but in order to make more perfect the only justification on which these other institutions may themselves rely. If the liberal arguments for a particular right are sound, then the right is an unqualified improvement in political morality, not a necessary but regrettable compromise of some other independent goal, like economic efficency.

Dworkin 'Liberalism' in S Hampshire (ed) *Public and Private Morality* 127–136

According to this argument, not only do the rights it is necessary to grant individuals function as trumps against collective goals; but it is also clear that their justification is not one that is goal-based. For individual rights are needed not because their existence makes the maximisation of happiness, or individual preferences, or of something else, possible, but because granting them ensures that the principle of equal concern and respect is upheld. Hence, Dworkin's claim that individual rights to goods and services are not something that can be traded off against an independently justifiable principle of efficiency—for to admit that the latter principle can be independently justified would be to admit goal-based considerations into his theory at a fundamental level. On the contrary, not only cannot individual rights be traded in this way,[4] but their justification is right-based; that is, they are to be justified 'not by some principle in competition with an independent justification of the political and economic institutions they

[4] It is something of a commonplace to speak of a trade-off between justice and efficiency. See Ch 13 on the economic interpretation of law for further discussion.

qualify, but in order to make more perfect the only justification on which these other institutions may themselves rely' ('Liberalism', 136). In other words, the justification ultimately rests on the principle of equal concern and respect.

(a) Dworkin and utilitarianism

Not surprisingly Dworkin's theory has a strong anti-utilitarian cast. Not only cannot individual rights be violated to further a collective goal, but their very justification is right-based not goal-based. However, it is not clear, at first sight, that the utilitarian has no defence against Dworkin's attack. For he can argue that utilitarianism itself attaches as much importance as does Dworkin to the principle of equal concern and respect, since it is a fundamental principle of utilitarianism that everyone is to count as one, and no more than one—in other words, it is a fundamental principle of utilitarianism that equal weight should be given to everyone's interests and preferences. This, of course, Dworkin has to accept; for, apart from anything else, as a version of classical liberalism utilitarianism must be committed to the principle of equal concern and respect.

However, though he acknowledges that this is so—so that thus far there is no disagreement between him and the utilitarian—Dworkin argues that the actual decision procedure which the utilitarian adopts to determine what is right is fatally flawed. Moreover, it is flawed in such a way that it leads to the violation of the principle of equal concern and respect, so that the implementation of utilitarianism is inconsistent with one of its own fundamental principles. One rather obvious way in which this might happen would be if special weight was given to the preferences of some, eg, if certain persons were given two votes in an election, while others had only one. But there is, Dworkin argues, a more subtle way in which this can and does happen. This involves failing to distinguish between two different kinds of preferences (*Taking Rights Seriously* 234); one of these can legitimately be counted by a utilitarian decision procedure, but the other should be excluded since counting it leads to violations of the principle of equal concern and respect. Examples of the first kind of preference, which Dworkin calls a *personal* preference, would be a preference for wine rather than beer, for town rather than country, and for the poetry of Eliot rather than that of Auden. Such preferences are personal in the sense that they rest on one's own tastes, and do not involve preferences about preferences. However, the second kind of preference, which Dworkin calls an *external preference*, does involve preferences about preferences. At first sight, such preferences look unusual; but reflection suggests that they are not uncommon. On the one hand, we prefer those we like and admire to get their personal preferences satisfied; whereas, on the other hand, we prefer those we dislike and despise not to get their preferences satisfied. Those who love Sarah have external preferences of the first kind about her personal preferences; while Nazis had external preferences of the second kind about the personal preferences of non-Aryans.

The distinction is important, Dworkin argues, because something goes badly wrong with the utilitarian's decision procedure if external preferences are allowed to count. It would, for instance, be obviously wrong to give Sarah-lovers two votes when everyone else has one, since that would violate the principle that everyone is to count as one and no more than one. But it is, Dworkin argues, equally wrong to count the external preferences of Sarah-lovers as well as their personal preferences, since 'if these special preferences are themselves allowed to count, therefore, Sarah will receive much more in the distribution of goods and services than she otherwise would' (R Dworkin, *A Matter of Principle* 361). So in this case too, there is a kind of double counting, and once again the principle of equal concern and respect is undermined. Indeed, this 'apparently neutral provision is then self-undermining because it gives critical weight, in deciding which distribution best promotes utility, to the views of those who hold the profoundly un-neutral (some would say anti-utilitarian) theory that the preferences of some should count for more than those of others' (ibid). This may not seem to matter that much in the case of the Sarah-lovers, since she is evidently so delightful; but it is easy to see how much it matters if extra weight is given, however unwittingly, to the external preferences of the Nazis.

It might seem that there is an easy way to save utilitarianism, namely, to identify and exclude external preferences. But Dworkin is right to point out that in practice it is very difficult to know whether an attitude rests on an external or a personal preference, so that one cannot exclude the first kind. But if external preferences cannot be excluded in practice, one way to protect individuals from their malign effects would be to take rights seriously:

> My argument, therefore, comes to this. If utilitarianism is to figure as part of an attractive working political theory, it must be qualified so as to restrict the preferences that count by excluding political [= external] preferences . . . One very practical way to achieve this restriction is provided by the idea of rights as trumps over unrestricted utilitarianism. A society committed to utilitarianism as a general background justification which does not in terms disqualify any preferences might achieve that disqualification by adopting a right to political independence.
>
> Dworkin *A Matter of Principle* 364

Hence, the case, or at least one case, for taking rights seriously points to a fundamental flaw in classical utilitarianism which can only be rectified by acknowledging the importance of individual rights as trumps over collective goals.

This subtle argument has, however, been challenged by Hart, not indeed because he wishes to defend an 'unpurified' version of utilitarianism—he too recognises the importance of rights—but because he thinks that the distinction between personal and external preferences will not bear the weight that Dworkin puts on it:

> What then is this element which may corrupt utilitarian argument or a democratic vote? Dworkin identifies it by a distinction between the personal and external preferences or satisfactions of individuals, both of which vulgar utilitarianism counts in assessments of general welfare and both of which may be represented in a majority vote. An individual's personal preferences (or satisfactions) are for (or arise from) the assignment of goods or advantages, including liberties, to himself, his external preferences are for such assignments to others. A utilitarianism refined or purified in the sense that it counted only personal preferences in assessing the balance of social welfare would for Dworkin be 'the only defensible form of Utilitarianism'[a] and indeed it is that which justifies the 'vast bulk of our laws diminishing liberty'.[b] It would, he thinks, genuinely treat persons as equals, even if the upshot was not

---

[a] *Taking Rights Seriously* at 276.
[b] Ibid at 269.

their equal treatment. So where the balance of personal self-interest preferences supported some restriction on freedom (as it did according to Dworkin in the labour contract cases) or reverse discrimination (as in *Bakke's* case), the restriction or discrimination may be justified, and the freedom restricted; or the claim not to be discriminated against is not a moral or political right. But the vulgar, corrupt form of utilitarianism counts both external and personal preferences and is not an acceptable decision procedure since (so Dworkin argues) by counting in external preferences it fails to treat individuals with equal concern and respect or as equals.[c]

Dworkin's ambitious strategy in this argument is to derive rights to specific liberties from nothing more controversial than the duty of governments to treat their subjects with equal concern and respect. His argument here has a certain Byzantine complexity and it is important in assessing it not to be misled by an ambiguity in the way in which a right may be an 'anti-utilitarian right'. There is a natural interpretation of this expression which is not Dworkin's sense; it may naturally be taken merely to mean that there are some liberties so precious for individual human life that they must not be overridden even in order to secure an advance in general welfare, because they are of greater value than any such increase of general welfare to be got by their denial, however fair the *procedure* for assessing the general welfare is and however genuinely as a procedure it treats persons as equals. Dworkin's sense is *not* that; his argument is not that these liberties must be safeguarded as rights because their value has been compared with that of the increase in general welfare and found to be greater than it, but because such liberties are likely to be defeated by an unfair form of utilitarian argument which by counting in external preferences fails to treat men as equals. So on this view the very identification of the liberties which are to rank as rights is dependent on the anticipated result of a majority vote or a utilitarian argument; whereas on the natural interpretation of an 'anti-utilitarian right' the liberties which are to rank as rights and prevail over general welfare are quite independently identified.

Dworkin's actual argument is more complicated[d] than this already complex story, but I do not think what is omitted is needed for its just assessment. I think both the general form of the argument and its detail are vulnerable to

[c] Ibid at 237, 275.

[d] The main complications are: (1) Personal and external preferences may be intertwined in two different ways. A personal preference, eg, for the segregated company of white men, may be parasitic on an external preference or prejudice against black men, and such 'parasitic' preferences are to rank as external preferences not to be counted (ibid at 236). They are however to be distinguished from certain personal preferences which, although they too involve a reference to others, do so only in an instrumental way, regarding others as a means to their personal ends. So a white man's preference that black men be excluded from law school because that will increase his own chances of getting in (ibid at 234–5) or a black man's preference for reverse discrimination against whites because that will increase the number of black lawyers, is to rank as a personal preference and is to be counted. (2) Though personal and external preferences are in principle distinguishable, in practical politics it will often be impossible to discriminate them and to know how many of each lie behind majority votes. Hence whenever external preferences are likely to influence a vote against some specific liberty, the liberty will need to be protected as an 'anti-utilitarian right'. So the 'anti-utilitarian' concept of a right is 'a response to the philosophical defects of a utilitarianism that counts external preferences and the practical impossibility of a utilitarianism that does not' (ibid at 277). Notwithstanding this 'practical impossibility', there are cases where according to Dworkin valid arguments may be made to show that external preferences are not likely to have tipped the balance. See his comments on *Lochner's* case (ibid at 278) and *Bakke's* case (see n 23 and accompanying text *supra*) and his view that most of the laws limiting liberties are justified on utilitarian grounds (R Dworkin, *supra* n 20, at 269).

many different objections. The most general objection is the following. What moral rights we have will, on this view, depend on what external preferences or prejudices are current and likely at any given time in any given society to dominate in a utilitarian decision procedure or majority vote. So as far as this argument for rights is concerned, with the progressive liberalization of a society from which prejudices against, say, homosexual behaviour or the expression of heterodox opinions have faded away, rights to these liberties will (like the State in Karl Marx) wither away. So the more tolerant a society is, the fewer rights there will be; there will not merely be fewer occasions for asserting rights. This is surely paradoxical even if we take Dworkin only to be concerned with rights against the State. But this paradox is compounded by another. Since Dworkin's theory is a response specifically to an alleged defect of utilitarian argument it only establishes rights against the outcome of utilitarian arguments concerning general welfare or a majority democratic vote in which external preferences are likely to tip the balance. This theory as it stands cannot provide support for rights against a tyranny or authoritative government which does not base its coercive legislation on considerations of general welfare or a majority vote. So this particular argument for rights helps to establish individual rights at neither extreme: neither in an extremely tolerant democracy nor in an extremely repressive tyranny. This of course narrows the scope of Dworkin's argument in ways which may surprise readers of his essay 'What Rights Do We Have?'[e] But of course he is entitled to reply that, narrow though it is, the reach of this particular argument extends to contemporary Western democracies in which the allegedly corrupting 'external preferences' hostile to certain liberties are rife as prejudices. He may say that *that* is good enough—for the time being.[f]

However, even if we accept this reply, a close examination of the detail of the argument shows it to be defective even within its limited scope; and the ways in which it is defective show an important general failing. In constructing his anti-utilitarian right-based theory Dworkin has sought to derive too much from the idea of equal concern and respect for persons, just as Nozick in constructing his theory sought to derive too much from the idea of the separateness of persons. Both of course appear to offer something comfortably firm and uncontroversial as a foundation for a theory of basic rights. But this appearance is deceptive: that it is so becomes clear if we press the question why, as Dworkin argues, does a utilitarian decision procedure or democratic vote which counts both personal and external preferences, *for that reason*, fail to treat persons as equals, so that when as he says it is 'antecedently likely' that external preferences may tip the balance against some individual's specific liberty, that liberty becomes clothed with the status of a moral right not to be overridden by such procedures. Dworkin's argument is that counting external preferences corrupts the utilitarian argument or a majority vote as a decision procedure, and this of course must be distinguished from any further independent moral objection there may be to the actual decision resulting

---

[e] R Dworkin, *supra* n 20, at 266–78.
[f] This argument from the defect of unreconstructed utilitarianism in counting external preferences is said to be 'only one possible ground of rights' (ibid at 272, and R Dworkin, *supra* n 20, at 356 (2nd printing 1977), and is stated to be applicable only in communities where the general collective justification of political decisions is the general welfare. Though Dworkin indicates that a different argument would be needed where collective justification is not utilitarian (ibid at 365), he does not indicate how in such a case the liberties to be preferred as rights are to be identified.

from the procedure. An obvious example of such a vice in utilitarian argument or in a majority vote procedure would of course be double counting, eg counting one individual's (a Brahmin's or a white man's) vote or preference twice while counting another's (an Untouchable's or a black man's) only once. This is, of course, the very vice excluded by the maxim 'everybody [is] to count for one, nobody for more than one' which Mill thought made utilitarianism so splendid. Of course an Untouchable denied some liberty, say liberty to worship, or a black student denied access to higher education as a result of such double counting would not have been treated as an equal, but the right needed to protect him against this is not a right to any specific liberty but simply a right to have his vote or preference count equally with the Brahmin's or the white man's. And of course the decision to deprive him of the liberty in question might also be morally objectionable for reasons quite independent of the unfairness in the procedure by which it was reached: if freedom of religion or access to education is something of which no one should be deprived whatever decision procedure, fair or unfair, is used, then a right to that freedom would be necessary for its protection. But it is vital to distinguish the specific alleged vice of unrefined utilitarianism or a democratic vote in failing, eg, through double counting, to treat persons as equals, from any independent objection to a particular decision reached through that procedure. It is necessary to bear this in mind in considering Dworkin's argument.

So, finally, why is counting external preferences thought to be, like the double counting of the Brahmin's or white man's preference, a vice of utilitarian argument or a majority vote? Dworkin actually says that 'the inclusion of external preference *is* a form of double counting'.[g] To understand this we must distinguish cases where the external preference is *favourable* to, and so supports, some personal preference or want for some good or advantage or liberty from cases where the external preference is hostile. Dworkin's simple example of the former is where one person wants the construction of a swimming-pool[h] for his use and others, non-swimmers, support this. But why is this a 'form of double counting'? No one's preference is counted twice as the Brahmin's is; it is only the case that the proposal for the allocation of some good to the swimmers is supported by the preferences both of the swimmer and (say) his disinterested non-swimmer neighbour. Each of the two preferences is counted only as one; and surely *not* to count the neighbour's disinterested preference on this issue would be to fail to treat the two as equals. It would be 'under-counting' and presumably as bad as double counting. Suppose—to widen the illustration—the issue is freedom for homosexual relationships, and suppose that (as may well have been the case at least in England when the old law was reformed in 1967[i]) it was the disinterested external preferences of liberal heterosexuals that homosexuals should have this freedom that tipped the balance against the external preferences of other heterosexuals who would deny this freedom. How in this situation could the defeated opponents of freedom or anyone else complain that the procedure, through counting external preferences (both those supporting the freedom for others and those denying it) as well as the personal preferences of homosexuals wanting it for themselves, had failed to treat persons as equals?

[g] Ibid at 235.
[h] Ibid.
[i] Sexual Offences Act, 1967, c 60.

It is clear that where the external preferences are hostile to the assignment of some liberty wanted by others, the phenomenon of one person's preferences being supported by those of another, which, as I think, Dworkin misdescribes as a 'form of double counting', is altogether absent. Why then, since the charge of double counting is irrelevant, does counting such hostile external preferences mean that the procedure does not treat persons as equals? Dworkin's answer seems to be that if, as a result of such preferences tipping the balance, persons are denied some liberty, say to form certain sexual relations, those so deprived suffer because by this result their concept of a proper or desirable form of life is despised by others, and this is tantamount to treating them as inferior to or of less worth than others, or not deserving equal concern and respect. So every denial of freedom on the basis of external preferences implies that those denied are not entitled to equal concern and respect, are not to be considered as equals. But even if we allow this most questionable interpretation of denials of freedom, still for Dworkin to argue in this way is altogether to change the argument. The objection is no longer that the utilitarian argument or a majority vote is, like double counting, unfair as a procedure because it counts in 'external preferences', but that a particular *upshot* of the procedure where the balance is tipped by *a particular kind* of external preference, one which denies liberty and is assumed to express contempt, fails to treat persons as equals. But this is a vice not of the mere externality of the preferences that have tipped the balance but of their content: that is, their liberty-denying and respect-denying content. But this is no longer to assign certain liberties the status of ('anti-utilitarian') rights simply as a response to the specific defects of utilitarianism, as Dworkin claims to do. Yet that is not the main weakness in his ingenious argument. What is fundamentally wrong is the suggested interpretation of denials of freedom as denials of equal concern or respect. This surely is mistaken. It is indeed least credible where the denial of a liberty is the upshot of a utilitarian decision procedure or majority vote in which the defeated minority's preferences or votes for the liberty were weighed equally with others and outweighed by number. Then the message need not be, as Dworkin interprets it, 'You and your views are inferior, not entitled to equal consideration, concern or respect', but 'You and your supporters are too few. You, like everyone else, are counted as one but no more than one. Increase your numbers and then your views may win out.' Where those who are denied by a majority vote the liberty they seek are able, as they are in a fairly working democracy, to continue to press their views in public argument and to attempt to change their opponents' minds, as they in fact with success did after several defeats when the law relating to homosexuality was changed in England, it seems quite impossible to construe every denial of liberty by a majority vote based on external preferences as a judgment that the minority whom it defeats are of inferior worth, not entitled to be treated as equals or with equal concern and respect. What is true is something different and quite familiar but no support for Dworkin's argument: namely that the procedural fairness of a voting system or utilitarian argument which weighs votes and preferences equally is no guarantee that all the requirements of fairness will be met in the actual working of the system in given social conditions. This is so because majority views may be, though they are not always, ill-informed and impervious to argument: a majority of theoretically independent voters may be consolidated by prejudice into a self-deafened or self-perpetuating bloc which affords no fair opportunities to a despised minority to publicize and argue its case. All that is possible and has sometimes been actual. But the moral unacceptability of the results in such cases is not traceable to the inherent vice of the decision procedure in counting external preferences, as if this was analogous to double counting. That, of course, would mean that every denial of liberty secured by the doubly counted votes or preferences would necessarily not only be a denial of liberty but also an instance of failing to treat those denied as equals.

Hart 'Between Utility and Rights' 79 Columbia Law Review (1979) 828–846

Certainly, the content of an external preference need not be objectionable simply because it is an external preference; indeed it would seem that much other-regarding action involves such preferences. So to exclude *all* external preferences, would be to exclude many which should in fact be encouraged. On the other hand, personal preferences, even though not objectionable in themselves, may, taken together, fall into a pattern which is tantamount to discrimination. For a preference for the company of the members of a favoured group X, rather than that of others, is presumably a personal preference; and whether or not it is itself objectionable, it is not difficult to see how it could be one of a set of personal preferences—for schools attended by members of X, for colleagues at work who are members, etc, whose combined effect is to discriminate seriously against non-members and to pay scant regard to their treatment as equals. Further, Hart is surely right to argue that, whether or not a vote is based on a personal or on an external preference, there cannot be any double counting in a decision procedure which allows everyone only one vote. So it is difficult to see that there is any general case for excluding external preferences.

Dworkin has replied to Hart's criticisms at length, and his reply now follows:

Hart's Objections

There are, then, good grounds for those who accept utilitarianism as a general background justification for political decisions also to accept, as part of the same package, a right of moral independence in the form that, I have just argued, would support or permit the major recommendations of the Williams Report. I shall end this essay by considering certain objections that H L A Hart made, in 1980,[a] to a similar argument that I made some years ago about the connection between utilitarianism and these rights.[b] Hart's objections show what I think is a comprehensive misunderstanding of this argument, which my earlier statement, as I now see, encouraged; it might therefore be helpful, as insurance against a similar misunderstanding now, to report these objections and my reasons for thinking that they misconceive my argument.

I suggested, in my earlier formulation of the present argument, that if a utilitarian counts preferences like the preferences of the Sarah-lovers, then this is a 'form' of double-counting because, in effect, Sarah's preferences are counted twice, once on her own account, and once through the second-order preferences of others that incorporate her preferences by reference. Hart says that this is a mistake, because in fact no one's preferences are counted twice, and it would *under*count the Sarah-lovers' preferences, and so fail to treat them as equals, if their preferences in her favor were discarded. There would be

[a] Hart, 'Between Utility and Rights,' 79 Columbia Law Review, 828, 836ff.
[b] See Dworkin, *Taking Rights Seriously*, introduction, ch 12, and app., pp 357–358. See also Dworkin, 'Liberalism,' in Stuart Hampshire, ed., *Public and Private Morality* (Cambridge, Eng.: Cambridge University Press, 1978), and Dworkin, 'Social Science and Constitutional Rights: the Consequences of Uncertainty,' 6 Journal of Law and Education, (1977) 3.

something in this last point if votes rather than preferences were in issue, because if someone wished to vote for Sarah's success rather than his own, his role in the calculation would be exhausted by this gift, and if his vote was then discarded, he might well complain that he had been cheated of his equal power over political decision. But preferences, as these figure in utilitarian calculations, are not like votes in that way. Someone who reports more preferences to the utilitarian computer does not (except trivially) diminish the impact of other preferences he also reports; he rather increases the role of his preferences overall, compared with the role of other people's preferences, in the giant calculation. So someone who prefers Sarah's success to the success of people generally, and through the contribution of that preference to an unrestricted utilitarian calculation secures more for her, does not have any less for himself—for the fulfillment of his more personal preferences—than someone else who is indifferent to Sarah's fortunes.

I do not think that my description, that counting his preferences in favor of Sarah is a form of double-counting, is misleading or unfair. But this description was meant to summarize the argument, not to make it, and I will not press that particular characterization. (As Hart notices, I made it only about some of the examples I gave in which unrestricted utilitarianism produced obviously inegalitarian results.) Hart makes more substantial points about a different example I used, which raised the question of whether homosexuals have the right to practice their sexual tastes in private. He thinks I want to say 'that if, as a result of [preferences that express moral disapproval of homosexuals] tipping the balance, persons are denied some liberty, say to form some sexual relations, those so deprived suffer because by this result their concept of a proper or desirable form of life is despised by others, and this is tantamount to treating them as inferior to or of less worth than others, or not deserving of equal concern and respect.'[c]

But this misstates my point. It is not the result (or, as Hart later describes it, the 'upshot') of the utilitarian calculation that causes or achieves the fact that homosexuals are despised by others. It is rather the other way round: if someone is denied liberty of sexual practice in virtue of a utilitarian justification that depends critically on other people's moralistic preferences, then he suffers disadvantage in virtue of the fact that his concept of a proper life is already despised by others. Hart says that the 'main weakness' in my argument—the feature that makes it 'fundamentally wrong'—is that I assume that if someone's liberty is restricted, this must be interpreted as a denial of his treatment as an equal. But my argument is that this is not inevitably or even usually so, but only when the constraint is justified in some way that depends on the fact that others condemn his convictions or values. Hart says that the interpretation of denial of liberty as a denial of equal concern is 'least credible' in exactly the case I discuss, that is, when the denial is justified through a utilitarian argument, because, he says, the message of that justification is not that the defeated minority or their moral convictions are inferior, but only that they are too few to outweigh the preferences of the majority, which can only be achieved if the minority is denied the liberty it wishes. But once again this ignores the distinction I want to make. If the utilitarian justification for denying liberty of sexual practice to homosexuals can succeed without counting the moralistic preferences of the majority in the balance (as it might if there was good reason to believe what is in fact incredible, that the spread of

[c] Hart, *Law, Liberty, and Morality*, p 842.

homosexuality fosters violent crime), then the message of prohibition would be only the message Hart finds, which might be put this way: 'It is impossible that everyone be protected in all his interests, and the interests of the minority must yield, regrettably, to the concern of the majority for its safety.' There is, at least in my present argument, no denial of treatment as an equal in that message. But if the utilitarian justification cannot succeed without relying on the majority's moralistic preferences about how the minority should live, and the government nevertheless urges that justification, then the message is very different and, in my view, nastier. It is exactly that the minority must suffer because others find the lives they propose to lead disgusting, which seems no more justifiable in a society committed to treating people as equals, than the proposition we earlier considered and rejected as incompatible with equality, that some people must suffer disadvantage under the law because others do not like them.

Hart makes further points. He suggests, for example, that it was the 'disinterested' political preferences of liberals that tipped the balance in favor of repealing laws against homosexual relationships in 1967 in England, and he asks how anyone could object that counting *those* preferences at that time offended anyone's right to be treated as an equal. But this question misunderstands my point in a fundamental way. I do not argue—how could anyone argue?—that citizens in a democracy should not campaign and vote for what they think is just. The question is not whether people should work for justice, but rather what test we and they should apply to determine what is just. Utilitarianism holds that we should apply this test: we should work to achieve the maximum possible satisfaction of the preferences we find distributed in our community. If we accepted this test in an unrestricted way, then we would count the attractive political convictions of the 1960s liberals simply as data, to be balanced against the less attractive convictions of others, to see which carried the day in the contest of number and intensity. Conceivably the liberal position would have won this contest. Probably it would not have.

But I have been arguing that this is a false test, which undermines the case for utilitarianism, if political preferences of either the liberals or their opponents are counted and balanced to determine what justice requires. That is why I recommended, as part of any overall political theory in which utilitarianism figures as a background justification, rights to political and moral independence. But the liberals who campaigned in the interests of homosexuals in England in the 1960s most certainly did not embrace the test I reject. They *expressed* their own political preferences in their votes and arguments, but they did not *appeal to* the popularity of these preferences as providing an argument in itself for what they wanted, as the unrestricted utilitarian argument I oppose would have encouraged them to do. Perhaps they appealed instead to something like the right of moral independence. In any case they did not rely on any argument inconsistent with that right. Nor is it necessary for us to rely on any such argument to say that what they did was right, and treated people as equals. The proof is this: the case for reform would have been just as strong in political theory even if there had been very few or no heterosexuals who wanted reform, though of course reform would not then have been practically possible. If so, then we cannot condemn the procedure that produced reform on the ground that that procedure offended anyone's right to independence.

Hart's misunderstanding here was no doubt encouraged by my own description of how rights like the right to moral independence function in a constitutional system, like that of the United States, which uses rights as a test of the legality of legislation. I said that a constitutional system of this sort is valuable when the community as a whole harbors prejudices against some minority or convictions that the way of life of that minority is offensive to people of good character. In that situation the ordinary political process is antecedently likely to reach decisions that would fail the test we have constructed, because these decisions would limit the freedom of the minority and yet could not be justified, in political theory, except by assuming that some ways of living are inherently wrong or degrading, or by counting the fact that the majority thinks them so as itself part of the justification. Since these *repressive* decisions would then be wrong, for the reasons I offer, the constitutional right forbids them in advance.

The decision for reform that Hart describes would not—could not—be a decision justified only on these offending grounds. Even if the benign liberal preferences figured as data rather than argument, as I think they should not, no one would be in a position to claim the right to moral or political independence as a shield against the decision that was in fact reached. But someone might have been led to suppose, by my discussion, that what I condemn is any political process that would allow any decision to be taken if people's reasons for supporting one decision rather than another are likely to lie beyond their own personal interests. I hope it is now plain why this is wrong. *That* position would not allow a democracy to vote for social welfare programs, or foreign aid, or conservation for later generations. Indeed, in the absence of an adequate constitutional system, the only hope for justice is precisely that people will vote with a disinterested sense of fairness. I condemn a political process that assumes that the fact that people have such reasons is itself part of the case in political morality for what they favor. Hart's heterosexual liberals may have been making the following argument to their fellow-citizens. 'We know that many of you find the idea of homosexual relationships troubling and even offensive. Some of us do as well. But you must recognize that it would deny equality, in the form of moral independence, to count the fact that we have these feelings as a justification for penal legislation. Since that is so, we in fact have no justification for the present law, and we ought, in all justice, to reform it.' Nothing in this argument counts the fact that either the liberals or those they address happen to have any particular political preferences or convictions as itself an argument: the argument is made by appeal to justice not to the fact that many people want justice. There is nothing in that argument that fails to treat homosexuals as equals. Quite the contrary. But that is just my point.

Dworkin 'Do We Have a Right to Pornography?' 1 Oxford Journal for Legal Studies (1981)

Dworkin is, of course, right that it is unlikely that anyone who argued for a liberalisation of the old laws relating to homosexuality did so simply on the grounds that the preferences of the majority favoured doing this. But his reply to Hart still seems to take it for granted that there is a fundamental difference between personal and external preferences, and that a utilitarian decision procedure which takes only the former into account is not objectionable in the way that one that admits the latter is; yet this is surely precisely what is at issue.

So any argument for taking rights seriously which appeals to the distinction, as does the argument of 'Liberalism', should be treated with caution. It may be, however, that the role the distinction plays in the argument is a relatively minor one in this case; and that the fundamental point is that if the basic right to equal concern and respect is to be taken seriously citizens must have other rights, otherwise the effects of prejudice would be to deny them their basic right. One can accept this, without accepting that there is any special connection between prejudice and external preferences.

THE RIGHTS WE HAVE

As we have seen, Dworkin argues that one of the rights that individuals have is pre-eminent. This is the right to *treatment as an equal*, that is, the right to be treated with the same degree of concern and respect as anyone else. He stresses that it is important to distinguish this abstract right from another, with which it might be confused, *the right to equal treatment*, that is the right to receive the same share of a distribution of goods or services as everyone else (*Taking Rights Seriously*, 227 and 273). Sometimes the only way an individual can be treated as an equal is by giving him or her equal treatment; the principle of one man one vote, for instance, treats everyone as an equal by giving each vote the same weight in the voting process. But usually treatment as an equal does not require equal treatment. If my two children are sick, one of them seriously, and one not, and I have a limited supply of a drug, then their right to treatment as equals does not entail that each should get half of the limited supply.

But how is the fundamental right of treatment as an equal to be justified? One can justify a derivative right on the grounds that the values protected by a fundamental right would be violated if the derivative right was not recognised; but clearly one cannot justify a fundamental right in that way, for there is no right more basic than it to appeal to. However, given the methodology that Dworkin adopts, there is a ground for treating the right to treatment as an equal as fundamental, namely, that this is the conclusion that the method of reflective equilibrium (cf Ch 6) leads to. And this argument would seem to be implicit in an important comment Dworkin makes on the status of Rawls's two principles of justice which recognise certain sorts of inequality as legitimate:

> Rawls makes plain that these inequalities are required, not by some competing notion of liberty or some overriding goal, but by a more basic sense of equality itself. He accepts a distinction between what he calls two conceptions of equality:
>
> > Some writers have distinguished between equality as it is invoked in connection with the distribution of certain goods, some of which will almost certainly give higher status or prestige to those who are more favored, and equality as it applies to the respect which is owed to persons irrespective of their social position. Equality of the first kind is defined by the second principle of justice . . . But equality of the second kind is fundamental.[a]
>
> We may describe a right to equality of the second kind, which Rawls says is fundamental, in this way. We might say that individuals have a right to equal concern and respect in the design and administration of the political

[a] J Rawls, *A Theory of Justice* 511.

institutions that govern them. This is a highly abstract right. Someone might argue, for example, that it is satisfied by political arrangements that provide equal opportunity for office and position on the basis of merit. Someone else might argue, to the contrary, that it is satisfied only by a system that guarantees absolute equality of income and status, without regard to merit. A third man might argue that equal concern and respect is provided by that system, whatever it is, that improves the average welfare of all citizens counting the welfare of each on the same scale. A fourth might argue, in the name of this fundamental equality, for the priority of liberty, and for the other apparent inequalities of Rawls's two principles.

The right to equal concern and respect, then, is more abstract than the standard conceptions of equality that distinguish different political theories. It permits arguments that this more basic right requires one or another of these conceptions as a derivative right or goal.

The original position may now be seen as a device for testing these competing arguments. It supposes, reasonably, that political arrangements that do not display equal concern and respect are those that are established and administered by powerful men and women who, whether they recognize it or not, have more concern and respect for members of a particular class, or people with particular talents or ideals, than they have for others. It relies on this supposition in shaping the ignorance of the parties to the contract. Men who do not know to which class they belong cannot design institutions, consciously or unconsciously, to favor their own class. Men who have no idea of their own conception of the good cannot act to favor those who hold one ideal over those who hold another. The original position is well designed to enforce the abstract right to equal concern and respect, which must be understood to be the fundamental concept of Rawls's deep theory.

If this is right, then Rawls must not use the original position to argue for this right in the same way that he uses it, for example, to argue for the rights to basic liberties embodied in the first principle. The text confirms that he does not. It is true that he once says that equality of respect is 'defined' by the first principle of justice.[b] But he does not mean, and in any case he does not argue, that the parties choose to be respected equally in order to advance some more basic right or goal. On the contrary, the right to equal respect is not, on his account, a product of the contract, but a condition of admission to the original position. This right, he says, is 'owed to human beings as moral persons', and follows from the moral personality that distinguishes humans from animals. It is possessed by all men who can give justice, and only such men can contract. This is one right, therefore, that does not emerge from the contract, but is assumed, as the fundamental right must be, in its design.

Dworkin *Taking Rights Seriously* 180–181

[b] Idem.

The right to treatment as an equal is, Dworkin argues, fundamental '. . . because it is the source both of the general authority of collective goals and of the special limitations on their authority that justify more particular rights' (*Taking Rights Seriously* xv). This raises two questions: what derivative rights do we have? And in what sense are they derivative? Dworkin's answer to these questions emerges from his discussion of whether we have a right to liberty.

Given the importance that liberal theorists have attached to liberty, it is, at first sight, surprising that he argues that we do not have a right to liberty. But as he points out there are many restrictions on individual liberty which are justifiable on utilitarian grounds; and if this is so, they cannot be restrictions of individual rights in the strong sense of trumps over collective goals. The natural response at this point is that if we do not have a right to liberty as such, we nevertheless have the right to certain basic liberties, such as the freedom of speech, worship, and political activity. This, of course, Dworkin does not deny; however, he argues that not only does the justification of these rights lend no support to the claim that we have a general right to liberty, but that it is clear that the justification cannot be on utilitarian grounds. On the contrary, the rights to specific liberties have to be justified on the grounds that they are derivative from the fundamental right to treatment as an equal:

I do not think that the right to liberty would come to very much, or have much power in political argument, if it relied on any sense of the right any weaker than that. If we settle on this concept of a right, however, then it seems plain that there exists no general right to liberty as such. I have no political right to drive up Lexington Avenue. If the government chooses to make Lexington Avenue one-way down town, it is a sufficient justification that this would be in the general interest, and it would be ridiculous for me to argue that for some reason it would nevertheless be wrong. The vast bulk of the laws which diminish my liberty are justified on utilitarian grounds, as being in the general interest or for the general welfare; if, as Bentham supposes, each of these laws diminishes my liberty, they nevertheless do not take away from me any thing that I have a right to have. It will not do, in the one-way street case, to say that although I have a right to drive up Lexington Avenue, nevertheless the government for special reasons is justified in overriding that right. That seems silly because the government needs no special justification—but only *a* justification—for this sort of legislation. So I can have a political right to liberty, such that every act of constraint diminishes or infringes that right, only in such a weak sense of right that the so called right to liberty is not competitive with strong rights, like the right to equality, at all. In any strong sense of right, which would be competitive with the right to equality, there exists no general right to liberty at all . . .

I propose that the right to treatment as an equal must be taken to be fundamental under the liberal conception of equality, and that the more restrictive right to equal treatment holds only in those special circumstances in which, for some special reason, it follows from the more fundamental right, as perhaps it does in the special circumstance of the Reapportionment Cases. I also propose that individual rights to distinct liberties must be recognized only when the fundamental right to treatment as an equal can be shown to require these rights. If this is correct, then the right to distinct liberties does not conflict with any supposed competing right to equality, but on the contrary follows from a conception of equality conceded to be more fundamental.

I must now show, however, how the familiar rights to distinct liberties— those established, for example, in the United States constitution—might be thought to be required by that fundamental conception of equality. I shall try to do this, for present purposes, only by providing a skeleton of the more elaborate argument that would have to be made to defend any particular liberty on this basis, and then show why it would be plausible to expect that the more familiar political and civil liberties would be supported by such an argument if it were in fact made.

A government that respects the liberal conception of equality may properly constrain liberty only on certain very limited types of justification. I shall adopt, for purposes of making this point, the following crude typology of political justifications. There are, first, arguments of principle, which support a particular constraint on liberty on the argument that the constraint is required to protect the distinct right of some individual who will be injured by the exercise of the liberty. There are, second, arguments of policy, which support constraints on the different ground that such constraints are required to reach some overall political goal, that is, to realize some state of affairs in which the community as a whole, and not just certain individuals, are better off by virtue of the constraint. Arguments of policy might be further subdivided in this way. Utilitarian arguments of policy argue that the community as a whole will be better off because (to put the point roughly) more of its citizens will have more of what they want overall, even though some of them will have less. Ideal arguments of policy, on the other hand, argue that the community will be better off, not because more of its members will have more of what they want, but because the community will be in some way closer to an ideal community, whether its members desire the improvement in question or not.

The liberal conception of equality sharply limits the extent to which ideal arguments of policy may be used to justify any constraint on liberty. Such arguments cannot be used if the idea in question is itself controversial within the community. Constraints cannot be defended, for example, directly on the ground that they contribute to a culturally sophisticated community, whether the community wants the sophistication or not, because that argument would violate the canon of the liberal conception of equality that prohibits a government from relying on the claim that certain forms of life are inherently more valuable than others.

Utilitarian arguments of policy, however, would seem secure from that objection. They do not suppose that any form of life is inherently more valuable than any other, but instead base their claim, that constraints on liberty are necessary to advance some collective goal of the community, just on the fact that that goal happens to be desired more widely or more deeply than any other. Utilitarian arguments of policy, therefore, seem not to oppose but on the contrary to embody the fundamental right of equal concern and respect, because they treat the wishes of each member of the community on a par with the wishes of any other, with no bonus or discount reflecting the view that that member is more or less worthy of concern, or his views more or less worthy of respect, than any other.

This appearance of egalitarianism has, I think, been the principal source of the great appeal that utilitarianism has had, as a general political philosophy, over the last century. In Chapter 9, however, I pointed out that the egalitarian character of a utilitarian argument is often an illusion. I will not repeat, but only summarize, my argument here.

Utilitarian arguments fix on the fact that a particular constraint on liberty will make more people happier, or satisfy more of their preferences, depending upon whether psychological or preference utilitarianism is in play. But people's overall preference for one policy rather than another may be seen to include, on further analysis, both preferences that are *personal*, because they state a preference for the assignment of one set of goods or opportunities to him and preferences that are *external*, because they state a preference for one assignment of goods or opportunities to others. But a utilitarian argument that assigns critical weight to the external preferences of members of the community will not be egalitarian in the sense under consideration. It will not respect the right of everyone to be treated with equal concern and respect.

Suppose, for example, that a number of individuals in the community holds racist rather than utilitarian political theories. They believe, not that each man is to count for one and no one for more than one in the distribution of goods, but rather that a black man is to count for less and a white man therefore to count for more than one. That is an external preference, but it is nevertheless a genuine preference for one policy rather than another, the satisfaction of which will bring pleasure. Nevertheless if this preference or pleasure is given the normal weight in a utilitarian calculation, and blacks suffer accordingly, then their own assignment of goods and opportunities will depend, not simply on the competition among personal preferences that abstract statements of utilitarianism suggest, but precisely on the fact that they are thought less worthy of concern and respect than others are.

Suppose, to take a different case, that many members of the community disapprove on moral grounds of homosexuality, or contraception, or pornography, or expressions of adherence to the Communist party. They prefer not only that they themselves do not indulge in these activities, but that no one else does so either, and they believe that a community that permits rather than prohibits these acts is inherently a worse community. These are external preferences, but, once again, they are no less genuine, nor less a source of pleasure when satisfied and displeasure when ignored, than purely personal preferences. Once again, however, if these external preferences are counted, so as to justify a constraint on liberty, then those constrained suffer, not simply because their personal preferences have lost in a competition for scarce resources with the personal preferences of others, but precisely because their conception of a proper or desirable form of life is despised by others.

These arguments justify the following important conclusion. If utilitarian arguments of policy are to be used to justify constraints on liberty, then care must be taken to insure that the utilitarian calculations on which the argument is based fix only on personal and ignore external preferences. That is an important conclusion for political theory because it shows, for example, why the arguments of John Stuart Mill in *On Liberty* are not counter-utilitarian but, on the contrary, arguments in service of the only defensible form of utilitarianism.

Important as that conclusion is at the level of political philosophy, however, it is in itself of limited practical significance, because it will be impossible to devise political procedures that will accurately discriminate between personal and external preferences. Representative democracy is widely thought to be the institutional structure most suited, in a complex and diverse society, to the identification and achievement of utilitarian policies. It works imperfectly at this, for the familiar reason that majoritarianism cannot sufficiently take account of the intensity, as distinct from the number, of particular preferences, and because techniques of political persuasion, backed by money, may corrupt the accuracy with which votes represent the genuine preferences of those who have voted. Nevertheless democracy seems to enforce utilitarianism more satisfactorily, in spite of these imperfections, than any alternative general political scheme would.

But democracy cannot discriminate, within the overall preferences imperfectly revealed by voting, distinct personal and external components, so as to provide a method for enforcing the former while ignoring the latter. An actual vote in an election or referendum must be taken to represent an overall preference rather than some component of the preference that a skillful cross-examination of the individual voter, if time and expense permitted, would reveal. Personal and external preferences are sometimes so inextricably combined, moreover, that the discrimination is psychologically as well as institutionally impossible. That will be true, for example, in the case of the associational preferences that many people have for members of one race, or people of one talent or quality, rather than another, for this is a personal preference so parasitic upon external preferences that it is impossible to say, even as a matter of introspection, what personal preferences would remain if the underlying external preference were removed. It is also true of certain self-denying preferences that many individuals have; that is preferences for less of a certain good on the assumption, or rather proviso, that other people will have more. That is also a preference, however noble, that is parasitic upon external preferences, in the shape of political and moral theories, and they may no more be counted in a defensible utilitarian argument than less attractive preferences rooted in prejudice rather than altruism.

I wish now to propose the following general theory of rights. The concept of an individual political right, in the strong anti-utilitarian sense I distinguished earlier, is a response to the philosophical defects of a utilitarianism that counts external preferences and the practical impossibility of a utilitarianism that does not. It allows us to enjoy the institutions of political democracy, which enforce overall or unrefined utilitarianism, and yet protect the fundamental right of citizens to equal concern and respect by prohibiting decisions that seem, antecedently, likely to have been reached by virtue of the external components of the preferences democracy reveals.

It should be plain how this theory of rights might be used to support the idea, which is the subject of this chapter, that we have distinct rights to certain liberties like the liberty of free expression and of free choice in personal and sexual relations. It might be shown that any utilitarian constraint on these liberties must be based on overall preferences in the community that we know, from our general knowlege of society, are likely to contain large components of external preferences, in the shape of political or moral theories, which the political process cannot discriminate and eliminate. It is not, as I said, my present purpose to frame the arguments that would have to be made to defend particular rights to liberty in this way, but only to show the general character such arguments might have.

Dworkin Taking Rights Seriously 269, 273–277

CRITIQUE

We have already discussed at length doubts whether Dworkin's distinction between external and personal preferences will bear the argumentative weight he puts on it. But even if it will not, we suggested that though the argument of 'Liberalism' appeals to the distinction it can perhaps be restated in a way which does not. Hence, the widespread doubts there are about the distinction between external and personal preferences is not necessarily fatal to Dworkin's position.

Even so, it might be felt that there are considerable problems with Dworkin's attempt to justify individual rights. For while it is easy enough to see what form an argument for a derived right has on his account—it will be an argument which eschews goal-based considerations, and shows that the derived right is necessary to ensure equality of respect and concern—it is difficult in practice to produce a *detailed* argument. Consequently, it is difficult to elicit from Dworkin's theoretical account any very precise list of the derived rights that individuals have. One reason why it is difficult to produce a detailed argument is that the right to equality of concern and respect is itself a highly abstract right, whereas the derived rights which are of interest to ordinary people are concrete institutional rights. These are of interest precisely because, unlike the abstract right to equal concern, they involve a remedy; and perhaps one of the dangers of Dworkin's proposed derivation of rights is that it promises more than it can deliver, that is, it promises a precisely defined list of concrete rights with remedies, whereas all it delivers is a poorly defined abstract right, and a sketch of the form of argument one has to construct to justify a derived right. As a recent writer says: 'background abstract "rights" dissolve into generalized moral values which cannot function as rights by giving us a relatively objective and politically uncontroversial way of determining entitlements by reference to an authoritative system of norms' (T Campbell *Justice* London MacMillan, 56).

A second difficulty with a detailed derivation is that though it must not be goal-based, nevertheless it has to include empirical premises about, for example, the relative degrees of deprivation of different groups within society, the extent and nature of prejudice, the means available to combat it, etc. Once again, the resulting argument is likely to seem complex and inconclusive. Moreover, we seem to be left with the rather paradoxical conclusion that what rights we should have is a contingent matter, depending on the particular prejudices and biases of our time and place (H L Hart, 'Between Utility and Rights', p 213).

Doubt has also been expressed whether the right which Dworkin treats as fundamental either is or could be. The problem is, Mackie argues, that the right to equal concern and respect is for Dworkin only a *political* right:

> It is governments that must treat those whom they govern with equal concern and respect, or, more generally, social and economic arrangements that must represent these in a concrete form. But this cannot be what is morally fundamental. The right to be treated in a certain way rests on a prior, even if somewhat indeterminate, right to certain opportunities of living.
>
> Mackie, 'Can There be a Right-Based Moral Theory?' in Waldron (ed) *Theories of Rights* 168

But while Dworkin would of course accept that governments ought to treat their citizens with equal concern and respect, it hardly follows that what he treats as fundamental is only a political right, or at least, that there is not a corresponding moral right. And in fact Dworkin's position seems to be that there is both a right to political independence and one to moral independence:

> People have the right not to suffer disadvantages in the distribution of social goods and opportunities, including disadvantages in the liberties permitted to them by the criminal law, just on the grounds that their officials or fellow-citizens think that their opinions about the right way for them to lead their own lives are ignoble or wrong. I shall call this putative right the right to moral independence.
>
> Dworkin *A Matter of Principle* 353

But behind Mackie's criticism there lies a deeper point, namely, a question of whether certain basic liberties must not be taken as fundamental, rather than an admittedly abstract conception of equality. This question is one which surfaces too in Hart's criticisms of Dworkin which we considered earlier. Nor is it surprising that it should be one that is often raised, given the very prominent position given to liberty in traditional liberal theories. We conclude this critique, therefore, with a critical discussion of Dworkin's views about liberty. This passage is one which follows an earlier section in which the author, Neil MacCormick, argues that Dworkin's concept of a right is insufficiently articulated given the importance he attaches to it:

These remarks are an essential preliminary to a consideration of Dworkin's political philosophy, which is an anti-utilitarian restatement of liberalism, in which he gives pride of place to every person's right to equal concern and respect with every other. So far indeed is he insistent upon the egalitarian aspect of his theory that he goes to the length of saying that 'In any strong sense of right, which would be competitive with the right to equality, there exists no general right to liberty at all'.[a] His argument for this view is that by his definition of 'right in the strong sense', there could be a right to liberty in general only if it were wrong for the state to limit any aspect of liberty on simple 'general interest' grounds. Yet laws restricting one's liberty to drive down Lexington Avenue and 'the vast bulk of the laws which diminish my liberty' are in fact justified 'as being in the general interest or welfare'.[b]

The point is dubitable on several counts: first, it turns on the inadequate analysis of 'right' already castigated above; secondly, it makes the somewhat facile assumption that the sole argument for a one-way street system, or other such legal restrictions, is a general interest one, whereas it might well be argued that traffic regulation systems, for example, are an attempt to balance such rights as the right to free and expeditious movement through cities and the right to bodily security (which is plainly put at some hazard by toleration of the motor car); and finally, most seriously, the argument does not treat on the same footing 'liberty' and 'equality'. Let us see how.

The argument concerning liberty is of the form: if there is a right to liberty in general, then no encroachment by government upon liberty can be justified simply on grounds of general interest. Some encroachments on liberty are justified simply on grounds of general interest. Therefore there is no right to liberty in general. To make out the case that 'equality in general' (which would be the relevant comparison) is the subject-matter of a right, Dworkin must therefore be prepared to argue that no departure by government from equality of treatment of citizens can ever be justified on grounds of general interest. I do not find him to make such an argument, and it would be difficult indeed to make and sustain the argument in relation to such matters as military conscription for defence of a nation, or taxation legislation, or legislation regulating different payment of different public-office-holders—and so on and so on.

Of course, Dworkin intends no such argument, for his contention is not that people have a right to equality of treatment in every respect, but only that people have a right to treatment as equally deserving an equal measure of concern and respect from the government. In short, he wishes to say that in this crucial matter, everyone has an equal right: an equal right to concern and respect.[c]

[a] *TRS*, p 269.
[b] Ibid.
[c] *TRS*, pp 180–3, 227, 272–8.

I agree with that, but at the cost of disagreeing with his assertion that the right to liberty cannot compete with the right to equality, for it turns out that they are by his lights on a similar footing: in *some* matters, people have a right to liberty; in *some* matters they have a right to equality.

Unlike Dworkin, I would be content with the traditional definition of liberty as what he tendentiously calls 'liberty as license'[d] rather than his 'liberty as independence'.[e] Liberty, in my judgment, is most simply to be understood as freedom from imposed constraint on one's actions, whether such constraints be normative (for example, laws imposing duties not to do this or that) or factual (for example, handcuffs on a prisoner's hands). To have liberty in some matters is to be free from constraint.

To establish that there is some right to liberty by my account of the matter, it is therefore necessary to establish that liberty is a good which individuals ought to have secured to them; and to establish that it is a fundamental right of everyone, it needs to be shown that liberty is a good for everyone, which ought to be secured to everyone.

There is one important reason why we should be inclined to think liberty both a good and a relatively basic good for everyone, namely, that people may have many various and mutually differing values, indeed they do; but whatever different things they value, they can pursue whatever values they have only on condition that they are not normatively or factually constrained against pursuing them. So, for everyone, liberty to pursue what they value is a good precisely because it is a condition of getting anything else they think good.

But to say that everyone ought to be free to pursue whatever he/she thinks good is evidently absurd because the satisfaction of some people's ideals or desires may result in the imposition of constraints by them on other people. Therefore it is necessary to stipulate that everyone's liberty should be constrained at least within such limits as prevent the imposition of unequal constraints on others.

This stipulation does indeed turn upon recognition that each person does have a right to equal respect with every other, has indeed an equal right to the conditions of self-respect and of the contentment which resides in the ability to pursue his or her own conception of what is a full and rewarding life. But that is a ground for prescribing the *universality* within a population of the right to liberty, not a ground for perceiving liberty as the subject-matter of right. Liberty is not good because people are to be treated as equals. Rather, it is because liberty is a good and because people ought to be treated as equals that there is, with certain qualifications, a right to equal liberty.

What then are the qualifications? First, there are exceptions for children and persons of unsound mind justified by reference to the interests of such persons. Secondly, there is the Rawlsian qualification that within a set of institutions designed for the protection of liberty, it may be legitimate to impose special restrictions on and to give special privileges to those who hold particular institutional offices: eg judges are (rightly) subjected to restrictions on their political activity and granted special privileges in relation to their utterances in their capacity as judges.[f] Thirdly, there are rights which compete with the right to liberty, especially those concerning fair shares in economic goods.

[d] *TRS*, pp 262, 267–8.
[e] *TRS*, p 263.
[f] J Rawls, *A Theory of Justice* (Oxford, 1971), p 302; cf ch 5 above.

The third of these points is worth pursuing. Liberty is one of the conditions of self-respect and the 'pursuit of contentment' as delineated above. But so is life, and so are the means essential to a tolerably commodious existence. A starving peasant may have the fullest possible freedom of speech, but writing letters to the editor of the local paper is not his foremost concern. For him to have an equal opportunity of self-respect with a well-heeled businessman, it is essential to him to have more money, more food, and the chance to sustain himself reasonably commodiously by his own work.

It is at least open to argument that a legal order which maximizes the freedom of property-owners to do what they will with their own and which encourages the fullest possible freedom of market transactions will fail to secure for the starving peasant the degree of equality with the businessman which has been postulated. To that extent and within such spheres the right to liberty collides or competes with the right to such a share in general economic resources as is a condition of one's self-respect and pursuit of contentment. Therefore there is good ground for arguing that liberty of property-owners and market liberties ought to be restricted to whatever extent is necessary to secure other no less basic rights to individuals.

This can be argued in a different way: the existence of a liberty to do X being defined solely in terms of the absence of constraints (normative or factual) against doing X, it is evident that one can be free to do X without being capable of doing it. I may be free to swim across the Atlantic without being capable of doing it. But a legal order may secure equality of liberty without in any degree securing an equal capability to exercise the liberties secured.[8] Black children of a given level of native intellectual capability may under a particular system of public education turn out to be incapable of exercising the liberty to enter a professional training which some white children may be capable of exercising, not because of greater native endowments but because of better schooling and greater environmental advantage. And so on.

On the basis of either of the foregoing arguments, or both of them, it is possible to argue for some restrictions either on the general scheme of legal liberty, or on the particular exercise of particular liberties, in the cause of securing economic fairness in general and of making fair allowance for socially induced differences of capability to exercise legal liberties. In constructing a fair legal and social order we inevitably find that there are goods other than the liberties of individuals which compete for recognition. But, so far as economic goods are concerned, the range of possible competition is restricted. Freedom of speech, freedom from arbitrary arrest and seizure, freedom of religion, conscience, and opinion, freedom to come and go in public places as one chooses, political rights of participation, and such like, are in principle neutral as between different systems of distribution and allocation of economic goods. Hence it is always a bogus argument that 'bourgeois liberties' such as these are inimical to a fair distribution of economic goods, or *a fortiori* that liberty in these respects is a mere adjunct of a bourgeois system of private ownership of the means of production, distribution, and exchange. It is an equally bad argument to contend, as some Conservatives appear to do, that liberty in the former respects is logically impossible without the liberties implicit in a private property system.

[8] This parallels Rawls's point about the distinction between the existence and the 'worth' of a liberty: ibid, pp 204 f; Cf Hart, 'Are there any Natural Rights?', 64 Philos Rev (1955), 175, and MacCormick, *H L A Hart* (London, 1981), pp 9–10.

The rhetoric of the indivisibility of liberty, to which Dworkin objects,[h] makes just that mistake. I wholeheartedly agree with him as to the absurdity of treating all liberties connected with property and the market as being essential to a just and liberal ordering of society, but I venture to think that the conclusion he reaches is preferable to the method of his argument for it. Liberty is a good, and people do have a right to it, but only within an order in which each has in principle an equal liberty, subject to the exception for children and other *incapaces*, subject to the Rawlsian qualification, and subject to other requirements of justice, especially economic fairness; but the last qualification operates only as against those aspects of liberty which can conflict with our favoured conception of economic fairness. Certainly, the idea of *equal* liberty for *everyone* requires as a prior postulate an equal right of everyone to self-respect and to respect from others. But to say, or even to seem to say, that that makes liberty in general subordinate to equality in general would be absurd.

Finally, one aspect of Dworkin's argument for the right to 'liberty as independence' should be challenged. He argues, in effect, that rights of self-expression always predominate over other rights. This he takes to follow from his interesting distinction between 'personal preferences' and 'external preferences'.[i] Preferences to the former kind concern how I want my life to be, preferences of the latter kind concern how I want other people to live, or what kind of relations I prefer to have with other people. If a person wants to be a lawyer, that is a personal preference. If a person wants all lawyers to be white men, that is an external preference.

One of the quarrels which Dworkin picks with utilitarianism is that in principle it equates personal and external preferences in prescribing principles of governmental action. Thus even if all blacks wanted to be lawyers, a scheme which admitted no blacks to the legal profession would satisfy more preferences if all the whites wanted there to be no black lawyers, and if whites were in the majority. But such a scheme would involve systematically refusing 'equal concern and respect' to the minority, in this case an ethnic minority. And so it would be wrong.

Dworkin argues that it would be wrong because it involves a kind of systematic double counting of majority preferences.[j] They get to be what they want to be (or at least get a chance of being it) in virtue of the weight of their personal preferences. But they also stop the minority, or some members of it, from getting to be what they want to be, in virtue of the weight of their external preferences. Since this is unfair, Dworkin argues that in principle all external preferences ought to be omitted in determining any public course of action. But since in a democratic system this is impossible in practice, the device of entrenched rights must be resorted to in order to secure minorities against the baneful restrictions entailed by majorities' external preferences. And, in turn, this leads to particular interpretations of the rights entrenched in the US Constitution.

Thus, in relation to the right of free speech Dworkin in effect argues that, short of inflicting physical danger on other people, demonstrators must have the right not only to say what they like but to express their position how they like, however that may be.

---

[h] *TRS*, pp 277–8.
[i] *TRS*, pp 234–8; also ch 11.
[j] Ibid.

It may be said that the anti-riot law leaves [a person] free to express [his] principles in a non-provocative way. But that misses the connection between expression and dignity. A man cannot express himself freely when he cannot match his rhetoric to his outrage, or when he must trim his sails to protect values he counts as nothing next to those he is trying to vindicate. It is true that some political dissenters speak in ways that shock the majority, but it is arrogant for the majority to suppose that the orthodox methods of expression are proper ways to speak, for this is a denial of equal concern and respect.[k]

This looks like an attractive argument. But how far does it go? What if the majority of people in a town prefer a beautiful old terrace to stand as it is, whereas a property-developer wants to tear it down to put up a new office block? The developer is also an architect, and claims that carrying out this piece of building here is essential to his self-expression. For my part, I would have no hesitation in saying that the property-developer has no absolute right worthy of entrenchment as against the wishes of the majority. Yet theirs are 'external preferences' and his are 'personal preferences', if I have the distinction aright.

The case seems to be one which casts doubt on the pleasing simplicity of the 'personal' versus 'external' distinction as between preferences. We all live in this town and necessarily share in the physical environment which it offers. Either the environment contains these historically interesting and aesthetically pleasing houses, or it contains the office block, but not both. There is as much risk that the property-developer will fail to show full and proper respect to his fellow citizens as vice versa. And somebody's preferences are going to lose out in the end.

I cannot bring myself to resist the belief that for each of us a physical and social environment which is pleasing to us is a good of the kind which may properly be the subject-matter of rights. So far as concerns public and visible additions to the environment or public actings which necessarily impinge upon all and sundry I cannot see the overwhelming justice of the view which says that everyone must always be free to choose whatever mode of self-expression he or she may choose. Thus for example it appears to me that some forms of obscenity law and of environmental protection law may be justified although they do impose limits on the manner of individuals' self-expression; but they must not limit the substance of what may be said or thought.

This requires an admission that environmental goods may be brought into the balance against the good of freedom of action, which is no doubt a dangerous admission which can readily be abused. But to the extent that constraints are placed only on actings in public and are placed equally on all, such constraints are not inimical to the essential equality of liberty for which I have argued.

TAKING THE 'RIGHTS THESIS' SERIOUSLY

With some caution, therefore, I would make that admission. In making it I am driven to conclude that Dworkin's distinction between external and personal preferences, at least as he has so far drawn it, is too crude to be acceptable. Applied to contexts other than those to which he applies it, it appears to yield unacceptable results.

MacCormick 'Taking the Rights Thesis Seriously' in *Legal Rights and Social Democracy*
145–153

---

[k] *TRS*, p 201.

Chapter 11
Nozick's theory of justice

The theory of justice presented in Robert Nozick's *Anarchy, State and Utopia* is inextricably intertwined with his political philosophy. This is so because he argues that *only* the so-called 'minimal' or 'nightwatchman' State is morally justified; for while the minimal State is preferable to anarchy, any State with powers stronger than those it has would violate principles of justice, and violate individual rights.

As we shall see, Nozick's theory develops the idea that justice is essentially a matter of *entitlement*; and since questions of entitlement are largely historical, his theory is in that sense an historical one. It is also a theory that is opposed to the forcible transfer of goods in order to achieve distributive justice. For instance, the kind of transfer in favour of the less well off that would be needed to implement Rawls's Difference Principle is not acceptable to Nozick, since such transfers would call for a State that is stronger than a minimal one. Not surprisingly, therefore, *Anarchy, State and Utopia* contains among other things a sustained critique of Rawls's *A Theory of Justice*.

The central question of political philosophy that Nozick raises is that of the legitimacy of a state of any kind:

> The fundamental question of political philosophy, one that precedes questions about how the state should be organized, is whether there should be any state at all. Why not have anarchy?

> Nozick *Anarchy, State and Utopia* 4

Though Nozick disagrees with the anarchist in thinking that there is a legitimate form of State, he shares a fundamental assumption with him, namely that 'Individuals have rights, and that there are things no person or group may do to them (without violating those rights)' (ix). But whereas the anarchist believes that any kind of State will violate the rights of individuals, Nozick argues that the minimal State does not. His demonstration that the minimal State does not violate fundamental rights is, therefore, also a refutation of anarchism.

This demonstration imagines that things are as the anarchist would wish them to be, and that men live in a state of nature very much like that described by Locke (10). In the state of nature individuals are free to pursue their interests so long as they do not harm the health, life, liberty or possessions of another. If, on the other hand, an individual is injured he is entitled to retaliate; though such retaliation should go no further than is necessary to secure compensation and restraint in the future. It is assumed that in this state people usually, though not invariably, respect each other's rights.

If this is an optimistic assumption, it is one the anarchist would make also. Moreover, it is a reasonable one given Nozick's overall strategy, which does not try to show that the state of nature is impossible, but rather that if such a state existed the minimal State would emerge from it in a morally permissible way under the pressure of rational self-interest. The anarchist can, therefore, have no rational objection to the minimal State, since not only does it have clear advantages over the state of nature, but its emergence from the latter sacrifices nothing that the anarchist values.

Clearly, to be morally permissible from the point of view of the anarchist the emergence of the minimal State should not violate any rights, and, of course, Nozick accepts that this is so. Indeed, he argues not only that individuals have rights, but that respect for them requires one to '. . . focus on the fact that there are distinct individuals, each with his own life *to lead*' (34). However, this 'libertarian constraint' is tempered by the fact that Nozick believes that there nevertheless are circumstances in which it is legitimate to restrict an individual's rights, even without his or her permission, provided that he or she is adequately compensated; and if there is a point at which the anarchist might be expected to be suspicious of Nozick's overall argument it is surely this! On the other hand, what Nozick concedes to the anarchist, the existence of full-blooded individual rights, is not something that can simply be taken for granted. So before we consider his account of how the minimal State would emerge from the state of nature in detail, we must consider three of the key ideas employed in that account, viz individual rights, compensation and the inviolability of persons.

RIGHTS, COMPENSATION AND PERSONS

(a) Rights and persons

The key idea which underpins Nozick's conception of a right is that of a moral side constraint, that is of a condition that has to be respected whatever the circumstances. Since they are side constraints the violation of an individual's rights can never be justified on the utilitarian ground that it would improve aggregate welfare; hence, the non-violation of rights has priority over the pursuit of any goal. But not only does the concept of rights as side constraints lead to the rejection of (i) traditional utilitarianism, it leads also to the rejection of (ii) Rawls's Difference Principle which forces some to contribute to the welfare of others, and (iii) to allowing any violation of rights because it results in a reduction in the total number of rights violations in a society—this would amount to a 'utilitarianism of rights' and should, according to Nozick, be rejected on the same grounds as utilitarianism.

But why suppose that there are any rights with the status of side constraints? Nozick's answer to this question appeals to the Kantian conception of persons as ends in themselves. Because persons are ends in themselves, they should never be used as means to achieve the goals of others without their consent. So that though it is of course desirable that someone who is well off makes voluntary donations to the poor, it is simply wrong from this perspective to make him do so if he does not wish to.

The following extract begins by developing the idea of rights as side constraints, and then goes on to ask why rights should be treated as side constraints. The opening sentence is an answer to the question whether someone would be consistent if he maintained that though it is right to purchase protection against rights violations for him or herself, it is wrong to provide protection for those who have not purchased it. For given the importance such a person attaches to rights, is it defensible for him to leave another person's rights unprotected?

344 Nozick's theory of justice

This question assumes that a moral concern can function only as a moral *goal*, as an end state for some activities to achieve as their result. It may, indeed, seem to be a necessary truth that 'right,' 'ought,' 'should,' and so on, are to be explained in terms of what is, or is intended to be, productive of the greatest good, with all goals built into the good.[1] Thus it is often thought that what is wrong with utilitarianism (which *is* of this form) is its too narrow conception of good. Utilitarianism doesn't, it is said, properly take rights and their nonviolation into account; it instead leaves them a derivative status. Many of the counterexample cases to utilitarianism fit under this objection, for example, punishing an innocent man to save a neighborhood from a vengeful rampage. But a theory may include in a primary way the nonviolation of rights, yet include it in the wrong place and the wrong manner. For suppose some condition about minimizing the total (weighted) amount of violations of rights is built into the desirable end state to be achieved. We then would have something like a 'utilitarianism of rights'; violations of rights (to be *minimized*) merely would replace the total happiness as the relevant end state in the utilitarian structure. (Note that we do not hold the nonviolation of our rights as our sole greatest good or even rank it first lexicographically to exclude trade-offs, if there is some desirable society we would choose to inhabit even though in it some rights of ours sometimes are violated, rather than move to a desert island where we could survive alone.) This still would require us to violate someone's rights when doing so minimizes the total (weighted) amount of the violation of rights in the society. For example, violating someone's rights might deflect others from *their* intended action of gravely violating rights, or might remove their motive for doing so, or might divert their attention, and so on. A mob rampaging through a part of town killing and burning *will* violate the rights of those living there. Therefore, someone might try to justify his punishing another *he* knows to be innocent of a crime that enraged a mob, on the grounds that punishing this innocent person would help to avoid even greater violations of rights by others, and so would lead to a minimum weighted score for rights violations in the society.

In contrast to incorporating rights into the end state to be achieved, one might place them as side constraints upon the actions to be done: don't violate constraints *C*. The rights of others determine the constraints upon your actions. (A *goal-directed* view with constraints added would be: among those acts available to you that don't violate constraints *C*, act so as to maximize goal *G*. Here, the rights of others would constrain your goal-directed behavior. I do not mean to imply that the correct moral view includes mandatory goals that must be pursued, even within the constraints.) This view differs from one that tries to build the side constraints *C into* the goal *G*. The side-constraint view forbids you to violate these moral constraints in the pursuit of your goals; whereas the view whose objective is to minimize the violation of these rights allows you to violate the rights (the constraints) in order to lessen their total violation in the society.[a]

[a] Unfortunately, too few models of the structure of moral views have been specified heretofore, though there are surely other interesting structures. Hence an argument for a side-constraint structure that consists largely in arguing against an end-state maximization structure is inconclusive, for these alternatives are not exhaustive. (On page 46 we describe a view which fits neither structure happily.) An array of structures must be precisely formulated and investigated; perhaps some novel structure then will seem most appropriate.

---

[1] For a clear statement that this view is mistaken, see John Rawls *A Theory of Justice* (Cambridge, Mass: Harvard University Press), pp 30, 565–566.

The claim that the proponent of the ultraminimal state is inconsistent, we now can see, assumes that he is a 'utilitarian of rights.' It assumes that his goal is, for example, to minimize the weighted amount of the violation of rights in the society, and that he should pursue this goal even through means that themselves violate people's rights. Instead, he may place the nonviolation of rights as a constraint upon action, rather than (or in addition to) building it into the end state to be realized. The position held by this proponent of the ultraminimal state will be a consistent one if his conception of rights holds that your being *forced* to contribute to another's welfare violates your rights, whereas someone else's not providing you with things you need greatly, including things essential to the protection of your rights, does not *itself* violate your rights, even though it avoids making it more difficult for someone else to violate them. (That conception will be consistent provided it does not construe the monopoly element of the ultraminimal state as itself a violation of rights.) That it is a consistent position does not, of course, show that it is an acceptable one.

WHY SIDE CONSTRAINTS?

Isn't it *irrational* to accept a side constraint C, rather than a view that directs minimizing the violations of C? (The latter view treats C as a condition rather than a constraint.) If nonviolation of C is so important, shouldn't that be the goal? How can a concern for the nonviolation of C lead to the refusal to violate C even when this would prevent other more extensive violations of C? What is the rationale for placing the nonviolation of rights as a side constraint upon action instead of including it solely as a goal of one's actions? Side constraints upon action reflect the underlying Kantian principle that individuals are ends and not merely means; they may not be sacrificed or used for the achieving of other ends without their consent. Individuals are inviolable. More should be said to illuminate this talk of ends and means. Consider a prime example of a means, a tool. There is no side constraint on how we may use a tool, other than the moral constraints on how we may use it upon others. There are procedures to be followed to preserve it for future use ('don't leave it out in the rain'), and there are more and less efficient ways of using it. But there is no limit on what we may do to it to best achieve our goals. Now imagine that there was an overrideable constraint C on some tool's use. For example, the tool might have been lent to you only on the condition that C not be violated unless the gain

---

The issue of whether a side-constraint view can be put in the form of the goal-without-side-contraint view is a tricky one. One might think, for example, that each person could distinguish in his goal between *his* violating rights and someone else's doing it. Give the former infinite (negative) weight in his goal, and no amount of stopping others from violating rights can outweigh his violating someone else's rights. In addition to a component of a goal receiving infinite weight, indexical expressions also appear, for example, '*my* doing something.' A careful statement delimiting 'constraint views' would exclude these gimmicky ways of transforming side constraints into the form of an end-state view as sufficient to constitute a view as end state. Mathematical methods of transforming a constrained minimization problem into a sequence of unconstrained minimizations of an auxiliary function are presented in Anthony Fiacco and Garth McCormick, *Nonlinear Programming: Sequential Unconstrained Minimization Techniques* (New York: Wiley, 1968). The book is interesting both for its methods and for their limitations in illuminating our area of concern; note the way in which the penalty functions include the constraints, the variation in weights of penalty functions (sec. 7.1), and so on.

The question of whether these side constraints are absolute, or whether they may be violated in order to avoid catastrophic moral horror, and if the latter, what the resulting structure might look like, is one I hope largely to avoid.

from doing so was above a certain specified amount, or unless it was necessary to achieve a certain specified goal. Here the object is not *completely* your tool, for use according to your wish or whim. But it is a tool nevertheless, even with regard to the overrideable constraint. If we add constraints on its use that may not be overridden, then the object may not be used as a tool *in those ways. In those respects*, it is not a tool at all. Can one add enough constraints so that an object cannot be used as a tool at all, in *any* respect?

Can behavior toward a person be constrained so that he is not to be used for any end except as he chooses? This is an impossibly stringent condition if it requires everyone who provides us with a good to approve positively of every use to which we wish to put it. Even the requirement that he merely should not object to any use we plan would seriously curtail bilateral exchange, not to mention sequences of such exchanges. It is sufficient that the other party stands to gain enough from the exchange so that he is willing to go through with it, even though he objects to one or more of the uses to which you shall put the good. Under such conditions, the other party is not being used solely as a means, in that respect. Another party, however, who would not choose to interact with you if he knew of the uses to which you *intend* to put his actions or good, *is* being used as a means, even if he receives enough to choose (in his ignorance) to interact with you. ('All along, you were just *using* me' can be said by someone who chose to interact only because he was ignorant of another's goals and of the uses to which he himself would be put.) Is it morally incumbent upon someone to reveal his intended uses of an interaction if he has good reason to believe the other would refuse to interact if he knew? Is he *using* the other person, if he does not reveal this? And what of the cases where the other does not choose to be of use at all? In getting pleasure from seeing an attractive person go by, does one use the other solely as a means?[b] Does someone so use an object of sexual fantasies? These and related questions raise very interesting issues for moral philosophy; but not, I think, for political philosophy.

Political philosophy is concerned only with *certain* ways that persons may not use others; primarily, physically aggressing against them. A specific side constraint upon action toward others expresses the fact that others may not be used in the specific ways the side constraint excludes. Side constraints express the inviolability of others, in the ways they specify. These modes of inviolability are expressed by the following injunction: 'Don't use people in specified ways.' An end-state view, on the other hand, would express the view that people are ends and not merely means (if it chooses to express this view at all), by a different injunction: 'Minimize the use in specified ways of persons as means.' Following this precept itself may involve using someone as a means in one of the ways specified. Had Kant held this view, he would have given the second formula of the categorical imperative as, 'So act as to minimize the use of humanity simply as a means,' rather than the one he actually used: 'Act in such a way that you always treat humanity, whether in your own person or in the person of any other, never simply as a means, but always at the same time as an end.'[c]

Side constraints express the inviolability of other persons. But why may not

[b] Which does which? Often a useful question to ask, as in the following:
—'What is the difference between a Zen master and an analytic philosopher?'
—'One talks riddles and the other riddles talks.'

[c] *Groundwork of the Metaphysic of Morals.* Translated by H. J. Paton, *The Moral Law* (London: Hutchinson, 1956), p 96.

one violate persons for the greater social good? Individually, we each sometimes choose to undergo some pain or sacrifice for a greater benefit or to avoid a greater harm: we go to the dentist to avoid worse suffering later; we do some unpleasant work for its results; some persons diet to improve their health or looks; some save money to support themselves when they are older. In each case, some cost is borne for the sake of the greater overall good. Why not, *similarly*, hold that some persons have to bear some costs that benefit other persons more, for the sake of the overall social good? But there is no *social entity* with a good that undergoes some sacrifice for its own good. There are only individual people, different individual people, with their own individual lives. Using one of these people for the benefit of others, uses him and benefits the others. Nothing more. What happens is that something is done to him for the sake of others. Talk of an overall social good covers this up. (Intentionally?) To use a person in this way does not sufficiently respect and take account of the fact that he is a separate person,[d] that his is the only life he has. *He* does not get some overbalancing good from his sacrifice, and no one is entitled to force this upon him—least of all a state or government that claims his allegiance (as other individuals do not) and that therefore scrupulously must be *neutral* between its citizens.

LIBERTARIAN CONSTRAINTS

The moral side constraints upon what we may do, I claim, reflect the fact of our separate existences. They reflect the fact that no moral balancing act can take place among us; there is no moral outweighing of one of our lives by others so as to lead to a greater overall *social* good. There is no justified sacrifice of some of us for others. This root idea, namely, that there are different individuals with separate lives and so no one may be sacrificed for others, underlies the existence of moral side constraints, but it also, I believe, leads to a libertarian side constraint that prohibits aggression against another.

The stronger the force of an end-state maximizing view, the more powerful must be the root idea capable of resisting it that underlies the existence of moral side constraints. Hence the more seriously must be taken the existence of distinct individuals who are not resources for others. An underlying notion sufficiently powerful to support moral side constraints against the powerful intuitive force of the end-state maximizing view will suffice to derive a libertarian constraint on aggression against another. Anyone who rejects *that particular* side constraint has three alternatives: (1) he must reject *all* side constraints; (2) he must produce a different explanation of why there are moral side constraints rather than simply a goal-directed maximizing structure, an explanation that doesn't itself entail the libertarian side constraint; or (3) he must accept the strongly put root idea about the separateness of individuals and yet claim that initiating aggression against another is compatible with this root idea. Thus we have a promising sketch of an argument from moral form to moral content: the form of morality includes F (moral side constraints); the best explanation[e] of morality's being F is p (a strong statement of the distinctness of individuals); and from p follows a particular moral content, namely, the libertarian constraint. The particular moral content gotten by this argument, which focuses upon the fact that there are distinct individuals each

[d] See John Rawls, *A Theory of Justice*, sects. 5, 6, 30.
[e] See Gilbert Harman, 'The Inference to the Best Explanation,' Philosophical Review, 1965, pp 88–95, and *Thought* (Princeton, NJ: Princeton University Press, 1973), chaps 8, 10.

with his *own* life to lead, will not be the *full* libertarian constraint. It will prohibit sacrificing one person to benefit another. Further steps would be needed to reach a prohibition on paternalistic aggression: using or threatening force for the benefit of the person against whom it is wielded. For this, one must focus upon the fact that there are distinct individuals, each with his own life *to lead*.

A nonaggression principle is often held to be an appropriate principle to govern relations among nations. What difference is there supposed to be between sovereign individuals and sovereign nations that makes aggression permissible among individuals? Why may individuals jointly, through their government, do to someone what no nation may do to another? If anything, there is a stronger case for nonaggression among individuals; unlike nations, they do not contain as parts individuals that others legitimately might intervene to protect or defend.

I shall not pursue here the details of a principle that prohibits physical aggression, except to note that it does not prohibit the use of force in defense against another party who is a threat, even though he is innocent and deserves no retribution. An *innocent threat* is someone who innocently is a causal agent in a process such that he would be an aggressor had he chosen to become such an agent. If someone picks up a third party and throws him at you down at the bottom of a deep well, the third party is innocent and a threat; had he chosen to launch himself at you in that trajectory he would be an aggressor. Even though the falling person would survive his fall onto you, may you use your ray gun to disintegrate the falling body before it crushes and kills you? Libertarian prohibitions are usually formulated so as to forbid using violence on innocent persons. But innocent threats, I think, are another matter to which different principles must apply.[f] Thus, a full theory in this area also must formulate the *different* constraints on response to innocent threats. Further complications concern *innocent shields of threats*, those innocent persons who themselves are nonthreats but who are so situated that they will be damaged by the only means available for stopping the threat. Innocent persons strapped onto the front of the tanks of aggressors so that the tanks cannot be hit without also hitting them are innocent shields of threats. (Some uses of force on people to get at an aggressor do not act upon innocent shields of threats; for example, an aggressor's innocent child who is tortured in order to get the aggressor to stop wasn't *shielding* the parent.) May one knowingly injure innocent shields? *If* one may attack an aggressor and injure an innocent shield, may the innocent shield fight back in self-defense (supposing that he cannot move against or fight the aggressor)? Do we get two persons battling each other in self-defense? Similarly, if you use force against an innocent threat to you, do you thereby become an innocent threat to him, so that he may now justifiably use additional force against you (supposing that he can do this, yet cannot prevent his original threateningness)? I tiptoe around these incredibly difficult issues here, merely noting that a view that says it makes nonaggression central must resolve them explicitly at some point.

Nozick *Anarchy, State and Utopia* 28–35

[f] 7. See Judith Jarvis Thomson, 'A Defense of Abortion,' 1 Philosophy and Public Affairs, no 2 (Fall 1971), 52–53. Since my discussion was written, John Hospers has discussed similar issues in a two-part essay, 'Some Problems about Punishment and the Retaliatory Use of Force,' Reason, November 1972 and January 1973.

(b) Compensation

Though Nozick believes that respect for a person requires that his interests should not be sacrificed to benefit another, he nevertheless thinks that there are circumstances in which it is legitimate to restrict someone's rights provided that he or she is compensated. The issues raised are clearly crucial ones for any rights theorist, for the fact that we often seem to restrict rights is difficult to reconcile with the view that they are side constraints, and the chapter in which Nozick discusses these issues is both subtle and complex.

The issue of compensation arises when the question is raised whether all activities likely to lead to the violations of an individual's rights should be prohibited. For to prohibit all such violations would have quite unacceptable consequences, since there are many things we do which are desirable in themselves, but which involve some degree of risk of the unintentional violation of the rights of another, eg the use of almost any form of transport. No doubt in some cases, eg cycling, the degree of risk is very small and the likely harm to others not great. In such cases there would be little justification for banning the activity, so the issue of compensation of those who can no longer do what they used to does not arise. But there are cases in which though the degree of risk is not large, the likely harm is great. Moreover, it is compounded by the fear that arises from the knowledge that the harm can arise in the way in question. For instance, what should a community do about epileptics who wish to drive cars? The likelihood of an attack while driving may be small, but the damage that could be caused by one is clearly very great. Nozick argues that it would be reasonable to restrict epileptics' rights to drive, provided that one compensated them for the restriction; but, as he makes clear at the end of the passage selected, it is not easy to formulate this principle in a satisfactory way:

THE PRINCIPLE OF COMPENSATION

Even when permitting an action provided compensation is paid . . . is prima facie more appropriate for a risky action than prohibiting it . . ., the issue of its being prohibited or permitted to someone still is not completely settled. For some persons will lack sufficient funds to pay the required compensation should the need arise; and they will not have purchased insurance to cover their obligations in that eventuality. May these persons be forbidden to perform the action? Forbidding an action to those not in a position to pay compensation differs from forbidding it unless compensation is paid to those actually harmed . . ., in that in the former case (but not in the latter) someone who lacks provision for paying compensation may be punished for his action even though it does not actually harm anyone or cross a boundary.

Does someone violate another's rights by performing an action without sufficient means or liability insurance to cover its risks? May he be forbidden to do this or punished for doing it? Since an enormous number of actions do increase risk to others, a society which prohibited such uncovered actions would ill fit a picture of a free society as one embodying a presumption in favor of liberty, under which people permissibly could perform actions so long as they didn't harm others in specified ways. Yet how can people be allowed to impose risks on others whom they are not in a position to compensate should the need arise? Why should some have to bear the costs of others' freedom? Yet to prohibit risky acts (because they are financially uncovered or because they are too risky) limits individuals' freedom to act, even though the actions actually might involve no cost at all to anyone else. Any given epileptic, for example, might drive throughout his lifetime without thereby harming anyone. Forbidding *him* to drive may not actually lessen the harm to others; and for all anyone knows, it doesn't. (It is true that we cannot identify in advance the individual who will turn out harmless, but why should he bear the full burden of our inability?) Prohibiting someone from driving in our automobile-dependent society, in order to reduce the risk to others, seriously disadvantages that person. It costs money to remedy these disadvantages— hiring a chauffeur or using taxis.

Consider the claim that a person must be compensated for the disadvantages imposed upon him by being forbidden to perform an activity for these sorts of reasons. Those who benefit from the reduction in risks to themselves have to 'make it up' to those who are restricted. So stated, the net has been cast too broadly. Must I really compensate someone when, in self-defense, I stop him from playing Russian roulette *on me*? If some person wishes to use a very risky but efficient (and if things go well *harmless*) process in manufacturing a product, must the residents near the factory compensate him for the economic loss he suffers from not being allowed to use the possibly dangerous process? Surely not.

. . . To arrive at an acceptable principle of compensation, we must delimit the class of actions covered by the claim. Some types of action are generally done, play an important role in people's lives, and are not forbidden to a person without seriously disadvantaging him. One principle might run: when an action of this type is forbidden to someone because it *might* cause harm to others and is especially dangerous when he does it, then those who forbid in order to gain increased security for themselves must compensate the person forbidden for the disadvantage they place him under. This principle is meant to cover forbidding the epileptic to drive while excluding the cases of involuntary Russian roulette and the special manufacturing process. The idea is to focus on important activities done by almost all, though some do them more dangerously than others. Almost everyone drives a car, whereas playing Russian roulette or using an especially dangerous manufacturing process is not a normal part of almost everyone's life.

Unfortunately this approach to the principle places a very great burden on the scheme used to classify actions. The fact that there is *one* description of a person's action that distinguishes it from the acts of others does *not* classify it as unusual and so outside the sphere of application of the principle. Yet it would be too strong to say, on the other hand, that any action falling under some description which almost every other person also instantiates is thereby shown to be usual and to fall within the compass of the principle. For unusual activities also fall under *some* descriptions that cover actions people normally do. Playing Russian roulette is a more dangerous way of 'having fun,' which others are allowed to do; and using the special manufacturing process is a more dangerous way of 'earning a living.' Almost any two actions can be construed as the same or different, depending upon whether they fall into the same or different subclasses in the background classification of actions. This possibility of diverse descriptions of actions prevents easy application of the principle as stated.

Nozick *Anarchy, State and Utopia* 78–82

THE DERIVATION OF THE MINIMAL STATE

For Nozick the minimal State is conceived of as

> The night-watchman state of classical liberal theory, limited to the functions of protecting all its citizens against violence, theft, fraud, and to the enforcement of contracts, and so on . . .
>
> Nozick *Anarchy, State and Utopia* 26

The aim of his derivation is, therefore, to show how such a State would emerge from the state of nature without violating any individual's rights by an invisible hand process, that is, a process which involves individuals pursuing their own self-interests which do not necessarily involve any collective goals. Thus, even if no one thought of bringing the minimal State into being, if Nozick is right, it would still have come into being as a result of each individual's pursuit of his or her own self-interest. The anarchist can, therefore, not object to the minimal State since the pursuit of individual self-interest leads to its emergence in a way which does not involve any rights violations.

Nozick's derivation is complex; and it is convenient to divide it into four stages.

(a) The inconveniences of the state of nature lead to the formation of protection agencies

Though it is assumed that in the state of nature people do generally respect each other's rights, there are inconveniences which stem from the lack of a legal system. For the understood natural law will not provide for every possible contingency, so that from time to time men and women will have to be judges in their own case. But it is difficult not to be partial in one's own case; as a result one is likely to overestimate the amount of harm done, and to try to exact excessive compensation:

> Thus private and personal enforcement of one's rights (including those rights that are violated when one is excessively punished) leads to feuds, to an endless series of acts of retaliation and exactions of compensation.
>
> Nozick *Anarchy, State and Utopia* 11

Since there is no agreed way of settling such disputes, they could be expected to go on interminably.

No doubt individuals will join mutual protection associations with family and friends, so that an individual does not have to rely just on himself to enforce his rights or to defend himself (p 12). But the basic problem emerges in a different form, since there will be many such associations each partial to its own side, and with no one to mediate between them, so that their feuds can be expected to be interminable like those of the Montagus and the Capulets. Further, the association will find it difficult to deal with disputes between its own members, or indeed with those of its members who are very disputatious. So because of these weaknesses of mutual protection associations there will emerge professional protection agencies which, in return for a fee, will arbitrate complaints made by its members, provide protection, and retaliate against those who violate the rights of its members.

(b)   One such agency becomes dominant in a given area

The way in which this happens, Nozick argues, is as follows:

Initially, several different protective associations or companies will offer their services in the same geographical area. What will occur when there is a conflict between clients of different agencies? Things are relatively simple if the agencies reach the same decision about the disposition of the case. (Though each might want to exact the penalty.) But what happens if they reach different decisions as to the merits of the case, and one agency attempts to protect its client while the other is attempting to punish him or make him pay compensation? Only three possibilities are worth considering:

1. In such situations the forces of the two agencies do battle. One of the agencies always wins such battles. Since the clients of the losing agency are ill protected in conflicts with clients of the winning agency, they leave their agency to do business with the winner.[a]
2. One agency has its power centered in one geographical area, the other in another. Each wins the battles fought close to its center of power, with some gradient being established.[b] People who deal with one agency but live under the power of the other either move closer to their own agency's home headquarters or shift their patronage to the other protective agency. (The border is about as conflict as one between states.)

In neither of these two cases does there remain very much geographical interspersal. Only one protective agency operates over a given geographical area.

3. The two agencies fight evenly and often. They win and lose about equally, and their interspersed members have frequent dealings and disputes with each other. Or perhaps without fighting or after only a few skirmishes the agencies realize that such battling will occur continually in the absence of preventive measures. In any case, to avoid frequent, costly, and wasteful battles the two agencies, perhaps through their executives, agree to resolve peacefully those cases about which they reach differing judgments. They agree to set up, and abide by the decisions of, some third judge or court to which they can turn when their respective judgments differ. (Or they might establish rules determining which agency has jurisdiction under which circumstances.)[c] Thus emerges a system of appeals courts and agreed upon rules about jurisdiction and the conflict of laws. Though different agencies operate, there is one unified federal judicial system of which they all are components.

In each of these cases, almost all the persons in a geographical area are under some common system that judges between their competing claims and *enforces* their rights. Out of anarchy, pressed by spontaneous groupings, mutual-protection associations, division of labor, market pressures,

---

[a] Exercise for the reader: describe how the considerations discussed here and below lead to each geographical area having one agency or a federal structure of agencies dominant within it, even if initially the area contains a group of agencies over which 'wins almost all the battles with' is a connected relation and a *nontransitive* one.

[b] See Kenneth B. Boulding, *Conflict and Defense* (New York: Harper, 1962), chap 12.

[c] For an indication of the complexity of such a body of rules, see American Law Institute, *Conflict of Laws; Second Restatement of the Law*, Proposed Official Draft, 1967–1969.

economies of scale, and rational self-interest there arises something very much resembling a minimal state or a group of geographically distinct minimal states. Why is this market different from all other markets? Why would a virtual monopoly arise in this market without the government intervention that elsewhere creates and maintains it?[d] The worth of the product purchased, protection against others, is *relative*: it depends upon how strong the others are. Yet unlike other goods that are comparatively evaluated, maximal competing protective services cannot coexist; the nature of the service brings different agencies not only into competition for customers' patronage, but also into violent conflict with each other. Also, since the worth of the less than maximal product declines disproportionately with the number who purchase the maximal product, customers will not stably settle for the lesser good, and competing companies are caught in a declining spiral. Hence the three possibilities we have listed.

Our story above assumes that each of the agencies attempts in good faith to act within the limits of Locke's law of nature.[e] But one 'protective association' might aggress against other persons. Relative to Locke's law of nature, it would be an outlaw agency. What actual counterweights would there be to its power? (What actual counterweights are there to the power of a state?) Other agencies might unite to act against it. People might refuse to deal with the outlaw agency's clients, boycotting them to reduce the probability of the agency's intervening in their own affairs. This might make it more difficult for the outlaw agency to get clients; but this boycott will seem an effective tool only on very optimistic assumptions about what cannot be kept secret, and about the costs to an individual of partial boycott as compared to the benefits of receiving the more extensive coverage offered by an 'outlaw' agency. If the 'outlaw' agency simply is an *open* aggressor, pillaging, plundering, and extorting under no plausible claim of justice, it will have a harder time than states. For the state's claim to legitimacy induces its citizens to believe they have some duty to obey its edicts, pay its taxes, fight its battles, and so on; and so some persons cooperate with it voluntarily. An openly aggressive agency could not depend upon, and would not receive, any such voluntary cooperation, since persons would view themselves simply as its victims rather than as its citizens.[f]

Nozick *Anarchy, State and Utopia* 15–17

[d] See Yale Brozen, 'Is Government the Source of Monopoly?' 5 The Intercollegiate Review, no 2 (1968–69), 67–78; Fritz Machlup, *The Political Economy of Monopoly* (Baltimore: Johns Hopkins Press, 1952).

[e] Locke assumed that the preponderant majority, though not all, of the persons living in the state of nature would accept the law of nature. See Richard Ashcroft, 'Locke's State of Nature,' American Political Science Review, September 1968, pp 898–915, especially pt I.

[f] See Morris and Linda Tannehill, *The Market for Liberty*; on the importance of voluntary cooperation to the functioning of governments see, for example, Adam Roberts, ed., *Civilian Resistance as National Defense* (Baltimore: Penguin Books, 1969) and Gene Sharp, *The Politics of Non-Violent Action* (Boston: Porter Sargent, 1973).

Is the emergence of a dominant protection agency tantamount to the emergence of the minimal State, the night-watchman State of classical liberal theory? Though a dominant protection agency performs many of the functions performed by such a State, there are, Nozick argues, two important differences; for the minimal State claims a monopoly of the use of force within its territory, and secondly, extends its protection to all of its citizens. But there seems no reason why a protection agency should claim a monopoly of the use of force; and even less reason why it should extend its services to those who judge they have no need of them and so do not purchase them.

So Nozick now has to show how a dominant protection agency could assume the functions of the minimal State; and the remaining two stages of his argument are devoted to explaining how this happens. However, the anarchist might be expected to peruse this part of the argument very carefully; for it has to meet two challenges which it is difficult to see can be met. First, the argument has to explain how in the process of making independents join (ie those who have not chosen to employ its services), it does not violate their rights. Second, how its provision of a universal service is not redistributive, since everyone gets the same service irrespective of his or her ability to pay. The way in which Nozick tries to meet these challenges is outlined in the following two sections.

(c) The dominant protection agency will only allow independents to enforce their rights against its clients if they judge that the procedures invoked are reliable and fair

Suppose an independent judges that his rights have been infringed by a member of an agency, and takes steps to enforce them. If the procedure the independent uses is one the agency judges to be reliable and fair, it can hardly object to what he does; but if it thinks it either unreliable or unfair it has a duty to protect its client. So in order to protect its clients the dominant agency will have in effect to approve all procedures adopted by an independent for enforcing his or her rights against its clients, so that it can stop the independent invoking procedures which are unreliable or unfair, and hence potentially damaging to its clients (p 108).

In so doing it does not claim a monopoly of power, since it does not prevent an independent from enforcing his or her own right, and so does not violate anyone's right. However, it does claim the right to approve any procedure invoked by anyone to enforce his or her rights. So though it does not have a *de jure* monopoly, it has a *de facto* one:

> There is no right the dominant protective association claims uniquely to possess. But its strength leads it to be the unique agent acting across the board to enforce a particular right. It is not merely that it *happens* to be the only exerciser of a right it grants that all possess; the nature of the right is such that once a dominant power emerges, it alone will actually exercise that right.
>
> Nozick *Anarchy, State and Utopia* 108

But given that the dominant agency does acquire a *de facto* monopoly of the procedures to be followed when enforcing a right in the way Nozick describes, two questions arise: Why should it in *addition* offer protection to independents who have not purchased it? And does not the *de facto* monopoly violate the rights of the independents to enforce their own rights?

(d) In return for the *de facto* monopoly of rights enforcement that it claims the dominant agency must offer the independents protection

The reason why it must is, of course, the principle of compensation; the risk of serious injustice arising if independents enforced their own rights is too great to allow them to do so, but they nevertheless must be compensated for the loss of their right:

PROTECTING OTHERS

If the protective agency deems the independents' procedures for enforcing their own rights insufficiently reliable or fair when applied to its clients, it will prohibit the independents from such self-help enforcement. The grounds for this prohibition are that the self-help enforcement imposes risks of danger on its clients. Since the prohibition makes it impossible for the independents credibly to threaten to punish clients who violate their rights, it makes them unable to protect themselves from harm and seriously disadvantages the independents in their daily activities and life. Yet it is perfectly possible that the independents' activities including self-help enforcement could proceed without anyone's rights being violated (leaving aside the question of procedural rights). According to our principle of compensation . . . in these circumstances those persons promulgating and benefiting from the prohibition must compensate those disadvantaged by it. The clients of the protective agency, then, must compensate the independents for the disadvantages imposed upon them by being prohibited self-help enforcement of their own rights against the agency's clients. Undoubtedly, the least expensive way to compensate the independents would be to *supply* them with protective services to cover those situations of conflict with the paying customers of the protective agency. This will be less expensive than leaving them unprotected against violations of their rights (by not punishing any client who does so) and then attempting to pay them afterwards to cover their losses through having (and being in a position in which they were exposed to having) their rights violated. If it were *not* less expensive, then instead of buying protective services, people would save their money and use it to cover their losses, perhaps by jointly pooling their money in an insurance scheme.

Nozick *Anarchy, State and Utopia* 110–111

Thus the dominant protection agency has assumed something very like the characteristics of the minimal State, for not only does it have a *de facto* monopoly of rights enforcement, it offers protection to all.

To the extent that the principle of compensation is questionable, then, of course, so is the final stage of Nozick's argument. Not only is the principle not an easy one to formulate (cf 1(b)) but it is far from clear that it excludes the kind of teleological considerations which appeal to utilitarians but which Nozick wishes to exclude (E Mack, 'Nozick on Unproductivity: the Unintended Consequences' in J Paul (ed) *Reading Nozick* 169). Moreover, does protection have to be offered irrespective of a person's ability to pay, so that even the minimal State is redistributive? Nozick argues that it is not; but there are many who remain unconvinced.

BEYOND THE MINIMAL STATE?

Since Nozick thinks that the minimal State is justified, so that anarchism has to be rejected, the question arises whether some stronger type of State is also justified, eg the Welfare State. Indeed, could we not in order to refute the proponent of the minimal State develop a similar type of argument to that employed by Nozick to refute the anarchist? Such an argument would show how the Welfare State could have emerged from the minimal State under the pressure of rational self-interest, and by a series of morally permissible steps. Since something like this seems to have happened in large parts of northern Europe, such an argument would not seem to be completely implausible. But plausible or not, Nozick thinks there is no such argument.[2] To see why he thinks this, it is necessary to turn to his theory of justice; for his objection to any State stronger than the minimal State is that it will inevitably violate principles of justice.

(a) Justice

We saw earlier that Nozick's theory of justice is an *entitlement* theory, and that moreover the kind of issues to do with entitlement it raises are historical ones, eg about the legitimacy of a person's title to something he possesses. Nozick contrasts entitlement theories with what he calls 'end state principles' (p 155). For instance, an egalitarian employs an end state principle when he assesses the justice of a state of affairs not in terms of the way in which people came to possess what they did, but in terms of the way in which the distribution is or is not an equal one. In other words, end state theorists are concerned with the structure of a certain distribution, rather than with the way it came about. Clearly, an end state principle is not historical, and so ignores entitlement. But there are, Nozick argues, historical principles of justice which are nevertheless not entitlement principles, so that they too have to be rejected:

PATTERNING

The entitlement principles of justice in holdings that we have sketched are historical principles of justice. To better understand their precise character, we shall distinguish them from another subclass of the historical principles. Consider, as an example, the principle of distribution according to moral merit. This principle requires that total distributive shares vary directly with moral merit; no person should have a greater share than anyone whose moral merit is greater. (If moral merit could be not merely ordered but measured on an interval or ratio scale, stronger principles could be formulated.) Or consider the principle that results by substituting 'usefulness to society' for 'moral merit' in the previous principle. Or instead of 'distribute according to moral merit,' or 'distribute according to usefulness to society,' we might consider 'distribute according to the weighted sum of moral merit, usefulness to society, and need,' with the weights of the different dimensions equal. Let us call a principle of distribution *patterned* if it specifies that a distribution is to vary along with some natural dimension, weighted sum of natural dimensions, or lexicographic ordering of natural dimensions. And let us say a distribution is patterned if it accords with some patterned principle. (I speak of natural dimensions, admittedly without a general criterion for them, because for any set of holdings some artificial dimensions can be gimmicked up to vary along with the distribution of the set.) The principle of distribution in accordance with moral merit is a patterned historical principle, which specifies a patterned distribution. 'Distribute according to I.Q.' is a patterned principle that looks to information not contained in distributional matrices. It is not historical, however, in that it does not look to any past actions creating differential entitlements to evaluate a distribution; it requires only distributional matrices whose columns are labeled by I.Q. scores. The distribution in a society, however, may be composed of such simple patterned distributions, without itself being simply patterned. Different sectors may operate different patterns, or some combination of patterns may operate in

[2] Nozick considers such a derivation, but since it involves somewhat arbitrary, not to say irrational, choices that people might have made, he does not think it is of any interest.

different proportions across a society. A distribution composed in this manner, from a small number of patterned distributions, we also shall term 'patterned.' And we extend the use of 'pattern' to include the overall designs put forth by combinations of end-state principles.

Almost every suggested principle of distributive justice is patterned: to each according to his moral merit, or needs, or marginal product, or how hard he tries, or the weighted sum of the foregoing, and so on. The principle of entitlement we have sketched is *not* patterned.[a] There is no one natural dimension or weighted sum or combination of a small number of natural dimensions that yields the distributions generated in accordance with the principle of entitlement. The set of holdings that results when some persons receive their marginal products, others win at gambling, others receive a share of their mate's income, others receive gifts from foundations, others receive interest on loans, others receive gifts from admirers, others receive returns on investment, others make for themselves much of what they have, others find things, and so on, will not be patterned.

Nozick Anarchy, State and Utopia 155–157

[a] One might try to squeeze a patterned conception of distributive justice into the framework of the entitlement conception, by formulating a gimmicky obligatory 'principle of transfer' that would lead to the pattern. For example, the principle that if one has more than the mean income one must transfer everything one holds above the mean to persons below the mean so as to bring them up to (but not over) the mean. We can formulate a criterion for a 'principle of transfer' to rule out such obligatory transfers, or we can say that no correct principle of transfer, no principle of transfer in a free society will be like this. The former is probably the better course, though the latter also is true.

Alternatively, one might think to make the entitlement conception instantiate a pattern, by using matrix entries that express the relative strength of a person's entitlements as measured by some real-valued function. But even if the limitation to natural dimensions failed to exclude this function, the resulting edifice would *not* capture our system of entitlements to *particular* things.

(b) Entitlement

Thus while almost every principle of distributive justice, whether historical or not, is patterned, taking into account such factors as ability to pay, merit and need, Nozick's theory is not patterned. The next extract expounds his theory in detail:

The term 'distributive justice' is not a neutral one. Hearing the term 'distribution,' most people presume that some thing or mechanism uses some principle or criterion to give out a supply of things. Into this process of distributing shares some error may have crept. So it is an open question, at least, whether *re*distribution should take place; whether we should do again what has already been done once, though poorly. However, we are not in the position of children who have been given portions of pie by someone who now makes last minute adjustments to rectify careless cutting. There is no *central* distribution, no person or group entitled to control all the resources, jointly deciding how they are to be doled out. What each person gets, he gets from others who give to him in exchange for something, or as a gift. In a free society, diverse persons control different resources, and new holdings arise out of the voluntary exchanges and actions of persons. There is no more a distributing or distribution of shares than there is a distributing of mates in a society in which persons choose whom they shall marry. The total result is the product of many individual decisions which the different individuals involved are entitled to make. Some uses of the term 'distribution,' it is true, do not imply a previous distributing appropriately judged by some criterion (for example, 'probability distribution'); nevertheless, despite the title of this chapter, it would be best to use a terminology that clearly is neutral. We shall speak of people's holdings; a principle of justice in holdings describes (part of) what justice tells us (requires) about holdings. I shall state first what I take to be the correct view about justice in holdings, and then turn to the discussion of alternate views.[a]

SECTION I

THE ENTITLEMENT THEORY

The subject of justice in holdings consists of three major topics. The first is the *original acquisition of holdings*, the appropriation of unheld things. This includes the issues of how unheld things may come to be held, the process, or processes, by which unheld things may come to be held, the things that may come to be held by these processes, the extent of what comes to be held by a particular process, and so on. We shall refer to the complicated truth about this topic, which we shall not formulate here, as the principle of justice in acquisition. The second topic concerns the *transfer of holdings* from one person to another. By what processes may a person transfer holdings to another? How may a person acquire a holding from another who holds it? Under this topic come general descriptions of voluntary exchange, and gift and (on the other hand) fraud, as well as reference to particular conventional details fixed upon in a given society. The complicated truth about this subject (with placeholders for conventional details) we shall call the principle of justice in transfer. (And we shall suppose it also includes principles governing how a person may divest himself of a holding, passing it into an unheld state.)

If the world were wholly just, the following inductive definition would exhaustively cover the subject of justice in holdings.

1. A person who acquires a holding in accordance with the principle of justice in acquisition is entitled to that holding.
2. A person who acquires a holding in accordance with the principle of justice in transfer, from someone else entitled to the holding, is entitled to the holding.
3. No one is entitled to a holding except by (repeated) applications of 1 and 2.

The complete principle of distributive justice would say simply that a distribution is just if everyone is entitled to the holdings they possess under the distribution.

A distribution is just if it arises from another just distribution by legitimate means. The legitimate means of moving from one distribution to another are specified by the principle of justice in transfer. The legitimate first 'moves' are specified by the principle of justice in acquisition.[b] Whatever arises from a just situation by just steps is itself just. The means of change specified by the principle of justice in transfer preserve justice. As correct rules of inference are truth-preserving, and any conclusion deduced via repeated application of such rules from only true premisses is itself true, so the means of transition from one situation to another specified by the principle of justice in transfer are

---

[a] The reader who has looked ahead and seen that the second part of this chapter discusses Rawls' theory mistakenly may think that every remark or argument in the first part against alternative theories of justice is meant to apply to, or anticipate, a criticism of Rawls' theory. This is not so; there are other theories also worth criticizing.

[b] Applications of the principle of justice in acquisition may also occur as part of the move from one distribution to another. You may find an unheld thing now and appropriate it. Acquisitions also are to be understood as included when, to simplify, I speak only of transitions by transfers.

justice-preserving, and any situation actually arising from repeated transitions in accordance with the principle from a just situation is itself just. The parallel between justice-preserving transformations and truth-preserving transformations illuminates where it fails as well as where it holds. That a conclusion could have been deduced by truth-preserving means from premises that are true suffices to show its truth. That from a just situation a situation *could* have arisen via justice-preserving means does *not* suffice to show its justice. The fact that a thief's victims voluntarily *could* have presented him with gifts does not entitle the thief to his ill-gotten gains. Justice in holdings is historical; it depends upon what actually has happened. We shall return to this point later.

Not all actual situations are generated in accordance with the two principles of justice in holdings: the principle of justice in acquisition and the principle of justice in transfer. Some people steal from others, or defraud them, or enslave them, seizing their product and preventing them from living as they choose, or forcibly exclude others from competing in exchanges. None of these are permissible modes of transition from one situation to another. And some persons acquire holdings by means not sanctioned by the principle of justice in acquisition. The existence of past injustice (previous violations of the first two principles of justice in holdings) raises the third major topic under justice in holdings: the rectification of injustice in holdings. If past injustice has shaped present holdings in various ways, some identifiable and some not, what now, if anything, ought to be done to rectify these injustices? What obligations do the performers of injustice have towards those whose position is worse than it would have been had the injustice not been done? Or, than it would have been had compensation been paid promptly? How, if at all, do things change if the beneficiaries and those made worse off are not the direct parties in the act of injustice, but, for example, their descendants? Is an injustice done to someone whose holding was itself based upon an unrectified injustice? How far back must one go in wiping clean the historical slate of injustices? What may victims of injustice permissibly do in order to rectify the injustices being done to them, including the many injustices done by persons acting through their government? I do not know of a thorough or theoretically sophisticated treatment of such issues.[c] Idealizing greatly, let us suppose theoretical investigation will produce a principle of rectification. This principle uses historical information about previous situations and injustices done in them (as defined by the first two principles of justice and rights against interference), and information about the actual course of events that flowed from these injustices, until the present, and it yields a description (or descriptions) of holdings in the society. The principle of rectification presumably will make use of its best estimate of subjunctive information about what would have occurred (or a probability distribution over what might have occurred, using the expected value) if the injustice had not taken place. If the actual description of holdings turns out not to be one of the descriptions yielded by the principle, then one of the descriptions yielded must be realized.[d]

[c] See, however, the useful book by Boris Bittker, *The Case for Black Reparations* (New York: Random House, 1973).

[d] If the principle of rectification of violations of the first two principles yields more than one description of holdings, then some choice must be made as to which of these is to be realized. Perhaps the sort of considerations about distributive justice and equality that I argue against play a legitimate role in *this* subsidiary choice. Similarly, there may be room for such considerations in deciding which otherwise arbitrary features a statute will embody, when such features are unavoidable because other considerations do not specify a precise line; yet a line must be drawn.

The general outlines of the theory of justice in holdings are that the holdings of a person are just if he is entitled to them by the principles of justice in acquisition and transfer, or by the principle of rectification of injustice (as specified by the first two principles). If each person's holdings are just, then the total set (distribution) of holdings is just.

Nozick *Anarchy, State and Utopia* 149–153

It is clear why Nozick's theory is not a patterned one. For the ways in which people may legitimately acquire their holdings are very diverse. For instance, I may have inherited my car, or received it as a present, or won it gambling or as a prize, or purchased it from a garage with money I have saved, etc. Moreover, Nozick argues, it is hard to see how someone who values liberty can object to the entitlement theory, whatever are the other principles of justice that he subscribes to:

For suppose a distribution favored by one of these non-entitlement conceptions is realized. Let us suppose it is your favorite one and let us call this distribution D_1; perhaps everyone has an equal share, perhaps shares vary in accordance with some dimension you treasure. Now suppose that Wilt Chamberlain is greatly in demand by basketball teams, being a great gate attraction. (Also suppose contracts run only for a year, with players being free agents.) He signs the following sort of contract with a team: In each home game, twenty-five cents from the price of each ticket of admission goes to him. (We ignore the question of whether he is 'gouging' the owners, letting them look out for themselves.) The season starts, and people cheerfully attend his team's games; they buy their tickets, each time dropping a separate twenty-five cents of their admission price into a special box with Chamberlain's name on it. They are excited about seeing him play; it is worth the total admission price to them. Let us suppose that in one season one million persons attend his home games, and Wilt Chamberlain winds up with $250,000, a much larger sum than the average income and larger even than anyone else has. Is he entitled to this income? Is this new distribution D_2, unjust? If so, why? There is *no* question about whether each of the people was entitled to the control over the resources they held in D_1; because that was the distribution (your favorite) that (for the purposes of argument) we assumed was acceptable. Each of these persons *chose* to give twenty-five cents of their money to Chamberlain. They could have spent it on going to the movies, or on candy bars, or on copies of *Dissent* magazine, or of *Monthly Review*. But they all, at least one million of them, converged on giving it to Wilt Chamberlain in exchange for watching him play basketball. If D_1 was a just distribution, and people voluntarily moved from it to D_2, transferring parts of their shares they were given under D_1 (what was it for if not to do something with?), isn't D_2 also just? If the people were entitled to dispose of the resources to which they were entitled (under D_1), didn't this include their being entitled to give it to, or exchange it with, Wilt Chamberlain? Can anyone else complain on grounds of justice? Each other person already has his legitimate share under D_1. Under D_1, there is nothing that anyone has that anyone else has a claim of justice against. After someone transfers something to Wilt Chamberlain, third parties *still* have their legitimate shares; *their* shares are not changed. By what process could such a transfer among two persons give rise to a legitimate claim of distributive justice on a portion of what was transferred, by a third party who had no claim of justice on any holding of the others *before* the transfer?[a] To cut off objections irrelevant here, we might imagine the exchanges occurring in a socialist society, after hours. After playing whatever basketball he does in his daily work, or doing whatever other daily work he does, Wilt Chamberlain decides to put in *overtime* to earn additional money. (First his work quota is set; he works time over that.) Or imagine it is a skilled juggler people like to see, who puts on shows after hours.

Why might someone work overtime in a society in which it is assumed their needs are satisfied? Perhaps because they care about things other than needs. I like to write in books that I read, and to have easy access to books for browsing at odd hours. It would be very pleasant and convenient to have the resources of Widener Library in my back yard. No society, I assume, will provide such resources close to each person who would like them as part of his regular allotment (under D_1). Thus, persons either must do without some extra things that they want, or be allowed to do something extra to get some of these things. On what basis could be the inequalities that would eventuate be forbidden? Notice also that small factories would spring up in a socialist society, unless forbidden. I melt down some of my personal possessions (under D_1) and build a machine out of the material. I offer you, and others, a philosophy lecture once a week in exchange for your cranking the handle on my machine, whose products I exchange for yet other things, and so on. (The raw materials used by the machine are given to me by others who possess them under D_1, in exchange for hearing lectures.) Each person might participate to gain things over and above their allotment under D_1. Some persons even might want to leave their job in socialist industry and work full time in this private sector. I shall say something more about these issues in the next chapter. Here I wish merely to note how private property even in means of production would occur in a socialist society that did not forbid people to use as they wished some of the resources they are given under the socialist distribution D_1.[b] The socialist society would have to forbid capitalist acts between consenting adults.

Nozick *Anarchy, State and Utopia* 160–163

[a] Might not a transfer have instrumental effects on a third party, changing his feasible options? (But what if the two parties to the transfer independently had used their holdings in this fashion?) I discuss this question below, but note here that this question concedes the point for distributions of ultimate intrinsic noninstrumental goods (pure utility experiences, so to speak) that are transferable. It also might be objected that the transfer might make a third party more envious because it worsens his position relative to someone else. I find it incomprehensible how this can be thought to involve a claim of justice. On envy, see Chapter 8.

Here and elsewhere in this chapter, a theory which incorporates elements of pure procedural justice might find what I say acceptable, *if* kept in its proper place; that is, if background institutions exist to ensure the satisfaction of certain conditions on distributive shares. But if these institutions are not themselves the sum or invisible-hand result of people's voluntary (nonaggressive) actions, the constraints they impose require justification. At no point does *our* argument assume any background institutions more extensive than those of the minimal night-watchman state, a state limited to protecting persons against murder, assault, theft, fraud, and so forth.

[b] See the selection from John Henry MacKay's novel, *The Anarchists*, reprinted in Leonard Krimmerman and Lewis Perry, eds., *Patterns of Anarchy* (New York: Doubleday Anchor Books, 1966), in which an individualist anarchist presses upon a communist anarchist the following question: 'Would you, in the system of society which you call "free Communism" prevent individuals from exchanging their labor among themselves by means of their own medium of exchange? And further: Would you prevent them from occupying land for the purpose of personal use?' The novel continues: '[The] question was not to be escaped. If he answered "Yes!" he admitted that society had the right of control over the individual and threw overboard the autonomy of the individual which he had always zealously defended; if on the other hand, he

(c) Acquisition

The account given to date of Nozick's theory of justice is radically incomplete: for without an account of what justice in acquisition, transfer, and rectification is we cannot tell what is just according to his theory. Therefore, though it certainly constitutes less than a full account, the remarks Nozick makes about the justice of acquisition are of great interest. They begin with a discussion of John Locke's view that one acquires a property right in an object by mixing his labour with it. There are, Nozick concedes, difficult questions about how much of an object or resource that one can acquire in this sort of way; if I take a bucket of water from a lake in a wilderness do I thereby acquire a property right in the lake, as well as the water in the bucket? In this context Nozick discusses an important proviso that Locke places on the acquisition of property, namely, that one must leave enough of the resource one has acquired for others. This proviso has, he argues, a stronger and a weaker version; and though it may not be clear how Locke himself interpreted the proviso, Nozick argues that any adequate theory of justice must include the weaker version of it. However, this places constraints on the theory of justice in transfer; for clearly if, as the weak version of the proviso entails, it was wrong for me to appropriate the only source of an essential commodity in the State of Nature and then deny others the use of it, it cannot be right for me to acquire by transfer the only source and then deny others the right to use it. The following extract begins with a discussion of Locke's proviso:

It will be implausible to view improving an object as giving full ownership to it, if the stock of unowned objects that might be improved is limited. For an object's coming under one person's ownership changes the situation of all others. Whereas previously they were at liberty (in Hohfeld's sense) to use the object, they now no longer are. This change in the situation of others (by removing their liberty to act on a previously unowned object) need not worsen their situation. If I appropriate a grain of sand from Coney Island, no one else may now do as they will with *that* grain of sand. But there are plenty of other grains of sand left for them to do the same with. Or if not grains of sand, then other things. Alternatively, the things I do with the grain of sand I appropriate might improve the position of others, counterbalancing their loss of the liberty to use that grain. The crucial point is whether appropriation of an unowned object worsens the situation of others.

Locke's proviso that there be 'enough and as good left in common for others' (sect. 27) is meant to ensure that the situation of others is not worsened. (If this proviso is met is there any motivation for his further condition of nonwaste?) It is often said that this proviso once held but now no longer does. But there appears to be an argument for the conclusion that if the proviso no longer holds, then it cannot ever have held so as to yield permanent and inheritable property rights. Consider the first person Z for whom there is not enough and

answered "No!" he admitted the right of private property which he had just denied so emphatically. . . . Then he answered "In Anarchy any number of men must have the right of forming a voluntary association, and so realizing their ideas in practice. Nor can I understand how any one could justly be driven from the land and house which he uses and occupies . . . every serious man must declare himself for Socialism, and thereby for force and against liberty, or for Anarchism, and thereby for liberty and against force."' In contrast, we find Noam Chomsky writing, 'Any consistent anarchist must oppose private ownership of the means of production,' 'the consistent anarchist then . . will be a socialist . . . of a particular sort.' Introduction to Daniel Guerin, *Anarchism: From Theory to Practice* (New York: Monthly Review Press, 1970), pages xiii, xv.

as good left to appropriate. The last person Y to appropriate left Z without his previous liberty to act on an object, and so worsened Z's situation. So Y's appropriation is not allowed under Locke's proviso. Therefore the next to last person X to appropriate left Y in a worse position, for X's act ended permissible appropriation. Therefore X's appropriation wasn't permissible. But then the appropriator two from last, W, ended permissible appropriation and so, since it worsened X's position, W's appropriation wasn't permissible. And so on back to the first person A to appropriate a permanent property right.

This argument, however, proceeds too quickly. Someone may be made worse off by another's appropriation in two ways: first, by losing the opportunity to improve his situation by a particular appropriation or any one; and second, by no longer being able to use freely (without appropriation) what he previously could. A *stringent* requirement that another not be made worse off by an appropriation would exclude the first way if nothing else counterbalances the diminution in opportunity, as well as the second. A *weaker* requirement would exclude the second way, though not the first. With the weaker requirement, we cannot zip back so quickly from Z to A, as in the above argument; for though person Z can no longer *appropriate*, there may remain some for him to *use* as before. In this case Y's appropriation would not violate the weaker Lockean condition. (With less remaining that people are at liberty to use, users might face more inconvenience, crowding, and so on; in that way the situation of others might be worsened, unless appropriation stopped far short of such a point.) It is arguable that no one legitimately can complain if the weaker provision is satisfied. However, since this is less clear than in the case of the more stringent proviso, Locke may have intended this stringent proviso by 'enough and as good' remaining, and perhaps he meant the non-waste condition to delay the end point from which the argument zips back . . .

THE PROVISO

Whether or not Locke's particular theory of appropriation can be spelled out so as to handle various difficulties, I assume that any adequate theory of justice in acquisition will contain a proviso similar to the weaker of the ones we have attributed to Locke. A process normally giving rise to a permanent bequeathable property right in a previously unowned thing will not do so if the position of others no longer at liberty to use the thing is thereby worsened. It is important to specify *this* particular mode of worsening the situation of others, for the proviso does not encompass other modes. It does not include the worsening due to more limited opportunities to appropriate (the first way above, corresponding to the more stringent condition), and it does not include how I 'worsen' a seller's position if I appropriate materials to make some of what he is selling, and then enter into competition with him. Someone whose appropriation otherwise would violate the proviso still may appropriate provided he compensates the others so that their situation is not thereby worsened; unless he does compensate these others, his appropriation will violate the proviso of the principle of justice in acquisition and will be an illegitimate one.[a] A theory of appropriation incorporating this Lockean

---

[a] Fourier held that since the process of civilization had deprived the members of society of certain liberties (to gather, pasture, engage in the chase), a socially guaranteed minimum provision for persons was justified as compensation for the loss (Alexander Gray, *The Socialist*

proviso will handle correctly the cases (objections to the theory lacking the proviso) where someone appropriates the total supply of something necessary for life.[b]

A theory which includes this proviso in its principle of justice in acquisition must also contain a more complex principle of justice in transfer. Some reflection of the proviso about appropriation constrains later actions. If my appropriating all of a certain substance violates the Lockean proviso, then so does my appropriating some and purchasing all the rest from others who obtained it without otherwise violating the Lockean proviso. If the proviso excludes someone's appropriating all the drinkable water in the world, it also excludes his purchasing it all. (More weakly, and messily, it may exclude his charging certain prices for some of his supply.) This proviso (almost?) never will come into effect; the more someone acquires of a scarce substance which others want, the higher the price of the rest will go, and the more difficult it will become for him to acquire it all. But still, we can imagine, at least, that something like this occurs: someone makes simultaneous secret bids to the separate owners of a substance, each of whom sells assuming he can easily purchase more from the other owners; or some natural catastrophe destroys all of the supply of something except that in one person's possession. The total supply could not be permissibly appropriated by one person at the beginning. His later acquisition of it all does not show that the original appropriation violated the proviso (even by a reverse argument similar to the one above that tried to zip back from Z to A). Rather, it is the combination of the original appropriation *plus* all the later transfers and actions that violates the Lockean proviso.

Each owner's title to his holding includes the historical shadow of the Lockean proviso on appropriation. This excludes his transferring it into an agglomeration that does violate the Lockean proviso and excludes his using it in a way, in coordination with others or independently of them, so as to violate the proviso by making the situation of others worse than their baseline situation. Once it is known that someone's ownership runs afoul of the Lockean proviso, there are stringent limits on what he may do with (what it is difficult any longer unreservedly to call) 'his property.' Thus a person may not appropriate the only water hole in a desert and charge what he will. Nor may he charge what he will if he possesses one, and unfortunately it happens that all the water holes in the desert dry up, except for his. This unfortunate circumstance, admittedly no fault of his, brings into operation the Lockean

---

Tradition (New York: Harper & Row, 1968), p 188). But this puts the point too strongly. This compensation would be due those persons, if any, for whom the process of civilization was a *net loss*, for whom the benefits of civilization did not counterbalance being deprived of these particular liberties.

[b] For example, Rashdall's case of someone who comes upon the only water in the desert several miles ahead of others who also will come to it and appropriates it all. Hastings Rashdall, 'The Philosophical Theory of Property,' in *Property, its Duties and Rights* (London: MacMillan, 1915).

We should note Ayn Rand's theory of property rights ('Man's Rights' in *The Virtue of Selfishness* (New York: New American Library, 1964), p 94), wherein these follow from the right to life, since people need physical things to live. But a right to life is not a right to whatever one needs to live; other people may have rights over these other things (see Chapter 3 of this book). At most, a right to life would be a right to have or strive for whatever one needs to live, provided that having it does not violate anyone else's rights. With regard to material things, the question is whether having it does violate any right of others. (Would appropriation of all unowned things do so? Would appropriating the water hole in Rashdall's example?) Since special considerations (such as the Lockean proviso) may enter with regard to material property, one *first* needs a theory of property rights before one can apply any supposed right to life (as amended above). Therefore the right to life cannot provide the foundation for a theory of property rights.

proviso and limits his property rights.^c Similarly, an owner's property right in the only island in an area does not allow him to order a castaway from a shipwreck off his island as a trespasser, for this would violate the Lockean proviso.

Nozick *Anarchy, State and Utopia* 175–180

^c The situation would be different if his water hole didn't dry up, due to special precautions he took to prevent this. Compare our discussion of the case in the text with Hayek, *The Constitution of Liberty*, p 136; and also with Ronald Hamowy, 'Hayek's Concept of Freedom; A Critique,' New Individualist Review, April 1961, pp 28–31.

(d) Why the minimal State is the only permissible one

The argument of 3(b) is a powerful one; for supposing that once a patterned distribution has been imposed, then, if Nozick is right, the only way of maintaining it would involve intolerable restrictions of the liberty of individuals, leading to the violation of fundamental human rights. Hence, his root and branch objection to any State stronger than the minimal State; such a State would have to employ patterned principles of justice, and thus would have constantly to interfere in private transactions between individuals which threaten to upset the pattern. This interference would inevitably violate fundamental human rights to liberty and property:

> Our main conclusions about the state are that a minimal state, limited to the narrow functions of protection against force, fraud, theft, enforcement of contracts, and so on, is justified; that any more extensive state will violate a person's rights not to be forced to do certain things, and is unjustified; and that the minimal state is inspiring as well as right. Two noteworthy implications are that the state may not use its coercive apparatus for the purpose of getting some citizens to aid others, or in order to prohibit activities to people for their *own* good or protection.

Nozick *Anarchy, State and Utopia* ix

Some of the consequences of Nozick's argument are, of course, radical ones. Not only is welfare economics rejected because it is an end state theory (p 153), but taxation is compared with forced labour:

> . . . taking the earnings of *n* hours labour is like taking *n* hours from the person; it is like forcing someone to work *n* hours for another's purpose

Nozick *Anarchy, State and Utopia* 169

Nozick argues that many find this claim absurd; but why then do they object to making unemployed hippies work to support the needy?

If Nozick is right, the State as such has no duty of care towards the needy or less well off; and the only grounds on which it can legitimately interfere with private transactions are protection against force, fraud, theft, and the enforcements of contracts and of rights, together with the rectification of injustices arising from the principles of the acquisition and transfer of holdings, in so far as they are not covered by any of the factors mentioned above. If the view that the State should not get involved in welfare provision for people however needy seems harsh, it is important to note that Nozick is not denying the importance of benevolence. On the contrary, voluntary giving to help the needy is desirable. What is wrong is the creation of welfarist institutions financed by taxation to assist the needy, since that involves the forced expropriation of one person's income to assist another and so violates his fundamental rights.

CRITIQUE

Though widely admired both as a defence of individual libertarianism and of the minimal State which, when it has provided protection for individual rights, leaves all other transactions to the operation of the market, *Anarchy, State and Utopia* has inevitably attracted much criticism; for when it appeared its position was a rather unfashionable one which at first sight appears to offer much comfort to the right, but none to the liberal centre or to the left.

However, this appearance is perhaps deceptive, for though *Anarchy, State and Utopia* seems to have been intended as a robust defence of libertarianism, it may well justify State intervention on a scale that few would welcome. As Bernard Williams points out, it offers little comfort to contemporary capitalism, because

> Mr. Nozick's derivation theory of justice does not imply that contemporary property holdings are just; on the contrary (though it is a matter of recoverable fact), it is 99 per cent probable that almost all of them are not. (Mr. Nozick may think that much of America rightfully belongs to the Indians.)

Williams in Paul (ed) *Reading Nozick* 27

The Nozickian case for saying that it does is, of course, that the Indians were unjustly deprived of land which they had justly acquired.[3] Perhaps it is not such a good idea to make justice solely a matter of entitlement.

Another difficulty is connected with the brilliance of Nozick's argument. For not only is it highly theoretical, but it would seem not to be subject in any way to the constraints of reflective equilibrium. So that if the argument leads to the conclusion that however great the inequalities in a society are the State as such should do nothing about them, that is the conclusion we should accept, *whatever* our intuitions are.

But what of the argument itself? There are a number of issues around which criticisms naturally cluster. As we have seen, one concerns the question whether the principle of compensation does not introduce the very kind of teleological considerations that Nozick wishes to exclude, thereby undermining his theory at a crucial step (E Mack 'Nozick on Unproductivity: The Unintended Consequences'). Another controversial issue concerns Nozick's claim that certain rights are fundamental, and have the status of side constraints. He suggests that the status of his fundamental rights as side constraints derives from the fact that a human being's capacity to shape his life enables him to give it meaning (p 50). But many doubt whether this basic intuition really supports his claim that the rights he lists are the fundamental ones; why for instance should the list not contain the right to relief from great suffering, or poverty? Others question whether it is plausible to suppose that the rights Nozick says are fundamental all have the same weight. We have seen that he thinks that certain kinds of rights can be restricted provided there is compensation; do these, nevertheless, have the same weight as rights which cannot be so compensated? In this connection the question arises whether property rights are really as inviolable as the right to life itself, and, connectedly, whether Nozick's Lockean account of how they are acquired show that they are. These are among the issues discussed by Hart and Scanlon in the following two extracts.

Hart's critique follows the valuable summary of the criticism of utilitarianism that it ignores the separateness of persons which was extracted at the end of Chapter 7 (p 277):

[3] For an interesting discussion of this issue see D Lyons 'The New Indian Claims and Original Rights to Land' in Paul (ed) *Reading Nozick*.

The modern insight that it is the arch-sin of unqualified utilitarianism to ignore in the ways I have mentioned the moral importance of the separateness of persons is, I think, in the main, a profound and penetrating criticism. It holds good when utilitarianism is restated in terms of maximum want or preference satisfaction and minimum want or preference frustration rather than in the Benthamite form of the balances of pleasure and pain as psychological states, and it holds good when the maximum is taken to be average rather than total general welfare. But it is capable of being abused to discredit all attempts to diminish inequalities and all arguments that one man's loss may be compensated by another's gain such as have inspired policies of social welfare; all these are discredited as if all necessarily committed the cardinal sin committed by maximizing utilitarianism of ignoring the separateness of individuals. This is I think the basis of the libertarian, strongly anti-utilitarian political theory developed by Robert Nozick in his influential book, *Anarchy, State and Utopia*.[a] For Nozick a strictly limited set of near-absolute individual rights constitute the foundations of morality. Such rights for him 'express the inviolability of persons[b] and 'reflect the fact of our separate existences'.[c] The rights are these: each individual, so long as he does not violate the same rights of others, has the right not to be killed or assaulted, to be free from all forms of coercion or limitation of freedom, and the right not to have property, legitimately acquired, taken, or the use of it limited. He has also the secondary right to punish and exact compensation for violation of his rights, to defend himself and others against such violation. He has the positive right to acquire property by making or finding things and by transfer or inheritance from others, and he has the right to make such transfers and binding contracts. The moral landscape which Nozick explicitly presents contains only rights and is empty of everything else except possibly the moral permissibility of avoiding what he terms catastrophe. Hence moral wrongdoing has only one form: the violation of rights, perpetrating a wrong to the holder of a right. So long as rights are not violated it matters not for morality, short of catastrophe, how a social system actually works, how individuals fare under it, what needs it fails to meet or what misery or inequalities it produces. In this scheme of things the basic rights which fill the moral landscape and express the inviolability of persons are few in number but are all equally stringent. The only legitimate State on this view is one to which individuals have transferred their right to punish or exact compensation from others, and the State may not go beyond the night-watchman functions of using the transferred rights to protect persons against force, fraud, and theft or breaches of contract. In particular the State may not impose burdens on the wealth or income or restraints on the liberty of some citizens to relieve the needs or suffering, however great, of others. So a State may only tax its citizens to provide the police, the law courts, and the armed forces necessary for defence and the performance of the night-watchman functions. Taxing earnings or profits for the relief of poverty or destitution, however dire the need, or for the general welfare such as public education, is on this view morally indefensible; it is said to be 'on a par with' forced labour[d] or making the government imposing such taxes into a 'part owner' of the persons taxed.[e]

[a] R Nozick, *Anarchy, State and Utopia* (1974).
[b] Ibid at 32.
[c] Ibid at 33.
[d] Ibid at 169.
[e] Ibid at 172.

Nozick's development of this extreme libertarian position is wide-ranging. It is full of original and ingenious argument splendidly designed to shake up any complacent interventionist into painful self-scrutiny. But it rests on the slenderest foundation. Indeed many critics have complained of the lack of any argument to show that human beings have the few and only the few but very stringent rights which Nozick assigns to them to support his conclusion that a morally legitimate government cannot have any more extensive functions than the night-watchman's. But the critics are wrong: there is argument of a sort, though it is woefully deficient. Careful scrutiny of his book shows that the argument consists of the assertion that if the functions of government are not limited to the protection of the basic stringent rights, then the arch-sin of ignoring the separateness of persons which modern critics impute to utilitarianism will have been committed. To sustain this argument Nozick at the start of his book envelops in metaphors all policies imposing burdens or restraints going beyond the functions of the night-watchman State, and the metaphors are in fact all drawn from a description of the arch-sin imputed to utilitarianism. Thus, not only is taxation said to be the equivalent of forced labour, but every limitation of property rights, every restriction of liberty for the benefit of others going beyond the constraints imposed by the basic rights, are described as *violating* a person,[f] as a *sacrifice* of that person,[g] or as an outweighing of *one life* by others,[h] or a treatment of a distinct individual as a *resource*[i] for others. So conceptions of justice permitting a graduated income tax to provide for basic needs or to diminish social or economic inequalities are all said to neglect the basic truth 'that each individual is a separate person, that his is the only life he has'.[j] To hold that a person should bear costs that benefit others more is represented as a '*sacrifice*' of that person and as implying what is false: namely that there is a single social entity with a life of which individual lives are merely part just as one individual's desires sacrificed for the sake of his other desires are only part of his life.[k] This imputation of the arch-sin committed by utilitarianism to any political philosophy which assigns functions to the State more extensive than the night-watchman's constitutes, I think, the foundation which Nozick offers for his system.

It is a paradoxical feature of Nozick's argument, hostile though it is to any form of utilitarianism, that it yields a result identical with one of the least acceptable conclusions of an unqualified maximizing utilitarianism, namely that given certain conditions there is nothing to choose between a society where few enjoy great happiness and very many very little, and a society where happiness is more equally spread. For the utilitarian the condition is that in both societies either aggregate or average welfare is the same. For Nozick the condition is a historical one: that the patterns of distribution of wealth which exist at any time in a society should have come about through exercise of the rights and powers of acquisition and voluntary transfer included in ownership and without any violation of the few basic rights. Given the satisfaction of this historical condition, how people fare under the resulting patterns of distribution, whether grossly inegalitarian or egalitarian, is of no moral significance. The only virtue of social institutions on this view is that they

[f] Ibid at 32.
[g] Ibid.
[h] Ibid.
[i] Ibid at 33.
[j] Ibid.
[k] Ibid at 32–3.

protect the few basic rights, and their only vice is failure to do this. Any consequence of the exercise of such rights is unobjectionable. It is as if the model for Nozick's basic moral rights were a legal one. Just as there can be no legal objection to the exercise of a legal right, so in a morality as empty as Nozick's is of everything except rights, there can be no moral objection to the exercise of a moral right.

Why should a critic of society thus assume that there is only one form of moral wrong, namely, violation of individual rights? Why should he turn his gaze away from the consequences in terms of human happiness or misery produced by the working of a system of such rights? The only answer apparent in Nozick's work is that to treat this misery as a matter of moral concern and to require some persons to contribute to the assistance of others only makes sense if one is prepared, like the maximizing utilitarian, to disregard the separateness of individuals and share the superstition that those required to make such contributions are merely part of the life of a single persisting social entity which both makes the contributions and experiences the balance of good that comes from such contributions. This of course simply assumes that utilitarianism is only intelligible if the satisfactions it seeks to maximize are regarded as those of a single social entity. It also assumes that the only alternative to the Nozickian philosophy of right is an unrestricted maximizing utilitarianism which respects not persons but only experiences of pleasure or satisfaction; and this is of course a false dilemma. The impression that we are faced with these two unpalatable alternatives dissolves if we undertake the no doubt unexciting but indispensable chore of confronting Nozick's misleading descriptive terms, such as 'sacrifice of one individual for others', 'treating one individual as a resource for others', 'making others a part owner of a man', 'forced labour', with the realities which these expressions are misused to describe. We must also substitute for the blindingly general use of concepts like 'interference with liberty' a discriminating catalogue which will enable us to distinguish those restrictions on liberty which can be imposed only at that intolerable cost of sacrificing an individual's life or depriving it of meaning, which according to Nozick is the cost of any restriction of liberty except the restriction on the violation of basic rights. How can it be right to lump together, and ban as equally illegitimate, things so different in their impact on individual life as taking some of a man's income to save others from some great suffering, and killing him or taking one of his vital organs for the same purpose? If we are to construct a tenable theory of rights for use in the criticism of law and society we must, I fear, ask such boring questions as: Is taxing a man's earnings or income, which leaves him free to choose whether to work and to choose what work to do, not altogether different in terms of the burden it imposes from forcing him to labour? Does it really sacrifice him or make him or his body just a resource for others? Does the admitted moral impermissibility of wounding or maiming others or the existence of an absolute moral right not to have one's vital organs taken for the benefit of others in any way support a conclusion that there exists an absolute moral right to retain untaxed all one's earnings or all the income accrued from inherited property except for taxes to support the army and the police? Can one man's great gain or relief from great suffering not outweigh a small loss of income imposed on another to provide it? Do such outweighings only make sense if the gain and the loss are of the same person or a single 'social entity'? Once we shake off that assumption and once we distinguish between the gravity of the different restrictions on different specific liberties and their importance for the conduct of a meaningful life or the development of the personality, the idea that they all, like unqualified maximizing utilitarianism, ignore the moral importance of the division of humanity into separate individuals, and threaten the proper inviolability of persons, disappears into the mist.

There is of course much of value to be learned from Nozick's ingenious and diverting pages, but there are also many quite different criticisms to be made of its foundations apart from the one which I have urged. But since other critics have been busy with many such criticisms I will here mention only one. Even if a social philosophy can draw its morality, as Nozick assumes, only from a single source; even if that source is individual rights, so that the only moral wrongdoing consists in wrongs done to individuals that violate their rights, and even if the foundation for such rights is respect for the separateness of persons, why should rights be limited as they are by Nozick to what Bentham called the negative services of others, that is to abstention from such things as murder, assault, theft, and breach of contract? Why should there not be included a basic right to the positive service of the relief of great needs or suffering or the provision of basic education and skills when the cost of these is small compared with both the need to be met and with the financial resources of those taxed to provide them? Why should property rights, to be morally legitimate, have an absolute, permanent, exclusive, inheritable, and unmodifiable character which leaves no room for this? Nozick is I think in particular called upon to answer this question because he is clear that though rights for him constitute the only source of constraint on action, they are not ends to be maximized,[1] the obligations they impose are, as Nozick insists, 'side constraints', so the rights form a protective bastion enabling an individual to achieve his own ends in a life he shapes himself; and *that*, Nozick thinks, is the individual's way of giving meaning to life.[m]

But it is of course an ancient insight that for a meaningful life not only the protection of freedom from deliberate restriction but opportunities and resources for its exercise are needed. Except for a few privileged and lucky persons, the ability to shape life for oneself and lead a meaningful life is something to be constructed by positive marshalling of social and economic resources. It is not something automatically guaranteed by a structure of negative rights. Nothing is more likely to bring freedom into contempt and so endanger it than failure to support those who lack, through no fault of their own, the material and social conditions and opportunities which are needed if a man's freedom is to contribute to his welfare.

Hart 'Between Utility and Rights' 79 Columbia Law Review (1979) 828–846

[1] Ibid at 28–9.
[m] Ibid, at 48–50.

The extract by Scanlon is a valuable discussion of the question whether property rights are natural rights. This question is an important one, because if they are not, then it is hard to see why they should have the kind of inviolability that Nozick accords them:

It is central to Nozick's argument that the rights with which he is concerned are claimed to be natural rights in the stronger sense. The objections I have raised to his examples almost all demand that he consider the consequences of enforcement of absolute property and contract rights and that he explain why the loss of liberty this involves for some people is not worse than that which is involved in the alternative systems which he deplores. Such objections suppose that the property rights enforced by the minimal state and those embodied in socialist institutions are two alternative social systems open to the same kind of objections and needing the same kind of defense. Nozick rejects this symmetrical picture. In his view, the particular property rights protected by the minimal state are not licensed or created by it and consequently do not need to be defended as part of its justification. These rights are ones that individuals have quite independently of the social institutions in which they live. In enforcing these rights the minimal state is only doing for them what they were already entitled to do for themselves. Consequently it is not doing anything that could be held to infringe anyone's liberty.

How plausible is the claim that the rights appealed to in Nozick's examples are ones that individuals would have in a state of nature? This claim has greatest initial plausibility with respect to the right of nonaggression. An unprovoked attack occurring today on the streets of New York seems to be wrong for the same reasons that would apply to a similar attack in the state of nature. But the right of nonaggression as Nozick interprets it covers more than this. It prohibits generally 'sacrificing one person to benefit another' (p 34). I take it that what Nozick wants to rule out here is any use of force or the threat of force to make one person contribute to the welfare of another who has no right to this contribution. This last qualification reduces the right considerably, but without it the right would be absurd. This shows that the right of nonaggression cannot be interpreted in isolation from other rights. Its invariance between the state of nature and other conditions will consequently depend on that of these other rights.

Chief among these is the right to one's property. A system of property is a set of rules defining the conditions under which a person owns an object and specifying the extent and character of the right of owners. What a person's property rights are will normally depend not only on what systems of property could be validly enforced under the conditions in which he lives but also on what system is actually in use. To the extent that this system is morally legitimate, its provisions determine his rights. But the provisions of this system may also be wrong. They may claim for him rights that no one could really have or they may fail to protect claims that any valid system would have to recognize. Surely we can imagine an incident, occurring in a state of nature, which strikes us intuitively as a violation of property rights. Imagine that a family is living in the wilderness when a group of strangers comes along and drives them off part of their land and takes their crops. This strikes us as a clear wrong. I take it that the point of saying that this happens 'in a state of nature' is just that the wrongness involved does not seem to depend on any system of law or social convention. But it is open to question whether what we feel to be violated in such examples is really a natural right to property.[a] For these cases strike us as clear wrongs only if we suppose, first, that what is taken is of use to the person who loses it (that is, that the taking actually constitutes an interference with his life and activities) and, second, that his appropriation and use of the thing did not already constitute an interference with others. (The notion of what constitutes an 'interference' will depend on, but perhaps

[a] *Anarchy, State and Utopia* 30n.

not be exhausted by, a historically varying notion of 'normal appetites.') When these conditions are satisfied, the taking infringes upon what might be called the natural right of noninterference. A system of property rights goes beyond this primitive right by specifying formal criteria of ownership. If a person is deprived of something to which he has acquired title in the specified way, then his property right has been violated whether the taking makes any difference to his life at all. Different systems of property carry out this extension in different ways, each specifying its own criteria of ownership and defining and limiting the rights of owners in its own way. These extended rights require justification since, as one's person's claims to forebearance cease to be limited by the requirements of a normal life, the justification for these claims becomes more attenuated and the threat they present to others grows more serious.

To support the claim that some property rights are natural rights we need to think of a state of nature example involving a clear wrong which seems to violate one of these rights without violating the primitive right of noninterference. But if we imagine such a case we may be open to the question of why we should imagine a state of nature containing *that* particular system of property, rather than some other system which would not be violated by the act in question.

This objection could be avoided if we could show that the primitive right of noninterference does not exhaust the common core of systems of property rights. Perhaps there are certain provisions falling outside this right which would be incorporated in any system of property rights that could plausibly be held to be valid in a state of nature. It could then be argued that the provisions which Nozick's examples turn on fall in this class, for example, that an unrestricted right of inheritance does so. But this is far from clear. Suppose the grandfather of the family we previously imagined lived on land a short distance away and that when he died he said, 'Now this is yours.' But they had all they could do to take care of their own place, and one day they noticed that someone else had moved onto their grandfather's old farm. Are they entitled (in the state of nature) to throw the people off or to demand payment? It is not obvious to me that they are. Even if there is 'as much land and as good' not far off, their claim to demand that the new people move to it is quite debatable. Furthermore, even if we were to be convinced by such examples that any system of property valid in a state of nature would have to include unrestricted inheritance, there would remain the question of how much this judgment is dependent upon our assessment of the consequences that this provision would have in a 'natural state.' These consequences are apt to be quite different from those that would result from the same provision under other social conditions.

It is of interest here that Locke clearly distinguishes between the natural property rights that he sees as holding in a state of nature antecedent to law or social convention and the systems of property that arise later with the introduction of money and the creation of government.[b] The system of natural property rights under which men can acquire title to things by laboring on them is held by Locke to be valid without consent. It is crucial to his argument for the validity of these rights that, under the conditions of the state of nature, the holdings to which people can be expected to acquire title will not extend beyond 'the conveniences of life.'[c] They will not do so because the right itself is

[b] Idem at 41.
[c] Idem (emphasis in original).

restricted by the proviso that things not be held if they will just go to waste and because the things men are interested in acquiring in a primitive state are generally 'of short duration.'[d] This limit on the extent of holdings is important to the positive case for the natural right of property since it means that the things the right protects are needed for a normal life. It also forestalls objections to the right by providing an important part of the reason for believing that acquisition under it will not allow one person to 'entrench upon' others but will leave them with 'enough and as good.'[e] Thus, under the conditions Locke believes to hold in the state of nature, his natural right of property will not significantly extend what I have called the right of noninterference, and Locke's argument for the validity of his right depends upon this fact.

Once the introduction of money gives men the means to store up, without spoilage, more than they can use, and commerce gives them a reason for doing so, there is no longer any reason to expect holdings to be limited to the conveniences of life. When this happens, the original moral foundation for property rights is no longer valid, and a new foundation is required. Locke takes consent to be this foundation. The 'disproportionate and unequal possession of the earth' which may obtain after money comes into use is legitimated, according to Locke, by the 'tacit and voluntary consent' which men give to the use of money and without which it would not work.[f] Later systems of property founded by positive legislation derive their authority from the consent men have given to their governments.

Nozick appears to reject both of these latter foundations for property rights. He avoids invoking a social contract, and he denies Locke's empirical claim that a functioning system of money requires consent, suggesting that it could arise instead through an 'invisible hand process' (p 18).[g] He faces the problem, then, of deriving an extended system of property rights involving money, commerce, and extensive holdings from something like Locke's original 'natural' foundation. This derivation faces two problems. The first is that the lack of natural bounds on acquisition means that others are likely to be threatened—there may not be enough and as good left for them. As I have already mentioned, Nozick's response here is that the increase in the stock of goods due to increasing productivity will keep pace with increased acquisition, making it unlikely that anyone will be made worse off relative to the baseline of expectations in the state of nature. The second problem is that, with holdings extending far beyond 'the conveniences of life' (certainly far beyond what these included in the state of nature), the case for absolute protection of these holdings becomes weaker. This makes even more controversial the choice of an extremely low baseline for determining whether the condition of others is worsened.

Scanlon 'Nozick on Rights, Liberty, and Property' 1 Philosophy and Public Affairs (1976)

---

[d] Or something like (*T*), for of course we shall want to allow for irrationality, preferences immorally inculcated, and so forth. I do not for a moment want to suggest that I think the proper spelling out of the thesis would be easy; it is merely that the difficulties are irrelevant for present purposes.

[e] Surely, however, it is not infinitely stringent: I should imagine it is overrideable, even if not overridden in the cases at which we are looking.

[f] See R Nozick *supra* note 1, at 152–53.

[g] See idem at 160–64, 168–72.

Chapter 12
Dworkin and the interpretive theory of law

In *Law's Empire* (1986) Dworkin presents an elaborate argument in support of a thesis which, he says, he has been 'developing piecemeal, in fits and starts, for several years: that legal reasoning is an exercise in constructive interpretation, that our law consists in the best justification of our legal practices as a whole, that it consists in the narrative story that makes of these practices the best they can be' (*Law's Empire* p vii). In this book we have Dworkin's most determined attempt to explain and justify his 'rights thesis' and the labours awaiting Hercules. We have already agonised over these matters when discussing the Dworkin/Hart debate (supra Chapter 4), but it is in this later book that Dworkin offers his first methodological understanding of the processes of legal reasoning that underpin the rights thesis—the interpretive theory of law. So, although we have already encountered many of the details of his argument when considering his views on adjudication, a new chapter is called for in order to set it within a methodological thesis of law as constructive interpretation.

THE SEMANTIC STING

Those who contend that a precondition of any reasoned debate is the agreement among the disputants on common definitions of terms exhibit the symptoms of the semantic sting, the cause 'of such great mischief in legal philosophy'. In fact all previous attempts to formulate a theory of law fall foul of the sting in attempting to furnish various criteria for the use of the word 'law'.

> They think we can argue sensibly with one another if, but only if, we all accept and follow the same criteria for deciding when our claims are sound, even if we cannot state exactly, as a philosopher might hope to do, what these criteria are. You and I can sensibly discuss how many books I have on my shelf, for example, only if we both agree, at least roughly, about what a book is. We can disagree over borderline cases: I may call something a slim book that you would call a pamphlet. But we cannot disagree over what I called pivotal cases. If you do not count my copy of *Moby Dick* as a book because in your view novels are not books, any disagreement is bound to be senseless.
>
> Dworkin *Law's Empire* 45

Such semantic-orientated approaches pose a dilemma.

> Either, in spite of first appearances, lawyers actually all do accept roughly the same criteria for deciding when a claim about the law is true or there can be no genuine agreement or disagreement about law at all, but only the idiocy of people thinking they disagree because they attach different meanings to the

same sound. The second leg of this dilemma seems absurd. So legal philosophers embrace the first and try to identify the hidden ground rules that must be there, embedded, though unrecognized, in legal practice. They produce and debate semantic theories of law.

Dworkin *Law's Empire* 45–46

Either the disputants offer or invent rival definitions of the word 'law', truly an exercise in vacuity, or they succumb to the first horn of the dilemma, the dreaded sting, which misrepresents the kinds of disagreements lawyers actually have. Dworkin's point is that the dispute is to be understood as conceptual and not merely semantic.

The only way to explain the kind of disagreements that do occur in hard cases is to recognise law as being an 'interpretive concept'.

CONSTRUCTIVE INTERPRETATION

The processes of interpretation pervade many different social contexts. The most common is conversation, where we interpret the noises made by someone in such a way so as to allow us to decide what he has said. The aim of the exercise is to articulate the intentions and purposes of the speaker from the data of his sounds, expressions, etc, as far as interpreting conversation is the rationale of the exercise. It is possible to characterise artistic interpretation in a similar fashion, reducing it to a species of conversational interpretation by making the intention of composer, poet, artist, etc, the priority issue. In championing constructive rather than conversational interpretation Dworkin moves the centre of gravity from the author to the interpreter himself. Social practices such as what is commonly called 'law', as well as artistic interpretation, are to be subjected to the machinations of constructive rather than conversational interpretation. The following extract sets out the ground rules of this process. Look out for these points:

(a)   the difference between the two approaches to interpretation;
(b)   the best possible light argument, central to understanding Dworkin;
(c)   the constraint on the interpreter going on an interpretive frolic of his own;
(d)   the interaction between purpose and object.

I defend a different solution: that creative interpretation is not conversational but constructive. Interpretation of works of art and social practices, I shall argue, is indeed essentially concerned with purpose not cause. But the purposes in play are not fundamentally those of some author but of the interpreter. Roughly, constructive interpretation is a matter of imposing purpose on an object or practice in order to make of it the best possible example of the form or genre to which it is taken to belong. It does not follow, even from that rough account, that an interpreter can make of a practice or work of art anything he would have wanted it to be . . . For the history or shape of a practice or object constrains the available interpretations of it, though the character of that constraint needs careful accounting, as we shall see. Creative interpretation, on the constructive view, is a matter of interaction between purpose and object.

A participant interpreting a social practice, according to that view, proposes value for the practice by describing some scheme of interests or goals or principles the practice can be taken to serve or express or exemplify.

Dworkin *Law's Empire* 52

In what follows, note the possibility of competing interpretations, despite the constraint on interpretation mentioned in the last excerpt, and reiteration of the best light thesis.

> Very often, perhaps even typically, the raw behavioral data of the practice—what people do in what circumstances—will undermine the ascription of value: those data will be consistent, that is, with different and competing ascriptions ... If the raw data do not discriminate between these competing interpretations, each interpreter's choice must reflect his view of which interpretation proposes the most value for the practice— which one shows it in the better light, all things considered.
>
> Dworkin *Law's Empire* 52–53

STAGES OF INTERPRETATION

The constructive interpretation of any social practice will manifest itself in three stages.

> We must begin to refine constructive interpretation into an instrument fit for the study of law as a social practice. We shall need an analytical distinction among the following three stages of an interpretation, noticing how different degrees of consensus within a community are needed for each stage if the interpretive attitude is to flourish there. First, there must be a 'preinterpretive' stage in which the rules and standards taken to provide the tentative content of the practice are identified. (The equivalent stage in literary interpretation is the stage at which discrete novels, plays, and so forth are identified textually, that is, the stage at which the text of *Moby Dick* is identified and distinguished from the text of other novels.) I enclose 'preinterpretive' in quotes because some kind of interpretation is necessary even at this stage. Social rules do not carry identifying labels. But a very great degree of consensus is needed— perhaps an interpretive community is usefully defined as requiring consensus at this stage—if the interpretive attitude is to be fruitful, and we may therefore abstract from this stage in our analysis by presupposing that the classifications it yields are treated as given in day-to-day reflection and argument.
>
> Second, there must be an interpretive stage at which the interpreter settles on some general justification for the main elements of the practice identified as the preinterpretive stage. This will consist of an argument why a practice of that general shape is worth pursuing, if it is. The justification need not fit every aspect or feature of the standing practice, but it must fit enough for the interpreter to be able to see himself as interpreting that practice, not inventing a new one.
>
> Finally, there must be a postinterpretive or reforming stage, at which he adjusts his sense of what the practice 'really' requires so as better to serve the justification he accepts at the interpretive stage.
>
> Dworkin *Law's Empire* 65–66

Having established the best light thesis for the interpretation of social practices, in the last extract Dworkin attempts to describe the process of interpretation. The first, 'preinterpretive' stage requires certain convictions about what counts as the thing to be interpreted. Notice why 'preinterpretive' is in quotation marks. The second stage, the actual stage of interpretation, provides a justification for the social practice. But such justification is constrained by a dimension of fact: the interpretive justification of the social practice must have some degree of fit with the data it interprets. However, as we see, the fit need not be perfect. Furthermore the dimension of value acts as a constraint upon interpretation, in that it tests the acceptability of certain convictions about the kinds of justification that show the data in the best light. In short, the constructive interpretation of a social practice means an attempt to offer the best possible justification of that practice. The operation of the third, postinterpretive stage is illustrated by Dworkin's discussion of the social practice of courtesy.

> An interpreter of courtesy, for example, may come to think that a consistent enforcement of the best justification of that practice would require people to tip their caps to soldiers returning from a crucial war as well as to nobles. Or that it calls for a new exception to an established pattern of deference making returning soldiers exempt from displays of courtesy, for example. Or perhaps even that an entire rule stipulating deference to an entire group or class or persons must be seen as a mistake in the light of that justification.
>
> Dworkin *Law's Empire* 66

In the next extract, using again the social practice of courtesy as an example, Dworkin re-attempts to describe the stages in the process by composing 'an inventory of the kinds of convictions or beliefs or assumptions someone needs to interpret something'. Whereas the first two convictions need to be approximately shared within the community, the third must be independent. Why?

> We can now look back through our analytical account to compose an inventory of the kind of convictions or beliefs or assumptions someone needs to interpret something. He needs assumptions or convictions about what counts as part of the practice in order to define the raw data of his interpretation at the preinterpretive stage; the interpretive attitude cannot survive unless members of the same interpretive community share at least roughly the same assumptions about this. He also needs convictions about how far the justification he proposes at the interpretive stage must fit the standing features of the practice to count as an interpretation of it rather than the invention of something new. Can the best justification of the practices of courtesy, which almost everyone else takes to be mainly about showing deference to social superiors, really be one that would require, at the reforming stage, no distinctions of social rank? Would this be too radical a reform, too ill-fitting a justification to count as an interpretation at all? Once again, there cannot be too great a disparity in different people's convictions about fit; but only history can teach us how much difference is too much. Finally, he will need more substantive convictions about which kinds of justification really would show the practice in the best light, judgments about whether social ranks are desirable or deplorable, for example. These substantive convictions must be independent of the convictions about fit just described, otherwise the latter could not constrain the former, and he could not, after all, distinguish interpretation from invention. But they need not be so much shared within his community, for the interpretive attitude to flourish, as his sense of preinterpretive boundaries or even his convictions about the required degree of fit.
>
> Dworkin *Law's Empire* 67–68

A further account of the three stages is offered in a footnote:

> We might summarize these three stages in the observation that interpretation
> seeks to establish an equilibrium between the preinterpretive account of a
> social practice and a suitable justification of that practice. I borrow
> 'equilibrium' from Rawls, but this account of interpretation is different from
> his account of reasoning about justice. He contemplates equilibrium between
> what he calls 'intuitions' about justice and a formal theory uniting these
> intuitions . . . Interpretation of a social practice seeks equilibrium between the
> justification of the practice and its post-interpretive requirement.
>
> > Dworkin *Law's Empire* 424

Before leaving his general theory of interpretation and applying it specifically to
law we need to mark his disclaimer.

> We need some account of how the attitude I call interpretive works from the
> inside, from the point of view of interpreters. Unfortunately, even a
> preliminary account will be controversial, for if a community uses interpretive
> concepts at all, the concept of interpretation itself will be one of them: a theory
> of interpretation is an interpretation of the higher-order practice of using
> interpretive concepts. (So any adequate account of interpretation must hold
> true of itself.)
>
> > Dworkin *Law's Empire* 49

CONSTRUCTIVE INTERPRETATION AND THE
THREE STAGES APPLIED TO LAW

It will be remembered that disputes about or indeed within law are not disputes
concerning the use of the word 'law': the semantic sting has been pulled. Rather
they represent differing constructive interpretations of the practices commonly
referred to as 'law'. In fact, different accounts of the best justification of the
practice are being tendered both by the jurist philosophising about the nature of
law and by the judge adjudicating the hard case.

> General theories of law, like general theories of courtesy and justice, must be
> abstract because they aim to interpret the main point and structure of
> legal practice, not some particular part or department of it. But for all
> their abstraction, they are constructive interpretations: they try to show
> legal practice as a whole in its best light, to achieve equilibrium between legal
> practice as they find it and the best justification of that practice.
>
> > Dworkin *Law's Empire* 90

Consequently the best justification will be that conception which fits most neatly
with empirical features of the practice (the dimension of fact) and which reveals
the practice in the most compelling moral light (the dimension of value). The
relevant criteria for furnishing an appropriate concept of law are its fit with the
factual data of the practice and its moral persuasiveness.

(a)   The preinterpretive stage and the plateau

We are to focus on law; it follows there needs to be a degree of consensus as to the practices that go to constitute law.

> Law cannot flourish as an interpretive enterprise in any community unless there is enough initial agreement about what practices are legal practices so that lawyers argue about the best interpretation of roughly the same data. That is a practical requirement of any interpretive enterprise; it would be pointless for two critics to argue over the best interpretation of a poem if one has in mind the text of 'Sailing to Byzantium' and the other the text of 'Mathilda Who Told Lies'. I do not mean that all lawyers everywhere and always must agree on exactly which practices should count as practices of law, but only that the lawyers of any culture where the interpretive attitude succeeds must largely agree at any one time. We all enter the history of an interpretive practice at a particular point; the necessary preinterpretive agreement is in that way contingent and local.
>
> In fact we have no difficulty identifying collectively the practices that count as legal practices in our own culture. We have legislatures and courts and administrative agencies and bodies, and the decisions these institutions make are reported in a canonical way. In the United States we have the Constitution as well. Each lawyer has joined the practice of law with that furniture in place and with a shared understanding that these institutions together form our legal system. It would be a mistake—another lingering infection from the semantic sting—to think that we identify these institutions through some shared and intellectually satisfying definition of what a legal system necessarily is and what institutions necessarily make it up. Our culture presents us with legal institutions and with the idea that they form a system. The question which features they have, in virtue of which they combine as a distinctly legal system, is part of the interpretive problem. It is part of the controversial and uncertain process of assigning meaning to what we find, not a given of the preinterpretive structure.
>
> Dworkin *Law's Empire* 90–91

Given this 'fairly uncontroversial preinterpretive identification of the domain of law', the possibility of a further initial assumption arises: it would be of assistance if jurists in the preinterpretive stage could agree upon an initial abstract description of the 'point' of the practice of law. Such an abstract account would provide a 'plateau' for further arguments about law's characteristics.

In what follows note what this abstract account actually is, but also that this sort of agreement on the point of the practice of law, very useful in providing a plateau as it is, is not in any way a precondition of the validity of Dworkin's thesis.

> Now the question arises whether he [a jurist] and his competitors might agree on what I called, in discussing courtesy and justice, a statement of the central concept of their institution that will allow them to see their arguments as having a certain structure, as arguments over rival conceptions of that concept. A conceptual statement of that sort would be useful in several ways. Just as we understood the practice of courtesy better at one stage in its career by finding general agreement about the abstract proposition that courtesy is a matter of respect, we might understand law better if we could find a similar

abstract description of the point of law most legal theorists accept so that their arguments take place on the plateau it furnishes.

Neither jurisprudence nor my own arguments later in this book depend on finding an abstract description of that sort. Political philosophy thrives, as I said, in spite of our difficulties in finding any adequate statement of the concept of justice. Nevertheless I suggest the following as an abstract account that organizes further argument about law's character. Governments have goals: they aim to make the nations they govern prosperous or powerful or religious or eminent; they also aim to remain in power. They use the collective force they monopolize to these and other ends. Our discussions about law by and large assume, I suggest, that the most abstract and fundamental point of legal practice is to guide and constrain the power of government in the following way. Law insists that force not be used or withheld, no matter how useful that would be to ends in view, no matter how beneficial or noble these ends, except as licensed or required by individual rights and responsibilities flowing from past political decisions about when collective force is justified.

The law of a community on this account is the scheme of rights and responsibilities that meet that complex standard: they license coercion because they flow from past decisions of the right sort. They are therefore 'legal' rights and responsibilities. This characterization of the concept of law sets out, in suitably airy form, what is sometimes called the 'rule' of law. It is compatible with a great many competing claims about exactly which rights and responsibilities, beyond the paradigms of the day, do follow from past political decisions of the right sort and for that reason do license or require coercive enforcement. It therefore seems sufficiently abstract and uncontroversial to provide, at least provisionally, the structure we seek. No doubt there are exceptions to this claim, theories that challenge rather than elaborate the connection it assumes between law and the justification of coercion. But not as many as there might seem to be at first glance.

Dworkin Law's Empire 92–94

This 'central concept' makes many appearances.

I am defending this suggestion about how we might describe our concept of law; for us, legal argument takes place on a plateau of rough consensus that if law exists it provides a justification for the use of collective force against individual citizens or groups. General conceptions of law . . . begin in some broad thesis about whether and why past political decisions do provide such a justification, and this thesis then provides a unifying structure for the conception as a whole.

Dworkin Law's Empire 108–109

(b) An interim summary

Pulling together the best light thesis, the three stages, and the abstract central account, we can set out Dworkin's criteria for an adequate theory of law.

(a) 'A conception of law is a general, abstract interpretation of legal practice as a whole. It offers to show the practice in its best light, to deploy some argument why law on that conception provides an adequate justification for coercion' (p 139).

(b)   A conception of law must fit our practice.
(c)   A conception of law must provide a sound justification of our legal practices. Does it provide a justification of legal practices that is morally respectable?

He discusses three rival conceptions of law as an interpretive concept. They are to fight one another on the above 'plateau'. Which one wins? Which one best satisfies the above criteria?

Before going to this battlefield we need to consider the third stage of the interpretive process.

(c)   The postinterpretive stage

First, refer back to the discussion of the social practice of courtesy in the postinterpretive stage (supra p 377). Let us apply that discussion to the social practice called 'law'.

The assumed abstract account considered above establishes a connection between a conception of law and coercion. Consequently, any of the rival conceptions of law must necessarily explain why legal practices that manifest themselves in past decisions of, for example, legislatures or courts, justify the use of force. Why should the past decisions of legislatures have a justifying power? Why should a previous judicial decision furnish justification for a similar use of force by different officials at a later date? Naturally enough, it would be far too sanguine to contemplate a conception that would furnish a hundred per cent justification. Not every feature of the practice will be justified by the conception of law arrived at through the processes of interpretation. In fact the conception can condemn some of the practice as being an aberration, a mistake, as being inconsistent with the justification that interprets the major part of the practice in the best possible light, satisfying the dimensions of fact and value. It is in the postinterpretive stage that such anomalies are to be rectified.

> Conceptions of law will be controversial just because they will differ in this way in their postinterpretive accounts of legal practice, in their opinions, that is, about the right way to expand or extend the practice in areas presently disputed or uncultivated. These controversial postinterpretive claims are the cutting edge of a conception of law, and that is why hard cases . . . provide the best theater for displaying their power.
>
> Dworkin *Law's Empire* 99

Hard cases confronting hard questions are irretrievably embedded in the postinterpretive stage: the controversies endemic in the postinterpretive stage are the fodder of examination papers in law.

> Each question raises hosts of others, and an interpretation of this kind is necessarily open-ended and incomplete. It must also be internally complex and crossreferenced. The different questions . . . and the vast variety of further questions for which they stand surrogate, must be answered together, in one complex though incomplete theory, if the answers are to stand coherent or even make any sense at all. Each part will in some way depend on the rest because they will be knit together by some unifying vision of the connection between legal practice and political justification. So any general conception

must also have external connections to other parts or departments of political morality and, through these, to more general ideological and even metaphysical convictions. I do not mean that any lawyer or philosopher who takes up a general conception of law will have already developed some explicit and articulate view about the point of law, or the large questions of personality, life, and community on which any such view must rest. I mean only that his conception of law, so far as he has developed it, will reveal some attitude towards these large topics whether or not he realizes this.

Dworkin Law's Empire 100–101

Eventually, then, the interpreter is catapulted straight into Plato's cave.

THREE RIVAL CONCEPTIONS BATTLING IT OUT ON THE PLATEAU

A concept of law is furnished by the initial, abstract and uncontroversial interpretation of law as constraining the use of collective force except as licensed by past decisions, legislative or judicial, about when the use of force is justified. It is argued that this is an interpretive and not a semantic claim having nothing to do with laying out linguistic ground rules everyone must follow in order to make sense. The various conceptions of law refine this initial abstraction. The difference between concept and conception is the difference between levels of abstraction at which the interpretation of a practice can be studied. The conceptions are competing positions about what the conceptual tie between law and coercion actually involves, they are the points where the controversies latent within the initial concept are taken up.

Three conceptions of law are to battle it out: conventionalism, resembling legal positivism minus semantic sting; pragmatism, resembling legal realism; and law as integrity which provides, according to Dworkin, the best interpretation of what lawyers, law teachers, and judges actually do and much of what they say.

However, he accepts the novelty of these conceptions because perhaps no legal philosopher would actually defend either of the first two conceptions, although each does capture some idea prominent in the literature, 'now organized as interpretive rather than semantic claims'. This concession goes some way to reducing the battle between the conceptions to something of a simulated affray between straw men.

Each conception faces up to three issues. First, a question prompted by the concept of law described above: is the supposed link between law and coercion, that collective force is to be used only in ways conforming to rights and duties 'that flow from' past legislative and judicial decisions, justified at all? Secondly, does the conception fit legal practice? What account of consistency with past decisions is required? Thirdly, what is the justification for law's constraint, the reason for requiring that force be used only in ways consistent with past decisions? What is the substance of the justification?

We shall call these, respectively, the conceptual question, the dimension of fit and the dimension of substance.

(a) Conventionalism

Within the practice of law there are a number of conventions about what is to be depicted as 'law'. This conception of law is basically backward-looking in that we conclude that rights and duties exist only when they are consistent with past statutes or case law. The negative side of conventionalism is that when the force of convention is spent, that is when past decisions fail to provide an answer, the judge will fall back on discretion and make the law himself.

On the conceptual question, does this conception recognise the abstract and foundational point of legal practice, that rights and duties license coercion because they flow from past decisions of the right sort? Yes, there is the idea of existing rights and duties to be upheld by the deployment of force, if necessary. Conventionalism accepts the idea of law (as described in the concept of law) and legal rights.

Does it fit? It is the negative side of conventionalism that is problematic.

> It proposes . . . a sharply restricted account of the form of consistency we should require with past decisions: a right or responsibility flows from past decisions only if it is explicit within them or can be made explicit through methods or techniques conventionally accepted by the legal profession as a whole. Political morality, according to conventionalism, requires no further respect for the past, so when the force of convention is spent judges must find some wholly forward-looking ground of decision.
>
> Dworkin *Law's Empire* 95

The conventionalist must argue that whenever we run out of explicit conventions the judge must then invoke discretion and make new law in the manner of a legislator. But this is not true of practice. Judges do not write this way; they continue to probe and worry the old statutes and cases.

> [Conventionalism] fails for the following paradoxical reason: our judges actually pay more attention to so-called conventional sources of law like statutes and precedents than conventionalism allows them to do. A self-consciously strict conventionalist judge would lose interest in legislation and precedent at just the point when it became clear that the explicit extension of these supposed conventions had run out. He would then acknowledge that there was no law, and he would have no further concern for consistency with the past; he would proceed to make new law by asking what law the present legislature would make or what the people want or what would be in the community's best interests for the future.
>
> Dworkin *Law's Empire* 130

The dimension of substance: can conventionalism provide 'a sound or even decent justification' of the practice? What is the normative value of this conception? It is the 'ideal of protected expectations' (p 117). The substance of this justification is contained in the requirements of predictability and of procedural fairness grounded on past decisions. However, given that the explicit rules and principles are unable to determine everything in advance, the best conventionalist is forced to balance the competing goals of 'reliance and flexibility'. Convention governs the straightforward case, judges' discretion determines what is the best rule for the future in cases which are not obviously governed by past decisions. In clear cases judges follow the obvious rule or principle, in other situations they act as legislators: the conception of law that better accounts for this balancing operation is pragmatism and not conventionalism. Conventionalism cannot accommodate the relevant dimension of flexibility without abandoning the ideal of protected expectations and therefore predictability and procedural fairness.

But Dworkin's argument against conventionalism is wider and more powerful than this. There will be occasions when it is necessary for a judge to overrule even clear cases, cases where a relevant past legal rule has been established, on pragmatic grounds. Even apparently easy cases collapse into hard ones, it seems.

It follows that conventionalism cannot be the 'best' interpretation along the dimension of substance.

(b)   Pragmatism

This conception is epitomised in the sceptical claim that there is no intrinsic value in maintaining any consistency with the past. Judges, like legislators, ought to make law solely by reference to certain social goals such as utility or efficiency. In effect, there is a denial of legal rights flowing from past legal decisions; the approach is essentially forward-looking where judges, untrammelled by legal history, decide what is the best solution for the community. Consistency with decisions already made by the legislature or courts is too expensive a luxury. However, there is a startling qualification which characterises judges as experts in deception: judges act and write as if they are vindicating preexisting rights enshrined in past decisions. This 'as if' sleight of hand constitutes the 'noble lie' which camouflages the true character of judicial reasoning, that is, handing down decisions that are best for the community without regard for past decisions.

The conceptual question is responded to by a brusque negative, denying any genuine benefit in requiring judges' decisions to be 'checked' by supposed rights of the litigants to consistency with the past. Both the concept of law, the tie between law and coercion and past decisions, and legal rights are rejected, except in so far as they appear in the noble lie.

Does it fit?

> So pragmatism can be rescued as a good explanation for our cross-section picture of adjudication only by procrustean machinery that seems wildly inappropriate. It can be rescued only if we do not take judicial opinions at face value at all; we must treat all the judges who worry about problematical statutes and precedents as practising some unmotivated form of deception. They must be seen as inventing new rules for the future in accordance with their convictions about what is best for society as a whole, freed from any supposed rights flowing from consistency, but presenting these for unknown reasons in the false uniform of rules dug out of the past.
>
> Dworkin *Law's Empire* 159–160

This can be accepted as a good explanation of practice only if 'pragmatism is so powerful along the second dimension of legal interpretation, so attractive as a political justification for state coercion, that it merits heroic life support. Does it?' There is an initial appeal about it.

> If judicial divisions and controversial judgments are in any case inevitable, the pragmatist asks, why should the controversy not be about what really matters, about what decision will produce the least inefficient practice or the fewest occasions of injustice in the future? How can that goal itself be unjust? How

can consistency in principle be important for its own sake, particularly when it is uncertain and controversial what consistency requires?

Dworkin *Law's Empire* 163

The noble lie means that the pragmatist judges must treat some past decisions as if they were rights-creating 'as a matter of strategy'. Therefore litigants, whose cases are indistinguishable from past cases or fit snugly under the umbrella of a statute, relying on such 'rights', must understand that what is best for the community today could well involve the trumping of such metaphorical rights. Why this is an inferior interpretation of the practice of law can be understood from the 'checkerboard' argument (infra p 387). In the meantime Dworkin concedes that this conception is the major challenge to the one he champions: law as integrity.

(c) Law as integrity

Politics, as well as political philosophy, argues for the virtues of fairness, justice, and procedural due process.

> Fairness in politics is a matter of finding political procedures—methods of electing officials and making their decisions responsive to the electorate—that distribute political power in the right way. That is now generally understood, in the United States and Britain at least, to mean procedures and practices that give all citizens more or less equal influence in the decisions that govern them. Justice, on the contrary, is concerned with the decisions that the standing political institutions, whether or not they have been chosen fairly, ought to make. If we accept justice as a political virtue we want our legislators and other officials to distribute material resources and protect civil liberties so as to secure a morally defensible outcome. Procedural due process is a matter of the right procedures for judging whether some citizen has violated laws laid down by the political procedures; if we accept it as a virtue, we want courts and similar institutions to use procedures of evidence, discovery, and review that promise the right level of accuracy and otherwise treat people accused of violation as people in that position ought to be treated.

Dworkin *Law's Empire* 164–165

There is an addition to these three ideals.

> This is sometimes described in the catch phrase that we must treat like cases alike. It requires government to speak with one voice, to act in a principled and coherent manner toward all its citizens, to extend to everyone the substantive standards of justice or fairness it uses for some. If government relies on principles of majoritarian democracy to justify its decisions about who may vote, it must respect the same principles in designing voting districts. If it appeals to the principle that people have a right to compensation from those who injure them carelessly, as its reason why manufacturers are liable for defective automobiles, it must give full effect to that principle in deciding whether accountants are liable for their mistakes as well. If government says that a unanimous verdict is necessary for criminal conviction because special moral harm is suffered when someone is unjustly convicted of a crime, then it must take that special moral harm into account in considering, for example, the admissibility of confessions under various circumstances.

This particular demand of political morality is not in fact well described in the catch phrase that we must treat like cases alike. I give it a grander title: it is the virtue of political integrity. I choose that name to show its connection to a parallel ideal of personal morality. We want our neighbors to behave, in their day-to-day dealings with us, in the way we think right. But we know that people disagree to some extent about the right principles of behavior, so we distinguish that requirement that they act in important matters with integrity, that is, according to convictions that inform and shape their lives as a whole, rather than capriciously or whimsically. The practical importance of this latter requirement among people who know they disagree about justice is evident. Integrity becomes a political ideal when we make the same demand of the state or community taken to be a moral agent, when we insist that the state act on a single, coherent set of principles even when its citizens are divided about what the right principles of justice and fairness really are. We assume, in both the individual and the political cases, that we can recognize other people's acts as expressing a conception of fairness or justice or decency even when we do not endorse that conception ourselves.

This ability is an important part of our more general ability to treat others with respect, and it is therefore a prerequisite of civilization.

Dworkin *Law's Empire* 165–166

What we are encountering in the virtue of integrity is a 'non strategic' account of legal rights.

I began this discussion of ordinary politics, and of its departments of political virtue, in the shadow of the pragmatist's challenge to the idea of legal rights. If we accept integrity as a distinct political virtue beside justice and fairness, then we have a general, nonstrategic argument for recognizing such rights. The integrity of a community's conception of fairness requires that the political principles necessary to justify the legislature's assumed authority be given full effect in deciding what a statute it has enacted means. The integrity of a community's conception of justice demands that the moral principles necessary to justify the substance of its legislature's decisions be recognized in the rest of the law. The integrity of its conception of procedural due process insists that trial procedures that are counted as striking the right balance between accuracy and efficiency in enforcing some part of the law be recognized throughout, taking into account differences in the kind and degree of moral harm an inaccurate verdict imposes. These several claims justify a commitment to consistency in principle valued for its own sake. They suggest what I shall argue: that integrity rather than some superstition of elegance is the life of law as we know it.

Dworkin *Law's Empire* 166–167

What of integrity and the conceptual question? From what he has already said, clearly, like conventionalism and in contrast to pragmatism, integrity endorses the concept of law and of legal rights. What of the dimension of fit?

[Integrity] argues that rights and responsibilities flow from past decisions and so count as legal, not just when they are explicit in these decisions but also when they follow from the principles of personal and political morality that explicit decisions presuppose by way of justification.

Dworkin *Law's Empire* 96

In going beyond explicit consistency with past legal decisions, law as integrity merges the strengths of conventionalism and pragmatism. The appeal of predictability and of procedural equity is acknowledged but is tempered by a dose of restrained pragmatism, restrained by the fact that the principles of personal and political morality are not to be grasped from the air but are the principles that can be unpacked from the explicit past decisions. Judges are not engaged in an untrammelled frolic of their own.

Why is this conception morally attractive? How does it fare in the dimension of substance? A new argument is introduced, which incidentally can also be employed when considering whether law as integrity has the appropriate dimension to fit. This is the 'checkerboard' argument and this is why law as integrity is morally more appealing than pragmatism. Most of us have an intuition that when strongly held, diametrically opposed opinions are held on issues of principle, any solution which would involve political compromise is completely unacceptable. However, the pragmatist would be attracted by such compromise, by a 'checkerboard' solution. Why should the legislature 'not forbid racial discrimination on buses but permit it in restaurants'? This would be a compromise giving something to both sides. It would be acceptable to the pragmatist but, Dworkin claims, not to the vast majority of us. 'Do the British divide on the morality of abortion? Why should Parliament not make abortion criminal for pregnant women who are born in even years but not for those born in odd ones?' Why should such a 'Solomonic' solution be morally unacceptable?

> Most of us, I think, would be dismayed by 'checkerboard' laws that treat similar accidents or occasions of racial discrimination or abortion differently on arbitrary grounds . . . we reject a division between parties of opinion when matters of principle are at stake. We follow a different model: that each point of view must be allowed a voice in the process of deliberation but that the collective decision must nevertheless aim to settle on some coherent principle whose influence then extends to the natural limits of its authority. If there must be compromise because people are divided about justice, then the compromise must be external, not internal; it must be compromise about which scheme of justice to adopt rather than a compromised scheme of justice.
>
> But there lies the puzzle. Why should we turn our back on checkerboard solutions as we do? Why should we not embrace them as a general strategy for legislation whenever the community is divided over some issue of principle? . . . What is the special defect we find in checkerboard solutions? It cannot be a failure in fairness (in our sense of a fair distribution of political power) because checkerboard laws are by hypothesis fairer than either of the two alternatives. Allowing each of two groups to choose some part of the law of abortion, in proportion to their numbers, is fairer (in our sense) than the winner-takes-all scheme our instincts prefer, which denies many people any influence at all over an issue they think desperately important.

Dworkin *Law's Empire* 179

The answer is predictable.

Astronomers postulated Neptune before they discovered it. They knew that only another planet, whose orbit lay beyond those already recognized, could explain the behavior of the nearest planets. Our instincts about internal compromise suggest another political ideal standing beside justice and fairness. Integrity is our Neptune. The most natural explanation of why we oppose checkerboard statutes appeals to that ideal: we say that a state that adopts these internal compromises is acting in an unprincipled way, even though no single official who voted for or enforces the compromise has done anything which, judging his individual actions by the ordinary standards of personal morality, he ought not to have done. The state lacks integrity because it must endorse principles to justify part of what it has done that it must reject to justify the rest. That explanation distinguishes integrity from the perverse consistency of someone who refuses to rescue prisoners because he cannot save all. If he had saved some, selected arbitrarily, he would not have violated any principle he needs to justify other acts. But a state does act that way when it accepts a Solomonic checkerboard solution; it is inconsistency in principle among the acts of the state personified that integrity condemns.

Dworkin *Law's Empire* 183–184

There seems to be no doubt that law as integrity is a conception of law that is most impressive on the dimension of substance. Indeed not only does it entail the most impressive foil to pragmatism and checkerboard solutions, it also furnishes a morally acceptable account of political obligation.

INTEGRITY AND POLITICAL OBLIGATION

The conception of law as integrity converts a political society into a special kind of community, 'special in a way that promotes its moral authority to assume and deploy a monopoly of coercive force'. In what follows it is the attitude of the citizen to those decisions that extend explicit past decisions that is so important.

Integrity expands and deepens the role individual citizens can play in developing the public standards of their community because it requires them to treat relations among themselves as characteristically, not just spasmodically, governed by these standards. If people understood formal legislation as only a matter of negotiated solutions to discrete problems, with no underlying commitment to any more fundamental public conception of justice, they would draw a sharp distinction between two kinds of encounters with fellow citizens: those that fall within and those that fall without the scope of some past political decision. Integrity, in contrast, insists that each citizen must accept demands on him, and may make demands on others, that share and extend the moral dimension of any explicit political decisions. Integrity therefore fuses citizens' moral and political lives: it asks the good citizen, deciding how to treat his neighbor when their interests conflict, to interpret the common scheme of justice to which they are both committed just in virtue of citizenship.

Dworkin *Law's Empire* 189–190

To arrive at the best account of political obligation and the obligation to obey, he wants us to consider the relationships between the members of a family and similar associations, such as universities, colleges, clubs, etc. In such, there will exist 'genuine fraternal obligations' when the members of the group exhibit certain attitudes concerning the responsibilities they owe one another. Most importantly, they accept the responsibilities as being personal, owed by one member to another, as not directed at the group as an entity. Furthermore, members must see these responsibilities 'as flowing from a more general responsibility each has of *concern* for the well-being of others in the group' (p 200). So the obligation to help a friend in financial trouble is to be treated as 'derivative from and expressing a more general responsibility active throughout the association in different ways' (p 200). Lastly, this concern needs to be an *equal* concern for all members.

> Fraternal associations are in that sense conceptually egalitarian. They may be structured, even hierarchical, in the way a family is, but the structure and hierarchy must reflect the group's assumption that its roles and rules are equally in the interests of all, that no one's life is more important than anyone else's.
>
> Dworkin *Law's Empire* 200

What is the relevance of this interesting excursion into the world of smaller associations when we are really discussing the larger political community and the obligation to obey?

> [The best account of political obligation] is to be found not in the hard terrain of contracts or duties of justice or obligations of fair play that might hold among strangers, where philosophers have hoped to find it, but in the more fertile ground of fraternity, community, and their attendant obligations. Political association, like family and friendship and other forms of association more local and intimate, is in itself pregnant of obligation.
>
> Dworkin *Law's Empire* 206

Such is 'the community of principle' where the conception of law as integrity acts as the bond that aspires to fraternity.

> It insists that people are members of a genuine political community only when they accept that their fates are linked in the following strong way: they accept that they are governed by common principles, not just by rules hammered out in political compromise. Politics has a different character for such people. It is a theater of debate about which principles the community should adopt as a system, which view it should take of justice, fairness, and due process, not the different story, appropriate to the other models, in which each person tries to plant the flag of his convictions over as large a domain of powers or rules as possible. Members of a society of principle accept that their political rights and duties are not exhausted by the particular decisions their political institutions have reached, but depend, more generally, on the scheme of principles those decisions presuppose and endorse. So each member accepts that others have rights and that he has duties flowing from that scheme, even though these have never been formally identified or declared. Nor does he suppose that these further rights and duties are conditional on his wholehearted approval of that scheme; these obligations arise from the historical fact that his community had adopted that scheme, which is then

special to it, not the assumption that he would have chosen it were the choice entirely his. In short, each accepts political integrity as a distinct political ideal and treats the general acceptance of that ideal, even among people who otherwise disagree about political morality, as constitutive of political community.

Dworkin *Law's Empire* 211

Therefore integrity is the best interpretation of 'a morally pluralistic society', superior to backward-looking conventionalism and forward-looking pragmatism. Unlike the latter conceptions, law as integrity 'commands that no one be left out, that we are all in politics together for better or worse, that no one may be sacrificed, like wounded left on the battlefield, to the crusade for justice overall' (p 213). In short, it manifests those conditions we saw in smaller associations which have responsibilities that amount to genuine fraternal obligations.

The result of this section on political obligation and the previous one on law as integrity is that the conception of law as integrity is not only basic to Dworkin's theory of adjudication but also as a solution to the problem of political obligation. The battle on the plateau ends with integrity putting to rout the evil forces of conventionalism and pragmatism.

LAW AS INTEGRITY

The main issue confronting Dworkin in his work before *Law's Empire* was to demonstrate how to determine legal rights in hard cases. In *Law's Empire* he has added the problem of showing how the imposition of collective force through the concept of law is justified. The first problem was previously discussed in terms of the rights thesis (supra Chapter 4). There is a 'right answer' or 'best interpretation' of past decisions, even in hard cases, and this is based on principle, not policy, in a manner that gives individual rights priority over collective goals. These arguments are preserved in *Law's Empire*. However, the name of the theory, or at least of the methodology, has changed to the metaphor of constructive interpretation. Where legal adjudication answers both the above problems it is now called 'law as integrity'.

Dworkin's discussion of law as integrity and his chain novel analogy is explained in the chapter on 'Positivism and Adjudication: H L A Hart v Ronald Dworkin' (supra pp 77ff).

Part Three
Critical Jurisprudence

Chapter 13

The economic theory of law

The economic interpretation of law advances a bold thesis: this is that many, if not all, areas of the law can be understood to be concerned with the promotion of efficiency.[1] The thesis has both a descriptive and a normative aspect. According to the former, analysis reveals that many legal rules in areas such as tort and contract in fact promote efficiency; while according to the latter, the theory forms a basis for the critique and evaluation of new legal rules and legislation.

It is, however, important to stress that the concept of efficiency that is in question is a technical one, namely, that of wealth maximisation. Wealth is maximised when goods and services are so distributed that aggregate social wealth—measured by the willingness of individuals to pay for the relevant goods and services—could not be increased. Hence, any additional benefit to a particular individual could only be at the expense of a loss to someone else which was greater—so that aggregate social wealth was less.[2]

It might seem an urgent question to ask why social wealth should have the importance given to it by the economic interpretation of law. After all, it is a familiar complaint against utilitarianism that an overall increase in aggregate utility is compatible with great injustice in its distribution, and a similar point can surely be made about an increase in social wealth. The pressing nature of this question about the importance given to social wealth seems to be further underlined by the fact that various writers on the subject recognise a distinction between efficiency, or social wealth, on the one hand, and equity, or justice, on the other. Polinsky, for instance, writes that 'efficiency corresponds to "the size of the pie", while equity has to do with how it is sliced. Economists traditionally concentrate on how to maximize the size of the pie, leaving to others—such as legislators—the decision how to divide it' (Polinsky *An Introduction to Law and Economics* 7). Since there are infinitely many different ways in which a pie can be sliced the distinction between efficiency and justice would seem to be transparent. However, Polinsky goes on to say that 'The attractiveness of efficiency as a goal is that, under some circumstances described below, everyone can be made better off if society is organized in an efficient manner.' This strongly suggests that he thinks that in certain circumstances efficiency and equity do not

---

[1] Two excellent introductory accounts to this topic are: J Murphy and J Coleman *The Philosophy of Law: an Introduction to Jurisprudence* New Jersey, Rowman and Allanheld, ch 5; and A M Polinksy *An Introduction to Law and Economics* Boston, Little Brown and Co.

[2] So the state of affairs would be what is called Pareto optimal, that is, one in which no one can gain an increase in welfare without someone else suffering a loss. This makes it tempting to identify the concept of efficiency in question with Pareto optimality, as do many writers on this subject. However, Dworkin argues that this would be a mistake (R Dworkin *A Matter of Principle* 239); and whether or not he is right, everyone agrees that the efficient solution is one which maximises wealth in the sense of producing the largest possible net balance of benefits over costs.

diverge. Anyway, it is important at this stage to keep an open mind on this issue, just as it is to remember that the concept of efficiency in question is a technical one.

THE COASE THEOREM

Some of the central ideas that inspired the economic interpretation of law are beautifully illustrated in the following extract which describes the seminal work of Ronald Coase.

One of the central ideas in the economic analysis of law was developed in an article by Ronald Coase in 1960.[a] This idea, which has since been named the *Coase Theorem*, is most easily described by an example. Consider a factory whose smoke causes damage to the laundry hung outdoors by five nearby residents. In the absence of any corrective action each resident would suffer $75 in damages, a total of $375. The smoke damage can be eliminated in either of two ways: A smokescreen can be installed on the factory's chimney, at a cost of $150, or each resident can be provided an electric dryer, at a cost of $50 per resident. The efficient solution is clearly to install the smokescreen since it eliminates total damages of $375 for an outlay of only $150, and it is cheaper than purchasing five dryers for $250.

ZERO TRANSACTION COSTS

The question asked by Coase was whether the efficient outcome would result if the right to clean air is assigned to the residents or if the right to pollute is given to the factory. If there is a right to clean air, then the factory has three choices: pollute and pay $375 in damages, install a smokescreen for $150, or purchase five dryers for the residents at a total cost of $250. Clearly, the factory would install the smokescreen, the efficient solution. If there is a right to pollute, then the residents face three choices: suffer their collective damages of $375, purchase five dryers for $250, or buy a smokescreen for the factory for $150. The residents would also purchase the smokescreen. In other words, the efficient outcome would be achieved regardless of the assignment of the legal right.

It was implicitly assumed in this example that the residents could costlessly get together and negotiate with the factory. In Coase's language, this is referred to as the assumption of *zero transaction costs*. In general, transaction costs include the costs of identifying the parties with whom one has to bargain, the costs of getting together with them, the costs of the bargaining process itself, and the costs of enforcing any bargain reached. With this general definition in mind, we can now state the simple version of the Coase Theorem: If there are zero transaction costs, the efficient outcome will occur regardless of the choice of legal rule.

Note that, although the choice of the legal rule does not affect the attainment of the efficient solution when there are zero transaction costs, it does affect the distribution of income. If the residents have the right to clean air, the factory pays $150 for the smokescreen, whereas if the factory has the right to pollute, the residents pay for the smokescreen. Thus, the choice of the legal rule redistributes income by the amount of the least-cost solution to the conflict.

[a] Ronald H Coase, The Problem of Social Costs, 3 J L & Econ 1 (1960).

Since it is assumed for now that income can be costlessly redistributed, this distributional effect is of no consequence—if it is not desired, it can be easily corrected.

POSITIVE TRANSACTION COSTS

The assumption of zero transaction costs obviously is unrealistic in many conflict situations. At the very least, the disputing parties usually would have to spend time and/or money to get together to discuss the dispute. To see the consequences of positive transaction costs, suppose in the example that it costs each resident $60 to get together with the others (due, say, to transportation costs and the value attached to time). If the residents have a right to clean air, the factory again faces the choice of paying damages, buying a smokescreen, or buying five dryers. The factory would again purchase the smokescreen, the efficient solution. If the factory has a right to pollute, each resident now has to decide whether to bear the losses of $75, buy a dryer for $50, or get together with the other residents for $60 to collectively buy a smokescreen for $150. Clearly, each resident will choose to purchase a dryer, an inefficient outcome. Thus, given the transaction costs described, a right to clean air is efficient, but a right to pollute is not.

Note that in the example the preferred legal rule minimized the effects of transaction costs in the following sense. Under the right to clean air, the factory had to decide whether to pay damages, install a smokescreen, or buy five dryers. Since it was not necessary for the factory to get together with the residents to decide what to do, the transaction costs considered—the costs of the residents to get together—did not have any effect. Under the right to pollute, the residents had to decide what to do. Since the residents were induced to choose an inefficient solution in order to avoid the cost of getting together, the transaction costs did have an effect. Thus, even though no transaction costs were actually incurred under the right to pollute since the residents did not get together, the effects of transaction costs were greater under that rule.

We can now state the more complicated version of the Coase Theorem: If there are positive transaction costs, the efficient outcome may not occur under every legal rule. In these circumstances, the preferred legal rule is the rule that minimizes the effects of transaction costs. These effects include the actual incurring of transaction costs and the inefficient choices induced by a desire to avoid transaction costs.

The distributional consequences of legal rules are somewhat more complicated when there are transaction costs. It is no longer true, as it was when there were zero transaction costs, that the choice of rule redistributes income by the amount of the least-cost solution. In the example, if the residents have the right to clean air, the factory pays $150 for the smokescreen, whereas if the factory has the right to pollute, the residents pay $250 for five dryers.

Although the simple version of the Coase Theorem makes an unrealistic assumption about transaction costs, it provides a useful way to begin thinking about legal problems because it suggests the kinds of transactions that would have to occur under each legal rule in order for that rule to be efficient. Once these required transactions are identified, it may be apparent that, given more realistic assumptions about transaction costs, one rule is clearly preferable to another on efficiency grounds. The more complicated version of the Coase Theorem provides a guide to choosing legal rules in this situation. All of the applications investigated in this book—nuisance law, breach of contract, automobile accidents, law enforcement, pollution control, and products liability—can be approached in this way, although some fit more naturally into the Coasian framework than others.

Polinsky *An Introduction to Law and Economics* 11–14

Let us concentrate our discussion to begin with on the case in which there are no transaction costs. Coase's result is a remarkable one, namely, that it makes no difference from the point of view of efficiency whether a right to clean air is awarded to the residents, or a right to pollute to the factory owner. In either case, assuming zero transaction costs, rationality, cooperativeness, and perfect information, the same efficient result will be reached—that is, the smokescreen will be purchased. One is tempted to argue that surely the polluter should pay so that, since the factory owner is the polluter, the right to claim damages should be awarded to the residents. Moreover, one wants to add, the alternative allocation of rights, which gives the factory owner the right to pollute, is doubly unjust, since in this case the costs of the smokescreen fall on the residents. But Coase rejects this argument. It is true that there would not be any harm if the chimney did not pour forth smoke; but it is equally true that there would not be any if the houses were not situated in close proximity to the factory. Consider an analogous situation: a rancher lives next door to a farmer who grows corn and, from time to time, the rancher's cattle trespass and eat some of the corn. Who then is to blame? Coase argues that the blame should be shared equally: 'It is true that there would be no crop damage without the cattle. It is equally true that there would be no crop damage without the crops . . . If we are to discuss the problem in terms of causation, both parties cause the damage. If we are to obtain an optimal allocation of resources, it is therefore desirable that both parties should take the harmful effects (the nuisance) into account in deciding on their course of action' (R Coase, 'The Problem of Social Cost' *The Journal of Law and Economics* 1960, 13).

To a non-economist at least, one assumption which the Coase theorem makes is striking, namely, that both parties can afford to pay the costs involved however the rights are allocated. But suppose that the residents are poor, so that if the right to pollute is awarded to the factory they cannot afford to do anything to protect themselves. If I have £10, then I may well be prepared to spend it to avoid a loss of £15; but if I have not got the £10, then I presumably must suffer the loss, and the efficient outcome will not be attainable by bargaining.

But supposing that the residents can afford to compensate the factory owner if the right to pollute is awarded to him, is there any sense in which the result reached is just either in this case, or in the case in which the right to clean air is awarded to the residents? Presumably, if there is, it is because of the way in which the result is reached in each case, that is, by cooperative bargaining in conditions of perfect information. And if it is felt that in one of these cases—the one in which the right to pollute is awarded to the factory owner—the initial assignment of rights is wrong, we have seen that Coase would reply that there is no reason to allocate causal blame uniquely.[3] Of course, even so, we could say that the result of the transaction is unqualifiedly just only if the initial holdings of the parties were just; to put the point in Nozickian terms, justice requires not only a just transfer

---

[3] But even if this were so, would it be right to allocate the costs of the nuisance arbitrarily? If the blame is shared, surely so should the costs.

but an original acquisition that was just. And while the Coase theorem may give us an account of the justice of transfer, it has nothing to say about the justice of acquisition.

Note, finally, that though from the point of view of efficiency it does not matter how rights are assigned to individuals, they do have to be assigned in one way or the other to enable the parties to bargain. However, Coase's point is that when transaction costs are zero, either assignment is efficient.

WHEN TRANSACTION COSTS ARE NOT ZERO

But of course transaction costs never are zero, so that practically speaking the question is what to do in such cases. Polinsky argues that the desired rule is the one which diminishes the effects of transaction costs; and that this being so it is no longer a matter of indifference how rights are assigned. Assigning a right to clean air to the residents both diminishes transaction costs, and reaches an efficient result; whereas assigning a right to pollute to the factory owner does neither of these things. A different suggestion about a procedure to follow when choosing a rule in such cases is that one should try to mimic the market, by producing the outcome that would have obtained had transaction costs been zero and the parties had bargained freely (R Posner *The Economic Analysis of Law*, Boston, 10–12). This would presumably produce the same result in the case in question, since, as Coase tells us, when transaction costs are zero a smokescreen would have been built however rights are assigned. So that when transaction costs are not zero we must mimic the market and ensure that a smokescreen is built; and the only way in which we can do this is by assigning the right to clean air to the residents.

Anyway, if transaction costs are not zero, then the question of who has the right to do what is not irrelevant from the point of view of efficiency; on the contrary, it is crucial. Furthermore, the nature of the right itself is important, as Calabresi and Melamed argue in the following extract, which distinguishes different kinds of rights or entitlements. A further complication is that, unlike Coase, they admit the possibility of taking distributional factors into account as well—so that a decision as to which entitlements to assign may involve not only efficiency, but also equity.

The first issue which must be faced by any legal system is one we call the problem of 'entitlement.' Whenever a state is presented with the conflicting interests of two or more people, or two or more groups of people, it must decide which side to favor. Absent such a decision, access to goods, services, and life itself will be decided on the basis of 'might makes right'— whoever is stronger or shrewder will win. Hence the fundamental thing that law does is to decide which of the conflicting parties will be entitled to prevail. The entitlement to make noise versus the entitlement to have silence, the entitlement to pollute versus the entitlement to breathe clean air, the entitlement to have children versus the entitlement to forbid them—these are the first order of legal decisions.

Having made its initial choice, society must enforce that choice. Simply setting the entitlement does not avoid the problem of 'might makes right'; a minimum of state intervention is always necessary. Our conventional notions make this easy to comprehend with respect to private property. If Taney owns a cabbage patch and Marshall, who is bigger, wants a cabbage, he will get it unless the state intervenes. But it is not so obvious that the state must also intervene if it chooses the opposite entitlement, communal property. If large Marshall has grown some communal cabbages and chooses to deny them to small Taney, it will take state action to enforce Taney's entitlement to the communal cabbages. The same symmetry applies with respect to bodily integrity. Consider the plight of the unwilling ninety-eight-pound weakling in a state which nominally entitles him to bodily integrity but will not intervene to enforce the entitlement against a lustful Juno. Consider then the plight—absent state intervention—of the ninety-eight-pounder who desires an unwilling Juno in a state which nominally entitles everyone to use everyone else's body. The need for intervention applies in a slightly more complicated way to injuries. When a loss is left where it falls in an auto accident, it is not because God so ordained it. Rather it is because the state has granted the injurer an entitlement to be free of liability and will intervene to prevent the yictim's friends, if they are stronger, from taking compensation from the injurer. The loss is shifted in other cases because the state has granted an entitlement to compensation and will intervene to prevent the stronger injurer from rebuffing the victim's requests for compensation.

The state not only has to decide whom to entitle, but it must also simultaneously make a series of equally difficult second order decisions. These decisions go to the manner in which entitlements are protected and to whether an individual is allowed to sell or trade the entitlement. In any given dispute, for example, the state must decide not only which side wins but also the kind of protection to grant. It is with the latter decisions, decisions which shape the subsequent relationship between the winner and the loser, that this article is primarily concerned. We shall consider three types of entitlements—entitlements protected by property rules, entitlements protected by liability rules, and inalienable entitlements. The categories are not, of course, absolutely distinct; but the categorization is useful since it reveals some of the reasons which lead us to protect certain entitlements in certain ways.

An entitlement is protected by a property rule to the extent that someone who wishes to remove the entitlement from its holder must buy it from him in a voluntary transaction in which the value of the entitlement is agreed upon by the seller. It is the form of entitlement which gives rise to the least amount of state intervention: once the original entitlement is decided upon, the state does not try to decide its value. It lets each of the parties say how much the entitlement is worth to him, and gives the seller a veto if the buyer does not offer enough. Property rules involve a collective decision as to who is to be given an initial entitlement but not as to the value of the entitlement.

Whenever someone may destroy the initial entitlement if he is willing to pay an objectively determined value for it, an entitlement is protected by a liability rule. This value may be what it is thought the original holder of the entitlement would have sold it for. But the holder's complaint that he would have demanded more will not avail him once the objectively determined value is set. Obviously, liability rules involve an additional stage of state intervention: not only are entitlements protected, but their transfer or destruction is allowed on the basis of a value determined by some organ of the state rather than by the parties themselves.

An entitlement is inalienable to the extent that its transfer is not permitted between a willing buyer and a willing seller. The state intervenes not only to determine who is initially entitled and to determine the compensation that must be paid if the entitlement is taken or destroyed, but also to forbid its sale under some or all circumstances. Inalienability rules are thus quite different from property and liability rules. Unlike those rules, rules of inalienability not only 'protect' the entitlement; they may also be viewed as limiting or regulating the grant of the entitlement itself.

It should be clear that most entitlements to most goods are mixed. Taney's house may be protected by a property rule in situations where Marshall wishes to purchase it, by a liability rule where the government decides to take it by eminent domain, and by a rule of inalienability in situations where Taney is drunk or incompetent. This article will explore two primary questions: (1) In what circumstances should we grant a particular entitlement? and (2) In what circumstances should we decide to protect that entitlement by using a property, liability, or inalienability rule?

THE SETTING OF ENTITLEMENTS

What are the reasons for deciding to entitle people to pollute or to entitle people to forbid pollution, to have children freely or to limit procreation, to own property or to share property? They can be grouped under three headings: economic efficiency, distributional preferences, and other justice considerations.

Economic Efficiency

Perhaps the simplest reason for a particular entitlement is to minimize the administrative costs of enforcement. This was the reason Holmes gave for letting the costs lie where they fall in accidents unless some clear societal benefit is achieved by shifting them. By itself this reason will never justify any result except that of letting the stronger win, for obviously that result minimizes enforcement costs. Nevertheless, administrative efficiency may be relevant to choosing entitlements when other reasons are taken into account. This may occur when the reasons accepted are indifferent between conflicting entitlements and one entitlement is cheaper to enforce than the others. It may also occur when the reasons are not indifferent but lead us only slightly to prefer one over another and the first is considerably more expensive to enforce than the second.

But administrative efficiency is just one aspect of the broader concept of economic efficiency. Economic efficiency asks that we choose the set of entitlements which would lead to that allocation of resources which could not be improved in the sense that a further change would not so improve the condition of those who gained by it that they could compensate those who lost from it and still be better off than before. This is often called Pareto optimality. To give two examples, economic efficiency asks for that combination of entitlements to engage in risky activities and to be free from harm from risky activities which will most likely lead to the lowest sum of accident costs and of costs of avoiding accidents. It asks for that form of property, private or communal, which leads to the highest product for the effort of producing.

Recently it has been argued that on certain assumptions, usually termed the absence of transaction costs, Pareto optimality or economic efficiency will occur regardless of the initial entitlement. For this to hold, 'no transaction costs' must be understood extremely broadly as involving both perfect knowledge and the absence of any impediments or costs of negotiating. Negotiation costs include, for example, the cost of excluding would-be freeloaders from the fruits of market bargains. In such a frictionless society, transactions would occur until no one could be made better off as a result of further transactions without making someone else worse off. This, we would suggest, is a necessary, indeed a tautological, result of the definitions of Pareto optimality and of transaction costs which we have given.

Such a result would not mean, however, that the *same* allocation of resources would exist regardless of the initial set of entitlements. Taney's willingness to pay for the right to make noise may depend on how rich he is; Marshall's willingness to pay for silence may depend on his wealth. In a society which entitles Taney to make noise and which forces Marshall to buy silence from Taney, Taney is wealthier and Marshall poorer than each would be in a society which had the converse set of entitlements. Depending on how Marshall's desire for silence and Taney's for noise vary with their wealth, an entitlement to noise will result in negotiations which will lead to a different quantum of noise than would an entitlement to silence. This variation in the quantity of noise and silence can be viewed as no more than an instance of the well accepted proposition that what is a Pareto optimal, or economically efficient, solution varies with the starting distribution of wealth. Pareto optimality is optimal *given* a distribution of wealth, but different distributions of wealth imply their own Pareto optimal allocation of resources. . . .

Distributional Goals

There are, we would suggest, at least two types of distributional concerns which may affect the choice of entitlements. These involve distribution of wealth itself and distribution of certain specific goods, which have sometimes been called merit goods.

All societies have wealth distribution preferences. They are, nonetheless, harder to talk about than are efficiency goals. For efficiency goals can be discussed in terms of a general concept like Pareto optimality to which exceptions—like paternalism—can be noted. Distributional preferences, on the other hand, cannot usefully be discussed in a single conceptual framework. There are some fairly broadly accepted preferences—caste preferences in one society, more rather than less equality in another society. There are also preferences which are linked to dynamic efficiency concepts—producers ought to be rewarded since they will cause everyone to be better off in the end. Finally, there are a myriad of highly individualized preferences as to who should be richer and who poorer which need not have anything to do with either equality or efficiency—silence lovers should be richer than noise lovers because they are worthier.

Difficult as wealth distribution preferences are to analyze, it should be obvious that they play a crucial role in the setting of entitlements. For the placement of entitlements has a fundamental effect on a society's distribution of wealth. It is not enough, if a society wishes absolute equality, to start everyone off with the same amount of money. A financially egalitarian society which gives individuals the right to make noise immediately makes the would-be noisemaker richer than the silence-loving hermit. Similarly, a society which entitles the person with brains to keep what his shrewdness gains him implies a different distribution of wealth from a society which demands from each according to his relative ability but gives to each according to his relative desire. One can go further and consider that a beautiful woman or handsome man is better off in a society which entitles individuals to bodily integrity than in one which gives everybody use of all the beauty available.

The consequence of this is that it is very difficult to imagine a society in which there is complete equality of wealth. Such a society either would have to consist of people who were all precisely the same, or it would have to compensate for differences in wealth caused by a given set of entitlements. The former is, of course, ridiculous, even granting cloning. And the latter would be very difficult; it would involve knowing what everyone's tastes were and taxing every holder of an entitlement at a rate sufficient to make up for the benefits the entitlement gave him. For example, it would involve taking from everyone with an entitlement to private use of his beauty or brains sufficiently to compensate those less favorably endowed but who nonetheless desired what beauty or brains could get.

If perfect equality is impossible, a society must choose what entitlements it wishes to have on the basis of criteria other than perfect equality. In doing this, a society often has a choice of methods, and the method chosen will have important distributional implications. Society can, for instance, give an entitlement away free and then, by paying the holders of the entitlement to limit their use of it, protect those who are injured by the free entitlement. Conversely, it can allow people to do a given thing only if they buy the right from the government. Thus a society can decide whether to entitle people to have children and then induce them to exercise control in procreating, or to require people to buy the right to have children in the first place. A society can also decide whether to entitle people to be free of military service and then induce them to join up, or to require all to serve but enable each to buy his way out. Which entitlement a society decides to sell, and which it decides to give away, will likely depend in part on which determination promotes the wealth distribution that society favors . . .

Property and Liability Rules

Why cannot a society simply decide on the basis of the already mentioned criteria who should receive any given entitlement, and then let its transfer occur only through a voluntary negotiation? Why, in other words, cannot society limit itself to the property rule? To do this it would need only to protect and enforce the initial entitlements from all attacks, perhaps through criminal sanctions, and to enforce voluntary contracts for their transfer. Why do we need liability rules at all?

In terms of economic efficiency the reason is easy enough to see. Often the cost of establishing the value of an initial entitlement by negotiation is so great that even though a transfer of the entitlement would benefit all concerned, such a transfer will not occur. If a collective determination of the value were available instead, the beneficial transfer would quickly come about.

Eminent domain is a good example. A park where Guidacres, a tract of land owned by 1,000 owners in 1,000 parcels, now sits would, let us assume, benefit a neighboring town enough so that the 100,000 citizens of the town would each be willing to pay an average of $100 to have it. The park is Pareto desirable if the owners of the tracts of land in Guidacres actually value their entitlements at less than $10,000,000 or an average of $10,000 a tract. Let us assume that in fact the parcels are all the same and all the owners value them at $8,000. On this assumption, the park is, in economic efficiency terms, desirable—in values foregone it costs $8,000,000 and is worth $10,000,000 to the buyers. And yet it may well not be established. If enough of the owners hold-out for more than $10,000 in order to get a share of the $2,000,000 that they guess the buyers are willing to pay over the value which the sellers in actuality attach, the price demanded will be more than $10,000,000 and no park will result. The sellers have an incentive to hide their true valuation and the market will not succeed in establishing it.

An equally valid example could be made on the buying side. Suppose the sellers of Guidacres have agreed to a sales price of $8,000,000 (they are all relatives and at a family banquet decided that trying to hold-out would leave them all losers). It does not follow that the buyers can raise that much even though each of 100,000 citizens *in fact* values the park at $100. Some citizens may try to freeload and say the park is only worth $50 or even nothing to them, hoping that enough others will admit to a higher desire and make up the $8,000,000 price. Again there is no reason to believe that a market, a decentralized system of valuing, will cause people to express their true valuations and hence yield results which all would *in fact* agree are desirable.

Whenever this is the case an argument can readily be made for moving from a property rule to a liability rule. If society can remove from the market the valuation of each tract of land, decide the value collectively, and impose it, then the holdout problem is gone. Similarly, if society can value collectively each individual citizen's desire to have a park and charge him a 'benefits' tax based upon it, the freeloader problem is gone. If the sum of the taxes is greater than the sum of the compensation awards, the park will result . . .

The Framework and Pollution Control Rules

Nuisance or pollution is one of the most interesting areas where the question of who will be given an entitlement, and how it will be protected, is in frequent issue. Traditionally, and very ably in the recent article by Professor Michelman, the nuisance-pollution problem is viewed in terms of three rules. First, Taney may not pollute unless his neighbor (his only neighbor let us assume), Marshall, allows it (Marshall may enjoin Taney's nuisance). Second, Taney may pollute but must compensate Marshall for damages caused (nuisance is found but the remedy is limited to damages). Third, Taney may pollute at will and can only be stopped by Marshall if Marshall pays him off (Taney's pollution is not held to be a nuisance to Marshall). In our terminology rules one and two (nuisance with injunction, and with damages only) are entitlements to Marshall. The first is an entitlement to be free from pollution and is protected by a property rule; the second is also an entitlement to be free from pollution but is protected only by a liability rule. Rule three (no nuisance) is instead an entitlement to Taney protected by a property rule, for only by buying Taney out at Taney's price can Marshall end the pollution.

The very statement of these rules in the context of our framework suggests that something is missing. Missing is a fourth rule representing an entitlement in Taney to pollute, but an entitlement which is protected only by a liability rule. The fourth rule, really a kind of partial eminent domain coupled with a benefits tax, can be stated as follows: Marshall may stop Taney from polluting, but if he does he must compensate Taney.

As a practical matter it will be easy to see why even legal writers as astute as Professor Michelman have ignored this rule. Unlike the first three it does not often lend itself to judicial imposition for a number of good legal process reasons. For example, even if Taney's injuries could practically be measured, apportionment of the duty of compensation among many Marshalls would present problems for which courts are not well suited. If only those Marshalls who voluntarily asserted the right to enjoin Taney's pollution were required to pay the compensation, there would be insuperable freeloader problems. If, on the other hand, the liability rule entitled one of the Marshalls alone to enjoin the pollution and required all the benefited Marshalls to pay their share of the compensation, the courts would be faced with the immensely difficult task of determining who was benefited how much and imposing a benefits tax accordingly, all the while observing procedural limits within which courts are expected to function.

The fourth rule is thus not part of the cases legal scholars read when they study nuisance law, and is therefore easily ignored by them. But it is available, and may sometimes make more sense than any of the three competing approaches. Indeed, in one form or another, it may well be the most frequent device employed. To appreciate the utility of the fourth rule and to compare it with the other three rules, we will examine why we might choose any of the given rules.

We would employ rule one (entitlement to be free from pollution protected by a property rule) from an economic efficiency point of view if we believed that the polluter, Taney, could avoid or reduce the costs of pollution more cheaply than the pollutee, Marshall. Or to put it another way, Taney would be enjoinable if he were in a better position to balance the costs of polluting against the costs of not polluting. We would employ rule three (entitlement to pollute protected by a property rule) again solely from an economic efficiency standpoint, if we made the converse judgment on who could best balance the harm of pollution against its avoidance costs. If we were wrong in our judgments and if transactions between Marshall and Taney were costless or even very cheap, the entitlement under rules one or three would be traded and an economically efficient result would occur in either case. If we entitled Taney to pollute and Marshall valued clean air more than Taney valued the pollution, Marshall would pay Taney to stop polluting even though no nuisance was found. If we entitled Marshall to enjoin the pollution and the right to pollute was worth more to Taney than freedom from pollution was to Marshall, Taney would pay Marshall not to seek an injunction or would buy Marshall's land and sell it to someone who would agree not to seek an injunction. As we have assumed no one else was hurt by the pollution, Taney could now pollute even though the initial entitlement, based on a wrong guess of who was the cheapest avoider of the costs involved, allowed the pollution to be enjoined. Wherever transactions between Taney and Marshall are easy, and wherever economic efficiency is our goal, we could employ entitlements protected by property rules even though we would not be sure that the entitlement chosen was the right one. Transactions as described above would cure the error. While the entitlement might have important distributional effects, it would not substantially undercut economic efficiency.

The moment we assume, however, that transactions are not cheap, the situation changes dramatically. Assume we enjoin Taney and there are 10,000 injured Marshalls. Now *even if* the right to pollute is worth more to Taney than the right to be free from pollution is to the sum of the Marshalls, the injunction will probably stand. The cost of buying out all the Marshalls, given holdout problems, is likely to be too great, and an equivalent of eminent domain in Taney would be needed to alter the initial injunction. Conversely, if we denied a nuisance remedy, the 10,000 Marshalls could only with enormous difficulty, given freeloader problems, get together to buy out even one Taney and prevent the pollution. This would be so even if the pollution harm was greater than the value to Taney of the right to pollute.

If, however, transaction costs are not symmetrical, we may still be able to use the property rule. Assume that Taney can buy the Marshalls' entitlements easily because holdouts are for some reason absent, but that the Marshalls have great freeloader problems in buying out Taney. In this situation the entitlement should be granted to the Marshalls unless we are sure the Marshalls are the cheapest avoiders of pollution costs. Where we do not know the identity of the cheapest cost avoider it is better to entitle the Marshalls to be free of pollution because, even if we are wrong in our initial placement of the entitlement, that is, even if the Marshalls are the cheapest cost avoiders, Taney will buy out the Marshalls and economic efficiency will be achieved. Had we chosen the converse entitlement and been wrong, the Marshalls could not have bought out Taney. Unfortunately, transaction costs are often high on both sides and an initial entitlement, though incorrect in terms of economic efficiency, will not be altered in the market place.

Under these circumstances—and they are normal ones in the pollution area—we are likely to turn to liability rules whenever we are uncertain whether the polluter or the pollutees can most cheaply avoid the cost of pollution. We are only likely to use liability rules where we are uncertain because, if we are certain, the costs of liability rules—essentially the costs of collectively valuing the damages to all concerned plus the cost in coercion to those who would not sell at the collectively determined figure—are unnecessary. They are unnecessary because transaction costs and bargaining barriers become irrelevant when we are certain who is the cheapest cost avoider; economic efficiency will be attained without transactions by making the correct initial entitlement.

As a practical matter we often are uncertain who the cheapest cost avoider is. In such cases, traditional legal doctrine tends to find a nuisance but imposes only damages on Taney payable to the Marshalls. This way, if the amount of damages Taney is made to pay is close to the injury caused, economic efficiency will have had its due; if he cannot make a go of it, the nuisance was not worth its costs. The entitlement to the Marshalls to be free from pollution unless compensated, however, will have been given *not* because it was thought that polluting was probably worth less to Taney than freedom from pollution was worth to the Marshalls, nor even because on some distributional basis we preferred to charge the cost to Taney rather than to the Marshalls. It was so placed *simply because we did not know* whether Taney desired to pollute more than the Marshalls desired to be free from pollution, and the only way we thought we could test out the value of the pollution was by the only liability rule we thought we had. This was rule two, the imposition of nuisance damages on Taney. At least this would be the position of a court concerned with economic efficiency which believed itself limited to rules one, two, and three.

Rule four gives at least the possibility that the opposite entitlement may also lead to economic efficiency in a situation of uncertainty. Suppose for the moment that a mechanism exists for collectively assessing the damage resulting to Taney from being stopped from polluting by the Marshalls, and a mechanism also exists for collectively assessing the benefit to each of the Marshalls from such cessation. Then—assuming the same degree of accuracy in collective valuation as exists in rule two (the nuisance damage rule)—the Marshalls would stop the pollution if it harmed them more than it benefited Taney. If this is possible, then even if we thought it necessary to use a liability rule, we would still be free to give the entitlement to Taney or Marshall for whatever reasons, efficiency or distributional, we desired.

Actually, the issue is still somewhat more complicated. For just as transaction costs are not necessarily symmetrical under the two converse property rule entitlements, so also the liability rule equivalents of transaction costs—the cost of valuing collectively and of coercing compliance with that valuation—may not be symmetrical under the two converse liability rules. Nuisance damages may be very hard to value, and the costs of informing all the injured of their rights and getting them into court may be prohibitive. Instead, the assessment of the objective damage to Taney from foregoing his pollution may be cheap and so might the assessment of the relative benefits to all Marshalls of such freedom from pollution. But the opposite may also be the case. As a result, just as the choice of which property entitlement may be based on the asymmetry of transaction costs and hence on the greater amenability of one property entitlement to market corrections, so might the choice between liability entitlements be based on the asymmetry of the costs of collective determination.

The introduction of distributional considerations makes the existence of the fourth possibility even more significant. One does not need to go into all the permutations of the possible tradeoffs between efficiency and distributional goals under the four rules to show this. A simple example should suffice. Assume a factory which, by using cheap coal, pollutes a very wealthy section of town and employs many low income workers to produce a product purchased primarily by the poor; assume also a distributional goal that favors equality of wealth. Rule one—enjoin the nuisance—would possibly have desirable economic efficiency results (if the pollution hurt the homeowners more than it saved the factory in coal costs), but it would have disastrous distribution effects. It would also have undesirable efficiency effects if the initial judgment on costs of avoidance had been wrong and transaction costs were high. Rule two—nuisance damages—would allow a testing of the economic efficiency of eliminating the pollution, even in the presence of high transaction costs, but would quite possibly put the factory out of business or diminish output and thus have the same income distribution effects as rule one. Rule three—no nuisance—would have favorable distributional effects since it might protect the income of the workers. But if the pollution harm was greater to the homeowners than the cost of avoiding it by using a better coal, and if transaction costs—holdout problems—were such that homeowners could not unite to pay the factory to use better coal, rule three would have unsatisfactory efficiency effects. Rule four—payment of damages to the factory after allowing the homeowners to compel it to use better coal, and assessment of the cost of these damages to the homeowners—would be the only one which would accomplish both the distributional and efficiency goals.

An equally good hypothetical for any of the rules can be constructed. Moreover, the problems of coercion may as a practical matter be extremely severe under rule four. How do the homeowners decide to stop the factory's use of low grade coal? How do we assess the damages and their proportional allocation in terms of benefits to the homeowners? But equivalent problems may often be as great for rule two. How do we value the damages to each of the many homeowners? How do we inform the homeowners of their rights to damages? How do we evaluate and limit the administrative expense of the court actions this solution implies?

The seriousness of the problem depends under each of the liability rules on the number of people whose 'benefits' or 'damages' one is assessing and the expense and likelihood of error in such assessment. A judgment on these questions is necessary to an evaluation of the possible economic efficiency benefits of employing one rule rather than another. The relative ease of making such assessments through different institutions may explain why we often employ the courts for rule two and get to rule four—when we do get there—only through political bodies which may, for example, prohibit pollution, or 'take' the entitlement to build a supersonic plane by a kind of eminent domain, paying compensation to those injured by these decisions. But all this does not, in any sense, diminish the importance of the fact that an awareness of the possibility of an entitlement to pollute, but one protected only by a liability rule, may in some instances allow us best to combine our distributional and efficiency goals.

Calabresi and Melamed 'Property Rules, Liability Rules and Inalienability: One View of the Cathedral' 85 Harvard Law Review (1972) 1089–1128

Calabresi and Melamed's distinctions between different kinds of entitlement is an important one. One advantage of an entitlement protected by a property rule is, of course, that since it can only be sold voluntarily, its value is determined by that transaction; whereas the value of an entitlement protected by a liability rule may be much harder to determine if others may breach it and then compensate for the breach. The possibility of both over- and under-compensation is obvious, either of which would, of course, be inefficient. Moreover, the conditions of the Coase theorem are significantly relaxed since bargaining need not have taken place. And though the result may be more efficient, there may well be a feeling that the loss of the right to bargain is itself an important loss, and that the outcome does not have the same legitimacy, since it is the process gone through, not the actual outcome, that makes it legitimate. Even so, Calabresi and Melamed's reasons for claiming that entitlements protected by liability rules rather than property rules are the most efficient in some cases are convincing; so the issue is not about the efficiency of such rules in these cases, but about their justice.

As they concede, Calabresi and Melamed's introduction of distributional factors into their account adds a further layer of complexity, and raises the question whether such factors can be traded off against efficiency as they suppose. Certainly, the lexical priority which Rawls gives to his first principle of justice over his second, denies the legitimacy of such trade-offs; and Calabresi and Melamed's position has been severely criticised by Dworkin (*A Matter of Principle* 267–289). So it is worth noting that other advocates of the economic interpretation of law would not agree that legal rules as such should be concerned with distributional matters or equity—however paradoxical that might sound—and that these are better taken care of by the tax system and transfer payments. Polinsky, for instance, argues that:

In disputes in which the parties are in a contractual or market relationship—as in the breach of contract and products liability examples—efficiency usually should be the only criterion because it is very difficult, if not impossible, to redistribute income. In disputes in which the parties are, in actuality or in effect, strangers—as in the nuisance law, automobile accident, and pollution control examples—it is possible to promote the equitable distribution of income through the legal system, but this can usually be done better through the government's tax and transfer system. Thus efficiency generally should be the primary criterion for evaluating legal rules.

Polinsky *An Introduction to Law and Economics* 115

The reason why in the first set of cases redistribution is not possible is, Polinsky argues, because the parties concerned will be able to compensate for any attempts to redistribute resources—for instance a polluter if made to pay for polluting will seek to recover his costs from his customers—and so will defeat the attempt to redistribute. While in cases in which it is possible, there are a variety of reasons why the law is in fact a very inefficient way of doing it.

Finally, it is important to note that if the bargaining parties indulge in strategic behaviour, that is, they adopt tactics designed to establish reputations as hard bargainers, then the result will very likely be an inefficient one, because transaction costs become very high. To overcome this problem Polinsky argues that if an injunction is granted 'it is necessary to choose an entitlement corresponding to the efficient outcome. This is because, starting from any other entitlement, the parties must reach some kind of agreement to get to the efficient outcome; strategic behavior may prevent this outcome being reached' (Polinsky *An Introduction to Law and Economics* 19). And if the remedy involves damages, then, Polinsky argues, it is crucially important that the liability should be equal to the actual damages. But clearly one cannot set an entitlement that corresponds to the efficient outcome if one does not know what that outcome is, any more than one can restrict liability to actual damages if one does not know what they are. In other words, Polinsky's solutions to the problem of strategic behaviour can be used only when courts have available to them information which often they clearly do not have. Moreover, his proposals would have the quite odd effect that quite different entitlements would have to be awarded in different cases because the efficient solution was different, even though they were relevantly similar in all other respects.

WEALTH AS A VALUE

At the beginning of this chapter we raised the question why the concept of efficiency should be given such a central position by the economic interpretation of law, and then postponed further discussion of it. Later we argued that in the circumstances described by the Coase theorem what, if anything, made the bargains struck just, and not merely efficient, was the fact that they were voluntarily entered into by cooperative, fully informed, and rational individuals—though we expressed some unease about the assumption that both parties were in a position to trade, and pointed out that the theorem can tell us nothing about the justice of the initial holdings of the parties concerned. However, in the discussion of pollution and nuisance by Calabresi and Melamed there are various relaxations of the conditions of the Coase theorem. Moreover, we noted that the admission of entitlements protected by liability rules seemed to undercut the defence of the justice of the outcome that was available in the circumstances of the Coase theorem. If what made the outcome just in the latter case was the fact that it was arrived at with the fully informed consent of the parties concerned, clearly some other account of the justice of an outcome when an entitlement is protected by a liability rule is needed. Is there, for instance, a virtue in efficiency as such, so that an efficient outcome is intrinsically valuable, or, at least, contains elements that are? In the next extract Posner argues that this is indeed so.

WEALTH MAXIMIZATION AS AN ETHICAL CONCEPT

Wealth versus Utility

Since Adam Smith, the term 'value' in economics has generally referred to value in exchange, value as measured or at least measurable in a market, whether explicit or implicit. From the concept of value derives the concept of the wealth of society as the sum of all goods and services in the society weighted by their values.

Although the concept of value is inseparable from that of markets, value is not the same thing as price. The market price of a good is its value to the marginal purchaser, and intramarginal purchasers will value it more in the sense that they would pay more for it if the price were higher. The wealth of society includes not only the market value in the sense of price times quantity of all goods and services produced in it, but also the total consumer and producer surplus generated by those goods and services.

The most important thing to bear in mind about the concept of value is that it is based on what people are willing to pay for something rather than on the happiness they would derive from having it. Value and happiness are of course related: a person would not buy something unless having it would give him more happiness, in the broad utilitarian sense, than the alternative goods or services (including leisure) that he must give up to have it. But while value necessarily implies utility, utility does not necessarily imply value. The individual who would like very much to have some good but is unwilling or unable to pay anything for it—perhaps because he is destitute—does not value the good in the sense in which I am using the term 'value'.

Equivalently, the wealth of society is the aggregate satisfaction of those preferences (the only ones that have ethical weight in a system of wealth maximization) that are backed up by money, that is, that are registered in a market. The market, however, need not be an explicit one. Much of economic life is still organized on barter principles. The 'marriage market,' child rearing, and a friendly game of bridge are examples. These services have value which could be monetized by reference to substitute services sold in explicit markets or in other ways. They illustrate the important point that wealth cannot be equated to the Gross National Product or any other actual pecuniary measure of welfare. A society is not necessarily wealthier because of an (involuntary) shift by women from household production to prostitution, or because a wealthy person who used to give money to charity (thereby increasing the consumption of others) now spends it on himself.

Another type of nonexplicit market, the hypothetical market, is also important in analyzing the wealth of society. Compare two situations. In one, I offer you $5 for a bag of oranges, you accept, and the exchange is consummated. The wealth of the society must now be greater. Before the transaction, you had a bag of oranges worth less than $5 to you and I had $5; after the transaction you have $5 and I have a bag of oranges worth more than $5 to me. However, suppose that instead of buying the oranges from you, I accidentally smash them. A court applying the Learned Hand formula of negligence liability would ask whether the expected cost to you of the accident was greater or less than the expected gain to me of whatever activity produced the accident as a by-product. To answer, the court would have to make a judgment as to how much those oranges were worth to you, how much walking fast was worth to me, and so on. The purist would insist that the relevant values are unknowable since they have not been revealed in an actual market transaction, but I believe that in many cases a court can make a reasonably accurate guess as to the allocation of resources that would maximize wealth. Since, however, the determination of value made by a court is less accurate than that made by a market, the hypothetical-market approach should be reserved for cases, such as the typical accident case, where market-transaction costs preclude use of an actual market to allocate resources efficiently.

Hypothetical-market analysis plays an important role in the economic analysis of the common law. Much of that law seems designed, consciously or not, to allocate resources as actual markets would, in circumstances where the costs of market transactions are so high that the market is not a feasible method of allocation. Hypothetical-market analysis also makes clear that maximizing wealth and maximizing happiness are not the same thing. Suppose a polluting factory lowers residential property values in an area by $2 million, but that it would cost the factory $3 million to relocate (the only way to eliminate the pollution), and on this basis the factory prevails in the property owners' nuisance action. The unhappiness of the property owners may exceed the happiness of the owners of the factory (who might consist of thousands of shareholders, each with only a small stake in the enterprise) at avoiding a $2 million judgment. Now reverse the numbers and assume that the property owners are wealthy people and that if the factory has to close down, its workers will suffer heavy relocation costs and many small local merchants will be pushed into bankruptcy. A judgment that forces the factory to close will be efficient but it will probably not maximize happiness.

As another example of why wealth maximization is not just a proxy for utility maximization in the sense of classical utilitarianism, consider a poor man who decides to steal a diamond necklace for his wife. The necklace has a market value of $10,000, which is also, let us assume, its subjective value to the owner. That is, the owner would be willing to sell it for any price above $10,000. The optimum fine for this theft (based on the value of the necklace, the probability of apprehending and convicting the thief, the costs of the criminal justice system, the costs of self-protection, and so on) is, let us say, $25,000; for the indigent thief, a term of imprisonment has been set that equals the disutility of a $25,000 fine to a thief who could pay it. In these circumstances, we can be reasonably confident that if our poor man goes ahead and commits the theft, the total happiness of society will rise, even though he cannot pay the fine. The thief must obtain greater utility than the disutility he imposes on society (in the cost to the victim, the costs of operating the criminal justice system, the insecurity generated by crime, and so on) since that disutility is brought to bear on him in the form of an expected disutility of imprisonment yet he commits the theft anyway. But the theft does not increase the wealth of society, because it is the outcome of neither a voluntary nor a hypothetical-market transaction. In actual-market terms the thief's unwillingness (based on inability) to pay for the necklace shows that the necklace is worth less to him than to the owner. Hypothetical-market analysis is unwarranted because there is no problem of high market transaction costs that would justify allowing the thief to circumvent the market. Even if the hypothetical-market approach were used in this example, it still would not result in awarding the necklace to the thief, for it is not worth more to him than the owner in a willingness-to-pay sense. The hypothetical-market approach would, however, be applicable if someone of monetary means broke into an unoccupied cabin and stole food in order to avert starvation. Transaction costs would be prohibitive and there would be reason to believe that the food was more valuable, in the economic sense of value, to the thief than to the owner.

The uncertainty of the relationship between wealth and happiness is further suggested by the fact that the inhabitants of wealthy countries appear to be no happier than those of poor countries, although within countries the wealthy seem to be happier than the poor. Adam Smith, who was not a utilitarian or a 'welfare economist,' thought people were deluded in believing that they would be happier if they were richer, though he had no doubt that this belief was prevalent and was an essential stimulant to human progress.

Not only can wealth not be equated to happiness, but, to state the same point in the language of economics, people are not just wealth maximizers. Wealth is an important element in most people's preferences, and wealth maximization thus resembles utilitarianism in assigning substantial weight to preferences, but it is not the sum total of those preferences. That is why positive economic theory assumes that people are utility maximizers in a broad, utilitarian sense, and is another reason for the frequent confusion of economics and utilitarianism as ethical systems.

Before concluding my exposition of the meaning of wealth maximization, I want to clarify an ambiguity in the critical concept of 'willingness to pay.' Suppose I own a home that has a market value of $100,000. It is possible that I would not sell the house for less than, say, $125,000 (the market value is the value to the marginal purchaser in the market, and I may not have the same preferences as he). But it is also possible that if I did not own the house—it is my principal asset—I would not be willing to pay more than $75,000 for it, because that is all I could 'afford' to pay. Is the house, then, worth $75,000 or $125,000? The answer depends on whether or not I own the house. But this does not conclude the analysis because, assuming I own the house, we must consider whether my ownership is consistent with ethically proper principles by which rights are assigned (the principles of distributive justice). As a dramatic example of this point, consider a totalitarian society in which a small group of government officials possesses immense amounts of that valuable commodity, power. If the price they would demand to surrender their power is considered an element in determining the wealth of the society, then it would be unclear whether introducing democratic institutions would increase that wealth. But except in the unlikely event that the bosses had obtained power through market or hypothetical-market transactions, the 'value' of their power to them would be no more relevant in measuring social wealth than the 'value' that the thief derives from the goods he steals.

Wealth Maximization, Morality, and Justice

If wealth is not just another name for happiness, and it surely is not, why should the pursuit of wealth be considered morally superior to the pursuit of happiness? That is the central question of this chapter and the next.

What makes so many moral philosophers queasy about utilitarianism is that it seems to invite gross invasions of individual liberty—whether in the name of animal happiness, or the happiness of Nozick's 'utility monster,' or Bentham's speculation on what really makes people happy. But uncompromising insistence on individual liberty or autonomy regardless of the consequences of the happiness or utility of the people of the society seems equally misplaced and unacceptable. Hence there is increasing interest in trying to combine utilitarianism and the Kantian tradition in some fashion, as in the recent work of Richard Epstein. The ethics of wealth maximization can be viewed as a blend of these rival philosophical traditions. Wealth is positively correlated, although imperfectly so, with utility, but the pursuit of wealth, based as it is on the model of the voluntary market transaction, involves greater respect for individual choice than in classical utilitarianism.

Compare once again the man who is willing to pay $10,000 for a necklace with the man who has no money but is willing to incur a nonpecuniary disutility equivalent to that of giving up such a sum. The position of the first man is morally superior because he seeks to increase his welfare by conferring a benefit on another, namely the owner. Moreover, the buyer's $10,000 was in all likelihood accumulated through productive activity—that is, activity beneficial to other people besides himself, whether to his employer, customers, or his father's customers. If we assume that a person's income is less than the total value of his production, it follows that the productive individual puts into society more than he takes out of it. Hence, not only does the buyer in our example confer a net benefit on the owner of the necklace (who would not accept $10,000 otherwise), but at every stage in the accumulation of that money through productive activity, net benefits were conferred on other people besides the producer. The thief, in contrast, provides no benefit to the owner of the necklace or to anyone else. His 'claim' to the necklace, which the utilitarian would honor, is based on a faculty—the capacity to experience pleasure—that may be worth nothing to other people. The term 'thief' is used pejoratively even in societies where theft, being punished very severely, is unlikely to occur unless the utility to the thief exceeds the victim's disutility; this fact is a datum about our ethical beliefs that utilitarianism cannot account for, and wealth maximization can.

This discussion is relevant to the question whether the utility that a thief obtains from theft should be taken into account in the design of an efficient system of penalties. If all thefts were pure coercive transfer payments extracted in a setting of low transaction costs, the utility of the thief would be entitled to no consideration, because such thefts do not create wealth. But not all thefts are of this type. Consider my earlier example of the person lost in the woods who breaks into an empty cabin and steals food that he must have to live. The cost of transacting with the owner would be prohibitive, and the theft is wealth maximizing because the food is worth more in a strict economic sense to the thief than to the owner. It follows not that the thief should go unpunished in this case—we may want to punish him to ensure that no one will commit a theft unless it really is wealth maximizing (that is, yields a gain to the thief greater than the loss of the victim)—but only that the punishment should be set at a level that deters stealing *unless* it is wealth maximizing. In contrast, if theft never had social value, the size of the penalty would be limited only by the costs of imposing it.

Economic liberty is another value that can be grounded more firmly in wealth maximization than in utilitarianism. It is the almost universal opinion of economists (including Marxist economists) that free markets, whatever objections can be made to them on grounds of equity, maximize a society's wealth. This is, to be sure, an empirical judgment, but it rests on firmer ground than the claim that free markets maximize happiness.

Most of the conventional pieties—keeping promises, telling the truth, and the like—can also be derived from the wealth-maximization principle. Adherence to these virtues facilitates transactions and so promotes trade and hence wealth by reducing the costs of policing markets through self-protection, detailed contracts, litigation, and so on. Even altruism (benevolence) is an economizing principle, because it can be a substitute for costly market and legal processes. And yet even the altruist might decide to sell his services to the highest bidder rather than donate them to the neediest supplicant. Because of the costs of determining need other than through willingness to pay, allocation by price may confer greater net benefits on the rest of society than allocation by 'need' or 'desert.' Allocation by price will also result in a greater accumulation of wealth. This wealth can be given away in whole or in part—though again the altruist will not want to spend so much time screening applicants for charity that he greatly reduces his productive work and the benefits it confers on other people.

To summarize, the wealth-maximization principle encourages and rewards the traditional 'Calvinist' or 'Protestant' virtues and capacities associated with economic progress. It may be doubted whether the happiness principle also implies the same constellation of virtues and capacities, especially given the degree of self-denial implicit in adherence to them. Utilitarians would have to give capacity for enjoyment, self-indulgence, and other hedonistic and epicurean values at least equal emphasis with diligence and honesty, which the utilitarian values only because they tend to increase wealth and hence *might* increase happiness.

Wealth maximization is a more defensible moral principle also in that it provides a firmer foundation for a theory of distributive and corrective justice. It has been argued that the source of rights exchanged in a market economy is itself necessarily external to the wealth-maximization principle. In fact the principle ordains the creation of a system of personal and property rights that ideally would extend to *all* valued things that are scarce—not only real and personal property but the human body and even ideas. Sometimes, to be sure, these rights have to be qualified because of the costs of protecting them—that is why the patent, copyright, and related laws protect only a subset of valuable ideas—or because of transaction costs or because of the problems of conflicting use (should I have the right to burn trash on my property or should my neighbor have the right to be free from smoke?) Nonetheless, the commitment of the economic approach to the principle of rights is stronger than that of most utilitarians—or, for that matter, of those Kantians who allow redistributive concerns to override property rights.

Posner *The Economics of Justice* ch 3

CRITIQUE

We begin with a question about the Coase theorem:[4] can one be sure that in the hypothetical circumstances described the parties will reach agreement? Why should they not indulge in the kind of strategic behaviour which, as we saw, can lead to an inefficient result? Coleman argues that Coase's view 'expresses an enormous amount of confidence in the ability of the negotiating parties to agree on a division of the stakes. For failure to do so blocks exchange and thus inhibits efficiency. This roadblock to efficiency, moreover, is not a function of high transaction costs' (J Murphy and J Coleman *The Philosophy of Law: an Introduction to Jurisprudence* 260). The reason why this is so is, Coleman argues, that high transaction costs put a premium on settling, while low costs make it easier to

---

[4] The point made here follows Coleman's excellent discussion.

drag out negotiations. An economist might, of course, count time spent bargaining as a transaction cost,

> But if we are to count every failure to reach agreement on the division of the spoils as necessarily resulting from transaction costs (I have no doubt that *sometimes* it does), then by transaction costs we must literally mean anything that threatens the efficiency of market exchange. In that case, it could hardly come as a surprise that in the absence of transaction costs, market exchange is efficient.
>
> Murphy and Coleman *The Philosophy of Law: an Introduction to Jurisprudence* 261

And, one might add, that anyway, *ex hypothesi*, bargaining has to be treated as costless for the purposes of the Coase theorem. Other responses would be that failure to reach agreement is a sign of lack of rationality, or of unwillingness to cooperate, so that the conditions laid down for the Coase theorem don't apply. But Coleman argues that this line of defence runs a grave risk of trivialising the theorem, so that it would be even less informative than it is normally taken to be. So perhaps the defender of the Coase theorem can be presented with the following dilemma: *either* there is bargaining which is costless, in which case there is no guarantee that agreement will be reached; *or* bargaining is never costless, so that the assumption that transaction costs are zero is one that can never be met.

Second, it is worth reiterating two points that have already been made. The first is that if the outcome reached in the circumstances of the Coase theorem is not only efficient but just, because of the way in which it is arrived at—by voluntary bargaining between rational, cooperative, and fully informed individuals—then any relaxation of the conditions may make the account of why the outcome is unjust unavailable. For if what makes the outcome just is not the fact that it is efficient, but the way in which it is reached by negotiation, then any change in the conditions which leads to the absence of negotiation—even though the most efficient outcome is reached—is one which leaves us with no account of the justice of the outcome. This important point has been forcibly made by Burrows and Veljanovski:

> The efficiency approach focuses exclusively on the efficiency of *outcomes*, and assumes that the processes by which they are achieved are not valued by individuals. The law is treated as a factor of production, like a machine, which is efficient if it maximizes the economic value of goods and services. The suppression of processes and other intangible factors in economics is largely the result of the economist's urge to make things commensurable in terms of the common denominator of money. But at a conceptual level the efficiency calculus cannot sustain this distinction between means and ends if both are independent sources of utility. If legal processes or the way of doing a thing yield utility, then individuals will be willing to pay for these (through the reduced efficiency of the outcome), and if they are not incorporated into the efficiency calculation it will be both incomplete and misleading. This is a very important point. It implies that if there are reasons to believe that a law or regulation is valued in itself because it is just, one cannot comment on its 'efficiency' by merely doing a cost-benefit analysis of its impact on the economic value of goods and services. The value people place on the legal processes must also be included in the efficiency calculus, despite the difficulties involved in placing monetary values on them. In cases where

procedural considerations are important the role of the usual efficiency analysis is elegantly summed up by Liebhafsky: 'A benefit-cost study ought to be recognized for what it is . . . a piece of evidence presented by one side or the other.' In an adjudicative or legislative adversary proceeding, evidence is not a substitute for the proceeding itself.

Burrows and Veljanovski *The Economic Approach to Law* 17

The second point worth reiterating is that the justice of the overall outcome in the circumstances of the Coase theorem is conditional on the justice of the initial holding of the parties. This is a further point which Burrows and Veljanovski make forcibly in the course of a powerful critique of the unclarity of the connection between efficiency and distributional matters:

A disappointing feature of the economic approach to law to date has been the tendency of many studies to ignore the relationship between *social efficiency* and the distribution of income and wealth. If a perfectly competitive market is to operate we require, in addition to the assumptions listed below, a clearly defined initial distribution of income and wealth which is legally protected by a set of property rights. The characteristics of a socially efficient market outcome are in part dependent on the initial distribution, because for each different distribution of income there is a different socially efficient outcome. Theoretically, therefore, there are an infinite number of socially efficient outcomes, each of which is just as good as any other in terms of efficiency alone. The desirability of social efficiency as a goal requires a value judgment as to the justness of the underlying distribution of income and property rights. As Sen stresses, efficiency itself is not such 'a momentous achievement from the point of view of social welfare. A person who starts off ill-endowed may stay poor and deprived even after . . . [trading] and if being . . . [efficient] . . . is all that competition offers, the propertyless may be forgiven for not regarding the achievement as a "big deal"'.

It is worth pursuing this point because of the confusion that has recently arisen in the literature. It has been asserted that legal rights should be assigned to those who value them most highly. This dictum is seen as establishing efficiency as a 'comprehensive and unitary theory of rights and duties'. But this claim fails for a number of reasons. First, the valuation of rights in terms of money is itself determined by the bundle of rights the individual already possesses, which in turn determines the individual's wealth. The willingness-to-pay criterion depends on the legal rights possessed by the individual, so that it is circular to argue that it can determine the 'efficient' set of rights. Secondly, the contention that corrective rights should mimic perfect market outcomes begs the question. If rights are to be assigned to mimic perfect market outcomes we must know what structure of rights that outcome was based on. The Coase Theorem tells us that *any* assignment of rights is efficient in the abstract, so that in the most favourable setting efficiency does not provide a theory of rights. The situation is not remedied by market failure, and an efficiency theory of rights is not possible unless some value judgment is made about the distribution of rights that defines the hypothetical market outcome one is attempting to replicate.

An efficiency theory of legal rights is admitted by its advocates to be a very limited theory: 'it [is] a theory that the law seeks to optimize the use and exchange of whatever rights people start out with' (Posner, 1979a, p.108). Yet even this is an exaggerated claim because it is not theory of rights at all, but a definition of allocative efficiency which assumes a pre-existing set of rights!

The exclusive concentration on efficiency in much of this literature associated with the 'Chicago school' clearly has normative connotations. It implies that efficiency is desirable, although this interpretation has been vigorously denied, for example by Posner: '"more efficient" is not a synonym for "better"' (Posner, 1973b, p.113). But this statement only elicits the reasonable response: if efficient does not necessarily mean better what is the use of an analysis which makes no attempt to specify the conditions under which it does? And should not analysts who are admittedly restricting their attention to only one of the objects of the legal system be a good deal more circumspect in the claims they make for their theory? Moreover, it is not surprising if people read into these analyses a total and unquestioning commitment to the market when the logical sequence 'the law pursues an efficiency objective→markets are efficient→the law should (and does!) seek to sustain and/or mimic the market' is relentlessly employed.

Burrows and Veljanovski *The Economic Approach to Law* 12–13

So when the conditions of the Coase theorem do not obtain, an account of why efficiency is important is badly needed. One such account, suggested by Posner's claim that in one sense of the word 'justice' just means efficiency, would be that efficiency is a good thing in its own right. Another account, also suggested by Posner, but in a different context, is that though it is not intrinsically good, it is instrumentally so, because the pursuit of efficiency requires people to cultivate ethically desirable ways of behaving. Both of these claims are discussed critically by Dworkin in our next extract:

THE QUESTION OF JUSTICE

Academic and Practical Theory

A successful interpretation must not only fit but also justify the practice it interprets. The judicial decisions we have been describing force some people to compensate others for losses suffered because their otherwise lawful activities conflicted, and since these decisions are made after the event, they are justified only if it is reasonable to suppose that people held in damages should have acted in some other way or should have accepted responsibility for the damage they caused. So the decisions can be justified only by deploying some general scheme of moral responsibility the members of a community might properly be deemed to have, about not injuring others or about taking financial responsibility for their acts. Can we find a plausible scheme of responsibility, a plausible account of how people should behave, that would suggest making liability turn on the market simulation test?

We need yet another distinction: between what we might call the academic and the practical elaboration of a moral theory. People self-consciously settling on a scheme of personal responsibility for accidents, guided by an abstract moral theory, would not try to define very concrete rules capturing exactly what the abstract theory would require in every imaginable circumstance if it were elaborated by an academic moral philosopher able to take account of every nuance of fact. If they did, they would produce too many rules to understand and master. They would have two options which they could combine. They could settle on rules using words like 'reasonable under the circumstances,' that call for more specific calculation on particular occasions, or they could construct crude rules, clear in themselves, that ignore subtleties. We are looking for a moral theory, then, whose practical rather than academic elaboration would require market-simulating rules of law. Nevertheless, when we come to inspect any such theory, to see whether it is sound *as* a moral theory, we must study its academic elaboration, because then we are concerned, not with the practical adjustments required to make that theory manageable and efficient in politics and daily life, but with the very different question whether we can accept that theory in the first place. If we cannot accept its academic elaboration because some part of this strikes us as morally wrong, the theory is not rescued because its practical elaboration would be different. For it is the academic elaboration that reveals the true nature or character of a moral theory. We shall see the importance of this distinction at once when we consider the most natural, because simplest, defense of market-simulating rules on moral grounds.

Do We Have a Duty to Maximize Wealth?

This defense lies in a two-step argument. (1) People have a moral duty to advance the good of the community as a whole in whatever they do and a corresponding moral right that others always act in that way. (2) The good of the community as a whole lies in its overall wealth according to the definition I described earlier; a community is always better when it is richer in that sense. The second step of this argument is absurd, as we learn by considering the academic elaboration of the claim that a richer society is necessarily a better society. Suppose a poor, sick man needs medicine and is therefore willing to sell a favored book, his sole source of pleasure, for the $5 the medicine costs. His neighbor is willing to pay $10 to have the book, if necessary, because he is the famous (and rich) grandson of the author, and if he autographs the book he can sell it for $11. The community is made richer, according to the economic definition of community wealth, if the police just take the book from the poor sick man and give it to his rich neighbor, leaving the poor man with neither book nor medicine. The community is richer because the book is worth $11 in the rich man's hands and only $5 to the poor man. The community's aggregate wealth is increased if the book is taken from the poor man, even beyond what it would gain if the two struck a bargain, because a forced transfer saves the transaction costs of that negotiation.

This solution would not be part of the *practical* elaboration of the thesis that people always have a duty to do whatever will make the community richer. A statesman anxious to provide rules of law reflecting that duty would avoid any rule permitting forced transfers even in circumstances like these. I assumed that we know the poor man would sell the book for $5 and the rich man would pay $10. But the best means of discovering how much people value things is to require them actually to conclude transactions. Otherwise we have no good means of testing whether they actually would do what they say they would. No doubt it costs the community more to allow the neighbors to haggle over the exact price of the book than it does to take the book from the poor man without wasting the time a bargain would take. But we gain more in accuracy over the long run by insisting that people do bargain, in order to make sure that wealth is actually increased by a transfer. So a statesman who thought people always have a duty to maximize community wealth would insist that the law refuse to allow forced transfers when negotiation is possible. Nevertheless our simple argument against the wealth-maximizing duty stands, because the argument is meant to show, not that the duty would produce horrifying results in practice, but that what it recommends, if this were feasible, is deeply wrong in principle. Even if we were *certain* that the rich man would pay more than the poor man would charge, so that social wealth would indeed be increased by just taking the book from the poor man and giving it to his rich neighbor, we would not think the situation in any way more just or the community in any way better after a transfer made in that way. So increasing social wealth does not in itself make the community better.

THE UTILITARIAN DUTY

A Utilitarian Argument

If there is a good moral argument for the wealth-maximizing, market-simulating approach to personal liability, therefore, it must be more complicated than the simple one we have now rejected. We should next consider whether an argument might be found in the popular moral theory of utilitarianism, which holds that political decisions should aim to improve average happiness (or average welfare on some other conception) in the community as a whole. The utilitarian argument we inspect recognizes the point I first emphasized, that any successful interpretation of accident and other unintended injury decisions at law must begin in some theory of individual responsibility for acts and risk. This argument has three steps. (1) Everyone has a general moral duty always to act, in each decision he makes including decisions about the use of his own property, as if the interests of all others were just as important as his own interests and those of people close to him like family and friends. (2) People act in that way when they make decisions that improve average happiness in the community as a whole, trading off losses in some people's happiness against gains to others. (3) The best practical elaboration of the duty that flows from these two first steps, the duty to maximize average happiness, takes the form of market-simulating rules of personal liability, that is, rules that require people to act as if they had made bargains in costless negotiations. . . . People should simulate markets and make the community richer in that way, not because a richer community is necessarily happier on average but because it generally is, and because no other practical code of responsibility could be expected to do better for average happiness. The utilitarian argument concedes that people have no ultimate or fundamental duty to maximize community wealth; it proposes that the best practical realization of the duty they do have, the duty to maximize happiness, is achieved by their acting as if they did have a duty to maximize wealth.

We must study this argument in stages, beginning with its third step. This declares that if citizens accept and follow market-simulating, and therefore wealth-maximizing, rules in deciding what risks to run of injuring others and when to take financial responsibility for the injuries they do cause, this practice will improve the average happiness of citizens in the long run. That is not a claim about the immediate consequences of particular acts considered one by one. Some market-simulating decisions, in and of themselves, will probably decrease overall happiness. But according to this view, general happiness is increased in the long run if everyone follows such rules in the cases we are considering. History provides no useful evidence for this supposition. It does not confirm that the best way to make a community happier on average is to make it richer on the whole with no direct constraints of distribution; that thesis remains an article of faith more popular among the rich than the poor. No doubt people on average have better lives, at least according to conventional views of what makes a life better, in prosperous nations than in very poor ones. But the present question is different. Do we have any reason to think that average happiness is generally improved in prosperous nations by still more prosperity, measured by the sums its citizens are collectively willing and able to pay for the goods they make and trade? Or that happiness could not be improved even more if citizens accepted other standards of personal responsibility, standards that sometimes ignored prosperity for other values? I think not; these claims may be true, but we have no persuasive evidence that they are.

We might, however, want to assume that they are true just for the sake of the utilitarian argument we are considering. We must then move back to the second step in that argument and ask whether its thesis is correct that treating people with equal concern means acting so as to improve average happiness. Critics of utilitarianism invent stories—sometimes very fanciful stories—that seem to cast doubt on that thesis. Suppose racial bigots are so numerous and so sadistic that torturing an innocent black man would improve the overall level of happiness in the community as a whole. Would this justify the torture? Utilitarian philosophers have a standard reply to these horrifying examples of what utilitarianism might require. They say that good moral reasoning proceeds on two levels. On the first, or theoretical, level we should aim to discover those rules or principles of morality which, as maxims of conduct, are likely to provide the greatest average happiness within the community over the long run. On the second, or practical, level we should apply the maxims so chosen in concrete cases. We should decide what to do on particular occasions, not by asking which particular decision seems likely to produce more happiness considered on its own, but by asking what the standards we chose at the first level would require us to do. Obviously, we chose at the first level of theory, rules that condemn torture and racial prejudice. This explains and justifies our 'intuition' that it would be wrong to pander to sadism or prejudice even in special circumstances when we thought a direct utilitarian calculation, applied only to the immediate facts, would require this.

But this standard defense of utilitarianism evades the hard question. Once again it mistakes a powerful criticism of its academic elaboration for an erroneous claim about its practical elaboration, about the moral intuitions it would encourage statesmen and philosophers to cultivate in ordinary people. It is not so difficult to imagine changes in the economic or social or psychological climate that would make our familiar intuitions not the best for a utilitarian to instill. Sadistic bigots *might* become so numerous among us, their capacity for delight so profound, and their tastes so ineradicable that even at the first level—when we are considering what rules would increase happiness in the very long run—we would be forced to make exceptions to our general rules and to permit the torture of blacks alone. It is not a good answer that luckily there is no genuine possibility of that situation arising. For once again the point of horrifying stories is not to provide a practical warning—that if we are seduced by utilitarianism we may well find ourselves advocating torture—but to expose defects in the academic elaboration of the theory by calling attention to moral convictions that remain powerful even in hypothetical form. If we believe that it would be unjust to torture blacks even in the (extremely improbable) circumstances when that would increase average happiness, if we think that that practice would not treat people as equals, then we reject the second step of our utilitarian argument.

Two Strategies

But let us once again, for the sake of the argument, assume that the second step is sound, that treating people with equal concern does mean maximizing average happiness. We now move back to the first step. Now we ask whether, even if we concede the last two steps, it is reasonable to suppose that everyone has a moral duty always to act in market-simulating ways when actual negotiation is for some reason not feasible. It is time to notice an intuitive connection between wealth of maximization and equality that might make that idea seem reasonable. The legal doctrines of negligence and nuisance I described strike a moral chord. It seems plausible that when accidents are likely, people ought to look out for each other's interests in the same way and to the same degree that they look after their own. We might try to explain that conviction in two ways. We might assume, first, that people always have that egalitarian responsibility, that they must always, in everything they do, consider the interests of all others to be as important as their own or those of their family and friends. Then the egalitarian responsibility that accident law enforces is only a special instance of a pervasive moral responsibility. Or we might try to show, second, that though people do not have that burdensome responsibility, generally, they do in the circumstances of negligence or nuisance cases, for a reason we must then disclose.

The present utilitarian argument, we now see, takes up the first of these strategies. It supposes that we must always, in everything we do, treat the interests of others as equally important to our own. It offers a debatable account of what that means in practice, but we are accepting that account, for the sake of the argument, by conceding the argument's second and third steps. We are now studying the first step which assumes that we each have a pervasive moral responsibility always to show equal concern for others. Most of us do not accept that pervasive responsibility. We think we are normally free, morally as well as legally, to prefer our own interests and projects, and those of a small number of other people to whom we feel special associative responsibilities and ties, in the day-to-day decisions we make using our own property. We accept that sometimes we must *not* favor ourselves and those close to us in that way, and in particular we accept that we must not do so in the circumstances of nuisance and negligence, but must instead count an injury to a stranger as equal in importance to an injury to ourselves. But we feel that these circumstances are for some reason special. We use, that is, the second strategy to explain them.

We think the circumstances of negligence and nuisance are special, moreover, in a particular way that makes our moral responsibilities parasitic on, and thus sensitive to, our legal responsibilities. I shall have to explain this connection in more detail and more apt language later in this chapter, when we consider a nonutilitarian account of accident and nuisance law I shall argue is superior. But the connection can be described informally in this way. Our legal practice recognizes what are often called prima facie legal rights in property, but which I shall call abstract rights. I have an abstract legal right to run my trains along the road bed I own, as you have to plant corn on your field next to it. I have an abstract right to use my apartment as I wish and therefore to play my trumpet, as you have to use yours as you wish and therefore to be free to study algebra in peace. We call these rights prima facie or abstract because we know that they can conflict: my exercise of my right may invade or restrict yours, in which case the question arises which of us has an actual or concrete right to do what he wishes. It is in these circumstances—the domain of negligence and nuisance and other forms of unintended damage law—that we believe the egalitarian responsibility arises. I must decide on my concrete rights—may I speed my train or blow my trumpet here and now?—in some way that respects your interests as much as my own, not because I must always act in that way, but because I must do so when our abstract rights compete. I have no such responsibility when they do not compete. I make most of the important decisions of my life on the premise that I am morally free to pay somewhat more attention to my life than to the lives of others, though of course that does not mean I am free to ignore others entirely.

That is a fair statement of ordinary moral attitudes, which someone who takes up the utilitarian argument we are testing must confront. He might say these attitudes are wrong because they display an indefensible selfishness. He might insist that, however radical this might seem, we must always, in everything we do, test our conduct by asking whether it treats everyone's interests as equally important to our own. But that is a very implausible claim, at least when joined to the market simulation theory of what it would require in practice. Almost any decision we make can be thought of as the subject of some hypothetical negotiation, so we should constantly have to consider whether others would pay more for our not doing something than we would or could pay for the privilege of doing it, and if they would, we should have to forbear (though of course without actually being paid to do so). I know, for example, that many conscientious professors of law feel a responsibility to read whatever is published in legal philosophy and therefore wish that much less were written. It seems reasonable to think that if such a negotiation were possible and costless, the academic community as a whole would pay me more to not publish this book than I could pay for the right to publish it, because I could not earn enough from royalties to meet their bid even if I wanted to do so. If I had a moral responsibility not to publish just for that reason, my life, in this respect and then in countless others, would collapse into only those activities I could and would want to outbid others for the privilege of performing. Personal autonomy would almost disappear in a society whose members accepted the market-simulating duty, because the duty would never sleep.

The utilitarian market simulator might want, therefore, to consider a different tack. He might want to fall back on the distinction I described between two levels of utilitarian argument; he might hope to show that overall happiness is best served in the long run if people do not accept his strict requirement always to consider other people's interests as equal in importance to their own but instead act in the more relaxed way they presently do. No such argument has ever been produced, and we must wait until one is to evaluate his chances of success. Any attempt, however, is likely to seem ad hoc. For the two-level argument must show not just that more utility would be produced by relaxing the strict requirement in practice, but that most utility is produced by relaxing that requirement in a particular way: by insisting on it when, and only when, abstract legal rights in property conflict. Perhaps this can be shown, but it is hardly evident, and the danger is lively that someone who attempts it will in fact be arguing backward, from the fact that our moral practices do make these discriminations to the

unwarranted conclusion that they must promote utility better in the long run
than other feasible schemes of responsibility.

Dworkin *Law's Empire* 285–295

In spite of these criticisms it might still seem reasonable, when tackling pollution,
for instance, to try to assign rights and entitlements in a way which both
minimises social costs, and mimics the market. But doubts about even this have
been forcibly expressed in a trenchant comment on Calabresi and Melamed's
important paper discussed earlier.[5] We do not have space to discuss these issues
here; however, the reader is urged to pursue them.

[5] From P Burrows, 'Nuisance, legal rules and decentralised decisions; a different view of the
cathedral crypt', in P Burrows and C G Veljanovski (eds) *The Economic Approach to Law* 12–13.

Chapter 14

Scandinavian legal realism

Scandinavian legal realism is the name given to the theories of a number of Scandinavian scholars of whom the most prominent are the Swedes, Axel Hägerström and Karl Olivecrona, and the Dane, Alf Ross. There is no doubt that the group derives its inspiration from Hägerström.

AXEL HÄGERSTRÖM (1868–1939)

Hägerström's work is conditioned by his denial of the existence of objective values. Here is the editor's preface to Hägerström's *Inquiries into the Nature of Law and Morals*—the editor being Olivecrona.

> So-called value-judgments, according to Hägerström, are judgments only with regard to the verbal form. If we say, eg, that a certain action is desirable, the property of being desirable is ascribed to the action, but no such property can be discovered in the action as belonging to the context of reality; nor can the property in question be identified with the fact that the action is desired. The utterance springs from an association of a feeling of pleasure with the idea of the actuality of the action. No real judgment lies behind the sentence; nevertheless, the sentence takes the indicative form. This form of language is the ground for the objectification of values.
>
> Olivecrona's Preface to Hägerström *Inquiries into the Nature of Law and Morals*, xi

This is a commitment to non-cognitivism (supra p 5). Consequently, all metaphysical concepts are pseudo-concepts which, when winnowed out, will leave a thoroughly realistic conception of law. 'Rights', 'duties', 'will of the State', 'binding quality of the law', these are all sham concepts whose apparent objectivity is just a trick of the form of language—the indicative mood. So, duty, for example, is but a feeling of compulsion when a particular action is contemplated. Again, 'justice' is only a matter of personal evaluation, not amenable to the scientific process. No science of the 'ought' is possible. What is required is the examination of the actual use of legal concepts. Metaphysical ideas are viewed as psychological facts. To understand his thesis we need to look at his analysis of a 'right'.

Look at the ordinary use of the word 'right'. Can it be identified with any facts? Hägerström argues that all attempts at this identification are doomed.

> Suppose I have the right of property to a certain house. The only fact seems to be that the state guarantees to me a certain protection in my possession, provided that I or my predecessors have not taken certain actions by which I have lost that protection, eg, if I have let the house and vacated it, or if I have

mortgaged it and have failed to pay the debt for which it was pledged. But at this point difficulties at once arise. Does the fact just mentioned really correspond to what we understand by a right of property? We must notice that the state does not step in as protector unless I have actually lost possession of the thing, ie, unless it is in the possession of another person who cannot base his case on any relevant legal act. But the right of property would seem to be a right to the thing itself, ie, a right to retain possession valid against every other person. Can the state guarantee this? Of course not. All that it can do is to enable me to regain the house if it should already be in the possession of another person. Moreover: Who would make the right of property dependent on the question of proving the title? Yet in a law-suit I can obtain legal protection only if I can bring forward proof. It should be noted that the child who asserts a right of property in his plaything certainly is not thinking of protection by the state, and not necessarily of protection by his parents. It is plain that he often wishes merely to exercise a certain influence over his playmate and to give to himself a certain strength in his possession. We find the same situation in inter-state relations. Every state is in the main without external protection, yet in cases of conflict it asserts its rights in order to weaken the moral force of the other state and to strengthen its own. One fights the better when one is standing up for one's rights. The assertion that private property in the juristic sense has nothing to do with this natural notion of right cannot be maintained, for the historical connection is palpable.

So, in order to find the fact in question, one is forced to view the matter in another light. It is now said that a person's property means the fact that the state commands all others, who are not entitled to the possession of this thing through special legal acts, to respect this person's possession; and that, in the event of disobedience to this command, it threatens to take coercive measures for the benefit of this person if he should so desire. But consider an ordinary dispute about property where both parties believe themselves to be in the right. No one here has been disobedient. For disobedience implies that one was aware of the command. But suppose I believe that I am in the right, and therefore that the state has not commanded me to give up the thing to my opponent. Then I am in no way disobedient. In this case I have never received a command addressed to me, and that is the same as if it had never been given to me. For an order which does not reach the person for whom it is intended is only an empty sound and not a real order. But although no disobedience to a command has occurred, and though none can even be alleged, yet the state-executive forces the party who has lost his case according to judicial decision to give up the thing if it is in his possession. And the ground which is given is that the *right* of the party who wins the suit was being infringed. So a person's right of property cannot consist in the fact that the state commands others to respect his possession, and threatens, in case of disobedience, to take coercive measures for the benefit of the proprietor, if he so desires.

It is plain that there are insuperable difficulties in determining the fact which corresponds to that which we call a right of property.

Hägerström *Inquiries into the Nature of Law and Morals* 1–3

Here is his conclusion on this preliminary question.

The factual basis which we are seeking cannot be found, then, either in *protection guaranteed* or *commands issued* by an external authority. But, on the other hand, we cannot find any other fact of which it could be said that it corresponds to our idea of a right of property or a rightful claim. This insuperable difficulty in finding the facts which correspond to our ideas of such rights forces us to suppose that there are no such facts and that we are here concerned with ideas which have nothing to do with reality.

Hägerström *Inquiries into the Nature of Law and Morals* 4

Given that no factual basis for the idea of a right can be found, he continues with his analysis of rights, and of the right of property in particular. What is meant is a power over something or somebody. But this power is no actual power.

It seems, then, that we mean, both by rights of property and rightful claims, actual forces, which exist quite apart from our natural powers; forces which belong to another world than that of nature, and which legislation or other forms of law-giving merely liberate. The authority of the state merely lends its help to carry these forces, so far as may be, over into reality. But they exist before such help is given. So we can understand why one fights better if one believes that one has right on one's side. We feel that here there are mysterious forces in the background from which we can derive support. Modern jurisprudence, under the sway of the universal demand which is now made upon science, seeks to discover facts corresponding to these supposed mysterious forces, and it lands in hopeless difficulties because there are no such facts. Traditional points of view overmaster us, which we try to fit into the framework of modern thinking, unsuccessfully because they are not adapted to it.

Hägerström *Inquiries into the Nature of Law and Morals* 5–6

We are left with the idea of a mystical power. His conclusion seems to be that when we talk of rights no concept can be found beyond the word itself but this is accompanied by a supernatural idea that the word manifests something which we believe to be a power.

This idea of mystical powers associated with certain words can be explained psychologically: for example, the idea of possessing a right to something gives rise to a feeling of power. The psychological explanation of the idea manifests itself in the feeling of strength and power associated with the idea of possessing a right.

The idea of a legal duty is subjected to a similar analysis.

From this point forward we are inevitably led to the view that the notion of legal duty cannot be defined by reference to any fact, but has a mystical basis, as is the case with right. Legal duty means, it would seem, an obligation in regard to a certain action which exists independently of any actual authority and which is crystallized out by legislation or other form of legal enactment. The interference of the legislative authority is a reaction which depends on one's neglecting to perform the action which is one's duty.

Hägerström *Inquiries into the Nature of Law and Morals* 8

Again there is a supernatural power that accompanies the word and this can be explained psychologically: the idea of being obliged to do something gives rise to a feeling of being under a pressure.

Hägerström looked to history for support for the contention that rights and duties are based on ideas of supernatural powers established through magical means. The aim of his detailed study of Roman law was to show that the *jus civile*, the civil law of the Roman citizens, was conceived of as a system of rules for establishing and maintaining supernatural powers by the use of 'magical' means. For example, the act of *mancipatio*, or buying: the buyer holds the slave, throws a piece of copper into a scale and recites a proclamation to the effect that the slave belongs to him at that moment, ie before the ceremony is over. So what?

> The curious thing is that the buyer is not reckoned to be owner until the seller has appropriated the piece of copper. Consequently, the utterance of the buyer is false in the moment when it is pronounced. Now the Romans were extremely careful in phrasing their legal formulas; it is inconceivable that they should have put a false statement into the mouth of the buyer—if its veracity was relevant. The phrase has therefore long puzzled interpreters. Hägerström's solution is the following. The purpose of the pronouncement was to *establish*, in the person of the buyer, the *dominium ex iure Quiritium* over the slave. This *dominium* was a power with regard to the slave. But how could a power be established by being *said* to be present? This depends on the nature of the power in question. True enough, the buyer would, in most cases, acquire an *actual* power. This power was, however, a consequence of the whole psychological situation in Roman society, including the general respect of the law, the importance attributed to such acts as the *mancipatio*, etc., briefly, by all the factors that caused surrounding people to regard the slave as belonging to the buyer and tended to reinforce the sense of power in himself. Every social power is a result of the interplay of such factors. Now, could the buyer proclaim the existence in himself of a power of this nature? Certainly not. This power was not even present when the words were spoken; moreover, it did not infallibly come into existence as the *dominium* was believed to do; finally, it was conditioned by the conviction that the buyer really had acquired *dominium*. The said power must have been of a supernatural kind. According to the Roman view, the formal words of the buyer in conjunction with the other elements of the ceremony had the effect of *producing* this power.
>
> Olivecrona's Preface to Hägerström *Inquiries into the Nature of Law and Morals*, xvii–xviii

Concepts employed by the law are rooted in such magical beliefs. They evolve from the primitive belief that through the observance of certain rituals, or through the recital of a set proclamation, powers are actually produced. Such powers have no real existence; they are magical ideas.

The word 'magic' has caused difficulty: 'In many minds, this word seems to evoke a vision of witches gathering around a boiling cauldron in the middle of the night.' Rather he uses the word to refer to an objective existence of powers or concepts where, in fact, such objectivity is an illusion based on the form of language used.

> It is of quite subordinate significance that I have characterized as mystical and magical the supersensible power with regard to things or persons that the Romans understood by [certain concepts and ideas]; or that I have characterized these ideas, as well as the belief in the gods being astringed by external ceremonies, as superstitious. I have called the power in question mystical because it is an ability to control things or persons—though this ability has no foundation in empirical reality—I have called it magical,

because in magic one handles such mysterious powers: and I have labelled the whole outlook superstitious because I hold belief in such powers—or in gods as being powers of such nature—can have no basis in reality.

Olivecrona's Preface to Hägerström *Inquiries into the Nature of Law and Morals*, xix

Hägerström's approach to Roman concepts, he believed, could be applied to the modern law and the influence of his claim can be seen in Olivecrona's discussion of legal language (infra pp 427ff).

But, before considering the arguments of the realists upon whom Hägerström has such an influence—Olivecrona and Ross—read this comment from another jurist, himself interested in the forms of legal language.

Hägerström himself had understood more clearly than his predecessors that certain uses of language within the law were anomalous compared with what was commonly assumed to be its normal function. For he saw that the verbal forms used both in ancient and modern legal systems to effect such legal transactions as the alienation of property, or the making of an offer, a will, or a contract, were not, as their indicative grammatical form often suggested, mere reports of the intention or the will of those entering into such transactions, and the conventional juristic classification of such verbal forms as 'declarations of intention' left unexplained their dynamic role in changing the legal situation of the parties. But Hägerström's explanation of this phenomenon in terms of beliefs in 'mystical bonds' and 'the magical' powers of language to produce changes in a supernatural world of rights and duties simply abandoned the task of serious analysis of an important dimension of language, the use of which is not confined to legal contexts, and led his followers into a blind alley.

Thus in Alf Ross, the most acute and best-equipped philosopher of this school, a narrow empiricist conception of rational meaningful discourse had bred a readiness to see 'superstition', 'fiction', or 'meaningless metaphysics' 'raising the law above the world of facts' as embodied in the normative concepts and modes of description customarily used by lawyers in representing the law. So he claimed that the only method of representation of the law fit to figure in a modern rational science of law was one which shared the structure and logic of statements of empirical science. In effect this involves an interpretation of propositions of law such as statements of legal validity or legal obligation or legal rights as essentially predictions of judicial behaviour accompanied by feelings of being bound by legal directives.

My main objection to this reduction of propositions of law which suppresses their normative aspect is that it fails to mark and explain the crucial distinction that there is between mere regularities of human behaviour and rule-governed behaviour. It thus jettisons something vital to the understanding not only of law but of any form of normative social structure. For the understanding of this the methodology of the empirical sciences is useless.

Hart *Essays in Jurisprudence and Philosophy* 12–13

What is needed, according to Hart, is to portray rule-governed behaviour as it appears to the participants. This would lead to an analysis of the 'internal aspect of rules', the idea of the 'acceptance of rules' (supra pp 34ff). Because of Hägerström's influence this dimension is lost.

KARL OLIVECRONA

It is regarded as an essential property of legal rules that they are 'valid', meaning that they are obligatory or have 'binding force'. Olivecrona is much exercised by explaining this 'binding force': what is the reason for it? By what criterion, if any, is it possible to ascertain whether a particular rule possesses this property of being binding? This problem has been the concern of most theories of law. So, it has been asserted that validity or the binding force of law resides in the idea of a natural law; according to Olivecrona this, however, is no more than an expression of faith. Can it be found in the consent of the governed? This would be far too artificial as a source of bindingness because subjects are not asked to consent to their system in any meaningful sense of the word and, furthermore, it is not the case, as it would be if the binding force of law could be found in consent, that the withdrawal of consent amounts to the end of the binding nature of the law. Similarly, theorists who try to find an explanation in law as the will of the State, or the command of the sovereign, are involved in an exercise in mythology. Kelsen tried to elucidate the idea of validity or being bound in ought norms. Ultimately, his theory depends upon a basic norm whose validity is presupposed. But this amounts to saying that no reason can be given for the validity of the basic norm. Consequently, no reason is given for the validity of the other norms that are supposed to derive their validity from this basic norm. The whole Kelsenite construct crumbles.

Is it acceptable to argue that the binding force of law is derived from the unpleasant consequences which are prompted by disobedience? This would be an inadequate explanation: unpleasant consequences ensue if we put our hands into the fire, but we do not conclude that there is a *binding* rule prohibiting us from putting our hands into the fire.

After this lengthy survey Olivecrona's conclusion will be obvious.

> Every attempt to maintain scientifically that law is binding in another sense than that of actually exerting a pressure on the population, necessarily leads to absurdities and contradictions. Here, therefore, is the dividing-line between realism and metaphysics, between scientific method and mysticism in the explanation of the law. The 'binding force' of the law is a reality merely as an idea in human minds. There is nothing in the outside world which corresponds to this idea.
>
> Olivecrona *Law as Fact* 17

From this it can be seen that the reality is what is made by men, 'actually exerting a pressure on the population'. The result is that most people have a *feeling of being bound* by the law, but this is certainly not the same thing as saying that there is a property called the binding force of law, or the validity of the law, existing outside the mind of man. More than a feeling of being bound it cannot be. It is the feeling of being bound that needs further analysis.

(a) Laws as commands?

The feeling of being bound is the psychological reaction to the fact that laws are couched in imperative terms. Although this is so it would be a fundamental mistake to conclude that Olivecrona is defining law as a set of commands.

A command presupposes one person who commands and another to whom the command is addressed. In true appreciation of this fact, the imperative theory has endeavoured to point out from whom the 'commands' emanate. Generally this has not been said to be any single individual. It would be hard indeed to maintain that the immense bulk of rules contained in the law of a modern state are the commands of any single human being. Such a being would undoubtedly require superhuman qualities. It is for this reason that the commands are ascribed to the *state*.

It is, however, impossible to maintain that the 'state', properly speaking, could issue commands. The state is an organization. But an organization cannot, as such, be said to command. If this is maintained, the expression is at best a loose one for the fact that commands are given by individuals active within the organization. Only in this sense is the statement at all reasonable.

Olivecrona *Law as Fact* 36

(b) Rules of law as 'independent imperatives'

Though not real commands, the rules of law, as has already been said, are given in the imperative form. The ideas about certain actions in certain situations, which form the contents of the rules, are not narratively described in the rules. The text of the law does not say that the law-givers or some other persons actually have conceived such and such imaginations in their minds. This would be absurd. The ideas are *imperatively* expressed. Whatever words are used, the meaning of a rule is always: this action *shall* be performed under such and such circumstances, this right *shall* arise from such and such facts, this official *shall* have this or that power, etc.

Now, does not this mean that the rules are, after all, commands? No, it does not. The term 'command' may, of course, be used by everybody according to his own pleasure, provided that the meaning is made clear. What is important is not the terminological question. But different *things* must be kept apart if the real nature of the law is to be made clear. Such imperative statements as are found, *eg* in the law, must be carefully distinguished from commands in the proper sense. They are something else. The imperative theory has neglected this distinction. For this reason it has been driven to unrealistic constructions in order to make the realities of the law fit in with the assumption that the rules are commands in the proper sense of the word.

A command in the proper sense implies a personal relationship. The command is given by one person to another by words or gestures meant to influence the will. Now the same kind of words are also used in many connexions where no personal relations whatever exist between the person who commands and the receiver of the command. The words can nevertheless have a similar, if not identical, effect. They function independently of any person who commands. We may in this case speak of '*independent imperatives*,' in order to get a convenient term.

As an example of independent imperatives may be cited the Decalogue. It cannot be said that Moses is commanding us to do this or that. Nor is this supposed to be so. The words are said to be the commands of God. In reality the Decalogue is a bundle of imperative sentences, formulated several thousand years ago and carried through the centuries by oral tradition and in writing. They are nobody's commands, though they have the form of language that is characteristic of a command.

The rules of law are of a similar character.

Olivecrona *Law as Fact* 42–43

[Rules of law are] imperative statements about imaginary actions, rights, duties, etc. As we have seen they cannot be defined as anybody's commands. Those who have drafted them or acted as formal law-givers have not at all acted in such a way as a person who commands. And to those who take cognizance of the rules, the law-givers are for the most part entirely unknown. They have only the imperative statements as such before them, isolated from the law-givers, who may have died a hundred years ago. Thus the statements function, independent of any person commanding, as guides for people's conduct.

Olivecrona *Law as Fact* 43–44

It is this imperative mode of expression and the consequent feeling of being bound that is the reality of the binding force of law.

(c) Force in the State organisation

Ultimately, Olivecrona's analysis is based on force. Surely this is an unquestionable social fact.

In every community force is consistently applied through the officials of the state, more particularly in three forms;—police measures against disturbances, infliction of punishment and execution of civil judgments. In all three cases physical violence or coercion is the ultimate expedient. It is used not only to disperse dangerous mobs if need be and to keep the peace generally. It is also an unavoidable instrument in the regular application of criminal and civil law. In criminal law, actual violence against the person of the criminal is used in the form of the death penalty and imprisonment. Even in civil law physical violence is sometimes used against a person, as *eg* when a tenant is ejected from the premises by means of force and when imprisonment for debt takes place. Generally, however, violence against a person is not needed in civil matters. Nevertheless, it must not be forgotten that physical force is the basis of execution in these cases too. Thus the goods of the debtor are seized by force if he does not deliver them peacefully when they are required in order to pay his debt. Physical force is resorted to in administrative law, also, when necessary. In the whole field therefore, the provisions of the law are ultimately carried out by physical force or violence.

Actual violence is, however, kept very much in the background. The more this is done, the smoother and more undisturbed is the working of the legal machinery. In this respect many modern states have been successful to an extent which is something of a miracle, considering the nature of man. Under suitable conditions the use of violence in the proper sense is so much reduced that it passes almost unnoticed.

Such a state of things is apt to create the belief that violence is alien to the law or of secondary importance. This is, however, a fatal illusion. One essential condition for reducing the application of violence to this extent is that there is to hand an organized force of overwhelming strength in comparison to that of any possible opponents. This is generally the case in every state organized on modern lines. Resistance is therefore known to be useless. Those who are engaged in applying force in criminal and civil matters of the ordinary kind are few in number, it is true. But they are thoroughly organized and they are in each case concerned with only a single individual, or a few individuals.

Olivecrona *Law as Fact* 124–125

ALF ROSS

The preface to Ross's *On Law and Justice* (1958) outlines his philosophical position.

> The leading idea of this work is to carry, in the field of law, the empirical principles to their ultimate conclusions. From this idea springs the methodological demand that the study of law must follow the traditional patterns of observation and verification which animate all modern empirical science; and the analytical demand that the fundamental legal notions must be interpreted as conceptions of social reality, the behaviour of man in society, and as nothing else. For this reason, I reject the idea of a specific *a priori* 'validity' which raises the law above the world of facts, and reinterpret validity in terms of social facts; I reject the idea of an *a priori* principle of justice as a guide for legislation (legal politics), and discuss the problems of legal politics in a relativistic spirit, that is, in relation to hypothetical values accepted by influential groups in the society; and, finally, I reject the idea that legal cognition constitutes a specific normative cognition, expressed in *ought*-propositions, and interpret legal thinking formally in terms of the same logic as that on which other empirical sciences are based (*is*-propositions).
>
> Ross *On Law and Justice* Preface, ix–x

The last part of this extract reveals his starting point: law is conceived of as a system of normative rules concerning social facts.

(a)   Ross's account of norms

At the centre of Ross's account is the separation of the *directive* or prescriptive function of norms from the *fact* of their existence. A statement to the effect that something ought to or may or must be done is the directive function; the existence of this directive is a separate factor.

> From the point of view of the social sciences a norm is to be defined neither merely as a linguistic phenomenon (the meaning content which is a directive) nor merely as a social fact.
>
> Ross *Directives and Norms* 78

From this it appears that this statement in his 1968 book qualifies the last part of the preface to the earlier book quoted above. This is considered below.

For the concept 'norm' to be useful its definition must meet two conditions: norms must be intrinsically connected with directives, and the explanation given of the concept of a norm must make it possible to say that certain norms actually *exist*, or *are in force*. The concept 'norm' cannot be identified with the concept 'directive' because when we talk of the existence of a norm we refer to a social *state of affairs*—we refer to conditions which, although changing, are of relative permanence.

> From this point of view many directives are ruled out as possible candidates for the norms studied in the social sciences. This holds with regard to all directives born out of a situation which is nothing more than an occurrence, or passing event. If, for example, a gangster orders the employees of a bank to hand over some money, they either do or do not comply with the directive. This is a

situation describable in psychological terms as an event happening, and leaving no room for a term which refers to a state of affairs, a lasting condition. What could it mean to say that in this situation a norm has come into existence in any permanent or lasting sense? . . .

We may provisionally conclude that the concept 'norm' cannot be identified with the concept 'directive'. This is so, briefly, because a directive is a *linguistic* phenomenon (of whatever category—semantic, grammatical, or pragmatic), and the factual contexts which define many directives are passing events to be described in terms of individual psychology.

Ross *Directives and Norms* 80

But what about the qualification, in the quotation that opened this section on norms, made to the preface of the 1958 book (supra p 430)? Is it possible to define the concept 'norm' in such a way that it designates not a linguistic phenomenon, that is a directive, but a factual social condition whose existence is established empirically? Why not define the term 'norm' as something that denotes a set of observable social facts, that is, a certain regularity of behaviour (as he did in 1958)?

But this definition is incompatible with certain other essential uses of the concept. One would not be able to say, for example, that a norm is *followed* or *applied*; that it is felt to be *binding*; or that it is *logically* connected with other norms which together make up a *system of norms*. These and other current uses of the concept 'norm' presuppose that a norm is a meaning content, and not a set of social facts . . . [He concludes by referring to the] impossibility of successfully defining 'norm' in such a way that it denotes simply a set of social facts.

Ross *Directives and Norms* 82–83

So the opening quotation can now be fully appreciated.

. . . it is not possible to define the concept 'norm' (in a way useful to the social sciences) so that it denotes either simply a kind of meaning content (which includes all or only some directives), or simply a set of social facts. Both approaches must founder as too one-sided.

Ross *Directives and Norms* 82

Therefore, he needs a definition which integrates both aspects of 'norm'.

On this basis, I put forward the following definition: *a norm is a directive which stands in a relation of correspondence to social facts*, the nature of the relation to be specified subsequently. The only directives which can stand in the required relation are the impersonal directives with the exclusion of the autonomous moral directives; that is, those directives which have been called in the above survey 'quasi-commands' and 'constitutive rules based on mutual agreement'.

Before I undertake the task of specifying what relation of correspondence is relevant, I want to stress the fundamental adequacy of the definition. The norm is said to be a directive, in the sense of a meaning content; to this extent the definition is adequate with regard to the use according to which a norm can be *followed* or *complied with*, felt to be *binding*, and *logically* related to other norms so that they together constitute a *system of norms*. But according to the definition a directive is a norm only if it corresponds to certain social facts, in a way to be specified. To say that a norm 'exists' means, then, that these facts exist; and to this extent the adequacy of the definition is secured with regard to that use of 'norm' which requires that norms can exist, and that statements to this effect form part of the description of societies.

Now, in undertaking the task of specifying how directives are related to social facts, I assume provisionally that we are concerned only with generally formulated directives, or rules. It is, then, barely questionable that the fundamental condition for the existence of a norm must be that *in the majority of cases the pattern of behaviour presented in the directive* $(s \rightarrow b)$ *is followed by the members of the society*. If a rule is not effective in this sense, then it would be misleading to say that it 'exists', if such a statement is meant to be part of a description of social facts.

That a pattern of behaviour is on the whole *followed* does not mean that every member of the society generally acts in the same way in given circumstances. Usually the description of s is so qualified that the norm will concern only certain categories of the members of the society. Thus the directive that shops are to be closed at a certain hour relates only to those members of society who are shopkeepers.

That the pattern is *on the whole* followed involves a certain vagueness which makes it difficult to decide in some circumstances whether or not a norm exists.

This condition, however, is not of itself sufficient to provide an adequate definition. For it is necessary for the establishment of a norm that it be followed not only with external regularity, that is with observable conformity to the rule, but also with the consciousness of following a rule and being bound to do so. If this requirement is not met (I shall subsequently return to the question of what it implies) then many patterns of social behaviour which differ essentially from those traditionally called norms would be included under the concept. I have in mind the following types of observable regularities of behaviour:

(1) *Patterns biologically or physically based.* Man's biological make-up and the general economy of nature effect conformity of behaviour in many ways. Most of us sleep during the night and are awake in daytime; we turn on the light when it becomes dark and wear more clothes when it is cold; we carry an umbrella or a raincoat if it looks like rain.

(2) *Technical patterns.* As we have mentioned earlier, some directives are offered as advice or directions for the most efficient performance of certain tasks and achievement of certain goals. When faced with similar tasks, people will to a great extent act uniformly and follow directions which are warranted by technology and tradition. This is especially true of professional undertakings. Bricklayers are trained in the time-honoured methods of building a wall or a chimney, gardeners learn how to graft and plant cuttings, tailors are taught the traditions of their profession.

(3) *Folkways* (habits which lack binding force). Because of uniform interests and traditions uniform habits grow up in the life of a people. In certain circles, under certain circumstances, it is usual to celebrate Christmas with a Christmas tree and gifts; to eat at set hours; to dance at the local inn on Saturday night; to get engaged before being married; to wear a wedding ring; to serve mustard with boiled cod; to have children baptized and confirmed. These patterns, without changing their substance, may become customs of a normative character merely by being deeply established.

These three and perhaps other classes of behaviour patterns are characterized by external conformity or regularity, without being internalized, that is, without being experienced as binding. This much is, I believe, commonly agreed.

Ross *Directives and Norms* 82–84

It should be noted that when he introduces the second condition—the consciousness of following a rule and being bound to do so—he refers, in a footnote, to Hart's discussion of the 'internal aspect of rules' in *The Concept of Law* (supra pp 34ff). We shall return to this cross-reference.

But what is it that transforms an external pattern of behaviour into something that is 'binding'? What does the second condition mean?

Two answers have usually been offered. Some jurists emphasise that the rule needs to be experienced *internally* as valid; others argue that the key feature is the *external* fact that any breach of the rule is regularly met by a sanction. On the former account, the criterion of a pattern of behaviour having binding force lies in mental experiences and reactions of the agent himself or of a spectator. The result is the feeling of a special impulse to act according to the pattern.

This impulse does not appear as a manifestation of his needs and interests; it may, indeed, conflict with these. Even though there exist no external hindrances to acting in violation of the pattern, and although his interests prompt him to act differently, the agent, under the influence of this impulse, does not feel free to do so. He feels himself to be subject to a peculiar kind of 'compulsion', but not a compulsion in the usual sense of a pressure stemming from the threat of sanctions—a threat of having inflicted on him some evil, which provides an incentive to act based on his interests and fears. The 'compulsion' that constitutes 'binding force' resembles the compulsion which arises out of the threat of sanctions in so far as the agent does not feel free, but rather feels under pressure to act in a way which conflicts with the way he would *like* to act. But it differs from external compulsion in that the impulse which prevents him from following his desires is not itself experienced as a manifestation of any need or interest; that is, it is not rooted in the fear of some evil or the desire for some good. For this reason, the compelling impulse has a stamp of unintelligibility and mystery, as if it did not arise from his own nature but was a dictate coming to him from outside.

Ross *Directives and Norms* 85

This feeling of being bound is usually expressed in terms of *duty*: when asked why he is acting against his interests the agent typically replies, 'because it is my duty so to do'.

Notice that what is emerging from this is the denial of an objective property of 'validity' or 'binding force of law'. We have already seen such a denial in Hägerström and Olivecrona.

I shall call any experience of obligation, rightness, wrongness, approval, or disapproval, the *experience of validity*. It must be made clear that this term designates certain psychological phenomena; 'validity' is nothing but the peculiar characteristic of these experiences. When I speak of the 'experience of validity', then, I am not referring to a recognition of 'validity' in the sense earlier discussed of a property inherent in moral principles, which cognitivists claim to exist and non-cognitivists deny. But it is not accidental that the word 'validity' is used to characterize these psychological experiences; for it is just the false interpretation of these experiences which has given rise to the idea of an objective quality of validity accessible to cognition.

Ross *Directives and Norms* 86

Now for the second account.

According to the rival account of the 'binding' character of a behaviour pattern, what distinguishes a binding norm from non-binding conformity, or internal regularity from external conformity, is a set of observable facts: if the pattern of behaviour is violated, there regularly follows a reaction on the part of the society.

Ross *Directives and Norms* 86

Therefore, the existence of a norm depends upon a threat of coercion guaranteeing compliance with the pattern of behaviour. The experience of the norm as 'binding' is the internal reflection of this external fact.

Is this second account, where the key is external observation of behaviour, feasible? Ross answers in the negative.

Not any disagreeable reaction is a sanction. The notion of a sanction is intimately connected with the feeling of disapproval. A merely external record of behaviour must lead to unacceptable results, by abstracting from the meaning of the reaction and its mental background. A person who earns a certain income is regularly met with the requirement to pay a certain sum to the Inland Revenue. Why do we not interpret this demand as a sanction (a fine) which shows the existence of a norm forbidding the earning of such an income? Why are customs duties not considered to be sanctions against imports, or the coercive measures taken with regard to the insane interpreted as sanctions against becoming insane? These and similar questions are not answerable on behaviouristic premises; and this proves that a behaviouristic account of what it is for a norm to exist cannot be sustained.

Ross *Directives and Norms* 87

The failure of the second, behaviouristic account is pronounced in the case of legal norms. Because legal sanctions are applied according to court decisions, the existence of a legal norm would have to be derived from an observed regularity in court decisions. But external observation is not sufficient to establish such regularity, the pattern of reaction of judges may change suddenly if a new law has been passed.

A behaviourist interpretation, then, achieves nothing. For the *change* in the judge's behaviour can be understood and predicted only by taking into account ideological facts, that is, only by assuming the existence of those feelings of validity, or ideology, which motivate the judge's decisions. Only on the hypothesis of the allegiance which the judge feels toward the constitution, its institutions and the traditionally recognized sources of law, is it possible to interpret changing judicial reactions as a coherent whole—as regularities constituted by an ideology.

Ross *Directives and Norms* 88

(b) Validity

The preceding section was concerned with Ross's analysis of the nature of a norm. Unavoidably this task caused us to discuss his views on the nature of 'validity' or the 'experience of validity' and, as we have seen, there are two necessary and sufficient conditions: that the norm is followed with observable, external regularity and that it is followed with the consciousness of following the rule and being bound to do so. In order to appreciate fully these conditions it is necessary to refer to his analysis of legal validity by considering the simpler case of the rules of chess. He drew such an analogy in his 1958 book.

> Let us imagine that two persons are playing chess, while a third person looks on.
>
> If the onlooker knows nothing about chess he will not understand what is going on. From his knowledge of other games he will probably conclude that it is some sort of game. But he will not be able to understand the individual moves or to see any connection between them. Still less will he have any notion of the problems involved in any particular disposition of the pieces on the board.
>
> Ross *On Law and Justice* 11

His contention is that the game of chess can be taken as a model of what we call a social phenomenon. He begins by highlighting certain features in a game of chess.

> If the onlooker knows the rules of chess, but beyond that not much about the theory of the game, his experience of the others' play changes character. He will understand that the horse's 'irregular' movement is the prescribed knight's move. He is in a position to recognize the movements of the pieces in turn as moves prescribed by the rules. Within limits he is even able to predict what will take place. For he knows that the players take turns to make a move, and that each move has to fall within the total of possibilities allowed by the rules in any given disposition of the pieces. But beyond that, especially if the players are more than mere beginners, a great deal will appear puzzling. He does not understand the players' strategy, and has no eye for the tactical problems of the situation. Why, for example, does White not take the bishop? For a complete understanding of the game a knowledge not only of the rules of chess but also of a certain amount of the theory of the game is essential. The likelihood of being able to predict the next move increases if account is taken not only of the rules of play but also of the theory of the game and the understanding each player has of it. Finally there must also be taken into account the purpose governing the play of the individual players. It is normally assumed that a player plays to win. But there are also other possibilities (for example, to let his opponent win, or to experiment and try out the value of a certain move).
>
> These considerations of the game of chess contain a peculiar and interesting lesson. Here before us we have a series of human actions (the movements of the hands to change the position of certain objects in space) and we may well suppose that these together with other bodily processes (breathing, psychophysical processes, etc.) constitute a course of events which follow certain biological and physiological laws. Nevertheless, it is obvious that it is beyond the limit of all reasonable possibility to give an account of this course of events in such a way that the individual moves of chess can be explained and predicted on a biological and physiological basis.

The problem presents a quite different aspect if we go to another level of observation and interpret the course of events in the light of the rules and theory of chess. Certain items of the whole series of events, namely, the moving of the pieces, stand out then as being actions relevant to chess or significant for chess. The movement of the pieces is not looked on as merely changing the position of objects in space, but as moves in the game, and the game becomes a significant coherent whole, because the moves reciprocally motivate each other and are construed as attack and defence in accordance with the theoretical principles of the game. If we watch the players we understand each move made by each player from the point of view of the consciousness of the rules of chess together with the knowledge we assume them to have of the theory of the game, and the goal they have set themselves in the game. Further it is also possible to ignore the persons of the players and understand the game on its own in its abstract significance (a game in a book of chess).

It must be noted that the 'understanding' we are thinking of here is of a kind other than causal. We are not operating here with laws of causation. The moves do not stand in any mutually causal relation. The connection between them is established by way of the rules and theory of chess. The connection is one of meaning.

It can further be stated that fellowship is an essential factor in a game of chess. By this I mean that the aims and interests pursued and the actions conditioned by these can only be conceived of as a link in a greater whole which includes the actions of another person. When two men dig a ditch together, they are doing nothing that each one of them could not equally well do on his own. It is quite otherwise in chess. It is not possible for one person on his own to set himself the goal of winning at chess. The actions which make up playing chess can only be performed when playing in turns with a second person. Each player has his part to play, but each part only achieves significance when the second player fulfils his role.

Fellowship is also revealed in the intersubjective character of the rules of chess. It is essential that they should be given the same interpretation, at least by the two players in a given game. Otherwise there would be no game, and the separate moves would remain in isolation with no coherent meaning.

Ross *On Law and Justice* 12–13

These features are also present in human social life, hence the usefulness of the analogy with chess.

Now all this shows that the game of chess can be taken as a simple model of that which we call a social phenomenon. Human social life in a community is not a chaos of mutually isolated individual actions. It acquires the character of community life from the very fact that a large number (not all) of individual actions are relevant and have significance in relation to a set of common conceptions of rules. They constitute a significant whole, bearing the same relation to one another as move and countermove. Here too, there is mutual interplay, motivated by and acquiring its significance from the common rules of the social 'game.' And it is the consciousness of these rules which makes it possible to understand and in some measure to predict the course of events.

Ross *On Law and Justice* 13–14

After these preliminaries he proceeds with the analogy, first by looking at the rules of chess and then looking at the concept of law.

I will now examine more closely what a rule of chess actually is, and in what way it is possible to establish what the rules are which govern the game of chess.

I have in mind here the primary rules of chess, those which determine the arrangement of the pieces, the moves, 'taking,' and the like, and not rules of chess theory.

As to the latter a few remarks will suffice. Like other technological rules they obviously are of the nature of hypothetical theoretical pronouncements. They assume the existence of the primary rules of chess and indicate the consequences which different openings and gambits will lead to in the game, judged in relation to the chance of winning. Like other technological rules their directive force is conditioned by an interest—in this example the interest in the winning of the game. If a player does not have this interest, then the theory of the game is without importance to him.

The primary rules of chess, on the other hand, are directives. Although they are formulated as assertions about the 'ability' or 'power' of the pieces to move and 'take' it is clear that they are intended to indicate how the game is to be played. They aim directly, that is, unqualified by any underlying objective, to motivate the player; they tell him, as it were: This is how it is played.

These directives are felt by each player to be socially binding; that is to say, a player not only feels himself spontaneously motivated ('bound') to a certain method of action but is at the same time certain that a breach of the rules will call forth a reaction (protest) on the part of his opponent. And in this way they are clearly distinguished from the rules of skill contained in the theory. A stupid move can arouse astonishment, but not a protest.

On the other hand, the rules of chess are not tinged with morality; this is the result of the fact that normally no one really wants to break them. The wish to cheat at a game must be due to the fact that a player has an aim other than merely to win according to the rules of the game; for example, he may want to be admired or to win a sum of money which is at stake. This latter aim is often present at a game of cards, and it is well known that the demand for honourable play here takes on a moral value.

How is it possible then to establish which rules (directives) govern the game of chess?

One could perhaps think of approaching the problem from the behaviourist angle—limiting oneself to what can be established by external observation of the actions and then finding certain regularities. But in this way an insight into the rules of the game would never be achieved. It would never be possible to distinguish actual custom, or even regularities conditioned by the theory of the game, from the rules of chess proper. Even after watching a thousand games it would still be possible to believe that it is against the rules to open with a rook's pawn.

The simplest thing, perhaps, would be to go by certain authoritative rulings, for example, rulings given at chess congresses, or information contained in recognized textbooks on chess. But even this might not be sufficient, since it is not certain that such declarations are adhered to in practice. Sometimes games are played in fact in many varying ways. Even in a classic game like chess variations of this kind can occur (for example, the rule about 'taking' *en passant* is not always adhered to). This problem of what rules govern 'chess' must therefore, strictly speaking, be understood to refer to the rules which govern an actual game between two specific persons. It is their actions, and theirs alone, which are bound up in a significant whole, and governed for both of them by the rules.

Thus we cannot but adopt an introspective method. The problem is to discover which rules are actually felt by the players to be socially binding, in the sense indicated above. The first criterion is that they are in fact effective in the game and are outwardly visible as such. But in order to decide whether rules that are observed are more than just customary usage or motivated by technical reasons, it is necessary to ask the players by what rules they feel themselves bound.

Accordingly we can say: a rule of chess 'is valid' means that within a given fellowship (which fundamentally comprises the two players of an actual game) this rule is effectively adhered to, because the players feel themselves to be socially bound by the directive contained in the rule. The concept of validity (in chess) involves two elements. The one refers to the actual effectiveness of the rule which can be established by outside observation. The other refers to the way in which the rule is felt to be motivating, that is, socially binding.

There is a certain ambiguity in the concept 'rule of chess.' The rules of chess have no reality and do not exist apart from the experience of the players, that is, their ideas of certain patterns of behaviour and, associated therewith, the emotional experience of the compulsion to obey. It is possible to abstract the meaning of an assertion purely as a thought content ('2 and 2 make 4') from the apprehension of the same by a given person at a given time; and in just the same way it is also possible to abstract the meaning of a directive ('the king has the power of moving one square in any direction') from the concrete experience of the directive. The concept 'rule of chess' must therefore in any accurate analysis be divided into two: the experienced ideas of certain patterns of behaviour (with the accompanying emotion) and the abstract content of those ideas, the norms of chess.

Thus the norms of chess are the abstract idea content (of a directive nature) which make it possible, as a scheme of interpretation, to understand the phenomena of chess (the actions of the moves and the experienced patterns of action) as a coherent whole of meaning and motivation, a game of chess; and, along with other factors, within certain limits to predict the course of the game.

The phenomena of chess and the norms of chess are not mutually independent, each of them having their own reality; they are different sides of the same thing. No biological-physical action is as such regarded as a move of chess. It acquires this quality only by being interpreted in relation to the norms of chess. And conversely, no directive idea content has as such the character of a valid norm of chess. It acquires this quality only by the fact that it can, along with others, be effectively applied as a scheme of interpretation for the phenomena of chess. The phenomena of chess become phenomena of chess only when placed in relation to the norms of chess and vice versa.

The purpose of this discussion of chess has undoubtedly become clear by now. It is a pointer toward the statement that the concept 'valid norm of chess' may function as the model for the concept 'valid law' which is the real object of our preliminary considerations.

The law too may be regarded as consisting partly of legal phenomena and partly of legal norms in mutual correlation.

Observing the law as its functions in society we find that a large number of human actions are interpreted as a coherent whole of meaning and motivation by means of legal norms as the scheme of interpretation. A purchases a house from B. It turns out that the house is full of termites. A asks B for a reduction in the purchase price, but B will not agree. A brings an action against B, and the judge in accordance with the law of contract orders B to pay to A a certain sum of money within a given time. B does not do this. A has the sheriff levy upon the personal property of B which is then sold in auction. This sequence of events comprises a whole series of human actions, from the establishment of the law of contract to the auction. A biological-physical consideration of these actions cannot reveal any causal connection between them. Such connections lie within each single individual. But we interpret them with the aid of the reference scheme 'valid law' as legal phenomena constituting a coherent whole of meaning and motivation. Each one of these actions acquires its legal character only when this is done. A's purchase of the house happens by word of mouth or with the aid of written characters. But these become a 'purchase' only when seen in relation to the legal norms. The various actions are mutually motivating just like the moves in chess. The judge, for example, is motivated by A's and B's parts in the deal (and the further circumstances in connection with it, the condition of the house), and by the precedents establishing the law of contract. The whole proceeding has the character of a 'game' only according to norms which are far more complicated than the norms of the game of chess.

On the basis of what has been said, the following hypothesis is advanced: The concept 'valid (Illinois, California, common) law' can be explained and defined in principle in the same manner as the concept 'valid (for any two players) norm of chess.' That is to say, 'valid law' means the abstract set of normative ideas which serve as a scheme of interpretation for the phenomena of law in action, which again means that these norms are effectively followed, and followed because they are experienced and felt to be socially binding.

This conclusion may perhaps be thought commonplace, and it may seem that a vast apparatus of reasoning has been employed to this end. This might be true if the problems were approached by a person with no preconceived notions. But it would not be true for an historical approach. By far the greater part of all writers on jurisprudence up to the present have maintained that the concept 'valid law' cannot be explained without recourse to the metaphysical. The law according to this view is not merely an empirical phenomenon. When we say that a rule of law is 'valid' we refer not only to something factual, that can be observed, but also to a 'validity' of a metaphysical character. This validity is alleged to be a pure concept of reason of divine origin or existing *a priori* (independent of experience) in the rational nature of man. And eminent writers on jurisprudence who deny such spiritual metaphysics have nevertheless been of the opinion that the 'validity' of the law can only be explained by means of specific postulates.

Seen in this light our preliminary conclusion will, I trust, not be called commonplace. This analysis of a simple model is calculated to raise doubts as to the necessity of metaphysical explanations of the concept of law. Who would ever think of tracing the valid norms of chess back to an *a priori* validity, a pure idea of chess, bestowed upon man by God or deduced by man's eternal reason? The thought is ridiculous, because we do not take chess as seriously as law— because stronger emotions are bound up with the concepts of law. But this is no reason for believing that logical analysis should adopt a fundamentally different attitude in each of the two cases.

Ross *On Law and Justice* 14–18

The rule, in both chess and law, serves, then, both as a 'scheme of interpretation' and a basis for prediction.

A national law system, considered as a valid system of norms, can accordingly be defined as the norms which actually are operative in the mind of the judge, because they are felt by him to be socially binding and therefore obeyed. The test of the validity is that on this hypothesis—that is, accepting the system of norms as a scheme of interpretation—we can comprehend the actions of the judge (the decisions of the courts) as meaningful responses to given conditions and within certain limits predict them—in the same way as the norms of chess enable us to understand the moves of the players as meaningful responses and predict them.

Ross *On Law and Justice* 35

At the basis of this analysis is the proposition that legal rules are essentially directives to courts to apply sanctions under certain circumstances. So take the provisions of the criminal law.

They say nothing about citizens being forbidden to commit homicide, but merely indicate to the judge what his judgment shall be in such a case . . . This shows that the real content of a norm of conduct is a directive to the judge, while the instruction to the private individual is a derived and figurative legal norm deduced from it.

Ross *On Law and Justice* 33

There is something seriously wrong in the contention that validity of law can only be considered as a scheme of interpretation enabling us to understand and to predict the actions of the judiciary and, consequently, to regard norms directed to individuals as merely derivative and metaphorical, as a sort of second-class norm, as it were.

Accordingly, as the consequence of much criticism, in *Directives and Norms*, 1968, he reconsiders the issue.

In the next extract notice that he starts by reaffirming the importance of the norms being directed to judges and that from a logical point of view any other type of norm has no independent existence. However, he is able to qualify his original position by recognising 'a psychological point of view'.

Legal rules are directed at those in authority, the organs of the state, and their source of effectiveness is the allegiance of officials toward the constitution and the institutions derived from it, together with the non-violent sanctions of disapproval and criticism which are implied in this attitude. Legal rules govern the structure and functioning of the legal machinery. By 'legal machinery' I mean the whole set of institutions and agencies through which the *actes juridiques* and the factual actions we ascribe to the state are undertaken. It includes the legislature, the courts, and the administrative apparatus, to which belong the agencies of enforcement (especially the police and the military). To know these rules is to know everything about the existence and content of the law. For example, if one knows that the courts are directed by these laws to imprison whoever is guilty of manslaugher, then, since imprisonment is a reaction of disapproval and, consequently, a sanction, one knows that it is forbidden to commit manslaughter. This last norm is implied in the first one directed to the courts; logically, therefore, it has no independent existence. The upshot is that, in describing a legal order, there is no need to employ a double set of norms, one demanding of citizens a certain type of behaviour (eg, not to commit manslaughter), and the other prescribing for the agencies of the legal machinery under what conditions coercive sanctions are to be applied (eg, if manslaughter has been committed). At times, those drafting statutes employ the device of formulating a legal rule as a directive to the courts, leaving it to the citizen to infer what conduct is required of him. The criminal code is drawn in exactly this way. Nowhere is it stated in so many words that manslaughter is prohibited. The prescription against this and other crimes is, rather, inferred from the appropriate rules of the criminal code which are directed to the judge. The Danish Criminal Code, section 237, thus simply states that 'he who kills another man shall be sentenced for manslaughter to imprisonment from 5 years and into lifetime'. More commonly, however, another device is employed. *Primary* rules (or substantive law) state how citizens are obliged to behave. It is impossible to infer from these rules alone how a judge is to decide in the case of a violation. According to the circumstances of the case, the judge may specify as a sentence some punishment (whose kind and severity is left unspecified by the primary law), or enjoin some performance or payment for damages. For this reason a set of *secondary* rules (the law of sanctions) is required to specify what sanctions may be exacted of those who violate the substantive law, and to make more precise the conditions under which various sanctions may be applied. Such rules are directed to the judge, instructing him how to decide different types of case. They are often expressed in terms of the *legal effects* that arise out of violations of substantive law; for example, when it is said that the legal effect of overdue delivery is to give the buyer a right to claim damages. This rule in fact amounts to a directive to the judge, requiring him to hold for the plaintiff when he sues in appropriate circumstances.

Are we to conclude from this that there are two sets of legal norms, one addressed to the citizens stating their obligations, and another addressed to judges, directing them to decide certain cases in certain ways?

From a logical point of view, we must answer in the negative: there exists only one set of rules, namely, the so called 'secondary' rules which prescribe how cases are to be decided, which, that is, basically prescribe the conditions under which violent coercion is to be exercised. For we have seen that primary norms, logically speaking, contain nothing not already implied in secondary norms, whereas the converse does not hold.

From a psychological point of view, however, there do exist two sets of norms. Rules addressed to citizens are felt psychologically to be independent entities which are grounds for the reactions of the authorities. If we apply our definition of the existence of a norm, primary rules must be recognized as actually existing norms, in so far as they are followed with regularity and experienced as being binding. It is immaterial to the question of the existence of these rules that they are, in addition, sanctioned by the threat of coercion and consequently obeyed from mixed motives, both interested (fear of sanctions) and disinterested (respect for law and order). Confusion on this point might lead to the mistaken objection that our logical thesis that there exists only one set of norms implies that the law is obeyed solely from fear of sanctions.

Ross *Directives and Norms* 90–92

(c) Ross's feeling of being bound and Hart's internal aspect of rules

Ross has been at pains to argue that a purely behaviouristic interpretation of the judges' actions would achieve nothing in the analysis of law. In his discussion of the idea of 'valid law' not only is there an external aspect, in the sense of outwardly observable compliance with a pattern of behaviour, but also an internal aspect. Ross's internal aspect, his second condition (supra p 431), is the 'experience of validity' or 'the feeling of being bound'. In Hart's analysis of rules, much reliance is placed on the difference between the external and internal aspects (supra pp 34ff). In their common insistence upon the importance of the relevance of an internal aspect, are they coming to similar conclusions? Is the 'feeling of being bound' synonymous with 'the internal aspect of rules'? Hart denies any possible compatibility between their common emphasis on some sort of internal aspect.

Ross is right in thinking that we must distinguish an *internal* as well as an external aspect of the phenomenon presented by the existence of social rules. This is true and very important for the understanding of any kind of rule. But unfortunately he draws the line between these aspects in the wrong places and misrepresents the internal aspect of rules as a matter of 'emotion' or 'feeling'—as a special psychological 'experience'. Only by doing this is he able to create the impression that what Kelsen terms 'ought-propositions' may be dispensed with in the analysis of legal thinking. In fact the elucidation of the internal aspect of any normative discourse requires such propositions, and if we carefully study them we shall see that there is nothing 'metaphysical' about them, though their 'logic' or structure is different from statements of fact or expressions of feeling.

The required distinction between external and internal is not one dividing physical behaviour from feeling, though of course that can be drawn; it is one dividing two radically different types of statement for which an opportunity is afforded whenever a social group conducts its affairs by rules. Thus an external observer of the group who does not accept or endorse the rules may report the fact that the group behaves in certain uniform ways and regularly reacts to deviations in adverse or hostile ways either through officials or private persons. He may predict both the future behaviour of the group and the future reaction of officials. Such statements are external statements of fact *about* the group and the efficacy of its rules. But if the group really has rules and not merely a set of convergent habits, members of the group display this by use of expressions of a different kind. These expressions do not state the fact that they follow or will follow regular patterns of behaviour; but members of the group use these expressions in the *criticism* of their own and each other's conduct by reference to the regular patterns of behaviour which they accept as a *standard*. They do not merely react to deviations from the regular pattern in a predictable adverse manner, but treat deviations as a *reason* for such reaction and demands for conformity as *justified*.

When a pattern of behaviour is thus taken as a standard the criticism of conduct in terms of it and the claims and justifications based on it are expressed by the distinctive normative vocabulary of 'ought', 'must', 'should', 'may', 'right', 'wrong', and special variants like 'duty' and 'obligation'. The forms 'I (you, he, they) ought to do that' and 'I (you, etc.) ought not to have done that' are the most general ones used to discharge these critical normative functions which indeed constitute their meaning. They are not external statements of fact predicting likely behaviour in accordance with the standards; they are internal statements in the sense that they manifest acceptance of the standards and use and appeal to them in various ways. But the internal character of these statements is not a mere matter of the speaker having certain 'feelings of compulsion'; for though these may indeed often accompany the making of such statements they are neither necessary nor sufficient conditions of their normative use in criticizing conduct, making claims and justifying hostile reactions by reference to the accepted standard.

Ross treats statements of legal validity (eg, 'this is a valid rule of Danish law') as an external statement of fact predicting judicial behaviour and feeling. Yet the normal central use of 'legally valid' is in an internal normative statement of a special kind, and Ross's failure to give a plausible account of the use of this expression in the mouth of a judge, where its internal character is clear, is due to his more general failure to allow for the internal non-factual, non-predictive uses of language inseparable from the use of rules. The internal statement 'This is a valid rule', as distinct from the external predictive statement 'In England they will follow this rule', is appropriate when a system of rules contains, as legal systems do, not only primary rules forming legal standards of behaviour, but also rules for recognizing, or general criteria identifying, the primary rules of the system by certain marks. So when a judge recognizes a statutory provision as 'valid' he identifies this as a primary rule, using for this purpose an unstated rule of recognition or criteria of identification which might be formulated as 'What the Queen in Parliament enacts is a legal standard of behaviour.'

The concept of legal validity is in some respects different from that of a chess rule to which Ross compares it and much more like that of a score in a game. When the scorer records a run or goal he is using an accepted, unstated rule in the recognition of critical phases of the game which count towards winning. He is not predicting his own or others' behaviour or feelings, nor making any other form of factual statement about the operation of the system. The temptation to misrepresent such internal statements in which use is made of an unstated, accepted rule or criterion of recognition as an external statement of fact predicting the regular operation of the system is due to the fact that the general acceptance of the rules and efficacy of the system is indeed the *normal context* in which such internal normative statements are made. It will *usually* be pointless to assess the validity of a rule (or the progress of a game) by reference to rules of recognition (scoring) which are not accepted by others in fact, or are not likely to be observed in future. We do, however, sometimes do this, in a semi-fictional mood, as a vivid way of teaching the law of a dead legal system like classical Roman law. But this normal *context* of efficacy presupposed in the making of internal statements must be distinguished from their normative meaning or content.

It is therefore vital if we are to understand social rules and the normative uses of language which are an inseparable part of this complex phenomenon of social life not to accept Ross's dilemma: 'Either construe these as predictions of judicial behaviour and feelings or as metaphysical assertions about unobservable entities above the world of facts.' The dimensions of legal language are far richer than this allows. It is, however, equally important to stress that though 'ought-propositions' and other forms of normative internal statements are both necessary and harmless in the analysis of legal thinking, it does not in the least follow that a legal system is 'a closed logical system' alleged to be dear to the formalist's heart, or that legal statements of rights and duties or validity are all deducible from clear determinate legal rules. Of course, it is here, as everywhere in law, a matter of a central core of certain meaning and a wide penumbra of uncertainty leaving room for judicial choice. Sometimes, where the rules are vague, all we can do is to predict what judges will say, and to do this we may use, in a guarded way, the word 'valid' or the cautious form 'I think this is valid.' Among the many good things in the first part of this book, none are better than Ross's discussion of judicial reasoning. But even here, even where the system's criteria for identifying particular rules of the system are vague or indeterminate, Ross's predictive analysis cannot hold good for 'This is a valid rule' said by a judge. And surely, until the central function of assertions of legal validity as a species of internal statements is recognized for what it is in the *clear* cases, we shall not understand their use in the more debatable area of the penumbra.

Hart *Essays in Jurisprudence and Philosophy* 165–169

Ross's response takes the form of an attack on an internal aspect which claims to be divorced from any psychological implications. When reading this response it must be remembered that Hart has conceded that he made a mistake in not recognising 'detached' statements as well as 'internal' and 'external' ones (supra p 52).

A recurrent theme of high interest is the distinction made by Hart between *internal* and *external* statements in our language referring to legal rules. This distinction is related to, but not identical with, a distinction between the *internal* and *external* aspect of a legal rule (or any social rule). The distinction between the two aspects of a rule is no new idea. It has often been pointed out that a social rule is more than a mere regularity in observable behavior and that legal rules for this reason cannot be ascertained and described merely by behavioristic methods. I myself have stressed this point in saying that a social rule presupposes not only an observable regularity but also that the rule be felt as 'socially binding' by the human beings following it. This means that a person not only will feel himself spontaneously motivated ('bound') to a certain pattern of behavior, but at the same time will expect that a breach of the rule will call forth a protest from his fellows in the group.

Hart objects that it is a misrepresentation to depict the internal aspect as a matter of feelings. Such feelings of being bound may occur but are neither necessary nor sufficient for the existence of 'binding' rules. 'What is necessary,' says Hart, 'is that there should be a critical reflective attitude to certain patterns of behavior as a common standard, and that this should display itself in criticism (including self criticism), demands for conformity, and in acknowledgements that such criticism and demands are justified, all of which find their characteristic expression in the normative terminology of "ought," "must," and "should," "right" and "wrong."' For my own part, however, I am unable to understand how it is possible that a person could have an attitude as described—criticize himself for breaking the rule, and acknowledge that criticism on the part of his fellows is justified—and still feel free to act as he likes. I believe that the attitude and reactions described by Hart are the overt manifestations of feelings engendered in the individual during his growth in the group. Hart uses the word 'acceptance' or even 'voluntary acceptance' to depict the internalization of the rule. In my view this is misleading, pointing too much in the direction of a deliberate decision. It may, in extraordinary situations—eg, under revolutions—happen that an attitude of allegiance is the outcome of a decision. But most people will feel themselves bound by the social norms of the group without ever being conscious of any choice or decision.

When a social group, says Hart, has certain rules of conduct, this fact affords an opportunity for many closely related, yet different, kinds of assertion; for it is possible to be concerned with the rules, either merely as an observer who does not himself accept them, or as a member of the group which accepts and uses them as guides to conduct. The two kinds of statements are called, respectively, external and internal statements. I believe this distinction to be very important as it seems to throw new light on controversies in the analysis of legal concepts. For my part I want to add that the internal language is not of a descriptive nature. Its function is not to state or describe facts, not to confer information of any kind, but to present claims, to admonish, to exhort. When I say 'You borrowed my car. It is your duty to take good care of it,' my intention is to claim a certain behavior from the borrower and to justify this claim by a reference to the (legal or moral) rules concerning borrowing. I don't inform him of the rules, I *apply* them. The external language, on the other hand, is descriptive in nature. It is concerned with facts, the description and prediction of facts.

Hart primarily is concerned with the internal language and it is his belief that most of the obscurities and distortions surrounding legal and political concepts will vanish if it is understood that they essentially involve reference to the internal point of view. He displays little concern with the external language. When he occasionally refers to it he seems to consider members of dissenting minorities within a group as the users of this language. Rejecting the rules, the dissenters talk about them only from the point of view of what probably will happen if the rules are broken. To me it is astonishing that Hart does not see, or at any rate does not mention, the most obvious use of the external language in the mouth of an observer who as such neither accepts nor rejects the rules but solely makes a report about them: the legal writer in so far as his job is to give a true statement of the law actually in force.

Ross, Book Review of Hart's *The Concept of Law* 71 Yale Law Journal 1188, 1188–1189

For a final assessment of Scandinavian jurisprudence generally and the arguments of Alf Ross in particular see the comments of Hart in his introduction to *Essays in Jurisprudence and Philosophy* (supra p 426).

Chapter 15
American legal realism

Although any generalisation about this movement would be fraught with the risk of requiring constant qualification and amendment, it clearly represents a break with the traditional approach to the definition of law. The emphasis is away from the idea of law as a body of rules and principles to be enforced by the courts, a perspective of the concept of law which this movement argues, with varying degrees of extremism, has been assigned a place of exaggerated significance in traditional jurisprudential thought. To understand the law it is necessary to understand the operation of the courts and to investigate what the lawyers actually do: look at what lawyers do and not at what they say they do. If this exercise is carried out it will soon be realised that rules, principles, statutes, and case-law are but a part of a cluster of factors working upon the process of decision-making. The personality of the judge, the politics of the judge, the social problems in a particular case, the possibility of corruption, these are some of the complex of factors which go towards making a judicial decision. Legal concepts used in the course of legal reasoning become a sort of supernatural superstructure built upon, and hiding from view, actual occurrences. Therefore concepts such as rights and duties, concepts employed by the court, need to be redefined in terms of the reality.

> You see how the vague circumference of the notion of duty shrinks and at the same time grows more precise when we wash it with cynical acid and expel everything except the object of our study, the operations of the law.

Holmes 'The Path of the Law' (1897) 10 Harvard Law Review 461–462

Oliver Wendell Holmes (1844–1935), a revered member of the United States' judiciary, wrote 'The Path of the Law' in 1897 and in it his liberal use of 'cynical acid' left behind an entirely sceptical and empirical definition of law. This was an inspirational message for those who followed, so much so that, in retrospect, Holmes can be seen as a precursor of the realist movement.

> My object is not so much to point out what seem to me to be fallacies in particular cases as to enforce by various examples and in various applications the need of scrutinizing the reasons for the rules which we follow, and of not being contented with hollow forms of words merely because they have been used very often and have been repeated from one end of the Union to the other. We must think things not words, or at least we must constantly translate our words into the facts for which they stand, if we are to keep to the real and the true.

Holmes *Collected Legal Papers* 238

His discussion of the concepts of rights and duties is important for two reasons: it emphasizes the need for an empirical basis for legal science and it argues for a predictive theory of law.

> The primary rights and duties with which jurisprudence busies itself again are nothing but prophecies. One of the many evil effects of the confusion between legal and moral ideas . . . is that theory is apt to get the cart before the horse, and to consider the right or the duty as something existing apart from and independent of the consequences of its breach, to which certain sanctions are added afterwards. But . . . a legal duty so called is nothing but a prediction that if a man does or omits certain things he will be made to suffer in this or that way by judgment of the court; and so of a legal right.
>
> Holmes 'The Path of the Law' (1897) Harvard Law Review 458

However, it is another passage from the same essay that has been treated as a catechism of realism.

> The confusion with which I am dealing besets confessedly legal conceptions. Take the fundamental question, What constitutes the law? You will find some text writers telling you that it is something different from what is decided by the courts of Massachusetts or England, that it is a system of reason, that it is a deduction from principles of ethics or admitted axioms or what not, which may or may not coincide with the decisions. But if we take the view of our friend the bad man we shall find that he does not care two straws for the axioms or deductions, but that he does want to know what the Massachusetts or English courts are likely to do in fact. I am much of his mind. The prophecies of what the courts will do in fact, and nothing more pretentious, are what I mean by the law.
>
>   Take again a notion which as popularly understood is the widest conception which the law contains;—the notion of legal duty, to which already I have referred. We fill the word with all the content which we draw from morals. But what does it mean to a bad man? Mainly, and in the first place, a prophecy that if he does certain things he will be subject to disagreeable consequences by way of imprisonment or compulsory payment of money.
>
> Holmes 'The Path of the Law' (1897) 10 Harvard Law Review 460–461

Several points need to be made. First, describing law in terms of 'prophecies' is a break with the traditional approach that seems to question not only the element of certainty in the process of decision-making, 'the notion that the only force at work in the development of the law is logic', but also the belief in any connection between law and morality. Secondly, the extract is very much in line with a basic tenet of realism, that we should study what the lawyers do and not what they say they do. Thirdly, it must be accepted that this was not intended as a neat, once-and-for-all-time, definition of law. Without more, the statement would be misleading and rather gross. In fact, he argues that we have too little legal theory and not too much, ending his essay with an eloquent plea for the 'command of ideas' and a roll call of philosophers that includes Kant and Descartes. Lastly, law is viewed through the eyes of the 'bad man'.

But 'the bad man' is a neat device for dramatizing the point that there are other ways of looking at law than as a logically consistent body of rules. For the purposes of the intending practitioner there is a more realistic way of viewing the subject-matter of his studies and this is inevitably linked to the idea of prediction. In the opening paragraph of 'The Path of the Law' Holmes made clear the significance of this for legal education:

> When we study law we are not studying a mystery but a well-known profession. We are studying what we shall want in order to appear before judges, or to advise people in such a way as to keep them out of court. The reason why it is a profession, why people will pay lawyers to argue for them or to advise them, is that in societies like ours the command of the public force is intrusted to the judges in certain cases, and the whole power of the state will be put forth, if necessary, to carry out their judgements and decrees. People want to know under what circumstances and how far they will run the risk of coming against what is so much stronger than themselves, and hence it becomes a business to find out when this danger is to be feared. The object of our study, then, is prediction, the prediction of the incidence of the public force through the instrumentality of the courts.

This passage clearly indicates that Holmes treated his audience as intending private practitioners, who would spend much of their time as office lawyers giving advice. In advocating that they should adopt the standpoint of the 'bad man', he was presumably not intending to suggest that they should be unethical or amoral, but rather that they should be clear thinking, hard-headed and realistic and that as law students they should look at law in the same way as they would look at it in practice.

Twining Karl Llewellyn and the Realist Movement 18

It is worth referring to Twining's conclusion on 'The Path of the Law'.

> The 'Path of the Law' is often treated as the *locus classicus* of the prediction theory of law. The theory, despite its ambiguity, is embryonic in character, and its vulnerability to elementary criticism seems to continue to attract at least two classes of persons: those who feel that the traditional approaches to law exhibited in juristic writing, legal literature, legal research, and legal education tend to be too academic or unrealistic or divorced from the realities of the law in action; and those who find that much of the theorizing of analytical jurists from Austin to Hart is narrow or sterile, or, again, remote from reality. Although demands for greater practicality and demands for a broader approach to law are by no means identical, they reflect a felt need for a theoretical framework which accords to such notions as purpose, role, function, official, institution, decision, and technique an important place in juristic analysis alongside traditional notions such as sovereignty, sanction, authority, rule, and duty.

Twining 'The Bad Man Revisited' (1973) 58 Cornell Law Review 292

Philosophical support for the realist movement was at hand in the 'pragmatism' of William James and John Dewey, whose work became popular at about the same time.

> A pragmatist turns away from abstraction and insufficiencies, from verbal solutions, from bad *a priori* reasons, from fixed principles, closed systems and

pretended absolutes and origins. He turns towards completeness and adequacy, towards facts, towards actions, towards powers. That means empiric temper regnant, and the rationalist temper sincerely given up, it means the open air and the possibilities of nature as against the dogma, artificiality and the pretence of finality in truth.

James Pragmatism 51

KARL LLEWELLYN

To understand the aims and nature of American legal realism we intend to take a detailed look at the work of Karl Llewellyn (1893–1962).

In an early article, 'A Realistic Jurisprudence—The Next Step', Llewellyn argues that legal doctrine, in the sense of legal rules, principles, rights and duties as embodied in case-law and statutes, is of restricted relevance for the understanding of the judicial process. His argument is based on the distinction between 'paper' rules and 'real' rules. The corollary is the distinction between 'paper' rights and 'real' rights. By 'substantive' rights, he means rights in the traditional sense, and it is these that on a descriptive level disappear. Note what is left in the realm of description.

> I should like to begin by distinguishing real 'rules' and rights from paper rules and rights. The former are conceived in terms of behavior; they are but other names, convenient shorthand symbols, for the remedies, the actions of the courts. They are descriptive, not prescriptive, except in so far as there may commonly be implied that courts *ought* to continue in their practices. 'Real rules,' then, if I had my way with words, would *by legal scientists* be called the practices of the courts, and not 'rules' at all. And for such scientists statements of 'rights' would be statements of likelihood that in a given situation a certain type of court action loomed in the offing. Factual terms. No more. This use of 'rights,' at least, has already considerable standing among the followers of Hohfeld. This concept of 'real rule' has been gaining favor since it was first put into clarity by Holmes. 'Paper rules' are what have been treated, traditionally, as rules of law: the accepted *doctrine* of the time and place—what the books there say 'the law' is. The 'real rules' and rights—'what the courts will do in a given case, and nothing more pretentious'—are then predictions. They are, I repeat, on the level of isness and not of oughtness; they seek earnestly to go no whit, in their suggestions, beyond the remedy actually available. Like all shorthand symbols, they are dangerous in connotation, when applied to situations which are not all quite alike. But their intent and effort is to describe. And one can adapt for them Max Weber's magnificent formulation in terms of probability: a right (or practice, or 'real rule') exists *to the extent that* a likelihood exists that *A* can induce a court to squeeze, out of *B*, *A*'s damages; more: *to the extent that* the likely collections will cover *A*'s damage. In this aspect *substantive* rights and 'rules,' as distinct from adjective, simply disappear—on the descriptive level. The measure of a 'rule,' the measure of a right, becomes what can be done about the situation. *Accurate* statement of a 'real rule' or of a right includes all procedural limitations on what can be done about the situation. What is left, in the realm of *description*, are at the one end the facts, the groupings of conduct (and demonstrable expectations [and/or needs]) which may be claimed to constitute an interest; and on the other the practices of courts in their effects upon the conduct and expectations of the laymen in

question. Facts, in the world of isness, to be compared directly with other facts, also in the world of isness.

Llewellyn *Jurisprudence* 21–22

His view is that although legal concepts are unreal, 'to attempt their excision from the field of law would be to fly in the face of fact'. So, although it is necessary to continue to use words such as rights, rules etc, these words need to be redefined in terms of the realities. In short, look at the actual activities of courts. Again the concern with predictability or 'likelihood' is evident.

In this extract the significance of the analysis of legal doctrine as an insight into understanding law, although not quite rendered nugatory, seems to be severely circumscribed. However it would be wrong to go too far on this tack. Despite the apparently pejorative adjective in 'paper' rules, legal doctrine, including of course rules, receives the following encouragement in a footnote to the same article.

It is along the same line that I feel strongly the unwisdom, when turning the spot light on behavior, of throwing overboard emphasis on rules, concepts, ideology, and ideological stereotypes or patterns. These last, as we have them, are, by themselves, confusing, misleading, inadequate to describe or explain. But a jurisprudence which was practically workable could not be built in terms of them, if they had not contained a goodly core of truth and sense.

Llewellyn *Jurisprudence* 37

What follows is the last section of the 1930 article.

In conclusion, then, may I repeat that I have been concerned not at all with marking a periphery of law, with defining 'it,' with *excluding* anything at all from its field. I have argued that the trend of the most fruitful thinking about law has run steadily toward regarding law as an engine (a heterogeneous multitude of engines) having purposes, not values in itself: and that the clearer visualization of the problems involved moves toward ever-decreasing emphasis on words, and ever-increasing emphasis on observable behavior (in which any demonstrably probable attitudes and thought-patterns should be included). Indeed that the focus of study, the point of reference for all things legal has been shifting, and should now be consciously shifted to the area of contact, of interaction, between official regulatory behavior and the behavior of those affecting or affected by official regulatory behavior; and that the rules and precepts and principles which have hitherto tended to keep the limelight should be displaced, and treated with severe reference to their bearing upon that area of contact—in order that paper rules may be revealed for what they are, and rules with real behavior correspondences come into due importance. That the complex phenomena which are lumped under the term 'law' have been too broadly treated in the past, and that a realistic understanding, possible only in terms of observable behavior, is again possible only in terms of study of the way in which persons and institutions are organized in our society, and of the cross-bearings of any particular *part* of law and of any particular *part* of the social in the social organization.

Included in the field of law under such an approach is everything currently included, and a vast deal more. At the very heart, I suspect, is the behavior of judges, peculiarly, that part of their behavior which marks them as judges—

those practices which establish the continuity of their office with their predecessors and successors, and which make official their contacts with other persons; but the suspicion on my part may be a relic of the case law tradition in which we American lawyers have been raised. Close around it on the one hand lies the behavior of other government officials. On the other, the sets of accepted formulae which judges recite, seek light from, try to follow. Distinguishing here the formulae with close behavior-correspondences from others; those of frequent application from those of infrequent. Close around these again, lie various persons' ideas of what the law is; and especially their views of what it or some part of it ought to accomplish. At first hand contact with officials' behavior, from another angle, lies the social set-up where the official's acts impinge directly on it; and behind that the social set-up which resists or furthers or reflects the impingement of his acts. Farther from the center lies legal and social philosophy—approaching that center more directly in proportion as the materials with which it deals are taken directly from the center. Part of law, in many aspects, is all of society, and all of man in society. But that is a question of periphery and not of center, of the reach of a specific problem in hands, not of a general discussion. As to the overlapping of the field as thus sketched with that of other social sciences, I should be sorry if no overlapping were observable. The social sciences are not staked out like real estate. Even in law the sanctions for harmless trespass are not heavy.

Llewellyn *Jurisprudence* 39–41

The overall message of the 1930 article ought to be clear: it does not argue for a root-and-branch expulsion of study of rule-orientated doctrine from jurisprudence; rather it issues a warning that a blinkered approach, concentrating solely on such doctrine and failing to look at the reality of law as practical activity, will lead to a distorted knowledge of law.

It is still worth studying Llewellyn's 1931 defence and manifesto of realism in 'Some Realism About Realism'. He begins part two of this article by asserting that there is no single credo, single programme, or, indeed, school of legal realism. There is only a *movement* in thought of jurists who are, as Jerome Frank— a fellow realist—says, related in their negations, and in their scepticism, and in their curiosity.

Llewellyn tabulates the 'common points of departure' of these jurists.

(1)   The conception of law in flux, of moving law, and of judicial creation of law.

(2)   The conception of law as a means to social ends and not as an end in itself; so that any part needs constantly to be examined for its purpose, and for its effect, and to be judged in the light of both and of their relation to each other.

(3)   The conception of society in flux, and in flux typically faster than the law, so that the probability is always given that any portion of law needs reexamination to determine how far it fits the society it purports to serve.

(4)   The *temporary* divorce of Is and Ought for purposes of study. By this I mean that whereas value judgments must always be appealed to in order to set objectives for inquiry, yet during the inquiry itself into what Is, the observation, the description, and the establishment of relations between the things described are to remain *as largely as possible* uncontaminated by the desires of the observer or by what he wishes might be or thinks ought

(ethically) to be. More particularly, this involves during the study of what courts are doing the effort to disregard the question what they ought to do. Such divorce of Is and Ought is, of course, not conceived as permanent. To men who begin with a suspicion that change is needed, a permanent divorce would be impossible. The argument is simply that no judgment of what Ought to be done in the future with respect to any part of law can be intelligently made without knowing objectively, as far as possible, what that part of law is now doing. And realists believe that experience shows the intrusion of Ought-spectacles *during the investigation of the facts* to make it very difficult to see what is being done . . .

(5)   Distrust of traditional legal rules and concepts insofar as they purport to *describe* what either courts or people are actually doing. Hence the constant emphasis on rules as 'generalized predictions of what courts will do.' This is much more widespread as yet than its counterpart: the careful severance of rules *for* doing (precepts) from rules *of* doing (practices).

(6)   Hand in hand with this distrust of traditional rules (on the descriptive side) goes a distrust of the theory that traditional prescriptive rule-formulations are *the* heavily operative factor in producing court decisions. This involves the tentative adoption [better: exploration] of the theory of rationalization for [what light it can give in] the study of opinions. It will be noted that 'distrust' in this and the preceding point is not at all equivalent to 'negation in any given instance.'

(7)   The belief in the worthwhileness of grouping cases and legal situations into narrower categories than has been the practice in the past. This is connected with the distrust of verbally simple rules—which so often cover dissimilar and non-simple fact situations (dissimilarity being tested partly by the way cases come out, and partly by the observer's judgment as to how they ought to come out; but a realist tries to indicate explicitly which criterion he is applying in any particular instance).

(8)   An insistence on evaluation of any part of law in terms of its effects, and an insistence on the worthwhileness of trying to find these effects.

(9)   Insistence on *sustained and programmatic attack* on the problems of law along any of these lines . . .

Llewellyn Jurisprudence 55–57

He admits that nothing in this inventory is new. What would be new would be for a 'goodly number' to pick up these ideas and to use them '*consistently, persistently, insistently to carry them through*'.

The first, second, third and fifth of the above items, while common to the workers of the newer movement, are not peculiar to them. But the other items (4, 6, 7, 8, and 9) are to me the characteristic marks of the movement. Men or work fitting those specifications are to me 'realistic' whatever label they may wear. Such, and none other, are the perfect fauna of this new land. Not all the work cited below fits my peculiar definition in all points. All such work fits most of the points.

Llewellyn Jurisprudence 57

Items (5) and (6) manifest the distrust of legal rules, principles and concepts. As has been pointed out, this distrust, for Llewellyn at least, suggests a diminution of the sway wielded by legal doctrine and not to its complete sublimation; there is a limit to the degree of the corrosiveness present in his cynical acid. But notice how the diminution of the significance of doctrine is relevant to predictability in item (6). The theory of rationalisation referred to in this item needs some explanation. As well as tabulating these nine attitudes of realism, he suggests a number of practical techniques to be utilised by the movement. Of these the most important is considered in the next extract.

> An early and fruitful line of attack borrowed from psychology the concept of *rationalization* already mentioned. To recanvass the opinions, viewing them no longer as mirroring the process of deciding cases, but rather as trained lawyers' arguments made by the judges (after the decision has been reached), intended to make the decision seem plausible, legally decent, legally right, to make it seem, indeed, legally inevitable—this was to open up new vision. It was assumed that the deductive logic of opinions need by no means be either a *description* of the process of decision, or an *explanation* of how the decision had been reached. Indeed over-enthusiasm has at times assumed that the logic of the opinion *could* be neither; and similar over-enthusiasm, perceiving case after case in which the opinion is clearly almost valueless as an indication of how that case came to decision, has worked at times almost as if the opinion were equally valueless in predicting what a later court will do.
>
> But the line of inquiry via rationalization has come close to demonstrating that in any case doubtful enough to make litigation respectable the available authoritative premises—*ie*, premises legitimate and impeccable under the traditional legal techniques—are at least two, and that the two are mutually contradictory as applied to the case in hand. Which opens the question of what made the court select the one available premise rather than the other. And which raises the greatest of doubts as to *how far* any supposed certainty in decision which may derive merely [or even chiefly] from the presence of accepted rules really goes.
>
> Llewellyn *Jurisprudence* 58

This argument can be traced back to the exhortation that we should look at what the courts do and not at what they say they do. Again, the result of this scepticism is a depreciation in the value of rules but also again, the scepticism needs to be qualified as we have seen. Item (7) accepts that legal concepts, like rules, cannot be eliminated. But it does express the belief that narrower and more significant categories are to be desired, categories that mirror the actual distinctions made in judicial practice.

> The suggestion then comes to this: that with the new purpose in mind one approach the data afresh, taking them in as raw a condition as possible, and discovering how far and how well the available traditional categories really cover the most relevant of the raw data. And that before proceeding one undertake such modifications in the categories as may be necessary or look promising. In view of the tendency toward over-generalization in the past this is likely to mean the making of smaller categories—which may either be sub-groupings inside the received categories, or may cut across them.
>
> Llewellyn *Jurisprudence* 27–28

By 1940 he was treating law as an *institution* organised around the idea of doing certain 'jobs'. An institution will manifest certain patterns of behaviour which themselves operate around the doing of certain jobs—'job-cluster'. In the case of a major institution, such as the law, the job-cluster is fundamental to the continuation of the society. Given that aiding the survival of the group is a function of the law, there are a number of 'law-jobs' which the institution of law manifests.

> The law-jobs are in their bare bones fundamental, they are eternal. Perhaps they can be summed up in a single formulation: such arrangement and adjustment of people's behavior that the society (or the group) remains a society (or a group) and gets enough energy unleashed and coordinated to keep on with its job as a society (or a group). But if the matter is put in that inclusive way, it sounds like mere tautology—almost as if one were saying that to be a group you must just be a group. Whereas what is being said is that to *stay* a group, you must manage to deal with the centrifugal tendencies, when they break out, and you must manage, preventively, to keep them from breaking out. And that you must *effect* organization, and that you must *keep* it effective. And that you must do all this by means which do not choke off, but elicit, your necessary flow of human energy.

> Llewellyn 'The Normative, The Legal and The Law-Jobs: The Problem of Juristic Method' (1940) 49 Yale Law Journal 1373

Law, as a complicated institution, comprises not only rules but also techniques, practices, and ideology. These affect the law-jobs which must be carried out if society is to survive and attempt to attain justice.

In what follows, he classifies these jobs into five categories. Note the two 'serviceable points of orientation' provided by looking on law as an institution.

> To begin, the viewing of law as a going institution provides two vitally serviceable points of orientation which freshen eyes and give a cross-check on what may be there to see. For, first, a going institution has jobs to do, and its function is to get them done effectively and well. This gives a pole of purpose and value to measure by. And, secondly, a going institution has results in life, and must be tested by them; and those results are capable of inquiry. The measure of the institution is, then, the measure of how its results check in fact, in regard to the actual doing of its jobs.
>
> The jobs on which law is focussed are not indeed accomplished wholly by law, nor will they ever be. For all that, they are well seen as peculiarly *law*-jobs, because law represents a phase and a machinery in their accomplishment which is peculiarly conscious, is often critical in its points of incidence, and is the area of action and thought in which conflicts and needed corrections come peculiarly to attention, with best hope of better solutions.
>
> The lines of 'law-job' around which it seems especially useful to group legal phenomena for study are five:
>
> 1.   The disposition of the trouble-case: a wrong, a grievance, a dispute. This is garage-repair work or the going concern of society, with (as case-law shows) its continuous effect upon the remaking of the order of that society.
>
> 2.   The preventive channeling of conduct and expectations so as to avoid trouble, and together with it, the effective reorientation of conduct and expectations in similar fashion. This does not mean merely, for instance, new legislation; it is, instead, what new legislation (among other things) is about, and is for.

3. The allocation of authority and the arrangement of procedures which mark action as being authoritative; which includes all of any constitution, and much more.

4. The positive side of law's work, seen as such, and seen not in detail, but as a net whole: the net organization of the society *as a whole* so as to provide integration, direction, and incentive.

5. 'Juristic method,' to use a single slogan to sum up the task of so handling, and of so building up effective traditions of handling, the legal materials and tools and people developed for the other jobs—to the end that those materials and tools and people are kept doing their law-jobs, and doing them better, until they become a source of revelation of new possibility and achievement.

Llewellyn My Philosophy of Law 185–187

Dispersed through his voluminous work there are more elaborate descriptions of these jobs. Here are some of them in numerical order.

(1) . . . there is the cleaning up of trouble-cases, which in various groups has been dealt with by tommy-gun or teargas, by legally binding compromise, by decree of a king or father or judge, by election or electrocution, revolution, oracle, or some combination or variation.

Llewellyn Jurisprudence 359

(2) *Preventive channeling and shift of orientation.* The second phase centers on the effective channeling, preventively and in advance, of people's conduct—and attitudes—toward one another. Its importance lies peculiarly in areas of patent or of latent conflict of interest: in the arrangement of participation in the scarce and desirable, from physical things on through to power and prestige. This—as in marriage, and property-rights—has always been easy to see. But no less important is the avoidance of hitches in the coordination of life and work; for in any organized action, a slip of expected performance, a break of rhythmed timing, can produce conflict by its mere disruptive disturbance. In general, the job is that of producing and maintaining a going order instead of a disordered series of collisions; it is this order on which the first job does garage-repair work. The function includes, to repeat, not only the channeling of overt behavior but the channeling of expectations, norms and claims.

Llewellyn (1940) 49 Yale Law Journal 1376

(3) The third phase which it seems convenient to mark off for special treatment centers on allocation and exercise of authority or jurisdiction, within a group, and of legitimatizing action as being authoritative; let me call it the job of *arranging the say, and its saying.* There occur doubts as to what to do, in drought, or war, or petty crisis; there occur disputes as to what to do, and as to whose say is to go. To get these matters settled in advance, and to get settled also what procedures must be gone through in order to legitimatize a decision and give it standing, and what the limits are on any person's authority—this is a matter of peculiar importance. It differs from ordinary channeling of conduct in looking to allocation rather of powers than of rights, to indication of the person and the procedure rather than the substance.

As the first job finds centered around its doing such institutional devices as tribunals, legal procedure, advocacy, peace-makers and jails; as the second finds centered about its doing such institutional devices as rules of substantive law, statute books, law publishing houses, sanitary inspection departments, traffic lights, preventive policing generally—and most of usage, and much of education; so this third task or function finds centered on its doing the 'constitutions' of states and of minor interest-groups, and in general the institutional devices for allocating authority to persons or bodies *and* for fixing the time or manner or procedure whereby their say, when said, is to gain standing as being *the* say: the legislature must be 'in session' (though with the clock turned back); the two houses must concur, by vote, and with a quorum; the bill must have been 'read' the proper number of times.

Llewellyn (1940) 49 Yale Law Journal 1383–1384

(4) *Integration, incentive, direction, net.* The fourth focus of law-jobs goes to the whole net effect of the other three, as performed. The reason for choosing it as a distinct focus is that to do so brings out into an emphasis otherwise too easy to let drift away, the *positive*, the constructive, side of the 'legal': the net organization around something, toward something: the Whither of the net Totality. It is doubly necessary to bring that into emphasis, because it is presupposed by the pervading, though implicit, drive of Law-officials (and indeed of political movements) for something felt, dimly or clearly, as Balance in the Total Legal, as well as for something felt as Health. Planning of the Whole has been too much for us, but tinkering is both furthered and fought, always, under the tug and torsion of some *feeling* for the Whole.

So that we can well take as a fourth focus the organization of the Entirety into some type of coordination which also unleashes enough incentive to get that enterprise carried on, and leaves the group-members sound enough to carry it on; along with which one must put the net shaping of direction of the enterprise toward one Whither rather than another.

However loose and vague such a description may appear, however joyous of infinite leeway and infinite variety, eluding all grasp, it nonetheless says something; as the seemingly tautologous statement of the total law-job said something; and as the statement that a society, or a Legal System, has its own variety of living unity says something. And I conceive it as peculiarly a *law*-job focus because the legal system of a group (not its Legal doctrine, merely, but its going whole) seems to me to be inescapably one place, and the main place, in which men face group-responsibility for shift in direction, and rekilter to achieve a readjusted net result or recapture of balance.

Llewellyn (1940) 49 Yale Law Journal 1387

(5) If what has been written above had been written with adequacy, there would be no point in continuing. Put it together, and the problem of juristic method is set. Men deviate from the anticipated, or anticipate what others do not think they have business to anticipate or clash otherwise, and there are cases of trouble. In furtherance of desire or interest, in the service of self or group or the Entirety concerned, to gain backing or to avoid pressure, men put forth normative generalizations which rest always in part on something in the culture, and move always to suppression or neglect of some other things in the culture. Decisions are reached, and some of those decisions become determinative of what can be expected. Out of them, out of action which they stimulate, out of the work of any specialists who emerge as men of

trouble-settlement or of governing, régimes of authority bud and grow, tending into some working unity. The pressure toward regularity, and the pressure of the anticipable to be felt as right, is steady. The law-jobs of trouble-handling, of channeling, of say-allocation, of the Net Drive, all need doing, and they all drive toward the emergence of some type of institutional machinery (ways *and* personnel *and* ideology about both) which can be seen as different from just who is there and just what is done and what is thought or felt, in general. With the emergence of the perceptibly 'legal,' as a body of ways, people and ideology, there emerges at once the problem raised by any institution and its staff: the problem of keeping the institution and its staff in hand and on their jobs. Institutional ways and ideology tend to grow hard, wooden, tend to crystallize upon their own premises, tend to be patterned in further operation on their own past rather than on their living function; or they tend to be turned to service of their staff rather than of the people. Exactly comparable tendencies bud in the staff, the personnel. In the main, machinery 'legal' in character, and personnel 'official' in character, have best potentiality for accomplishing the 'law-jobs.' But rarely, in any culture, and never in a culture both developed and mobile, can official 'legal' machinery and personnel accomplish the whole of those jobs. What is wanted is an on-going optimum balance, keeping in the hands of the official 'legal' machinery and personnel, and well-handled by them, so much as they can best handle. This problem, seen as reaching over all the law-job foci, or seen if you will as one phase of the play of the fourth upon the first three, I take in any event to be worth isolation for study. I shall call it the problem of *juristic method*, that of the *ways* of handling 'legal' tools to law-job ends, and of the on-going upkeep and improvement of both ways and tools.

Llewellyn (1940) 49 Yale Law Journal 1392

So societies will develop institutions to perform these law-jobs and he often calls such institutions 'law-and-government'. But it is to be noted that law-and-government is the main but not the only institution for performing the jobs. Twining expands on this theme.

> . . . by emphasizing that the institution of law-government is not the only device for doing the law-jobs, Llewellyn provides a useful reminder that there are other devices which assist in performing the same functions. Writers on law sometimes seem to forget that courts are not the only, nor are they necessarily the most important, dispute-settlement mechanisms in society; similarly it is useful to be reminded from time to time that legal rules are only one of a number of types of device that can be used for channelling conduct and expectations. Whole areas of enquiry are suggested by this kind of approach. In what circumstances do disputants choose to resort to the courts rather than to some other type of mechanism? What percentage of accidents of type X ever reach the courts? To what extent are the results of disputes settled 'out of court' in conformity with established legal doctrine, in so far as this is clear? In respect of some particular example of 'law reform', to what extent did the legislators envisage a change in the legal rules as being in itself sufficient to produce a change in the relevant patterns of behaviour? To what extent did they explore the whole range of possible devices for channelling or rechannelling this type of conduct?

Twining *Karl Llewellyn and the Realist Movement* 183

He proceeds to look more carefully at what is involved, and what are the consequences of doing these jobs. After distinguishing the 'bare-bones' from the 'ideal' aspects, he considers the activities that develop around the doing of the law-jobs.

In the doing of each of these law-jobs one can distinguish a bare-bones aspect which runs no further than the keeping of a society (or indeed of any group) together and alive; and, in addition, two ideal aspects. The one ideal aspect has to do with efficiency of operation. The other has to do with the realization of man's aspirations.

Around the law-jobs (which are inherent in the nature of any group, big or little) there develop (in any group) activities. When these activities become distinct enough to be recognizable as such, the stuff of law has thereby become observable as such. When men specialize in such activities, the men of law become recognizable. Both the men and the stuff show, as distinguishing marks, a more-or-less regularity of action, and show felt standards, more or less articulate, as to the manner and direction of such action. It is ill-advised to take either the practices or the standards, to take either the men or the practices-and-standards, as being alone somehow the substance of law. The going institution takes them in, all together: 'Precept' and 'principle,' *eg* to be part of a legal system, must be somehow actually at work in that system, and only in and through men and ideas *held* by men can they be at work. Practice, again, is the bony structure of a legal system. Yet practice is no part of *law* except as it comes wrapped in and is measured constantly against the held norm or felt ideal. Men are the life blood of a legal system, yet men are not even of it, save as bedded in a context of tradition, both existent and becoming, which shapes the men even as it is being shaped by them.

Llewellyn *My Philosophy of Law* 187–188

We have the evolution of the 'stuff of the law' and the 'men of the law'. It is this that takes him on to his notion of 'craft'.

Out of the conjunction of activities and men around the law-jobs there arise the crafts of the law, and so the craftsmen. Advocacy, counselling, judging, law-making, administering—these are major groupings of the law-crafts. But meditation, organization, policing, teaching, scholarship, and others. At the present juncture, the fresh study of these crafts and the manner of their best doing is one of the major needs of jurisprudence.

Llewellyn *My Philosophy of Law* 188

Not surprisingly, 'craft' includes lawyers' skills, but it is far wider: tradition, professional ethics, specialisation and training, fall under its ambit. In this context he considers the nature of rules. In the next extract notice the emphasis on the 'reckonability' or predictability of result—a theme that becomes paramount in his *Common Law Tradition*.

Among other things, only a clear perspective of the crafts of the quite different tasks of different crafts leads to a clear view of the manifold nature of legal rules themselves. Rules are measures based on ideals, practices, standards or commands, measures cast into verbal form, authoritative verbal form, with sharp-edged consequences. They add thus a tremendous power at once of communication, of rigidification over time, and of flexibility. They are a well-nigh indispensable precondition to any degree of standardization of law-work across space and the generations. They stand with such relative conspicuousness to observation, they accumulate so easily, they can be gathered so conveniently, and they are so easy to substitute for either thought or investigation, that they have drawn the attention of jurisprudes too largely to themselves; to the rules—as if rules stood and could stand alone. A first evil has been the attribution to the rules of many results, *eg* of court decisions— which rest instead on phases of judicial tradition. Not the least of that tradition is the ideal of justice to be reached, an ideal equipped with a whole set of *janus- faced* techniques for handling rules to keep them out of the way of justice. Reckonability of result here lies only sometimes in the rules; it lies with some consistency in the tradition. The crass instance is the 'correctness,' both in doctrine and in sense, of either emasculating a silly statute by treating it as in 'derogation,' or of expanding a wise but ill-drawn statute as 'remedial.' The polite convention that the results in both cases are drawn from the rule alone produces conflicting doctrine on the correct method of handling statutes, which proceeds in other cases, where an answer right in substance, is not quite so clear, to lead to trouble. The same holds of the equally multiform and mutually inconsistent 'correct' doctrines on how to handle precedent principle, or standard. But let this situation be seen as a problem in the ways of a going institution, and the craft of judging must at once come in for study. The quest becomes then one for guidance, first, as to when a court will use some particular one of such 'correct' techniques rather than any other; and second, as to when it ought to.

Llewellyn My Philosophy of Law 188–189

'Craft', among a group of specialists who are involved in doing the law-jobs, is a portmanteau of skills passed on from one generation to the next. It is in *The Common Law Tradition* that he details his views on 'craft'. In fact 'craft' itself becomes a minor institution with judicial reasoning becoming the pre-eminent craft.

What he does in *The Common Law Tradition* is to analyse the meaning and use of precedent. This analysis results in working rules for 'reckonability', consequently, there is a large measure of predictability in the work of US appellate courts. He can claim such reckonability because the common law tradition depends on the legal rule fitting into the needs of the particular society in which it is applied. This conformance between legal rule and needs can be expressed only by a reasoning process; it has a basis in rationality. It follows that Llewellyn refutes the idea that courts are merely engaged in providing rationalistic camouflage for what in reality are *ad hoc* decisions grounded on the nonintellectual reflex actions of specific judges. The *ex post facto* rationalisation view of legal reasoning succumbs to the process of stable decision-making.

'Reckonability' is usually attainable because of the craft of decision-making in the common law tradition: there are patterns of uniformity in judicial decision- making. In fact there are fourteen 'steadying factors' in the appellate courts. In Rumble's summary of these note the pre-eminence given to 'professional judicial office'. The quotations are from Llewellyn *The Common Law Tradition* pp 19–51.

. . . [He attempts] to explain the patterns of uniformity in judicial decision- making by reference to fourteen 'major steadying factors in our appellate courts.' Supposedly, they furnish the basis upon which reliable predictions of future decisions can be made. The fourteen are the existence of 'law-conditioned officials,' personnel who are 'all trained and in the main rather experienced lawyers'; the presence of 'legal doctrine' and 'known doctrinal techniques'; the responsibility of the judiciary for 'justice'; the tradition of 'one single right answer' for each case; the existence of written opinions 'which tell any interested person what the cause is and why the decision—under the authorities—is right, and perhaps why it is wise,' and which may also 'show how like cases are properly to be decided in the future'; the existence of 'a frozen record from below' and the fact that the issues before the court are 'limited, sharpened, and phrased in advance'; the presentation, oral and written, of adversary argument by counsel; the practice of group decisions; the security for independent judgment which life tenure makes possible; a 'known bench'; the 'general period style and its Promise'; and, finally, 'professional judicial office.' To be sure, 'there is neither magic nor any assumption of the absolute in this "fourteen."' Still, these are the 'factors which if they have any power should be expected to produce a degree of depersonizing in the deciding far beyond that when such flywheel factors are not present.'

For Llewellyn, the most important of the fourteen factors is professional judicial office. 'Office' means, essentially, the role which the judge is expected to play in our judicial system. No single word can precisely delineate the nature of this role.

> The typical word, used as a sufficient word, is 'impartial,' which describes a condition: 'not on either side, and without personal interest or desire re the outcome' is about as far as that word really takes you, though the dictionaries tend to add 'just.' But we mean when we use the word about a man in judicial *office* a great deal more. We mean, and definitely in addition, 'upright.' We also mean—and if we stop to think we know that we mean—not a passive but a positive and active attitude: the judge must be *seeking*, as best he can, to see the matter fairly, and with an eye not to the litigants merely, but to All-of-Us as well. We mean further, and importantly, still another attitude: 'Open, truly open, to listen, to get informed, to be persuaded, to respond to good reason.' Nay, more; we gather into this one weak, bleak word 'impartial' a drive: an idea of effort, of self-denying labor, toward patience, toward understanding sympathy, toward quest for wisdom in the result.

'Professional judicial office' is such an important factor because it is the major restraint upon the *use* of judicial freedom. The human element is not eliminated. 'The factor of person is still important, even when we limit observation to that overwhelming bulk of the appellate judges to whom improper conduct in office would be unthinkable.' If this factor were not significant, then the existence of appeals or dissenting opinions could not be justified. The function of the judicial office is, instead, to create a tradition which 'grips them [the judges], shapes them, limits them, guides them; not for nothing do we speak of *ingrained* ways of work or thought, of men *experienced* or case-hardened, of *habits* of mind.'

Rumble American Legal Realism 151–153

The result: reckonability.

> You cannot listen to the dirges of lawyers about the death of *stare decisis* (of the nature of which lovely institution the dirge-chanters have little inkling)

without realizing that one great group at the bar are close to losing their faith. You cannot listen to the cynicism about the appellate courts that is stock conversation of the semi- or moderately successful lawyer in his middle years without realizing that his success transmutes into gall even as it comes to him. You cannot watch generations of law students assume, two thirds of them, as of course and despite all your effort, that *if* the outcome of an appeal is not foredoomed in logic it *therefore* is the product of uncontrolled will which is as good as wayward, without realizing that our *machinery for communicating* the facts of life about the work of our central and vital symbol of The Law: the appellate courts, has become frighteningly deficient.

For the fact is that the work of our appellate courts all over the country is reckonable. It is reckonable first, and on a relative scale, far beyond what any sane man has any business expecting from a machinery devoted to settling disputes self-selected for their toughness. It is reckonable second, and on an absolute scale, quite sufficiently for skilled craftsmen to make usable and valuable judgments about likelihoods, and quite sufficiently to render the handling of an appeal a fitting subject for effective and satisfying craftsmanship.

It is in the contrast between these joyous facts and the therefore needless but truly perilous crisis in confidence that the book takes its start.

Llewellyn *The Common Law Tradition* 4

One of the fourteen steadying factors comes in for extended treatment in the book: the 'period style' of judicial reasoning. He contrasts the late-nineteenth-century 'formal style', in which the real grounds for a decision are hidden behind rationalisation, with the 'grand style' of the common law, in which judges know that the roots of the law are in social needs. In their judgments they try to relate the rules of law to the needs that they have unearthed. Whereas the formal style tends towards the blind following of precedent, the grand style epitomises the appeal to reason. His claim is not that either period is ever one hundred per cent present; rather there is, in different periods, movement between these two polar positions. Writing in 1960, his conclusion is that, at least in US appellate courts, there has been a resurgence of the grand style which itself has led the legal profession to the erroneous conclusion that the law is an unpredictable, unstable entity. The gist of what follows is that the grand style, with its reliance upon principle and policy (on this note the different meanings of 'principle' in the two 'styles' and how 'policy' is classified differently according to which style is in the ascendant), is more likely to produce 'rules that make sense'.

There is a further cluster of conditioning and steadying factors in the work of the appellate courts (and commonly at the same time of other branches of legal work) which has been curiously disregarded. It is the general and pervasive manner over the country at large, at any given time, of going about the job, the general outlook, the ways of professional knowhow, the kind of thing the men of law are sensitive to and strive for, the tone and flavor of the working and of the results. It is well described as a 'period-style'; it corresponds to what we have long known as period-style in architecture or the graphic arts or furniture or music or drama. Its slowish movement but striking presence remind me also of shifting 'types' of economy ('agricultural,' 'industrial,' eg) and of the cycles or spirals many sociologists and historians discover in the history of political aggregations or of whole cultures.

Thus, for instance, the outlook and manner of Mansfield, or of Marshall, Kent, Cowen, Parker, Tilghman, Gibson, are in no wise peculiar to these giants; both are shared unmistakably by most of the lesser men of the period. The *type*-thinking of the time is to view precedents as welcome and *very* persuasive, but it is to test a precedent almost always against three types of reason before it is accepted. The reputation of the opinion-writing judge counts heavily (and it is right reason to listen carefully to the wise). Secondly, 'principle' is consulted to check up on precedent, and at this period and in this way of work 'principle' means no mere verbal tool for bringing large-scale order into the rules, it means a broad generalization which must yield patent sense as well as order, if it is to be 'principle.' Finally, 'policy,' in terms of prospective consequences of the rule under consideration, comes in for explicit examination by reason in a further test of both the rule in question and its application. The tone and mark consist in an as-of-courseness in the constant questing for better and best law to guide the future, but the better and best law is to be built on and out of what the past can offer; the quest consists in a constant re-examination and reworking of a heritage, that the heritage may yield not only solidity but comfort for the new day and for the morrow.

This is the Grand Style of the Common Law. I am referring to a way of thought and work, not to a way of writing. It is a way of on-going renovation of doctrine, but touch with the past is too close, the mood is too craft-conscious, the need for the clean line is too great, for the renovation to smell of revolution or, indeed, of campaigning reform. Of the judges named above, Mansfield and Gibson stand out from the others in that in each an impatience to built *fast* sometimes stirs strongly enough to permit breaks with the past that jar the rhythm of the law and of the work. To that degree and on those occasions they are out of key with the Grand Style at its peak. There will of course always be an opposition, and some of it will be factious and fractious; and contemporary criticism and abuse are inherent in the controversy which produces law. But some of the sparks caused by Mansfield and Gibson, great judges though both were, were struck by a brusqueness of manner and language toward men and toward tradition which is no part of that grace in work which is the Grand Style at its best. For let me repeat: 'style' refers in this connection not to literary quality or tone, but to the manner of doing the job, to the way of craftsmanship in office, to a functioning harmonization of vision with tradition, of continuity with growth, of machinery with purpose, of measure with need. This can conceivably work out into florid words or into ponderous Elizabethan euphuism; if so, I am prepared to be laden with the language if I may have the thing. But it is worthy of note (and it is perhaps some evidence that style grips in one fist more phases of man and culture than we always realize) that work in the Grand Style has, historically, tended into simplicity of verbal form and of sentence and paragraph structure, in combination with a certain pungency.

It will also be obvious that in this reference to the early nineteenth-century work in this country I have in mind something greater, deeper, and of more far-reaching implication than the 'formative' character of the early American era as discussed by Roscoe Pound. His other phrasing, 'our classic period,' comes much closer to what is here in mind. With 'formative' his eye was on the effective creation of needed doctrine—by selection, by modification, by invention. That was indeed in process, in say 1820–1860, and the Grand Style is peculiarly apt to such a task. But the matter goes much further: the Grand Style is *always* the best style, even though the cabin of doctrine may seem for the moment complete, with only chinks and leaks left to attend to.

On reckonability of result, three points cry for attention: first, the Grand Style is the best device ever invented by man for drying up that free-flowing spring of uncertainty, conflict between the seeming commands of the authorities and the felt demands of justice. Second, when a frozen text happens to be the crux, to insist that an acceptable answer shall satisfy the reason *as well as* the language is not only to escape much occasion for divergence, but to radically reduce the degree thereof . . . Third, the future-directed quest for ever better formulations for guidance, which is inherent in the Grand Style, means the on-going production and improvement of rules which make sense on their face, and which can be understood and reasonably well applied even by mediocre men. *Such* rules have a fair chance to get the same results out of very different judges, and so in truth to hit close to the ancient target of 'laws and not men.' Of the results of such rules, handled in such a manner, one can rightly say what Carter pungently but most wrongly said of the common law of his own day: 'forefelt, if not foreseen.'

That was not true in Carter's day because the Formal Style which was coming into dominance when he began his writing and froze his views in the early '80's can yield reckonable results only when the rules of law are clear; and whatever one may say in praise of Our Lady of the Common Law (to whom I do bow), clarity and precise outline of her rules of law are not the chief jewel in her crown. Moreover, to thicken the obscurity, the statutes of Carter's day had come to approach the involuted sloppiness of drafting which is too familiar still, and the courts had also opened that war of guerrilla raids on statutes by way of 'strict construction' in unforeseeable spots which made a faro game of every statutory case.

The Formal Style is of peculiar interest to us because it set the picture against which all modern thinking has played—call it, as of the last eighty or ninety years, 'the orthodox ideology.' That picture is clean and clear: the rules of law are to decide the cases; policy is for the legislature, not for the courts, and so is change even in pure common law. Opinions run in deductive form with an air or expression of single-line inevitability. 'Principle' is a generalization producing order which can and should be used to prune away those 'anomalous' cases or rules which do not fit, such cases or rules having no function except, in places where the supposed 'principle' does not work well, to accomplish sense—but sense is no official concern of a formal-style court.

Langdell's dazzling contract-construct is the American archetype of such a set of principles: without consideration, no legal obligation on a promise; consideration is *only* a bargained-for detriment (this planes off, for example, all enforcement via reliance, and all matters already past when a promise is made); the detriment can move *only* from the promisee (this chops off all enforcement by beneficiaries); an offer requires communication in order to be capable of acceptance (this prunes away the old sensible 'unknown reward' cases); acceptance must be by *either* a promise *or* 'an act,' the very promise *or* the very act 'called for' by the 'master of the offer'—a jealous master, who has no desire to close a deal (this puts the axe to any expectation of alternative or even reasonable modes of acceptance, glorifies last-minute revocation in the continuing performance cases, and crowns verbal ribbon-matching between communications with a kind of ponderous dignity). Sense, the ways of men with words, the ways of businessmen in dealing, these are irrelevant and literally inadmissible: they do not get into the hall, to be heard or considered. Generations of law students were introduced to their profession by way of these strange ideas, and courts have in consequence made actual decisions in their image, sometimes with a touch of patent Parkeian pleasure as the pretty little puzzle-pieces lock together to leave for hundreds of good business promises no legal container but the garbage can. But in the ideal of the Formal Style, as has been said, thus to prune away anomaly is to vindicate Principle: large-scale Order. And it is a good judge's business to steel himself against emotion, and against deflection by sense or sense of justice which may run counter to 'the law,' lest such should lead him to neglect of his stern duty; in the titans of the style there develops a perverse drive for the 'strong' opinion dear to Parke. Finally, even as the common law is thus moved with sweat toward a simpler and more peacefully life-remote structural system, the disturbing statute (inconsistently with 'Policy for the Legislature') is dealt with as an enemy invader.

This deeply etched and revered picture or idea-pattern did not, as the labor injunction cases and the familiar Constitutional cases remind us, in fact bar out innovations of doctrine as far-reaching as they could be sudden; far less did it bar out those more gradual and less noticed cumulative changes which have been with us throughout our history. But it did, in its devotees (and that means by say 1885 practically the bar and bench entire) drive *conscious* creation all but underground, make change and growth things to be ignored in opinions, and to be concealed not only from a public but from a self. Meanwhile, the available doctrinal material (then even more grievously afflicted than today with preindustrial concepts and flavor, while major reformatory statutes were being knocked out again and again)—that material lagged further and further behind conditions which were remodeling with increasing speed, and the urge for felt right which no judge of conscience can ever wholly escape tended more and more into clash with prevailing doctrine and with the death's-head duties of the prevailing pattern of judicial ideal. It is true that a widespread public revolt put on the bench a great body of State court judges to replace many whose feeling for justice had merged in peace with obsolete or otherwise unhappy doctrine. But note: whatever their political or economic or social outlook, these new appellate judges, too, had grown up in and into the formal-style picture of how to go about their work. Pound's famous American Bar Association speech of 1906 had sounded warnings and blown the charge, but it had died out on the inert resistant air. What was left in the State courts at large was an astounding decrease in reckonability of result: judges who wanted to go right, and did not know how to; other judges who more often than not, though felt justice cried loud, could yet deafen their ears as they remembered duty to 'the law,' but who nevertheless with frequent, persistent, and almost random irregularity jumped 'legal' traces and coursed to fulfillment of their other duty by way of bad logic, or by distortion of authority or fact, or by main strength. The effects not only on reckonability but on 'the law,' during the early decades of the twentieth century, were devastating.

Such generalizations as the foregoing can offer light and perspective; they cannot offer basis for conclusion to any particular, re either jurisdiction or era. What, for example, is true in general of Massachusetts, New York, Ohio, and Pennsylvania in the first half of the nineteenth century holds much less for Illinois until the advent of Breese in 1857; and in New York the Supreme Court can show the Grand Style in perfection in the same volume in which the Court for the Correction of Errors is bogged in wordy senators. Similarly, the Formal Style, which had begun to lose control of the New York Court of Appeals before 1920, continued to dominate the Supreme Court of Maryland (both in manner of writing and manner of deciding) for more than a generation thereafter; and while the Supreme Courts of Massachusetts were in 1939 still writing largely in the strict Formal Style, there can be no question that their process of actual deciding had already materially departed therefrom; indeed, even in 1939 Chief Justice Field was casting the Opinions of the Justices in a manner strongly reminiscent of the Grand Style, and within a few years thereafter the Formal Style had completely lost control of the law opinions, too. No, a 'prevailing' style does not mean a uniformity. Indeed, just as some judges can become almost an ideal embodiment of the prevailing style, others can and do stand out in powerful idiosyncratic contrast to their surroundings: for instance, Doe.

It is of course when this type of contrast ceases to seem idiosyncratic that 'change of style' has begun. This showed in the New York Court of Appeals and in the Second Circuit before 1920; the work of Burch and Mason showed clearly in Kansas by 1905. Long before the movement became characteristic of the Supreme Court of the United States its mark had become clear upon the State courts in general; the Supreme Court—save for some dissenters—was indeed amazingly slow in responding to the tide. During the last three decades it has become clear that the Formal Style, though still of influence and moment, has yet lost its grip. It offers still one of the standard styles for the writing of opinions, but I do not believe that it anywhere wholly dominates opinion-writing style today, nor do I believe that in any of our appellate courts it retains its ancient aspect of a deep, unquestioned, and powerful faith. Today's typical appellate judge is interested first of all in getting the case decided *right*—within the authorities; and however he writes, it is the goal of rightness which gives the main drive and direction to his labors. The danger, as has been said above, has become one of giving too little attention to continuity and to guidesomeness of legal doctrine.

What now of the effects of this shift on reckonability of outcome?

(i) *Re statutes*, the gain has been great. Today's appellate courts have long made their peace with the legislatures. Today, nine times out of ten, or better, legislative policy is not resisted, but is accepted cheerfully, and the court works with it. This obviously aids prediction of result.

Not yet, however, has the Grand Style of statutory treatment been recaptured. The courts do not yet regularly and as of course face up to their job of integrating the particular statute into the doctrinal whole; and while the sound principle 'where the reason stops, there stops even the enacted rule (*lex*)' is receiving attention half the time or more, often even when the statutory language makes it difficult, yet the courts at large are still caught in the theories of the '90's on the equally important matter of implementing the clear purposes of a statute with the full resources of a court or the matter of recognizing a clear and broad statutory policy in an apt area even though that area is not embraced by the literal language.

(ii) *Re the bar:* To the degree that the appellate courts have—as they have—resorted to conscious consideration of right and wisdom in order to guide choice between or among the permissible doctrinal possibilities, a tool for producing much more reckonable regularity has been added to their actual working kit. But to the degree that such consideration fails to be unmistakable on the face of the opinion, most of the bar remains in the dark about what is happening, and accordingly is troubled in prediction.

Moreover, *occasional* display of process and reason in *occasional* opinions does not do the necessary work for the bar in general, as contrasted with the really good appellate lawyer. For the bar in general, in the first place, does not read the current local reports, as such. Most of the bar *read* (I am not saying 'note' or 'skim') almost exclusively the cases whose *subject matter* is of interest to the individual reading lawyer, and so will never see most of such indications as have been referred to. In the second place, the bar in general reads to discover what the last authoritative statement or decision is about 'the law' of a point; it does *not* read to get light on how the court is, in general, going about its perplexing job of deciding tough cases. And in the third place, the bulk of the bar reads still with the spectacles of 'orthodox ideology,' so that a court's remarks about the reason and wisdom of the decision just do not come through. At best: '*mere* dicta.'

It is of first importance to observe that any such general ignorance and confusion of the bar does more than yield worry and distress, does more than undermine that confidence in the law and in the appellate bench which every lawyer needs for his soul's health. It also drives into a vicious circle. For it produces appeals based not on sound judgment but on wild speculation, therefore vastly too many appeals, half or more of them those footless, 'foredoomed' ones of which Cardozo wrote. These proceed to heap waste-work on the appellate court until that court's time gives out and the full job which is the court's function must, in most instances, be scanted or passed over. Meantime, an American advocate's nature being to acquire belief in his cause, the appealing lawyer finds himself once again kicked in the teeth 'without ground'; the slow bleeding of his faith *and* of his judgment continues—fertilizing a new crop of footless appeals.

(iii)   *Re the judges themselves:* Meantime the inarticulateness of the vast body of appellate judges about how they do their work and why—their inarticulateness even to themselves—leaves them man by man somewhat soul-troubled, albeit their consciences are clear. This tells against reckonability of result; case by case, a troubled man is less certain in his action than a man who, like James Stephens' salmon, 'is all one piece from his head to his tail.' There obviously results some waste of effort, some waste of energy in internal friction, and especially an unevenness in operation which lessens predictability for the most skilled observer, whether at the bar or outside.

But the biggest single effect of the inarticulateness is that it tends to focus the court's known duty to justice—to what is right and fair—on the particular case and on the particular parties who happen to be in hand. This is a better way of going at decision than to discard the earthy concreteness of the case and to ignore the starry-eyed or knave-fool equities; but it is for all that a half-baked technique and one which strains toward both discontinuity and unwisdom. The wise place to search thoroughly for what is a right and fair solution is *the recurrent problem-situation* of which the instant case is *typical*. For in the first place this presses, this drives, toward formulating a solving *and guiding rule*; and to address oneself to the rule side of the puzzle is of necessity both to look back upon the heritage of doctrine and also to look forward into prospective consequences and prospective further problems—and to account to each. In that work, the tang of the case at bar gives feel and flavor, and stimulates the imagination; but the immediate equities fall into a wider, paler frame which renders it much easier both to feel and to see how much and what parts of them are typical and so are proper shapers of policy, how much and what part on the other hand is too individual for legal cognizance or appeals rather to sentimentality than to the sensitivity and sense proper to a legal-governmental scheme. It is not to appellate courts that our polity commits the pardoning power, nor yet the dispensing power, to be exercised along any lines which cannot be put into a form significantly general.

It seems to me obvious at sight that this order of approach to the problem of deciding an appellate case *must* materially raise the level of reckonability, make results more even, make the operating factors easier to foresee and forefeel, make the ways of handling prior doctrine stand forth, make the new formulations so reached increase in adequacy both of content and of phrasing. It seems to me no less obvious at sight that this same order of approach *must* at the same time raise the level of wisdom of result. At the moment it is a procedure employed from time to time by every court, employed consistently by none that I have studied.

Some of what has just been said may suggest heavy uncertainty of result to be today's condition. I mean no such suggestion. I hold that from the beginning of this century to say 1950, there occurred in the State supreme courts a rise in reckonability of result (and, let me add, of wisdom of result as well) which resembles the percentage rise in national production. It was, as I see it, an outgrowth of groping, not of plan; it was uncoordinated; it just happened, over fifty years of cumulative drift, with many men worried and independently at work. In process, as in impact on the particular case, such a change is irregular and unreckonable; but its net can and slowly has thrust the whole of operation up into a higher and much more even plateau of forecastability. I do not spot heavy influence of any particular leading figures unless it be Cardozo. I incline to believe, moreover, that until rather recently the ferment among the intellectuals which was discussed at the outset of this paper has been of minor moment. Today, taking the close of the trial as a base line, my judgment (this is much more than a guess or a 'guesstimate') is that a skilled man careful of the lines of factor here discussed ought even in the present state of our knowledge to average correct prediction of outcome eight times out of ten, and better than that if he knows the appeal counsel on both sides or sees the briefs. This, of course, presupposes the existence of that half or so of the cases which really are foredoomed.

Meantime the position is one to put to shame the ancient friendly cynic: the leopard of the appellate court *can* change his spots, and the courts *can* by taking thought add more than a cubit to their stature.

Llewellyn *The Common Law Tradition* 35–45

It has been pointed out by Cotterrell that it is the idea of a 'period-style' that makes it possible for Llewellyn to fuse the behavioural analysis of judicial work with the normative analysis of legal doctrine (Cotterrell *The Politics of Jurisprudence* 198).

A key concept in his work, and the most important characteristic of the ground style, is 'situation sense'. His explanation of this concept would not win any prize for clarity of exposition.

Situation sense will serve well enough to indicate the type-facts in their context and at the same time in their pressure for a satisfying working result, coupled with whatever the judge or court brings and adds to the evidence, in the way of knowledge and experience and values to see with, and to judge with.

Llewellyn *The Common Law Tradition* 60

This must mean the attempt to view the issue at hand not as a one-off affair but as a 'type' requiring a rule that will govern the future. But the major difficulty, articulated by Twining, remains.

'Situation sense' appears to involve 'true understanding' of the facts and 'right evaluation' of them. But how does one recognize 'true understanding' of the facts and 'right evaluation' of them? What are the criteria for determining 'right evaluation', 'right fashioning', 'a sound rule'?

Twining *Karl Llewellyn and the Realist Movement* 217

The best discussion of this troublesome concept is Twining's. In the following summary, the phrase 'fireside equities' is used by Llewellyn as shorthand for the factors peculiar to the particular case that may provoke sympathy.

Situation sense (summary)
Facts: (a)   In interpreting a reported case, or in approaching a current case, start by studying the facts as a layman familiar with their general context might see them. Try to grasp what would have happened if things had been working smoothly and what it was that brought the dispute about. Analyse what interests are in conflict and formulate statements of policy that may be relevant.

(b)   Try to fit the facts into some socially significant category or pattern, separating clearly irrelevant 'fireside equities' peculiar to this case from potentially relevant elements in the situation. In seeking for appropriate categories the following guidelines should be observed: (1) in categorizing the facts choose 'situational concepts'—ie categories which clearly refer to fact situations only and do not straddle facts and legal consequences; (ii) terms used and distinctions drawn by persons familiar with the context of the dispute (either as experts, observers or participants) may provide appropriate categories; (iii) the practices and expectations of such persons may also be of use; (iv) one aspect of the problem is to characterize the facts at an appropriate level of generality. No general formula exists for this but: (a) the facts should be characterized as a type; (b) in first instance, the facts should be characterized fairly narrowly (eg hospital employing a doctor rather than employer-employee) and movement up the ladder of abstraction to broader categories should proceed with awareness of the dangers of lumping together disparate social situations under one head.

Values: (a)   Sometimes it will be found that after the facts have been categorized, there may be a consensus within the affected group or within society as a whole respecting applicable policies or principles. In such cases the selection of an appropriate situational concept may be sufficient to resolve the problem.

(b)   in other instances, a conflict of principles or policies may be found. In such cases the process of categorization should have assisted in identification of the issues of policy, etc. but will not in itself resolve such conflict. However, even if reasonable men might disagree on the choice of conflicting policies, they might share common ground in limiting the range of choices.

Measures: (a)   Determine what you consider to be the most appropriate line or direction of treatment and only then; (b) decide on what specific prescription is appropriate.

This procedure provides no cure-all for finding 'appropriate' categories or choosing between competing values. 'No technique or method can ever be a cure-all.' It will not assist in the disposition of marginal cases. Nevertheless it provides a broad framework which should maximize the role of reason in solving problems presented to appellate courts.

Twining *Karl Llewellyn and the Realist Movement* 226–227

The common law tradition is, in essence, the making of law in response to social needs and it is to be found in the opinions of appellate judges, accessible to all who can read and understand the jargon. The reward of such study is reckonability.

Before we again pick up the forecasting problem, let us make quick audit of this last assertion: Are the lines of inquiry we have been exploring indeed available to ordinary lawyers? Or do these leads or devices go dumb or incoherent in the absence of some peculiar psychological or other technical training, or in the absence of some elaborate and inaccessible data, or in the absence of some intransmissible native knack? I submit that the signs to be looked for, though wholly unstandardized, are nonetheless as gross and unmistakable as road signs, and that there are obvious and valuable procedures of interpretation and use which are well-nigh as simple and communicable as the driving of a nail. Road signs *can* secrete themselves behind hedges, *can* break or fade, *can* be misleading; and nails *can* be hammered on the thumb; but for daily living the signs suffice to guide most folk and the process to rough-carpenter boards into some utility. I submit that the average lawyer has only to shift his focus for a few hours from 'what was held' in a series of opinions to what those opinions suggest or show about *what was bothering and what was helping the court* as it decided. If he will take that as his subject matter, I submit that the average lawyer can provide himself, and rather speedily, with the kit of coarse tools we have been discussing and with evidence, too, of his own ability to use that kit to immediate advantage.

Is the effort worth while? Leave intellectual curiosity on one side, and the fun that comes from sudden novel cross-lighting of scenes otherwise too familiar to notice. Look, if you will, to bald practicality: does this proposed way of reading opinions, this proposed focus on the *How* of the court's deciding, substantially increase the reader's forecasting power, as contrasted with a forecasting based merely on a search for the prevailing doctrine, or with a forecasting based chiefly on feel, hunch, or guess, or with a forecasting based on some unanalyzed cross-play of those two? For the ordinary lawyer I submit that there can be no question as to the gain in predictive power. Spend a single thoughtful weekend with a couple of recent volumes of reports from your own supreme court, read this way, and you can never again, with fervor or despair, make that remark about never knowing where an appellate court will hang its hat. Spend five such weekends, and you will be getting a workable idea of the local geography of hat-racks.

Llewellyn *The Common Law Tradition* 178–179

'Reckonability' is determined by three 'laws'.

(a)   A *law of compatibility*. The application of an appropriate rule is compatible with sense; this 'narrows the spread of possible decision and significantly increases the reckonability not only of the upshot but also of the direction which will be taken by the ground on which the decision will be rested. To know this both limits the field of doubt and sharpens the eyes of inquiry' (*The Common Law Tradition* 180). It seems to come down to this: if the court assesses the rule against the *situation* from which it initially emanates, considers it good, and, when reassessing it against the present situation, continues to find it good, one may predict that the rule will remain.

(b)   A *law of incompatibility*. The application of a seemingly apposite rule is incompatible with sense so that the 'reckonability of either upshot or direction of the ground of decision depends on factors apart from the rule, sense, or both' (*The Common Law Tradition* 180). If one can see that the rule is only just about workable, then the court will be unhappy with it and change towards a more workable rule will be on the cards.

(c)   A *law of regularity and reason*. This applies where there is a rule with 'a singing reason'. Such a rule yields regularity, reckonability and justice. This is the sort of rule that evolves latest in any particular area in a mature legal system. It furnishes not only a readily understood standard but also allows enough discretion for flexibility in reaching good decisions in the largest number of situations. Such a rule will possess maximum predictability. Rules containing such words as 'reasonable', 'just and equitable' etc, are 'singing rules' allowing for flexible but referable standards.

A rule which wears both a right situation-sense and a clear scope-criterion on its face yields regularity, reckonability, and justice all together. We may add that such a rule is a staff and a comfort to any court, as well as to any counsellor.

Llewellyn *The Common Law Tradition* 183

Needless to say, it is the grand style which is likely to produce more of such decisions than any other style.

In the next chapter we consider a modern movement of radical jurisprudence that claims to be the descendant of jurists such as Karl Llewellyn.

Chapter 16

Critical legal studies

The critical legal studies movement is a species of radical scepticism that surfaced in the United States in the 1970s.

> The invitation to the first annual Conference on Critical Legal Studies in 1977 gave little hint as to what the organizers thought 'critical legal studies' (CLS) was or might become. In a sense I suppose this was perfectly natural, since only those organizers long associated with the empiricist, generally politically reformist Law and Society movement had done much of their work yet. It seems that the organizers were simply seeking to *locate* those people working either at law schools or in closely related academic settings (legal sociology, legal anthropology) with a certain vaguely perceived, general political or cultural predisposition and a relatively better defined relationship to ordinary legal academic life. At the general level they sought something akin to New Leftists, in an obviously inexact sense: people on the left at least relatively skeptical of the State Socialist regimes (although many were undoubtedly more or less sympathetic with revolutionaries arguably seeking to establish such regimes), egalitarian, in a more far-reaching sense than those committed to tax-and-transfer-based income redistribution, culturally radical, or at least unsympathetic to the furious New Right assaults on permissiveness. In terms of the cultural politics of the law schools, the people the organizers were seeking were those appalled by the routine Socratic discussions of appellate court decisions, repelled by their sterility and thorough disconnection from actual social life (their mainstream fellow teachers seemed barely to care or notice whether either arguments or case results had any impact on actual practice); repelled by the supposition that neutral and apolitical *legal* reasoning could resolve charged controversies; impatient with the idea that people freed by Rigor from a stereotypically feminized or infantilized pre-professional sentimentality must ultimately share some sober centrist ideals; put off by the hierarchical classroom style in which phony priests first crush and then bless each new group of initiates.
>
> Kelman *A Guide to Critical Legal Studies* 1

CLS is regarded as a descendant of American legal realism (supra, Chapter 15) and we start with this apparent connection between the two movements.

> If the legal Realists were simply scholars who believed it important to focus attention on the law 'in action,' 'to try to describe as honestly and clearly as possible what is to be seen,' most modern legal academics would qualify as heirs of the Realists. Legal Realism was not simply a clarion call for energetic empiricism, however, but also the herald of a characteristic critical

471

methodology oriented toward pragmatic policy reform. Today's critical legal scholar can claim a particularly close kinship to Realist forebears in adoption of the Realists' twin orientations toward an iconoclastic historiography and a rigorous analytic jurisprudence. The work of the critical legal scholars can be understood as the maturation of these Realist methodologies—a maturation in which critical scholars explore incoherences at the level of social or political theory and critical scholarship is linked, not to reformist policy programs, but to a radical political agenda.

A Mature Historiography

Unlike the Realists, the critical legal scholars no longer claim novelty for their recognition that legal phenomena are not simple products of an interplay between precedent and interpretive technique. With the demise of formalism, post-Realist historiography inevitably incorporates some vision of the external influences that affect legal development—whether social, economic, political, or psychological. The most promising work of the critical legal scholars is distinguished from that of their colleagues in matters of emphasis—in a stress on the open-ended charter of the social and political context in which substantive law is shaped and in attention to the formative import of a legal consciousness with internal dynamics distinct from social, political, or economic influences.

For example, Karl Klare's commentary on judicial interpretation of the Wagner Act begins by asserting that the statute was an open-ended document upon enactment—that the indeterminacy of the text and political circumstances surrounding the Act's passage meant that no coherent set of principles provided a conclusive guide to its initial interpretation. Klare argues that the judiciary's interpretation of the Act was ultimately guided by an emerging legal consciousness—'social conceptualism'—that set new boundaries on the issues and outcomes appropriate to labor cases. This new framework assured the truncation of the Act's potential as a mandate for radical restructuring of the workplace by abandoning redistribution, equality of bargaining power, and industrial democracy 'as serious components of national labor policy.'

By demonstrating that first principles, not only doctrinal details, are products of historical circumstances and historically specific modes of legal reasoning, the critical legal scholar uses history to disclose that the underlying assumptions of doctrinal fields lack the necessity sometimes claimed for them—to demonstrate that such assumptions represent mere choices of one set of values over another. Whether or not the critical scholars are correct in contending that recognition of the historical contingency of law represents a 'perpetual threat' to the aims of traditional legal scholarship, their emphasis on contingency does serve as an appropriate prelude to proposals for the radical transformation of basic institutions. Similarly, if more subtly, the critical scholars' emphasis on the significance of transitory modes of legal consciousness in the construction of past socio-legal orders—when combined with the suggestion that a legal consciousness that sees itself as historically specific has taken the first step toward its own transformation—suggests potential for the reconstruction of the present order.

The critical legal scholar's twin stresses on social contingency and the influences of legal ideology implicate broader areas of social and political life than did the Realists' emphasis on historical circumstance. Llewellyn's study of sales law was discrete, limited in scope and unproblematically oriented toward the simple reform of outdated policies. In contrast, the critical legal scholar's historical analysis posits the malleability of fundamental legal ideas and simultaneously suggests that legal thought both directs legal change and legitimates the present social order in much more subtle and pervasive ways than the Realists would have recognized. The maturation of the Realists' critique elevates the level of generative speculation from specific legal categories to social theory.

Doctrinalism

If the critical legal historians have erected substantial barriers to faith in any conception of a continuous, steadily evolving legal universe, the critical doctrinalists—the systematic 'trashers' who most strikingly resemble Llewellyn's frenzied locust eaters—are perhaps most overtly responsible for the unease characteristic of modern legal scholarship. Their oft-repeated demonstration that abstract principles like liberty, freedom of contract, and property can ground contradictory arguments in any given case are, however, but one facet of the critical enterprise. After employing the analytic techniques of the Realists at a higher level of abstraction to expose the assumptions underlying traditional legal discourse as contradictory and incoherent, the contemporary scholars also employ an amalgam of sociological, philosophical, anthropological, and psychological techniques to dissect the presuppositions and ideologies immanent in the legal order.

The first stage of the critical scholar's critique of legal theory differs from the Realists' approach in its explicit recognition that tensions endemic to particular doctrinal fields pervade whole systems of legal discourse. While the Realists used analytic critique selectively, to discredit existing dogmas and suggest specific avenues of law reform, the critical legal scholar is more concerned with the entire framework of liberal thought. He explores the 'tension between normative ideals and social structure' and the repercussive effects of a belief in liberalism's particular articulation of boundaries between self and community, fact and value, civil society and sovereign. Critical scholarship, in seeking focuses for its attack on liberalism, is often drawn to a criticism of legal scholarship as a cloaking of the systematic tensions in liberal theory.

The second component of the doctrinal project—recourse to the methodologies of other disciplines—is the natural consequence of an unremitting critique of legal theory. Once criticism has challenged the explanatory power of legal scholarship by attacking its premises at higher and higher levels of generality, critical scholarship inquires into reasons for the persistence of legal theories that provide inadequate explanations for legal phenomena. Positioning themselves outside the basic assumptions of the existing legal order, the critical scholars seek, however, to characterize, not participate in, the ways in which law contributes to the stabilization of a social world. The interpretive devices for this exploration are necessarily borrowed from outside a legal scholarship that is part of the process of stabilization.

For example, Duncan Kennedy's *The Structure of Blackstone's Commentaries* adopts structuralist techniques to dissect the *Commentaries* on the basis of an overarching theoretical assumption that the ideas, practices, and beliefs of a legal community are structured by the need to mediate tension between community and autonomy. Expanding on the Realist insight that legal categorization creates emphases that assume an appearance of 'solidity, reality and inherent value,' Kennedy anatomizes the ways in which the *Commentaries* legitimated existing social practices in Blackstone's England through the creation of artificial legal categories that gradually assumed an appearance of necessity. The structural analysis of the *Commentaries* is, in effect, an indirect inquiry into the ways in which the boundaries and groupings of modern legal thought contribute to stabilization of an existing social order.

The Critical Scholar and Social Transformation

While the critical legal scholars are direct heirs to the Realists in methodology—in recognition of the subversive role of history and in skepticism concerning conceptualisms that purport to explain legal phenomena—modern criticism emerges from a distinct political tradition. Rejecting a legacy of social engineering and liberal reform, the critical legal scholars ground their political vision in participatory democracy, civic republicanism, or decentralized socialism. Animated by utopian aspirations that demand the transformation of social, political, and economic processes, these scholars cannot link their critique to discrete doctrinal change.

By seeking the realization of a social order not accessible via traditional avenues of legal reform, the critical legal scholars place novel and troublesome demands on their scholarship. The contemporary scholars must develop a theory for critical scholarship that can search out the transformative potential of law and society. Because the critical scholars self-consciously embrace the advancement of their political vision as one criterion for scholarly endeavor, political utility and depth of insight into the mechanisms of social transformation are proper standards for assessing their three predominant methodological approaches—textual explication, social theory, and pure critique.

Explication of legal texts, using the interpretive techniques of other disciplines—semiology, phenomenology, and structuralism, for instance—provides the critical legal scholar one possible means of studying legal phenomena that escapes the framework of doctrinal elaboration. Following intellectual currents in literary criticism, a discipline in which radical skepticism concerning the surface meaning of texts has led some critics to increasingly hermetic modes of interpretation, the critical school is searching for a methodology that does not reinforce the legitimacy of the concepts and processes that the scholar addresses. Such a methodology would permit the radical scholar to depict legal phenomena—to discuss ideology, structure, and content—in a manner that would reveal underlying truths about the legal order.

Losing oneself entirely to literary criticism of legal texts would, however, preclude inquiry into law's social context and limit knowledge of the legal order's potential for radical change. Engaged in labyrinthine textual explorations easily dismissed as the interpretive idiosyncrasies of individual writers, the critical legal scholars might find themselves increasingly segregated from both their academic contemporaries and the political realities to which their scholarship is addressed. Although such methodologies may be appropriate in the humanities, textual techniques divorced from social context raise the specter of a hybrid formalism that limits knowledge of socio-legal phenomena.

Recognizing the inadequacies of a single-minded textual project, the critical legal scholar could turn to social theory and speculative, even utopian, inquiry. Legal scholarship, like economics, could begin with a set of simplifying normative assumptions—assumptions concerning, for instance, the individual's active desire to participate in community life or the value of an institutional framework that systematically reduces economic inequalities. These assumptions, by removing barriers posed by present legal and social acculturation, would allow the critical scholar to suggest reconstructions of, for example, labor law, investment banking, or judicial decision-making. Such scholarship would generate radical political alternatives to existing institutions and challenge the legal culture with alternative theories suggesting that current orderings are neither necessary nor eternal.

Speculative inquiry, however, is prey to ensnarement in historical circumstance, an ensnarement that destines most theory to oscillate between phantasmic utopia and peregrine detail. While the abstract outlines of a general social theory are often too far removed from the present to generate either prescriptions for legal practice or focused doctrinal proposals, greater specificity ignores the relativity of social knowledge—knowledge that is bounded by its present historical setting and unaware of unpredictable alterations in a utopian objective that are outgrowths of intermediate stages on the path to the objective's realization. A wholesale move into social theory would divorce the critical scholars from their specialty—the investigation of legal phenomena—and might leave them with a potpourri of incommensurable ideas, only tangentially related to possibilities for transformation of an existing social reality.

Rejecting textual construction and social theory, the critical legal scholars could conclude that the critical project, the constant demonstration of indeterminacy, incoherence, and contradiction, is, at present, the most politically effective form of radical legal scholarship. Though perhaps initially dismissed as so much tilting at windmills, criticism would eventually challenge complacency by increasing self-consciousness in the discipline and making each scholar aware of the problematic character of his political assumptions. Demystification, 'exposure of the contingency of events as cultural constructions rather than natural conditions,' might engender social and political change simply by removing the sense of necessity inherent in perceptions of the present social order. Demonstration that current legal doctrines are ineffective, class-biased, or undetermined by shared moral judgments would be even more effective motors of social transformation.

The pursuit of a pure critical project, however, risks the persistence of an intractable gap between critical theory and legal practice. Abstract doctrinal criticism, particularly if disassociated from demonstrations of existing social injustice and unaccompanied by a substantive vision that suggests avenues for its implementation, is likely to be disregarded. Relentlessly pursued, contradiction can be self-perpetuating—the end product of a scholarship that disables the critic from utopian speculation, prey to his own devices. Indeed, critical scholarship could reinforce cynicism in the profession without generating the social and legal change the radical scholars would advocate.

Faced with the limitations of textual analysis, social theory, and criticism, the critical scholar must assess the boundaries of current methodological approaches. Textual explication is divorced from the society to which the study of law is directed. Speculation enmeshes the theorist in pendulations between amorphous fancy and exotic detail. Criticism, unconnected to practical alternatives, is easily dismissed as the senseless derision of social reality. The scholar must conclude that current understanding of scholarship and social change are inadequate. The critical school, as academic and political movement, requires an additional component to complement existing avenues of knowledge and transformation.

LEGAL SCHOLARSHIP: A REALISTIC RECONCEPTION

The emergence of a mature school of critical legal studies, evocative of self-reflection in the discipline, heralds a change in the character of legal scholarship. The critical legal school, arriving at the boundaries of its current methodologies, must find additional means for fulfilling its political program and ensuring that radical legal scholarship is more than a reenactment of legal Realism. Traditional scholarship, implicated in the revival of the Realist critique, must consciously reevaluate its scholarly purposes and intellectual claims. For both critical and traditional scholars, the maturation of Realist methodologies finally demands a reconception of the undertaking, a rethinking of the meaning of legal scholarship itself.

The Critical Legal Scholars

Confounded by the inadequacies of textual explication, social theory, and criticism, the critical legal scholars should complement existing methodologies with more widespread resort to social experimentation and inquiry, to a scholarship that effaces the line between theoretical speculation and practical activity. A radical scholarship of practice presupposes that knowledge concerning the mechanisms of legal transformation is inextricably tied to the exploration of a broader social transformation. Radical scholarship must involve the academic in prodding social circumstance toward utopian objectives, in creating conditions in which collective interests can legitimate radical and innovative social and political visions.

A radical scholarship of practice would enmesh legal scholars in activity, in endeavors that, beginning with a transformative objective, would explore the capacity of social structure to respond to efforts toward fundamental change. Scholars might, for example, create situations that would blur the boundary between political and legal discourse by setting up conflict-resolution mechanisms in which community members served as arbitrators of neighborhood disputes. Community organization, perhaps inviting the participation of law students, would involve scholars in the implementation of participatory democracy and place them in environments in which property, contract, or tort doctrines could be imaginatively recast. Total environments—prisons, hospitals, or workplaces—could provide unique opportunities for the involvement of relatively homogeneous populations in activities that would explore the possibilities for sustained social and political engagement.

Situationally specific, social involvement would not unmask immutable laws of social and legal change, but would produce a socially oriented literature that might suggest further paths for social transformation. For instance, experimentation with informal dispute-resolution processes might generate a scholarship that would suggest ways in which the mechanisms of dispute resolution can engender community cohesion and participation. Inquiry into the effects of corporate law firm practice, legal education, or public interest advocacy on the values, self-perception, and ideals of lawyers might provide the most effective criticism of prevailing practice in the legal community. Social practice and inquiry would also offer the scholars an opportunity for collaboration with academics in other disciplines, collaboration that is part of the critical school's utopian vision for post-Realist scholarship.

Isolated activity in factory, classroom, neighborhood, or prison moves outside traditional conceptions of the legal scholar's activities, but only because the critical scholars have chosen a more ambitious political vision than those visions embraced by their academic contemporaries. Relentlessly iconoclastic, critical scholarship refuses to accept the legal, social, or political suppositions of traditional academia. By challenging traditional theory with a social reality incommensurate with the theory's own presuppositions, the critical theorist suggests that correspondence with the realities of social and political life must provide the criterion of acceptance of any alternative vision. Though the attempt to communicate the vision inherent in the critical enterprise will encounter charges of contradiction, chaos, and conundrum, the effort to reach beyond the university is a first step toward realization of a transformed social order. If the critical scholars meet unanticipated defeats in their attempts to create new social and political realities, at least they risk the incoherences of a new vision, a vision yet unexplored.

Traditional Scholarship

While the critical legal scholars pursue one vision of legal scholarship, a vision encompassing various methodologies, traditional scholarship waits at a crossroads, without a clear sense of its mission. By forcing the legal scholar to consider the framework of assumptions that structure problems and solutions in the discipline, criticism has increased self-consciousness and deflated the scholar's implicit claims to objectivity. Self-awareness could engender two reconceptions of legal scholarship.

Conscious of the political assumptions that animate his scholarship, the legal scholar could decide that partisan advocacy is, indeed, the aim of academic law. Deprived of any recourse to unchallenged objectivity or prereflective social and political preference, the scholar could continue in his present enterprise, but recognize scholarship as a dialogical process shaped by political or aesthetic preference. Legal scholarship, so conceived, would be a self-conscious exchange between scholars with particular notions of social good, doctrinal purity, or economic rationality. This exchange would be directed toward political actors outside the academic community, actors who adopt the arguments of academic counterparts in their own political endeavors. The utility of such scholarship is contingent upon its ability to influence, an ability that may be undercut as those outside the university become increasingly aware of the nonlegal value choices that underlie the legal scholar's recommendations.

A more radical reconception of legal academia would focus on the legal order's integration in social processes and conceive of the law school as the repository of knowledge concerning law's past and present meaning to the social order. Such a reconception would require the law school to reach outward, to provide sociologist, historian, and economist with integral roles in legal institutions. Extensive interdisciplinary collaboration would be intellectually mandated by an affirmative recognition of law's integration in the social whole. Rigorous, nonrandom collaboration might be required to ensure the usefulness of legal scholarship directed to the external political actor. The promise of this conception hinges on the legal scholar's ability to mesh the languages and insights of other professions with his particular expertise in legal research and doctrinal elaboration.

Conclusion

Even if legal Realism was simply a methodology, a tool of legal actors dissatisfied with particular aspects of the social order, its effectiveness in challenging the assumed fixity of accepted social and political realities raised troublesome questions concerning the purposes of legal scholarship. For the critical legal scholar, the maturation of Realist methodologies is an implicit challenge to rise above them, to imagine new and transformative discourses for radical scholarship. The reemergence of criticism also evokes a reassessment in traditional legal scholarship, a troublesome reevaluation of institutional competence, intellectual claim, academic and professional orientation. Facing a reevaluation of their tasks, both critical and traditional legal scholars must look to society and ponder on the proper contours of a discipline whose defining characteristic is its role in shaping an existing social world.

'Round and Round the Bramble Bush: From Legal Realism to Critical Legal Studies' a note in (1982) 95 Harvard Law Review 1676–1690

THE DOMINANT THEMES OF THE CLS MOVEMENT

Although CLS writers cannot be shoehorned into one united body of thought, David Andrew Price has detected a certain consensus as regards a number of propositions.

1. Indeterminacy

CLS writings reject the view that legal doctrines can determine the outcome of a case. Unger suggests that 'a doctrinal practice that puts its hope in the contrast of legal reasoning to ideology, philosophy, and political prophecy ends up as a collection of makeshift apologies.' Harking back to the Legal Realists, the CLS writers argue that much of what lawyers know as 'legal reasoning' is simply the manipulation of abstract categories, with no particular manipulation being demonstrably correct or incorrect. In their analysis, a judge who tries to 'apply' the controlling doctrine may believe that his conclusion follows from doctrine, but in fact the judge could also have reached a different result using the same materials.

It is a common observation that one can make an argument on both sides of a question. Yet most lawyers surely believe from experience that legal rules often do yield determinate answers. Lawyers routinely advise their clients about the 'answers' to any number of legal issues, from the tax consequences of a transaction under the US Internal Revenue Code to the availability of legal remedies to enforce a child support order. One CLS author anticipates this objection, acknowledging that 'there are plenty of short- and medium-run stable regularities in social life, including regularities in the interpretation and application, in given contexts, of legal rules.' The practitioner's error, he explains, is in believing that the regularities are dictated by what the written law says. 'The Critical claim of indeterminacy is simply that none of these regularities are *necessary* consequences of the adoption of a given regime of rules.'

Numerous CLS writings, including the passages quoted above, imply that legal doctrines have no content at all; in other words, the doctrinally proper outcome of every legal question is fully indeterminate. The indeterminacy thesis stakes out an extreme position, and one that is almost trivially easy to disprove. It is rebutted, as Lawrence Solum notes, by 'even a single example of a case whose results are determined by the body of legal doctrine.' Such counter-examples are simple to identify. If a state enacts a law restricting suffrage to white males, the law is unconstitutional under the Fifteenth and Nineteenth Amendments. No doubt about it. If a man threatens someone with a gun and demands money, he has committed armed robbery. No question.

Legal doctrines are often underdeterminate, foreclosing some results while leaving others open. This much has long been conceded by mainstream theorists. Indeed, much of contemporary Anglo-American legal theory has been concerned with the question of how judges ought to resolve 'hard cases'—cases in which the formal legal materials apparently fail to direct the interpreter toward a single answer. Underdeterminate legal doctrines do not, however, lead to the situation portrayed by CLS writers in which the fetters imposed upon judges by 'legal' argument are spurious and artificial. Lawyers may indeed be able to make arguments in support of either side of an issue, but this does not imply that each side is equally valid.

The indeterminacy thesis of CLS would have troubling implications if it were true. It would leave the boundaries of lawful behaviour unpredictable. It would also leave the power of judges, and of government as a whole, unconstrained by limiting rules. CLS authors appear unconcerned by this possibility. One of them writes:

> But people do not want just to be beastly to each other. People want freedom to pursue happiness. But they also want not to harm others or be harmed themselves. The evidence is all around us that people are often caring, supportive, loving, and altruistic, both in their family lives and in their relations with strangers.
>
> It is also not true that, if left to do 'just what they like,' government officials will necessarily harm us or oppress us. They may do these things if that is what they want to do. But it is simply not the case that all government officials admire Hitler and Stalin and use them as role models.
>
> [Singer (1984) 94 Yale Law Journal 1, 54–55]

This statement is not strictly false—government officials do not necessarily want to harm others—but it is revealing for what it omits. This passage, like much of the corpus of CLS literature, downplays the potential for ill- or well-intended abuse of government power and downplays the role of legal rules in restraining that power.

2. *Contradiction*

The contradiction thesis in CLS thought is a rejection of the idea that a legal doctrine 'contains a single, coherent, and justifiable view of human relations; rather, CLS authors see doctrine as reflecting two or even more different and often competing views, no one of which is either coherent or pervasive enough to be called dominant.' Unger gives a broad example of the interplay between contradictory principles in legal doctrine:

> The generalization of contract theory revealed, alongside the dominant principles of freedom to choose the partner and the terms, the counterprinciples: that freedom to contract would not be allowed to undermine the communal aspects of social life and that grossly unfair bargains would not be enforced. Though the counterprinciples might be

pressed to the corner, they could neither be driven out completely nor subjected to a system of metaprinciples that would settle, once and for all, their relation to the dominant principles.

[Unger (1983) 46 Harvard Law Review 569]

Further, CLS writers contend that recognition of the contradictory nature of the principles underlying legal doctrine poses a threat to the established order. By making contradiction explicit, a scholar can thwart the ability of doctrine to serve its purpose of maintaining privilege. Doctrine can be seen as rightful and legitimate, Unger asserts, only if it embodies such a 'coherent and justifiable view of human relations.' Unger writes:

Every stabilized social world depends, for its serenity, upon the redefinition of power and preconception as legal right or practical necessity. The mundane and visionary struggles must be stopped or circumscribed, and the truce lines reinterpreted as a plausible though flawed version of the rightful order of society. This simple and uncontroversial idea can be restated with greater specificity. Legal rules and doctrines . . . must be intepreted and elaborated as expressions of a more or less coherent normative order, not just as a disconnected series of trophies with which different factions mark their victories in the effort to enlist government power in the service of private advantage. Otherwise, the restatement of power and preconception as right would not have been fully accomplished.

[ibid p 582]

Unger's claim about the potentially destructive effect of contradiction is unpersuasive. Contrary to his assertion, there is no apparent reason why legal doctrine can be legitimate only if it forms a seamless theoretical web. As far as statutory law is concerned, for example, few lay persons could be unaware of the compromise and exchanges that occur in the lawmaking process. There are probably few people who would require that laws exhibit a coherent and justifiable view of human relations in the demanding sense put forward by the CLS writers. Even under Dworkin's thesis of 'law as integrity,' in which judges are called upon to interpret the law *as if* it exhibited a uniform set of principles, there is no question but that the law's 'integrity' is a *post hoc* construction that must be developed by a judge in the process of interpretation, rather than a pre-existing feature of the law itself. The fact that legal rules embrace contradictory aims and assumptions, and thus do not perfectly serve any one of them, poses no threat to legal liberalism. Even if a rule is not consistently grounded in a coherent body of ideas about society, it can still accord with an individual's rights, and it can still be administered in a regular and general way.

Like the indeterminacy thesis, the contradiction thesis can be weakened and made more realistic if a distinction is drawn between *un*constrained and *under*constrained choices. To return to Unger's argument about the principles and counterprinciples in contract, it is true that most contract cases involve neither a canonical instance of a freely-made agreement between equals nor an extortionate, grossly unfair one. The presence of the two competing principles in contract cases does not imply, however, that the two principles are always in perfect equipoise. Not every case presents a hard choice between competing aims and assumptions, one in which different principles are always equally applicable and thus must be resolved politically or arbitrarily. If the contract is a routine business agreement between sophisticated enterprises, for example, then the freedom of choice principle identified by Unger will most likely dominate, rather than his paternalistic counterprinciple.

The contradiction thesis has no greater force when it is restated on a more abstract level—that is, as an assertion of the existence of contradictory theories *about* doctrines, not just the existence of contradictory aims and assumptions *within* doctrines. Consider this passage from Unger:

> In the most contested areas of contract law, two different views of the sources of obligation still contend. One . . . identifies the fully articulated act of will and the unilateral imposition of a duty by the state as the two exhaustive sources of obligation. The other view . . . finds the standard sources of obligations in the only partly deliberative ties of mutual dependence and redefines the two conventional sources as extreme, limiting cases. Which of these clashing conceptions provides the real theory of contract?'
>
> [ibid, 582]

Here again, Unger has overstated the contestability of the two choices. While Unger's description of the second view is ambiguous we might interpret 'the only partly deliberative ties of mutual dependence' to refer to obligations derived from relations based on reliance and reciprocity without an exchange of promises. If we have defined the second view accurately, then it is obvious that the first view of a contract is closer to the mark. More important, even if these two views about contract doctrine actually did have an equal hold on the thinking of lawyers, this fact would not threaten liberalism any more than the existence of contradictory aims and assumptions within contract doctrines. As a critic of Unger has pointed out,

> Unger fails to see that one might reasonably defend a set of rules and doctrines authoritatively established in the 'legal materials' (say, the current rules and doctrines of an American law of contract), and defend them as 'embodying' and 'sustaining' a 'defensible' conception (say, of 'fair' market relationships), without claiming that, in all or even most respects, they are the *uniquely* reasonable rules and doctrines available for such embodiment and sustenance, or that such a conception is the *only* 'defensible' conception of a fair market.
>
> . . . [T]he other indispensable component(s) of legal reasoning, and the only component that could begin to 'contrast' legal with any other form of practical reasoning about social life, is carefully omitted by Unger here and virtually throughout: the *fiat* of legislation, precedent, or custom . . .
>
> [Finnis (1985) 30 American Journal of Jurisprudence 23–25]

In other words, it does not matter that neither of Unger's 'clashing conceptions' represents 'the real theory of contract' in the rigorous sense considered by Unger. If a 'real theory' is understood to refer to a unitary theory behind the actual doctrines, then there *is* no 'real theory' of contract in practice because the statutes and precedents—the formal materials—do not embody one. The conclusion to draw from this fact is not that the legal system is on the brink of destruction from without or within, but instead that legal doctrines are made by imperfect human institutions, are the result of high-minded and low-minded compromises, and must continually be elaborated further and revised in response to new situations. The argument that competing conceptions exist in the law has neither the novelty nor the destructive significance that the CLS adherents claim.

The contradiction thesis may have some utility as a critique, not of liberalism, but of 'law-review-ism'—that is, the Langdellian tendency of academic law review articles to attribute an extraordinary degree of theoretical unity to masses of varied court decisions. Even here, however, the effect of the contradiction thesis is limited. Despite occasional over-reaching, it is entirely legitimate for a work of legal scholarship to advance a unified theory about an area of doctrine. If such a theory is advanced as a normative argument about how an area of doctrine should be revised, then the presence of competing concepts in the *current* doctrine obviously does not defeat the theory. Alternatively, if the theory is advanced as a description of the current doctrine, it is still a legitimate enterprise as long as the author honestly identifies contrary or divergent elements of the doctrine.

3. *Legitimation and false consciousness*

Rejecting the idea that formal sources of law can account for judicial decisions, CLS adherents disagree about the actual function served by laws. One work associated with the CLS movement, Professor Horwitz's *The Transformation of American Law*, has advanced an instrumentalist view in which legal doctrines are developed to subsidise industrial growth and, as a result, directly serve the economic interests of the wealthiest segments of society. This view, although popularly ascribed to the CLS movement as a whole, is actually atypical of CLS writings. It has the logical consequence of affirming the possibility that law can be a tool to achieve policy objectives, whether those objectives happen to be liberal and reformist (the project of the Legal Realists) or exploitative and reactionary (according to Horwitz, the project of the dominant classes in the nineteenth century). Perhaps because it lends support to the possibility of the liberal reform approach that the CLS adherents reject—and, perhaps because the asserted quasi-conspiracy between the judiciary and a supposedly monolithic capitalist class is not entirely plausible—CLS adherents have generally not embraced the Horwitz thesis.

By far the predominant view within the CLS movement is that law serves the powerful, not in an immediate and direct way, but instead through 'legitimation.' In other words, the rhetoric of legal rights and the rule of law leads people to think that the existing order, despite its inequitable aspects, is just or at least that it is better than any alternative. Unlike the conception of law advanced by Professor Horwitz, which can arguably be drawn from 'orthodox' or 'scientific' Marxism, the idea of legitimation extends the work of a school of thought that rejects much of Marx's thinking while still seeing itself as within the Marxist tradition. This neo-Marxist school of thought, commonly known as 'critical' Marxism, is based on the work of Antonio Gramsci, a leader of the Italian communist movement in the early twentieth century. Gramsci argued that the capitalist class does not maintain its power exclusively or even primarily through force, but also through a complex variety of widespread moral and social beliefs that lead people to assume that the *status quo* is basically good. These beliefs serve to reinforce, and are reinforced by, institutions such as the church, the corporation, and the family.

CLS adherents take Gramsci's argument and apply it to the law in particular. To them, the legal system (including legal doctrine) buttresses the hegemony of the capitalists by propagating a range of everyday ideas about property and contract as well as a range of broader notions about individual rights and the rule of law. In this way, the legal system is said to elicit the co-operation of the oppressed without routinely using force or the threat of force. For example, the legal system protects landholders not just by enforcing laws against trespass, but also by instilling into other people a general respect for property rights—by making it seem ordinary, natural, and socially beneficial that one person should be able to exclude others from a tract of land.

In the CLS view, the legitimating forces of the legal system contribute to 'false consciousness,' the erroneous belief that one is benefiting from the current system. False consciousness is a failure to see the exploitative aspects of the current system. It is a useful concept of CLS adherents for a number of reasons. It accounts for the continual failure of Marxist prophecies in which workers were supposed to rise against capitalism—that is, the workers don't know any better. It also enables CLS writers to claim tacitly that they have privileged access to hidden truths about society and human nature. Finally, as one critic of CLS has wondered, 'Is not "false consciousness" an expression . . . that gives others the authority to treat the victim as if he lacks humanity, autonomy, or will?'

Some writers have questioned the CLS assertion of a link between the legal system and people's attitudes; they suggest that the effects of the legal system may be too marginal to legitimate anything. This critique of the legitimation thesis has some force. Clearly, beliefs about respect for property, bodily integrity, and so on find their way into people's attitudes based on the teachings of parents, religion, and other sources apart from the legal system. Without trying to venture too deeply into the province of social scientists, it seems plausible that a person's acceptance of such concepts as 'mine' and 'yours' might precede even the influence of those sources.

Despite the above qualifications, however, there is no reason to doubt that the legal system does have a legitimating effect, in the sense that it is one of many important influences upon general attitudes about what is ordinary, natural, and beneficial. Whether this effect is desirable or not depends on whether one agrees with the values that the legal system is inculcating. To the extent that legal doctrine leads people to believe that it is wrong to trespass, steal, assault, or kill, this seems like a good result. Likewise, if legal norms against racial discrimination have aided the formation of social norms against racism, as I suspect they have, then this too is a good result.

If the legitimation thesis meant only that law affects people's attitudes, then it would not be especially problematic. The greatest difficulty arises from the CLS claim that law can, and in fact currently does, legitimate an unjust order. To put the legitimation thesis in a modest form, one could say that the backing of the legal system will make people slightly more willing to accept (again, in the sense of intellectual acceptance, not mere acquiescence to the threat of force) a somewhat unjust aspect of the current system. Whether or not the legitimation thesis is true in this weak form, CLS adherents go considerably further.

The one proposition uniting CLS authors most clearly is that 'liberalism' in its various forms plays a central role in shoring up the current system, a system that they see as pervasively unjust. But for the legitimating effect of law, they claim, people could and would invent a different way of ordering society. This view implies a much stronger version of the legitimation thesis: that the legitimating effect of law is powerful enough to maintain people's acceptance of an otherwise intolerable system. More precisely, it is powerful enough to maintain the *victim's* acceptance. This claim is unfounded. The slave regime of the American South was backed by elaborate, legalistic slave codes, but I doubt that such doctrines led the slaves to believe that their servitude was in any way rightful, necessary, or desirable. The segregation of buses, trains, and public schools was long required by state law, but that plainly did not lead blacks to think it was legitimate.

CLS adherents contend that the present system continuously oppresses and exploits people and that legal doctrine keeps them unaware of their true interests. A more persuasive counter-thesis is that when people are victims, they usually know it. When they do not know it, legal doctrine is not the reason why. History is replete with instances of people who denounced, protested against, or disobeyed laws that they believed unjust, notwithstanding the 'false consciousness' supposedly generated by the 'legitimating' effects of the legal order.

Price (1989) 48 Cambridge Law Journal 283–291

DUNCAN KENNEDY: RULES AND STANDARDS

A fundamental tenet of CLS writing is to uncover and highlight the presence of ambiguity in legal directives. All legal controversies manifest a common theme: there will exist a tension between resolving the dispute either by the mechanical application of formal rules or by using some less formal standards which leave room for the use of judicial discretion in order to side-step the consequences of a too rigid adherence to the rules.

> There are . . . two supposed modes of dealing with questions of the form in which legal solutions to the substantive problems should be cast. One formal mode favors the use of clearly defined, highly administerable, general rules; the other supports the use of equitable standards producing ad hoc decisions with relatively little precedential value.

> Kennedy 'Form and Substance in Private Law Adjudication' (1976) 89 Harvard Law Review 1685

Legal reasoning is simultaneously committed to both modes, with the consequence that all legal arguments exhibit instability and conflict. He proceeds by describing what he calls 'the jurisprudence of rules' or the body of thought that deals with questions of legal form. This is based on the idea that the choice between standards and rules of varying degrees of generality can be analysed as a separate issue from the actual substantive issues that the rules or standards respond to. He argues that there are three dimensions of form.

1. Formal Realizability.—The first dimension of rules is that of formal realizability. I will use this term, borrowed from Rudolph von Ihering's classic *Spirit of Roman Law*, to describe the degree to which a legal directive has the quality of 'ruleness.' The extreme of formal realizability is a directive to an official that requires him to respond to the presence together of each of a list of easily distinguishable factual aspects of a situation by intervening in a determinate way. Ihering used the determination of legal capacity by sole reference to age as a prime example of a formally realizable definition of liability; on the remedial side, he used the fixing of money fines of definite amounts as a tariff of damages for particular offenses.

At the opposite pole from a formally realizable rule is a standard or principle or policy. A standard refers directly to one of the substantive objectives of the legal order. Some examples are good faith, due care, fairness, unconscionability, unjust enrichment, and reasonableness. The application of a standard requires the judge both to discover the facts of a particular situation and to assess them in terms of the purposes or social values embodied in the standard.

It has been common ground, at least since Ihering, that the two great social virtues of formally realizable rules, as opposed to standards or principles, are the restraint of official arbitrariness and certainty. The two are distinct but overlapping. Official arbitrariness means the sub rosa use of criteria of decision that are inappropriate in view of the underlying purposes of the rule. These range from corruption to political bias. Their use is seen as an evil in itself, quite apart from their impact on private activity.

Certainty, on the other hand, is valued for its effect on the citizenry: if private actors can know in advance the incidence of official intervention, they will adjust their activities in advance to take account of them. From the point of view of the state, this increases the likelihood that private activity will follow a desired pattern. From the point of view of the citizenry, it removes the inhibiting effect on action that occurs when one's gains are subject to sporadic legal catastrophe.

It has also been common ground, at least since Ihering, that the virtues of formal realizability have a cost. The choice of rules as the mode of intervention involves the sacrifice of precision in the achievement of the objectives lying behind the rules. Suppose that the reason for creating a class of persons who lack capacity is the belief that immature people lack the faculty of free will. Setting the age of majority at 21 years will incapacitate many but *not all* of those who lack this faculty. And it will incapacitate some who actually possess it. From the point of view of the purpose of the rules, this combined over- and underinclusiveness amounts not just to licensing but to requiring official arbitrariness. If we adopt the rule, it is because of a judgment that this kind of arbitrariness is less serious than the arbitrariness and uncertainty that would result from empowering the official to apply the standard of 'free will' directly to the facts of each case.

2. *Generality.*—The second dimension that we commonly use in describing legal directives is that of generality vs. particularity. A rule setting the age of legal majority at 21 is more general than a rule setting the age of capacity to contract at 21. A standard of reasonable care in the use of firearms is more particular than a standard of reasonable care in the use of 'any dangerous instrumentality.' Generality means that the framer of the legal directive is attempting to kill many birds with one stone. The wide scope of the rule or standard is an attempt to deal with as many as possible of the different imaginable fact situations in which a substantive issue may arise.

The dimensions of generality and formal realizability are logically independent: we can have general or particular standards, and general or particular rules. But there are relationships between the dimensions that commonly emerge in practice. First, a general rule will be more over- and underinclusive than a particular rule. Every rule involves a measure of imprecision vis-à-vis its purpose (this is definitional), but the wider the scope of the rule, the more serious the imprecision becomes.

Second, the multiplication of particular rules undermines their formal realizability by increasing the number of 'jurisdictional' questions. Even where the scope of each particular rule is defined in terms of formally realizable criteria, if we have a different age of capacity for voting, drinking, driving, contracting, marrying and tortfeasing, there are likely to be contradictions and uncertainty in borderline cases. One general rule of legal capacity at age 18 eliminates all these at a blow, and to that extent makes the system more formally realizable.

Third, a regime of general rules should reduce to a minimum the occasions of judicial lawmaking. Generality in statement guarantees that individual decisions will have far reaching effects. There will be fewer cases of first impression, and because there are fewer rules altogether, there will be fewer occasions on which a judge is free to choose between conflicting lines of authority. At the same time, formal realizability eliminates the sub rosa lawmaking that is possible under a regime of standards. It will be clear what the rule is, and everyone will know whether the judge is applying it. In such a situation, the judge is forced to confront the extent of his power, and this alone should make him more wary of using it than he would otherwise be.

Finally, the application of a standard to a particular fact situation will often generate a particular rule much narrower in scope than that standard. One characteristic mode of ordering a subject matter area including a vast number of possible situations is through the combination of a standard with an ever increasing group of particular rules of this kind. The generality of the standard means that there are no gaps: it is possible to find out something about how judges will dispose of cases that have not yet arisen. But no attempt is made to formulate a formally realizable general rule. Rather, case law gradually fills in the area with rules so closely bound to particular facts that they have little or no precedential value.

3.   *Formalities vs. Rules Designed to Deter Wrongful Behavior.*—There is a third dimension for the description of legal directives that is as important as formal realizability and generality. In this dimension, we place at one pole legal institutions whose purpose is to prevent people from engaging in particular activities because those activities are morally wrong or otherwise flatly undesirable. Most of the law of crimes fits this pattern: laws against murder aim to eliminate murder. At the other pole are legal institutions whose stated object is to facilitate private ordering. Legal institutions at this pole, sometimes called formalities, are supposed to help parties in communicating clearly to the judge which of various alternatives they want him to follow in dealing with disputes that may arise later in their relationship. The law of conveyancing is the paradigm here.

Formalities are premised on the lawmaker's indifference as to which of a number of alternative relationships the parties decide to enter. Their purpose is to make sure, first, that the parties know what they are doing, and, second, that the judge will know what they did. These are often referred to as the cautionary and evidentiary functions of formalities. Thus the statute of frauds is supposed both to make people take notice of the legal consequences of a writing and to reduce the occasions on which judges enforce non-existent contracts because of perjured evidence.

Although the premise of formalities is that the law has no preference as between alternative private courses of action, they operate through the contradiction of private intentions. This is true whether we are talking about the statute of frauds, the parol evidence rule, the requirement of an offer and acceptance, of definiteness, or whatever. In every case, the formality means that unless the parties adopt the prescribed mode of manifesting their wishes, they will be ignored. The reason for ignoring them, for applying the sanction of nullity, is to force them to be self conscious and to express themselves clearly, not to influence the substantive choice about whether or not to contract, or what to contract for.

By contrast, legal institutions aimed at wrongdoing attach sanctions to courses of conduct in order to discourage them. There is a wide gamut of possibilities, ranging from outright criminalization to the mere refusal to enforce contracts to perform acts 'contrary to public policy' (eg, contracts not to marry). In this area, the sanction of nullity is adopted not to force the parties to adopt a prescribed form, but to discourage them by making it more difficult to achieve a particular objective.

While the two poles are quite clear in theory, it is often extremely difficult to decide how the concepts involved apply in practice. One reason for this is that, whatever its purpose, the requirement of a formality imposes some cost on those who must use it, and it is often unclear whether the lawmaker intended this cost to have deterrent effect along with its cautionary and evidentiary functions. Thus the requirement that promises of bequests be in writing may have been aimed to discourage the descent of property outside of the normal family channel, as well as to decrease the probability of perjurious claims.

Another source of difficulty is that there exists an intermediate category of legal institutions that partakes simultaneously of the nature of formalities and of rules designed to deter wrongdoing. In this category falls a vast number of directives applied in situations where one party has injured another, but has not done something that the legal system treats as intrinsically immoral or antisocial. It is generally the case that the parties could have, but have not made an agreement that would have determined the outcome under the circumstances. In the absence of prior agreement, it is up to the court to decide what to do. The following are examples of rules of this kind:

(a) Rules defining nonconsensual duties of care to another, imposed by the law of torts, property, quasi-contract or fiduciary relations, or through the 'good faith' requirement in the performance of contractual obligations.

(b) Rules defining the circumstances in which violations of legal duty will be excused (eg, for mistake, impossibility, assumption of risk, contributory negligence, laches).

(c) Rules for the interpretation of contracts and other legal instruments, insomuch as those rules go beyond attempting to determine the actual intent of the parties (eg, interpretation of form contracts against the drafting party).

(d) The law of damages.

The ambiguity of the legal directives in this category is easiest to grasp in the cases of interpretation and excuses. For example, the law of impossibility allocates risks that the parties might have allocated themselves. Doctrines of this kind, which I will call suppletive, can be interpreted as merely facilitative. In other words, we can treat them *not* as indicating a preference for particular conduct (sharing of losses when unexpected events occur within a contractual context), but as cheapening the contracting process by making it known in advance that particular terms need not be explicitly worked out and written in. The parties remain free to specify to the contrary whenever the suppletive term does not meet their purposes.

On the other hand, it may be clear that the terms in question *are* designed to induce people to act in particular ways, and that the lawmaker is not indifferent as to whether the parties adopt them. This approach may be signaled by a requirement of 'clear and unambiguous statement' of contrary intent, or by other rules of interpretation, like that in favor of bilateral rather than unilateral contracts. But it is only when the courts refuse to allow even an explicit disclaimer or modification of the term that we know that we are altogether out of the realm of formalities.

The same kind of obscurity of purpose is present in the legal rules defining liability and fixing damages in tort, property and contract. *Sometimes* it is quite clear that the legal purpose is to eradicate a particular kind of behavior. By granting punitive damages or specific performance, for example, the lawmaker indicates that he is not indifferent as between the courses of action open to the parties. But where damages are merely compensatory, and perhaps even then not *fully* compensatory, there is a problem. The problem is aggravated when these damages are exacted both for breaches or torts involving some element of fault and for those that are innocent (nonnegligent injury; involuntary breach).

It is nonetheless possible to take a determinedly moralistic view of tort and breach of contract. The limitation of damages to compensation may be seen not as condoning the conduct involved, but as recognizing the deterrent effect that higher damages would have on activity in general, including innocent and desirable activity. It may also reflect qualms about windfall gains to the victims. Liability for involuntary breach and for some nonnegligent injuries are overinclusive from the moralistic point of view, but may be justified by the need to avoid hopelessly difficult factual issues.

The contrary view is that contract and tort liability reflect a decision that, so long as compensation is paid, the lawmaker is indifferent as between 'wrongful' and 'innocent' behavior. Legal directives defining breach of contract and tortious activity, and fixing damage measures, are then in a special class situated midway between formalities and rules punishing crimes that are *mala in se*. Unlike the rules of offer and acceptance, for example, they reflect a moral objective; that private actors should internalize particular costs of their activities, and have some security that they will not have to bear the costs of the activities of others. But the moral objective is a limited one, implying no judgment about the qualities of tort or breach of contract in themselves. The wrong involved is the failure to compensate, not the infliction of damage.

Along with a limited substantive content, these legal doctrines have limited cautionary and evidentiary functions. They define in advance a tariff that the private actor must pay if he wishes to behave in a particular way. The lawmaker does not care what choice the actor makes within this structure, but has an interest in the choice being made knowingly and deliberately, and in the accuracy of the judicial processes that will assess liability to pay the tariff and determine its amount. Since he is not trying to discourage torts or breaches of contract, it is important to define liability and its consequences in such a way as to facilitate private choice.

Kennedy 'Form and Substance in Private Law Adjudication' (1976) 89 Harvard Law Review, 1687–1694

CLS writers argue that many legal controversies can be seen as instances of this rules-standards dilemma. The conclusion is that there is no inherent logic within the law. Decision-makers in the legal system are constrained in their reasoning to the mechanical application of rules to facts. However, at the same time, they are committed to the use of formal standards and the dictates of policy which leave room for one-off decisions tuned to the specific facts.

> Because all actors are simultaneously committed to both positions, and because the arguments for one are ultimately counterbalanced by opposing ones, we should, as a purely predictive matter, expect instability, oscillation, and unsettled conclusions on every significant issue along the purely *formal* dimension—that is, along this dimension of whether to cope with any issue by imprecise rule or by imperfectly administrable standard. This is not to say that we could not posit hypothetical rules that are *excessively* inapt or posit standards that are *excessively* nonadministrable, as some imply when they attack claims that the choice of form poses a contradiction rather than a soluble problem of balancing. It *is* to say, though, that there will remain in any legal dispute a logically or empirically unanswerable formal problem, that granting substantially greater discretion or limiting discretion through significantly greater rule boundedness in the formation of the prevailing legal command is always perfectly plausible.

> Kelman *A Guide to Critical Legal Studies* 15–16

(a) The deeper meaning

The ambivalence over choice of form mirrors an even deeper contradiction over substantive political ideals.

> The first is that altruistic views on substantive private law issues lead to willingness to resort to standards in administration, while individualism seems to harmonize with an insistence on rigid rules rigidly applied.

> Kennedy 'Form and Substance in Private Adjudication' (1976) 89 Harvard Law Review 1685

When rule-orientation manifests the ideals of individualism and self-reliance, this signifies that one's own ends and purposes are primary. Altruism, manifested in the standard form, on the other hand, signifies that no priority is allocated to one's own interest.

> Whatever their status may have been at different points over the last hundred years, individualism and altruism are now strikingly parallel in their conflicting claims. The individualist attempt at a comprehensive rational theory of the form and content of private law was a failure. But altruism has not emerged as a comprehensive rational counter theory able to accomplish the task which has defeated its adversary.

> Nonetheless, the two positions live on and even flourish. The individualist who accepts the (at least temporary) impossibility of constructing a truly neutral judicial role still insists that there is a rational basis for a presumption of non-intervention or judicial passivity. The altruist, who can do no better with the problem of neutrality, is an activist all the same, arguing that the judge should accept the responsibility of enforcing communitarian, paternalist and regulatory standards wherever possible.

> In this section, I will argue that the persistence of these attitudes as organizing principles of legal discourse is derived from the fact that they reflect

not only practical and moral dispute, but also conflict about the nature of humanity, economy and society. There are two sets of conflicting fundamental premises that are available when we attempt to reason abstractly about the world, and these are linked with the positions that are available to us on the more mundane level of substantive and formal issues in the legal system.

Individualism is associated with the body of thought about man and society sometimes very generally described as liberalism. It is not necessary (in a logical or any other sense of necessity) for an individualist to hold to the liberal theory. It is possible to believe passionately in the intrinsic moral rightness of self-reliance and in the obvious validity of the practical arguments for an individualist bias in law, and yet reject the liberal premises. It is a fact, however, that liberal theory has been an important component of individualism in our political culutre at least since Hobbes. The whole enterprise of Classical individualist conceptualism was to show that a determinate legal regime could be deduced from liberal premises, as well as derived from individualist morality and practicality.

The same is true on the altruist side. The organicist premises with which the altruist responds to the liberal political argument are on another level altogether from the moral and practical assertions we have dealt with up to now. Yet, as is the case with individualism, there is both an historical connection and a powerful modern resonation between the levels of argument.

The importance of adding this theoretical dimension to the moral and practical is that it leads to a new kind of understanding of the conflict of individualism and altruism. In particular, it helps to explain what I called earlier the sticking points of the two sides—the moments at which the individualist, in his movement toward the state of nature, suddenly reverses himself and becomes an altruist, and the symmetrical moment at which the altruist becomes an advocate of rules and self-reliance rather than slide all the way to total collectivism or anarchism.

Fundamental Premises of Individualism

The characteristic structure of individualist social order consists of two elements. First, there are areas within which actors (groups or individuals) have total arbitrary discretion (often referred to as total freedom) to pursue their ends (purposes, values, desires, goals, interests) without regard to the impact of their actions on others. Second, there are rules, of two kinds: those defining the spheres of freedom or arbitrary discretion, and those governing the cooperative activities of actors—that is, their activity outside their spheres of arbitrariness. A full individualist order is the combination of (a) property rules that establish, with respect to everything valued, a legal owner with arbitrary control within fixed limits, and (b) contract rules—part supplied by the parties acting privately and part by the group as a whole acting legislatively—determining how the parties shall interact when they choose to do so.

The most important characteristic of an order with this structure is that individuals encounter one another in only three situations.

(a) *A* is permitted to ignore *B* and carry on within the sphere of his discretion as though *B* did not exist. *A* can let *B* starve, or, indeed, kill him, so long as this can be accomplished without running afoul of one of the limits of discretion.

(b) *A* and *B* are negotiating, either as private contracting parties or as public legislators, the establishment of some rules to govern their future relations. These rules will be binding whether or not based on agreement between *A* and *B* about what ends they should pursue or even about what ends the rules are designed to serve. *A* and *B* are working only toward binding directives that will benefit each *according to his own view of desirable outcomes*.

(c) *A* and *B* are once again permitted to ignore one another, so long as each follows the rules that govern their cooperative behavior. Although they are working together, neither need have the slightest concern for the other's ends, or indeed for the other's person, so long as he executes the plan.

Thus an individualist social order eliminates any necessity for *A* and *B* to engage in a discussion of ends or values. They can achieve the most complex imaginable interdependence in the domains of production and consumption, without acknowledging any interdependence whatever as moral beings. If we define freedom as the ability to choose for oneself the ends one will pursue, then an individualist order maximizes freedom, within the constraints of whatever substantive regime is in force.

The creation of an order within which there are no occasions on which it is necessary for group members to achieve a consensus about the ends they are to pursue, or indeed for group members to make the slightest effort toward the achievement of other ends than their own, makes perfect sense if one operates on the premise that values, as opposed to facts, are inherently arbitrary and subjective. Like the relationship between the other components of individualism (or of Romanticism, Classicism, etc.), the link between the two sets of ideas is more complicated than one of logical implication. But it is enough for our purposes to mention briefly some of the ways in which the idea of the subjectivity and arbitrariness of values reinforces or resonates the rule/discretion structure.

The *subjectivity* of values means that it is, by postulate, impossible to verify directly another person's statement about his experience of ends. That is, when *A* asserts that for him a particular state of affairs involves particular values in particular ways, *B* must choose between accepting the statement or challenging the good faith of the report. *B* knows about the actual state of affairs only through the medium of *A*'s words and actions. She cannot engage *A* in an argument about *A*'s values except on the basis of that information.

The postulate of the *arbitrariness* of values means that there is little basis for discussing them. Even supposing that values were objective, so that we could all agree which ones were involved in a particular situation, and how they were involved, it would still be impossible to show by any rational process how one ought to change that objective situation. Our understanding of the existence of values, according to the postulate, is not founded on rational deductive or inductive processes. Values are simply *there* in the psyche as the springs of all action. And since we cannot explain—except by appeal to behavioristic notions like those of learning theory—why or how they *are* there, we cannot expect to converse intelligently about what they ought to be or become.

Given these conditions, it seems likely that mechanisms of social order dependent on consensus about ends will run into terrible trouble. If, by providential arrangement (or perhaps by conditioning) everyone's values turn out to be identical (or to produce identical effects), then all is well; if there is disagreement, chaos ensues. This expectation is reinforced by the other major postulate of liberal theory: that people enter groups in order to achieve ends that pre-exist the group, so that the group is a means or instrument of its members considered as individuals.

Once again, this idea is *logically* connected neither with the postulate of
the arbitrariness of values nor with the characteristic rule/discretion
structure of an individualist social order. It merely 'resonates' these allied
conceptions. Thus, if the state is only an instrument each party adopts to
achieve his individual purposes, it is hard to see how it would ever make
sense to set up state processes founded on the notions of changing or
developing values. If the state is truly only a means to values, and all values
are inherently arbitrary and subjective, the only legitimate state institutions
are *facilitative*. The instant the state adopts change or development of values
as a purpose, we will suspect that it does so in opposition to certain
members whose values other members desire to change. The state then
becomes not a means to the ends of all, but an instrument of some in their
struggle with others, supposing that those others desire to retain and pursue
their disfavored purposes.

The individualist theory of the judicial role follows directly from these
premises. In its pure form, that theory makes the judge a simple rule applier,
and rules are defined as directives whose predicates are always facts and never
values. So long as the judge refers only to facts in deciding the question of
liability, and the remedial consequences, he is in the realm of the objective.
Since facts are objective rather than subjective, they can be determined, and
one can assert that the judge is right or wrong in what he does. The result is
both the certainty necessary for private maximization and the exclusion of
arbitrary use of state power to further some ends (values) at the expense of
others.

Classical late nineteenth century individualism had to deal with the
argument that it was impossible to formulate a code of laws that would deal
with all situations in advance through formally realizable rules. The response
was that the truly common, though minimal, ends that led to the creation of
the state could be formulated as concepts from which formally realizable rules
could be deduced. The judge could then deal with gaps in the legal order—
with new situations—by deductivity elaborating new rules. The process of
elaboration would be objective, because rational, just as the application of
rules was objective because referring only to facts.

Modern individualism accepts that this enterprise was a failure, but it does
not follow that the judge is totally at large. There is still a rational
presumption in favor of nonintervention, based on the fundamental liberal
premises. These have been strengthened rather than weakened by the failure
of the Classical enterprise, which asserted that there was at least enough
consensus about values to found an aggressive theory of the 'right', if not of
the good.

Nonintervention is consistent with the liberal premise because it means the
refusal of the group to use the state to enforce its vision of altruistic duty against
the conflicting visions of individuals pursuing their self-interest. The judge
should be intensely aware of the subjectivity and arbitrariness of values, and of
the instrumental character of the state he represents. He may not be able to
frame a coherent theory of what it means to be neutral, and in this sense the
legitimacy of everything he does is problematic. All reason can offer him in this
dilemma is the injunction to respect autonomy, to facilitate rather than to
regulate, to avoid paternalism, and to favor formal realizability and generality
in his decisions. If nothing else, his action should be relatively predictable, and
subject to democratic review through the alteration or prospective legislative
overruling of his decisions.

Fundamental Premises of Altruism

The utopian counter-program of altruist justice is collectivism. It asserts that justice consists of order according to shared ends. Everything else is rampant or residual injustice. The state, and with it the judge, are destined to disappear as people come to feel their brotherhood; it will be unnecessary to make them act 'as if.' The direct application of moral norms through judicial standards is therefore far preferable to a regime of rules based on moral agnosticism. But it still leaves us far from anything worthy of the name of altruistic order. The judge, after all, is there because we feel that force is necessary. Arbitrators are an improvement; mediators even better. But we attain the goal only when we surmount our alienation from one another and share ends to such an extent that contingency provides occasions for ingenuity but never for dispute.

Altruism denies the arbitrariness of values. It asserts that we understand our own goals and purposes and those of others to be at all times in a state of evolution, progress or retrogression, in terms of a universal ideal of human brotherhood. The laws of this evolution are reducible neither to rules of cause and effect, nor to a logic, nor to arbitrary impulses of the actor. We do not control our own moral development in the sense that the mechanic controls his machine or legal rules control the citizen, but we do participate in it rather than simply undergoing it. It follows that we can speak meaningfully about values, perhaps even that this is the highest form of discourse.

Altruism also denies the subjectivity of values. My neighbor's experience is anything but a closed book to me. Economists make the simplifying assumption of the 'independence of utility functions,' by which they suppose that A's welfare is unaffected by B's welfare. This notion is at *two* removes from reality: A's utility function is not only dependent on B's, it cannot truthfully be distinguished from B's. Quite true that we suffer *for* the suffering of others; more important that we suffer directly the suffering of others.

For the altruist, it is simply wrong to imagine the state as a means of the pre-existing ends of the citizens. Ends are collective and in process of development. It follows that the purposes that form a basis for moral decision are those of man-in-society rather than those of individuals. The administration of justice is more than a means to the ends of this whole. It is a part of it. In other words, judging is not something we have to *tolerate*; it is not a *cost* unavoidable if we are to achieve the various individual benefits of living together in groups.

Good judging, in this view, means the creation and development of values, not just the more efficient attainment of whatever we may already want. The parties and the judge are bound together, because their disputes derive an integral part of their meaning from his participation, first imagined, later real. It is desirable rather than not that they should see their negotiations as part of a collective social activity from which they cannot, short of utopia, exclude a representative of the group. A theory that presents the judge as an instrument denies this. Recognizing it means accepting that private citizens do or do not practice justice. It is an illusion to think that they only submit to or evade it.

Perhaps as important, an instrumental theory of judging lies to the judge himself, telling him that he has two kinds of existence. He is a private citizen, a *subject*, a cluster of ends 'consuming' the world. And he is an official, an *object*, a service consumed by private parties. As an instrument, the judge is not implicated in the legislature's exercise of force through him. Only when he chooses to make his own rules, rather than blindly apply those given him, must he take moral responsibility. And then, that responsibility is asserted to be altogether individual, his alone, and therefore fatally close to tyranny. The judge must choose alienation from his judgment (rule application) or the role of God (rule making).

By contrast, altruism denies the judge the right to apply rules without looking over his shoulder at the results. Altruism also denies that the only alternative to the passive stance is the claim of total discretion as creator of the legal universe. It asserts that we can gain an understanding of the values people have woven into their particular relationships, and of the moral tendency of their acts. These sometimes permit the judge to reach a decision, after the fact, on the basis of all the circumstances, as a person-in-society rather than as an individual. Though these faculties do not permit him to make rules for the future, that they permit him to decide is enough to make decision his duty. He must accept that his official life is personal, just as his private life, as manipulator of the legal order and as litigant, is social. The dichotomy of the private and the official is untenable, and the judge must undertake to practice justice, rather than merely transmit or invent it.

Altruism offers its own definitions of legal certainty, efficiency, and freedom. The certainty of individualism is perfectly embodied in the calculations of Holmes' 'bad man,' who is concerned with law only as a means or an obstacle to the accomplishment of his antisocial ends. The essence of individualist certainty-through-rules is that because it identifies for the bad man the precise limits of toleration for his badness, it authorizes him to hew as close as he can to those limits. To the altruist this is a kind of collective insanity by which we traduce our values while pretending to define them. Of what possible benefit can it be that the bad man calculates with certainty the contours within which vice is unrestrained? Altruism proposes an altogether different standard: the law is certain when not the bad but the *good* man is secure in the expectation that if he goes forward in good faith, with due regard for his neighbor's interest as well as his own, and a suspicious eye to the temptations of greed, then the law will not turn up as a dagger in his back. As for the bad man, let him beware; the good man's security and his own are incompatible.

'Efficiency' in the resolution of disputes is a pernicious objective unless it includes in the calculus of benefits set against the costs of administering justice the moral development of society through deliberation on the problem of our apparently disparate ends. Indeed, attempts to achieve the efficiency celebrated by individualism are likely to make these true benefits of judging unattainable, and end in a cheaper and cheaper production of injustice and social disintegration.

The 'freedom' of individualism is negative, alienated and arbitrary. It consists in the absence of restraint on the individual's choice of ends, and has no moral content whatever. When the group creates an order consisting of spheres of autonomy separated by (property) and linked by (contract) rules, each member declares her indifference to her neighbor's salvation—washes her hands of him the better to 'deal' with him. The altruist asserts that the staccato alternation of mechanical control and obliviousness is destructive of every value that makes freedom a thing to be desired. We can achieve real freedom only collectively, through *group* self-determination. We are simply too weak to realize ourselves in isolation. True, collective self-determination, short of utopia, implies the use of force against the individual. But we experience and accept the use of physical and psychic coercion every day, in family life, education and culture. We experience it indirectly, often unconsciously, in political and economic life. The problem is the conversion of force into moral force, in the face of the experience of moral indeterminacy. A definition of freedom that ignores this problem is no more than a rationalization of indifference, or the velvet glove for the hand of domination through rules.

The Implications of Contradictions Within Consciousness

The explanation of the sticking points of the modern individualist and altruist is that both believe quite firmly in both of these sets of premises, in spite of the fact that they are radically contradictory. The altruist critique of liberalism rings true for the individualist who no longer believes in the possibility of generating concepts that will in turn generate rules defining a just social order. The liberal critique of anarchy or collectivism rings true for the altruist, who acknowledges that after all we have not overcome the fundamental dichotomy of subject and object. So long as others are, to some degree, independent and unknowable beings, the slogan of shared values carries a real threat of a tyranny more oppressive than alienation in an at least somewhat altruistic liberal state.

The acknowledgment of contradiction does not abate the moral and practical conflict, but it does permit us to make some progress in characterizing it. At an elementary level, it makes it clear that it is futile to imagine that moral and practical conflict will yield to analysis in terms of higher level concepts. The meaning of contradiction at the level of abstraction is that there is no metasystem that would, if only we could find it, key us into one mode or the other as circumstances 'required.'

Second, the acknowledgment of contradiction means that we cannot 'balance' individualist and altruist values or rules against equitable standards, except in the tautological sense that we can, as a matter of fact, decide if we have to. The imagery of balancing presupposes exactly the kind of more abstract unit of measurement that the sense of contradiction excludes. The only kind of imagery that conveys the process by which we act and act and act in one direction, but then reach the sticking point, is that of existentialist philosophy. We make commitments, and pursue them. The moment of abandonment is not more rational than that of beginning, and equally a moment of terror.

Third, the recognition that both participants in the rhetorical struggle of individualism and altruism operate from premises that they accept only in this problematic fashion weakens the individualist argument that result orientation is dynamically unstable. Given contradiction at the level of pure theory, the open recognition of the altruist element in the legal system does not mean an irrevocable slide down the slope of totalitarianism, any more than it would lead to the definitive establishment of substantive justice in the teeth of the individualist rule structure.

Individualism, whether in the social form of private property or in that of rules, is *not* an heroically won, always precariously held symbol of man's fingernail grip on civilized behavior. That is a liberal myth. In any developed legal system, individualist attitudes, and especially the advocacy of rules, respond to a host of concrete interests having everything to lose by their erosion. Lawyers are necessary because of rules; the prestige of the judge is professional and technical, as well as charismatic and arcane, because of them; litigants who have mastered the language of form can dominate and oppress others, or perhaps simply prosper because of it; academics without number hitch their wagonloads of words to the star of technicality. Individualism is the structure of the status quo.

But there is more to it even than that. In elites, it responds to fear of the masses. In the masses, it responds to fear of the caprice of rulers. In small groups, it responds to fear of intimacy. In the psyche, it responds to the ego's primordial fear of being overwhelmed by the id. Its roots are deep enough so that one suspects an element of the paranoid in the refusal to recognize its contradictory sibling within consciousness.

Finally, the acknowledgment of contradiction makes it easier to understand judicial behavior that offends the ideal of the judge as a supremely rational being. The judge cannot, any more than the analyst, avoid the moment of truth in which one simply shifts modes. In place of the apparatus of rule making and rule application, with its attendant premises and attitudes, we come suddenly on a gap, a balancing test, a good faith standard, a fake or incoherent rule, or the enthusiastic adoption of a train of reasoning all know will be ignored in the next case. In terms of individualism, the judge has suddenly begun to act in bad faith. In terms of altruism *she has found herself.* The only thing that counts is this change in attitude, but it is hard to imagine anything more elusive of analysis.

Kennedy 'Form and Substance in Private Law Adjudication' (1976) 89 Harvard Law Review 1766–1777

Kennedy offers an extended note on the individualism-altruism dichotomy.

There are many problems with the use of concepts like individualism and altruism. Both positions have been assembled from diverse legal, moral, economic, and political writings, and I can give no plausible description of the principle of selection at work. As a result, it is impossible to 'prove' or 'disprove' the validity of the two constructs. They are neither falsifiable empirical statements about a determinate mass of data, nor logically pure 'models' totally abstracted from reality.

Nonetheless, I hope that the reader will find that the bits and pieces fit together into two intuitively familiar, easily recognizable wholes. Not being a systematic nominalist, I believe that there really *is* an altruist and an individualist mode of argument. More, I believe that the rhetorical modes are responsive to real issues in the real world. They are opposed concepts like Romanticism *vs.* Classicism, Gothic *vs.* Renaissance, toughminded *vs.* tenderminded, shame culture *vs.* guilt culture, or *Gemeinschaft vs. Gesellschaft.* As with Romanticism, we can believe in the usefulness of the notion of altruism without being able to demonstrate its existence experimentally, or show the inevitability of the association of the elements that compose it.

Methodological difficulties of this kind color all of the analysis that follows. One must keep constantly in mind that the individualist arguments are drawn from the same basic resources as the altruist ones. The same judge may, in a single opinion, provide examples of each mode. Over time, a single judge may provide complete statements of both positions. In other words, a person can use the arguments that compose the individualist set without being an 'individualist character.' When I speak of 'altruist judges' or 'altruist legislators', I mean only the proponents of particular arguments that fall within one set or the other. I have no intention of characterizing these proponents as *personalities.*

When we set out to analyze an action, and especially a judicial opinion, it is only rarely possible to make a direct inference from the rhetoric employed to the real motives or ideals that animate the judge. And it is even harder to characterize outcomes when it is personalities or opinions. It will almost always be possible to argue that, if we look hard at its actual effects on significant aspects of the real world, a particular decision will further both altruist and individualist values, or neither. I will therefore avoid talking about 'altruist outcomes' as much as possible.

Given that individualism and altruism are sets of stereotyped pro and con arguments, it is hard to see how either of them can ever be 'responsible' for a decision. First, each argument is applied, in almost identical form, to hundreds or thousands of fact situations. When the shoe fits, it is obviously not because it was designed for the wearer. Second, for each pro argument there is a con twin. Like Llewellyn's famous set of contradictory 'canons on statutes,' the opposing positions seem to cancel each other out. Yet somehow this is not *always* the case in practice. Although each argument has an absolutist, imperialist ring to it, we find that we are able to distinguish particular fact situations in which one side is much more plausible than the other. The difficulty, the mystery, is that there are no available metaprinciples to explain just what it is about these particular situations that makes them ripe for resolution. And there are many, many cases in which confidence in intuition turns out to be misplaced.

These are problems of a kind familiar in some other fields. Lawyers don't usually confront them, because lawyers usually believe that their analytic skills can produce explanations of legal rules and decisions more convincing than any that employ such vague, 'value laden' concepts. The typical legal argument at least pretends that it is possible to get from some universally agreed or positively enacted premise (which may be the importance of protecting a 'social interest') to some particular desirable outcome through a combination of logic and 'fact finding' (or, more likely, 'fact asserting').

Yet most contemporary students of legal thought seem to agree that an account of adjudication limited to the three dimensions of authoritative premises, facts and analysis is incomplete. One way to express this is to say that 'policy' plays a large though generally unacknowledged part in decisionmaking. The problem is to find a way to describe this part. My hope is that the substantive and formal categories I describe can help in rendering the contribution of 'policy' intelligible. Although individualism and altruism can be reduced neither to facts nor to logic, although they cannot be used with any degree of consistency to characterize personalities or opinions or the outcomes of lawsuits, they may nonetheless be helpful in this enterprise.

The ultimate goal is to break down the sense that legal argument is autonomous from moral, economic, and political discourse in general. There is nothing innovative about this. Indeed, it has been a premise of legal scholars for several generations that it is impossible to construct an autonomous logic of legal rules. What is new in this piece is the attempt to show an orderliness to the debates about 'policy' with which we are left after abandonment of the claim of neutrality.

Kennedy 'Form and Substance in Private Law Adjudication' (1976) 89 Harvard Law Review 1722–1724

Kelman gives some examples.

Kennedy may well have drawn this close connection because he most carefully analyzed the body of law in which the claim probably fits best: contract law. It seems to be the case that most of the formally vaguer positions are associated with enacting greater degrees of solicitude from one contracting party for the other than the stricter rules demand. The standard that one can't enforce an unconscionable contract makes each of us responsible for ensuring that we don't take advantage of improvident fellow contractors, while the rule that a judge will look only for formal consideration, not a substantively fair bargain, allows us to celebrate when we find a chump to contract with. The standard that one must bargain in good faith demands that one watch out for the interests of a trading partner to ensure that he doesn't hurt himself courting one's business; the rule that enables one to skirt obligations until the contract is fully formalized enables one to get what one can from someone eager to please before committing oneself at all. The traditional mechanically applicable parol evidence rule congratulates the successful individualist on memorializing the contract as he desires, even if he gives (unenforceable) verbal assurances that he will do things unmentioned in the text; the more standardlike exceptions or counterrules demand that the less wary party be taken care of as well as the more wary one.

Kelman *A Guide to Critical Legal Studies* 55

It is important not to misread Kennedy. He is not saying that a commitment to rules logically entails individualism; nor is there any factual prediction in the sense that the use of a rule in a specific controversy will inevitably be the work of political individualism.

One might attempt to link the substantive and formal dimensions at the level of social reality. This would involve investigating, from the points of view of individualism and altruism, the actual influence of private law decisions on economic, social, and political life. One could then ask how the form in which the judge chooses to cast his decision contributes to these effects, being careful to determine the *actual* degree of formal realizability and generality of the rule or standard in question. This method is hopelessly difficult, given the current limited state of the art of assessing either actual effects of decisions or their actual formal properties. *Theories* of the practical importance of deciding private law disputes in one way or another abound, but ways to test those theories do not. This gives most legal argument a distinctly unreal, even fantastic quality that this essay will do nothing to dispel. Rather, my subject is that often unreal and fantastic rhetoric itself. This is no more than a first step, but it may be an important one.

Kennedy 'Form and Substance in Private Law Adjudication' (1976) 89 Harvard Law Review 1738

Again it is instructive to refer to Kelman.

The connection between form and substance has never been said to be one of either logical entailment or material necessity. In some ways it is difficult to interpret the critical articles to make any claim at all about the nature of the connection other than that it *exists*. My argument is that to the extent Kennedy's point is interpreted (wrongly, but frequently) as an empirical prediction (for example that rule orientation in particular controversies will inevitably be the program of political individualists), it will often be simply wrong, other times simply irrelevant. To the extent, though, that there is supposed to be a *cultural connection* between a fuzzy ideal of a world of rule-grounded persons (rather than an unbending commitment to the use of rules in all cases) and both political individualism and a personal or philosophical commitment to the privacy of some asocial self, I believe that this insight of 'Form and Substance' remains invaluable.

Kelman *A Guide to Critical Legal Studies* 17

(b) The deepest meaning

In his later article which analyses Blackstone's *Commentaries*, this deep ambivalence over political visions reflects a 'fundamental contradiction' between the desire to merge with others and yet to remain separate from them.

The Fundamental Contradiction

Here is an initial statement of the fundamental contradiction: Most participants in American legal culture believe that the goal of individual freedom is at the same time dependent on and incompatible with the communal coercive action that is necessary to achieve it. Others (family, friends, bureaucrats, cultural figures, the state) are necessary if we are to become persons at all—they provide us the stuff of our selves and protect us in crucial ways against destruction. Even when we seem to ourselves to be most alone, others are with us, incorporated in us through processes of language, cognition and feeling that are, simply as a matter of biology, collective aspects of our individuality. Moreover, we are not always alone. We sometimes experience fusion with others, in groups of two or even two million, and it is a good rather than a bad experience.

But at the same time that it forms and protects us, the universe of others (family, friendship, bureaucracy, culture, the state) threatens us with annihilation and urges upon us forms of fusion that are quite plainly bad rather than good. A friend can reduce me to misery with a single look. Numberless conformities, large and small abandonments of self to others, are the price of what freedom we experience in society. And the price is a high one. Through our existence as members of collectives, we impose on others and have imposed on us hierarchical structures of power, welfare, and access to enlightenment that are illegitimate, whether based on birth into a particular social class or on the accident of genetic endowment.

The kicker is that the abolition of these illegitimate structures, the fashioning of an unalienated collective existence, appears to imply such a massive increase of collective control over our lives that it would defeat its purpose. Only collective force seems capable of destroying the attitudes and institutions that collective force has itself imposed. Coercion of the individual by the group appears to be inextricably bound up with the liberation of that same individual. If one accepts that collective norms weigh so heavily in favor of the status quo that purely 'voluntary' movement is inconceivable, then the only alternative is the assumption of responsibility for the totalitarian domination of other people's minds—for 'forcing them to be free.'

Even this understates the difficulty. It is not just that the world of others is intractable. The very structures against which we rebel are necessarily within us as well as outside of us. We are implicated in what we would transform, and it in us. This critical insight is not compatible with that sense of the purity of one's intention which seems often to have animated the enterprise of remaking the social world. None of this renders political practice impossible, or even problematic: we can identify oppression without having overcome the fundamental contradiction, and do something against it. But it does mean proceeding on the basis of faith and hope in humanity, without the assurances of reason.

The fundamental contradiction—that relations with others are both necessary to and incompatible with our freedom—is not only intense. It is also pervasive. First, it is an aspect of our experience of every form of social life. It arises in the relations of lovers, spouses, parents and children, neighbours, employers and employees, trading partners, colleagues, and so forth. Second, within law, as law is commonly defined, it is not only an aspect, but the very *essence* of every problem. There simply are no legal issues that do not involve directly the problem of the legitimate content of collective coercion, since there is by definition no legal problem until someone has at least imagined that he might invoke the force of the state. And it is not just a matter of definition. The more sophisticated a person's legal thinking, regardless of her political stance, the more likely she is to believe that all issues within a doctrinal field reduce to a single dilemma of the degree of collective as opposed to individual self-determination that is appropriate. And analyses of particular fields tend themselves to collapse into a single analysis as soon as the thinker attempts to understand together, say, free speech and economic due process, or contracts and torts.

Kennedy 'The Structure of Blackstone's Commentaries' (1979) 28 Buffalo Law Review
211–213

ROBERTO UNGER AND THE THREE LEVELS

The tone is set in the opening words to Unger's massive article, 'The Critical Legal Studies Movement', (1983) 96 Harvard Law Review 563: the movement has 'undermined the central ideas of modern legal thought and put another conception of law in their place'. In this work he sets out to 'exemplify the spirit of our movement' and begins by 'placing critical legal studies within the tradition of leftist tendencies in modern legal thought and practice' (p 564). His overriding concern, within this leftist tradition, is the critique of *formalism* and of *objectivity*.

In the following extract, note:

(a)   he argues that by formalism he means something other than what the term is usually taken to signify;
(b)   he targets two basic formalist theses—the contention that legal reasoning, being determinate and rational and relying on 'impersonal' purposes, policies and principles, is to be distinguished from indeterminate reasoning in open-ended ideological disputes in, for example, philosophy and the view that legal doctrine is only possible through this method of arguing;
(c)   his restatement of the second contention in terms of the difference between lawmaking and law application;
(d)   his definition of objectivism—the idea of a defensible scheme of 'human association'.

The first concern has been the critique of formalism and objectivism. Let me pause to define formalism and objectivism carefully, for these ideas will play an important role in later stages of my argument. By formalism I do not mean what the term is usually taken to describe: belief in the availability of a deductive or quasi-deductive method capable of giving determinate solutions to particular problems of legal choice. What I mean by formalism in this context is a commitment to, and therefore also a belief in the possibility of, a method of legal justification that can be clearly contrasted to open-ended disputes about the basic terms of social life, disputes that people call ideological, philosophical, or visionary. Though such conflicts may not be entirely bereft of criteria, they fall far short of the rationality that the formalist claims for legal analysis. The formalism I have in mind characteristically invokes impersonal purposes, policies, and principles as an indispensable component of legal reasoning. Formalism in the conventional sense—the search for a method of deduction from a gapless system of rules—is merely the anomalous, limiting case of this jurisprudence.

You might add a second distinctive formalist thesis: that only through such a restrained, relatively apolitical method of analysis is legal doctrine possible. By legal doctrine or legal analysis, in turn, I mean a form of conceptual practice that combines two characteristics: the willingness to work from the institutionally defined materials of a given collective tradition and the claim to speak authoritatively within this tradition, to elaborate it from within in a way that is meant, at least ultimately, to affect the application of state power. Doctrine can exist—the formalist says or assumes—because of a contrast between the more determinate rationality of legal analysis and the less determinate rationality of ideological contests.

This thesis can be restated as the belief that lawmaking and law application differ fundamentally, as long as legislation is seen to be guided only by the looser rationality of ideological conflict. Lawmaking and law application diverge in both how they work and how their results may properly be justified. To be sure, law application may have an important creative element. But in the politics of lawmaking the appeal to principle and policy—when it exists at all—is supposed to be both more controversial in its foundations and more indeterminate in its implications than the corresponding features of legal analysis. Other modes of justification allegedly compensate for the diminished force and precision of the ideal element in lawmaking. Thus, legislative decisions may be validated as results of procedures that are themselves legitimate because they allow all interest groups to be represented and to compete for influence or, more ambitiously, because they enable the wills of citizens to count equally in choosing the laws that will govern them.

By objectivism I mean the belief that the authoritative legal materials—the system of statutes, cases, and accepted legal ideas—embody and sustain a defensible scheme of human association. They display, though always imperfectly, an intelligible moral order. Alternatively they show the results of practical constraints upon social life—constraints such as those of economic efficiency—that, taken together with constant human desires, have a normative force. The laws are not merely the outcome of contingent power struggles or of practical pressures lacking in rightful authority.

Unger 'The Critical Legal Studies Movement' (1983) 96 Harvard Law Review 564–565

According to Unger both formalism and objectivity fail; but can they be divorced from one another?

The modern lawyer may wish to keep his formalism while avoiding objectivist assumptions. He may feel happy to switch from talk about interest group politics in a legislative setting to invocations of impersonal purpose, policy, and principle in an adjudicative or professional one. He is plainly mistaken;

formalism presupposes at least a qualified objectivism. For if the impersonal purposes, policies, and principles on which all but the most mechanical versions of the formalist thesis must rely do not come, as objectivism suggests, from a moral or practical order exhibited, however partially and ambiguously, by the legal materials themselves, where could they come from? They would have to be supplied by some normative theory extrinsic to the law. Even if such a theory could be convincingly established on its own ground, it would be a sheer miracle for its implications to coincide with a large portion of the received doctrinal understandings. At least it would be a miracle unless you had already assumed the truth of objectivism. But if the results of this alien theory failed to overlap with the greater part of received understandings of the law, you would need to reject broad areas of established law and legal doctrine as 'mistaken.' You would then have trouble maintaining the contrast of doctrine to ideology and political prophecy that represents an essential part of the formalist creed: you would have become a practitioner of the free-wheeling criticism of established arrangements and received ideas. No wonder theorists committed to formalism and the conventional view of doctrine have always fought to retain some remnant of the objectivist thesis. They have done so even at a heavy cost to their reputation among the orthodox, narrow-minded lawyers who otherwise provide their main constituency.

Unger 'The Critical Legal Studies Movement' (1983) 96 Harvard Law Review 565–566

There is a second tenet of leftist thought.

If the criticism of formalism and objectivism is the first characteristic theme of leftist movements in modern legal thought, the purely instrumental use of legal practice and legal doctrine to advance leftist aims is the second. The connection between these two activities—the skeptical critique and the strategic militancy—seems both negative and sporadic. It is negative because it remains almost entirely limited to the claim that nothing in the nature of law or in the conceptual structure of legal thought—neither objectivist nor formalist assumptions—constitutes a true obstacle to the advancement of leftist aims. It is sporadic because short-run leftist goals might occasionally be served by the transmutation of political commitments into delusive conceptual necessities.

Unger 'The Critical Legal Studies Movement' (1983) 96 Harvard Law Review 566–567

(a)   The critique of objectivism

Note what the critique upon objectivism amounts to and the two fronts upon which this attack has been launched. The second front introduces the distinction between principles and counterprinciples. His description of contract law, for example, is of legal principles and their counterprinciples, the main point being that both sets of principles represent competing visions of 'human association'.

What are the two competing visions? Can the counterprinciples be trumped comprehensibly by the principles? In contract law, what are the two competing sources of legal obligation?

The critique of objectivism that we have undertaken is essentially the critique of the idea of types of social organization with a built-in legal structure and of the more subtle but still powerful successors of this idea in current conceptions of substantive law and doctrine. We have conducted this assault on more than one front.

Historical study has repeatedly shown that every attempt to find the universal legal language of the democracy and the market revealed the falsehood of the original idea. An increasing part of doctrinal analysis and legal theory has been devoted to containing the subversive implications of this discovery.

The general theory of contract and property provided the core domain for the objectivist attempt to disclose the built-in legal content of the market just as the theory of protected constitutional interests and of the legitimate ends of state action was designed to reveal the intrinsic legal structure of a democratic republic. But the execution kept belying the intention. As the property concept was generalized and decorporealized, it faded into the generic conception of right, which in turn proved to be systematically ambiguous (eg, Hohfeld) if not entirely indeterminate. Contract, the dynamic counterpart to property, could do no better. The generalization of contract theory revealed, alongside the dominant principles of freedom to choose the partner and the terms, the counterprinciples: that freedom to contract would not be allowed to undermine the communal aspects of social life and that grossly unfair bargains would not be enforced. Though the counterprinciples might be pressed to the corner, they could be neither driven out completely nor subjected to some system of metaprinciples that would settle, once and for all, their relation to the dominant principles. In the most contested areas of contract law, two different views of the sources of obligation still contend. One, which sees the counterprinciples as mere ad hoc qualifications to the dominant principles, identifies the fully articulated act of will and the unilateral imposition of a duty by the state as the two exhaustive sources of obligation. The other view, which treats the counterprinciples as possible generative norms of the entire body of law and doctrine, finds the standard source of obligations in the only partially deliberate ties of mutual dependence and redefines the two conventional sources as extreme, limiting cases. Which of these clashing conceptions provides the real theory of contract? Which describes the institutional structure inherent in the very nature of a market?

Unger 'The Critical Legal Studies Movement' (1983) 96 Harvard Law Review 568–569

(b) The critique of formalism

We have approached the critique of formalism from an angle equally specific. The starting point of our argument is the idea that every branch of doctrine must rely tacitly if not explicitly upon some picture of the forms of human association that are right and realistic in the areas of social life with which it deals. If, for example, you are a constitutional lawyer, you need a theory of the democratic republic that would describe the proper relation between state and society or the essential features of social organization and individual entitlement that government must protect come what may.

Without such a guiding vision, legal reasoning seems condemned to a game of easy analogies. It will always be possible to find, retrospectively, more or less convincing ways to make a set of distinctions, or failures to distinguish, look credible. A common experience testifies to this possibility; every thoughtful law student or lawyer has had the disquieting sense of being able to argue too well or too easily for too many conflicting solutions. Because everything can be defended nothing can; the analogy-mongering must be brought to a halt. It must be possible to reject some of the received understandings and decisions as mistaken and to do so by appealing to some background normative theory of the branch of law in question or of the realm of social practice governed by that part of the law.

Suppose that you could determine on limited grounds of institutional propriety how much a style of doctrinal practice may regularly reject as mistaken. With too little rejection, the lawyer fails to avoid the suspect quality of endless analogizing. With too much, he forfeits his claim to be doing doctrine as opposed to ideology, philosophy, or prophecy. For any given level of revisionary power, however, different portions of the received understandings in any extended field of law may be repudiated.

To determine which part of established opinion about the meaning and applicability of legal rules you should reject, you need a background prescriptive theory of the relevant area of social practice, a theory that does for the branch of law in question what a doctrine of the republic or of the political process does for constitutional argument. This is where the trouble arises. No matter what the content of this background theory, it is, if taken seriously and pursued to its ultimate conclusions, unlikely to prove compatible with a broad range of the received understandings. Yet just such a compatibility seems to be required by a doctrinal practice that defines itself by contrast to open-ended ideology. For it would be strange if the results of a coherent, richly developed normative theory were to coincide with a major portion of any extended branch of law. The many conflicts of interest and vision that lawmaking involves, fought out by countless minds and wills working at cross-purposes, would have to be the vehicle of an immanent moral rationality whose message could be articulated by a single cohesive theory. This daring and implausible sanctification of the actual is in fact undertaken by the dominant legal theories and tacitly presupposed by the unreflective common sense of orthodox lawyers. Most often, the sanctification takes the form of treating the legal order as a repository of intelligible purposes, policies, and principles, in abrupt contrast to the standard disenchanted view of legislative politics.

Unger 'The Critical Legal Studies Movement' (1983) 96 Harvard Law Review 570–571

The result of this is that no line can be drawn between legal justification and open-ended disputes about the basic terms of life. The critique of formalism demonstrates that a 'doctrinal practice that puts its hope in the contrast of legal reasoning to ideology, philosophy, and political prophecy ends up as a collection of makeshift apologies' (p 573).

(c) The triadic scheme

The legal scholar who is convinced by these views, according to Unger, must engage in political activity to change the society: he needs to engage in 'deviationist doctrine'. In demonstrating the failure of formalism and objectivism in specific areas of the law there are three levels of legal doctrine: the first are the authoritative rules and the second are the ideal purposes, principles underlying these rules. Therefore the jurist needs to show that underpinning the specific rules there are matching principles and counterprinciples with the result that no recourse to principle can guarantee one interpretation of a rule in preference to another.

On another description the crucial feature of deviationist doctrine is the willingness to recognize and develop the disharmonies of the law: the conflicts between principles and counterprinciples that can be found in any body of law. Critical doctrine does this by finding in these disharmonies the elements of broader contests among prescriptive conceptions of society.

Unger 'The Critical Legal Studies Movement' (1983) 96 Harvard Law Review 578

It is the last sentence to this extract that introduces the third level. The deviationist doctrine must show that on a third level below both the rules and their underlying principles there are conflicting ideological assumptions about social life. This is the level of conceptions of the possible and desirable human associations to be enacted in different areas of social practice.

The dominant styles of legal doctrine often included all three levels of analysis: the authoritative rules and precedents; the ideal purposes, policies, and principles; and the conceptions of possible and desirable human associations to be enacted in different areas of social practice. Each such set of conceptions made a particular version of society stand in the place of the indefinite possibilities of human connection. To identify this set is to see how power-ridden and manipulable materials gain a semblance of authority, necessity, and determinacy and thus how formalism and objectivism seem plausible. It is to illuminate the mental world within which impersonal purposes, policies, and principles make sense and claim authority.

Most legal traditions of the past incorporated the final level of legal argument by relying upon a secular or sacred vision of the one right and necessary order of social life. Modern legal doctrine, however, works in a social context in which society has increasingly been forced open to transformative conflict. It exists in a cultural context in which, to an unprecedented extent, society is understood to be made and imagined rather than merely given. To incorporate the final level of legal analysis in this new setting would be to transform legal doctrine into one more arena for continuing the fight over the right and possible forms of social life. Modern jurists and their philosophers have generally wanted to avoid this result. They have avoided it at the cost of a series of violent and arbitrary intellectual restrictions whose ultimate effect is to turn legal doctrine into an endless array of argumentative tricks. Through its constructive attempts to devise a less confined genre of legal analysis, the critical legal studies movement has insisted upon avoiding this avoidance.

The rationality for which this expanded version of legal doctrine can hope is nothing other than the minimal but perhaps still significant potential rationality of the normal modes of moral and political controversy. You start from the conflicts between the available ideals of social life in your own social world or legal tradition and their flawed actualizations in present society. You imagine the actualizations transformed, or you transform them in fact, perhaps only by extending an ideal to some area of social life from which it had previously been excluded. Then you revise the ideal conceptions in the light of their new practical embodiments. You might call this process internal development. To engage in it self-reflectively you need make only two crucial assumptions: that no one scheme of association has conclusive authority and that the mutual correction of abstract ideals and their institutional realizations represents the last best hope of the standard forms of normative controversy. The weakness of such a method is obviously its dependence upon the starting points provided by a particular tradition; its strength, the richness of reference to a concrete collective history of ideas and institutions. Legal doctrine rightly understood and practised is the conduct of internal development through legal materials.

Unger 'The Critical Legal Studies Movement (1983) 96 Harvard Law Review 579–580

From the last extract it is clear that Unger envisages that the three levels will be present in critical legal doctrine as well as in existing doctrine. In this extract does he succeed in showing how the three levels will differ in these two different doctrines?
He argues for the existence of two 'deviationist doctrines'.

The Two Models Compared.—Compare now the two models of deviationist doctrine. The first model begins by analyzing the major thematic commitments of a particular branch of law and legal doctrine as well as the specific categories that serve these commitments. It then makes explicit the assumptions about social fact and the social ideal on which those categories rest and subjects them to criticism by the light of more or less widely accepted ideals and understandings. The concealment of these assumptions is vital to the persuasive authority of the dominant legal ideas; seemingly uncontroversial technical conceptions commonly depend upon highly controversial, nontechnical premises. At this point the first model of deviationist doctrine switches to a different and independently justified view of how the area of social life with which it deals should be ordered. This view implies the institutional reconstruction of major aspects of present society. Finally, the model shows how this programmatic conception can be taken as a regulative ideal for the development of current doctrine.

The second model of critical doctrine starts by conceiving a broad field of law as the expression of a system of principles and counterprinciples whose actual or proper relation to each other can be represented in clashing ways. It then shows how these rival approaches appear in a series of instances of exemplary difficulty. The countervision worked out through the analysis of these foci of controversy brings a changed understanding of the proper relation between counterprinciples and principles. This understanding can be clarified through generalization into a more comprehensive legal theory. Once generalized it may be applied, and revised through its application, to other related branches of law. Finally, the larger justifications and implications of the suggested developments can be made explicit.

Both models of doctrine begin from the same view of the relations among the three levels of law and legal analysis: authoritative rules and precedents expressed today mainly by statutes and judicial decisions, organizing principles and counterprinciples, and imaginative schemes of social life that assign distinct models of human association to different sectors of social practice. The attempt to reassert and reexamine a set of legal norms and ideas in the face of fresh problems highlights two sources of permanent though often latent uncertainty and conflict and thus demonstrates once again how the effort to reproduce a practical or imaginative order in society supplies instruments and occasions for the demolition of that order. The interpretation of large bodies of rules and precedents must rely tacitly if not explicitly upon principles and counterprinciples, and the understanding of principles and counterprinciples must in turn presuppose conceptions of what the dealings among people can and should be like in each sphere of social life, even if these conceptions are said to be somehow embodied in the law rather than imported into it from outside. Each time the next deepest level is exposed, the exposure produces a twofold destabilizing effect. The more superficial level (the rules and precedents in relation to the principles and counterprinciples, the principles and counterprinciples in relation to the models of possible and desirable association) is shown to be but a flawed realization of the deeper one, while the empirical and normative beliefs that constitute this deeper level are made controversial if not implausible in the very process of being exposed. Alongside these vertical tensions between levels of legal analysis, the reconsideration of law in untried contexts generates horizontal conflicts within each level. For each is revealed as the stage for a contest among ideals, a contest that becomes fiercer as we move down the sequence of levels.

Conventional legal doctrine, and the legal theories that propose to refine it the better to support it, try to suppress or minimize both the horizontal and the vertical conflicts. Deviationist doctrine, on the contrary, wants to bring these instabilities to the surface: first, because this is the form subversion takes in the domain of legal ideas and, second, because if insight and justification can be achieved at all in legal doctrine or any other field of normative argument, they can be achieved only through the repeated practice of such subversion, under its double aspect of internal development and visionary thought.

Though the two kinds of instability implicate and reinforce each other, one may temporarily receive pride of place. The first style of doctrine emphasizes the vertical conflicts; the second style, the horizontal ones. But the two emphases can be effected and combined in any number of ways; the methods suggested here exemplify an approach that might follow a different tack while remaining faithful to the same central conception. Yet even these limited versions of deviationist doctrine can be successfully applied to every branch of law.

Unger 'The Critical Legal Studies Movement' (1983) 96 Harvard Law Review 646–648

(d) The law of contract

Unger's discussion of contract law reveals the methods of critical legal doctrine. First, he wishes to show that existing legal doctrine hides the connection between the second level principles and the third level conceptions of desirable forms of human association and that the third level conceptions are treated uncritically, their status being assumed to be 'given' or 'natural'. Secondly, his argument is that on the second level contract is comprised of principles and counterprinciples.

Principle and Counterprinciple: Freedom to Contract and Community.—The initial stage in this variant of deviationist doctrine is the effort to understand the better part of contract law and doctrine as an expression of a small number of opposing ideas: principles and counterprinciples. These ideas connect the more concrete legal rules and standards to a set of background assumptions about the kinds of human association that can and should prevail in different areas of social life. The principles and counterprinciples are more than artifacts of theoretical curiosity. They provisionally settle what would otherwise be pervasive ambiguities in the more concrete legal materials. But they themselves can be understood and justified only as expressions of background schemes of possible and desirable human association. For only this deeper context can offer guidance about the relative reach and the specific content of the opposing principles and counterprinciples. Because the conventional methods of legal analysis are committed to the contrast between doctrine and ideology or philosophy, they almost invariably prefer to leave implicit the reference to the larger imaginative foundations of rules and principles. Thus, I have argued, they gain a semblance of higher certainty at the cost of an arbitrary dogmatism.

But why should the controlling ideas come in the form of antagonistic principles and counterprinciples? Such an opposition can alone generate a body of law and legal thought that applies different models of human association to distinct areas of social life. At a minimum the counterprinciples keep the principles in place and prevent them from extending, imperialistically, to all social life. Once the crucial role of counterprinciples has been recognized, the appeal to a larger vision of the possible and desirable models of human connection becomes inevitable. Because conventional analysis wants to avoid, if not the reality, at least the appearance of such an appeal, it also systematically downplays the counterprinciples.

Unger 'The Critical Legal Studies Movement' (1983) 96 Harvard Law Review 618–619

What are the principles and counterprinciples? He discusses two pairs.

The structure of reigning ideas about contract and its adjacent fields can be stated with the greatest possible simplicity, in the form of only two pairs of principles and counterprinciples. If we were concerned with a specific contract problem, many intermediate levels of generalization might be warranted.

The first principle is that of the freedom to enter or to refuse to enter into contracts. More specifically, it is the faculty of choosing your contract partners. It might be called, for short, the freedom to contract. The qualifications that the law of assignment imposes upon the doctrine of privity show that the principle of freedom of contract is marked by a certain complexity of meaning even when the currently dominant forms of market organization are taken for granted. In a system that treats the consolidated property right as the exemplary form of right itself and that conceives property in part as that which can be freely bought and sold in an impersonal market, restraints upon assignability must be limited. The law must treat contractual relations as if they were powerless to imprint a permanent character upon the tangible or intangible things (including the labor of other people) that these relations concern. Any way you look at it—from the perspective of the common meaning of freedom to contract, or the practical demands of the existing kinds of markets, or the actual behavior and motivations of economic agents—the interplay of the ideals of personality and impersonality, manifested respectively in doctrines of privity and assignability, represents less a conflict between the first principle and a counterprinciple than a disharmony within that principle itself. This disharmony can be resolved by any number of practical compromises.

Other areas of law and doctrine, however, do circumscribe the principle of freedom to contract on behalf of an entirely different idea. They embody a counterprinciple: that the freedom to choose the contract partner will not be allowed to work in ways that subvert the communal aspects of social life.

Unger 'The Critical Legal Studies Movement' (1983) 96 Harvard Law Review 619–620

So, Unger sees the law of contract as a conflict at the third level between two different forms of human association.

The relation of principle and counterprinciple in contract law can be interpreted as an expression of two different views of how people can and should interact in the areas of social life touched by contract law: one crude and easy to criticize, the other more subtle and justifiable. The crude view is the one displayed most clearly by the rules that try to keep contract out of the realm of 'social arrangements.' It contrasts an ideal of private community, meant to be realized chiefly in the life of family and friendship, to the ideal of contractual freedom, addressed to the world of self-interested commerce. The social realm is pictured as rich in precisely the attributes that are thought to be almost wholly absent from the economic realm. The communal forms in which it abounds, islands of reciprocal loyalty and support, neither need much law nor are capable of tolerating it. For law in this conception is the regime of rigidly defined rights that demarcate areas for discretionary action.

The idea that there is an area of experience outside the serious world of work, in which communal relations flourish, can be made to justify the devolution of practical life to the harshest self-interest. The premises to this devolution recall the contrast between Venice and Belmont in *The Merchant of Venice*. In Venice people make contracts; in Belmont they exchange wedding rings. In Venice they are held together by combinations of interest; in Belmont by mutual affection. The wealth and power of Venice depend upon the willingness of its courts to hold men to their contracts. The charm of Belmont is to provide its inhabitants with a community in which contracts remain for the most part superfluous. Venice is tolerable because its citizens can flee occasionally to Belmont and appeal from Venetian justice to Belmontine mercy. But the very existence of Belmont presupposes the prosperity of Venice, from which the denizens of Belmont gain their means of livelihood. This is the form of life classical contract theory claims to describe and seeks to define—an existence separated into a sphere of trade supervised by the state and an area of private family and friendship largely though not wholly beyond the reach of contract. Each half of this life both denies the other and depends upon it. Each is at once the other's partner and its enemy.

The larger imaginative background to this contrast is a vision of social life that distinguishes more or less sharply among separate models of human connection. These models are meant to be realized in separate areas of social life: democracy for the state and citizenship, private community for family and friendship, and an amalgam of contract and impersonal technical hierarchy for the everyday world of work and exchange. The most remarkable feature of this vision is its exclusion of the more morally ambitious models of human connection from the prosaic activities and institutions that absorb most people most of the time. These models are democracy and private community. Their moral ambition consists in their promise of a partial reconciliation between the competing claims of self-assertion and attachment to other people—a reconciliation, in fact, between two competing sides of the experience of self-assertion itself. According to the logic of the vision, any attempt to extend these ideals beyond their proper realm of application into everyday life will meet with disaster. Not only will the extension fail, but the practical and psychological conditions that enable the higher ideals to flourish on their own ground may also be destroyed in the course of the attempt.

Unger 'The Critical Legal Studies Movement' (1983) 96 Harvard Law Review 622–623

The second of the two principles in the law of contract is freedom of contract, as distinguished from freedom to contract: 'the parties must be free to choose the terms of their agreement. Save in special circumstances, they will not be second-guessed by a court, not at least as long as they stay within the ground rules that define a regime of free contract' (p 625). Of course this principle has its own matching counterprinciple: 'that unfair bargains should not be enforced'.

Pre-critical, conventional law and doctrines try 'to suppress or minimize' these conflicts on the third level. However, on the contrary, deviationist doctrine wants to 'bring these instabilities to the surface'. Refer back to the two deviationist models (supra p 506).

He describes in detail a constructive programme that comes after the critique.

> The program I have described is neither just another variant of the mythic, antiliberal republic nor much less some preposterous synthesis of the established democracies with their imaginary opposite. Instead, it represents a superliberalism. It pushes the liberal premises about state and society, about freedom from dependence and governance of social relations by the will, to the point at which they merge into a larger ambition: the building of a social world less alien to a self that can always violate the generative rules of its own mental or social constructs and put other rules and other constructs in their place.
>
> A less contentious way to define the superliberalism of the program is to say that it represents an effort to make social life resemble more closely what politics (narrowly and traditionally defined) are already largely like in the liberal democracies: a series of conflicts and deals among more or less transitory and fragmentary groups. These groups constitute parties of opinion, by which I mean not only political parties in the narrow sense, but also whoever may coalesce round the defense of an interest or a cause that he wants to see advanced by the assertion or withdrawal of governmental power. All this stands in contrast to a mode of social organization that to a significant extent pegs people at fixed stations in a more or less pacified division of labor. To remake social life in the image of liberal politics it is necessary, among other things, to change the liberal conception and practice of politics.

Unger 'The Critical Legal Studies Movement' (1983) 96 Harvard Law Review 602

He writes of 'reinventing democracy', a democracy that would not be constrained in its job of removing social hierarchies and redistributing resources. This entails a new concept of law, the most important feature of which would be 'destabilization rights': 'claims to the disruption of established institutions and forms of social practice that have achieved the very sort of insulation and have contributed to the very kind of crystallized plan of social hierarchy and division that the entire constitution wants to avoid' (p 600).

What of the role of the lawyer?

> As legal analysis approached deviationist doctrine and society came to execute the institutional program described earlier, the character of professional expertise in law would change. The contrast between lawyers and laymen would give way to a situation of multiple points of entry into the more or less authoritative resolution of problems that we now define as legal. If legal doctrine is acknowledged to be continuous with other modes of normative argument if the institutional plan that decrees the existence of a distinct judiciary alongside only one or two other branches of government is reconstructed, and if long before this reconstruction the belief in a logic of inherent institutional roles is abandoned, legal expertise can survive only as a

loose collection of different types of insight and responsibility. Each type would combine elements of current legal professionalism with allegedly nonlegal forms of special knowledge and experience as well as with varieties of political representation. This disintegration of the bar might serve as a model for what would happen in a more democratic and less superstitious society to all claims to monopolize in the name of expert knowledge an instrument of power.

Unger 'The Critical Legal Studies Movement' (1983) 96 Harvard Law Review 668

(e) Critique of Unger's critique

In the next extract, J W Harris's reference to his recent article is to 'Legal Doctrine and Interests in Land' in *Oxford Essays in Jurisprudence* (3rd series, eds Eekelaar and Bell).

In a recent essay, I investigated the part played in modern English land law by two subspecies of doctrinal reasoning, distinguished within Max Weber's sociology of law. Weber claimed that it was of the essence of legal reasoning that it is 'formal' in one or other of two ways. It might be 'casuistic,' in the sense that support for a legal proposition was based on precedent or analogy; and such casuistry will be empirical or conceptual, depending on whether precedential or analogical force is thought to reside in similarity of facts or the meaning of concepts. Alternatively, legal reasoning might be 'logically formal' in that a proposition was derived from a notionally gapless set of abstract conceptual definitions. I argued that English land law exhibited formalism of both these kinds. I further maintained that there was nothing fundamentally irreconcilable, at the level of sociological analysis, between Weber's and Unger's depiction of law. For both, the concept of law (as we have it) encompasses doctrinal, including formalistic, reasoning. It is for that reason that the critical legal studies movement, as Unger interprets it, seeks to replace what we have with a new conception of law.

I sought to highlight the implications of deviationist doctrine by inventing a scholar (named Hero) who applies it to contemporary English land law. Hero shares Unger's social vision and accepts his methodology. In particular, he accepts two programmatic restraints which Unger places upon deviationist doctrine. Firstly, scorn for institutional deference: it is, for Hero, no objection to a frankly political analysis of doctrine that it is the sort of argument which could not be advanced before a court or adopted by a judge. It is of no moment that deviationist doctrine could not be employed in conventional courts:

'We have no stake in finding a pre-established harmony between moral compulsions and institutional constraints.'

[Unger, ibid 1]

Secondly, disdain for the conventional doctrinal crutch: Hero will not employ a conventional doctrinal argument even to support a legal interpretation which would favour the socially disadvantaged. Hero must resist any temptation to manipulate doctrine even to serve good ends, because to do so would only encourage the false formalist belief that sufficient reasons can be found in given legal materials to settle a question of law without reference to full-blown ideological debate.

'The appeal to a spurious conceptual necessity may prove tactically expedient. In the end, however, it always represents a defeat for our cause.'

[Unger, ibid 616]

Of course, Hero could never accept judicial office; and it is doubtful whether he, or any of his disciples, could even enter the legal profession. There might be a case for joining a law firm as a covert saboteur, hoping that there he could disrupt cases by showing that no legal argument could be advanced without an equally strong competitor argument. But that would be a risky adventure. He might be tempted to use doctrinal reasoning, including formalism, to the advantage of some socially oppressed client, and thereby to bolster up the spurious formality or objectivity of the law. His motto must be: 'joining them only encourages them.' Hero's true role is that of the critical scholar. He engages in politics, but he disengages himself and his pupils from legal practice.

In the field of property law, for example, Hero will not take the course advocated by some Marxist-revisionist scholars. He will not, as C B Macpherson argues we should, build on the prestige already accorded by liberal society to private property by seeking to expand the concept of property to include such social goods as welfare rights or rights to employment. Instead, as Unger puts it, he will seek the 'disaggregation of the consolidated property right.'

As things are, English land law doctrine, in the manner of Weberian logically formal rationality, admits two abstract definitional limitations on the recognition of novel interests in land. I have called these 'the doctrinal cleavage' and 'the doctrinal prescription.' According to the former, a right must avail either against a land-owner personally, or it must be enforceable against all-comers to the land (with whatever qualifications are allowed by equitable doctrines and systems of registration). According to the latter, a fully-fledged interest in land must have three characteristics: enjoyment-content relating to land, general protection against allcomers, and transmissibility by the person entitled to it. Hero will subvert these aspects of doctrine in the following way. He will begin by emphasising the emergence of informal putative interests in land, such as equitable co-ownership interests and interests arising from proprietary estoppel, and reject all those efforts made by conventional scholars to accommodate them within familiar categories. Then he will point to matched principles and counterprinciples underlying such case law developments—for example, security of homes versus more efficient conveyancing. Beyond these, he will bring to light irreconcilable social visions—allocation according to need versus individualist market freedom. Nothing can be done, he will claim, to dissipate these contradictions. We must unpack the elements in the consolidated property right, not only for novel putative interests, but for all the more familiar estates and interests in land; and we must bring to bear on all transactions involving land-use the destabilisation right, wielded by the new lawyer in the service of new communitarian institutions. When that day comes, whether I can exercise my 'provisional market right' to sell or lease my house to you, and whether or not you may expel squatters who wish to share your dwelling, or erect fences to prevent the public taking a short cut through your garden, will be at the mercy of destabilisation rights. If (in the opinion of the new institutions, advised by the new lawyer) such transactions would foster social hierarchy and differentiation, they will not be permitted.

Harris 'Unger's Critique of Formalism in Legal Reasoning: Hero, Hercules, and Humdrum' (1989) 52 Modern Law Review 46–48

CLS AND LEGAL LIBERALISM

Critical Legal Studies writers deprecate 'liberalism,' by which they usually mean 'legal liberalism'. The more familiar sense of 'liberalism', of course, is that of an eclectic political programme hovering around the centre-left of the American political spectrum. The coincidence in terminology is perhaps unfortunate, because the CLS writers also inveigh against liberalism in this everyday sense. In the CLS view, the reformist objectives of Democratic Party style liberalism alleviate only a small part of the problems in American society while affirming and strengthening a broad range of pernicious practices. For example, employment laws requiring that men and women receive equal pay for equal work are said to have diverted attention from the need for radical change in the societal roles of men and women. The United States Supreme Court's decisions limiting the ability of a state to forbid contraception and abortion are said to have promoted exploitation in society 'by legitimating the notion that there are naturally separate private and public spheres of human existence.'

Legal liberalism refers instead to a pair of distinct but closely related sets of ideas. The first is concerned with the proper scope of governmental activity. This set of ideas, associated pre-eminently with the writings of John Locke, is also known as 'classical liberalism' or 'individualism.' In this view, individuals have rights over themselves and their property; the rights of an individual define a private zone into which neither the government nor other individuals can forcibly intrude. Within this zone, individuals are legally free to conduct themselves as they choose. Classical liberal writers argued that a person's rights are divinely sanctioned and that the protection of those rights is therefore an important end in itself. They also believed that the protection of rights would create prosperity, promote intellectual advancement, and reduce civil conflict, especially the religious strife with which they were familiar.

While present-day political conservatives and liberals differ both from each other and among themselves on the nature and extent of individual rights, all would agree that distinct private and public zones should exist and that the government must respect a person's rights, including various property rights, within his or her private zone. They would also agree that rights are needed to define the permissible behaviour of individuals in their dealings with one another. This consensus view acknowledges that the definition and application of individual rights is often difficult, but maintains that the difficulties do not render the project impossible or undesirable.

The CLS movement generally disparages the quest for a system of rights. CLS adherents dispute the possibility that such a system can be made coherent—that is, its application to particular cases must be arbitrary. Moreover, they argue that the protection of individual rights has undesirable effects. First, it exalts the autonomy of the individual over the needs of the community. Second, it neglects the individual's own need to be part of the community. Finally, the existing system of rights, like the 'liberal' political programme, deflects any fundamental changes in the structure of society:

> This is the essence of the problem with rights discourse. People don't realize that what they're doing is recasting the real existential feelings that led them to become political people into an ideological framework that coopts them into adopting the very consciousness they want to transform. Without even knowing it, they start talking as if 'we' were rights-bearing citizens who are 'allowed' to do this or that by something

called 'the state,' which is a passivizing illusion—actually a hallucination which establishes the presumptive political legitimacy of the status quo.

*   *   *

Exactly what people don't need is their *rights*. What they need are the actual forms of social life that have to be created through the building of movements that can overcome illusions about the nature of what is political, like the illusion that there is an entity called the state, that people possess rights. It may be necessary to use the rights argument in the course of political struggle, in order to make gains. But the thing to be understood is the extent to which it is enervating to use it.

[Gabel and Kennedy (1984) 36 Stanford Law Review 1, 26, 33]

As expressed in this quotation, the CLS account depicts a focus on rights as a diversion from more urgent kinds of change. Needless to add, not all leftists subscribe to the CLS disparagement of individual rights. On the contrary, this aspect of CLS has provoked alarm in a number of leftist writers. One such writer, while taking care to offer effusive praise for the theoretical contributions of the CLS movement, noted that the CLS account

is not directed simply at the theories used to justify rights. Rather, it is primarily an attack on the notion of legal rights as basic instruments of human freedom and welfare. On this point, I believe that Critical legal theorists have built an argument of great force and yet one which encompasses dangerous distortion . . . It is sometimes blind to the significance of legal protections for certain fundamental human rights. This attack leads not to 'transformative' social activity but to a nihilistic perspective which can encourage repression and tyranny.

[Sparer (1984) 36 Stanford Law Review 509, 512]

Another leftist writer has focused on the failure of CLS adherents to recognise the importance of individual rights as a means of protecting racial minorities from government:

Even if rights and rights-talk paralyze us and induce a false sense of security, as CLS scholars maintain, might they not have a comparable effect on public officials, such as the police? Rights do, at times, give pause to those who would otherwise oppress us . . .

Second, CLS scholars are often hazy about what would provide minorities comparable protection if rights no longer existed . . .

Third, Crits argue that rights separate and alienate the individual from the rest of the human community. This may be so for the hard-working Crits who spend much of their time in their studies and law offices. For minorities, however, rights serve as a rallying point and bring us closer together. On the other hand, any distance rights place between us and others may be beneficial; there is at least safety in distance.

[Delgado (1987) 22 Harv. C.R.–C.L.L. Rev, 301, 305]

Much of the CLS account would have the effect of removing vital barriers to government oppression. I do not know of any CLS author who would regard Stalinist totalitarianism as a desirable form of government, but the rejection of individual rights and the rejection of any distinction between public and private concerns would nonetheless contribute powerfully, if unintentionally, toward that outcome. To the extent that CLS authors recognise this possibility, they alternatively imply either that government officials can be trusted to act benevolently or that the liberal notion of liberty should be subordinated to other ends.

The second set of ideas to which legal liberalism refers is that associated with the rule of law. Like the notion of a system of rights, the notion of the rule of law is shared by both political conservatives and liberals. The rule of law entails that the actions of government in general, and of judges in particular, are constrained by authoritative sources of law such as statutes and common law precedents. The rights and entitlements specified by the law therefore exist apart from the arbitrary will of the government officials who interpret and administer the law. Government officials must obey the law in carrying out governmental activities, and judges must abide by the law in deciding cases.

Most contemporary lawyers, recognising that the law contains gaps, conflicts, and ambiguities, would disavow the rigid formalism exemplified by the work of nineteenth century American legal scholars such as Christopher Columbus Langdell. That is, they no longer see legal reasoning as a scientific domain in which a conscientious interpreter will always find one and only one correct answer to every problem. They would still agree, however, that there is good legal reasoning and bad legal reasoning and that the law significantly limits the results that a judge can properly reach. In short, a judge is obliged to try to interpret the law. While the proper way for a judge to fulfil this obligation is itself controversial, the parties to this controversy agree that the difficulties and disagreements entailed do not undermine the validity of the assumptions behind the rule of law.

The Critical Legal Studies adherents go much further. Just as CLS adherents reject the individual rights aspects of legal liberalism, they also reject the desirability and possibility of the rule of law. Like a system of individual rights, the rule of law is said to thwart social change and the formation of community. As Morton Horwitz expressed it, 'I do not see how a Man of the Left can describe the rule of law as "an unqualified human good"! It undoubtedly restrains power, but it also prevents power's benevolent exercise. . . . [I]t ratifies and legitimates an adversarial, competitive, and atomistic conception of human relations.'

In rejecting the possibility of the rule of law, at least some CLS writings have claimed that laws can provide no guidance at all to judges deciding cases. Because the law is wholly indeterminate, the claim runs, a judge's decisions must be entirely political. For example, Duncan Kennedy has asserted that

> Legal reasoning is not distinct, *as a method for reaching correct results*, from ethical and political discourse in general (ie, from policy analysis). It is true that there is a distinctive lawyers' body of knowledge of the rules in force. It is true that there are distinctive lawyers' argumentative techniques for spotting gaps, conflicts, and ambiguities in the rules, for arguing broad and narrow holdings of cases, and for generating pro and con policy arguments. But these are *only* argumentative techniques. There is never a 'correct legal solution' that is other than the correct ethical and political solution to that legal problem.

> [*Legal Education and the Reproduction of Hierarchy* p 20]

Similarly, Roberto Unger has identified the notion of judicial decisions governed by legal rules as one important object of criticism by the movement. In particular, he criticises the consensus view of law for having a commitment to, and therefore also a belief in the possibility of, a method of legal justification that contrasts with open-ended disputes about the basic terms of social life, disputes that people call ideological, philosophical, or visionary . . . Formalism in the conventional sense—the search for a method of deduction from a gapless system of rules—is merely the anomalous, limiting case of this jurisprudence.

Although CLS adherents reject the idea that case holdings are determined by legal reasoning, they do not mean to imply that judges actually dissemble when they decide cases, pretending to employ legal reasoning to cover the fact that they are greedily promoting the interests of their own economic and social class in every case. Few CLS adherents, if any, appear to believe that judges do so. What, then, determines the outcome of a case? CLS adherents differ on this point. In some CLS writings, the results of a case follow from the desire of judges to promote certain economic objectives, such as industrial growth; to promote these objectives, the argument runs, judges tend to embrace doctrines that operate in favour of capitalists at the expense of the poor and weak. The law thus serves the interests of capitalists as a general matter even if it does not benefit capitalist litigants in each particular lawsuit. Proponents of this view hold that the law directly serves the interests of society's dominant classes at any given stage in history. This instrumental view of the relation between class interests and the legal system harks back to the social analysis of Marx.

Most CLS writings find the claim of a direct instrumental link implausible. They argue instead that the law serves the dominant classes in a more diffuse way by propagating a set of general ideas about society itself. According to this view, the process of deciding a case under the rule of law is simply incoherent, rather than always favouring the dominant classes; the legal order as a whole, however, is said to reinforce the ideas that private property should be respected, that certain hierarchies among people in the workplace are necessary, and so on. This view of the relation between class interests and the legal system is influenced by a neo-Marxist school of thought known as 'critical Marxism.'

The two parts of legal liberalism that I have described—individual rights and the rule of law—are inextricably related. The protection of individual rights requires a system in which judges and administrators comply with the prescribed body of legal rules. Without the rule of law, there is by definition no legal obligation upon government officials to respect the rights and entitlements that the law sets forth.

Most people of the left and right no doubt see individual rights and the rule of law, not as *flaws* in the American and British political orders, but instead as important virtues, even if sometimes achieved incompletely. Racial minorities and other vulnerable groups would be especially ill-served if legal liberalism's requirements of governmental generality and regularity were abandoned; indeed, many of the triumphs of the American civil rights movement called for the application of legal liberal notions in new domains. It may therefore seem all the more puzzling that a movement claiming to identify with the interests of the vulnerable would find individual rights and the rule of law objectionable.

The puzzle cannot be resolved with the suggestion that the CLS writers are simply reporting what they believe a sound analysis of the law dictates. Their writings make clear that they are not only reporting, but also applauding. The CLS writers do not purport to offer merely technical, apolitical criticism— which, for them, is a non-existent category of scholarship anyway. Rather, the impossibility of individual rights and the rule of law is seen as fortunate; the eventual discrediting of those ideas is to be welcomed. As I suggested earlier, CLS writers uniformly find these aspects of legal liberalism disagreeable because they are said to stand in the way of communitarian goals and other urgently needed changes in society.

Price 'Taking Rights Cynically: A Review of Critical Legal Studies' [1989] Cambridge Law Journal 272–278

A CRITIQUE OF CLS'S CRITIQUE OF LIBERALISM

The diverse writings of the CLS movement have an overarching motif: namely, that the pursuit of individual rights and the rule of law acts as an obstacle to various goals. One of these goals is to change the present institutions and forms of social relations. Another is to make people's relations with one another more 'communitarian.' While the concept of community appears in diverse forms itself in CLS writings, it can be understood as encompassing a greater degree of altruism, or mutual sharing and sacrifice; an increase in popular participation in social decisions; and even a heightened sense of emotional bonds or common purposes among people.

The precise relationship between the goals of change and community can vary. For most CLS authors, social change is a route to the end of making relations more communitarian; for Unger, on the other hand, change is an end in itself that fulfils certain needs of human nature. Whatever the connection to be drawn between change and community, the CLS authors uniformly find liberalism objectionable because it legitimates the *status quo* and makes the self-seeking individual supreme.

Contrary to the CLS critique, liberalism itself permits ample sources of change and community. The most obvious, to the point of making it banal to bother mentioning, is democratic self-government. While there are a variety of models for democratic governance, such as the direct participation afforded by the referendum or the more common 'representative' form, each gives the members of the community some opportunity to take part in the shaping of the rules by which the community will live.

Another source of change and community permitted by liberalism is voluntary co-operation among individuals. Economic exchanges under capitalism are one example, but far from the only one. Voluntary co-operation of all kinds, whether economic, social, or otherwise, can bring about changes in institutions and social relations and it has done so extensively. Those who value communal experience can seek it in a liberal society; those who value distance can seek that. In a system of individual rights, people can rely on a sphere of legal autonomy from others and from the state, but they do not necessarily have to remain separated from others. While the CLS writers are undoubtedly correct in asserting that individuals need relations with others for fulfilment, it is simply a *non sequitur* to conclude that the abandonment of liberalism is necessary to foster those relations.

As suggested earlier with regard to Frug's programme of decentralisation, the CLS rejection of the rule of law defeats its own communitarian objectives. Unless those who administer the community's decisions can be expected to carry out and abide by its decisions, communal decision-making becomes pointless. The rule of law—the separation of an official's own moral or political preferences from the laws that he is called upon to administer—is thus a *prerequisite* for popular participation in social decisions, not a barrier to it.

It is true that a system of individual rights inevitably limits the possibilities for change and community under liberalism. In seeking to demarcate a realm in which the community cannot rightfully dominate, it forbids the state from insisting upon certain kinds of assent or conformity. The liberal society has only a limited ability to make the dissenting individual serve as an instrument of change, whether economic or artistic, religious or sexual. This aspect of liberalism is not a drawback, however, because not all forms of change and community are equally desirable.

The CLS scholars focus only on *imposed* change and *imposed* community— that is, the forms of change and community that can be created by the law. Conversely, they give little attention to *voluntary* change and *voluntary* community. Under the CLS thesis of false consciousness, people are incapable of determining their own interests accurately, so there is no reason for the law to respect their voluntary choices. In that view, the zone of autonomy created by a liberal system of individual rights is unsupportable: it upholds individual decisions that are unworthy of respect while preventing society from imposing better decisions. On the other hand, if one believes that individual liberty is desirable—if one believes that a person's own choices should generally be respected—then voluntary relations are preferable to imposed relations.

The very features of liberalism that limit imposed relations also promote voluntary relations. The rule of law, by making legal norms general and regular, encourages people to enter into voluntary relations without having to fear unexpected legal consequences. Individual rights, by maintaining a zone of autonomy in which people can avoid unwelcome intrusions, likewise provide the security that encourages people to enter into relations with others. A society without the rule of law or individual rights, one in which all decisions are vested in the judgment (or caprice) of certain individuals, would not exhibit much community and change except to the extent that they could be imposed coercively. As far as voluntary relations are concerned, such a society would in all likelihood prove relentlessly distant and stagnant.

One could even question whether imposed community is a form of community at all. On the subject of community, Kennedy writes,

> The 'freedom' of individualism is negative, alienated, and arbitrary. . . . We can achieve real freedom only collectively, through *group* self-determination. We are simply too weak to realize ourselves in isolation. True, collective self-determination, short of utopia, implies the use of force against the individual. But we experience and accept the use of physical and psychic coercion every day, in family life, education, and culture.
> ['Form and Substance in Private Law Adjudication' (1976) 89 Harvard Law Review 1774]

Thus, Kennedy identifies freedom with community, and then identifies community with imposed community. Elsewhere in his discussion, he mentions the possible objection that it may be 'nonsense to speak of forcing someone to behave altruistically.' That is, true community or true altruism *means* voluntary sacrifice. Under a regime of imposed community, the individual who engages in sharing and sacrifice may well be acting out of nothing more than a self-seeking desire to avoid legal sanctions. That hardly fits the usual understanding of 'altruism'. After acknowledging this objection, Kennedy simply answers,

One idea of justice is the organization of society so that the outcomes of interaction are equivalent to those that would occur *if* everyone behaved altruistically. I take this as a given for the rest of the discussion.

[Ibid 1722]

Kennedy's answer begs the question. If an individual engages in sharing and sacrifice only because the law commands it, then the person is not an altruist, but is instead the same calculating 'bad man' that Kennedy decries for being 'concerned with law only as a means or an obstacle to the accomplishment of his antisocial ends.' The altruism urged by Kennedy and the other CLS writers is the altruism of *A Clockwork Orange*; the form of community urged by the CLS writers is the antithesis of true community.

Liberalism, in its classical sense of embodying individual rights and the rule of law, offers the possibility of security in distance while permitting community in voluntary co-operation as well. It makes true community possible by making toleration and ordered liberty possible. If the CLS authors have found liberalism difficult to escape, perhaps it is because freedom has a strong gravitational pull.

Price 'Taking Rights Cynically: A Review of Critical Legal Studies' [1989] Cambridge Law Journal 298–301

Index